Math 266
Introduction to Calculus II

Custom Publication of Stewart:
Single Variable Calculus, 5e

Student Solutions Manual

NELSON / E D U C A T I O N

COPYRIGHT © 2009 by
Nelson Education Limited.

Printed and bound in Canada

25 26 27 28 19 18 17 16

For more information contact
Nelson Education Limited 1120
Birchmount Road, Toronto,
Ontario, M1K 5G4. Or you can
visit our internet site at http://
www.nelson.com

ALL RIGHTS RESERVED.
No part of this work covered by the copyright
hereon may be reproduced, transcribed, or used in
any form or by any means – graphic, electronic, or
mechanical, including photocopying, recording,
taping, web distribution or information storage and
retrieval systems – without the written permission
of the publisher.

For permission to use material from this text or
product, submit all requests online at
www.cengage.com/permissions.

Further questions about permissions can be emailed
to permissionrequest@cengage.com.

Every effort has been made to trace ownership of
all copyrighted material and to secure permission
from copyright holders. In the event of any
question arising as to the use of any material, we
will be pleased to make the necessary corrections
in future printings.

This textbook is a Nelson custom publication.
Because your instructor has chosen to produce a
custom publication, you pay only for material that
you will use in your course.

ISBN-13: 978-0-17-643558-5
ISBN-10: 0-17-643558-1

Consists of:

*Student Solutions Manual for
Single Variable Calculus,
Fifth Edition*
Daniel Anderson, Jeffery Cole,
Daniel Drucker, James Stewart
ISBN-10: 0-534-39369-1, © 2003

Contents

....

Selected Chapters from
Student Solution Manual for Single Variable Calculus, 5th Edition

....

6.2 Volumes

1. A cross-section is circular with radius x^2, so its area is $A(x) = \pi \left(x^2\right)^2$.

$$V = \int_0^1 A(x)\,dx = \int_0^1 \pi\left(x^2\right)^2 dx = \pi \int_0^1 x^4 dx = \pi \left[\tfrac{1}{5}x^5\right]_0^1 = \tfrac{\pi}{5}$$

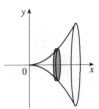 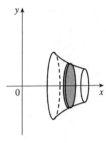

3. A cross-section is a disk with radius $1/x$, so its area is $A(x) = \pi(1/x)^2$.

$$V = \int_1^2 A(x)\,dx = \int_1^2 \pi\left(\frac{1}{x}\right)^2 dx = \pi \int_1^2 \frac{1}{x^2}\,dx = \pi\left[-\frac{1}{x}\right]_1^2 = \pi\left[-\tfrac{1}{2} - (-1)\right] = \tfrac{\pi}{2}$$

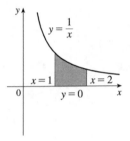

5. A cross-section is a disk with radius $\sqrt{y}$, so its area is $A(y) = \pi\left(\sqrt{y}\right)^2$.

$$V = \int_0^4 A(y)\,dy = \int_0^4 \pi\left(\sqrt{y}\right)^2 dy = \pi \int_0^4 y\,dy = \pi\left[\tfrac{1}{2}y^2\right]_0^4 = 8\pi$$

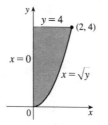 

7. A cross-section is a washer (annulus) with inner radius x^2 and outer radius $\sqrt{x}$, so its area is

$$A(x) = \pi(\sqrt{x})^2 - \pi\left(x^2\right)^2 = \pi\left(x - x^4\right).$$

$$V = \int_0^1 A(x)\,dx = \pi \int_0^1 \left(x - x^4\right) dx = \pi\left[\tfrac{1}{2}x^2 - \tfrac{1}{5}x^5\right]_0^1 = \pi\left(\tfrac{1}{2} - \tfrac{1}{5}\right) = \tfrac{3\pi}{10}$$

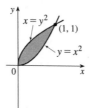 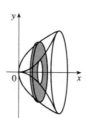

9. A cross-section is a washer with inner radius y^2 and outer radius $2y$, so its area is

$$A(y) = \pi(2y)^2 - \pi\left(y^2\right)^2 = \pi\left(4y^2 - y^4\right).$$

$$V = \int_0^2 A(y)\,dy = \pi \int_0^2 \left(4y^2 - y^4\right) dy = \pi\left[\tfrac{4}{3}y^3 - \tfrac{1}{5}y^5\right]_0^2 = \pi\left(\tfrac{32}{3} - \tfrac{32}{5}\right) = \tfrac{64\pi}{15}$$

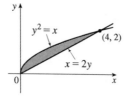 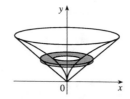

11. A cross-section is a washer with inner radius $1 - \sqrt{x}$ and outer radius $1 - x$, so its area is

$$A(x) = \pi(1 - x)^2 - \pi(1 - \sqrt{x})^2 = \pi\left[(1 - 2x + x^2) - (1 - 2\sqrt{x} + x)\right] = \pi\left(-3x + x^2 + 2\sqrt{x}\right).$$

$$V = \int_0^1 A(x)\, dx = \pi \int_0^1 \left(-3x + x^2 + 2\sqrt{x}\right) dx$$

$$= \pi\left[-\tfrac{3}{2}x^2 + \tfrac{1}{3}x^3 + \tfrac{4}{3}x^{3/2}\right]_0^1 = \pi\left(-\tfrac{3}{2} + \tfrac{5}{3}\right) = \tfrac{\pi}{6}$$

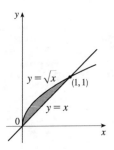 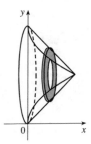

13. A cross-section is an annulus with inner radius $2 - 1$ and outer radius $2 - x^4$, so its area is

$$A(x) = \pi\left(2 - x^4\right)^2 - \pi(2 - 1)^2 = \pi\left(3 - 4x^4 + x^8\right).$$

$$V = \int_{-1}^1 A(x)\, dx = 2\int_0^1 A(x)\, dx = 2\pi \int_0^1 \left(3 - 4x^4 + x^8\right) dx = 2\pi\left[3x - \tfrac{4}{5}x^5 + \tfrac{1}{9}x^9\right]_0^1$$

$$= 2\pi\left(3 - \tfrac{4}{5} + \tfrac{1}{9}\right) = \tfrac{208}{45}\pi$$

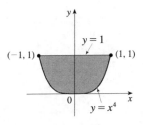 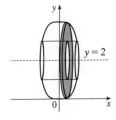

15. $V = \int_{-1}^1 \pi\left(1 - y^2\right)^2 dy = 2\int_0^1 \pi\left(1 - y^2\right)^2 dy = 2\pi \int_0^1 \left(1 - 2y^2 + y^4\right) dy$

$$= 2\pi\left[y - \tfrac{2}{3}y^3 + \tfrac{1}{5}y^5\right]_0^1 = 2\pi \cdot \tfrac{8}{15} = \tfrac{16}{15}\pi$$

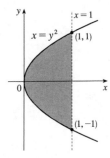 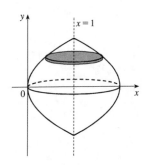

17. $y = x^2 \;\Rightarrow\; x = \sqrt{y}$ for $x \geq 0$. The outer radius is the distance from $x = -1$ to $x = \sqrt{y}$ and the inner radius is the distance from $x = -1$ to $x = y^2$.

$$V = \int_0^1 \pi \left\{ \left[\sqrt{y} - (-1)\right]^2 - \left[y^2 - (-1)\right]^2 \right\} dy = \pi \int_0^1 \left[\left(\sqrt{y} + 1\right)^2 - \left(y^2 + 1\right)^2\right] dy$$

$$= \pi \int_0^1 \left(y + 2\sqrt{y} + 1 - y^4 - 2y^2 - 1\right) dy = \pi \int_0^1 \left(y + 2\sqrt{y} - y^4 - 2y^2\right) dy$$

$$= \pi \left[\tfrac{1}{2}y^2 + \tfrac{4}{3}y^{3/2} - \tfrac{1}{5}y^5 - \tfrac{2}{3}y^3\right]_0^1 = \pi\left(\tfrac{1}{2} + \tfrac{4}{3} - \tfrac{1}{5} - \tfrac{2}{3}\right) = \tfrac{29}{30}\pi$$

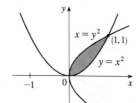 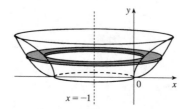

19. $\mathscr{R}_1$ about OA (the line $y = 0$): $V = \int_0^1 A(x)\,dx = \int_0^1 \pi(x^3)^2\,dx = \pi \int_0^1 x^6\,dx = \pi\left[\tfrac{1}{7}x^7\right]_0^1 = \tfrac{\pi}{7}$

21. $\mathscr{R}_1$ about AB (the line $x = 1$):

$$V = \int_0^1 A(y)\,dy = \int_0^1 \pi\left(1 - \sqrt[3]{y}\right)^2 dy = \pi \int_0^1 \left(1 - 2y^{1/3} + y^{2/3}\right) dy$$

$$= \pi\left[y - \tfrac{3}{2}y^{4/3} + \tfrac{3}{5}y^{5/3}\right]_0^1 = \pi\left(1 - \tfrac{3}{2} + \tfrac{3}{5}\right) = \tfrac{\pi}{10}$$

23. $\mathscr{R}_2$ about OA (the line $y = 0$):

$$V = \int_0^1 A(x)\,dx = \int_0^1 \left[\pi(1)^2 - \pi(\sqrt{x})^2\right] dx = \pi \int_0^1 (1 - x)\,dx = \pi\left[x - \tfrac{1}{2}x^2\right]_0^1 = \pi\left(1 - \tfrac{1}{2}\right) = \tfrac{\pi}{2}$$

25. $\mathscr{R}_2$ about AB (the line $x = 1$):

$$V = \int_0^1 A(y)\,dy = \int_0^1 \left[\pi(1)^2 - \pi(1 - y^2)^2\right] dy = \pi \int_0^1 \left[1 - (1 - 2y^2 + y^4)\right] dy$$

$$= \pi \int_0^1 (2y^2 - y^4)\,dy = \pi\left[\tfrac{2}{3}y^3 - \tfrac{1}{5}y^5\right]_0^1 = \pi\left(\tfrac{2}{3} - \tfrac{1}{5}\right) = \tfrac{7\pi}{15}$$

27. $\mathscr{R}_3$ about OA (the line $y = 0$):

$$V = \int_0^1 A(x)\,dx = \int_0^1 \left[\pi(\sqrt{x})^2 - \pi(x^3)^2\right] dx = \pi \int_0^1 (x - x^6)\,dx = \pi\left[\tfrac{1}{2}x^2 - \tfrac{1}{7}x^7\right]_0^1 = \pi\left(\tfrac{1}{2} - \tfrac{1}{7}\right) = \tfrac{5\pi}{14}.$$

Note: Let $\mathscr{R} = \mathscr{R}_1 + \mathscr{R}_2 + \mathscr{R}_3$. If we rotate $\mathscr{R}$ about any of the segments OA, OC, AB, or BC, we obtain a right circular cylinder of height 1 and radius 1. Its volume is $\pi r^2 h = \pi(1)^2 \cdot 1 = \pi$. As a check for Exercises 19, 23, and 27, we can add the answers, and that sum must equal π. Thus, $\tfrac{\pi}{7} + \tfrac{\pi}{2} + \tfrac{5\pi}{14} = \left(\tfrac{2+7+5}{14}\right)\pi = \pi$.

29. $\mathscr{R}_3$ about AB (the line $x = 1$):

$$V = \int_0^1 A(y)\,dy = \int_0^1 \left[\pi(1 - y^2)^2 - \pi\left(1 - \sqrt[3]{y}\right)^2\right] dy = \pi \int_0^1 \left[(1 - 2y^2 + y^4) - (1 - 2y^{1/3} + y^{2/3})\right] dy$$

$$= \pi \int_0^1 \left(-2y^2 + y^4 + 2y^{1/3} - y^{2/3}\right) dy = \pi\left[-\tfrac{2}{3}y^3 + \tfrac{1}{5}y^5 + \tfrac{3}{2}y^{4/3} - \tfrac{3}{5}y^{5/3}\right]_0^1$$

$$= \pi\left(-\tfrac{2}{3} + \tfrac{1}{5} + \tfrac{3}{2} - \tfrac{3}{5}\right) = \tfrac{13\pi}{30}$$

Note: See the note in Exercise 27. For Exercises 21, 25, and 29, we have $\tfrac{\pi}{10} + \tfrac{7\pi}{15} + \tfrac{13\pi}{30} = \left(\tfrac{3 + 14 + 13}{30}\right)\pi = \pi$.

31. $V = \pi \int_0^{\pi/4} (1 - \tan^3 x)^2\, dx$

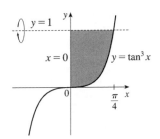

33. $V = \pi \int_0^{\pi} \left[(1-0)^2 - (1 - \sin x)^2 \right] dx$

$\quad = \pi \int_0^{\pi} \left[1^2 - (1 - \sin x)^2 \right] dx$

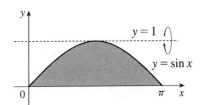

35. $V = \pi \int_{-\sqrt{8}}^{\sqrt{8}} \left\{ [3 - (-2)]^2 - \left[\sqrt{y^2 + 1} - (-2) \right]^2 \right\} dy$

$\quad = \pi \int_{-2\sqrt{2}}^{2\sqrt{2}} \left[5^2 - \left(\sqrt{1 + y^2} + 2 \right)^2 \right] dy$

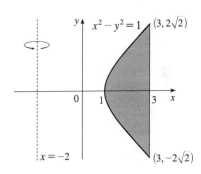

37. We see from the graph in Exercise 6.1.35 that the x-coordinates of the points of intersection are $x = a \approx -0.72$ and $x = b \approx 1.22$, with $\sqrt{x + 1} > x^2$ on the interval (a, b), so the volume of revolution is

$\pi \int_a^b \left[\left(\sqrt{x+1} \right)^2 - \left(x^2 \right)^2 \right] dx = \pi \int_a^b \left(x + 1 - x^4 \right) dx = \pi \left[\frac{1}{2}x^2 + x - \frac{1}{5}x^5 \right]_a^b \approx 5.80.$

39. $V = \pi \int_0^{\pi} \left\{ \left[\sin^2 x - (-1) \right]^2 - [0 - (-1)]^2 \right\} dx$

$\quad \overset{CAS}{=} \frac{11}{8}\pi^2$

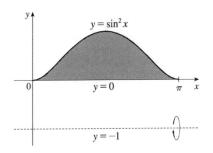

41. $\pi \int_0^{\pi/2} \cos^2 x\, dx$ describes the volume of the solid obtained by rotating the region

$\mathcal{R} = \left\{ (x, y) \mid 0 \le x \le \frac{\pi}{2}, 0 \le y \le \cos x \right\}$ of the xy-plane about the x-axis.

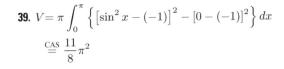

43. $\pi \displaystyle\int_0^1 (y^4 - y^8)\,dy = \pi \int_0^1 \left[\left(y^2\right)^2 - \left(y^4\right)^2\right]\,dy$ describes the volume of the solid obtained by rotating the region

$\mathcal{R} = \left\{(x,y) \mid 0 \le y \le 1, y^4 \le x \le y^2\right\}$ of the xy-plane about the y-axis.

45. There are 10 subintervals over the 15-cm length, so we'll use $n = 10/2 = 5$ for the Midpoint Rule.

$$V = \int_0^{15} A(x)\,dx \approx M_5 = \tfrac{15-0}{5}[A(1.5) + A(4.5) + A(7.5) + A(10.5) + A(13.5)]$$
$$= 3(18 + 79 + 106 + 128 + 39) = 3 \cdot 370 = 1110 \text{ cm}^3$$

47. We'll form a right circular cone with height h and base radius r by revolving the line $y = \frac{r}{h}x$ about the x-axis.

$$V = \pi \int_0^h \left(\frac{r}{h}x\right)^2 dx = \pi \int_0^h \frac{r^2}{h^2} x^2\,dx = \pi \frac{r^2}{h^2}\left[\frac{1}{3}x^3\right]_0^h$$
$$= \pi \frac{r^2}{h^2}\left(\frac{1}{3}h^3\right) = \frac{1}{3}\pi r^2 h$$

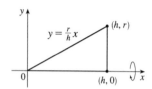

Another solution: Revolve $x = -\dfrac{r}{h}y + r$ about the y-axis.

$$V = \pi \int_0^h \left(-\frac{r}{h}y + r\right)^2 dy \overset{*}{=} \pi \int_0^h \left[\frac{r^2}{h^2}y^2 - \frac{2r^2}{h}y + r^2\right] dy$$
$$= \pi \left[\frac{r^2}{3h^2}y^3 - \frac{r^2}{h}y^2 + r^2 y\right]_0^h = \pi\left(\tfrac{1}{3}r^2 h - r^2 h + r^2 h\right) = \tfrac{1}{3}\pi r^2 h$$

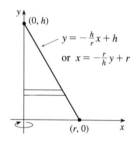

* Or use substitution with $u = r - \dfrac{r}{h}y$ and $du = -\dfrac{r}{h}\,dy$ to get

$$\pi \int_r^0 u^2\left(-\frac{h}{r}\,du\right) = -\pi\frac{h}{r}\left[\frac{1}{3}u^3\right]_r^0 = -\pi\frac{h}{r}\left(-\frac{1}{3}r^3\right) = \frac{1}{3}\pi r^2 h.$$

49. $x^2 + y^2 = r^2 \quad \Leftrightarrow \quad x^2 = r^2 - y^2$

$$V = \pi \int_{r-h}^r (r^2 - y^2)\,dy = \pi\left[r^2 y - \frac{y^3}{3}\right]_{r-h}^r$$
$$= \pi\left\{\left[r^3 - \frac{r^3}{3}\right] - \left[r^2(r-h) - \frac{(r-h)^3}{3}\right]\right\}$$
$$= \pi\left\{\tfrac{2}{3}r^3 - \tfrac{1}{3}(r-h)\left[3r^2 - (r-h)^2\right]\right\}$$
$$= \tfrac{1}{3}\pi\left\{2r^3 - (r-h)\left[3r^2 - (r^2 - 2rh + h^2)\right]\right\}$$
$$= \tfrac{1}{3}\pi\left\{2r^3 - (r-h)\left[2r^2 + 2rh - h^2\right]\right\}$$
$$= \tfrac{1}{3}\pi\left(2r^3 - 2r^3 - 2r^2 h + rh^2 + 2r^2 h + 2rh^2 - h^3\right)$$
$$= \tfrac{1}{3}\pi\left(3rh^2 - h^3\right) = \tfrac{1}{3}\pi h^2(3r - h), \text{ or, equivalently, } \pi h^2\left(r - \frac{h}{3}\right)$$

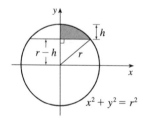

51. For a cross-section at height y, we see from similar triangles that $\dfrac{\alpha/2}{b/2} = \dfrac{h-y}{h}$, so $\alpha = b\left(1 - \dfrac{y}{h}\right)$.

Similarly, for cross-sections having $2b$ as their base and β replacing α, $\beta = 2b\left(1 - \dfrac{y}{h}\right)$. So

$$V = \int_0^h A(y)\,dy = \int_0^h \left[b\left(1 - \frac{y}{h}\right)\right]\left[2b\left(1 - \frac{y}{h}\right)\right] dy$$

$$= \int_0^h 2b^2\left(1 - \frac{y}{h}\right)^2 dy = 2b^2 \int_0^h \left(1 - \frac{2y}{h} + \frac{y^2}{h^2}\right) dy$$

$$= 2b^2\left[y - \frac{y^2}{h} + \frac{y^3}{3h^2}\right]_0^h = 2b^2\left[h - h + \tfrac{1}{3}h\right]$$

$$= \tfrac{2}{3}b^2 h \quad [\,= \tfrac{1}{3}Bh \text{ where } B \text{ is the area of the base, as with any pyramid.}]$$

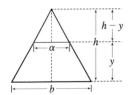

53. A cross-section at height z is a triangle similar to the base, so we'll multiply the legs of the base triangle, 3 and 4, by a proportionality factor of $(5 - z)/5$. Thus, the triangle at height z has area

$$A(z) = \frac{1}{2} \cdot 3\left(\frac{5-z}{5}\right) \cdot 4\left(\frac{5-z}{5}\right) = 6\left(1 - \frac{z}{5}\right)^2, \text{ so}$$

$$V = \int_0^5 A(z)\,dz = 6\int_0^5 (1 - z/5)^2\,dz$$

$$= 6\int_1^0 u^2(-5\,du) \quad \left[u = 1 - z/5,\ du = -\tfrac{1}{5}dz\right]$$

$$= -30\left[\tfrac{1}{3}u^3\right]_1^0 = -30\left(-\tfrac{1}{3}\right) = 10 \text{ cm}^3$$

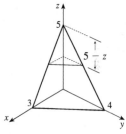

55. If l is a leg of the isosceles right triangle and $2y$ is the hypotenuse,

then $l^2 + l^2 = (2y)^2 \ \Rightarrow\ 2l^2 = 4y^2 \ \Rightarrow\ l^2 = 2y^2$.

$$V = \int_{-2}^2 A(x)\,dx = 2\int_0^2 A(x)\,dx = 2\int_0^2 \tfrac{1}{2}(l)(l)\,dx = 2\int_0^2 y^2\,dx$$

$$= 2\int_0^2 \tfrac{1}{4}(36 - 9x^2)\,dx = \tfrac{9}{2}\int_0^2 (4 - x^2)\,dx$$

$$= \tfrac{9}{2}\left[4x - \tfrac{1}{3}x^3\right]_0^2 = \tfrac{9}{2}\left(8 - \tfrac{8}{3}\right) = 24$$

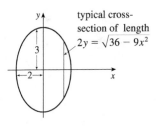

typical cross-section of length $2y = \sqrt{36 - 9x^2}$

57. The cross-section of the base corresponding to the coordinate y has length $2x = 2\sqrt{y}$. The square has area $A(y) = \left(2\sqrt{y}\right)^2 = 4y$, so

$$V = \int_0^1 A(y)\,dy = \int_0^1 4y\,dy = \left[2y^2\right]_0^1 = 2.$$

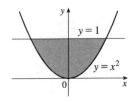

59. A typical cross-section perpendicular to the y-axis in the base has length

$\ell(y) = 3 - \frac{3}{2}y$. This length is the leg of an isosceles right triangle, so

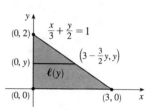

$$A(y) = \tfrac{1}{2}\left[\ell(y)\right]^2 \quad \left[\tfrac{1}{2}bh \text{ with base} = \text{height}\right]$$

$$= \tfrac{1}{2}\left[3\left(1 - \tfrac{1}{2}y\right)\right]^2 = \tfrac{9}{2}\left(1 - \tfrac{1}{2}y\right)^2$$

Thus,

$$V = \int_0^2 A(y)\,dy = \tfrac{9}{2}\int_1^0 u^2(-2\,du) \quad \left[u = 1 - \tfrac{1}{2}y,\ du = -\tfrac{1}{2}\,dy\right]$$

$$= -9\left[\tfrac{1}{3}u^3\right]_1^0 = -9\left(-\tfrac{1}{3}\right) = 3$$

61. (a) The torus is obtained by rotating the circle $(x - R)^2 + y^2 = r^2$

about the y-axis. Solving for x, we see that the right half of the

circle is given by $x = R + \sqrt{r^2 - y^2} = f(y)$ and the left half by

$x = R - \sqrt{r^2 - y^2} = g(y)$. So

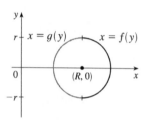

$$V = \pi \int_{-r}^{r} \left\{[f(y)]^2 - [g(y)]^2\right\} dy$$

$$= 2\pi \int_0^r \left[\left(R^2 + 2R\sqrt{r^2 - y^2} + r^2 - y^2\right) - \left(R^2 - 2R\sqrt{r^2 - y^2} + r^2 - y^2\right)\right] dy$$

$$= 2\pi \int_0^r 4R\sqrt{r^2 - y^2}\,dy = 8\pi R \int_0^r \sqrt{r^2 - y^2}\,dy$$

(b) Observe that the integral represents a quarter of the area of a circle with radius r, so

$$8\pi R \int_0^r \sqrt{r^2 - y^2}\,dy = 8\pi R \cdot \tfrac{1}{4}\pi r^2 = 2\pi^2 r^2 R.$$

63. (a) Volume$(S_1) = \int_0^h A(z)\,dz =$ Volume(S_2) since the cross-sectional area $A(z)$ at height z is the same for both

solids.

(b) By Cavalieri's Principle, the volume of the cylinder in the figure is the same as that of a right circular cylinder

with radius r and height h, that is, $\pi r^2 h$.

65. The volume is obtained by rotating the area common to two circles of

radius r, as shown. The volume of the right half is

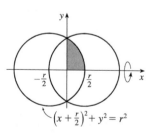

$$V_{\text{right}} = \pi \int_0^{r/2} y^2\,dx = \pi \int_0^{r/2} \left[r^2 - \left(\tfrac{1}{2}r + x\right)^2\right] dx$$

$$= \pi\left[r^2 x - \tfrac{1}{3}\left(\tfrac{1}{2}r + x\right)^3\right]_0^{r/2} = \pi\left[\left(\tfrac{1}{2}r^3 - \tfrac{1}{3}r^3\right) - \left(0 - \tfrac{1}{24}r^3\right)\right] = \tfrac{5}{24}\pi r^3$$

So by symmetry, the total volume is twice this, or $\tfrac{5}{12}\pi r^3$.

Another solution: We observe that the volume is the twice the volume of a cap of a sphere, so we can use the

formula from Exercise 49 with $h = \tfrac{1}{2}r$: $V = 2 \cdot \tfrac{1}{3}\pi h^2(3r - h) = \tfrac{2}{3}\pi\left(\tfrac{1}{2}r\right)^2\left(3r - \tfrac{1}{2}r\right) = \tfrac{5}{12}\pi r^3.$

67. Take the x-axis to be the axis of the cylindrical hole of radius r. A quarter of the cross-section through y, perpendicular to the y-axis, is the rectangle shown. Using the Pythagorean Theorem twice, we see that the dimensions of this rectangle are

$x = \sqrt{R^2 - y^2}$ and $z = \sqrt{r^2 - y^2}$, so

$\frac{1}{4}A(y) = xz = \sqrt{r^2 - y^2}\,\sqrt{R^2 - y^2}$, and

$$V = \int_{-r}^{r} A(y)\,dy = \int_{-r}^{r} 4\sqrt{r^2 - y^2}\,\sqrt{R^2 - y^2}\,dy$$

$$= 8\int_{0}^{r} \sqrt{r^2 - y^2}\,\sqrt{R^2 - y^2}\,dy$$

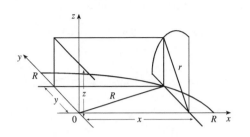

69. (a) The radius of the barrel is the same at each end by symmetry, since the function $y = R - cx^2$ is even. Since the barrel is obtained by rotating the graph of the function y about the x-axis, this radius is equal to the value of y at $x = \frac{1}{2}h$, which is $R - c\left(\frac{1}{2}h\right)^2 = R - d = r$.

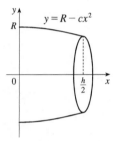

(b) The barrel is symmetric about the y-axis, so its volume is twice the volume of that part of the barrel for $x > 0$. Also, the barrel is a volume of rotation, so

$$V = 2\int_{0}^{h/2} \pi y^2\,dx = 2\pi \int_{0}^{h/2} \left(R - cx^2\right)^2 dx = 2\pi\left[R^2 x - \frac{2}{3}Rcx^3 + \frac{1}{5}c^2 x^5\right]_{0}^{h/2}$$

$$= 2\pi\left(\frac{1}{2}R^2 h - \frac{1}{12}Rch^3 + \frac{1}{160}c^2 h^5\right)$$

Trying to make this look more like the expression we want, we rewrite it as

$V = \frac{1}{3}\pi h\left[2R^2 + \left(R^2 - \frac{1}{2}Rch^2 + \frac{3}{80}c^2 h^4\right)\right]$. But

$R^2 - \frac{1}{2}Rch^2 + \frac{3}{80}c^2 h^4 = \left(R - \frac{1}{4}ch^2\right)^2 - \frac{1}{40}c^2 h^4 = \left(R - d\right)^2 - \frac{2}{5}\left(\frac{1}{4}ch^2\right)^2 = r^2 - \frac{2}{5}d^2$.

Substituting this back into V, we see that $V = \frac{1}{3}\pi h\left(2R^2 + r^2 - \frac{2}{5}d^2\right)$, as required.

6.3 Volumes by Cylindrical Shells

1.

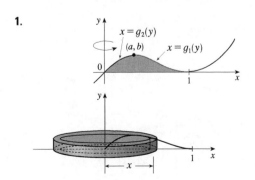

If we were to use the "washer" method, we would first have to locate the local maximum point (a, b) of $y = x(x - 1)^2$ using the methods of Chapter 4. Then we would have to solve the equation $y = x(x - 1)^2$ for x in terms of y to obtain the functions $x = g_1(y)$ and $x = g_2(y)$ shown in the first figure. This step would be difficult because it involves the cubic formula. Finally we would find the volume using

$$V = \pi \int_{0}^{b} \left\{[g_1(y)]^2 - [g_2(y)]^2\right\} dy.$$

Using shells, we find that a typical approximating shell has radius x, so its circumference is $2\pi x$. Its height is y, that is, $x(x-1)^2$. So the total volume is

$$V = \int_0^1 2\pi x[x(x-1)^2]\,dx = 2\pi \int_0^1 (x^4 - 2x^3 + x^2)\,dx = 2\pi\left[\frac{x^5}{5} - 2\frac{x^4}{4} + \frac{x^3}{3}\right]_0^1 = \frac{\pi}{15}$$

3. $V = \displaystyle\int_1^2 2\pi x \cdot \frac{1}{x}\,dx = 2\pi \int_1^2 1\,dx$

$\qquad = 2\pi\,[x]_1^2 = 2\pi(2-1) = 2\pi$

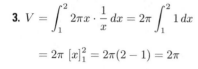 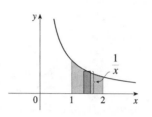

5. $V = \int_0^2 2\pi x\left(4 - x^2\right)dx = 2\pi \int_0^2 \left(4x - x^3\right)dx$

$\qquad = 2\pi\left[2x^2 - \frac{1}{4}x^4\right]_0^2 = 2\pi\left(8 - 4\right)$

$\qquad = 8\pi$

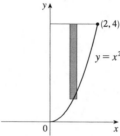 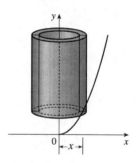

7. The curves intersect when $4(x-2)^2 = x^2 - 4x + 7 \iff 4x^2 - 16x + 16 = x^2 - 4x + 7 \iff$

$3x^2 - 12x + 9 = 0 \iff 3(x^2 - 4x + 3) = 0 \iff 3(x-1)(x-3) = 0$, so $x = 1$ or 3.

$V = 2\pi \int_1^3 \left\{x\left[(x^2 - 4x + 7) - 4(x-2)^2\right]\right\}dx = 2\pi \int_1^3 \left[x(x^2 - 4x + 7 - 4x^2 + 16x - 16)\right]dx$

$\quad = 2\pi \int_1^3 \left[x(-3x^2 + 12x - 9)\right]dx = 2\pi(-3)\int_1^3 (x^3 - 4x^2 + 3x)\,dx = -6\pi\left[\frac{1}{4}x^4 - \frac{4}{3}x^3 + \frac{3}{2}x^2\right]_1^3$

$\quad = -6\pi\left[\left(\frac{81}{4} - 36 + \frac{27}{2}\right) - \left(\frac{1}{4} - \frac{4}{3} + \frac{3}{2}\right)\right] = -6\pi\left(20 - 36 + 12 + \frac{4}{3}\right) = -6\pi\left(-\frac{8}{3}\right) = 16\pi$

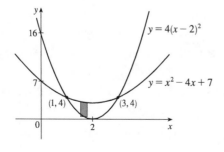 

9. $V = \int_1^2 2\pi y\left(1 + y^2\right) dy = 2\pi \int_1^2 \left(y + y^3\right) dy = 2\pi\left[\frac{1}{2}y^2 + \frac{1}{4}y^4\right]_1^2$

$\quad = 2\pi\left[(2+4) - \left(\frac{1}{2} + \frac{1}{4}\right)\right] = 2\pi\left(\frac{21}{4}\right) = \frac{21\pi}{2}$

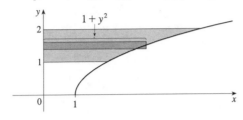

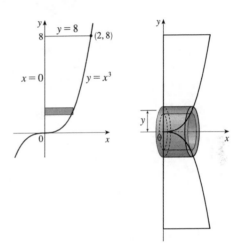

11. $V = 2\pi \int_0^8 \left[y\left(\sqrt[3]{y} - 0\right)\right] dy$

$\quad = 2\pi \int_0^8 y^{4/3}\, dy = 2\pi\left[\frac{3}{7}y^{7/3}\right]_0^8$

$\quad = \frac{6\pi}{7}\left(8^{7/3}\right) = \frac{6\pi}{7}\left(2^7\right) = \frac{768\pi}{7}$

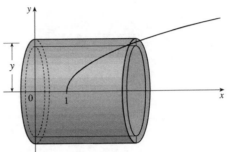

13. The curves intersect when $4x^2 = 6 - 2x \iff 2x^2 + x - 3 = 0 \iff (2x+3)(x-1) = 0 \iff x = -\frac{3}{2}$ or 1.

Solving the equations for x gives us $y = 4x^2 \Rightarrow x = \pm\frac{1}{2}\sqrt{y}$ and $2x + y = 6 \Rightarrow x = -\frac{1}{2}y + 3$.

$V = 2\pi \int_0^4 \left\{y\left[\left(\frac{1}{2}\sqrt{y}\right) - \left(-\frac{1}{2}\sqrt{y}\right)\right]\right\} dy + 2\pi \int_4^9 \left\{y\left[\left(-\frac{1}{2}y + 3\right) - \left(-\frac{1}{2}\sqrt{y}\right)\right]\right\} dy$

$\quad = 2\pi \int_0^4 \left(y\sqrt{y}\right) dy + 2\pi \int_4^9 \left(-\frac{1}{2}y^2 + 3y + \frac{1}{2}y^{3/2}\right) dy = 2\pi\left[\frac{2}{5}y^{5/2}\right]_0^4 + 2\pi\left[-\frac{1}{6}y^3 + \frac{3}{2}y^2 + \frac{1}{5}y^{5/2}\right]_4^9$

$\quad = 2\pi\left(\frac{2}{5} \cdot 32\right) + 2\pi\left[\left(-\frac{243}{2} + \frac{243}{2} + \frac{243}{5}\right) - \left(-\frac{32}{3} + 24 + \frac{32}{5}\right)\right]$

$\quad = \frac{128}{5}\pi + 2\pi\left(\frac{433}{15}\right) = \frac{1250}{15}\pi = \frac{250}{3}\pi$

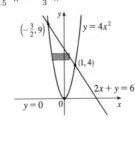

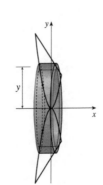

15. $V = \int_1^2 2\pi(x-1)x^2\,dx = 2\pi\left[\frac{1}{4}x^4 - \frac{1}{3}x^3\right]_1^2$

$\qquad = 2\pi\left[\left(4 - \frac{8}{3}\right) - \left(\frac{1}{4} - \frac{1}{3}\right)\right] = \frac{17}{6}\pi$

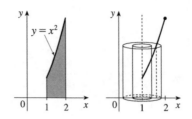

17. $V = \int_1^2 2\pi(4-x)x^2\,dx = 2\pi\left[\frac{4}{3}x^3 - \frac{1}{4}x^4\right]_1^2$

$\qquad = 2\pi\left[\left(\frac{32}{3} - 4\right) - \left(\frac{4}{3} - \frac{1}{4}\right)\right] = \frac{67}{6}\pi$

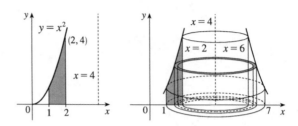

19. $V = \int_0^2 2\pi(3-y)(5-x)\,dy$

$\qquad = \int_0^2 2\pi(3-y)\left(5 - y^2 - 1\right)\,dy$

$\qquad = \int_0^2 2\pi\left(12 - 4y - 3y^2 + y^3\right)\,dy$

$\qquad = 2\pi\left[12y - 2y^2 - y^3 + \frac{1}{4}y^4\right]_0^2$

$\qquad = 2\pi(24 - 8 - 8 + 4) = 24\pi$

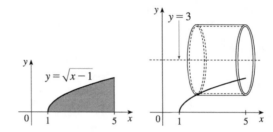

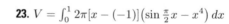

21. $V = \int_{2\pi}^{3\pi} 2\pi x \sin x\,dx$

23. $V = \int_0^1 2\pi[x - (-1)]\left(\sin\frac{\pi}{2}x - x^4\right)\,dx$

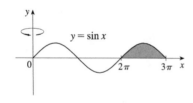

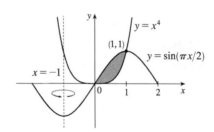

25. $V = \int_0^\pi 2\pi(4-y)\sqrt{\sin y}\,dy$

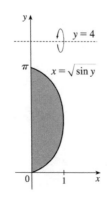

27. $\Delta x = \dfrac{\pi/4 - 0}{4} = \dfrac{\pi}{16}$.

$V = \int_0^{\pi/4} 2\pi x \tan x \, dx \approx 2\pi \cdot \frac{\pi}{16}\left(\frac{\pi}{32}\tan\frac{\pi}{32} + \frac{3\pi}{32}\tan\frac{3\pi}{32} + \frac{5\pi}{32}\tan\frac{5\pi}{32} + \frac{7\pi}{32}\tan\frac{7\pi}{32}\right) \approx 1.142$

29. $\int_0^3 2\pi x^5 \, dx = 2\pi \int_0^3 x(x^4)\, dx$. The solid is obtained by rotating the region $0 \le y \le x^4$, $0 \le x \le 3$ about the y-axis using cylindrical shells.

31. $\int_0^1 2\pi(3-y)(1-y^2)\, dy$. The solid is obtained by rotating the region bounded by (i) $x = 1 - y^2$, $x = 0$, and $y = 0$ or (ii) $x = y^2$, $x = 1$, and $y = 0$ about the line $y = 3$ using cylindrical shells.

33.

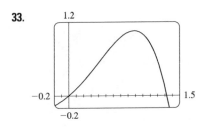

From the graph, the curves intersect at $x = 0$ and at $x = a \approx 1.32$, with $x + x^2 - x^4 > 0$ on the interval $(0, a)$. So the volume of the solid obtained by rotating the region about the y-axis is

$$V = 2\pi \int_0^a \left[x(x + x^2 - x^4)\right] dx = 2\pi \int_0^a (x^2 + x^3 - x^5)\, dx$$

$$= 2\pi\left[\tfrac{1}{3}x^3 + \tfrac{1}{4}x^4 - \tfrac{1}{6}x^6\right]_0^a \approx 4.05$$

35. $V = 2\pi \displaystyle\int_0^{\pi/2}\left[\left(\tfrac{\pi}{2} - x\right)\left(\sin^2 x - \sin^4 x\right)\right] dx$

$\overset{\text{CAS}}{=} \tfrac{1}{32}\pi^3$

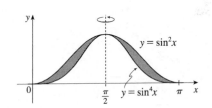

37. Use disks:

$$V = \int_{-2}^1 \pi\left(x^2 + x - 2\right)^2 dx = \pi \int_{-2}^1 \left(x^4 + 2x^3 - 3x^2 - 4x + 4\right) dx$$

$$= \pi\left[\tfrac{1}{5}x^5 + \tfrac{1}{2}x^4 - x^3 - 2x^2 + 4x\right]_{-2}^1 = \pi\left[\left(\tfrac{1}{5} + \tfrac{1}{2} - 1 - 2 + 4\right) - \left(-\tfrac{32}{5} + 8 + 8 - 8 - 8\right)\right]$$

$$= \pi\left(\tfrac{33}{5} + \tfrac{3}{2}\right) = \tfrac{81}{10}\pi$$

39. Use shells:

$$V = \int_1^4 2\pi\left[x - (-1)\right]\left[5 - \left(x^2 - 5x + 9\right)\right] dx$$

$$= 2\pi \int_1^4 (x+1)\left(-x^2 + 5x - 4\right) dx$$

$$= 2\pi \int_1^4 \left(-x^3 + 4x^2 + x - 4\right) dx = 2\pi\left[-\tfrac{1}{4}x^4 + \tfrac{4}{3}x^3 + \tfrac{1}{2}x^2 - 4x\right]_1^4$$

$$= 2\pi\left[\left(-64 + \tfrac{256}{3} + 8 - 16\right) - \left(-\tfrac{1}{4} + \tfrac{4}{3} + \tfrac{1}{2} - 4\right)\right]$$

$$= 2\pi\left(\tfrac{63}{4}\right) = \tfrac{63\pi}{2}$$

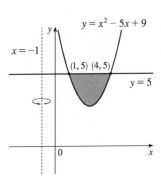

41. Use disks: $V = \pi \int_0^2 \left[\sqrt{1 - (y-1)^2} \right]^2 dy = \pi \int_0^2 \left(2y - y^2 \right) dy = \pi \left[y^2 - \frac{1}{3}y^3 \right]_0^2 = \pi \left(4 - \frac{8}{3} \right) = \frac{4}{3}\pi$

43. $V = 2 \int_0^r 2\pi x \sqrt{r^2 - x^2}\, dx = -2\pi \int_0^r \left(r^2 - x^2 \right)^{1/2}(-2x)\, dx = \left[-2\pi \cdot \frac{2}{3} \left(r^2 - x^2 \right)^{3/2} \right]_0^r$

$= -\frac{4}{3}\pi \left(0 - r^3 \right) = \frac{4}{3}\pi r^3$

45. $V = 2\pi \int_0^r x \left(-\frac{h}{r}x + h \right) dx = 2\pi h \int_0^r \left(-\frac{x^2}{r} + x \right) dx = 2\pi h \left[-\frac{x^3}{3r} + \frac{x^2}{2} \right]_0^r = 2\pi h\, \frac{r^2}{6} = \frac{\pi r^2 h}{3}$

6 Review

1. (a) See Section 6.1, Figure 2 and Equations 6.1.1 and 6.1.2.

(b) Instead of using "top minus bottom" and integrating from left to right, we use "right minus left" and integrate from bottom to top. See Figures 11 and 12 in Section 6.1.

2. The numerical value of the area represents the number of meters by which Sue is ahead of Kathy after 1 minute.

3. (a) See the discussion in Section 6.2, near Figures 2 and 3, ending in the Definition of Volume.

(b) See the discussion between Examples 5 and 6 in Section 6.2. If the cross-section is a disk, find the radius in terms of x or y and use $A = \pi(\text{radius})^2$. If the cross-section is a washer, find the inner radius r_{in} and outer radius r_{out} and use $A = \pi(r_{\text{out}}^2) - \pi(r_{\text{in}}^2)$.

4. (a) $V = 2\pi r h \, \Delta r = (\text{circumference})(\text{height})(\text{thickness})$

(b) For a typical shell, find the circumference and height in terms of x or y and calculate
$V = \int_a^b (\text{circumference})(\text{height})\,(dx \text{ or } dy)$, where a and b are the limits on x or y.

(c) Sometimes slicing produces washers or disks whose radii are difficult (or impossible) to find explicitly. On other occasions, the cylindrical shell method leads to an easier integral than slicing does.

5. $\int_0^6 f(x)\,dx$ represents the amount of work done. Its units are newton-meters, or joules.

6. (a) The average value of a function f on an interval $[a, b]$ is $f_{\text{ave}} = \dfrac{1}{b-a}\int_a^b f(x)\,dx$.

(b) The Mean Value Theorem for Integrals says that there is a number c at which the value of f is exactly equal to the average value of the function, that is, $f(c) = f_{\text{ave}}$. For a geometric interpretation of the Mean Value Theorem for Integrals, see Figure 2 in Section 6.5 and the discussion that accompanies it.

EXERCISES
---

1. $0 = x^2 - x - 6 = (x-3)(x+2) \quad \Leftrightarrow \quad x = 3 \text{ or } -2.$ So

$$A = \int_{-2}^{3} \left[0 - \left(x^2 - x - 6 \right) \right] dx = \int_{-2}^{3} \left(-x^2 + x + 6 \right) dx$$

$$= \left[-\tfrac{1}{3}x^3 + \tfrac{1}{2}x^2 + 6x \right]_{-2}^{3}$$

$$= \left(-9 + \tfrac{9}{2} + 18 \right) - \left(\tfrac{8}{3} + 2 - 12 \right)$$

$$= \tfrac{125}{6}$$

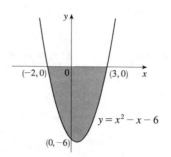

3. $1 - x^2 = 1 - \sqrt{x} \quad \Leftrightarrow \quad -x^2 = -\sqrt{x} \quad \Leftrightarrow \quad x^2 = \sqrt{x} \quad \Rightarrow \quad x^4 = x$

$\Rightarrow \quad x^4 - x = 0 \quad \Rightarrow \quad x\left(x^3 - 1 \right) = 0 \quad \Rightarrow$

$x(x-1)\left(x^2 + x + 1 \right) = 0 \quad \Rightarrow \quad x = 0 \text{ or } 1.$ So

$$A = \int_{0}^{1} \left[\left(1 - x^2 \right) - \left(1 - \sqrt{x} \right) \right] dx = \int_{0}^{1} \left(\sqrt{x} - x^2 \right) dx$$

$$= \left[\tfrac{2}{3}x^{3/2} - \tfrac{1}{3}x^3 \right]_{0}^{1} = \tfrac{2}{3} - \tfrac{1}{3} = \tfrac{1}{3}$$

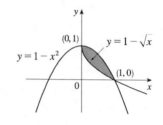

5. $A = \displaystyle\int_{0}^{2} \left[\sin\left(\tfrac{\pi x}{2} \right) - \left(x^2 - 2x \right) \right] dx$

$$= \left[-\tfrac{2}{\pi} \cos\left(\tfrac{\pi x}{2} \right) - \tfrac{1}{3}x^3 + x^2 \right]_{0}^{2}$$

$$= \left(\tfrac{2}{\pi} - \tfrac{8}{3} + 4 \right) - \left(-\tfrac{2}{\pi} - 0 + 0 \right) = \tfrac{4}{3} + \tfrac{4}{\pi}$$

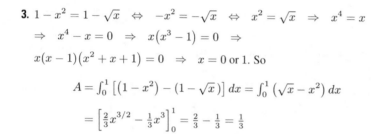

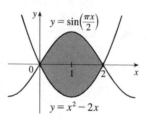

7. Using washers with inner radius x^2 and outer radius $2x$, we have

$$V = \pi \int_{0}^{2} \left[(2x)^2 - \left(x^2 \right)^2 \right] dx = \pi \int_{0}^{2} \left(4x^2 - x^4 \right) dx$$

$$= \pi \left[\tfrac{4}{3}x^3 - \tfrac{1}{5}x^5 \right]_{0}^{2} = \pi \left(\tfrac{32}{3} - \tfrac{32}{5} \right) = 32\pi \cdot \tfrac{2}{15}$$

$$= \tfrac{64\pi}{15}$$

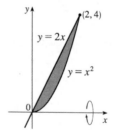

9. $V = \pi \displaystyle\int_{-3}^{3} \left\{ \left[\left(9 - y^2 \right) - (-1) \right]^2 - \left[0 - (-1) \right]^2 \right\} dy$

$$= 2\pi \int_{0}^{3} \left[\left(10 - y^2 \right)^2 - 1 \right] dy$$

$$= 2\pi \int_{0}^{3} \left(100 - 20y^2 + y^4 - 1 \right) dy$$

$$= 2\pi \int_{0}^{3} \left(99 - 20y^2 + y^4 \right) dy = 2\pi \left[99y - \tfrac{20}{3}y^3 + \tfrac{1}{5}y^5 \right]_{0}^{3}$$

$$= 2\pi \left(297 - 180 + \tfrac{243}{5} \right) = \tfrac{1656\pi}{5}$$

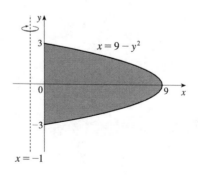

11. The graph of $x^2 - y^2 = a^2$ is a hyperbola with right and left branches. Solving for y gives us $y^2 = x^2 - a^2 \implies y = \pm\sqrt{x^2 - a^2}$. We'll use shells and the height of each shell is $\sqrt{x^2 - a^2} - \left(-\sqrt{x^2 - a^2}\right) = 2\sqrt{x^2 - a^2}$.

The volume is $V = \int_a^{a+h} 2\pi x \cdot 2\sqrt{x^2 - a^2}\, dx$. To evaluate, let $u = x^2 - a^2$, so $du = 2x\, dx$ and $x\, dx = \frac{1}{2}\, du$. When $x = a$, $u = 0$, and when $x = a + h$,
$u = (a + h)^2 - a^2 = a^2 + 2ah + h^2 - a^2 = 2ah + h^2$.

Thus, $V = 4\pi \int_0^{2ah+h^2} \sqrt{u}\left(\frac{1}{2}\, du\right) = 2\pi\left[\frac{2}{3}u^{3/2}\right]_0^{2ah+h^2} = \frac{4}{3}\pi\left(2ah + h^2\right)^{3/2}$.

13. $V = \int_0^1 \pi\left[\left(1 - x^3\right)^2 - \left(1 - x^2\right)^2\right] dx$

15. (a) A cross-section is a washer with inner radius x^2 and outer radius x.

$V = \int_0^1 \pi\left[(x)^2 - \left(x^2\right)^2\right] dx = \int_0^1 \pi\left(x^2 - x^4\right) dx = \pi\left[\frac{1}{3}x^3 - \frac{1}{5}x^5\right]_0^1 = \pi\left[\frac{1}{3} - \frac{1}{5}\right] = \frac{2\pi}{15}$

(b) A cross-section is a washer with inner radius y and outer radius $\sqrt{y}$.

$V = \int_0^1 \pi\left[\left(\sqrt{y}\right)^2 - y^2\right] dy = \int_0^1 \pi\left(y - y^2\right) dy = \pi\left[\frac{1}{2}y^2 - \frac{1}{3}y^3\right]_0^1 = \pi\left[\frac{1}{2} - \frac{1}{3}\right] = \frac{\pi}{6}$

(c) A cross-section is a washer with inner radius $2 - x$ and outer radius $2 - x^2$.

$V = \int_0^1 \pi\left[\left(2 - x^2\right)^2 - (2 - x)^2\right] dx = \int_0^1 \pi\left(x^4 - 5x^2 + 4x\right) dx = \pi\left[\frac{1}{5}x^5 - \frac{5}{3}x^3 + 2x^2\right]_0^1$

$= \pi\left[\frac{1}{5} - \frac{5}{3} + 2\right] = \frac{8\pi}{15}$

17. (a) Using the Midpoint Rule on $[0, 1]$ with $f(x) = \tan\left(x^2\right)$ and $n = 4$, we estimate

$A = \int_0^1 \tan\left(x^2\right) dx \approx \frac{1}{4}\left[\tan\left(\left(\frac{1}{8}\right)^2\right) + \tan\left(\left(\frac{3}{8}\right)^2\right) + \tan\left(\left(\frac{5}{8}\right)^2\right) + \tan\left(\left(\frac{7}{8}\right)^2\right)\right] \approx \frac{1}{4}(1.53) \approx 0.38$

(b) Using the Midpoint Rule on $[0, 1]$ with $f(x) = \pi\tan^2\left(x^2\right)$ (for disks) and $n = 4$, we estimate

$V = \int_0^1 f(x)\, dx \approx \frac{1}{4}\pi\left[\tan^2\left(\left(\frac{1}{8}\right)^2\right) + \tan^2\left(\left(\frac{3}{8}\right)^2\right) + \tan^2\left(\left(\frac{5}{8}\right)^2\right) + \tan^2\left(\left(\frac{7}{8}\right)^2\right)\right] \approx \frac{\pi}{4}(1.114) \approx 0.87$

19. The solid is obtained by rotating the region $\mathcal{R} = \left\{(x, y) \mid 0 \le x \le \frac{\pi}{2}, 0 \le y \le \cos x\right\}$ about the y-axis.

21. The solid is obtained by rotating the region $\mathcal{R} = \left\{(x, y) \mid 0 \le y \le 2, 0 \le x \le 4 - y^2\right\}$ about the x-axis.

23. Take the base to be the disk $x^2 + y^2 \le 9$. Then $V = \int_{-3}^3 A(x)\, dx$, where $A(x_0)$ is the area of the isosceles right triangle whose hypotenuse lies along the line $x = x_0$ in the xy-plane. The length of the hypotenuse is $2\sqrt{9 - x^2}$ and the length of each leg is $\sqrt{2}\sqrt{9 - x^2}$. $A(x) = \frac{1}{2}\left(\sqrt{2}\sqrt{9 - x^2}\right)^2 = 9 - x^2$, so

$V = 2\int_0^3 A(x)\, dx = 2\int_0^3 \left(9 - x^2\right) dx = 2\left[9x - \frac{1}{3}x^3\right]_0^3 = 2(27 - 9) = 36$.

25. Equilateral triangles with sides measuring $\frac{1}{4}x$ meters have height $\frac{1}{4}x\sin 60° = \frac{\sqrt{3}}{8}x$. Therefore,

$$A(x) = \frac{1}{2}\cdot\frac{1}{4}x\cdot\frac{\sqrt{3}}{8}x = \frac{\sqrt{3}}{64}x^2. \quad V = \int_0^{20} A(x)\,dx = \frac{\sqrt{3}}{64}\int_0^{20} x^2\,dx = \frac{\sqrt{3}}{64}\left[\frac{1}{3}x^3\right]_0^{20} = \frac{8000\sqrt{3}}{64\cdot 3} = \frac{125\sqrt{3}}{3}\ \text{m}^3.$$

27. $f(x) = kx \quad\Rightarrow\quad 30\,\text{N} = k(15-12)\,\text{cm} \quad\Rightarrow\quad k = 10\,\text{N/cm} = 1000\,\text{N/m}.\ 20\,\text{cm} - 12\,\text{cm} = 0.08\,\text{m} \quad\Rightarrow$

$$W = \int_0^{0.08} kx\,dx = 1000\int_0^{0.08} x\,dx = 500\left[x^2\right]_0^{0.08} = 500(0.08)^2 = 3.2\ \text{N-m} = 3.2\ \text{J}.$$

29. (a) The parabola has equation $y = ax^2$ with vertex at the origin and passing

through $(4,4)$. $\ 4 = a\cdot 4^2 \ \Rightarrow\ a = \frac{1}{4} \ \Rightarrow\ y = \frac{1}{4}x^2 \ \Rightarrow\ x^2 = 4y$

$\Rightarrow\ x = 2\sqrt{y}$. Each circular disk has radius $2\sqrt{y}$ and is moved $4-y$ ft.

$$W = \int_0^4 \pi\left(2\sqrt{y}\right)^2 62.5\,(4-y)\,dy = 250\pi\int_0^4 y(4-y)\,dy$$

$$= 250\pi\left[2y^2 - \tfrac{1}{3}y^3\right]_0^4 = 250\pi\left(32 - \tfrac{64}{3}\right) = \frac{8000\pi}{3} \approx 8378\ \text{ft-lb}$$

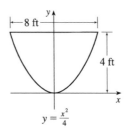

(b) In part (a) we knew the final water level (0) but not the amount of work

done. Here we use the same equation, except with the work fixed, and the

lower limit of integration (that is, the final water level — call it h)

unknown: $W = 4000 \ \Leftrightarrow\ 250\pi\left[2y^2 - \tfrac{1}{3}y^3\right]_h^4 = 4000 \ \Leftrightarrow$

$\frac{16}{\pi} = \left[\left(32 - \tfrac{64}{3}\right) - \left(2h^2 - \tfrac{1}{3}h^3\right)\right] \ \Leftrightarrow\ h^3 - 6h^2 + 32 - \frac{48}{\pi} = 0.$

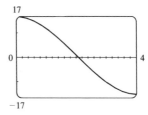

We graph the function $f(h) = h^3 - 6h^2 + 32 - \frac{48}{\pi}$ on the interval $[0,4]$ to see where it is 0. From the graph,

$f(h) = 0$ for $h \approx 2.1$. So the depth of water remaining is about 2.1 ft.

31. $\displaystyle\lim_{h\to 0} f_{\text{ave}} = \lim_{h\to 0}\frac{1}{(x+h)-x}\int_x^{x+h} f(t)\,dt = \lim_{h\to 0}\frac{F(x+h)-F(x)}{h}$, where $F(x) = \int_a^x f(t)\,dt$. But we

recognize this limit as being $F'(x)$ by the definition of a derivative. Therefore, $\displaystyle\lim_{h\to 0} f_{\text{ave}} = F'(x) = f(x)$

by FTC1.

☐ PROBLEMS PLUS

1. (a) The area under the graph of f from 0 to t is equal to $\int_0^t f(x)\,dx$, so the requirement is that $\int_0^t f(x)\,dx = t^3$ for all t. We differentiate both sides of this equation with respect to t (with the help of FTC1) to get $f(t) = 3t^2$. This function is positive and continuous, as required.

(b) The volume generated from $x = 0$ to $x = b$ is $\int_0^b \pi[f(x)]^2\,dx$. Hence, we are given that $b^2 = \int_0^b \pi[f(x)]^2\,dx$ for all $b > 0$. Differentiating both sides of this equation with respect to b using the Fundamental Theorem of Calculus gives $2b = \pi[f(b)]^2 \;\Rightarrow\; f(b) = \sqrt{2b/\pi}$, since f is positive. Therefore, $f(x) = \sqrt{2x/\pi}$.

3. Let a and b be the x-coordinates of the points where the line intersects the curve. From the figure, $R_1 = R_2 \;\Rightarrow\;$

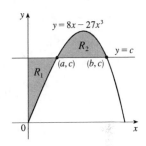

$y = 8x - 27x^3$

$\int_0^a \left[c - (8x - 27x^3) \right] dx = \int_a^b \left[(8x - 27x^3) - c \right] dx$

$\left[cx - 4x^2 + \tfrac{27}{4}x^4 \right]_0^a = \left[4x^2 - \tfrac{27}{4}x^4 - cx \right]_a^b$

$ac - 4a^2 + \tfrac{27}{4}a^4 = \left(4b^2 - \tfrac{27}{4}b^4 - bc \right) - \left(4a^2 - \tfrac{27}{4}a^4 - ac \right)$

$0 = 4b^2 - \tfrac{27}{4}b^4 - bc = 4b^2 - \tfrac{27}{4}b^4 - b\left(8b - 27b^3\right)$

$= 4b^2 - \tfrac{27}{4}b^4 - 8b^2 + 27b^4 = \tfrac{81}{4}b^4 - 4b^2$

$= b^2\left(\tfrac{81}{4}b^2 - 4\right)$

So for $b > 0$, $b^2 = \tfrac{16}{81} \;\Rightarrow\; b = \tfrac{4}{9}$. Thus, $c = 8b - 27b^3 = 8\left(\tfrac{4}{9}\right) - 27\left(\tfrac{64}{729}\right) = \tfrac{32}{9} - \tfrac{64}{27} = \tfrac{32}{27}$.

5. (a) $V = \pi h^2(r - h/3) = \tfrac{1}{3}\pi h^2(3r - h)$. See the solution to Exercise 6.2.49.

(b) The smaller segment has height $h = 1 - x$ and so by part (a) its volume is $V = \tfrac{1}{3}\pi(1-x)^2\left[3(1) - (1-x)\right] = \tfrac{1}{3}\pi(x-1)^2(x+2)$. This volume must be $\tfrac{1}{3}$ of the total volume of the sphere, which is $\tfrac{4}{3}\pi(1)^3$. So $\tfrac{1}{3}\pi(x-1)^2(x+2) = \tfrac{1}{3}\left(\tfrac{4}{3}\pi\right) \;\Rightarrow\; (x^2 - 2x + 1)(x+2) = \tfrac{4}{3} \;\Rightarrow\; x^3 - 3x + 2 = \tfrac{4}{3} \;\Rightarrow\; 3x^3 - 9x + 2 = 0$. Using Newton's method with $f(x) = 3x^3 - 9x + 2$, $f'(x) = 9x^2 - 9$, we get $x_{n+1} = x_n - \dfrac{3x_n^3 - 9x_n + 2}{9x_n^2 - 9}$. Taking $x_1 = 0$, we get $x_2 \approx 0.2222$, and $x_3 \approx 0.2261 \approx x_4$, so, correct to four decimal places, $x \approx 0.2261$.

(c) With $r = 0.5$ and $s = 0.75$, the equation $x^3 - 3rx^2 + 4r^3s = 0$ becomes $x^3 - 3(0.5)x^2 + 4(0.5)^3(0.75) = 0$ $\;\Rightarrow\; x^3 - \tfrac{3}{2}x^2 + 4\left(\tfrac{1}{8}\right)\tfrac{3}{4} = 0 \;\Rightarrow\; 8x^3 - 12x^2 + 3 = 0$. We use Newton's method with

$f(x) = 8x^3 - 12x^2 + 3$, $f'(x) = 24x^2 - 24x$, so $x_{n+1} = x_n - \dfrac{8x_n^3 - 12x_n^2 + 3}{24x_n^2 - 24x_n}$. Take $x_1 = 0.5$. Then

$x_2 \approx 0.6667$, and $x_3 \approx 0.6736 \approx x_4$. So to four decimal places the depth is 0.6736 m.

(d) (i) From part (a) with $r = 5$ in., the volume of water in the bowl is

$$V = \tfrac{1}{3}\pi h^2(3r - h) = \tfrac{1}{3}\pi h^2(15 - h) = 5\pi h^2 - \tfrac{1}{3}\pi h^3.$$ We are given that $\dfrac{dV}{dt} = 0.2$ m^3/s and we want to

find $\dfrac{dh}{dt}$ when $h = 3$. Now $\dfrac{dV}{dt} = 10\pi h \dfrac{dh}{dt} - \pi h^2 \dfrac{dh}{dt}$, so $\dfrac{dh}{dt} = \dfrac{0.2}{\pi(10h - h^2)}$. When $h = 3$, we have

$$\frac{dh}{dt} = \frac{0.2}{\pi(10 \cdot 3 - 3^2)} = \frac{1}{105\pi} \approx 0.003 \text{ in/s}.$$

(ii) From part (a), the volume of water required to fill the bowl from the instant that the water is 4 in. deep is

$$V = \tfrac{1}{2} \cdot \tfrac{4}{3}\pi(5)^3 - \tfrac{1}{3}\pi(4)^2(15 - 4) = \tfrac{2}{3} \cdot 125\pi - \tfrac{16}{3} \cdot 11\pi = \tfrac{74}{3}\pi.$$ To find the time required to fill the

bowl we divide this volume by the rate: Time $= \dfrac{74\pi/3}{0.2} = \dfrac{370\pi}{3} \approx 387$ s ≈ 6.5 min

7. We are given that the rate of change of the volume of water is $\dfrac{dV}{dt} = -kA(x)$, where k is some positive constant

and $A(x)$ is the area of the surface when the water has depth x. Now we are concerned with the rate of change of

the depth of the water with respect to time, that is, $\dfrac{dx}{dt}$. But by the Chain Rule, $\dfrac{dV}{dt} = \dfrac{dV}{dx}\dfrac{dx}{dt}$, so the first equation

can be written $\dfrac{dV}{dx}\dfrac{dx}{dt} = -kA(x)$ ($\star$). Also, we know that the total volume of water up to a depth x is

$V(x) = \int_0^x A(s)\,ds$, where $A(s)$ is the area of a cross-section of the water at a depth s. Differentiating this

equation with respect to x, we get $dV/dx = A(x)$. Substituting this into equation $\star$, we get

$A(x)(dx/dt) = -kA(x) \;\Rightarrow\; dx/dt = -k$, a constant.

9. We must find expressions for the areas A and B, and then set them equal and see what this says about the curve C.

If $P = (a, 2a^2)$, then area A is just $\int_0^a \left(2x^2 - x^2\right) dx = \int_0^a x^2\,dx = \tfrac{1}{3}a^3$. To find area B, we use y as the variable

of integration. So we find the equation of the middle curve as a function of y: $y = 2x^2 \;\Leftrightarrow\; x = \sqrt{y/2}$,

since we are concerned with the first quadrant only. We can express area B as

$\int_0^{2a^2} \left[\sqrt{y/2} - C(y)\right] dy = \left[\tfrac{4}{3}(y/2)^{3/2}\right]_0^{2a^2} - \int_0^{2a^2} C(y)\,dy = \tfrac{4}{3}a^3 - \int_0^{2a^2} C(y)\,dy$, where $C(y)$ is the function

with graph C. Setting $A = B$, we get $\tfrac{1}{3}a^3 = \tfrac{4}{3}a^3 - \int_0^{2a^2} C(y)\,dy \;\Leftrightarrow\; \int_0^{2a^2} C(y)\,dy = a^3$. Now we

differentiate this equation with respect to a using the Chain Rule and the Fundamental Theorem:

$C(2a^2)(4a) = 3a^2 \;\Rightarrow\; C(y) = \tfrac{3}{4}\sqrt{y/2}$, where $y = 2a^2$. Now we can solve for y: $x = \tfrac{3}{4}\sqrt{y/2} \;\Rightarrow$

$x^2 = \tfrac{9}{16}(y/2) \;\Rightarrow\; y = \tfrac{32}{9}x^2$.

11. (a) Stacking disks along the y-axis gives us $V = \int_0^h \pi \, [f(y)]^2 \, dy$.

(b) Using the Chain Rule, $\dfrac{dV}{dt} = \dfrac{dV}{dh} \cdot \dfrac{dh}{dt} = \pi \, [f(h)]^2 \, \dfrac{dh}{dt}$.

(c) $kA\sqrt{h} = \pi[f(h)]^2 \dfrac{dh}{dt}$. Set $\dfrac{dh}{dt} = C$: $\pi[f(h)]^2 \, C = kA\sqrt{h} \;\Rightarrow\; [f(h)]^2 = \dfrac{kA}{\pi C}\sqrt{h} \;\Rightarrow$

$f(h) = \sqrt{\dfrac{kA}{\pi C}}\, h^{1/4}$; that is, $f(y) = \sqrt{\dfrac{kA}{\pi C}}\, y^{1/4}$. The advantage of having $\dfrac{dh}{dt} = C$ is that the markings on the

container are equally spaced.

13. We assume that P lies in the region of positive x. Since $y = x^3$ is an odd

function, this assumption will not affect the result of the calculation. Let

$P = \left(a, a^3\right)$. The slope of the tangent to the curve $y = x^3$ at P is $3a^2$, and so

the equation of the tangent is $y - a^3 = 3a^2(x - a) \;\Leftrightarrow\; y = 3a^2 x - 2a^3$.

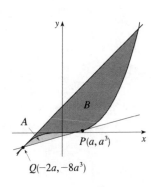

We solve this simultaneously with $y = x^3$ to find the other point of intersection:

$x^3 = 3a^2 x - 2a^3 \;\Leftrightarrow\; (x - a)^2(x + 2a) = 0$. So $Q = \left(-2a, -8a^3\right)$ is

the other point of intersection. The equation of the tangent at Q is

$y - \left(-8a^3\right) = 12a^2[x - (-2a)] \;\Leftrightarrow\; y = 12a^2 x + 16a^3$. By symmetry,

this tangent will intersect the curve again at $x = -2(-2a) = 4a$. The curve lies above the first tangent, and below

the second, so we are looking for a relationship between $A = \int_{-2a}^{a} \left[x^3 - \left(3a^2 x - 2a^3\right)\right] dx$ and

$B = \int_{-2a}^{4a} \left[\left(12a^2 x + 16a^3\right) - x^3\right] dx$. We calculate $A = \left[\tfrac{1}{4}x^4 - \tfrac{3}{2}a^2 x^2 + 2a^3 x\right]_{-2a}^{a} = \tfrac{3}{4}a^4 - \left(-6a^4\right) = \tfrac{27}{4}a^4$,

and $B = \left[6a^2 x^2 + 16a^3 x - \tfrac{1}{4}x^4\right]_{-2a}^{4a} = 96a^4 - \left(-12a^4\right) = 108a^4$. We see that $B = 16A = 2^4 A$. This is

because our calculation of area B was essentially the same as that of area A, with a replaced by $-2a$, so if we

replace a with $-2a$ in our expression for A, we get $\tfrac{27}{4}(-2a)^4 = 108a^4 = B$.

7 □ INVERSE FUNCTIONS:
Exponential, Logarithmic, and Inverse Trigonometric Functions

7.1 Inverse Functions

1. (a) See Definition 1.

(b) It must pass the Horizontal Line Test.

3. f is not one-to-one because $2 \neq 6$, but $f(2) = 2.0 = f(6)$.

5. No horizontal line intersects the graph of f more than once. Thus, by the Horizontal Line Test, f is one-to-one.

7. The horizontal line $y = 0$ (the x-axis) intersects the graph of f in more than one point. Thus, by the Horizontal Line Test, f is not one-to-one.

9. The graph of $f(x) = \frac{1}{2}(x + 5)$ is a line with slope $\frac{1}{2}$. It passes the Horizontal Line Test, so f is one-to-one.

Algebraic solution: If $x_1 \neq x_2$, then $x_1 + 5 \neq x_2 + 5 \Rightarrow \frac{1}{2}(x_1 + 5) \neq \frac{1}{2}(x_2 + 5) \Rightarrow f(x_1) \neq f(x_2)$, so f is one-to-one.

11. $x_1 \neq x_2 \Rightarrow \sqrt{x_1} \neq \sqrt{x_2} \Rightarrow g(x_1) \neq g(x_2)$, so g is 1-1.

13. $h(x) = x^4 + 5 \Rightarrow h(1) = 6 = h(-1)$, so h is not 1-1.

15. A football will attain every height h up to its maximum height twice: once on the way up, and again on the way down. Thus, even if t_1 does not equal t_2, $f(t_1)$ may equal $f(t_2)$, so f is not 1-1.

17. f does not pass the Horizontal Line Test, so f is not 1-1.

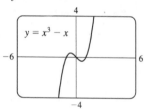

19. Since $f(2) = 9$ and f is 1-1, we know that $f^{-1}(9) = 2$. Remember, if the point $(2, 9)$ is on the graph of f, then the point $(9, 2)$ is on the graph of f^{-1}.

21. $h(x) = x + \sqrt{x} \Rightarrow h'(x) = 1 + 1/(2\sqrt{x}) > 0$ on $(0, \infty)$. So h is increasing and hence, 1-1. By inspection, $h(4) = 4 + \sqrt{4} = 6$, so $h^{-1}(6) = 4$.

23. We solve $C = \frac{5}{9}(F - 32)$ for F: $\frac{9}{5}C = F - 32 \Rightarrow F = \frac{9}{5}C + 32$. This gives us a formula for the inverse function, that is, the Fahrenheit temperature F as a function of the Celsius temperature C. $F \geq -459.67 \Rightarrow \frac{9}{5}C + 32 \geq -459.67 \Rightarrow \frac{9}{5}C \geq -491.67 \Rightarrow C \geq -273.15$, the domain of the inverse function.

25. $y = f(x) = 3 - 2x \Rightarrow 2x = 3 - y \Rightarrow x = \dfrac{3 - y}{2}$. Interchange x and y: $y = \dfrac{3 - x}{2}$. So $f^{-1}(x) = \dfrac{3 - x}{2}$.

27. $f(x) = \sqrt{10 - 3x} \Rightarrow y = \sqrt{10 - 3x} \quad (y \geq 0) \Rightarrow y^2 = 10 - 3x \Rightarrow 3x = 10 - y^2 \Rightarrow x = -\frac{1}{3}y^2 + \frac{10}{3}$. Interchange x and y: $y = -\frac{1}{3}x^2 + \frac{10}{3}$. So $f^{-1}(x) = -\frac{1}{3}x^2 + \frac{10}{3}$. Note that the domain of f^{-1} is $x \geq 0$.

29. For $f(x) = \dfrac{1 - \sqrt{x}}{1 + \sqrt{x}}$, the domain is $x \geq 0$. $f(0) = 1$ and as x increases, y decreases. As $x \to \infty$,

$\dfrac{1 - \sqrt{x}}{1 + \sqrt{x}} \cdot \dfrac{1/\sqrt{x}}{1/\sqrt{x}} = \dfrac{1/\sqrt{x} - 1}{1/\sqrt{x} + 1} \to \dfrac{-1}{1} = -1$, so the range of f is $-1 < y \leq 1$. Thus, the domain of f^{-1} is

$-1 < x \leq 1$.

$y = \dfrac{1 - \sqrt{x}}{1 + \sqrt{x}} \quad \Rightarrow \quad y(1 + \sqrt{x}) = 1 - \sqrt{x} \quad \Rightarrow \quad y + y\sqrt{x} = 1 - \sqrt{x} \quad \Rightarrow \quad \sqrt{x} + y\sqrt{x} = 1 - y \quad \Rightarrow$

$\sqrt{x}(1 + y) = 1 - y \quad \Rightarrow \quad \sqrt{x} = \dfrac{1 - y}{1 + y} \quad \Rightarrow \quad x = \left(\dfrac{1 - y}{1 + y}\right)^2$. Interchange x and y: $y = \left(\dfrac{1 - x}{1 + x}\right)^2$. So

$f^{-1}(x) = \left(\dfrac{1 - x}{1 + x}\right)^2$ with $-1 < x \leq 1$.

31. $y = f(x) = 1 - \dfrac{2}{x^2} \quad \Rightarrow \quad 1 - y = \dfrac{2}{x^2} \quad \Rightarrow \quad x^2 = \dfrac{2}{1 - y} \quad \Rightarrow$

$x = \sqrt{\dfrac{2}{1 - y}}$, since $x > 0$. Interchange x and y: $y = \sqrt{\dfrac{2}{1 - x}}$.

So $f^{-1}(x) = \sqrt{\dfrac{2}{1 - x}}$.

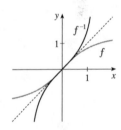

33. The function f is one-to-one, so its inverse exists and the graph of its inverse can be obtained by reflecting the graph of f about the line $y = x$.

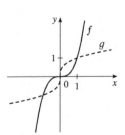

35. (a) $x_1 \neq x_2 \quad \Rightarrow \quad x_1^3 \neq x_2^3 \quad \Rightarrow \quad f(x_1) \neq f(x_2)$, so f is one-to-one.

(b) $f'(x) = 3x^2$ and $f(2) = 8 \quad \Rightarrow \quad g(8) = 2$, so $g'(8) = 1/f'(g(8)) = 1/f'(2) = \frac{1}{12}$.

(c) $y = x^3 \quad \Rightarrow \quad x = y^{1/3}$. Interchanging x and y gives $y = x^{1/3}$,

so $f^{-1}(x) = x^{1/3}$. Domain$(g) = $ range$(f) = \mathbb{R}$.

Range$(g) = $ domain$(f) = \mathbb{R}$.

(d) $g(x) = x^{1/3} \quad \Rightarrow \quad g'(x) = \frac{1}{3}x^{-2/3} \quad \Rightarrow \quad g'(8) = \frac{1}{3}\left(\frac{1}{4}\right) = \frac{1}{12}$

as in part (b).

(e)

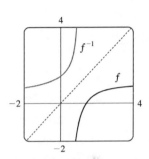

37. (a) Since $x \geq 0$, $x_1 \neq x_2 \quad \Rightarrow \quad x_1^2 \neq x_2^2 \quad \Rightarrow \quad 9 - x_1^2 \neq 9 - x_2^2 \quad \Rightarrow \quad f(x_1) \neq f(x_2)$, so f is 1-1.

(b) $f'(x) = -2x$ and $f(1) = 8 \quad \Rightarrow \quad g(8) = 1$, so $g'(8) = \dfrac{1}{f'(g(8))} = \dfrac{1}{f'(1)} = \dfrac{1}{(-2)} = -\dfrac{1}{2}$.

(c) $y = 9 - x^2 \Rightarrow x^2 = 9 - y \Rightarrow x = \sqrt{9 - y}$. Interchange x
and y: $y = \sqrt{9 - x}$, so $f^{-1}(x) = \sqrt{9 - x}$.

Domain $(g) =$ range $(f) = [0, 9]$.

Range $(g) =$ domain $(f) = [0, 3]$.

(d) $g'(x) = -1/(2\sqrt{9 - x}) \Rightarrow g'(8) = -\frac{1}{2}$ as in part (b).

(e)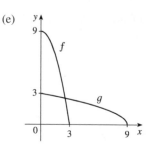

39. $f(0) = 1 \Rightarrow f^{-1}(1) = 0$, and $f(x) = x^3 + x + 1 \Rightarrow f'(x) = 3x^2 + 1$ and $f'(0) = 1$. Thus,
$(f^{-1})'(1) = \dfrac{1}{f'(f^{-1}(1))} = \dfrac{1}{f'(0)} = \dfrac{1}{1} = 1$.

41. $f(0) = 3 \Rightarrow f^{-1}(3) = 0$, and $f(x) = 3 + x^2 + \tan(\pi x/2) \Rightarrow f'(x) = 2x + \frac{\pi}{2}\sec^2(\pi x/2)$ and
$f'(0) = \frac{\pi}{2} \cdot 1 = \frac{\pi}{2}$. Thus, $(f^{-1})'(3) = 1/f'(f^{-1}(3)) = 1/f'(0) = 2/\pi$.

43. $f(4) = 5 \Rightarrow g(5) = 4$. Thus, $g'(5) = \dfrac{1}{f'(g(5))} = \dfrac{1}{f'(4)} = \dfrac{1}{2/3} = \dfrac{3}{2}$.

45. We see that the graph of $y = f(x) = \sqrt{x^3 + x^2 + x + 1}$ is increasing, so
f is 1-1. Enter $x = \sqrt{y^3 + y^2 + y + 1}$ and use your CAS to solve the
equation for y. Using Derive, we get two (irrelevant) solutions involving
imaginary expressions, as well as one which can be simplified to the
following:

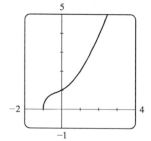

$$y = f^{-1}(x) = -\frac{\sqrt[3]{4}}{6}\left(\sqrt[3]{D - 27x^2 + 20} - \sqrt[3]{D + 27x^2 - 20} + \sqrt[3]{2}\right)$$

where $D = 3\sqrt{3}\sqrt{27x^4 - 40x^2 + 16}$. Maple and Mathematica each give two complex expressions and one real
expression, and the real expression is equivalent to that given by Derive. For example, Maple's expression simplifies
to $\dfrac{1}{6}\dfrac{M^{2/3} - 8 - 2M^{1/3}}{2M^{1/3}}$, where $M = 108x^2 + 12\sqrt{48 - 120x^2 + 81x^4} - 80$.

47. (a) If the point (x, y) is on the graph of $y = f(x)$, then the point $(x - c, y)$ is that point shifted c units to the left.
Since f is 1-1, the point (y, x) is on the graph of $y = f^{-1}(x)$ and the point corresponding to $(x - c, y)$ on the
graph of f is $(y, x - c)$ on the graph of f^{-1}. Thus, the curve's reflection is shifted *down* the same number of
units as the curve itself is shifted to the left. So an expression for the inverse function is $g^{-1}(x) = f^{-1}(x) - c$.

(b) If we compress (or stretch) a curve horizontally, the curve's reflection in the line $y = x$ is compressed (or
stretched) *vertically* by the same factor. Using this geometric principle, we see that the inverse of $h(x) = f(cx)$
can be expressed as $h^{-1}(x) = (1/c)\,f^{-1}(x)$.

7.2 Exponential Functions and Their Derivatives

1. (a) $f(x) = a^x$, $a > 0$ (b) $\mathbb{R}$

(c) $(0, \infty)$ (d) See Figures 6(c), 6(b), and 6(a), respectively.

3. All of these graphs approach 0 as $x \to -\infty$, all of them pass through the point $(0, 1)$, and all of them are increasing and approach ∞ as $x \to \infty$. The larger the base, the faster the function increases for $x > 0$, and the faster it approaches 0 as $x \to -\infty$.

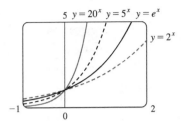

5. The functions with bases greater than 1 (3^x and 10^x) are increasing, while those with bases less than 1 $\left[\left(\frac{1}{3}\right)^x \text{ and } \left(\frac{1}{10}\right)^x\right]$ are decreasing. The graph of $\left(\frac{1}{3}\right)^x$ is the reflection of that of 3^x about the y-axis, and the graph of $\left(\frac{1}{10}\right)^x$ is the reflection of that of 10^x about the y-axis. The graph of 10^x increases more quickly than that of 3^x for $x > 0$, and approaches 0 faster as $x \to -\infty$.

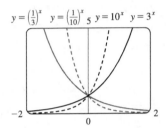

7. We start with the graph of $y = 4^x$ (Figure 3) and then shift 3 units downward. This shift doesn't affect the domain, but the range of $y = 4^x - 3$ is $(-3, \infty)$. There is a horizontal asymptote of $y = -3$.

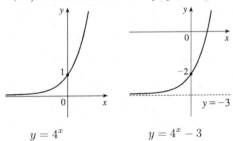

9. We start with the graph of $y = 2^x$ (Figure 3), reflect it about the y-axis, and then about the x-axis (or just rotate $180°$ to handle both reflections) to obtain the graph of $y = -2^{-x}$. In each graph, $y = 0$ is the horizontal asymptote.

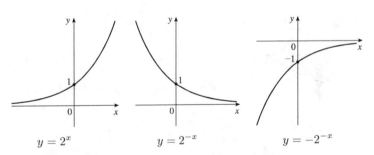

11. We start with the graph of $y = e^x$ (Figure 12), reflect it about the x-axis, and then shift 3 units upward. Note the horizontal asymptote of $y = 3$.

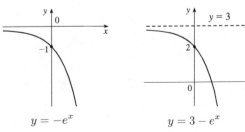

13. (a) To find the equation of the graph that results from shifting the graph of $y = e^x$ 2 units downward, we subtract 2 from the original function to get $y = e^x - 2$.

(b) To find the equation of the graph that results from shifting the graph of $y = e^x$ 2 units to the right, we replace x with $x - 2$ in the original function to get $y = e^{(x-2)}$.

(c) To find the equation of the graph that results from reflecting the graph of $y = e^x$ about the x-axis, we multiply the original function by -1 to get $y = -e^x$.

(d) To find the equation of the graph that results from reflecting the graph of $y = e^x$ about the y-axis, we replace x with $-x$ in the original function to get $y = e^{-x}$.

(e) To find the equation of the graph that results from reflecting the graph of $y = e^x$ about the x-axis and then about the y-axis, we first multiply the original function by -1 (to get $y = -e^x$) and then replace x with $-x$ in this equation to get $y = -e^{-x}$.

15. (a) The denominator $1 + e^x$ is never equal to zero because $e^x > 0$, so the domain of $f(x) = 1/(1 + e^x)$ is $\mathbb{R}$.

(b) $1 - e^x = 0 \iff e^x = 1 \iff x = 0$, so the domain of $f(x) = 1/(1 - e^x)$ is $(-\infty, 0) \cup (0, \infty)$.

17. Use $y = Ca^x$ with the points $(1, 6)$ and $(3, 24)$. $6 = Ca^1$ $\left[C = \frac{6}{a} \right]$ and $24 = Ca^3 \Rightarrow 24 = \left(\dfrac{6}{a} \right) a^3 \Rightarrow$ $4 = a^2 \Rightarrow a = 2$ [since $a > 0$] and $C = \frac{6}{2} = 3$. The function is $f(x) = 3 \cdot 2^x$.

19. 2 ft $= 24$ in, $f(24) = 24^2$ in $= 576$ in $= 48$ ft. $g(24) = 2^{24}$ in $= 2^{24}/(12 \cdot 5280)$ mi ≈ 265 mi

21. The graph of g finally surpasses that of f at $x \approx 35.8$.

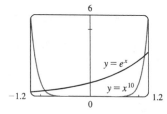
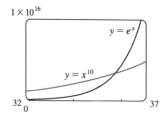

23. $\lim\limits_{x \to \infty} (1.001)^x = \infty$ by (3), since $1.001 > 1$.

25. Divide numerator and denominator by e^{3x}: $\lim\limits_{x \to \infty} \dfrac{e^{3x} - e^{-3x}}{e^{3x} + e^{-3x}} = \lim\limits_{x \to \infty} \dfrac{1 - e^{-6x}}{1 + e^{-6x}} = \dfrac{1 - 0}{1 + 0} = 1$

27. Let $t = 3/(2 - x)$. As $x \to 2^+$, $t \to -\infty$. So $\lim\limits_{x \to 2^+} e^{3/(2-x)} = \lim\limits_{t \to -\infty} e^t = 0$ by (11).

29. By the Product Rule, $f(x) = x^2 e^x \Rightarrow f'(x) = x^2 \dfrac{d}{dx}(e^x) + e^x \dfrac{d}{dx}(x^2) = x^2 e^x + e^x (2x) = xe^x(x + 2)$.

31. By (10), $y = e^{ax^3} \Rightarrow y' = e^{ax^3} \dfrac{d}{dx}(ax^3) = 3ax^2 e^{ax^3}$.

33. $f(u) = e^{1/u} \Rightarrow f'(u) = e^{1/u} \cdot \dfrac{d}{du}\left(\dfrac{1}{u} \right) = e^{1/u} \left(\dfrac{-1}{u^2} \right) = \left(\dfrac{-1}{u^2} \right) e^{1/u}$

35. By (10), $F(t) = e^{t \sin 2t} \Rightarrow$
$F'(t) = e^{t \sin 2t}(t \sin 2t)' = e^{t \sin 2t}(t \cdot 2\cos 2t + \sin 2t \cdot 1) = e^{t \sin 2t}(2t \cos 2t + \sin 2t)$

37. $y = \sqrt{1 + 2e^{3x}} \Rightarrow y' = \dfrac{1}{2}(1 + 2e^{3x})^{-1/2} \dfrac{d}{dx}(1 + 2e^{3x}) = \dfrac{1}{2\sqrt{1 + 2e^{3x}}}(2e^{3x} \cdot 3) = \dfrac{3e^{3x}}{\sqrt{1 + 2e^{3x}}}$

39. $y = e^{e^x} \Rightarrow y' = e^{e^x} \cdot \dfrac{d}{dx}(e^x) = e^{e^x} \cdot e^x$ or $e^{e^x + x}$

41. By the Quotient Rule, $y = \dfrac{ae^x + b}{ce^x + d}$ $\Rightarrow$

$$y' = \frac{(ce^x + d)(ae^x) - (ae^x + b)(ce^x)}{(ce^x + d)^2} = \frac{(ace^x + ad - ace^x - bc)e^x}{(ce^x + d)^2} = \frac{(ad - bc)e^x}{(ce^x + d)^2}.$$

43. $y = e^{2x}\cos\pi x$ $\Rightarrow$ $y' = e^{2x}(-\pi\sin\pi x) + (\cos\pi x)(2e^{2x}) = e^{2x}(2\cos\pi x - \pi\sin\pi x)$.

At $(0, 1)$, $y' = 1(2 - 0) = 2$, so an equation of the tangent line is $y - 1 = 2(x - 0)$, or $y = 2x + 1$.

45. $\dfrac{d}{dx}\left(e^{x^2 y}\right) = \dfrac{d}{dx}(x + y)$ $\Rightarrow$ $e^{x^2 y}(x^2 y' + y\cdot 2x) = 1 + y'$ $\Rightarrow$ $x^2 e^{x^2 y}y' + 2xye^{x^2 y} = 1 + y'$ $\Rightarrow$

$x^2 e^{x^2 y}y' - y' = 1 - 2xye^{x^2 y}$ $\Rightarrow$ $y'(x^2 e^{x^2 y} - 1) = 1 - 2xye^{x^2 y}$ $\Rightarrow$ $y' = \dfrac{1 - 2xye^{x^2 y}}{x^2 e^{x^2 y} - 1}$

47. $y = e^x + e^{-x/2}$ $\Rightarrow$ $y' = e^x - \tfrac{1}{2}e^{-x/2}$ $\Rightarrow$ $y'' = e^x + \tfrac{1}{4}e^{-x/2}$, so

$$2y'' - y' - y = 2\left(e^x + \tfrac{1}{4}e^{-x/2}\right) - \left(e^x - \tfrac{1}{2}e^{-x/2}\right) - \left(e^x + e^{-x/2}\right) = 0.$$

49. $y = e^{rx}$ $\Rightarrow$ $y' = re^{rx}$ $\Rightarrow$ $y'' = r^2 e^{rx}$, so if $y = e^{rx}$ satisfies the differential equation $y'' + 6y' + 8y = 0$,

then $r^2 e^{rx} + 6re^{rx} + 8e^{rx} = 0$; that is, $e^{rx}(r^2 + 6r + 8) = 0$. Since $e^{rx} > 0$ for all x, we must have

$r^2 + 6r + 8 = 0$, or $(r + 2)(r + 4) = 0$, so $r = -2$ or -4.

51. $f(x) = e^{2x}$ $\Rightarrow$ $f'(x) = 2e^{2x}$ $\Rightarrow$ $f''(x) = 2\cdot 2e^{2x} = 2^2 e^{2x}$ $\Rightarrow$

$f'''(x) = 2^2 \cdot 2e^{2x} = 2^3 e^{2x}$ $\Rightarrow$ $\cdots$ $\Rightarrow$ $f^{(n)}(x) = 2^n e^{2x}$

53. (a) $f(x) = e^x + x$ is continuous on $\mathbb{R}$ and $f(-1) = e^{-1} - 1 < 0 < 1 = f(0)$, so by the Intermediate Value

Theorem, $e^x + x = 0$ has a root in $(-1, 0)$.

(b) $f(x) = e^x + x$ $\Rightarrow$ $f'(x) = e^x + 1$, so $x_{n+1} = x_n - \dfrac{e^{x_n} + x_n}{e^{x_n} + 1}$. Using $x_1 = -0.5$, we get

$x_2 \approx -0.566311$, $x_3 \approx -0.567143 \approx x_4$, so the root is -0.567143 to six decimal places.

55. (a) $m(t) = 24 \cdot 2^{-t/25}$ $\Rightarrow$

$m(40) = 24 \cdot 2^{-40/25} \approx 7.92$ mg

(b) $m'(t) = 24 \dfrac{d}{dt}\left(2^{-t/25}\right)$

$\approx 24(0.69)2^{-t/25} \dfrac{d}{dt}\left(-\dfrac{t}{25}\right)$ [(7) and (10)]

$= 24(0.69)\left(-\tfrac{1}{25}\right) 2^{-t/25}$

so $m'(40) \approx -\tfrac{24}{25}(0.69)2^{-40/25} \approx -0.22$ mg/yr.

(c)

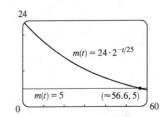

From the graph, we can determine that

$m(t) = 5$ $\Rightarrow$ $t \approx 56.6$ yr.

57. (a) $\displaystyle\lim_{t\to\infty} p(t) = \lim_{t\to\infty} \frac{1}{1 + ae^{-kt}} = \frac{1}{1 + a\cdot 0} = 1$, since $k > 0$ $\Rightarrow$ $-kt \to -\infty$ $\Rightarrow$ $e^{-kt} \to 0$.

(b) $p(t) = \left(1 + ae^{-kt}\right)^{-1}$ $\Rightarrow$ $\dfrac{dp}{dt} = -\left(1 + ae^{-kt}\right)^{-2}\left(-kae^{-kt}\right) = \dfrac{kae^{-kt}}{\left(1 + ae^{-kt}\right)^2}$

(c)

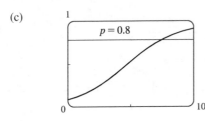

From the graph of $p(t) = \left(1 + 10e^{-0.5t}\right)^{-1}$, it seems that

$p(t) = 0.8$ (indicating that 80% of the population has heard the

rumor) when $t \approx 7.4$ hours.

59. (a) Using a calculator or CAS, we obtain the model $Q = ab^t$ with $a = 100.0124369$ and $b = 0.000045145933$.

We can change this model to one with base e and exponent $\ln b$ [$b^t = e^{t \ln b}$ from precalculus mathematics or

from Section 7.3]: $Q = ae^{t \ln b} = 100.012437e^{-10.005531t}$.

(b) Use $Q'(t) = ab^t \ln b$ or the calculator command $\texttt{nDeriv(Y}_1\texttt{,X,.04)}$ with $\texttt{Y}_1\texttt{=ab}^x$ to get

$Q'(0.04) \approx -670.63 \ \mu\text{A}$. The result of Example 2 in Section 2.1 was $-670 \ \mu\text{A}$.

61. $f(x) = x - e^x \ \Rightarrow \ f'(x) = 1 - e^x = 0 \ \Leftrightarrow \ e^x = 1 \ \Leftrightarrow \ x = 0$. Now $f'(x) > 0$ for all $x < 0$ and

$f'(x) < 0$ for all $x > 0$, so the absolute maximum value is $f(0) = 0 - 1 = -1$.

63. (a) $f(x) = xe^x \ \Rightarrow \ f'(x) = e^x + xe^x = e^x(1+x) > 0 \ \Leftrightarrow \ 1 + x > 0 \ \Leftrightarrow \ x > -1$, so f is increasing on
$(-1, \infty)$ and decreasing on $(-\infty, -1)$.

(b) $f''(x) = e^x(1+x) + e^x = e^x(2+x) > 0 \ \Leftrightarrow \ 2 + x > 0 \ \Leftrightarrow \ x > -2$, so f is CU on $(-2, \infty)$ and
CD on $(-\infty, -2)$.

(c) f has an inflection point at $\left(-2, -2e^{-2}\right)$.

65. $y = f(x) = e^{-1/(x+1)}$ **A.** $D = \{x \mid x \neq -1\} = (-\infty, -1) \cup (-1, \infty)$ **B.** No x-intercept;

y-intercept $= f(0) = e^{-1}$ **C.** No symmetry   **D.** $\displaystyle\lim_{x \to \pm\infty} e^{-1/(x+1)} = 1$ since $-1/(x+1) \to 0$, so $y = 1$ is

a HA. $\displaystyle\lim_{x \to -1^+} e^{-1/(x+1)} = 0$ since $-1/(x+1) \to -\infty$, $\displaystyle\lim_{x \to -1^-} e^{-1/(x+1)} = \infty$ since $-1/(x+1) \to \infty$, so

$x = -1$ is a VA.   **E.** $f'(x) = e^{-1/(x+1)}/(x+1)^2 \ \Rightarrow \ f'(x) > 0$ for all x except 1, so

f is increasing on $(-\infty, -1)$ and $(-1, \infty)$.   **F.** No extreme values   **H.**

G. $f''(x) = \dfrac{e^{-1/(x+1)}}{(x+1)^4} + \dfrac{e^{-1/(x+1)}(-2)}{(x+1)^3} = -\dfrac{e^{-1/(x+1)}(2x+1)}{(x+1)^4}$

$\Rightarrow \ f''(x) > 0 \ \Leftrightarrow \ 2x + 1 < 0 \ \Leftrightarrow \ x < -\frac{1}{2}$, so f is CU on

$(-\infty, -1)$ and $\left(-1, -\frac{1}{2}\right)$, and CD on $\left(-\frac{1}{2}, \infty\right)$. f has an IP

at $\left(-\frac{1}{2}, e^{-2}\right)$.

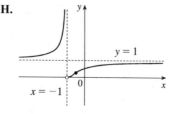

67. $y = f(x) = e^{3x} + e^{-2x}$ **A.** $D = \mathbb{R}$ **B.** y-intercept $= f(0) = 2$;   **H.**

no x-intercept   **C.** No symmetry   **D.** No asymptotes

E. $f'(x) = 3e^{3x} - 2e^{-2x}$, so $f'(x) > 0 \ \Leftrightarrow \ 3e^{3x} > 2e^{-2x}$

[multiply by e^{2x}] $\ \Leftrightarrow \ e^{5x} > \frac{2}{3}$ $(*)$ $\ \Leftrightarrow \ 5x > \ln\frac{2}{3} \ \Leftrightarrow$

$x > \frac{1}{5}\ln\frac{2}{3} \approx -0.081$. Similarly, $f'(x) < 0 \ \Leftrightarrow \ x < \frac{1}{5}\ln\frac{2}{3}$.

f is decreasing on $\left(-\infty, \frac{1}{5}\ln\frac{2}{3}\right)$ and increasing on $\left(\frac{1}{5}\ln\frac{2}{3}, \infty\right)$.

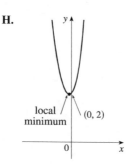

F. Local minimum value $f\left(\frac{1}{5}\ln\frac{2}{3}\right) = \left(\frac{2}{3}\right)^{3/5} + \left(\frac{2}{3}\right)^{-2/5} \approx 1.96$; no local maximum.

G. $f''(x) = 9e^{3x} + 4e^{-2x}$, so $f''(x) > 0$ for all x, and f is CU on $(-\infty, \infty)$. No IP

$(*)$ If you have not yet learned about logarithms, graph $y = e^{5x}$ and $y = \frac{2}{3}$, find the point of intersection, and use

decimal approximations for the rest of the solution.

69. $f(x) = e^{x^3 - x} \to 0$ as $x \to -\infty$, and $f(x) \to \infty$ as $x \to \infty$. From the graph, it appears that f has a local minimum of about $f(0.58) = 0.68$, and a local maximum of about $f(-0.58) = 1.47$. To find the exact values, we calculate

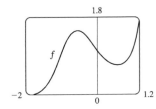 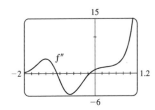

$f'(x) = (3x^2 - 1)e^{x^3 - x}$, which is 0 when $3x^2 - 1 = 0 \iff x = \pm\frac{1}{\sqrt{3}}$. The negative root corresponds to the local maximum $f\left(-\frac{1}{\sqrt{3}}\right) = e^{(-1/\sqrt{3})^3 - (-1/\sqrt{3})} = e^{2\sqrt{3}/9}$, and the positive root corresponds to the local minimum $f\left(\frac{1}{\sqrt{3}}\right) = e^{(1/\sqrt{3})^3 - (1/\sqrt{3})} = e^{-2\sqrt{3}/9}$. To estimate the inflection points, we calculate and graph

$$f''(x) = \frac{d}{dx}\left[(3x^2 - 1)e^{x^3 - x}\right] = (3x^2 - 1)e^{x^3 - x}(3x^2 - 1) + e^{x^3 - x}(6x) = e^{x^3 - x}(9x^4 - 6x^2 + 6x + 1).$$

From the graph, it appears that $f''(x)$ changes sign (and thus f has inflection points) at $x \approx -0.15$ and $x \approx -1.09$. From the graph of f, we see that these x-values correspond to inflection points at about $(-0.15, 1.15)$ and $(-1.09, 0.82)$.

71. Let $u = -3x$. Then $du = -3\,dx$, so

$\int_0^5 e^{-3x}\,dx = -\frac{1}{3}\int_0^{-15} e^u\,du = -\frac{1}{3}[e^u]_0^{-15} = -\frac{1}{3}\left(e^{-15} - e^0\right) = \frac{1}{3}\left(1 - e^{-15}\right)$.

73. Let $u = 1 + e^x$. Then $du = e^x\,dx$, so $\int e^x\sqrt{1 + e^x}\,dx = \int \sqrt{u}\,du = \frac{2}{3}u^{3/2} + C = \frac{2}{3}(1 + e^x)^{3/2} + C$.

75. $\int \frac{e^x + 1}{e^x}\,dx = \int (1 + e^{-x})\,dx = x - e^{-x} + C$

77. Let $u = \sqrt{x}$. Then $du = \frac{1}{2\sqrt{x}}\,dx$, so $\int \frac{e^{\sqrt{x}}}{\sqrt{x}}\,dx = 2\int e^u\,du = 2e^u + C = 2e^{\sqrt{x}} + C$.

79. Area $= \int_0^1 (e^{3x} - e^x)\,dx = \left[\frac{1}{3}e^{3x} - e^x\right]_0^1 = \left(\frac{1}{3}e^3 - e\right) - \left(\frac{1}{3} - 1\right) = \frac{1}{3}e^3 - e + \frac{2}{3} \approx 4.644$

81. $V = \int_0^1 \pi(e^x)^2\,dx = \pi\int_0^1 e^{2x}\,dx = \frac{1}{2}\pi[e^{2x}]_0^1 = \frac{\pi}{2}(e^2 - 1)$

83. We use Theorem 7.1.7. Note that $f(0) = 3 + 0 + e^0 = 4$, so $f^{-1}(4) = 0$. Also $f'(x) = 1 + e^x$. Therefore,

$$\left(f^{-1}\right)'(4) = \frac{1}{f'(f^{-1}(4))} = \frac{1}{f'(0)} = \frac{1}{1 + e^0} = \frac{1}{2}.$$

85. (a) Let $f(x) = e^x - 1 - x$. Now $f(0) = e^0 - 1 = 0$, and for $x \geq 0$, we have $f'(x) = e^x - 1 \geq 0$. Now, since $f(0) = 0$ and f is increasing on $[0, \infty)$, $f(x) \geq 0$ for $x \geq 0 \implies e^x - 1 - x \geq 0 \implies e^x \geq 1 + x$.

(b) For $0 \leq x \leq 1$, $x^2 \leq x$, so $e^{x^2} \leq e^x$ [since e^x is increasing]. Hence [from (a)] $1 + x^2 \leq e^{x^2} \leq e^x$. So $\frac{4}{3} = \int_0^1 (1 + x^2)\,dx \leq \int_0^1 e^{x^2}\,dx \leq \int_0^1 e^x\,dx = e - 1 < e \implies \frac{4}{3} \leq \int_0^1 e^{x^2}\,dx \leq e$.

87. (a) By Exercise 85(a), the result holds for $n = 1$. Suppose that $e^x \geq 1 + x + \dfrac{x^2}{2!} + \cdots + \dfrac{x^k}{k!}$ for $x \geq 0$.

Let $f(x) = e^x - 1 - x - \dfrac{x^2}{2!} - \cdots - \dfrac{x^k}{k!} - \dfrac{x^{k+1}}{(k+1)!}$. Then $f'(x) = e^x - 1 - x - \cdots - \dfrac{x^k}{k!} \geq 0$

by assumption. Hence $f(x)$ is increasing on $(0, \infty)$. So $0 \leq x$ implies that

$$0 = f(0) \leq f(x) = e^x - 1 - x - \cdots - \frac{x^k}{k!} - \frac{x^{k+1}}{(k+1)!}, \text{ and hence } e^x \geq 1 + x + \cdots + \frac{x^k}{k!} + \frac{x^{k+1}}{(k+1)!}$$

for $x \geq 0$. Therefore, for $x \geq 0$, $e^x \geq 1 + x + \dfrac{x^2}{2!} + \cdots + \dfrac{x^n}{n!}$ for every positive integer n, by mathematical induction.

(b) Taking $n = 4$ and $x = 1$ in (a), we have $e = e^1 \geq 1 + \frac{1}{2} + \frac{1}{6} + \frac{1}{24} = 2.708\overline{3} > 2.7$.

(c) $e^x \geq 1 + x + \cdots + \dfrac{x^k}{k!} + \dfrac{x^{k+1}}{(k+1)!} \quad \Rightarrow \quad \dfrac{e^x}{x^k} \geq \dfrac{1}{x^k} + \dfrac{1}{x^{k-1}} + \cdots + \dfrac{1}{k!} + \dfrac{x}{(k+1)!} \geq \dfrac{x}{(k+1)!}$.

But $\lim\limits_{x \to \infty} \dfrac{x}{(k+1)!} = \infty$, so $\lim\limits_{x \to \infty} \dfrac{e^x}{x^k} = \infty$.

7.3 Logarithmic Functions

1. (a) It is defined as the inverse of the exponential function with base a, that is, $\log_a x = y \iff a^y = x$.

(b) $(0, \infty)$ (c) $\mathbb{R}$ (d) See Figure 1.

3. (a) $\log_{10} 1000 = 3$ because $10^3 = 1000$. *Or:* $\log_{10} 1000 = \log_{10} 10^3 = 3$ by (2).

(b) $\log_{16} 4 = \frac{1}{2}$ because $16^{1/2} = 4$. *Or:* $\log_{16} 4 = \log_{16} 16^{1/2} = \frac{1}{2}$ by (2).

5. (a) $\log_5 \frac{1}{25} = \log_5 5^{-2} = -2$ by (2).   (b) $e^{\ln 15} = 15$ by (6).

7. (a) $\log_{12} 3 + \log_{12} 48 = \log_{12}(3 \cdot 48) = \log_{12} 144 = 2$ since $12^2 = 144$.

(b) $\log_2 5 - \log_2 90 + 2\log_2 3 = \log_2 5 + \log_2 3^2 - \log_2 90 = \log_2(5 \cdot 9) - \log_2 90$

$$= \log_2\left(\tfrac{45}{90}\right) = \log_2\left(\tfrac{1}{2}\right) = -1 \text{ since } 2^{-1} = \tfrac{1}{2}.$$

9. $\log_2\left(\dfrac{x^3 y}{z^2}\right) = \log_2(x^3 y) - \log_2 z^2 = \log_2 x^3 + \log_2 y - \log_2 z^2 = 3\log_2 x + \log_2 y - 2\log_2 z$

(assuming that the variables are positive)

11. $\ln(uv)^{10} = 10\ln(uv) = 10(\ln u + \ln v) = 10\ln u + 10\ln v$

13. $\log_{10} a - \log_{10} b + \log_{10} c = \log_{10} \dfrac{a}{b} + \log_{10} c = \log_{10}\left(\dfrac{a}{b} \cdot c\right) = \log_{10} \dfrac{ac}{b}$

15. $2\ln 4 - \ln 2 = \ln 4^2 - \ln 2 = \ln 16 - \ln 2 = \ln \frac{16}{2} = \ln 8$

17. $\frac{1}{2}\ln x - 5\ln(x^2 + 1) = \ln x^{1/2} - \ln(x^2 + 1)^5 = \ln \dfrac{\sqrt{x}}{(x^2 + 1)^5}$

19. (a) $\log_{12} e = \dfrac{\ln e}{\ln 12} = \dfrac{1}{\ln 12} \approx 0.402430$ (b) $\log_6 13.54 = \dfrac{\ln 13.54}{\ln 6} \approx 1.454240$

(c) $\log_2 \pi = \dfrac{\ln \pi}{\ln 2} \approx 1.651496$

21. To graph these functions, we use $\log_{1.5} x = \dfrac{\ln x}{\ln 1.5}$ and

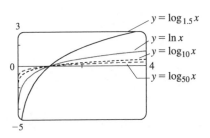

$\log_{50} x = \dfrac{\ln x}{\ln 50}$. These graphs all approach $-\infty$ as $x \to 0^+$, and they all pass through the point $(1, 0)$. Also, they are all increasing, and all approach ∞ as $x \to \infty$. The functions with larger bases increase extremely slowly, and the ones with smaller bases do so somewhat more quickly. The functions with large bases approach the y-axis more closely as $x \to 0^+$.

23. Shift the graph of $y = \log_{10} x$ five units to the left to obtain the graph of $y = \log_{10}(x + 5)$. Note the vertical asymptote of $x = -5$.

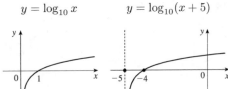

25. Reflect the graph of $y = \ln x$ about the x-axis to obtain the graph of $y = -\ln x$.

$$y = \ln x \qquad\qquad y = -\ln x$$

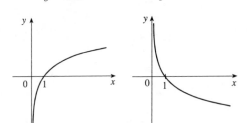

27. $y = 5 + \ln(x - 2)$: Start with the graph of $y = \ln x$, shift 2 units to the right and then shift 5 units upward.

$$y = \ln x \qquad\qquad y = \ln(x - 2) \qquad\qquad y = 5 + \ln(x - 2)$$

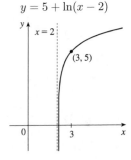

29. (a) $2 \ln x = 1 \;\Rightarrow\; \ln x = \tfrac{1}{2} \;\Rightarrow\; x = e^{1/2} = \sqrt{e}$

(b) $e^{-x} = 5 \;\Rightarrow\; -x = \ln 5 \;\Rightarrow\; x = -\ln 5$

31. (a) $5^{x-3} = 10 \;\Leftrightarrow\; \log_{10} 5^{x-3} = \log_{10} 10 \;\Leftrightarrow\; (x - 3) \log_{10} 5 = 1 \;\Leftrightarrow\; x - 3 = 1/\log_{10} 5 \;\Leftrightarrow\;$
$x = 3 + 1/\log_{10} 5$

(b) $\log_{10}(x + 1) = 4 \;\Leftrightarrow\; x + 1 = 10^4 \;\Leftrightarrow\; x = 10{,}000 - 1 = 9999$

33. $\ln(\ln x) = 1 \;\Leftrightarrow\; e^{\ln(\ln x)} = e^1 \;\Leftrightarrow\; \ln x = e^1 = e \;\Leftrightarrow\; e^{\ln x} = e^e \;\Leftrightarrow\; x = e^e$

35. $2 \ln x = \ln 2 + \ln(3x - 4) \;\Rightarrow\; \ln x^2 = \ln\left[2(3x - 4)\right] \;\Rightarrow\; \ln x^2 = \ln(6x - 8) \;\Rightarrow\; x^2 = 6x - 8 \;\Rightarrow\;$
$x^2 - 6x + 8 = 0 \;\Rightarrow\; (x - 2)(x - 4) = 0 \;\Rightarrow\; x = 2 \text{ or } x = 4$, both are valid solutions.

37. $e^{ax} = Ce^{bx} \;\Leftrightarrow\; \ln e^{ax} = \ln[C(e^{bx})] \;\Leftrightarrow\; ax = \ln C + bx + \ln e^{bx} \;\Leftrightarrow\; ax = \ln C + bx \;\Leftrightarrow\;$
$ax - bx = \ln C \;\Leftrightarrow\; (a - b)x = \ln C \;\Leftrightarrow\; x = \dfrac{\ln C}{a - b}$

39. $e^{2+5x} = 100 \quad\Rightarrow\quad \ln\left(e^{2+5x}\right) = \ln 100 \quad\Rightarrow\quad 2 + 5x = \ln 100 \quad\Rightarrow\quad 5x = \ln 100 - 2 \quad\Rightarrow$
$x = \frac{1}{5}(\ln 100 - 2) \approx 0.5210$

41. $\ln(e^x - 2) = 3 \quad\Rightarrow\quad e^x - 2 = e^3 \quad\Rightarrow\quad e^x = e^3 + 2 \quad\Rightarrow\quad x = \ln(e^3 + 2) \approx 3.0949$

43. (a) $e^x < 10 \quad\Rightarrow\quad \ln e^x < \ln 10 \quad\Rightarrow\quad x < \ln 10 \quad\Rightarrow\quad x \in (-\infty, \ln 10)$

(b) $\ln x > -1 \quad\Rightarrow\quad e^{\ln x} > e^{-1} \quad\Rightarrow\quad x > e^{-1} \quad\Rightarrow\quad x \in (1/e, \infty)$

45. 3 ft $= 36$ in, so we need x such that $\log_2 x = 36 \quad\Leftrightarrow\quad x = 2^{36} = 68{,}719{,}476{,}736$. In miles, this is
$68{,}719{,}476{,}736 \text{ in} \cdot \dfrac{1 \text{ ft}}{12 \text{ in}} \cdot \dfrac{1 \text{ mi}}{5280 \text{ ft}} \approx 1{,}084{,}587.7 \text{ mi.}$

47. If I is the intensity of the 1989 San Francisco earthquake, then $\log_{10}(I/S) = 7.1 \quad\Rightarrow$
$\log_{10}(16I/S) = \log_{10} 16 + \log_{10}(I/S) = \log_{10} 16 + 7.1 \approx 8.3.$

49. (a) $n = 100 \cdot 2^{t/3} \quad\Rightarrow\quad \dfrac{n}{100} = 2^{t/3} \quad\Rightarrow\quad \log_2\left(\dfrac{n}{100}\right) = \dfrac{t}{3} \quad\Rightarrow\quad t = 3\log_2\left(\dfrac{n}{100}\right)$. Using formula (7), we
can write this as $t = 3 \cdot \dfrac{\ln(n/100)}{\ln 2}$. This function tells us how long it will take to obtain n bacteria (given the number n).

(b) $n = 50{,}000 \quad\Rightarrow\quad t = 3\log_2 \dfrac{50{,}000}{100} = 3\log_2 500 = 3\left(\dfrac{\ln 500}{\ln 2}\right) \approx 26.9$ hours

51. Let $t = 2 - x$. As $x \to 2^-$, $t \to 0^+$. $\displaystyle\lim_{x \to 2^-} \ln(2 - x) = \lim_{t \to 0^+} \ln t = -\infty$ by (8).

53. $\displaystyle\lim_{x \to 0} \ln(\cos x) = \ln 1 = 0.$ [$\ln(\cos x)$ is continuous at $x = 0$ since it is the composite of two continuous functions.]

55. $\displaystyle\lim_{x \to \infty} \left[\ln(1 + x^2) - \ln(1 + x)\right] = \lim_{x \to \infty} \ln \dfrac{1 + x^2}{1 + x} = \ln\left(\lim_{x \to \infty} \dfrac{1 + x^2}{1 + x}\right) = \ln\left(\lim_{x \to \infty} \dfrac{\frac{1}{x} + x}{\frac{1}{x} + 1}\right) = \infty$, since the
limit in parentheses is ∞.

57. The domain of $f(x) = \log_2(5x - 3)$ is $\{x \mid 5x - 3 > 0\} = \{x \mid x > \frac{3}{5}\} = \left(\frac{3}{5}, \infty\right)$. Since $5x - 3$ takes on all positive values for x in $\left(\frac{3}{5}, \infty\right)$, the range of f is $\mathbb{R}$.

59. (a) For $f(x) = \sqrt{3 - e^{2x}}$, we must have $3 - e^{2x} \geq 0 \quad\Rightarrow\quad e^{2x} \leq 3 \quad\Rightarrow\quad 2x \leq \ln 3 \quad\Rightarrow\quad x \leq \frac{1}{2}\ln 3$.
Thus, the domain of f is $(-\infty, \frac{1}{2}\ln 3]$.

(b) $y = f(x) = \sqrt{3 - e^{2x}}$ [note that $y \geq 0$] $\quad\Rightarrow\quad y^2 = 3 - e^{2x} \quad\Rightarrow\quad e^{2x} = 3 - y^2 \quad\Rightarrow\quad 2x = \ln(3 - y^2)$
$\quad\Rightarrow\quad x = \frac{1}{2}\ln(3 - y^2)$. Interchange x and y: $y = \frac{1}{2}\ln(3 - x^2)$. So $f^{-1}(x) = \frac{1}{2}\ln(3 - x^2)$. For the domain of
f^{-1}, we must have $3 - x^2 > 0 \quad\Rightarrow\quad x^2 < 3 \quad\Rightarrow\quad |x| < \sqrt{3} \quad\Rightarrow\quad -\sqrt{3} < x < \sqrt{3} \quad\Rightarrow\quad 0 \leq x < \sqrt{3}$
since $x \geq 0$. Note that the domain of f^{-1}, $[0, \sqrt{3})$, equals the range of f.

61. $y = \ln(x + 3) \quad\Rightarrow\quad e^y = e^{\ln(x+3)} = x + 3 \quad\Rightarrow\quad x = e^y - 3$.
Interchange x and y: the inverse function is $y = e^x - 3$.

63. $f(x) = e^{x^3} \quad\Rightarrow\quad y = e^{x^3} \quad\Rightarrow\quad \ln y = x^3 \quad\Rightarrow\quad x = \sqrt[3]{\ln y}$. Interchange x and y: $y = \sqrt[3]{\ln x}$.
So $f^{-1}(x) = \sqrt[3]{\ln x}$.

65. $y = \dfrac{10^x}{10^x + 1} \quad\Rightarrow\quad 10^x y + y = 10^x \quad\Rightarrow\quad 10^x(1 - y) = y \quad\Rightarrow\quad 10^x = \dfrac{y}{1 - y} \quad\Rightarrow\quad x = \log_{10}\left(\dfrac{y}{1 - y}\right)$.

Interchange x and y: $y = \log_{10}\left(\dfrac{x}{1 - x}\right)$ is the inverse function.

67. $f(x) = e^{3x} - e^x \Rightarrow f'(x) = 3e^{3x} - e^x$. Thus, $f'(x) > 0 \Leftrightarrow 3e^{3x} > e^x \Leftrightarrow \dfrac{3e^{3x}}{e^x} > \dfrac{e^x}{e^x} \Leftrightarrow$

$3e^{2x} > 1 \Leftrightarrow e^{2x} > \frac{1}{3} \Leftrightarrow 2x > \ln\left(\frac{1}{3}\right) = -\ln 3 \Leftrightarrow x > -\frac{1}{2}\ln 3$, so f is increasing on $\left(-\frac{1}{2}\ln 3, \infty\right)$.

69. (a) We have to show that $-f(x) = f(-x)$.

$$-f(x) = -\ln\left(x + \sqrt{x^2 + 1}\right) = \ln\left(\left(x + \sqrt{x^2 + 1}\right)^{-1}\right) = \ln\dfrac{1}{x + \sqrt{x^2 + 1}}$$

$$= \ln\left(\dfrac{1}{x + \sqrt{x^2 + 1}} \cdot \dfrac{x - \sqrt{x^2 + 1}}{x - \sqrt{x^2 + 1}}\right) = \ln\dfrac{x - \sqrt{x^2 + 1}}{x^2 - x^2 - 1}$$

$$= \ln\left(\sqrt{x^2 + 1} - x\right) = f(-x)$$

Thus, f is an odd function.

(b) Let $y = \ln\left(x + \sqrt{x^2 + 1}\right)$. Then $e^y = x + \sqrt{x^2 + 1} \Leftrightarrow (e^y - x)^2 = x^2 + 1 \Leftrightarrow$

$e^{2y} - 2xe^y + x^2 = x^2 + 1 \Leftrightarrow 2xe^y = e^{2y} - 1 \Leftrightarrow x = \dfrac{e^{2y} - 1}{2e^y} = \frac{1}{2}(e^y - e^{-y})$. Thus, the inverse

function is $f^{-1}(x) = \frac{1}{2}(e^x - e^{-x})$.

71. $x^{1/\ln x} = 2 \Rightarrow \ln(x^{1/\ln x}) = \ln(2) \Rightarrow \dfrac{1}{\ln x} \cdot \ln x = \ln 2 \Rightarrow 1 = \ln 2$, a contradiction, so the given

equation has no solution. The function $f(x) = x^{1/\ln x} = (e^{\ln x})^{1/\ln x} = e^1 = e$ for all $x > 0$, so the function

$f(x) = x^{1/\ln x}$ is the constant function $f(x) = e$.

73. (a) Let $\varepsilon > 0$ be given. We need N such that $|a^x - 0| < \varepsilon$ when $x < N$. But $a^x < \varepsilon \Leftrightarrow x < \log_a \varepsilon$.

Let $N = \log_a \varepsilon$. Then $x < N \Rightarrow x < \log_a \varepsilon \Rightarrow |a^x - 0| = a^x < \varepsilon$, so $\lim\limits_{x \to -\infty} a^x = 0$.

(b) Let $M > 0$ be given. We need N such that $a^x > M$ when $x > N$. But $a^x > M \Leftrightarrow x > \log_a M$.

Let $N = \log_a M$. Then $x > N \Rightarrow x > \log_a M \Rightarrow a^x > M$, so $\lim\limits_{x \to \infty} a^x = \infty$.

75. $\ln(x^2 - 2x - 2) \leq 0 \Rightarrow 0 < x^2 - 2x - 2 \leq 1$. Now $x^2 - 2x - 2 \leq 1$ gives $x^2 - 2x - 3 \leq 0$ and hence

$(x - 3)(x + 1) \leq 0$. So $-1 \leq x \leq 3$. Now $0 < x^2 - 2x - 2 \Rightarrow x < 1 - \sqrt{3}$ or $x > 1 + \sqrt{3}$. Therefore,

$\ln(x^2 - 2x - 2) \leq 0 \Leftrightarrow -1 \leq x < 1 - \sqrt{3}$ or $1 + \sqrt{3} < x \leq 3$.

7.4 Derivatives of Logarithmic Functions

1. The differentiation formula for logarithmic functions, $\dfrac{d}{dx}(\log_a x) = \dfrac{1}{x \ln a}$, is simplest when $a = e$ because

$\ln e = 1$.

3. $f(\theta) = \ln(\cos\theta) \Rightarrow f'(\theta) = \dfrac{1}{\cos\theta}\dfrac{d}{d\theta}(\cos\theta) = \dfrac{-\sin\theta}{\cos\theta} = -\tan\theta$

5. $f(x) = \log_2(1 - 3x) \Rightarrow f'(x) = \dfrac{1}{(1 - 3x)\ln 2}\dfrac{d}{dx}(1 - 3x) = \dfrac{-3}{(1 - 3x)\ln 2}$ or $\dfrac{3}{(3x - 1)\ln 2}$

7. $f(x) = \sqrt[5]{\ln x} = (\ln x)^{1/5} \Rightarrow f'(x) = \frac{1}{5}(\ln x)^{-4/5}\dfrac{d}{dx}(\ln x) = \dfrac{1}{5(\ln x)^{4/5}} \cdot \dfrac{1}{x} = \dfrac{1}{5x\sqrt[5]{(\ln x)^4}}$

9. $f(x) = \sqrt{x}\ln x \Rightarrow f'(x) = \sqrt{x}\left(\dfrac{1}{x}\right) + (\ln x) \cdot \dfrac{1}{2\sqrt{x}} = \dfrac{1}{\sqrt{x}} + \dfrac{\ln x}{2\sqrt{x}} = \dfrac{2 + \ln x}{2\sqrt{x}}$

34

11. $F(t) = \ln\dfrac{(2t+1)^3}{(3t-1)^4} = \ln(2t+1)^3 - \ln(3t-1)^4 = 3\ln(2t+1) - 4\ln(3t-1) \quad \Rightarrow$

$F'(t) = 3 \cdot \dfrac{1}{2t+1} \cdot 2 - 4 \cdot \dfrac{1}{3t-1} \cdot 3 = \dfrac{6}{2t+1} - \dfrac{12}{3t-1}$, or combined, $\dfrac{-6(t+3)}{(2t+1)(3t-1)}$.

13. $g(x) = \ln\dfrac{a-x}{a+x} = \ln(a-x) - \ln(a+x) \quad \Rightarrow$

$g'(x) = \dfrac{1}{a-x}(-1) - \dfrac{1}{a+x} = \dfrac{-(a+x) - (a-x)}{(a-x)(a+x)} = \dfrac{-2a}{a^2 - x^2}$

15. $f(u) = \dfrac{\ln u}{1 + \ln(2u)} \quad \Rightarrow$

$f'(u) = \dfrac{[1 + \ln(2u)] \cdot \frac{1}{u} - \ln u \cdot \frac{1}{2u} \cdot 2}{[1 + \ln(2u)]^2} = \dfrac{\frac{1}{u}[1 + \ln(2u) - \ln u]}{[1 + \ln(2u)]^2}$

$= \dfrac{1 + (\ln 2 + \ln u) - \ln u}{u\,[1 + \ln(2u)]^2} = \dfrac{1 + \ln 2}{u\,[1 + \ln(2u)]^2}$

17. $h(t) = t^3 - 3^t \quad \Rightarrow \quad h'(t) = 3t^2 - 3^t \ln 3$

19. $y = \ln\left|2 - x - 5x^2\right| \quad \Rightarrow \quad y' = \dfrac{1}{2 - x - 5x^2} \cdot (-1 - 10x) = \dfrac{-10x - 1}{2 - x - 5x^2} \quad \text{or} \quad \dfrac{10x + 1}{5x^2 + x - 2}$

21. $y = \ln\left(e^{-x} + xe^{-x}\right) = \ln\left(e^{-x}(1 + x)\right) = \ln\left(e^{-x}\right) + \ln(1 + x) = -x + \ln(1 + x) \quad \Rightarrow$

$y' = -1 + \dfrac{1}{1 + x} = \dfrac{-1 - x + 1}{1 + x} = -\dfrac{x}{1 + x}$

23. Using Formula 7 and the Chain Rule, $y = 5^{-1/x} \quad \Rightarrow \quad y' = 5^{-1/x}(\ln 5)\left[-1 \cdot \left(-x^{-2}\right)\right] = 5^{-1/x}(\ln 5)/x^2$

25. $y = x\ln x \quad \Rightarrow \quad y' = x(1/x) + (\ln x) \cdot 1 = 1 + \ln x \quad \Rightarrow \quad y'' = 1/x$

27. $y = \log_{10} x \quad \Rightarrow \quad y' = \dfrac{1}{x\ln 10} = \dfrac{1}{\ln 10}\left(\dfrac{1}{x}\right) \quad \Rightarrow \quad y'' = \dfrac{1}{\ln 10}\left(-\dfrac{1}{x^2}\right) = -\dfrac{1}{x^2 \ln 10}$

29. $f(x) = \dfrac{x}{1 - \ln(x - 1)} \quad \Rightarrow$

$f'(x) = \dfrac{[1 - \ln(x-1)] \cdot 1 - x \cdot \frac{-1}{x-1}}{[1 - \ln(x-1)]^2} = \dfrac{\frac{(x-1)[1 - \ln(x-1)] + x}{x-1}}{[1 - \ln(x-1)]^2} = \dfrac{x - 1 - (x-1)\ln(x-1) + x}{(x-1)[1 - \ln(x-1)]^2}$

$= \dfrac{2x - 1 - (x-1)\ln(x-1)}{(x-1)[1 - \ln(x-1)]^2}$

$\text{Dom}(f) = \{x \mid x - 1 > 0 \quad \text{and} \quad 1 - \ln(x-1) \neq 0\} = \{x \mid x > 1 \quad \text{and} \quad \ln(x-1) \neq 1\}$

$= \{x \mid x > 1 \quad \text{and} \quad x - 1 \neq e^1\} = \{x \mid x > 1 \quad \text{and} \quad x \neq 1 + e\} = (1, 1 + e) \cup (1 + e, \infty)$

31. $f(x) = x^2 \ln(1 - x^2) \quad \Rightarrow \quad f'(x) = 2x\ln(1 - x^2) + \dfrac{x^2(-2x)}{1 - x^2} = 2x\ln(1 - x^2) - \dfrac{2x^3}{1 - x^2}$.

$\text{Dom}(f) = \{x \mid 1 - x^2 > 0\} = \{x \mid |x| < 1\} = (-1, 1)$.

33. $f(x) = \dfrac{x}{\ln x} \quad \Rightarrow \quad f'(x) = \dfrac{\ln x - x(1/x)}{(\ln x)^2} = \dfrac{\ln x - 1}{(\ln x)^2} \quad \Rightarrow \quad f'(e) = \dfrac{1 - 1}{1^2} = 0$

35. $y = f(x) = \ln\ln x \quad \Rightarrow \quad f'(x) = \dfrac{1}{\ln x}\left(\dfrac{1}{x}\right) \quad \Rightarrow \quad f'(e) = \dfrac{1}{e}$, so an equation of the tangent line at $(e, 0)$ is

$y - 0 = \dfrac{1}{e}(x - e)$, or $y = \dfrac{1}{e}x - 1$, or $x - ey = e$.

37. $f(x) = \sin x + \ln x \;\Rightarrow\; f'(x) = \cos x + 1/x.$ This is reasonable, because the graph shows that f increases when f' is positive, and $f'(x) = 0$ when f has a horizontal tangent.

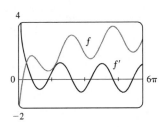

39. $y = (2x+1)^5 (x^4 - 3)^6 \;\Rightarrow\; \ln y = \ln\!\left((2x+1)^5 (x^4-3)^6\right) \;\Rightarrow$

$\ln y = 5\ln(2x+1) + 6\ln(x^4 - 3) \;\Rightarrow\; \dfrac{1}{y}\, y' = 5 \cdot \dfrac{1}{2x+1} \cdot 2 + 6 \cdot \dfrac{1}{x^4 - 3} \cdot 4x^3 \;\Rightarrow$

$y' = y\left(\dfrac{10}{2x+1} + \dfrac{24x^3}{x^4 - 3}\right) = (2x+1)^5 (x^4-3)^6 \left(\dfrac{10}{2x+1} + \dfrac{24x^3}{x^4-3}\right).$

[The answer could be simplified to $y' = 2(2x+1)^4 (x^4-3)^5 (29x^4 + 12x^3 - 15)$, but this is unnecessary.]

41. $y = \dfrac{\sin^2 x \tan^4 x}{(x^2+1)^2} \;\Rightarrow\; \ln y = \ln(\sin^2 x \tan^4 x) - \ln(x^2+1)^2 \;\Rightarrow$

$\ln y = \ln(\sin x)^2 + \ln(\tan x)^4 - \ln(x^2+1)^2 \;\Rightarrow\; \ln y = 2\ln|\sin x| + 4\ln|\tan x| - 2\ln(x^2+1) \;\Rightarrow$

$\dfrac{1}{y}\, y' = 2 \cdot \dfrac{1}{\sin x} \cdot \cos x + 4 \cdot \dfrac{1}{\tan x} \cdot \sec^2 x - 2 \cdot \dfrac{1}{x^2+1} \cdot 2x \;\Rightarrow$

$y' = \dfrac{\sin^2 x \tan^4 x}{(x^2+1)^2}\left(2\cot x + \dfrac{4\sec^2 x}{\tan x} - \dfrac{4x}{x^2+1}\right)$

43. $y = x^x \;\Rightarrow\; \ln y = \ln x^x \;\Rightarrow\; \ln y = x\ln x \;\Rightarrow\; y'/y = x(1/x) + (\ln x) \cdot 1 \;\Rightarrow$

$y' = y(1 + \ln x) \;\Rightarrow\; y' = x^x(1 + \ln x)$

45. $y = x^{\sin x} \;\Rightarrow\; \ln y = \ln x^{\sin x} \;\Rightarrow\; \ln y = \sin x \ln x \;\Rightarrow\; \dfrac{y'}{y} = (\sin x) \cdot \dfrac{1}{x} + (\ln x)(\cos x) \;\Rightarrow$

$y' = y\left(\dfrac{\sin x}{x} + \ln x \cos x\right) \;\Rightarrow\; y' = x^{\sin x}\left(\dfrac{\sin x}{x} + \ln x \cos x\right)$

47. $y = (\ln x)^x \;\Rightarrow\; \ln y = \ln(\ln x)^x \;\Rightarrow\; \ln y = x \ln \ln x \;\Rightarrow\; \dfrac{y'}{y} = x \cdot \dfrac{1}{\ln x} \cdot \dfrac{1}{x} + (\ln \ln x) \cdot 1 \;\Rightarrow$

$y' = y\left(\dfrac{x}{x\ln x} + \ln \ln x\right) \;\Rightarrow\; y' = (\ln x)^x\left(\dfrac{1}{\ln x} + \ln \ln x\right)$

49. $y = x^{e^x} \;\Rightarrow\; \ln y = e^x \ln x \;\Rightarrow\; \dfrac{y'}{y} = e^x \cdot \dfrac{1}{x} + (\ln x) \cdot e^x \;\Rightarrow\; y' = x^{e^x} e^x\left(\ln x + \dfrac{1}{x}\right)$

51. $y = \ln(x^2 + y^2) \;\Rightarrow\; y' = \dfrac{1}{x^2 + y^2} \dfrac{d}{dx}(x^2 + y^2) \;\Rightarrow\; y' = \dfrac{2x + 2yy'}{x^2 + y^2} \;\Rightarrow\; x^2 y' + y^2 y' = 2x + 2yy'$

$\Rightarrow\; x^2 y' + y^2 y' - 2yy' = 2x \;\Rightarrow\; (x^2 + y^2 - 2y)y' = 2x \;\Rightarrow\; y' = \dfrac{2x}{x^2 + y^2 - 2y}$

53. $f(x) = \ln(x-1) \;\Rightarrow\; f'(x) = 1/(x-1) = (x-1)^{-1} \;\Rightarrow\; f''(x) = -(x-1)^{-2} \;\Rightarrow$

$f'''(x) = 2(x-1)^{-3} \;\Rightarrow\; f^{(4)}(x) = -2 \cdot 3(x-1)^{-4} \;\Rightarrow\; \cdots \;\Rightarrow$

$f^{(n)}(x) = (-1)^{n-1} \cdot 2 \cdot 3 \cdot 4 \cdot \;\cdots\; \cdot (n-1)(x-1)^{-n} = (-1)^{n-1}\dfrac{(n-1)!}{(x-1)^n}$

55.

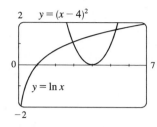

From the graph, it appears that the curves $y = (x-4)^2$ and $y = \ln x$ intersect just to the left of $x = 3$ and to the right of $x = 5$, at about $x = 5.3$. Let $f(x) = \ln x - (x-4)^2$. Then $f'(x) = 1/x - 2(x-4)$, so Newton's Method says that

$$x_{n+1} = x_n - f(x_n)/f'(x_n) = x_n - \frac{\ln x_n - (x_n - 4)^2}{1/x_n - 2(x_n - 4)}.$$ Taking

$x_0 = 3$, we get $x_1 \approx 2.957738$, $x_2 \approx 2.958516 \approx x_3$, so the first root is 2.958516, to six decimal places. Taking $x_0 = 5$, we get $x_1 \approx 5.290755$, $x_2 \approx 5.290718 \approx x_3$, so the second (and final) root is 5.290718, to six decimal places.

57. $f(x) = \dfrac{\ln x}{\sqrt{x}} \quad \Rightarrow \quad f'(x) = \dfrac{\sqrt{x}\,(1/x) - (\ln x)[1/(2\sqrt{x})]}{x} = \dfrac{2 - \ln x}{2x^{3/2}} \quad \Rightarrow$

$f''(x) = \dfrac{2x^{3/2}(-1/x) - (2 - \ln x)(3x^{1/2})}{4x^3} = \dfrac{3\ln x - 8}{4x^{5/2}} > 0 \quad \Leftrightarrow \quad \ln x > \frac{8}{3} \quad \Leftrightarrow \quad x > e^{8/3}$, so f is CU

on $\left(e^{8/3}, \infty\right)$ and CD on $\left(0, e^{8/3}\right)$. The inflection point is $\left(e^{8/3}, \frac{8}{3}e^{-4/3}\right)$.

59. $y = f(x) = \ln(\sin x)$

A. $D = \{x \text{ in } \mathbb{R} \mid \sin x > 0\} = \bigcup\limits_{n=-\infty}^{\infty} (2n\pi, (2n+1)\pi)$

$$= \cdots \cup (-4\pi, -3\pi) \cup (-2\pi, -\pi) \cup (0, \pi) \cup (2\pi, 3\pi) \cup \cdots$$

B. No y-intercept; x-intercepts: $f(x) = 0 \quad \Leftrightarrow \quad \ln(\sin x) = 0 \quad \Leftrightarrow \quad \sin x = e^0 = 1 \quad \Leftrightarrow \quad x = 2n\pi + \frac{\pi}{2}$ for

each integer n.   **C.** f is periodic with period 2π.   **D.** $\lim\limits_{x \to (2n\pi)^+} f(x) = -\infty$ and $\lim\limits_{x \to [(2n+1)\pi]^-} f(x) = -\infty$, so

the lines $x = n\pi$ are VAs for all integers n.   **E.** $f'(x) = \frac{\cos x}{\sin x} = \cot x$, so $f'(x) > 0$ when $2n\pi < x < 2n\pi + \frac{\pi}{2}$

for each integer n, and $f'(x) < 0$ when $2n\pi + \frac{\pi}{2} < x < (2n+1)\pi$. Thus, f is increasing on $\left(2n\pi, 2n\pi + \frac{\pi}{2}\right)$ and

decreasing on $\left(2n\pi + \frac{\pi}{2}, (2n+1)\pi\right)$ for each integer n.   **F.** Local maximum values $f\left(2n\pi + \frac{\pi}{2}\right) = 0$, no local

minimum.   **G.** $f''(x) = -\csc^2 x < 0$, so f is CD on $(2n\pi, (2n+1)\pi)$ for each integer n. No IP

H.

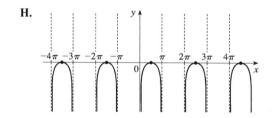

61. $y = f(x) = \ln(1 + x^2)$ **A.** $D = \mathbb{R}$ **B.** Both intercepts are 0.   **C.** $f(-x) = f(x)$, so the curve is symmetric

about the y-axis.   **D.** $\lim\limits_{x \to \pm\infty} \ln(1 + x^2) = \infty$, no asymptotes.   **E.** $f'(x) = \dfrac{2x}{1 + x^2} > 0 \quad \Leftrightarrow$

$x > 0$, so f is increasing on $(0, \infty)$ and decreasing on $(-\infty, 0)$.

F. $f(0) = 0$ is a local and absolute minimum.

H.

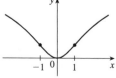

G. $f''(x) = \dfrac{2(1 + x^2) - 2x(2x)}{(1 + x^2)^2} = \dfrac{2(1 - x^2)}{(1 + x^2)^2} > 0 \quad \Leftrightarrow$

$|x| < 1$, so f is CU on $(-1, 1)$, CD on $(-\infty, -1)$ and $(1, \infty)$. IP

$(1, \ln 2)$ and $(-1, \ln 2)$.

63. We use the CAS to calculate $f'(x) = \dfrac{2 + \sin x + x \cos x}{2x + x \sin x}$ and

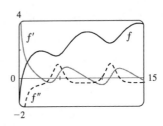

$f''(x) = \dfrac{2x^2 \sin x + 4 \sin x - \cos^2 x + x^2 + 5}{x^2(\cos^2 x - 4 \sin x - 5)}$. From the graphs, it

seems that $f' > 0$ (and so f is increasing) on approximately the intervals
$(0, 2.7)$, $(4.5, 8.2)$ and $(10.9, 14.3)$. It seems that f'' changes sign
(indicating inflection points) at $x \approx 3.8, 5.7, 10.0$ and 12.0.

Looking back at the graph of $f(x) = \ln(2x + x \sin x)$, this implies that the inflection points have approximate
coordinates $(3.8, 1.7)$, $(5.7, 2.1)$, $(10.0, 2.7)$, and $(12.0, 2.9)$.

65. $\displaystyle\int_2^4 \frac{3}{x}\, dx = 3 \int_2^4 \frac{1}{x}\, dx = 3 \Big[\ln |x|\Big]_2^4 = 3(\ln 4 - \ln 2) = 3 \ln \frac{4}{2} = 3 \ln 2$

67. $\displaystyle\int_1^2 \frac{dt}{8 - 3t} = \left[-\frac{1}{3} \ln |8 - 3t|\right]_1^2 = -\frac{1}{3} \ln 2 - \left(-\frac{1}{3} \ln 5\right) = \frac{1}{3}(\ln 5 - \ln 2) = \frac{1}{3} \ln \frac{5}{2}$

Or: Let $u = 8 - 3t$. Then $du = -3\, dt$, so

$\displaystyle\int_1^2 \frac{dt}{8 - 3t} = \int_5^2 \frac{-\frac{1}{3}\, du}{u} = \left[-\frac{1}{3} \ln |u|\right]_5^2 = -\frac{1}{3} \ln 2 - \left(-\frac{1}{3} \ln 5\right) = \frac{1}{3}(\ln 5 - \ln 2) = \frac{1}{3} \ln \frac{5}{2}$.

69. $\displaystyle\int_1^e \frac{x^2 + x + 1}{x}\, dx = \int_1^e \left(x + 1 + \frac{1}{x}\right) dx = \left[\tfrac{1}{2}x^2 + x + \ln x\right]_1^e = \left(\tfrac{1}{2}e^2 + e + 1\right) - \left(\tfrac{1}{2} + 1 + 0\right)$

$\qquad = \tfrac{1}{2}e^2 + e - \tfrac{1}{2}$

71. Let $u = 6x - x^3$. Then $du = (6 - 3x^2)\, dx = 3(2 - x^2)\, dx$, so

$\displaystyle\int \frac{2 - x^2}{6x - x^3}\, dx = \int \frac{\frac{1}{3}\, du}{u} = \frac{1}{3} \ln |u| + C = \frac{1}{3} \ln |6x - x^3| + C.$

73. Let $u = \ln x$. Then $du = \dfrac{dx}{x} \ \Rightarrow\ \displaystyle\int \frac{(\ln x)^2}{x}\, dx = \int u^2\, du = \frac{1}{3}u^3 + C = \frac{1}{3}(\ln x)^3 + C.$

75. $\displaystyle\int_1^2 10^t\, dt = \left[\frac{10^t}{\ln 10}\right]_1^2 = \frac{10^2}{\ln 10} - \frac{10^1}{\ln 10} = \frac{100 - 10}{\ln 10} = \frac{90}{\ln 10}$

77. (a) $\dfrac{d}{dx}(\ln |\sin x| + C) = \dfrac{1}{\sin x} \cos x = \cot x$

(b) Let $u = \sin x$. Then $du = \cos x\, dx$, so $\displaystyle\int \cot x\, dx = \int \frac{\cos x}{\sin x}\, dx = \int \frac{du}{u} = \ln |u| + C = \ln |\sin x| + C.$

79. The cross-sectional area is $\pi\left(1/\sqrt{x + 1}\right)^2 = \pi/(x + 1)$. Therefore, the volume is

$\displaystyle\int_0^1 \frac{\pi}{x + 1}\, dx = \pi[\ln(x + 1)]_0^1 = \pi(\ln 2 - \ln 1) = \pi \ln 2.$

81. $W = \int_{V_1}^{V_2} P\, dV = \displaystyle\int_{600}^{1000} \frac{C}{V}\, dV = C \int_{600}^{1000} \frac{1}{V}\, dV = C \Big[\ln |V|\Big]_{600}^{1000}$

$\qquad = C(\ln 1000 - \ln 600) = C \ln \frac{1000}{600} = C \ln \frac{5}{3}$

Initially, $PV = C$, where $P = 150$ kPa and $V = 600$ cm^3, so $C = (150)(600) = 90{,}000$. Thus,

$W = 90{,}000 \ln \frac{5}{3} \approx 45{,}974$ kPa $\cdot$ cm$^3 = 45{,}974(10^3$ Pa$)(10^{-6}$ m$^3) = 45{,}974$ Pa$\cdot$m$^3 = 45{,}974$ N$\cdot$m

$[$Pa $=$ N/m$^2]\quad = 45{,}974$ J

83. $f(x) = 2x + \ln x \ \Rightarrow\ f'(x) = 2 + 1/x$. If $g = f^{-1}$, then $f(1) = 2 \ \Rightarrow\ g(2) = 1$, so

$g'(2) = 1/f'(g(2)) = 1/f'(1) = \frac{1}{3}.$

85. The curve and the line will determine a region when they intersect at

two or more points. So we solve the equation $x/(x^2 + 1) = mx$ $\Rightarrow$

$x = 0$ or $mx^2 + m - 1 = 0$ $\Rightarrow$ $x = 0$ or

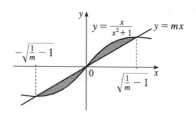

$x = \dfrac{\pm\sqrt{-4(m)(m-1)}}{2m} = \pm\sqrt{\dfrac{1}{m} - 1}$. Note that if $m = 1$, this

has only the solution $x = 0$, and no region is determined. But if

$1/m - 1 > 0$ $\Leftrightarrow$ $1/m > 1$ $\Leftrightarrow$ $0 < m < 1$, then there are two

solutions. [Another way of seeing this is to observe that the slope of the tangent to $y = x/(x^2 + 1)$ at the origin is

$y' = 1$ and therefore we must have $0 < m < 1$.] Note that we cannot just integrate between the positive and

negative roots, since the curve and the line cross at the origin. Since mx and $x/(x^2 + 1)$ are both odd functions,

the total area is twice the area between the curves on the interval $\left[0, \sqrt{1/m - 1}\right]$. So the total area enclosed is

$$2\int_0^{\sqrt{1/m-1}} \left[\frac{x}{x^2+1} - mx\right] dx = 2\left[\tfrac{1}{2}\ln(x^2+1) - \tfrac{1}{2}mx^2\right]_0^{\sqrt{1/m-1}}$$

$$= \left[\ln\left(\frac{1}{m} - 1 + 1\right) - m\left(\frac{1}{m} - 1\right)\right] - (\ln 1 - 0)$$

$$= \ln\left(\frac{1}{m}\right) + m - 1 = m - \ln m - 1$$

87. If $f(x) = \ln(1 + x)$, then $f'(x) = \dfrac{1}{1 + x}$, so $f'(0) = 1$.

Thus, $\displaystyle\lim_{x\to 0} \frac{\ln(1+x)}{x} = \lim_{x\to 0}\frac{f(x)}{x} = \lim_{x\to 0}\frac{f(x) - f(0)}{x - 0} = f'(0) = 1.$

7.2* The Natural Logarithmic Function

1. $\ln\dfrac{x^3 y}{z^2} = \ln x^3 y - \ln z^2 = \ln x^3 + \ln y - \ln z^2 = 3\ln x + \ln y - 2\ln z$

3. $\ln(uv)^{10} = 10\ln(uv) = 10(\ln u + \ln v) = 10\ln u + 10\ln v$

5. $2\ln 4 - \ln 2 = \ln 4^2 - \ln 2 = \ln 16 - \ln 2 = \ln\frac{16}{2} = \ln 8$

7. $\tfrac{1}{2}\ln x - 5\ln(x^2 + 1) = \ln x^{1/2} - \ln(x^2 + 1)^5 = \ln\dfrac{\sqrt{x}}{(x^2+1)^5}$

9. Reflect the graph of $y = \ln x$ about the x-axis to obtain the graph of $y = -\ln x$.

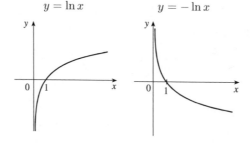

11. $y = \ln x$ $y = \ln(x + 3)$

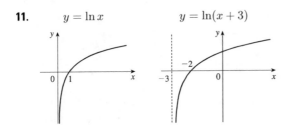

13. $f(x) = \sqrt{x} \ln x \;\;\Rightarrow\;\; f'(x) = \dfrac{1}{2\sqrt{x}} \ln x + \sqrt{x}\left(\dfrac{1}{x}\right) = \dfrac{\ln x + 2}{2\sqrt{x}}$

15. $f(\theta) = \ln(\cos\theta) \;\;\Rightarrow\;\; f'(\theta) = \dfrac{1}{\cos\theta}\dfrac{d}{d\theta}(\cos\theta) = \dfrac{-\sin\theta}{\cos\theta} = -\tan\theta$

17. $f(x) = \sqrt[5]{\ln x} = (\ln x)^{1/5} \;\;\Rightarrow\;\; f'(x) = \tfrac{1}{5}(\ln x)^{-4/5}\dfrac{d}{dx}(\ln x) = \dfrac{1}{5(\ln x)^{4/5}} \cdot \dfrac{1}{x} = \dfrac{1}{5x\sqrt[5]{(\ln x)^4}}$

19. $g(x) = \ln\dfrac{a-x}{a+x} = \ln(a-x) - \ln(a+x) \;\;\Rightarrow$

$\quad g'(x) = \dfrac{1}{a-x}(-1) - \dfrac{1}{a+x} = \dfrac{-(a+x) - (a-x)}{(a-x)(a+x)} = \dfrac{-2a}{a^2 - x^2}$

21. $f(u) = \dfrac{\ln u}{1 + \ln(2u)} \;\;\Rightarrow$

$\quad f'(u) = \dfrac{[1 + \ln(2u)] \cdot \frac{1}{u} - \ln u \cdot \frac{1}{2u} \cdot 2}{[1 + \ln(2u)]^2} = \dfrac{\frac{1}{u}[1 + \ln(2u) - \ln u]}{[1 + \ln(2u)]^2}$

$\quad = \dfrac{1 + (\ln 2 + \ln u) - \ln u}{u\,[1 + \ln(2u)]^2} = \dfrac{1 + \ln 2}{u\,[1 + \ln(2u)]^2}$

23. $F(t) = \ln\dfrac{(2t+1)^3}{(3t-1)^4} = \ln(2t+1)^3 - \ln(3t-1)^4 = 3\ln(2t+1) - 4\ln(3t-1) \;\;\Rightarrow$

$\quad F'(t) = 3 \cdot \dfrac{1}{2t+1} \cdot 2 - 4 \cdot \dfrac{1}{3t-1} \cdot 3 = \dfrac{6}{2t+1} - \dfrac{12}{3t-1}$, or combined, $\dfrac{-6(t+3)}{(2t+1)(3t-1)}$.

25. $y = \ln\left|2 - x - 5x^2\right| \;\;\Rightarrow\;\; y' = \dfrac{1}{2 - x - 5x^2} \cdot (-1 - 10x) = \dfrac{-10x - 1}{2 - x - 5x^2}$ or $\dfrac{10x + 1}{5x^2 + x - 2}$

27. $y = \ln\left(\dfrac{x+1}{x-1}\right)^{3/5} = \tfrac{3}{5}[\ln(x+1) - \ln(x-1)] \;\;\Rightarrow\;\; y' = \dfrac{3}{5}\left(\dfrac{1}{x+1} - \dfrac{1}{x-1}\right) = \dfrac{-6}{5(x^2-1)}$

29. $y = \tan[\ln(ax+b)] \;\;\Rightarrow\;\; y' = \sec^2[\ln(ax+b)] \cdot \dfrac{1}{ax+b} \cdot a = \sec^2[\ln(ax+b)]\dfrac{a}{ax+b}$

31. $y = \ln\ln x \;\;\Rightarrow\;\; y' = \dfrac{1}{\ln x}\dfrac{d}{dx}(\ln x) = \dfrac{1}{\ln x} \cdot \dfrac{1}{x} = \dfrac{1}{x\ln x} \;\;\Rightarrow$

$\quad y'' = -\dfrac{\dfrac{d}{dx}(x\ln x)}{(x\ln x)^2} \quad \text{[Reciprocal Rule]} \quad = -\dfrac{x \cdot \frac{1}{x} + \ln x \cdot 1}{(x\ln x)^2} = -\dfrac{1 + \ln x}{(x\ln x)^2}$

33. $f(x) = \dfrac{x}{1 - \ln(x - 1)} \quad \Rightarrow$

$$f'(x) = \frac{[1 - \ln(x-1)] \cdot 1 - x \cdot \dfrac{-1}{x-1}}{[1 - \ln(x-1)]^2} = \frac{\dfrac{(x-1)[1 - \ln(x-1)] + x}{x-1}}{[1 - \ln(x-1)]^2} = \frac{x - 1 - (x-1)\ln(x-1) + x}{(x-1)[1 - \ln(x-1)]^2}$$

$$= \frac{2x - 1 - (x-1)\ln(x-1)}{(x-1)[1 - \ln(x-1)]^2}$$

$\text{Dom}(f) = \{x \mid x - 1 > 0 \quad \text{and} \quad 1 - \ln(x-1) \neq 0\} = \{x \mid x > 1 \quad \text{and} \quad \ln(x-1) \neq 1\}$

$\qquad = \{x \mid x > 1 \quad \text{and} \quad x - 1 \neq e^1\} = \{x \mid x > 1 \quad \text{and} \quad x \neq 1 + e\} = (1, 1+e) \cup (1+e, \infty)$

35. $f(x) = \sqrt{1 - \ln x}$ is defined $\quad \Leftrightarrow \quad x > 0$ [so that $\ln x$ is defined] and $1 - \ln x \geq 0$

$\Leftrightarrow \quad x > 0$ and $\ln x \leq 1 \quad \Leftrightarrow \quad 0 < x \leq e$, so the domain of f is $(0, e]$. Now

$$f'(x) = \frac{1}{2}(1 - \ln x)^{-1/2} \cdot \frac{d}{dx}(1 - \ln x) = \frac{1}{2\sqrt{1 - \ln x}} \cdot \left(-\frac{1}{x}\right) = \frac{-1}{2x\sqrt{1 - \ln x}}.$$

37. $f(x) = \dfrac{x}{\ln x} \quad \Rightarrow \quad f'(x) = \dfrac{\ln x - x(1/x)}{(\ln x)^2} = \dfrac{\ln x - 1}{(\ln x)^2} \quad \Rightarrow \quad f'(e) = \dfrac{1 - 1}{1^2} = 0$

39. $f(x) = \sin x + \ln x \quad \Rightarrow \quad f'(x) = \cos x + 1/x$. This is reasonable,

because the graph shows that f increases when f' is positive, and

$f'(x) = 0$ when f has a horizontal tangent.

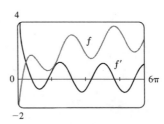

41. $y = \sin(2\ln x) \quad \Rightarrow \quad y' = \cos(2\ln x) \cdot \dfrac{2}{x}$. At $(1, 0)$, $y' = \cos 0 \cdot \dfrac{2}{1} = 2$, so an equation of the tangent line is

$y - 0 = 2 \cdot (x - 1)$, or $y = 2x - 2$.

43. $y = \ln(x^2 + y^2) \quad \Rightarrow \quad y' = \dfrac{1}{x^2 + y^2} \dfrac{d}{dx}(x^2 + y^2) \quad \Rightarrow \quad y' = \dfrac{2x + 2yy'}{x^2 + y^2} \quad \Rightarrow \quad x^2 y' + y^2 y' = 2x + 2yy'$

$\Rightarrow \quad x^2 y' + y^2 y' - 2yy' = 2x \quad \Rightarrow \quad (x^2 + y^2 - 2y)y' = 2x \quad \Rightarrow \quad y' = \dfrac{2x}{x^2 + y^2 - 2y}$

45. $f(x) = \ln(x - 1) \quad \Rightarrow \quad f'(x) = 1/(x - 1) = (x - 1)^{-1} \quad \Rightarrow \quad f''(x) = -(x - 1)^{-2} \quad \Rightarrow$

$f'''(x) = 2(x - 1)^{-3} \quad \Rightarrow \quad f^{(4)}(x) = -2 \cdot 3(x - 1)^{-4} \quad \Rightarrow \quad \cdots \quad \Rightarrow$

$f^{(n)}(x) = (-1)^{n-1} \cdot 2 \cdot 3 \cdot 4 \cdot \cdots \cdot (n - 1)(x - 1)^{-n} = (-1)^{n-1} \dfrac{(n-1)!}{(x-1)^n}$

47.

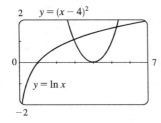

From the graph, it appears that the curves $y = (x - 4)^2$ and $y = \ln x$

intersect just to the left of $x = 3$ and to the right of $x = 5$, at about

$x = 5.3$. Let $f(x) = \ln x - (x - 4)^2$. Then $f'(x) = 1/x - 2(x - 4)$,

so Newton's Method says that

$$x_{n+1} = x_n - f(x_n)/f'(x_n) = x_n - \frac{\ln x_n - (x_n - 4)^2}{1/x_n - 2(x_n - 4)}. \text{ Taking}$$

$x_0 = 3$, we get $x_1 \approx 2.957738$, $x_2 \approx 2.958516 \approx x_3$, so the first root is

2.958516, to six decimal places. Taking $x_0 = 5$, we get $x_1 \approx 5.290755$, $x_2 \approx 5.290718 \approx x_3$, so the second

(and final) root is 5.290718, to six decimal places.

49. $y = f(x) = \ln(\sin x)$

A. $D = \{x \text{ in } \mathbb{R} \mid \sin x > 0\} = \bigcup_{n=-\infty}^{\infty} (2n\pi, (2n+1)\pi)$

$$= \cdots \cup (-4\pi, -3\pi) \cup (-2\pi, -\pi) \cup (0, \pi) \cup (2\pi, 3\pi) \cup \cdots$$

B. No y-intercept; x-intercepts: $f(x) = 0 \Leftrightarrow \ln(\sin x) = 0 \Leftrightarrow \sin x = e^0 = 1 \Leftrightarrow x = 2n\pi + \frac{\pi}{2}$ for each integer n. **C.** f is periodic with period 2π. **D.** $\lim\limits_{x \to (2n\pi)^+} f(x) = -\infty$ and $\lim\limits_{x \to [(2n+1)\pi]^-} f(x) = -\infty$, so the lines $x = n\pi$ are VAs for all integers n. **E.** $f'(x) = \frac{\cos x}{\sin x} = \cot x$, so $f'(x) > 0$ when $2n\pi < x < 2n\pi + \frac{\pi}{2}$ for each integer n, and $f'(x) < 0$ when $2n\pi + \frac{\pi}{2} < x < (2n+1)\pi$. Thus, f is increasing on $\left(2n\pi, 2n\pi + \frac{\pi}{2}\right)$ and decreasing on $\left(2n\pi + \frac{\pi}{2}, (2n+1)\pi\right)$ for each integer n. **F.** Local maximum values $f\left(2n\pi + \frac{\pi}{2}\right) = 0$, no local minimum. **G.** $f''(x) = -\csc^2 x < 0$, so f is CD on $(2n\pi, (2n+1)\pi)$ for each integer n. No IP

H.

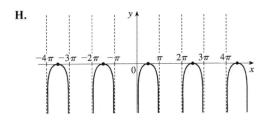

51. $y = f(x) = \ln(1 + x^2)$ **A.** $D = \mathbb{R}$ **B.** Both intercepts are 0. **C.** $f(-x) = f(x)$, so the curve is symmetric about the y-axis. **D.** $\lim\limits_{x \to \pm\infty} \ln(1 + x^2) = \infty$, no asymptotes. **E.** $f'(x) = \dfrac{2x}{1 + x^2} > 0 \Leftrightarrow$ $x > 0$, so f is increasing on $(0, \infty)$ and decreasing on $(-\infty, 0)$.

F. $f(0) = 0$ is a local and absolute minimum.

G. $f''(x) = \dfrac{2(1 + x^2) - 2x(2x)}{(1 + x^2)^2} = \dfrac{2(1 - x^2)}{(1 + x^2)^2} > 0 \Leftrightarrow$

$|x| < 1$, so f is CU on $(-1, 1)$, CD on $(-\infty, -1)$ and $(1, \infty)$. IP $(1, \ln 2)$ and $(-1, \ln 2)$.

H.

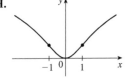

53. We use the CAS to calculate $f'(x) = \dfrac{2 + \sin x + x \cos x}{2x + x \sin x}$ and

$f''(x) = \dfrac{2x^2 \sin x + 4 \sin x - \cos^2 x + x^2 + 5}{x^2(\cos^2 x - 4 \sin x - 5)}$. From the graphs, it

seems that $f' > 0$ (and so f is increasing) on approximately the intervals $(0, 2.7)$, $(4.5, 8.2)$ and $(10.9, 14.3)$. It seems that f'' changes sign (indicating inflection points) at $x \approx 3.8, 5.7, 10.0$ and 12.0.

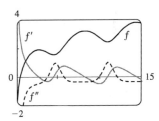

Looking back at the graph of $f(x) = \ln(2x + x \sin x)$, this implies that the inflection points have approximate coordinates $(3.8, 1.7)$, $(5.7, 2.1)$, $(10.0, 2.7)$, and $(12.0, 2.9)$.

55. $y = (2x + 1)^5 (x^4 - 3)^6 \Rightarrow \ln y = \ln\left((2x + 1)^5 (x^4 - 3)^6\right) \Rightarrow$

$\ln y = 5 \ln(2x + 1) + 6 \ln(x^4 - 3) \Rightarrow \dfrac{1}{y} y' = 5 \cdot \dfrac{1}{2x + 1} \cdot 2 + 6 \cdot \dfrac{1}{x^4 - 3} \cdot 4x^3 \Rightarrow$

$$y' = y\left(\frac{10}{2x+1} + \frac{24x^3}{x^4-3}\right) = (2x+1)^5(x^4-3)^6\left(\frac{10}{2x+1} + \frac{24x^3}{x^4-3}\right).$$

[The answer could be simplified to $y' = 2(2x+1)^4(x^4-3)^5(29x^4 + 12x^3 - 15)$, but this is unnecessary.]

57. $y = \dfrac{\sin^2 x \tan^4 x}{(x^2+1)^2} \quad \Rightarrow \quad \ln y = \ln(\sin^2 x \tan^4 x) - \ln(x^2+1)^2 \quad \Rightarrow$

$\ln y = \ln(\sin x)^2 + \ln(\tan x)^4 - \ln(x^2+1)^2 \quad \Rightarrow \quad \ln y = 2\ln|\sin x| + 4\ln|\tan x| - 2\ln(x^2+1) \quad \Rightarrow$

$\dfrac{1}{y} y' = 2 \cdot \dfrac{1}{\sin x} \cdot \cos x + 4 \cdot \dfrac{1}{\tan x} \cdot \sec^2 x - 2 \cdot \dfrac{1}{x^2+1} \cdot 2x \quad \Rightarrow$

$y' = \dfrac{\sin^2 x \tan^4 x}{(x^2+1)^2}\left(2\cot x + \dfrac{4\sec^2 x}{\tan x} - \dfrac{4x}{x^2+1}\right)$

59. $\displaystyle\int_2^4 \frac{3}{x}\, dx = 3\int_2^4 \frac{1}{x}\, dx = 3\Big[\ln|x|\Big]_2^4 = 3(\ln 4 - \ln 2) = 3\ln\frac{4}{2} = 3\ln 2$

61. $\displaystyle\int_1^2 \frac{dt}{8-3t} = \left[-\frac{1}{3}\ln|8-3t|\right]_1^2 = -\frac{1}{3}\ln 2 - \left(-\frac{1}{3}\ln 5\right) = \frac{1}{3}(\ln 5 - \ln 2) = \frac{1}{3}\ln\frac{5}{2}$

Or: Let $u = 8 - 3t$. Then $du = -3\,dt$, so

$\displaystyle\int_1^2 \frac{dt}{8-3t} = \int_5^2 \frac{-\frac{1}{3}\,du}{u} = \left[-\frac{1}{3}\ln|u|\right]_5^2 = -\frac{1}{3}\ln 2 - \left(-\frac{1}{3}\ln 5\right) = \frac{1}{3}(\ln 5 - \ln 2) = \frac{1}{3}\ln\frac{5}{2}.$

63. $\displaystyle\int_1^e \frac{x^2+x+1}{x}\, dx = \int_1^e \left(x + 1 + \frac{1}{x}\right) dx = \left[\tfrac{1}{2}x^2 + x + \ln x\right]_1^e = \left(\tfrac{1}{2}e^2 + e + 1\right) - \left(\tfrac{1}{2} + 1 + 0\right)$

$\qquad\qquad = \tfrac{1}{2}e^2 + e - \tfrac{1}{2}$

65. Let $u = 6x - x^3$. Then $du = (6 - 3x^2)\,dx = 3(2 - x^2)\,dx$, so

$\displaystyle\int \frac{2-x^2}{6x-x^3}\, dx = \int \frac{\frac{1}{3}\,du}{u} = \frac{1}{3}\ln|u| + C = \frac{1}{3}\ln|6x - x^3| + C.$

67. Let $u = \ln x$. Then $du = \dfrac{dx}{x} \quad \Rightarrow \quad \displaystyle\int \frac{(\ln x)^2}{x}\, dx = \int u^2\, du = \frac{1}{3}u^3 + C = \frac{1}{3}(\ln x)^3 + C.$

69. (a) $\dfrac{d}{dx}\left(\ln|\sin x| + C\right) = \dfrac{1}{\sin x}\cos x = \cot x$

(b) Let $u = \sin x$. Then $du = \cos x\, dx$, so $\displaystyle\int \cot x\, dx = \int \frac{\cos x}{\sin x}\, dx = \int \frac{du}{u} = \ln|u| + C = \ln|\sin x| + C.$

71. The cross-sectional area is $\pi\left(1/\sqrt{x+1}\right)^2 = \pi/(x+1)$. Therefore, the volume is

$\displaystyle\int_0^1 \frac{\pi}{x+1}\, dx = \pi[\ln(x+1)]_0^1 = \pi(\ln 2 - \ln 1) = \pi\ln 2.$

73. $W = \displaystyle\int_{V_1}^{V_2} P\, dV = \int_{600}^{1000} \frac{C}{V}\, dV = C\int_{600}^{1000} \frac{1}{V}\, dV = C\Big[\ln|V|\Big]_{600}^{1000}$

$\qquad = C(\ln 1000 - \ln 600) = C\ln\frac{1000}{600} = C\ln\frac{5}{3}$

Initially, $PV = C$, where $P = 150$ kPa and $V = 600$ cm^3, so $C = (150)(600) = 90{,}000$. Thus,

$W = 90{,}000\ln\frac{5}{3} \approx 45{,}974$ kPa $\cdot$ cm$^3 = 45{,}974(10^3$ Pa$)(10^{-6}$ m$^3) = 45{,}974$ Pa$\cdot$m$^3 = 45{,}974$ N$\cdot$m

[Pa = N/m^2] $= 45{,}974$ J

75. $f(x) = 2x + \ln x \quad \Rightarrow \quad f'(x) = 2 + 1/x$. If $g = f^{-1}$, then $f(1) = 2 \quad \Rightarrow \quad g(2) = 1$, so

$g'(2) = 1/f'(g(2)) = 1/f'(1) = \frac{1}{3}.$

77. (a)

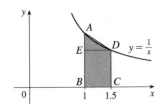

We interpret $\ln 1.5$ as the area under the curve $y = 1/x$ from $x = 1$ to $x = 1.5$. The area of the rectangle $BCDE$ is $\frac{1}{2} \cdot \frac{2}{3} = \frac{1}{3}$. The area of the trapezoid $ABCD$ is $\frac{1}{2} \cdot \frac{1}{2}\left(1 + \frac{2}{3}\right) = \frac{5}{12}$. Thus, by comparing areas, we observe that $\frac{1}{3} < \ln 1.5 < \frac{5}{12}$.

(b) With $f(t) = 1/t$, $n = 10$, and $\Delta t = 0.05$, we have

$$\ln 1.5 = \int_1^{1.5}(1/t)\,dt \approx (0.05)[f(1.025) + f(1.075) + \cdots + f(1.475)]$$

$$= (0.05)\left[\tfrac{1}{1.025} + \tfrac{1}{1.075} + \cdots + \tfrac{1}{1.475}\right] \approx 0.4054$$

79.

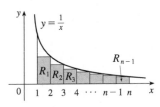

The area of R_i is $\dfrac{1}{i+1}$ and so $\dfrac{1}{2} + \dfrac{1}{3} + \cdots + \dfrac{1}{n} < \displaystyle\int_1^n \dfrac{1}{t}\,dt = \ln n$.

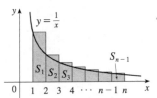

The area of S_i is $\dfrac{1}{i}$ and so $1 + \dfrac{1}{2} + \cdots + \dfrac{1}{n-1} > \displaystyle\int_1^n \dfrac{1}{t}\,dt = \ln n$.

81. The curve and the line will determine a region when they intersect at two or more points. So we solve the equation $x/(x^2 + 1) = mx \Rightarrow$
$x = 0$ or $mx^2 + m - 1 = 0 \Rightarrow x = 0$ or
$x = \dfrac{\pm\sqrt{-4(m)(m-1)}}{2m} = \pm\sqrt{\dfrac{1}{m} - 1}$. Note that if $m = 1$, this

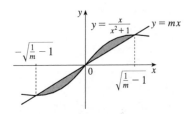

has only the solution $x = 0$, and no region is determined. But if
$1/m - 1 > 0 \Leftrightarrow 1/m > 1 \Leftrightarrow 0 < m < 1$, then there are two
solutions. [Another way of seeing this is to observe that the slope of the tangent to $y = x/(x^2 + 1)$ at the origin is
$y' = 1$ and therefore we must have $0 < m < 1$.] Note that we cannot just integrate between the positive and
negative roots, since the curve and the line cross at the origin. Since mx and $x/(x^2 + 1)$ are both odd functions,
the total area is twice the area between the curves on the interval $\left[0, \sqrt{1/m - 1}\right]$. So the total area enclosed is

$$2\int_0^{\sqrt{1/m-1}}\left[\frac{x}{x^2 + 1} - mx\right]dx = 2\left[\tfrac{1}{2}\ln(x^2 + 1) - \tfrac{1}{2}mx^2\right]_0^{\sqrt{1/m-1}}$$

$$= \left[\ln\left(\frac{1}{m} - 1 + 1\right) - m\left(\frac{1}{m} - 1\right)\right] - (\ln 1 - 0)$$

$$= \ln\left(\frac{1}{m}\right) + m - 1 = m - \ln m - 1$$

83. If $f(x) = \ln(1+x)$, then $f'(x) = \dfrac{1}{1+x}$, so $f'(0) = 1$.

Thus, $\displaystyle\lim_{x\to 0} \frac{\ln(1+x)}{x} = \lim_{x\to 0} \frac{f(x)}{x} = \lim_{x\to 0} \frac{f(x) - f(0)}{x - 0} = f'(0) = 1$.

7.3* The Natural Exponential Function

1. (a) e is the number such that $\ln e = 1$.

(b) $e \approx 2.71828$

(c)

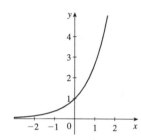

The function value at $x = 0$ is 1 and the slope at $x = 0$ is 1.

3. (a) $\ln e^{\sqrt{2}} = \sqrt{2}$ (b) $e^{3\ln 2} = \left(e^{\ln 2}\right)^3 = 2^3 = 8$

5. (a) $2\ln x = 1 \;\Rightarrow\; \ln x = \frac{1}{2} \;\Rightarrow\; x = e^{1/2} = \sqrt{e}$

(b) $e^{-x} = 5 \;\Rightarrow\; -x = \ln 5 \;\Rightarrow\; x = -\ln 5$

7. $\ln(\ln x) = 1 \;\Leftrightarrow\; e^{\ln(\ln x)} = e^1 \;\Leftrightarrow\; \ln x = e^1 = e \;\Leftrightarrow\; e^{\ln x} = e^e \;\Leftrightarrow\; x = e^e$

9. $2\ln x = \ln 2 + \ln(3x - 4) \;\Rightarrow\; \ln x^2 = \ln[2(3x-4)] \;\Rightarrow\; \ln x^2 = \ln(6x - 8) \;\Rightarrow\; x^2 = 6x - 8 \;\Rightarrow$
$x^2 - 6x + 8 = 0 \;\Rightarrow\; (x-2)(x-4) = 0 \;\Rightarrow\; x = 2$ or $x = 4$, both are valid solutions.

11. $e^{ax} = Ce^{bx} \;\Leftrightarrow\; \ln e^{ax} = \ln[C(e^{bx})] \;\Leftrightarrow\; ax = \ln C + bx + \ln e^{bx} \;\Leftrightarrow\; ax = \ln C + bx \;\Leftrightarrow$
$ax - bx = \ln C \;\Leftrightarrow\; (a-b)x = \ln C \;\Leftrightarrow\; x = \dfrac{\ln C}{a - b}$

13. $e^{2+5x} = 100 \;\Rightarrow\; \ln\left(e^{2+5x}\right) = \ln 100 \;\Rightarrow\; 2 + 5x = \ln 100 \;\Rightarrow\; 5x = \ln 100 - 2 \;\Rightarrow$
$x = \frac{1}{5}(\ln 100 - 2) \approx 0.5210$

15. $\ln(e^x - 2) = 3 \;\Rightarrow\; e^x - 2 = e^3 \;\Rightarrow\; e^x = e^3 + 2 \;\Rightarrow\; x = \ln(e^3 + 2) \approx 3.0949$

17. (a) $e^x < 10 \;\Rightarrow\; \ln e^x < \ln 10 \;\Rightarrow\; x < \ln 10 \;\Rightarrow\; x \in (-\infty, \ln 10)$

(b) $\ln x > -1 \;\Rightarrow\; e^{\ln x} > e^{-1} \;\Rightarrow\; x > e^{-1} \;\Rightarrow\; x \in (1/e, \infty)$

19.

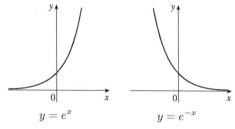

21. We start with the graph of $y = e^x$ (Figure 2), reflect it about the x-axis, and then shift 3 units upward. Note the horizontal asymptote of $y = 3$.

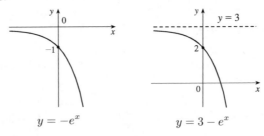

$$y = -e^x \qquad\qquad y = 3 - e^x$$

23. (a) To find the equation of the graph that results from shifting the graph of $y = e^x$ 2 units downward, we subtract 2 from the original function to get $y = e^x - 2$.

(b) To find the equation of the graph that results from shifting the graph of $y = e^x$ 2 units to the right, we replace x with $x - 2$ in the original function to get $y = e^{(x-2)}$.

(c) To find the equation of the graph that results from reflecting the graph of $y = e^x$ about the x-axis, we multiply the original function by -1 to get $y = -e^x$.

(d) To find the equation of the graph that results from reflecting the graph of $y = e^x$ about the y-axis, we replace x with $-x$ in the original function to get $y = e^{-x}$.

(e) To find the equation of the graph that results from reflecting the graph of $y = e^x$ about the x-axis and then about the y-axis, we first multiply the original function by -1 (to get $y = -e^x$) and then replace x with $-x$ in this equation to get $y = -e^{-x}$.

25. $\lim\limits_{x \to \infty} e^{1-x^3} = \lim\limits_{x \to \infty} (e^1 \cdot e^{-x^3}) = e \lim\limits_{x \to \infty} \dfrac{1}{e^{x^3}} = e \cdot 0 = 0$

27. Divide numerator and denominator by e^{3x}: $\lim\limits_{x \to \infty} \dfrac{e^{3x} - e^{-3x}}{e^{3x} + e^{-3x}} = \lim\limits_{x \to \infty} \dfrac{1 - e^{-6x}}{1 + e^{-6x}} = \dfrac{1 - 0}{1 + 0} = 1$

29. Let $t = 3/(2 - x)$. As $x \to 2^+$, $t \to -\infty$. So $\lim\limits_{x \to 2^+} e^{3/(2-x)} = \lim\limits_{t \to -\infty} e^t = 0$ by (6).

31. By the Product Rule, $f(x) = x^2 e^x \;\Rightarrow\; f'(x) = x^2 \dfrac{d}{dx}(e^x) + e^x \dfrac{d}{dx}(x^2) = x^2 e^x + e^x(2x) = x e^x (x + 2)$.

33. By (9), $y = e^{ax^3} \;\Rightarrow\; y' = e^{ax^3} \dfrac{d}{dx}(ax^3) = 3ax^2 e^{ax^3}$.

35. $f(u) = e^{1/u} \;\Rightarrow\; f'(u) = e^{1/u} \cdot \dfrac{d}{du}\left(\dfrac{1}{u}\right) = e^{1/u}\left(\dfrac{-1}{u^2}\right) = \left(\dfrac{-1}{u^2}\right) e^{1/u}$

37. By (9), $F(t) = e^{t \sin 2t} \;\Rightarrow\;$
$F'(t) = e^{t \sin 2t}(t \sin 2t)' = e^{t \sin 2t}(t \cdot 2 \cos 2t + \sin 2t \cdot 1) = e^{t \sin 2t}(2t \cos 2t + \sin 2t)$

39. $y = \sqrt{1 + 2e^{3x}} \;\Rightarrow\; y' = \dfrac{1}{2}(1 + 2e^{3x})^{-1/2} \dfrac{d}{dx}(1 + 2e^{3x}) = \dfrac{1}{2\sqrt{1 + 2e^{3x}}}(2e^{3x} \cdot 3) = \dfrac{3e^{3x}}{\sqrt{1 + 2e^{3x}}}$

41. $y = e^{e^x} \;\Rightarrow\; y' = e^{e^x} \cdot \dfrac{d}{dx}(e^x) = e^{e^x} \cdot e^x$ or $e^{e^x + x}$

43. By the Quotient Rule, $y = \dfrac{ae^x + b}{ce^x + d} \;\Rightarrow\;$
$$y' = \dfrac{(ce^x + d)(ae^x) - (ae^x + b)(ce^x)}{(ce^x + d)^2} = \dfrac{(ace^x + ad - ace^x - bc)e^x}{(ce^x + d)^2} = \dfrac{(ad - bc)e^x}{(ce^x + d)^2}.$$

45. $y = e^{2x} \cos \pi x \;\; \Rightarrow \;\; y' = e^{2x}(-\pi \sin \pi x) + (\cos \pi x)(2e^{2x}) = e^{2x}(2 \cos \pi x - \pi \sin \pi x)$.

At $(0, 1)$, $y' = 1(2 - 0) = 2$, so an equation of the tangent line is $y - 1 = 2(x - 0)$, or $y = 2x + 1$.

47. $\dfrac{d}{dx}\left(e^{x^2 y}\right) = \dfrac{d}{dx}(x + y) \;\; \Rightarrow \;\; e^{x^2 y}(x^2 y' + y \cdot 2x) = 1 + y' \;\; \Rightarrow \;\; x^2 e^{x^2 y} y' + 2xye^{x^2 y} = 1 + y' \;\; \Rightarrow$

$x^2 e^{x^2 y} y' - y' = 1 - 2xye^{x^2 y} \;\; \Rightarrow \;\; y'(x^2 e^{x^2 y} - 1) = 1 - 2xye^{x^2 y} \;\; \Rightarrow \;\; y' = \dfrac{1 - 2xye^{x^2 y}}{x^2 e^{x^2 y} - 1}$

49. $y = e^{rx} \;\; \Rightarrow \;\; y' = re^{rx} \;\; \Rightarrow \;\; y'' = r^2 e^{rx}$, so if $y = e^{rx}$ satisfies the differential equation $y'' + 6y' + 8y = 0$,

then $r^2 e^{rx} + 6re^{rx} + 8e^{rx} = 0$; that is, $e^{rx}(r^2 + 6r + 8) = 0$. Since $e^{rx} > 0$ for all x, we must have

$r^2 + 6r + 8 = 0$, or $(r + 2)(r + 4) = 0$, so $r = -2$ or -4.

51. $f(x) = e^{2x} \;\; \Rightarrow \;\; f'(x) = 2e^{2x} \;\; \Rightarrow \;\; f''(x) = 2 \cdot 2e^{2x} = 2^2 e^{2x} \;\; \Rightarrow$

$f'''(x) = 2^2 \cdot 2e^{2x} = 2^3 e^{2x} \;\; \Rightarrow \;\; \cdots \;\; \Rightarrow \;\; f^{(n)}(x) = 2^n e^{2x}$

53. (a) $f(x) = e^x + x$ is continuous on $\mathbb{R}$ and $f(-1) = e^{-1} - 1 < 0 < 1 = f(0)$, so by the Intermediate Value

Theorem, $e^x + x = 0$ has a root in $(-1, 0)$.

(b) $f(x) = e^x + x \;\; \Rightarrow \;\; f'(x) = e^x + 1$, so $x_{n+1} = x_n - \dfrac{e^{x_n} + x_n}{e^{x_n} + 1}$. Using $x_1 = -0.5$, we get

$x_2 \approx -0.566311$, $x_3 \approx -0.567143 \approx x_4$, so the root is -0.567143 to six decimal places.

55. (a) $m(t) = 24 \cdot e^{-(\ln 2)t/25} = 24 \cdot 2^{-t/25} \;\; \Rightarrow \;\; m(40) = 24 \cdot 2^{-40/25} \approx 7.92$ mg.

(b) $m'(t) = 24\dfrac{d}{dt}\left[e^{-(\ln 2)t/25}\right] = 24 \cdot e^{-(\ln 2)t/25}\left(-\dfrac{\ln 2}{25}\right)$, so

$m'(40) = 24e^{-(\ln 2)(40)/25}\left(-\dfrac{\ln 2}{25}\right) \approx -0.22$ mg/yr

(c) $m(t) = 5 \;\; \Rightarrow \;\; 24e^{-(\ln 2)t/25} = 5 \;\; \Rightarrow \;\; e^{-(\ln 2)t/25} = \dfrac{5}{24} \;\; \Rightarrow \;\; -(\ln 2)t/25 = \ln \dfrac{5}{24} \;\; \Rightarrow$

$t = -25\dfrac{\ln \frac{5}{24}}{\ln 2} \approx 56.6$ yr

57. (a) $\displaystyle\lim_{t \to \infty} p(t) = \lim_{t \to \infty} \dfrac{1}{1 + ae^{-kt}} = \dfrac{1}{1 + a \cdot 0} = 1$, since $k > 0 \;\; \Rightarrow \;\; -kt \to -\infty \;\; \Rightarrow \;\; e^{-kt} \to 0$.

(b) $p(t) = \left(1 + ae^{-kt}\right)^{-1} \;\; \Rightarrow \;\; \dfrac{dp}{dt} = -\left(1 + ae^{-kt}\right)^{-2}\left(-kae^{-kt}\right) = \dfrac{kae^{-kt}}{\left(1 + ae^{-kt}\right)^2}$

(c)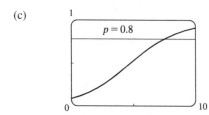

From the graph of $p(t) = \left(1 + 10e^{-0.5t}\right)^{-1}$, it seems that

$p(t) = 0.8$ (indicating that 80% of the population has heard the

rumor) when $t \approx 7.4$ hours.

59. $f(x) = x - e^x \;\; \Rightarrow \;\; f'(x) = 1 - e^x = 0 \;\; \Leftrightarrow \;\; e^x = 1 \;\; \Leftrightarrow \;\; x = 0$. Now $f'(x) > 0$ for all $x < 0$ and

$f'(x) < 0$ for all $x > 0$, so the absolute maximum value is $f(0) = 0 - 1 = -1$.

61. $y = xe^{3x} \;\; \Rightarrow \;\; y' = xe^{3x} \cdot 3 + e^{3x} \cdot 1 = (3x + 1)e^{3x} \;\; \Rightarrow \;\; y'' = (3x + 1)e^{3x} \cdot 3 + e^{3x} \cdot 3 = (9x + 6)e^{3x}$. The

curve is concave upward at $x \;\; \Leftrightarrow \;\; y'' > 0$ at $x \;\; \Leftrightarrow \;\; 9x + 6 > 0 \;\; \Leftrightarrow \;\; x > -\frac{2}{3}$. Thus, the curve is concave

upward on $\left(-\frac{2}{3}, \infty\right)$.

63. $y = f(x) = e^{-1/(x+1)}$ **A.** $D = \{x \mid x \neq -1\} = (-\infty, -1) \cup (-1, \infty)$ **B.** No x-intercept;

y-intercept $= f(0) = e^{-1}$ **C.** No symmetry   **D.** $\lim\limits_{x \to \pm\infty} e^{-1/(x+1)} = 1$ since $-1/(x+1) \to 0$, so $y = 1$ is

a HA. $\lim\limits_{x \to -1^+} e^{-1/(x+1)} = 0$ since $-1/(x+1) \to -\infty$, $\lim\limits_{x \to -1^-} e^{-1/(x+1)} = \infty$ since $-1/(x+1) \to \infty$, so

$x = -1$ is a VA.   **E.** $f'(x) = e^{-1/(x+1)}/(x+1)^2 \implies f'(x) > 0$ for all x except 1, so

f is increasing on $(-\infty, -1)$ and $(-1, \infty)$.   **F.** No extreme values   **H.**

G. $f''(x) = \dfrac{e^{-1/(x+1)}}{(x+1)^4} + \dfrac{e^{-1/(x+1)}(-2)}{(x+1)^3} = -\dfrac{e^{-1/(x+1)}(2x+1)}{(x+1)^4}$

$\implies f''(x) > 0 \iff 2x + 1 < 0 \iff x < -\frac{1}{2}$, so f is CU on

$(-\infty, -1)$ and $\left(-1, -\frac{1}{2}\right)$, and CD on $\left(-\frac{1}{2}, \infty\right)$. f has an IP

at $\left(-\frac{1}{2}, e^{-2}\right)$.

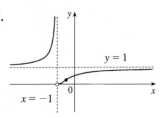

65. $y = f(x) = e^{3x} + e^{-2x}$ **A.** $D = \mathbb{R}$ **B.** y-intercept $= f(0) = 2$;   **H.**

no x-intercept   **C.** No symmetry   **D.** No asymptotes

E. $f'(x) = 3e^{3x} - 2e^{-2x}$, so $f'(x) > 0 \iff 3e^{3x} > 2e^{-2x}$

[multiply by e^{2x}] $\iff e^{5x} > \frac{2}{3} \iff 5x > \ln\frac{2}{3} \iff$

$x > \frac{1}{5}\ln\frac{2}{3} \approx -0.081$. Similarly, $f'(x) < 0 \iff x < \frac{1}{5}\ln\frac{2}{3}$.

f is decreasing on $\left(-\infty, \frac{1}{5}\ln\frac{2}{3}\right)$ and increasing on $\left(\frac{1}{5}\ln\frac{2}{3}, \infty\right)$.

F. Local minimum value $f\left(\frac{1}{5}\ln\frac{2}{3}\right) = \left(\frac{2}{3}\right)^{3/5} + \left(\frac{2}{3}\right)^{-2/5} \approx 1.96$; no local maximum.

G. $f''(x) = 9e^{3x} + 4e^{-2x}$, so $f''(x) > 0$ for all x, and f is CU on $(-\infty, \infty)$. No IP

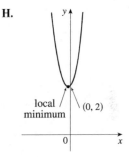

local
minimum $(0, 2)$

67. $f(x) = e^{x^3 - x} \to 0$ as $x \to -\infty$, and

$f(x) \to \infty$ as $x \to \infty$. From the graph,

it appears that f has a local minimum of

about $f(0.58) = 0.68$, and a local

maximum of about $f(-0.58) = 1.47$.

To find the exact values, we calculate

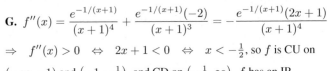

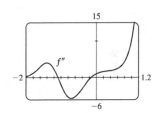

$f'(x) = (3x^2 - 1)e^{x^3 - x}$, which is 0 when $3x^2 - 1 = 0 \iff x = \pm\frac{1}{\sqrt{3}}$. The negative root corresponds to the

local maximum $f\left(-\frac{1}{\sqrt{3}}\right) = e^{(-1/\sqrt{3})^3 - (-1/\sqrt{3})} = e^{2\sqrt{3}/9}$, and the positive root corresponds to the local

minimum $f\left(\frac{1}{\sqrt{3}}\right) = e^{(1/\sqrt{3})^3 - (1/\sqrt{3})} = e^{-2\sqrt{3}/9}$. To estimate the inflection points, we calculate and graph

$f''(x) = \dfrac{d}{dx}\left[(3x^2 - 1)e^{x^3 - x}\right] = (3x^2 - 1)e^{x^3 - x}(3x^2 - 1) + e^{x^3 - x}(6x) = e^{x^3 - x}(9x^4 - 6x^2 + 6x + 1)$.

From the graph, it appears that $f''(x)$ changes sign (and thus f has inflection points) at $x \approx -0.15$ and

$x \approx -1.09$. From the graph of f, we see that these x-values correspond to inflection points at about $(-0.15, 1.15)$

and $(-1.09, 0.82)$.

69. Let $u = -3x$. Then $du = -3\,dx$, so

$$\int_0^5 e^{-3x}\,dx = -\tfrac{1}{3}\int_0^{-15} e^u\,du = -\tfrac{1}{3}[e^u]_0^{-15} = -\tfrac{1}{3}\left(e^{-15} - e^0\right) = \tfrac{1}{3}\left(1 - e^{-15}\right).$$

71. Let $u = 1 + e^x$. Then $du = e^x\,dx$, so $\int e^x\sqrt{1 + e^x}\,dx = \int \sqrt{u}\,du = \tfrac{2}{3}u^{3/2} + C = \tfrac{2}{3}(1 + e^x)^{3/2} + C.$

73. $\displaystyle\int \frac{e^x + 1}{e^x}\,dx = \int\left(1 + e^{-x}\right)dx = x - e^{-x} + C$

75. Let $u = \sqrt{x}$. Then $du = \dfrac{1}{2\sqrt{x}}\,dx$, so $\displaystyle\int \frac{e^{\sqrt{x}}}{\sqrt{x}}\,dx = 2\int e^u\,du = 2e^u + C = 2e^{\sqrt{x}} + C.$

77. Area $= \int_0^1 \left(e^{3x} - e^x\right)dx = \left[\tfrac{1}{3}e^{3x} - e^x\right]_0^1 = \left(\tfrac{1}{3}e^3 - e\right) - \left(\tfrac{1}{3} - 1\right) = \tfrac{1}{3}e^3 - e + \tfrac{2}{3} \approx 4.644$

79. $V = \int_0^1 \pi(e^x)^2\,dx = \pi\int_0^1 e^{2x}\,dx = \tfrac{1}{2}\pi[e^{2x}]_0^1 = \tfrac{\pi}{2}\left(e^2 - 1\right)$

81. $y = \ln(x + 3) \;\Rightarrow\; e^y = x + 3 \;\Rightarrow\;$

$x = e^y - 3$. Interchanging x and y, we get

$y = e^x - 3$, so $f^{-1}(x) = e^x - 3$.

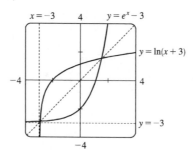

83. We use Theorem 7.1.7. Note that $f(0) = 3 + 0 + e^0 = 4$, so $f^{-1}(4) = 0$. Also $f'(x) = 1 + e^x$. Therefore,

$$\left(f^{-1}\right)'(4) = \frac{1}{f'(f^{-1}(4))} = \frac{1}{f'(0)} = \frac{1}{1 + e^0} = \frac{1}{2}.$$

85. Using the second law of logarithms and Equation 5, we have $\ln(e^x/e^y) = \ln e^x - \ln e^y = x - y = \ln(e^{x - y})$. Since $\ln$ is a one-to-one function, it follows that $e^x/e^y = e^{x - y}$.

87. (a) Let $f(x) = e^x - 1 - x$. Now $f(0) = e^0 - 1 = 0$, and for $x \geq 0$, we have $f'(x) = e^x - 1 \geq 0$. Now, since $f(0) = 0$ and f is increasing on $[0, \infty)$, $f(x) \geq 0$ for $x \geq 0 \;\Rightarrow\; e^x - 1 - x \geq 0 \;\Rightarrow\; e^x \geq 1 + x.$

(b) For $0 \leq x \leq 1$, $x^2 \leq x$, so $e^{x^2} \leq e^x$ [since e^x is increasing]. Hence [from (a)] $1 + x^2 \leq e^{x^2} \leq e^x.$

So $\tfrac{4}{3} = \int_0^1 \left(1 + x^2\right)dx \leq \int_0^1 e^{x^2}\,dx \leq \int_0^1 e^x\,dx = e - 1 < e \;\Rightarrow\; \tfrac{4}{3} \leq \int_0^1 e^{x^2}\,dx \leq e.$

89. (a) By Exercise 87(a), the result holds for $n = 1$. Suppose that $e^x \geq 1 + x + \dfrac{x^2}{2!} + \cdots + \dfrac{x^k}{k!}$ for $x \geq 0$.

Let $f(x) = e^x - 1 - x - \dfrac{x^2}{2!} - \cdots - \dfrac{x^k}{k!} - \dfrac{x^{k+1}}{(k+1)!}$. Then $f'(x) = e^x - 1 - x - \cdots - \dfrac{x^k}{k!} \geq 0$

by assumption. Hence $f(x)$ is increasing on $(0, \infty)$. So $0 \leq x$ implies that

$$0 = f(0) \leq f(x) = e^x - 1 - x - \cdots - \frac{x^k}{k!} - \frac{x^{k+1}}{(k+1)!}, \text{ and hence } e^x \geq 1 + x + \cdots + \frac{x^k}{k!} + \frac{x^{k+1}}{(k+1)!}$$

for $x \geq 0$. Therefore, for $x \geq 0$, $e^x \geq 1 + x + \dfrac{x^2}{2!} + \cdots + \dfrac{x^n}{n!}$ for every positive integer n, by mathematical induction.

(b) Taking $n = 4$ and $x = 1$ in (a), we have $e = e^1 \geq 1 + \tfrac{1}{2} + \tfrac{1}{6} + \tfrac{1}{24} = 2.708\overline{3} > 2.7.$

(c) $e^x \geq 1 + x + \cdots + \dfrac{x^k}{k!} + \dfrac{x^{k+1}}{(k+1)!} \;\Rightarrow\; \dfrac{e^x}{x^k} \geq \dfrac{1}{x^k} + \dfrac{1}{x^{k-1}} + \cdots + \dfrac{1}{k!} + \dfrac{x}{(k+1)!} > \dfrac{x}{(k+1)!}.$

But $\displaystyle\lim_{x \to \infty} \frac{x}{(k+1)!} = \infty$, so $\displaystyle\lim_{x \to \infty} \frac{e^x}{x^k} = \infty.$

7.4* General Logarithmic and Exponential Functions

1. (a) $a^x = e^{x \ln a}$

(b) The domain of $f(x) = a^x$ is $\mathbb{R}$.

(c) The range of $f(x) = a^x$ $(a \neq 1)$ is $(0, \infty)$.

(d) (i) See Figure 1.   (ii) See Figure 3.   (iii) See Figure 2.

3. $5^{\sqrt{7}} = \left(e^{\ln 5}\right)^{\sqrt{7}} = e^{\sqrt{7} \ln 5}$ **5.** $(\cos x)^x = \left(e^{\ln \cos x}\right)^x = e^{x \ln(\cos x)}$.

7. (a) $\log_{10} 1000 = 3$ because $10^3 = 1000$.

(b) $\log_2 \frac{1}{16} = -4$ since $2^{-4} = \frac{1}{16}$.   [*Or:* $\log_2 \frac{1}{16} = \log_2 2^{-4} = -4$]

9. (a) $\log_{12} 3 + \log_{12} 48 = \log_{12}(3 \cdot 48) = \log_{12} 144 = 2$ since $12^2 = 144$.

(b) $\log_5 5^{\sqrt{2}} = \sqrt{2}$ by the cancellation property $\log_a a^x = x$.

[*Or:* $\log_5 5^{\sqrt{2}} = \sqrt{2} \log_5 5 = \sqrt{2} \cdot 1 = \sqrt{2}$]

11. All of these graphs approach 0 as $x \to -\infty$, all of them pass

through the point $(0, 1)$, and all of them are increasing and

approach ∞ as $x \to \infty$. The larger the base, the faster the

function increases for $x > 0$, and the faster it approaches 0 as

$x \to -\infty$.

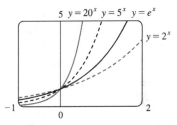

13. (a) $\log_{12} e = \dfrac{\ln e}{\ln 12} = \dfrac{1}{\ln 12} \approx 0.402430$ (b) $\log_6 13.54 = \dfrac{\ln 13.54}{\ln 6} \approx 1.454240$

(c) $\log_2 \pi = \dfrac{\ln \pi}{\ln 2} \approx 1.651496$

15. To graph these functions, we use $\log_{1.5} x = \dfrac{\ln x}{\ln 1.5}$ and

$\log_{50} x = \dfrac{\ln x}{\ln 50}$. These graphs all approach $-\infty$ as $x \to 0^+$, and

they all pass through the point $(1, 0)$. Also, they are all increasing,

and all approach ∞ as $x \to \infty$. The functions with larger bases

increase extremely slowly, and the ones with smaller bases do so

somewhat more quickly. The functions with large bases approach the

y-axis more closely as $x \to 0^+$.

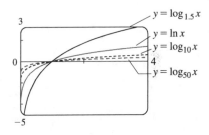

17. Use $y = Ca^x$ with the points $(1, 6)$ and $(3, 24)$. $6 = Ca^1$ $\left[C = \frac{6}{a}\right]$ and $24 = Ca^3$ $\Rightarrow$ $24 = \left(\dfrac{6}{a}\right)a^3$ $\Rightarrow$

$4 = a^2$ $\Rightarrow$ $a = 2$ [since $a > 0$] and $C = \frac{6}{2} = 3$. The function is $f(x) = 3 \cdot 2^x$.

19. (a) 2 ft = 24 in, $f(24) = 24^2$ in = 576 in = 48 ft. $g(24) = 2^{24}$ in = $2^{24}/(12 \cdot 5280)$ mi ≈ 265 mi

(b) 3 ft = 36 in, so we need x such that $\log_2 x = 36$ $\Leftrightarrow$ $x = 2^{36} = 68{,}719{,}476{,}736$. In miles, this is

$68{,}719{,}476{,}736$ in $\cdot \dfrac{1 \text{ ft}}{12 \text{ in}} \cdot \dfrac{1 \text{ mi}}{5280 \text{ ft}} \approx 1{,}084{,}587.7$ mi.

21. $\displaystyle\lim_{t \to \infty} 2^{-t^2} = \lim_{u \to -\infty} 2^u$ [where $u = -t^2$] $= 0$

23. $h(t) = t^3 - 3^t \quad \Rightarrow \quad h'(t) = 3t^2 - 3^t \ln 3$

25. Using Formula 4 and the Chain Rule, $y = 5^{-1/x} \quad \Rightarrow \quad y' = 5^{-1/x}(\ln 5)\left[-1 \cdot (-x^{-2})\right] = 5^{-1/x}(\ln 5)/x^2$

27. $f(u) = (2^u + 2^{-u})^{10} \quad \Rightarrow$

$$f'(u) = 10(2^u + 2^{-u})^9 \frac{d}{du}(2^u + 2^{-u}) = 10(2^u + 2^{-u})^9 \left[2^u \ln 2 + 2^{-u} \ln 2 \cdot (-1)\right]$$
$$= 10 \ln 2(2^u + 2^{-u})^9(2^u - 2^{-u})$$

29. $f(x) = \log_3(x^2 - 4) \quad \Rightarrow \quad f'(x) = \frac{1}{(x^2 - 4) \ln 3}(2x) = \frac{2x}{(x^2 - 4) \ln 3}$

31. $y = x^x \quad \Rightarrow \quad \ln y = x \ln x \quad \Rightarrow \quad y'/y = \ln x + x(1/x) \quad \Rightarrow \quad y' = x^x(\ln x + 1)$

33. $y = x^{\sin x} \quad \Rightarrow \quad \ln y = \sin x \ln x \quad \Rightarrow \quad \frac{y'}{y} = \cos x \ln x + \frac{\sin x}{x} \quad \Rightarrow \quad y' = x^{\sin x}\left(\cos x \ln x + \frac{\sin x}{x}\right)$

35. $y = (\ln x)^x \quad \Rightarrow \quad \ln y = x \ln \ln x \quad \Rightarrow \quad \frac{y'}{y} = \ln \ln x + x \cdot \frac{1}{\ln x} \cdot \frac{1}{x} \quad \Rightarrow \quad y' = (\ln x)^x\left(\ln \ln x + \frac{1}{\ln x}\right)$

37. $y = x^{e^x} \quad \Rightarrow \quad \ln y = e^x \ln x \quad \Rightarrow \quad \frac{y'}{y} = e^x \ln x + \frac{e^x}{x} \quad \Rightarrow \quad y' = x^{e^x} e^x\left(\ln x + \frac{1}{x}\right)$

39. $y = 10^x \quad \Rightarrow \quad y' = 10^x \ln 10$, so at $(1, 10)$, the slope of the tangent line is $10^1 \ln 10 = 10 \ln 10$, and its equation is $y - 10 = 10 \ln 10(x - 1)$, or $y = (10 \ln 10)x + 10(1 - \ln 10)$.

41. $\displaystyle\int_1^2 10^t \, dt = \left[\frac{10^t}{\ln 10}\right]_1^2 = \frac{10^2}{\ln 10} - \frac{10^1}{\ln 10} = \frac{100 - 10}{\ln 10} = \frac{90}{\ln 10}$

43. $\displaystyle\int \frac{\log_{10} x}{x} \, dx = \int \frac{(\ln x)/(\ln 10)}{x} \, dx = \frac{1}{\ln 10}\int \frac{\ln x}{x} \, dx$. Now put $u = \ln x$, so $du = \frac{1}{x}\, dx$, and the expression

becomes $\dfrac{1}{\ln 10}\displaystyle\int u \, du = \frac{1}{\ln 10}\left(\tfrac{1}{2}u^2 + C_1\right) = \frac{1}{2 \ln 10}(\ln x)^2 + C$.

Or: The substitution $u = \log_{10} x$ gives $du = \dfrac{dx}{x \ln 10}$ and we get $\displaystyle\int \frac{\log_{10} x}{x} \, dx = \tfrac{1}{2} \ln 10(\log_{10} x)^2 + C$.

45. Let $u = \sin \theta$. Then $du = \cos \theta \, d\theta$ and $\displaystyle\int 3^{\sin \theta} \cos \theta \, d\theta = \int 3^u \, du = \frac{3^u}{\ln 3} + C = \frac{1}{\ln 3} 3^{\sin \theta} + C$.

47.
$$A = \int_{-1}^0 (2^x - 5^x) \, dx + \int_0^1 (5^x - 2^x) \, dx$$
$$= \left[\frac{2^x}{\ln 2} - \frac{5^x}{\ln 5}\right]_{-1}^0 + \left[\frac{5^x}{\ln 5} - \frac{2^x}{\ln 2}\right]_0^1$$
$$= \left(\frac{1}{\ln 2} - \frac{1}{\ln 5}\right) - \left(\frac{1/2}{\ln 2} - \frac{1/5}{\ln 5}\right) + \left(\frac{5}{\ln 5} - \frac{2}{\ln 2}\right) - \left(\frac{1}{\ln 5} - \frac{1}{\ln 2}\right)$$
$$= \frac{16}{5 \ln 5} - \frac{1}{2 \ln 2}$$

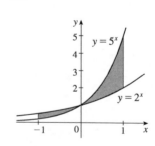

49. We see that the graphs of $y = 2^x$ and $y = 1 + 3^{-x}$ intersect at $x \approx 0.6$. We let $f(x) = 2^x - 1 - 3^{-x}$ and calculate $f'(x) = 2^x \ln 2 + 3^{-x} \ln 3$, and using the formula $x_{n+1} = x_n - f(x_n)/f'(x_n)$ (Newton's Method), we get $x_1 = 0.6$, $x_2 \approx x_3 \approx 0.600967$. So, correct to six decimal places, the root occurs at $x = 0.600967$.

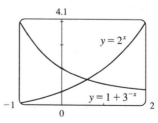

51. $y = \dfrac{10^x}{10^x + 1}$ $\Leftrightarrow$ $(10^x + 1)y = 10^x$ $\Leftrightarrow$ $10^x \cdot y + y = 10^x$ $\Leftrightarrow$ $y = 10^x - 10^x y$ $\Leftrightarrow$

$y = 10^x(1 - y)$ $\Leftrightarrow$ $10^x = \dfrac{y}{1 - y}$ $\Leftrightarrow$ $\log_{10} 10^x = \log_{10}\left(\dfrac{y}{1 - y}\right)$ $\Leftrightarrow$ $x = \log_{10} y - \log_{10}(1 - y)$.

Interchange x and y: $y = \log_{10} x - \log_{10}(1 - x)$ is the inverse function.

53. If I is the intensity of the 1989 San Francisco earthquake, then $\log_{10}(I/S) = 7.1$ $\Rightarrow$

$\log_{10}(16I/S) = \log_{10} 16 + \log_{10}(I/S) = \log_{10} 16 + 7.1 \approx 8.3$.

55. We find I with the loudness formula from Exercise 55, substituting $I_0 = 10^{-12}$ and $L = 50$:

$50 = 10\log_{10}\dfrac{I}{10^{-12}}$ $\Leftrightarrow$ $5 = \log_{10}\dfrac{I}{10^{-12}}$ $\Leftrightarrow$ $10^5 = \dfrac{I}{10^{-12}}$ $\Leftrightarrow$ $I = 10^{-7}$ watt/m^2. Now we

differentiate L with respect to I: $L = 10\log_{10}\dfrac{I}{I_0}$ $\Rightarrow$ $\dfrac{dL}{dI} = 10\dfrac{1}{(I/I_0)\ln 10}\left(\dfrac{1}{I_0}\right) = \dfrac{10}{\ln 10}\left(\dfrac{1}{I}\right)$.

Substituting $I = 10^{-7}$, we get $L'(50) = \dfrac{10}{\ln 10}\left(\dfrac{1}{10^{-7}}\right) = \dfrac{10^8}{\ln 10} \approx 4.34 \times 10^7\,\dfrac{\text{dB}}{\text{watt/m}^2}$.

57. (a) Using a calculator or CAS, we obtain the model $Q = ab^t$ with $a = 100.0124369$ and $b = 0.000045145933$.

We can change this model to one with base e and exponent $\ln b$ [$b^t = e^{t\ln b}$ from precalculus mathematics or

from Section 7.3]: $Q = ae^{t\ln b} = 100.012437e^{-10.005531t}$.

(b) Use $Q'(t) = ab^t \ln b$ or the calculator command nDeriv(Y$_1$,X,.04) with Y$_1$=ab^x to get

$Q'(0.04) \approx -670.63\ \mu\text{A}$. The result of Example 2 in Section 2.1 was $-670\ \mu\text{A}$.

59. Using Definition 1 and the second law of exponents for e^x, we have

$$a^{x-y} = e^{(x-y)\ln a} = e^{x\ln a - y\ln a} = \dfrac{e^{x\ln a}}{e^{y\ln a}} = \dfrac{a^x}{a^y}.$$

61. Let $\log_a x = r$ and $\log_a y = s$. Then $a^r = x$ and $a^s = y$.

(a) $xy = a^r a^s = a^{r+s}$ $\Rightarrow$ $\log_a(xy) = r + s = \log_a x + \log_a y$

(b) $\dfrac{x}{y} = \dfrac{a^r}{a^s} = a^{r-s}$ $\Rightarrow$ $\log_a\dfrac{x}{y} = r - s = \log_a x - \log_a y$

(c) $x^y = (a^r)^y = a^{ry}$ $\Rightarrow$ $\log_a(x^y) = ry = y\log_a x$

7.5 Inverse Trigonometric Functions

1. (a) $\sin^{-1}\left(\dfrac{\sqrt{3}}{2}\right) = \dfrac{\pi}{3}$ since $\sin\dfrac{\pi}{3} = \dfrac{\sqrt{3}}{2}$ and $\dfrac{\pi}{3}$ is in $\left[-\dfrac{\pi}{2}, \dfrac{\pi}{2}\right]$.

(b) $\cos^{-1}(-1) = \pi$ since $\cos\pi = -1$ and π is in $[0, \pi]$.

3. (a) $\tan^{-1}\sqrt{3} = \dfrac{\pi}{3}$ since $\tan\dfrac{\pi}{3} = \sqrt{3}$ and $\dfrac{\pi}{3}$ is in $\left(-\dfrac{\pi}{2}, \dfrac{\pi}{2}\right)$.

(b) $\arcsin\left(-\dfrac{1}{\sqrt{2}}\right) = -\dfrac{\pi}{4}$ since $\sin\left(-\dfrac{\pi}{4}\right) = -\dfrac{1}{\sqrt{2}}$ and $-\dfrac{\pi}{4}$ is in $\left[-\dfrac{\pi}{2}, \dfrac{\pi}{2}\right]$.

5. (a) $\arccos(\cos 2\pi) = \arccos(1) = 0$

(b) $\tan(\tan^{-1} 5) = 5$

7. Let $\theta = \sin^{-1}\left(\frac{2}{3}\right)$.

Then $\tan\left(\sin^{-1}\left(\frac{2}{3}\right)\right) = \tan\theta = \dfrac{2}{\sqrt{5}}$.

9. Let $\theta = \tan^{-1}\sqrt{2}$. Then

$$\sin\left(2\tan^{-1}\sqrt{2}\right) = \sin(2\theta) = 2\sin\theta\cos\theta$$
$$= 2\left(\frac{\sqrt{2}}{\sqrt{3}}\right)\left(\frac{1}{\sqrt{3}}\right) = \frac{2\sqrt{2}}{3}$$

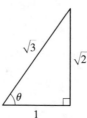

11. Let $y = \sin^{-1}x$. Then $-\frac{\pi}{2} \leq y \leq \frac{\pi}{2}$ $\Rightarrow$ $\cos y \geq 0$, so $\cos(\sin^{-1}x) = \cos y = \sqrt{1 - \sin^2 y} = \sqrt{1 - x^2}$

13. Let $y = \tan^{-1}x$. Then $\tan y = x$, so from the triangle we see that $\sin(\tan^{-1}x) = \sin y = \dfrac{x}{\sqrt{1 + x^2}}$.

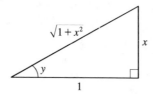

15.

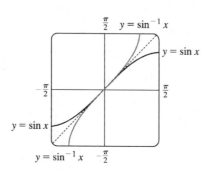

The graph of $\sin^{-1}x$ is the reflection of the graph of $\sin x$ about the line $y = x$.

17. Let $y = \cos^{-1}x$. Then $\cos y = x$ and $0 \leq y \leq \pi$ $\Rightarrow$ $-\sin y \dfrac{dy}{dx} = 1$ $\Rightarrow$

$\dfrac{dy}{dx} = -\dfrac{1}{\sin y} = -\dfrac{1}{\sqrt{1 - \cos^2 y}} = -\dfrac{1}{\sqrt{1 - x^2}}$. [Note that $\sin y \geq 0$ for $0 \leq y \leq \pi$.]

19. Let $y = \cot^{-1}x$. Then $\cot y = x$ $\Rightarrow$ $-\csc^2 y \dfrac{dy}{dx} = 1$ $\Rightarrow$ $\dfrac{dy}{dx} = -\dfrac{1}{\csc^2 y} = -\dfrac{1}{1 + \cot^2 y} = -\dfrac{1}{1 + x^2}$.

21. Let $y = \csc^{-1}x$. Then $\csc y = x$ $\Rightarrow$ $-\csc y \cot y \dfrac{dy}{dx} = 1$ $\Rightarrow$

$\dfrac{dy}{dx} = -\dfrac{1}{\csc y \cot y} = -\dfrac{1}{\csc y \sqrt{\csc^2 y - 1}} = -\dfrac{1}{x\sqrt{x^2 - 1}}$. Note that $\cot y \geq 0$ on the domain of $\csc^{-1}x$.

23. $y = \tan^{-1}\sqrt{x}$ $\Rightarrow$ $y' = \dfrac{1}{1 + (\sqrt{x})^2} \cdot \dfrac{d}{dx}(\sqrt{x}) = \dfrac{1}{1 + x}\left(\frac{1}{2}x^{-1/2}\right) = \dfrac{1}{2\sqrt{x}(1 + x)}$

25. $y = \sin^{-1}(2x + 1)$ $\Rightarrow$

$$y' = \frac{1}{\sqrt{1 - (2x+1)^2}} \cdot \frac{d}{dx}(2x+1) = \frac{1}{\sqrt{1 - (4x^2 + 4x + 1)}} \cdot 2 = \frac{2}{\sqrt{-4x^2 - 4x}} = \frac{1}{\sqrt{-x^2 - x}}$$

27. $H(x) = (1 + x^2)\arctan x$ $\Rightarrow$ $H'(x) = (1 + x^2)\dfrac{1}{1 + x^2} + (\arctan x)(2x) = 1 + 2x\arctan x$

29. $y = \cos^{-1}(e^{2x})$ $\Rightarrow$ $y' = -\dfrac{1}{\sqrt{1 - (e^{2x})^2}} \cdot \dfrac{d}{dx}(e^{2x}) = -\dfrac{2e^{2x}}{\sqrt{1 - e^{4x}}}$

31. $y = \arctan(\cos\theta)$ $\Rightarrow$ $y' = \dfrac{1}{1 + (\cos\theta)^2}(-\sin\theta) = -\dfrac{\sin\theta}{1 + \cos^2\theta}$

33. $h(t) = \cot^{-1}(t) + \cot^{-1}(1/t)$ $\Rightarrow$

$$h'(t) = -\frac{1}{1 + t^2} - \frac{1}{1 + (1/t)^2} \cdot \frac{d}{dt}\frac{1}{t} = -\frac{1}{1 + t^2} - \frac{t^2}{t^2 + 1} \cdot \left(-\frac{1}{t^2}\right) = -\frac{1}{1 + t^2} + \frac{1}{t^2 + 1} = 0.$$

Note that this makes sense because $h(t) = \dfrac{\pi}{2}$ for $t > 0$ and $h(t) = -\dfrac{\pi}{2}$ for $t < 0$.

35. $y = \arccos\left(\dfrac{b + a\cos x}{a + b\cos x}\right)$ $\Rightarrow$

$$y' = -\frac{1}{\sqrt{1 - \left(\dfrac{b + a\cos x}{a + b\cos x}\right)^2}} \frac{(a + b\cos x)(-a\sin x) - (b + a\cos x)(-b\sin x)}{(a + b\cos x)^2}$$

$$= \frac{1}{\sqrt{a^2 + b^2\cos^2 x - b^2 - a^2\cos^2 x}} \frac{(a^2 - b^2)\sin x}{|a + b\cos x|}$$

$$= \frac{1}{\sqrt{a^2 - b^2}\sqrt{1 - \cos^2 x}} \frac{(a^2 - b^2)\sin x}{|a + b\cos x|} = \frac{\sqrt{a^2 - b^2}}{|a + b\cos x|} \frac{\sin x}{|\sin x|}$$

But $0 \le x \le \pi$, so $|\sin x| = \sin x$. Also $a > b > 0$ $\Rightarrow$ $b\cos x \ge -b > -a$, so $a + b\cos x > 0$.

Thus $y' = \dfrac{\sqrt{a^2 - b^2}}{a + b\cos x}$.

37. $g(x) = \cos^{-1}(3 - 2x)$ $\Rightarrow$ $g'(x) = -\dfrac{1}{\sqrt{1 - (3 - 2x)^2}}(-2) = \dfrac{2}{\sqrt{1 - (3 - 2x)^2}}$.

Domain$(g) = \{x \mid -1 \le 3 - 2x \le 1\} = \{x \mid -4 \le -2x \le -2\} = \{x \mid 2 \ge x \ge 1\} = [1, 2]$.

Domain$(g') = \{x \mid 1 - (3 - 2x)^2 > 0\} = \{x \mid (3 - 2x)^2 < 1\} = \{x \mid |3 - 2x| < 1\}$

$\qquad = \{x \mid -1 < 3 - 2x < 1\} = \{x \mid -4 < -2x < -2\} = \{x \mid 2 > x > 1\} = (1, 2)$

39. $g(x) = x\sin^{-1}\left(\dfrac{x}{4}\right) + \sqrt{16 - x^2}$ $\Rightarrow$ $g'(x) = \sin^{-1}\left(\dfrac{x}{4}\right) + \dfrac{x}{4\sqrt{1 - (x/4)^2}} - \dfrac{x}{\sqrt{16 - x^2}} = \sin^{-1}\left(\dfrac{x}{4}\right)$ $\Rightarrow$

$g'(2) = \sin^{-1}\frac{1}{2} = \frac{\pi}{6}$

41. $f(x) = e^{-x}\arctan x$ $\Rightarrow$

$f'(x) = \dfrac{e^{-x}}{1 + x^2} - e^{-x}\arctan x$. The answer is reasonable

since f' is positive where f is increasing and f' is negative

where f is decreasing.

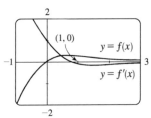

43. $\displaystyle\lim_{x \to -1^+} \sin^{-1} x = \sin^{-1}(-1) = -\frac{\pi}{2}$

45. Let $t = e^x$. As $x \to \infty$, $t \to \infty$. $\displaystyle\lim_{x \to \infty} \arctan(e^x) = \lim_{t \to \infty} \arctan t = \frac{\pi}{2}$ by (8).

47.

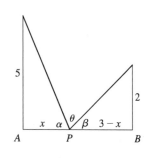

From the figure, $\tan \alpha = \dfrac{5}{x}$ and $\tan \beta = \dfrac{2}{3 - x}$. Since

$$\alpha + \beta + \theta = 180° = \pi, \ \theta = \pi - \tan^{-1}\left(\frac{5}{x}\right) - \tan^{-1}\left(\frac{2}{3 - x}\right) \ \Rightarrow$$

$$\frac{d\theta}{dx} = -\frac{1}{1 + \left(\dfrac{5}{x}\right)^2}\left(-\frac{5}{x^2}\right) - \frac{1}{1 + \left(\dfrac{2}{3 - x}\right)^2}\left[\frac{2}{(3 - x)^2}\right]$$

$$= \frac{x^2}{x^2 + 25} \cdot \frac{5}{x^2} - \frac{(3 - x)^2}{(3 - x)^2 + 4} \cdot \frac{2}{(3 - x)^2}.$$

Now $\dfrac{d\theta}{dx} = 0 \ \Rightarrow \ \dfrac{5}{x^2 + 25} = \dfrac{2}{x^2 - 6x + 13} \ \Rightarrow \ 2x^2 + 50 = 5x^2 - 30x + 65 \ \Rightarrow$

$3x^2 - 30x + 15 = 0 \ \Rightarrow \ x^2 - 10x + 5 = 0 \ \Rightarrow \ x = 5 \pm 2\sqrt{5}$. We reject the root with the $+$ sign,

since it is larger than 3. $d\theta/dx > 0$ for $x < 5 - 2\sqrt{5}$ and $d\theta/dx < 0$ for $x > 5 - 2\sqrt{5}$, so θ is maximized

when $|AP| = x = 5 - 2\sqrt{5} \approx 0.53$.

49.

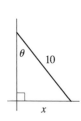

$\dfrac{dx}{dt} = 2 \ \text{ft/s}, \ \sin \theta = \dfrac{x}{10} \ \Rightarrow \ \theta = \sin^{-1}\left(\dfrac{x}{10}\right), \ \dfrac{d\theta}{dx} = \dfrac{1/10}{\sqrt{1 - (x/10)^2}},$

$$\frac{d\theta}{dt} = \frac{d\theta}{dx}\frac{dx}{dt} = \frac{1/10}{\sqrt{1 - (x/10)^2}}(2) \ \text{rad/s},$$

$$\left.\frac{d\theta}{dt}\right]_{x = 6} = \frac{2/10}{\sqrt{1 - (6/10)^2}} \ \text{rad/s} = \tfrac{1}{4} \ \text{rad/s}$$

51. $y = f(x) = \sin^{-1}(x/(x + 1))$ **A.** $D = \{x \mid -1 \le x/(x + 1) \le 1\}$. For $x > -1$ we have

$-x - 1 \le x \le x + 1 \ \Leftrightarrow \ 2x \ge -1 \ \Leftrightarrow \ x \ge -\frac{1}{2}$, so $D = \left[-\frac{1}{2}, \infty\right)$.   **B.** Intercepts are 0   **C.** No

symmetry   **D.** $\displaystyle\lim_{x \to \infty} \sin^{-1}\left(\frac{x}{x + 1}\right) = \lim_{x \to \infty} \sin^{-1}\left(\frac{1}{1 + 1/x}\right) = \sin^{-1} 1 = \frac{\pi}{2}$, so $y = \frac{\pi}{2}$ is a HA.

E. $f'(x) = \dfrac{1}{\sqrt{1 - [x/(x + 1)]^2}} \dfrac{(x + 1) - x}{(x + 1)^2} = \dfrac{1}{(x + 1)\sqrt{2x + 1}} > 0,$ **H.**

so f is increasing on $\left(-\frac{1}{2}, \infty\right)$.   **F.** No local maximum or minimum,

$f\left(-\frac{1}{2}\right) = \sin^{-1}(-1) = -\frac{\pi}{2}$ is an absolute minimum

G. $f''(x) = -\dfrac{\sqrt{2x + 1} + (x + 1)/\sqrt{2x + 1}}{(x + 1)^2(2x + 1)}$

$= -\dfrac{3x + 2}{(x + 1)^2(2x + 1)^{3/2}} < 0$ on D, so f is CD on $\left(-\frac{1}{2}, \infty\right)$.

53. $y = f(x) = x - \tan^{-1} x$ **A.** $D = \mathbb{R}$ **B.** Intercepts are 0   **C.** $f(-x) = -f(x)$, so the curve is symmetric about the origin.   **D.** $\lim\limits_{x \to \infty} (x - \tan^{-1} x) = \infty$ and $\lim\limits_{x \to -\infty} (x - \tan^{-1} x) = -\infty$, no HA.

But $f(x) - \left(x - \frac{\pi}{2}\right) = -\tan^{-1} x + \frac{\pi}{2} \to 0$ as $x \to \infty$, and

$f(x) - \left(x + \frac{\pi}{2}\right) = -\tan^{-1} x - \frac{\pi}{2} \to 0$ as $x \to -\infty$, so $y = x \pm \frac{\pi}{2}$ are

slant asymptotes.   **E.** $f'(x) = 1 - \dfrac{1}{x^2 + 1} = \dfrac{x^2}{x^2 + 1} > 0$, so f is

increasing on $\mathbb{R}$.   **F.** No extrema

G. $f''(x) = \dfrac{(1 + x^2)(2x) - x^2(2x)}{(1 + x^2)^2} = \dfrac{2x}{(1 + x^2)^2} > 0 \quad \Leftrightarrow \quad x > 0$, so

f is CU on $(0, \infty)$, CD on $(-\infty, 0)$. IP at $(0, 0)$.

H.

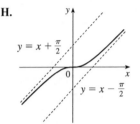

55. $f(x) = \arctan(\cos(3 \arcsin x))$. We use a CAS to compute f' and f'', and to graph f, f', and f'':

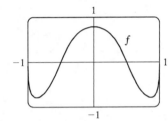 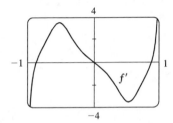 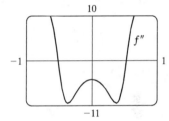

From the graph of f', it appears that the only maximum occurs at $x = 0$ and there are minima at $x = \pm 0.87$. From the graph of f'', it appears that there are inflection points at $x = \pm 0.52$.

57. $f(x) = 2x + 5(1 - x^2)^{-1/2} = 2x + 5/\sqrt{1 - x^2} \quad \Rightarrow \quad F(x) = x^2 + 5 \sin^{-1} x + C$

59. $\displaystyle\int_{1/2}^{\sqrt{3}/2} \frac{6}{\sqrt{1 - t^2}}\, dt = 6 \int_{1/2}^{\sqrt{3}/2} \frac{1}{\sqrt{1 - t^2}}\, dt = 6\left[\sin^{-1} t\right]_{1/2}^{\sqrt{3}/2} = 6\left[\sin^{-1}\left(\frac{\sqrt{3}}{2}\right) - \sin^{-1}\left(\frac{1}{2}\right)\right]$

$\qquad = 6\left(\frac{\pi}{3} - \frac{\pi}{6}\right) = 6\left(\frac{\pi}{6}\right) = \pi$

61. Let $u = 4x$. Then $du = 4\, dx$, so

$\displaystyle\int_0^{\sqrt{3}/4} \frac{dx}{1 + 16x^2} = \frac{1}{4} \int_0^{\sqrt{3}} \frac{1}{1 + u^2}\, du = \frac{1}{4}\left[\tan^{-1} u\right]_0^{\sqrt{3}} = \frac{1}{4}\left(\tan^{-1} \sqrt{3} - \tan^{-1} 0\right) = \frac{1}{4}\left(\frac{\pi}{3} - 0\right) = \frac{\pi}{12}.$

63. Let $u = \sin^{-1} x$. Then $du = \dfrac{1}{\sqrt{1 - x^2}}\, dx$, so $\displaystyle\int_0^{1/2} \frac{\sin^{-1} x}{\sqrt{1 - x^2}}\, dx = \int_0^{\pi/6} u\, du = \left.\frac{u^2}{2}\right]_0^{\pi/6} = \frac{1}{2}\left(\frac{\pi}{6}\right)^2 = \frac{\pi^2}{72}.$

65. $\displaystyle\int \frac{x + 9}{x^2 + 9}\, dx = \int \frac{x}{x^2 + 9}\, dx + 9 \int \frac{1}{x^2 + 9}\, dx = \frac{1}{2} \ln(x^2 + 9) + 3 \tan^{-1} \frac{x}{3} + C$

(Let $u = x^2 + 9$ in the first integral; use Equation 14 in the second.)

67. Let $u = t^3$. Then $du = 3t^2\, dt$ and $\displaystyle\int \frac{t^2}{\sqrt{1 - t^6}}\, dt = \int \frac{\frac{1}{3}\, du}{\sqrt{1 - u^2}} = \frac{1}{3} \sin^{-1} u + C = \frac{1}{3} \sin^{-1}(t^3) + C.$

69. Let $u = \sqrt{x}$. Then $du = \dfrac{dx}{2\sqrt{x}}$ and $\displaystyle\int \frac{dx}{\sqrt{x}(1 + x)} = \int \frac{2\, du}{1 + u^2} = 2 \tan^{-1} u + C = 2 \tan^{-1} \sqrt{x} + C.$

71. Let $u = x/a$. Then $du = dx/a$, so

$$\int \frac{dx}{\sqrt{a^2 - x^2}} = \int \frac{dx}{a\sqrt{1 - (x/a)^2}} = \int \frac{du}{\sqrt{1 - u^2}} = \sin^{-1} u + C = \sin^{-1} \frac{x}{a} + C.$$

73.

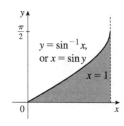

The integral represents the area below the curve $y = \sin^{-1} x$ on the interval $x \in [0, 1]$. The bounding curves are $y = \sin^{-1} x \Leftrightarrow x = \sin y$, $y = 0$ and $x = 1$. We see that y ranges between $\sin^{-1} 0 = 0$ and $\sin^{-1} 1 = \frac{\pi}{2}$. So we have to integrate the function $x = 1 - \sin y$ between $y = 0$ and $y = \frac{\pi}{2}$:

$$\int_0^1 \sin^{-1} x \, dx = \int_0^{\pi/2} (1 - \sin y) \, dy = \left(\frac{\pi}{2} + \cos \frac{\pi}{2}\right) - (0 + \cos 0) = \frac{\pi}{2} - 1.$$

75. (a) $\arctan \frac{1}{2} + \arctan \frac{1}{3} = \arctan\left(\dfrac{\frac{1}{2} + \frac{1}{3}}{1 - \frac{1}{2} \cdot \frac{1}{3}}\right) = \arctan 1 = \dfrac{\pi}{4}$

(b) $2\arctan \frac{1}{3} + \arctan \frac{1}{7} = \left(\arctan \frac{1}{3} + \arctan \frac{1}{3}\right) + \arctan \frac{1}{7} = \arctan\left(\dfrac{\frac{1}{3} + \frac{1}{3}}{1 - \frac{1}{3} \cdot \frac{1}{3}}\right) + \arctan \frac{1}{7}$

$$= \arctan \frac{3}{4} + \arctan \frac{1}{7} = \arctan\left(\dfrac{\frac{3}{4} + \frac{1}{7}}{1 - \frac{3}{4} \cdot \frac{1}{7}}\right) = \arctan 1 = \dfrac{\pi}{4}$$

77. Let $f(x) = 2\sin^{-1} x - \cos^{-1}(1 - 2x^2)$. Then

$$f'(x) = \frac{2}{\sqrt{1 - x^2}} - \frac{4x}{\sqrt{1 - (1 - 2x^2)^2}} = \frac{2}{\sqrt{1 - x^2}} - \frac{4x}{2x\sqrt{1 - x^2}} = 0 \qquad \text{[since } x \geq 0\text{]}$$

Thus $f'(x) = 0$ for all $x \in [0, 1)$. Thus $f(x) = C$. To find C let $x = 0$. Thus $2\sin^{-1}(0) - \cos^{-1}(1) = 0 = C$. Therefore we see that $f(x) = 2\sin^{-1} x - \cos^{-1}(1 - 2x^2) = 0 \Rightarrow 2\sin^{-1} x = \cos^{-1}(1 - 2x^2)$.

79. $y = \sec^{-1} x \Rightarrow \sec y = x \Rightarrow \sec y \tan y \dfrac{dy}{dx} = 1 \Rightarrow \dfrac{dy}{dx} = \dfrac{1}{\sec y \tan y}$. Now

$\tan^2 y = \sec^2 y - 1 = x^2 - 1$, so $\tan y = \pm\sqrt{x^2 - 1}$. For $y \in \left[0, \frac{\pi}{2}\right)$, $x \geq 1$, so $\sec y = x = |x|$ and $\tan y \geq 0$

$\Rightarrow \dfrac{dy}{dx} = \dfrac{1}{x\sqrt{x^2 - 1}} = \dfrac{1}{|x|\sqrt{x^2 - 1}}$. For $y \in \left(\frac{\pi}{2}, \pi\right]$, $x \leq -1$, so $|x| = -x$ and $\tan y = -\sqrt{x^2 - 1} \Rightarrow$

$$\frac{dy}{dx} = \frac{1}{\sec y \tan y} = \frac{1}{x\left(-\sqrt{x^2 - 1}\right)} = \frac{1}{(-x)\sqrt{x^2 - 1}} = \frac{1}{|x|\sqrt{x^2 - 1}}$$

7.6 Hyperbolic Functions

1. (a) $\sinh 0 = \frac{1}{2}\left(e^0 - e^0\right) = 0$

(b) $\cosh 0 = \frac{1}{2}\left(e^0 + e^0\right) = \frac{1}{2}(1 + 1) = 1$

3. (a) $\sinh(\ln 2) = \dfrac{e^{\ln 2} - e^{-\ln 2}}{2} = \dfrac{e^{\ln 2} - \left(e^{\ln 2}\right)^{-1}}{2} = \dfrac{2 - 2^{-1}}{2} = \dfrac{2 - \frac{1}{2}}{2} = \dfrac{3}{4}$

(b) $\sinh 2 = \frac{1}{2}\left(e^2 - e^{-2}\right) \approx 3.62686$

5. (a) $\operatorname{sech} 0 = \dfrac{1}{\cosh 0} = \dfrac{1}{1} = 1$

(b) $\cosh^{-1} 1 = 0$ because $\cosh 0 = 1$.

7. $\sinh(-x) = \frac{1}{2}\left[e^{-x} - e^{-(-x)}\right] = \frac{1}{2}\left(e^{-x} - e^x\right) = -\frac{1}{2}\left(e^x - e^{-x}\right) = -\sinh x$

9. $\cosh x + \sinh x = \frac{1}{2}\left(e^x + e^{-x}\right) + \frac{1}{2}\left(e^x - e^{-x}\right) = \frac{1}{2}\left(2e^x\right) = e^x$

11. $\sinh x \cosh y + \cosh x \sinh y = \left[\frac{1}{2}\left(e^x - e^{-x}\right)\right]\left[\frac{1}{2}\left(e^y + e^{-y}\right)\right] + \left[\frac{1}{2}\left(e^x + e^{-x}\right)\right]\left[\frac{1}{2}\left(e^y - e^{-y}\right)\right]$

$\qquad = \frac{1}{4}\left[\left(e^{x+y} + e^{x-y} - e^{-x+y} - e^{-x-y}\right) + \left(e^{x+y} - e^{x-y} + e^{-x+y} - e^{-x-y}\right)\right]$

$\qquad = \frac{1}{4}\left(2e^{x+y} - 2e^{-x-y}\right) = \frac{1}{2}\left[e^{x+y} - e^{-(x+y)}\right] = \sinh(x+y)$

13. Divide both sides of the identity $\cosh^2 x - \sinh^2 x = 1$ by $\sinh^2 x$:

$$\frac{\cosh^2 x}{\sinh^2 x} - \frac{\sinh^2 x}{\sinh^2 x} = \frac{1}{\sinh^2 x} \quad \Leftrightarrow \quad \coth^2 x - 1 = \operatorname{csch}^2 x.$$

15. Putting $y = x$ in the result from Exercise 11, we have

$\sinh 2x = \sinh(x + x) = \sinh x \cosh x + \cosh x \sinh x = 2 \sinh x \cosh x.$

17. $\tanh(\ln x) = \dfrac{\sinh(\ln x)}{\cosh(\ln x)} = \dfrac{\left(e^{\ln x} - e^{-\ln x}\right)/2}{\left(e^{\ln x} + e^{-\ln x}\right)/2} = \dfrac{x - \left(e^{\ln x}\right)^{-1}}{x + \left(e^{\ln x}\right)^{-1}} = \dfrac{x - x^{-1}}{x + x^{-1}}$

$\qquad = \dfrac{x - 1/x}{x + 1/x} = \dfrac{\left(x^2 - 1\right)/x}{\left(x^2 + 1\right)/x} = \dfrac{x^2 - 1}{x^2 + 1}$

19. By Exercise 9, $(\cosh x + \sinh x)^n = (e^x)^n = e^{nx} = \cosh nx + \sinh nx.$

21. $\tanh x = \frac{4}{5} > 0$, so $x > 0$. $\coth x = 1/\tanh x = \frac{5}{4}$, $\operatorname{sech}^2 x = 1 - \tanh^2 x = 1 - \left(\frac{4}{5}\right)^2 = \frac{9}{25} \Rightarrow$
$\operatorname{sech} x = \frac{3}{5}$ (since $\operatorname{sech} x > 0$), $\cosh x = 1/\operatorname{sech} x = \frac{5}{3}$, $\sinh x = \tanh x \cosh x = \frac{4}{5} \cdot \frac{5}{3} = \frac{4}{3}$, and
$\operatorname{csch} x = 1/\sinh x = \frac{3}{4}$.

23. (a) $\displaystyle\lim_{x\to\infty} \tanh x = \lim_{x\to\infty} \frac{e^x - e^{-x}}{e^x + e^{-x}} \cdot \frac{e^{-x}}{e^{-x}} = \lim_{x\to\infty} \frac{1 - e^{-2x}}{1 + e^{-2x}} = \frac{1-0}{1+0} = 1$

(b) $\displaystyle\lim_{x\to -\infty} \tanh x = \lim_{x\to -\infty} \frac{e^x - e^{-x}}{e^x + e^{-x}} \cdot \frac{e^x}{e^x} = \lim_{x\to -\infty} \frac{e^{2x} - 1}{e^{2x} + 1} = \frac{0-1}{0+1} = -1$

(c) $\displaystyle\lim_{x\to\infty} \sinh x = \lim_{x\to\infty} \frac{e^x - e^{-x}}{2} = \infty$

(d) $\displaystyle\lim_{x\to -\infty} \sinh x = \lim_{x\to -\infty} \frac{e^x - e^{-x}}{2} = -\infty$

(e) $\displaystyle\lim_{x\to\infty} \operatorname{sech} x = \lim_{x\to\infty} \frac{2}{e^x + e^{-x}} = 0$

(f) $\displaystyle\lim_{x\to\infty} \coth x = \lim_{x\to\infty} \frac{e^x + e^{-x}}{e^x - e^{-x}} \cdot \frac{e^{-x}}{e^{-x}} = \lim_{x\to\infty} \frac{1 + e^{-2x}}{1 - e^{-2x}} = \frac{1+0}{1-0} = 1$ [*Or:* Use part (a)]

(g) $\displaystyle\lim_{x\to 0^+} \coth x = \lim_{x\to 0^+} \frac{\cosh x}{\sinh x} = \infty$, since $\sinh x \to 0$ through positive values and $\cosh x \to 1$.

(h) $\displaystyle\lim_{x\to 0^-} \coth x = \lim_{x\to 0^-} \frac{\cosh x}{\sinh x} = -\infty$, since $\sinh x \to 0$ through negative values and $\cosh x \to 1$.

(i) $\displaystyle\lim_{x\to -\infty} \operatorname{csch} x = \lim_{x\to -\infty} \frac{2}{e^x - e^{-x}} = 0$

25. Let $y = \sinh^{-1} x$. Then $\sinh y = x$ and, by Example 1(a), $\cosh^2 y - \sinh^2 y = 1 \Rightarrow$ [with $\cosh y > 0$]
$\cosh y = \sqrt{1 + \sinh^2 y} = \sqrt{1 + x^2}$. So by Exercise 9, $e^y = \sinh y + \cosh y = x + \sqrt{1 + x^2} \Rightarrow$
$y = \ln\left(x + \sqrt{1 + x^2}\right).$

27. (a) Let $y = \tanh^{-1} x$. Then $x = \tanh y = \dfrac{\sinh y}{\cosh y} = \dfrac{(e^y - e^{-y})/2}{(e^y + e^{-y})/2} \cdot \dfrac{e^y}{e^y} = \dfrac{e^{2y} - 1}{e^{2y} + 1} \quad \Rightarrow$

$xe^{2y} + x = e^{2y} - 1 \quad \Rightarrow \quad 1 + x = e^{2y} - xe^{2y} \quad \Rightarrow \quad 1 + x = e^{2y}(1 - x) \quad \Rightarrow$

$e^{2y} = \dfrac{1 + x}{1 - x} \quad \Rightarrow \quad 2y = \ln\left(\dfrac{1 + x}{1 - x}\right) \quad \Rightarrow \quad y = \tfrac{1}{2}\ln\left(\dfrac{1 + x}{1 - x}\right).$

(b) Let $y = \tanh^{-1} x$. Then $x = \tanh y$, so from Exercise 18 we have

$e^{2y} = \dfrac{1 + \tanh y}{1 - \tanh y} = \dfrac{1 + x}{1 - x} \quad \Rightarrow \quad 2y = \ln\left(\dfrac{1 + x}{1 - x}\right) \quad \Rightarrow \quad y = \tfrac{1}{2}\ln\left(\dfrac{1 + x}{1 - x}\right).$

29. (a) Let $y = \cosh^{-1} x$. Then $\cosh y = x$ and $y \geq 0 \quad \Rightarrow \quad \sinh y \dfrac{dy}{dx} = 1 \quad \Rightarrow$

$\dfrac{dy}{dx} = \dfrac{1}{\sinh y} = \dfrac{1}{\sqrt{\cosh^2 y - 1}} = \dfrac{1}{\sqrt{x^2 - 1}}$ (since $\sinh y \geq 0$ for $y \geq 0$). *Or:* Use Formula 4.

(b) Let $y = \tanh^{-1} x$. Then $\tanh y = x \quad \Rightarrow \quad \text{sech}^2 y \dfrac{dy}{dx} = 1 \quad \Rightarrow \quad \dfrac{dy}{dx} = \dfrac{1}{\text{sech}^2 y} = \dfrac{1}{1 - \tanh^2 y} = \dfrac{1}{1 - x^2}.$

Or: Use Formula 5.

(c) Let $y = \text{csch}^{-1} x$. Then $\text{csch}\, y = x \quad \Rightarrow \quad -\text{csch}\, y \coth y \dfrac{dy}{dx} = 1 \quad \Rightarrow \quad \dfrac{dy}{dx} = -\dfrac{1}{\text{csch}\, y \coth y}.$

By Exercise 13, $\coth y = \pm\sqrt{\text{csch}^2 y + 1} = \pm\sqrt{x^2 + 1}$. If $x > 0$, then $\coth y > 0$, so $\coth y = \sqrt{x^2 + 1}$.

If $x < 0$, then $\coth y < 0$, so $\coth y = -\sqrt{x^2 + 1}$. In either case we have

$\dfrac{dy}{dx} = -\dfrac{1}{\text{csch}\, y \coth y} = -\dfrac{1}{|x|\sqrt{x^2 + 1}}.$

(d) Let $y = \text{sech}^{-1} x$. Then $\text{sech}\, y = x \quad \Rightarrow \quad -\text{sech}\, y \tanh y \dfrac{dy}{dx} = 1 \quad \Rightarrow$

$\dfrac{dy}{dx} = -\dfrac{1}{\text{sech}\, y \tanh y} = -\dfrac{1}{\text{sech}\, y \sqrt{1 - \text{sech}^2 y}} = -\dfrac{1}{x\sqrt{1 - x^2}}.$ (Note that $y > 0$ and so $\tanh y > 0$.)

(e) Let $y = \coth^{-1} x$. Then $\coth y = x \quad \Rightarrow \quad -\text{csch}^2 y \dfrac{dy}{dx} = 1 \quad \Rightarrow$

$\dfrac{dy}{dx} = -\dfrac{1}{\text{csch}^2 y} = \dfrac{1}{1 - \coth^2 y} = \dfrac{1}{1 - x^2}$ by Exercise 13.

31. $f(x) = x \cosh x \quad \Rightarrow \quad f'(x) = x(\cosh x)' + (\cosh x)(x)' = x \sinh x + \cosh x$

33. $h(x) = \sinh(x^2) \quad \Rightarrow \quad h'(x) = \cosh(x^2) \cdot 2x = 2x \cosh(x^2)$

35. $G(x) = \dfrac{1 - \cosh x}{1 + \cosh x} \quad \Rightarrow$

$G'(x) = \dfrac{(1 + \cosh x)(-\sinh x) - (1 - \cosh x)(\sinh x)}{(1 + \cosh x)^2}$

$= \dfrac{-\sinh x - \sinh x \cosh x - \sinh x + \sinh x \cosh x}{(1 + \cosh x)^2} = \dfrac{-2\sinh x}{(1 + \cosh x)^2}$

37. $h(t) = \coth\sqrt{1 + t^2} \quad \Rightarrow \quad h'(t) = -\text{csch}^2\sqrt{1 + t^2} \cdot \tfrac{1}{2}(1 + t^2)^{-1/2}(2t) = -\dfrac{t\,\text{csch}^2\sqrt{1 + t^2}}{\sqrt{1 + t^2}}$

39. $H(t) = \tanh(e^t) \quad \Rightarrow \quad H'(t) = \text{sech}^2(e^t) \cdot e^t = e^t \,\text{sech}^2(e^t)$

41. $y = e^{\cosh 3x} \quad \Rightarrow \quad y' = e^{\cosh 3x} \cdot \sinh 3x \cdot 3 = 3e^{\cosh 3x} \sinh 3x$

43. $y = \tanh^{-1}\sqrt{x} \quad \Rightarrow \quad y' = \dfrac{1}{1 - (\sqrt{x})^2} \cdot \tfrac{1}{2}x^{-1/2} = \dfrac{1}{2\sqrt{x}(1 - x)}$

45. $y = x\sinh^{-1}(x/3) - \sqrt{9 + x^2}$ $\Rightarrow$

$$y' = \sinh^{-1}\left(\frac{x}{3}\right) + x\frac{1/3}{\sqrt{1 + (x/3)^2}} - \frac{2x}{2\sqrt{9 + x^2}} = \sinh^{-1}\left(\frac{x}{3}\right) + \frac{x}{\sqrt{9 + x^2}} - \frac{x}{\sqrt{9 + x^2}} = \sinh^{-1}\left(\frac{x}{3}\right)$$

47. $y = \coth^{-1}\sqrt{x^2 + 1}$ $\Rightarrow$ $y' = \frac{1}{1 - (x^2 + 1)}\frac{2x}{2\sqrt{x^2 + 1}} = -\frac{1}{x\sqrt{x^2 + 1}}$

49. (a) $y = 20\cosh(x/20) - 15$ $\Rightarrow$ $y' = 20\sinh(x/20)\cdot\frac{1}{20} = \sinh(x/20)$. Since the right pole is positioned at $x = 7$, we have $y'(7) = \sinh\frac{7}{20} \approx 0.3572$.

(b) If α is the angle between the tangent line and the x-axis, then $\tan\alpha = $ slope of the line $= \sinh\frac{7}{20}$, so $\alpha = \tan^{-1}\left(\sinh\frac{7}{20}\right) \approx 0.343$ rad $\approx 19.66°$. Thus, the angle between the line and the pole is $\theta = 90° - \alpha \approx 70.34°$.

51. (a) $y = A\sinh mx + B\cosh mx$ $\Rightarrow$ $y' = mA\cosh mx + mB\sinh mx$ $\Rightarrow$
$y'' = m^2 A\sinh mx + m^2 B\cosh mx = m^2(A\sinh mx + B\cosh mx) = m^2 y$

(b) From part (a), a solution of $y'' = 9y$ is $y(x) = A\sinh 3x + B\cosh 3x$. So
$-4 = y(0) = A\sinh 0 + B\cosh 0 = B$, so $B = -4$. Now $y'(x) = 3A\cosh 3x - 12\sinh 3x$ $\Rightarrow$
$6 = y'(0) = 3A$ $\Rightarrow$ $A = 2$, so $y = 2\sinh 3x - 4\cosh 3x$.

53. The tangent to $y = \cosh x$ has slope 1 when $y' = \sinh x = 1$ $\Rightarrow$ $x = \sinh^{-1} 1 = \ln(1 + \sqrt{2})$, by Equation 3. Since $\sinh x = 1$ and $y = \cosh x = \sqrt{1 + \sinh^2 x}$, we have $\cosh x = \sqrt{2}$. The point is $(\ln(1 + \sqrt{2}), \sqrt{2})$.

55. Let $u = \cosh x$. Then $du = \sinh x\, dx$, so $\int \sinh x\cosh^2 x\, dx = \int u^2\, du = \frac{1}{3}u^3 + C = \frac{1}{3}\cosh^3 x + C$.

57. Let $u = \sqrt{x}$. Then $du = \frac{dx}{2\sqrt{x}}$ and $\int \frac{\sinh\sqrt{x}}{\sqrt{x}}\, dx = \int \sinh u\cdot 2\, du = 2\cosh u + C = 2\cosh\sqrt{x} + C$.

59. $\int \frac{\cosh x}{\cosh^2 x - 1}\, dx = \int \frac{\cosh x}{\sinh^2 x}\, dx = \int \frac{\cosh x}{\sinh x}\cdot\frac{1}{\sinh x}\, dx = \int \coth x\, \text{csch}\, x\, dx = -\text{csch}\, x + C$

61. Let $t = 3u$. Then $dt = 3\, du$ and
$$\int_4^6 \frac{1}{\sqrt{t^2 - 9}}\, dt = \int_{4/3}^2 \frac{1}{\sqrt{9u^2 - 9}}3\, du = \int_{4/3}^2 \frac{du}{\sqrt{u^2 - 1}} = \left[\cosh^{-1} u\right]_{4/3}^2 = \cosh^{-1} 2 - \cosh^{-1}\left(\frac{4}{3}\right) \quad \text{or}$$
$$= \left[\cosh^{-1} u\right]_{4/3}^2 = \left[\ln\left(u + \sqrt{u^2 - 1}\right)\right]_{4/3}^2$$
$$= \ln(2 + \sqrt{3}) - \ln\left(\frac{4 + \sqrt{7}}{3}\right) = \ln\left(\frac{6 + 3\sqrt{3}}{4 + \sqrt{7}}\right)$$

63. Let $u = e^x$. Then $du = e^x\, dx$ and $\int \frac{e^x}{1 - e^{2x}}\, dx = \int \frac{du}{1 - u^2} = \tanh^{-1} u + C = \tanh^{-1}(e^x) + C$
$\left[\text{or }\frac{1}{2}\ln\left(\frac{1 + e^x}{1 - e^x}\right) + C\right]$.

65. (a) From the graphs, we estimate that the two curves $y = \cosh 2x$ and $y = 1 + \sinh x$ intersect at $x = 0$ and at $x = a \approx 0.481$.

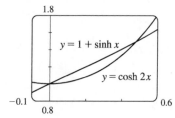
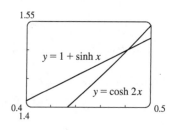

(b) We have found the two roots of the equation $\cosh 2x = 1 + \sinh x$ to be $x = 0$ and $x = a \approx 0.481$. Note from the first graph that $1 + \sinh x > \cosh 2x$ on the interval $(0, a)$, so the area between the two curves is

$$A = \int_0^a (1 + \sinh x - \cosh 2x)\, dx = \left[x + \cosh x - \tfrac{1}{2} \sinh 2x \right]_0^a$$

$$= \left[a + \cosh a - \tfrac{1}{2} \sinh 2a \right] - \left[0 + \cosh 0 - \tfrac{1}{2} \sinh 0 \right] \approx 0.0402$$

67. If $ae^x + be^{-x} = \alpha \cosh(x + \beta)$ [or $\alpha \sinh(x + \beta)$], then

$ae^x + be^{-x} = \tfrac{\alpha}{2}\left(e^{x+\beta} \pm e^{-x-\beta} \right) = \tfrac{\alpha}{2}\left(e^x e^\beta \pm e^{-x} e^{-\beta} \right) = \left(\tfrac{\alpha}{2} e^\beta \right) e^x \pm \left(\tfrac{\alpha}{2} e^{-\beta} \right) e^{-x}$. Comparing coefficients of e^x and e^{-x}, we have $a = \tfrac{\alpha}{2} e^\beta$ **(1)** and $b = \pm \tfrac{\alpha}{2} e^{-\beta}$ **(2)**. We need to find α and β. Dividing equation **(1)** by equation **(2)** gives us $\dfrac{a}{b} = \pm e^{2\beta} \;\Rightarrow\; (*)\;\; 2\beta = \ln\!\left(\pm \tfrac{a}{b} \right) \;\Rightarrow\; \beta = \tfrac{1}{2} \ln\!\left(\pm \tfrac{a}{b} \right)$. Solving equations **(1)** and **(2)** for e^β gives us $e^\beta = \dfrac{2a}{\alpha}$ and $e^\beta = \pm \dfrac{\alpha}{2b}$, so $\dfrac{2a}{\alpha} = \pm \dfrac{\alpha}{2b} \;\Rightarrow\; \alpha^2 = \pm 4ab \;\Rightarrow\; \alpha = 2\sqrt{\pm ab}$.

$(*)$ If $\dfrac{a}{b} > 0$, we use the $+$ sign and obtain a cosh function, whereas if $\dfrac{a}{b} < 0$, we use the $-$ sign and obtain a sinh function.

In summary, if a and b have the same sign, we have $ae^x + be^{-x} = 2\sqrt{ab} \cosh\!\left(x + \tfrac{1}{2} \ln \tfrac{a}{b} \right)$, whereas, if a and b have the opposite sign, then $ae^x + be^{-x} = 2\sqrt{-ab} \sinh\!\left(x + \tfrac{1}{2} \ln\!\left(-\tfrac{a}{b} \right) \right)$.

7.7 Indeterminate Forms and L'Hospital's Rule

The use of l'Hospital's Rule is indicated by an **H** above the equal sign: $\overset{H}{=}$.

1. (a) $\displaystyle\lim_{x \to a} \frac{f(x)}{g(x)}$ is an indeterminate form of type $\dfrac{0}{0}$.

(b) $\displaystyle\lim_{x \to a} \frac{f(x)}{p(x)} = 0$ because the numerator approaches 0 while the denominator becomes large.

(c) $\displaystyle\lim_{x \to a} \frac{h(x)}{p(x)} = 0$ because the numerator approaches a finite number while the denominator becomes large.

(d) If $\displaystyle\lim_{x \to a} p(x) = \infty$ and $f(x) \to 0$ through positive values, then $\displaystyle\lim_{x \to a} \frac{p(x)}{f(x)} = \infty$. [For example, take $a = 0$,

$p(x) = 1/x^2$, and $f(x) = x^2$.] If $f(x) \to 0$ through negative values, then $\displaystyle\lim_{x \to a} \frac{p(x)}{f(x)} = -\infty$. [For example,

take $a = 0$, $p(x) = 1/x^2$, and $f(x) = -x^2$.] If $f(x) \to 0$ through both positive and negative values, then the limit might not exist. [For example, take $a = 0$, $p(x) = 1/x^2$, and $f(x) = x$.]

(e) $\displaystyle\lim_{x \to a} \frac{p(x)}{q(x)}$ is an indeterminate form of type $\dfrac{\infty}{\infty}$.

3. (a) When x is near a, $f(x)$ is near 0 and $p(x)$ is large, so $f(x) - p(x)$ is large negative. Thus, $\displaystyle\lim_{x \to a} [f(x) - p(x)] = -\infty$.

(b) $\displaystyle\lim_{x \to a} [p(x) - q(x)]$ is an indeterminate form of type $\infty - \infty$.

(c) When x is near a, $p(x)$ and $q(x)$ are both large, so $p(x) + q(x)$ is large. Thus, $\displaystyle\lim_{x \to a} [p(x) + q(x)] = \infty$.

5. This limit has the form $\tfrac{0}{0}$. We can simply factor the numerator to evaluate this limit.

$$\lim_{x \to -1} \frac{x^2 - 1}{x + 1} = \lim_{x \to -1} \frac{(x + 1)(x - 1)}{x + 1} = \lim_{x \to -1} (x - 1) = -2$$

7. This limit has the form $\frac{0}{0}$. $\displaystyle\lim_{x\to1}\frac{x^9-1}{x^5-1}\overset{\text{H}}{=}\lim_{x\to1}\frac{9x^8}{5x^4}=\frac{9}{5}\lim_{x\to1}x^4=\frac{9}{5}(1)=\frac{9}{5}$

9. This limit has the form $\frac{0}{0}$. $\displaystyle\lim_{x\to(\pi/2)^+}\frac{\cos x}{1-\sin x}\overset{\text{H}}{=}\lim_{x\to(\pi/2)^+}\frac{-\sin x}{-\cos x}=\lim_{x\to(\pi/2)^+}\tan x=-\infty.$

11. This limit has the form $\frac{0}{0}$. $\displaystyle\lim_{t\to0}\frac{e^t-1}{t^3}\overset{\text{H}}{=}\lim_{t\to0}\frac{e^t}{3t^2}=\infty$ since $e^t\to1$ and $3t^2\to0^+$ as $t\to0$.

13. This limit has the form $\frac{0}{0}$. $\displaystyle\lim_{x\to0}\frac{\tan px}{\tan qx}\overset{\text{H}}{=}\lim_{x\to0}\frac{p\sec^2 px}{q\sec^2 qx}=\frac{p(1)^2}{q(1)^2}=\frac{p}{q}$

15. This limit has the form $\frac{\infty}{\infty}$. $\displaystyle\lim_{x\to\infty}\frac{\ln x}{x}\overset{\text{H}}{=}\lim_{x\to\infty}\frac{1/x}{1}=0$

17. $\displaystyle\lim_{x\to0^+}[(\ln x)/x]=-\infty$ since $\ln x\to-\infty$ as $x\to0^+$ and dividing by small values of x just increases the magnitude of the quotient $(\ln x)/x$. L'Hospital's Rule does not apply.

19. This limit has the form $\frac{0}{0}$. $\displaystyle\lim_{t\to0}\frac{5^t-3^t}{t}\overset{\text{H}}{=}\lim_{t\to0}\frac{5^t\ln5-3^t\ln3}{1}=\ln5-\ln3=\ln\frac{5}{3}$

21. This limit has the form $\frac{0}{0}$. $\displaystyle\lim_{x\to0}\frac{e^x-1-x}{x^2}\overset{\text{H}}{=}\lim_{x\to0}\frac{e^x-1}{2x}\overset{\text{H}}{=}\lim_{x\to0}\frac{e^x}{2}=\frac{1}{2}$

23. This limit has the form $\frac{\infty}{\infty}$. $\displaystyle\lim_{x\to\infty}\frac{e^x}{x^3}\overset{\text{H}}{=}\lim_{x\to\infty}\frac{e^x}{3x^2}\overset{\text{H}}{=}\lim_{x\to\infty}\frac{e^x}{6x}\overset{\text{H}}{=}\lim_{x\to\infty}\frac{e^x}{6}=\infty$

25. This limit has the form $\frac{0}{0}$. $\displaystyle\lim_{x\to0}\frac{\sin^{-1}x}{x}\overset{\text{H}}{=}\lim_{x\to0}\frac{1/\sqrt{1-x^2}}{1}=\lim_{x\to0}\frac{1}{\sqrt{1-x^2}}=\frac{1}{1}=1$

27. This limit has the form $\frac{0}{0}$. $\displaystyle\lim_{x\to0}\frac{1-\cos x}{x^2}\overset{\text{H}}{=}\lim_{x\to0}\frac{\sin x}{2x}\overset{\text{H}}{=}\lim_{x\to0}\frac{\cos x}{2}=\frac{1}{2}$

29. $\displaystyle\lim_{x\to0}\frac{x+\sin x}{x+\cos x}=\frac{0+0}{0+1}=\frac{0}{1}=0$. L'Hospital's Rule does not apply.

31. This limit has the form $\frac{\infty}{\infty}$. $\displaystyle\lim_{x\to\infty}\frac{x}{\ln(1+2e^x)}\overset{\text{H}}{=}\lim_{x\to\infty}\frac{1}{\dfrac{1}{1+2e^x}\cdot2e^x}=\lim_{x\to\infty}\frac{1+2e^x}{2e^x}\overset{\text{H}}{=}\lim_{x\to\infty}\frac{2e^x}{2e^x}=1$

33. This limit has the form $\frac{0}{0}$. $\displaystyle\lim_{x\to1}\frac{1-x+\ln x}{1+\cos\pi x}\overset{\text{H}}{=}\lim_{x\to1}\frac{-1+1/x}{-\pi\sin\pi x}\overset{\text{H}}{=}\lim_{x\to1}\frac{-1/x^2}{-\pi^2\cos\pi x}=\frac{-1}{-\pi^2(-1)}=-\frac{1}{\pi^2}$

35. This limit has the form $\frac{0}{0}$. $\displaystyle\lim_{x\to1}\frac{x^a-ax+a-1}{(x-1)^2}\overset{\text{H}}{=}\lim_{x\to1}\frac{ax^{a-1}-a}{2(x-1)}\overset{\text{H}}{=}\lim_{x\to1}\frac{a(a-1)x^{a-2}}{2}=\frac{a(a-1)}{2}$

37. This limit has the form $0\cdot(-\infty)$. We need to write this product as a quotient, but keep in mind that we will have to differentiate both the numerator and the denominator. If we differentiate $\dfrac{1}{\ln x}$, we get a complicated expression that results in a more difficult limit. Instead we write the quotient as $\dfrac{\ln x}{x^{-1/2}}$.

$\displaystyle\lim_{x\to0^+}\sqrt{x}\ln x=\lim_{x\to0^+}\frac{\ln x}{x^{-1/2}}\overset{\text{H}}{=}\lim_{x\to0^+}\frac{1/x}{-\frac{1}{2}x^{-3/2}}\cdot\frac{-2x^{3/2}}{-2x^{3/2}}=\lim_{x\to0^+}(-2\sqrt{x})=0$

39. This limit has the form $\infty\cdot0$. We'll change it to the form $\frac{0}{0}$.

$\displaystyle\lim_{x\to0}\cot2x\sin6x=\lim_{x\to0}\frac{\sin6x}{\tan2x}\overset{\text{H}}{=}\lim_{x\to0}\frac{6\cos6x}{2\sec^22x}=\frac{6(1)}{2(1)^2}=3$

41. This limit has the form $\infty \cdot 0$. $\lim\limits_{x\to\infty} x^3 e^{-x^2} = \lim\limits_{x\to\infty} \dfrac{x^3}{e^{x^2}} \overset{\text{H}}{=} \lim\limits_{x\to\infty} \dfrac{3x^2}{2xe^{x^2}} = \lim\limits_{x\to\infty} \dfrac{3x}{2e^{x^2}} \overset{\text{H}}{=} \lim\limits_{x\to\infty} \dfrac{3}{4xe^{x^2}} = 0$

43. This limit has the form $0 \cdot (-\infty)$.

$$\lim_{x\to 1^+} \ln x \, \tan(\pi x/2) = \lim_{x\to 1^+} \frac{\ln x}{\cot(\pi x/2)} \overset{\text{H}}{=} \lim_{x\to 1^+} \frac{1/x}{(-\pi/2)\csc^2(\pi x/2)} = \frac{1}{(-\pi/2)(1)^2} = -\frac{2}{\pi}$$

45. $\lim\limits_{x\to 0}\left(\dfrac{1}{x} - \csc x\right) = \lim\limits_{x\to 0}\left(\dfrac{1}{x} - \dfrac{1}{\sin x}\right) = \lim\limits_{x\to 0} \dfrac{\sin x - x}{x \sin x}$

$$\overset{\text{H}}{=} \lim_{x\to 0} \frac{\cos x - 1}{x\cos x + \sin x} \overset{\text{H}}{=} \lim_{x\to 0} \frac{-\sin x}{2\cos x - x\sin x} = \frac{0}{2} = 0$$

47. We will multiply and divide by the conjugate of the expression to change the form of the expression.

$$\lim_{x\to\infty}\left(\sqrt{x^2+x} - x\right) = \lim_{x\to\infty}\left(\frac{\sqrt{x^2+x} - x}{1} \cdot \frac{\sqrt{x^2+x} + x}{\sqrt{x^2+x} + x}\right) = \lim_{x\to\infty} \frac{(x^2+x) - x^2}{\sqrt{x^2+x} + x}$$

$$= \lim_{x\to\infty} \frac{x}{\sqrt{x^2+x} + x} = \lim_{x\to\infty} \frac{1}{\sqrt{1 + 1/x} + 1} = \frac{1}{\sqrt{1} + 1} = \frac{1}{2}.$$

As an alternate solution, write $\sqrt{x^2+x} - x$ as $\sqrt{x^2+x} - \sqrt{x^2}$, factor out $\sqrt{x^2}$, rewrite as $(\sqrt{1+1/x} - 1)/(1/x)$, and apply l'Hospital's Rule.

49. The limit has the form $\infty - \infty$ and we will change the form to a product by factoring out x.

$$\lim_{x\to\infty}(x - \ln x) = \lim_{x\to\infty} x\left(1 - \frac{\ln x}{x}\right) = \infty \text{ since } \lim_{x\to\infty} \frac{\ln x}{x} \overset{\text{H}}{=} \lim_{x\to\infty} \frac{1/x}{1} = 0.$$

51. $y = x^{x^2} \quad \Rightarrow \quad \ln y = x^2 \ln x$, so

$$\lim_{x\to 0^+} \ln y = \lim_{x\to 0^+} x^2 \ln x = \lim_{x\to 0^+} \frac{\ln x}{1/x^2} \overset{\text{H}}{=} \lim_{x\to 0^+} \frac{1/x}{-2/x^3} = \lim_{x\to 0^+}\left(-\frac{1}{2}x^2\right) = 0 \quad \Rightarrow$$

$$\lim_{x\to 0^+} x^{x^2} = \lim_{x\to 0^+} e^{\ln y} = e^0 = 1.$$

53. $y = (1 - 2x)^{1/x} \quad \Rightarrow \quad \ln y = \dfrac{1}{x}\ln(1 - 2x)$, so $\lim\limits_{x\to 0} \ln y = \lim\limits_{x\to 0} \dfrac{\ln(1 - 2x)}{x} \overset{\text{H}}{=} \lim\limits_{x\to 0} \dfrac{-2/(1 - 2x)}{1} = -2 \quad \Rightarrow$

$$\lim_{x\to 0}(1 - 2x)^{1/x} = \lim_{x\to 0} e^{\ln y} = e^{-2}.$$

55. $y = \left(1 + \dfrac{3}{x} + \dfrac{5}{x^2}\right)^x \quad \Rightarrow \quad \ln y = x\ln\left(1 + \dfrac{3}{x} + \dfrac{5}{x^2}\right) \quad \Rightarrow$

$$\lim_{x\to\infty} \ln y = \lim_{x\to\infty} \frac{\ln\left(1 + \dfrac{3}{x} + \dfrac{5}{x^2}\right)}{1/x} \overset{\text{H}}{=} \lim_{x\to\infty} \frac{\left(-\dfrac{3}{x^2} - \dfrac{10}{x^3}\right)\Big/\left(1 + \dfrac{3}{x} + \dfrac{5}{x^2}\right)}{-1/x^2} = \lim_{x\to\infty} \frac{3 + \dfrac{10}{x}}{1 + \dfrac{3}{x} + \dfrac{5}{x^2}} = 3,$$

so $\lim\limits_{x\to\infty}\left(1 + \dfrac{3}{x} + \dfrac{5}{x^2}\right)^x = \lim\limits_{x\to\infty} e^{\ln y} = e^3.$

57. $y = x^{1/x} \quad \Rightarrow \quad \ln y = (1/x)\ln x \quad \Rightarrow \quad \lim\limits_{x\to\infty} \ln y = \lim\limits_{x\to\infty} \dfrac{\ln x}{x} \overset{\text{H}}{=} \lim\limits_{x\to\infty} \dfrac{1/x}{1} = 0 \quad \Rightarrow$

$$\lim_{x\to\infty} x^{1/x} = \lim_{x\to\infty} e^{\ln y} = e^0 = 1$$

59. $y = \left(\dfrac{x}{x+1}\right)^x \;\Rightarrow\; \ln y = x \ln\left(\dfrac{x}{x+1}\right) \;\Rightarrow$

$$\lim_{x\to\infty} \ln y = \lim_{x\to\infty} x \ln\left(\frac{x}{x+1}\right) = \lim_{x\to\infty} \frac{\ln x - \ln(x+1)}{1/x} \overset{\text{H}}{=} \lim_{x\to\infty} \frac{1/x - 1/(x+1)}{-1/x^2}$$

$$= \lim_{x\to\infty}\left(-x + \frac{x^2}{x+1}\right) = \lim_{x\to\infty} \frac{-x}{x+1} = -1$$

so $\displaystyle\lim_{x\to\infty}\left(\frac{x}{x+1}\right)^x = \lim_{x\to\infty} e^{\ln y} = e^{-1}$

Or: $\displaystyle\lim_{x\to\infty}\left(\frac{x}{x+1}\right)^x = \lim_{x\to\infty}\left[\left(\frac{x+1}{x}\right)^{-1}\right]^x = \left[\lim_{x\to\infty}\left(1+\frac{1}{x}\right)^x\right]^{-1} = e^{-1}$

61. $y = (\cos x)^{1/x^2} \;\Rightarrow\; \ln y = \dfrac{1}{x^2}\ln\cos x \;\Rightarrow$

$$\lim_{x\to 0^+} \ln y = \lim_{x\to 0^+} \frac{\ln\cos x}{x^2} \overset{\text{H}}{=} \lim_{x\to 0^+} \frac{-\tan x}{2x} \overset{\text{H}}{=} \lim_{x\to 0^+} \frac{-\sec^2 x}{2} = -\frac{1}{2} \;\Rightarrow$$

$$\lim_{x\to 0^+}(\cos x)^{1/x^2} = \lim_{x\to 0^+} e^{\ln y} = e^{-1/2} = 1/\sqrt{e}$$

63.

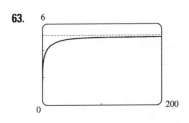

From the graph, it appears that $\displaystyle\lim_{x\to\infty} x\,[\ln(x+5) - \ln x] = 5$.

To prove this, we first note that

$$\ln(x+5) - \ln x = \ln\frac{x+5}{x} = \ln\left(1+\frac{5}{x}\right) \to \ln 1 = 0 \text{ as } x\to\infty. \text{ Thus,}$$

$$\lim_{x\to\infty} x\,[\ln(x+5) - \ln x] = \lim_{x\to\infty} \frac{\ln(x+5) - \ln x}{1/x} \overset{\text{H}}{=} \lim_{x\to\infty} \frac{\dfrac{1}{x+5} - \dfrac{1}{x}}{-1/x^2}$$

$$= \lim_{x\to\infty}\left[\frac{x - (x+5)}{x(x+5)}\cdot\frac{-x^2}{1}\right] = \lim_{x\to\infty}\frac{5x^2}{x^2+5x} = 5$$

65.

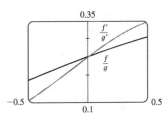

From the graph, it appears that

$$\lim_{x\to 0}\frac{f(x)}{g(x)} = \lim_{x\to 0}\frac{f'(x)}{g'(x)} = 0.25. \text{ We calculate}$$

$$\lim_{x\to 0}\frac{f(x)}{g(x)} = \lim_{x\to 0}\frac{e^x - 1}{x^3 + 4x} \overset{\text{H}}{=} \lim_{x\to 0}\frac{e^x}{3x^2 + 4} = \frac{1}{4}.$$

67. $y = f(x) = xe^{-x}$ **A.** $D = \mathbb{R}$ **B.** Intercepts are 0   **C.** No symmetry   **H.**

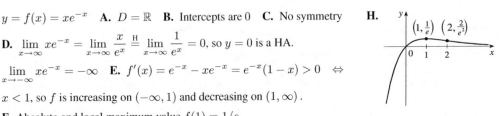

D. $\displaystyle\lim_{x\to\infty} xe^{-x} = \lim_{x\to\infty}\frac{x}{e^x} \overset{\text{H}}{=} \lim_{x\to\infty}\frac{1}{e^x} = 0$, so $y = 0$ is a HA.

$\displaystyle\lim_{x\to-\infty} xe^{-x} = -\infty$ **E.** $f'(x) = e^{-x} - xe^{-x} = e^{-x}(1-x) > 0 \;\Leftrightarrow$

$x < 1$, so f is increasing on $(-\infty, 1)$ and decreasing on $(1, \infty)$.

F. Absolute and local maximum value $f(1) = 1/e$.

G. $f''(x) = e^{-x}(x-2) > 0 \;\Leftrightarrow\; x > 2$, so f is CU on $(2, \infty)$ and CD on $(-\infty, 2)$. IP at $\left(2, 2/e^2\right)$

69. $y = f(x) = xe^{-x^2}$ **A.** $D = \mathbb{R}$ **B.** Intercepts are 0   **C.** $f(-x) = -f(x)$, so the curve is symmetric

about the origin.   **D.** $\displaystyle\lim_{x \to \pm\infty} xe^{-x^2} = \lim_{x \to \pm\infty} \frac{x}{e^{x^2}} \overset{\text{H}}{=} \lim_{x \to \pm\infty} \frac{1}{2xe^{x^2}} = 0$, so $y = 0$ is a HA.

E. $f'(x) = e^{-x^2} - 2x^2 e^{-x^2} = e^{-x^2}(1 - 2x^2) > 0 \iff x^2 < \frac{1}{2} \iff |x| < \frac{1}{\sqrt{2}}$, so f is increasing on

$\left(-\frac{1}{\sqrt{2}}, \frac{1}{\sqrt{2}}\right)$ and decreasing on $\left(-\infty, -\frac{1}{\sqrt{2}}\right)$ and $\left(\frac{1}{\sqrt{2}}, \infty\right)$.   **F.** Local maximum value $f\left(\frac{1}{\sqrt{2}}\right) = 1/\sqrt{2e}$, local

minimum value $f\left(-\frac{1}{\sqrt{2}}\right) = -1/\sqrt{2e}$ **G.** $f''(x) = -2xe^{-x^2}(1 - 2x^2) - 4xe^{-x^2} = 2xe^{-x^2}(2x^2 - 3) > 0$

$\iff x > \sqrt{\frac{3}{2}}$ or $-\sqrt{\frac{3}{2}} < x < 0$, so f is CU on $\left(\sqrt{\frac{3}{2}}, \infty\right)$ **H.**

and $\left(-\sqrt{\frac{3}{2}}, 0\right)$ and CD on $\left(-\infty, -\sqrt{\frac{3}{2}}\right)$ and $\left(0, \sqrt{\frac{3}{2}}\right)$.

IP are $(0, 0)$ and $\left(\pm\sqrt{\frac{3}{2}}, \pm\sqrt{\frac{3}{2}}\, e^{-3/2}\right)$.

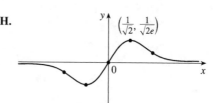

71. $y = f(x) = x - \ln(1 + x)$ **A.** $D = \{x \mid x > -1\} = (-1, \infty)$ **B.** Intercepts are 0   **C.** No symmetry

D. $\displaystyle\lim_{x \to -1^+} [x - \ln(1 + x)] = \infty$, so $x = -1$ is a VA. $\displaystyle\lim_{x \to \infty} [x - \ln(1 + x)] = \lim_{x \to \infty} x\left[1 - \frac{\ln(1 + x)}{x}\right] = \infty$,

since $\displaystyle\lim_{x \to \infty} \frac{\ln(1 + x)}{x} \overset{\text{H}}{=} \lim_{x \to \infty} \frac{1/(1 + x)}{1} = 0$.   **H.**

E. $f'(x) = 1 - \frac{1}{1 + x} = \frac{x}{1 + x} > 0 \iff x > 0$ since $x + 1 > 0$.

So f is increasing on $(0, \infty)$ and decreasing on $(-1, 0)$.

F. $f(0) = 0$ is an absolute minimum.

G. $f''(x) = 1/(1 + x)^2 > 0$, so f is CU on $(-1, \infty)$.

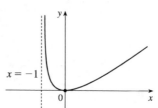

73. (a)

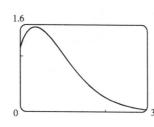

(b) $y = f(x) = x^{-x}$. We note that

$\ln f(x) = \ln x^{-x} = -x \ln x = -\dfrac{\ln x}{1/x}$, so

$\displaystyle\lim_{x \to 0^+} \ln f(x) \overset{\text{H}}{=} \lim_{x \to 0^+} -\frac{1/x}{-x^{-2}} = \lim_{x \to 0^+} x = 0$. Thus

$\displaystyle\lim_{x \to 0^+} f(x) = \lim_{x \to 0^+} e^{\ln f(x)} = e^0 = 1$.

(c) From the graph, it appears that there is a local and absolute maximum of about

$f(0.37) \approx 1.44$. To find the exact value, we differentiate: $f(x) = x^{-x} = e^{-x \ln x} \implies$

$f'(x) = e^{-x \ln x}\left[-x\left(\frac{1}{x}\right) + \ln x(-1)\right] = -x^{-x}(1 + \ln x)$. This is 0 only when $1 + \ln x = 0 \iff$

$x = e^{-1}$. Also $f'(x)$ changes from positive to negative at e^{-1}. So the maximum value is

$f(1/e) = (1/e)^{-1/e} = e^{1/e}$.

(d) We differentiate again to get

$$f''(x) = -x^{-x}(1/x) + (1 + \ln x)^2 (x^{-x})$$

$$= x^{-x} \left[(1 + \ln x)^2 - 1/x \right]$$

From the graph of $f''(x)$, it seems that $f''(x)$ changes from negative to positive at $x = 1$, so we estimate that f has an IP at $x = 1$.

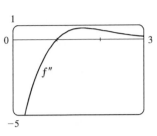

75. (a) $f(x) = x^{1/x}$

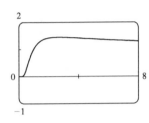

(b) Recall that $a^b = e^{b \ln a}$. $\displaystyle \lim_{x \to 0^+} x^{1/x} = \lim_{x \to 0^+} e^{(1/x) \ln x}$. As $x \to 0^+$,

$\dfrac{\ln x}{x} \to -\infty$, so $x^{1/x} = e^{(1/x) \ln x} \to 0$. This indicates that there is a hole at $(0, 0)$. As $x \to \infty$, we have the indeterminate form ∞^0.

$\displaystyle \lim_{x \to \infty} x^{1/x} = \lim_{x \to \infty} e^{(1/x) \ln x}$, but $\displaystyle \lim_{x \to \infty} \frac{\ln x}{x} \overset{H}{=} \lim_{x \to \infty} \frac{1/x}{1} = 0$, so

$\displaystyle \lim_{x \to \infty} x^{1/x} = e^0 = 1$. This indicates that $y = 1$ is a HA.

(c) Estimated maximum: $(2.72, 1.45)$. No estimated minimum. We use logarithmic differentiation to find any

critical numbers. $y = x^{1/x} \quad \Rightarrow \quad \ln y = \dfrac{1}{x} \ln x \quad \Rightarrow \quad \dfrac{y'}{y} = \dfrac{1}{x} \cdot \dfrac{1}{x} + (\ln x) \left(-\dfrac{1}{x^2} \right) \quad \Rightarrow$

$y' = x^{1/x} \left(\dfrac{1 - \ln x}{x^2} \right) = 0 \quad \Rightarrow \quad \ln x = 1 \quad \Rightarrow \quad x = e$. For $0 < x < e$, $y' > 0$ and for $x > e$, $y' < 0$, so

$f(e) = e^{1/e}$ is a local maximum value. This point is approximately $(2.7183, 1.4447)$, which agrees with our estimate.

(d)

From the graph, we see that $f''(x) = 0$ at $x \approx 0.58$ and $x \approx 4.37$. Since f'' changes sign at these values, they are x-coordinates of inflection points.

77. If $c < 0$, then $\displaystyle \lim_{x \to -\infty} f(x) = \lim_{x \to -\infty} \frac{x}{e^{cx}} \overset{H}{=} \lim_{x \to -\infty} \frac{1}{ce^{cx}} = 0$, and $\displaystyle \lim_{x \to \infty} f(x) = \infty$.

If $c > 0$, then $\displaystyle \lim_{x \to -\infty} f(x) = -\infty$, and $\displaystyle \lim_{x \to \infty} f(x) \overset{H}{=} \lim_{x \to \infty} \frac{1}{ce^{cx}} = 0$.

If $c = 0$, then $f(x) = x$, so $\displaystyle \lim_{x \to \pm\infty} f(x) = \pm\infty$ respectively.

So we see that $c = 0$ is a transitional value. We now exclude the case $c = 0$, since we know how the function behaves in that case. To find the maxima and minima of f, we differentiate: $f(x) = xe^{-cx} \quad \Rightarrow$

$f'(x) = x(-ce^{-cx}) + e^{-cx} = (1 - cx)e^{-cx}$. This is 0 when $1 - cx = 0 \quad \Leftrightarrow \quad x = 1/c$. If $c < 0$ then this

represents a minimum value of $f(1/c) = 1/(ce)$, since $f'(x)$ changes from negative to positive at $x = 1/c$;

and if $c > 0$, it represents a maximum value. As $|c|$ increases, the maximum or minimum point gets closer to the origin. To find the inflection points, we differentiate again: $f'(x) = e^{-cx}(1 - cx)$ $\Rightarrow$ $f''(x) = e^{-cx}(-c) + (1 - cx)(-ce^{-cx}) = (cx - 2)ce^{-cx}$. This changes sign when $cx - 2 = 0$ $\Leftrightarrow$ $x = 2/c$. So as $|c|$ increases, the points of inflection get closer to the origin.

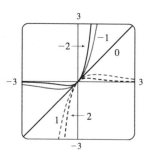

79. First we will find $\lim\limits_{n \to \infty} \left(1 + \dfrac{i}{n}\right)^{nt}$, which is of the form 1^{∞}. $y = \left(1 + \dfrac{i}{n}\right)^{nt}$ $\Rightarrow$ $\ln y = nt \ln\left(1 + \dfrac{i}{n}\right)$, so

$$\lim_{n \to \infty} \ln y = \lim_{n \to \infty} nt \ln\left(1 + \frac{i}{n}\right) = t \lim_{n \to \infty} \frac{\ln(1 + i/n)}{1/n} \overset{\text{H}}{=} t \lim_{n \to \infty} \frac{(-i/n^2)}{(1 + i/n)(-1/n^2)} = t \lim_{n \to \infty} \frac{i}{1 + i/n} = ti$$

$\Rightarrow$ $\lim\limits_{n \to \infty} y = e^{it}$. Thus, as $n \to \infty$, $A = A_0\left(1 + \dfrac{i}{n}\right)^{nt} \to A_0 e^{it}$.

81. Both numerator and denominator approach 0 as $x \to 0$, so we use l'Hospital's Rule (and FTC1):

$$\lim_{x \to 0} \frac{S(x)}{x^3} = \lim_{x \to 0} \frac{\int_0^x \sin(\pi t^2/2)dt}{x^3} \overset{\text{H}}{=} \lim_{x \to 0} \frac{\sin(\pi x^2/2)}{3x^2} \overset{\text{H}}{=} \lim_{x \to 0} \frac{\pi x \cos(\pi x^2/2)}{6x} = \frac{\pi}{6} \cdot \cos 0 = \frac{\pi}{6}$$

83. Since $f(2) = 0$, the given limit has the form $\frac{0}{0}$.

$$\lim_{x \to 0} \frac{f(2 + 3x) + f(2 + 5x)}{x} \overset{\text{H}}{=} \lim_{x \to 0} \frac{f'(2 + 3x) \cdot 3 + f'(2 + 5x) \cdot 5}{1} = f'(2) \cdot 3 + f'(2) \cdot 5 = 8f'(2) = 8 \cdot 7 = 56$$

85. Since $\lim\limits_{h \to 0}[f(x + h) - f(x - h)] = f(x) - f(x) = 0$ (f is differentiable and hence continuous) and $\lim\limits_{h \to 0} 2h = 0$, we use l'Hospital's Rule:

$$\lim_{h \to 0} \frac{f(x + h) - f(x - h)}{2h} \overset{\text{H}}{=} \lim_{h \to 0} \frac{f'(x + h)(1) - f'(x - h)(-1)}{2} = \frac{f'(x) + f'(x)}{2} = \frac{2f'(x)}{2} = f'(x)$$

$\dfrac{f(x + h) - f(x - h)}{2h}$ is the slope of the secant line between $(x - h, f(x - h))$ and $(x + h, f(x + h))$. As $h \to 0$, this line gets closer to the tangent line and its slope approaches $f'(x)$.

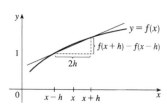

87. $\lim\limits_{x \to \infty} \dfrac{e^x}{x^n} \overset{\text{H}}{=} \lim\limits_{x \to \infty} \dfrac{e^x}{nx^{n-1}} \overset{\text{H}}{=} \lim\limits_{x \to \infty} \dfrac{e^x}{n(n - 1)x^{n-2}} \overset{\text{H}}{=} \cdots \overset{\text{H}}{=} \lim\limits_{x \to \infty} \dfrac{e^x}{n!} = \infty$

89. $\lim\limits_{x \to 0^+} x^{\alpha} \ln x = \lim\limits_{x \to 0^+} \dfrac{\ln x}{x^{-\alpha}} \overset{\text{H}}{=} \lim\limits_{x \to 0^+} \dfrac{1/x}{-\alpha x^{-\alpha - 1}} = \lim\limits_{x \to 0^+} \dfrac{x^{\alpha}}{-\alpha} = 0$ since $\alpha > 0$.

91. Let the radius of the circle be r. We see that $A(\theta)$ is the area of the whole figure (a sector of the circle with radius 1), minus the area of $\triangle OPR$. But the area of the sector of the circle is $\frac{1}{2}r^2\theta$ (see Reference Page 1), and the area of the triangle is $\frac{1}{2}r\,|PQ| = \frac{1}{2}r(r\sin\theta) = \frac{1}{2}r^2\sin\theta$. So we have

$A(\theta) = \frac{1}{2}r^2\theta - \frac{1}{2}r^2\sin\theta = \frac{1}{2}r^2(\theta - \sin\theta)$. Now by elementary trigonometry,

$B(\theta) = \frac{1}{2}|QR|\,|PQ| = \frac{1}{2}(r - |OQ|)\,|PQ| = \frac{1}{2}(r - r\cos\theta)(r\sin\theta) = \frac{1}{2}r^2(1 - \cos\theta)\sin\theta$.

So the limit we want is

$$\lim_{\theta\to 0^+}\frac{A(\theta)}{B(\theta)} = \lim_{\theta\to 0^+}\frac{\frac{1}{2}r^2(\theta - \sin\theta)}{\frac{1}{2}r^2(1 - \cos\theta)\sin\theta} \stackrel{\text{H}}{=} \lim_{\theta\to 0^+}\frac{1 - \cos\theta}{(1 - \cos\theta)\cos\theta + \sin\theta\,(\sin\theta)}$$

$$= \lim_{\theta\to 0^+}\frac{1 - \cos\theta}{\cos\theta - \cos^2\theta + \sin^2\theta} \stackrel{\text{H}}{=} \lim_{\theta\to 0^+}\frac{\sin\theta}{-\sin\theta - 2\cos\theta\,(-\sin\theta) + 2\sin\theta\,(\cos\theta)}$$

$$= \lim_{\theta\to 0^+}\frac{\sin\theta}{-\sin\theta + 4\sin\theta\,\cos\theta} = \lim_{\theta\to 0^+}\frac{1}{-1 + 4\cos\theta} = \frac{1}{-1 + 4\cos 0} = \frac{1}{3}$$

93. (a) We show that $\displaystyle\lim_{x\to 0}\frac{f(x)}{x^n} = 0$ for every integer $n \geq 0$. Let $y = \dfrac{1}{x^2}$. Then

$$\lim_{x\to 0}\frac{f(x)}{x^{2n}} = \lim_{x\to 0}\frac{e^{-1/x^2}}{(x^2)^n} = \lim_{y\to\infty}\frac{y^n}{e^y} \stackrel{\text{H}}{=} \lim_{y\to\infty}\frac{ny^{n-1}}{e^y} \stackrel{\text{H}}{=} \cdots \stackrel{\text{H}}{=} \lim_{y\to\infty}\frac{n!}{e^y} = 0 \quad\Rightarrow$$

$$\lim_{x\to 0}\frac{f(x)}{x^n} = \lim_{x\to 0}x^n\frac{f(x)}{x^{2n}} = \lim_{x\to 0}x^n\lim_{x\to 0}\frac{f(x)}{x^{2n}} = 0. \text{ Thus, } f'(0) = \lim_{x\to 0}\frac{f(x) - f(0)}{x - 0} = \lim_{x\to 0}\frac{f(x)}{x} = 0.$$

(b) Using the Chain Rule and the Quotient Rule we see that $f^{(n)}(x)$ exists for $x \neq 0$. In fact, we prove by induction that for each $n \geq 0$, there is a polynomial p_n and a non-negative integer k_n with $f^{(n)}(x) = p_n(x)f(x)/x^{k_n}$ for $x \neq 0$. This is true for $n = 0$; suppose it is true for the nth derivative. Then $f'(x) = f(x)(2/x^3)$, so

$$f^{(n+1)}(x) = \left[x^{k_n}\left[p_n'(x)f(x) + p_n(x)f'(x)\right] - k_n x^{k_n - 1}p_n(x)f(x)\right]x^{-2k_n}$$

$$= \left[x^{k_n}p_n'(x) + p_n(x)(2/x^3) - k_n x^{k_n - 1}p_n(x)\right]f(x)x^{-2k_n}$$

$$= \left[x^{k_n + 3}p_n'(x) + 2p_n(x) - k_n x^{k_n + 2}p_n(x)\right]f(x)x^{-(2k_n + 3)}$$

which has the desired form.

Now we show by induction that $f^{(n)}(0) = 0$ for all n. By part (a), $f'(0) = 0$. Suppose that $f^{(n)}(0) = 0$. Then

$$f^{(n+1)}(0) = \lim_{x\to 0}\frac{f^{(n)}(x) - f^{(n)}(0)}{x - 0} = \lim_{x\to 0}\frac{f^{(n)}(x)}{x} = \lim_{x\to 0}\frac{p_n(x)f(x)/x^{k_n}}{x} = \lim_{x\to 0}\frac{p_n(x)f(x)}{x^{k_n + 1}}$$

$$= \lim_{x\to 0}p_n(x)\lim_{x\to 0}\frac{f(x)}{x^{k_n + 1}} = p_n(0)\cdot 0 = 0$$

7 Review

1. (a) See Definition 1 in Section 7.1. It must pass the Horizontal Line Test.

(b) See Definition 2 in Section 7.1. The graph of f^{-1} is obtained by reflecting the graph of f about the line $y = x$.

(c) $g'(a) = \left(f^{-1}\right)'(a) = \dfrac{1}{f'(g(a))}$

2. (a) The function $f(x) = e^x$ has domain $\mathbb{R}$ and range $(0, \infty)$.

(b) The function $f(x) = \ln x$ has domain $(0, \infty)$ and range $\mathbb{R}$.

(c) The graphs are reflections of one another about the line $y = x$. See Figure 7.3.3 or Figure 7.3*.1.

(d) $\log_a x = \dfrac{\ln x}{\ln a}$

3. (a) See Definition 7.5.1. Domain $= [-1, 1]$, Range $= \left[-\frac{\pi}{2}, \frac{\pi}{2}\right]$

(b) See Definition 7.5.4. Domain $= [-1, 1]$, Range $= [0, \pi]$

(c) See Definition 7.5.7. Domain $= \mathbb{R}$, Range $= \left(-\frac{\pi}{2}, \frac{\pi}{2}\right)$. See Figure 10 in Section 7.5.

4. $\sinh x = \dfrac{e^x - e^{-x}}{2}$, $\cosh x = \dfrac{e^x + e^{-x}}{2}$, $\tanh x = \dfrac{\sinh x}{\cosh x} = \dfrac{e^x - e^{-x}}{e^x + e^{-x}}$

5. (a) $y = e^x \;\Rightarrow\; y' = e^x$ (b) $y = a^x \;\Rightarrow\; y' = a^x \ln a$

(c) $y = \ln x \;\Rightarrow\; y' = 1/x$ (d) $y = \log_a x \;\Rightarrow\; y' = 1/(x \ln a)$

(e) $y = \sin^{-1} x \;\Rightarrow\; y' = 1/\sqrt{1 - x^2}$ (f) $y = \cos^{-1} x \;\Rightarrow\; y' = -1/\sqrt{1 - x^2}$

(g) $y = \tan^{-1} x \;\Rightarrow\; y' = 1/(1 + x^2)$ (h) $y = \sinh x \;\Rightarrow\; y' = \cosh x$

(i) $y = \cosh x \;\Rightarrow\; y' = \sinh x$ (j) $y = \tanh x \;\Rightarrow\; y' = \operatorname{sech}^2 x$

(k) $y = \sinh^{-1} x \;\Rightarrow\; y' = 1/\sqrt{1 + x^2}$ (l) $y = \cosh^{-1} x \;\Rightarrow\; y' = 1/\sqrt{x^2 - 1}$

(m) $y = \tanh^{-1} x \;\Rightarrow\; y' = 1/(1 - x^2)$

6. (a) e is the number such that $\displaystyle\lim_{h \to 0} \dfrac{e^h - 1}{h} = 1$.

(b) $e = \displaystyle\lim_{x \to 0} (1 + x)^{1/x}$

(c) The differentiation formula for $y = a^x$ $[y' = a^x \ln a]$ is simplest when $a = e$ because $\ln e = 1$.

(d) The differentiation formula for $y = \log_a x$ $[y' = 1/(x \ln a)]$ is simplest when $a = e$ because $\ln e = 1$.

7. (a) See l'Hospital's Rule and the three notes that follow it in Section 7.7.

(b) Write fg as $\dfrac{f}{1/g}$ or $\dfrac{g}{1/f}$.

(c) Convert the difference into a quotient using a common denominator, rationalizing, factoring, or some other method.

(d) Convert the power to a product by taking the natural logarithm of both sides of $y = f^g$ or by writing f^g as $e^{g \ln f}$.

───────── TRUE-FALSE QUIZ ─────────

1. True.   If f is one-to-one, with domain $\mathbb{R}$, then $f^{-1}(f(6)) = 6$ by the first cancellation equation [see (4) in Section 7.1].

3. False.   For example, $\cos \frac{\pi}{2} = \cos\left(-\frac{\pi}{2}\right)$, so $\cos x$ is not 1-1.

5. True, since $\ln x$ is an increasing function on $(0, \infty)$.

7. True.   We can divide by e^x since $e^x \neq 0$ for every x.

9. False.   Let $x = e$. Then $(\ln x)^6 = (\ln e)^6 = 1^6 = 1$, but $6 \ln x = 6 \ln e = 6 \cdot 1 = 6 \neq 1 = (\ln x)^6$.

11. False. $\ln 10$ is a constant, so its derivative is 0.

13. False.   The "-1" is not an exponent; it is an indication of an inverse function.

15. True.   See Figure 2 in Section 7.6.

17. True. $\int_2^{16} (1/x)\, dx = \ln x\big]_2^{16} = \ln 16 - \ln 2 = \ln \frac{16}{2} = \ln 8 = \ln 2^3 = 3 \ln 2$

───────── EXERCISES ─────────

1. No. f is not 1-1 because the graph of f fails the Horizontal Line Test.

3. (a) $f^{-1}(3) = 7$ since $f(7) = 3$.   (b) $(f^{-1})'(3) = \dfrac{1}{f'(f^{-1}(3))} = \dfrac{1}{f'(7)} = \dfrac{1}{8}$

5.
$$y = 5^x - 1$$

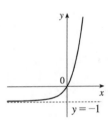

7. Reflect the graph of $y = \ln x$ about the x-axis to obtain the graph of $y = -\ln x$.

$$y = \ln x \qquad\qquad y = -\ln x$$

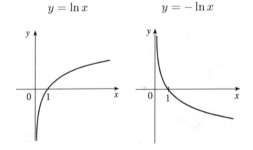

9.
$$y = 2\arctan x$$

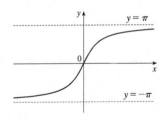

11. (a) $e^{2\ln 3} = \left(e^{\ln 3}\right)^2 = 3^2 = 9$

(b) $\log_{10} 25 + \log_{10} 4 = \log_{10}(25 \cdot 4) = \log_{10} 100 = \log_{10} 10^2 = 2$

13. $\ln x = \frac{1}{3}$ $\Leftrightarrow$ $\log_e x = \frac{1}{3}$ $\Rightarrow$ $x = e^{1/3}$

15. $e^{e^x} = 17$ $\Rightarrow$ $\ln e^{e^x} = \ln 17$ $\Rightarrow$ $e^x = \ln 17$ $\Rightarrow$ $\ln e^x = \ln(\ln 17)$ $\Rightarrow$ $x = \ln \ln 17$

17. $\ln(x+1) + \ln(x-1) = 1$ $\Rightarrow$ $\ln[(x+1)(x-1)] = 1$ $\Rightarrow$ $\ln(x^2 - 1) = \ln e$ $\Rightarrow$ $x^2 - 1 = e$ $\Rightarrow$
$x^2 = e + 1$ $\Rightarrow$ $x = \sqrt{e+1}$ since $\ln(x-1)$ is defined only when $x > 1$.

19. $\tan^{-1} x = 1$ $\Rightarrow$ $\tan \tan^{-1} x = \tan 1$ $\Rightarrow$ $x = \tan 1$ (≈ 1.5574)

21. $f(t) = t^2 \ln t$ $\Rightarrow$ $f'(t) = t^2 \cdot \frac{1}{t} + (\ln t)(2t) = t + 2t \ln t$ or $t(1 + 2 \ln t)$

23. $h(\theta) = e^{\tan 2\theta}$ $\Rightarrow$ $h'(\theta) = e^{\tan 2\theta} \cdot \sec^2 2\theta \cdot 2 = 2 \sec^2 2\theta \, e^{\tan 2\theta}$

25. $y = \ln|\sec 5x + \tan 5x|$ $\Rightarrow$

$$y' = \frac{1}{\sec 5x + \tan 5x}(\sec 5x \tan 5x \cdot 5 + \sec^2 5x \cdot 5) = \frac{5 \sec 5x \, (\tan 5x + \sec 5x)}{\sec 5x + \tan 5x} = 5 \sec 5x$$

27. $y = e^{cx}(c \sin x - \cos x)$ $\Rightarrow$ $y' = ce^{cx}(c \sin x - \cos x) + e^{cx}(c \cos x + \sin x) = (c^2 + 1)e^{cx} \sin x$

29. $y = \ln(\sec^2 x) = 2 \ln|\sec x|$ $\Rightarrow$ $y' = (2/\sec x)(\sec x \tan x) = 2 \tan x$

31. $y = xe^{-1/x}$ $\Rightarrow$ $y' = e^{-1/x} + xe^{-1/x}(1/x^2) = e^{-1/x}(1 + 1/x)$

33. $y = 2^{-t^2}$ $\Rightarrow$ $y' = 2^{-t^2}(\ln 2)(-2t) = (-2 \ln 2)t \, 2^{-t^2}$

35. $H(v) = v \tan^{-1} v$ $\Rightarrow$ $H'(v) = v \cdot \frac{1}{1+v^2} + \tan^{-1} v \cdot 1 = \frac{v}{1+v^2} + \tan^{-1} v$

37. $y = x \sinh(x^2)$ $\Rightarrow$ $y' = x \cosh(x^2) \cdot 2x + \sinh(x^2) \cdot 1 = 2x^2 \cosh(x^2) + \sinh(x^2)$

39. $y = \ln \sin x - \frac{1}{2} \sin^2 x$ $\Rightarrow$ $y' = \frac{1}{\sin x} \cdot \cos x - \frac{1}{2} \cdot 2 \sin x \cdot \cos x = \cot x - \sin x \cos x$

41. $y = \ln \dfrac{1}{x} + \dfrac{1}{\ln x} = \ln x^{-1} + (\ln x)^{-1} = -\ln x + (\ln x)^{-1}$ $\Rightarrow$

$$y' = -1 \cdot \frac{1}{x} + (-1)(\ln x)^{-2} \cdot \frac{1}{x} = -\frac{1}{x} - \frac{1}{x(\ln x)^2}$$

43. $y = \ln(\cosh 3x)$ $\Rightarrow$ $y' = (1/\cosh 3x)(\sinh 3x)(3) = 3 \tanh 3x$

45. $y = \cosh^{-1}(\sinh x)$ $\Rightarrow$ $y' = (\cosh x)/\sqrt{\sinh^2 x - 1}$

47. $f(x) = e^{\sin^3(\ln(x^2+1))}$ $\Rightarrow$

$$f'(x) = e^{\sin^3(\ln(x^2+1))} \cdot 3 \sin^2(\ln(x^2+1)) \cdot \cos(\ln(x^2+1)) \cdot \frac{1}{x^2+1} \cdot 2x$$

$$= \frac{6x}{x^2+1} \sin^2(\ln(x^2+1)) \cdot \cos(\ln(x^2+1)) \cdot e^{\sin^3(\ln(x^2+1))}$$

49. $f(x) = e^{g(x)}$ $\Rightarrow$ $f'(x) = e^{g(x)} g'(x)$

51. $f(x) = \ln|g(x)|$ $\Rightarrow$ $f'(x) = \frac{1}{g(x)} g'(x) = \frac{g'(x)}{g(x)}$

53. $f(x) = 2^x$ $\Rightarrow$ $f'(x) = 2^x \ln 2$ $\Rightarrow$ $f''(x) = 2^x(\ln 2)^2$ $\Rightarrow$ $\cdots$ $\Rightarrow$ $f^{(n)}(x) = 2^x(\ln 2)^n$

55. We first show it is true for $n = 1$: $f'(x) = e^x + xe^x = (x + 1)e^x$. We now assume it is true for $n = k$:

$f^{(k)}(x) = (x + k)e^x$. With this assumption, we must show it is true for $n = k + 1$:

$$f^{(k+1)}(x) = \frac{d}{dx}\left[f^{(k)}(x)\right] = \frac{d}{dx}\left[(x + k)e^x\right] = e^x + (x + k)e^x = \left[x + (k + 1)\right]e^x.$$

Therefore, $f^{(n)}(x) = (x + n)e^x$ by mathematical induction.

57. $y = (2 + x)e^{-x} \Rightarrow y' = (2 + x)(-e^{-x}) + e^{-x} \cdot 1 = e^{-x}[-(2 + x) + 1] = e^{-x}(-x - 1)$. At $(0, 2)$,

$y' = 1(-1) = -1$, so an equation of the tangent line is $y - 2 = -1(x - 0)$, or $y = -x + 2$.

59. $y = [\ln(x + 4)]^2 \Rightarrow y' = 2\dfrac{\ln(x + 4)}{x + 4} = 0 \Leftrightarrow \ln(x + 4) = 0 \Leftrightarrow x + 4 = 1 \Leftrightarrow x = -3$, so the

tangent is horizontal at $(-3, 0)$.

61. (a) The line $x - 4y = 1$ has slope $\frac{1}{4}$. The tangent to $y = e^x$ has slope $\frac{1}{4}$ when $y' = e^x = \frac{1}{4} \Rightarrow$

$x = \ln \frac{1}{4} = -\ln 4$, so an equation is $y - \frac{1}{4} = \frac{1}{4}(x + \ln 4)$ or $y = \frac{1}{4}x + \frac{1}{4}(\ln 4 + 1)$.

(b) The slope of the tangent at the point (a, e^a) is $\dfrac{d}{dx}e^x\bigg]_{x = a} = e^a$. An equation of the tangent line is thus

$y - e^a = e^a(x - a)$. We substitute $x = 0$, $y = 0$ into this equation, since we want the line to pass through the

origin: $0 - e^a = e^a(0 - a) \Leftrightarrow -e^a = e^a(-a) \Leftrightarrow a = 1$. So an equation of the tangent is

$y - e = e(x - 1)$, or $y = ex$.

63. $\lim\limits_{x \to \infty} e^{-3x} = 0$ since $-3x \to -\infty$ as $x \to \infty$ and $\lim\limits_{t \to -\infty} e^t = 0$.

65. Let $t = 2/(x - 3)$. As $x \to 3^-$, $t \to -\infty$. $\lim\limits_{x \to 3^-} e^{2/(x-3)} = \lim\limits_{t \to -\infty} e^t = 0$

67. Let $t = \sinh x$. As $x \to 0^+$, $t \to 0^+$. $\lim\limits_{x \to 0^+} \ln(\sinh x) = \lim\limits_{t \to 0^+} \ln t = -\infty$

69. $\lim\limits_{x \to \infty} \dfrac{(1 + 2^x)/2^x}{(1 - 2^x)/2^x} = \lim\limits_{x \to \infty} \dfrac{1/2^x + 1}{1/2^x - 1} = \dfrac{0 + 1}{0 - 1} = -1$

71. $\lim\limits_{x \to 0} \dfrac{\tan \pi x}{\ln(1 + x)} \overset{\text{H}}{=} \lim\limits_{x \to 0} \dfrac{\pi \sec^2 \pi x}{1/(1 + x)} = \dfrac{\pi \cdot 1^2}{1/1} = \pi$

73. $\lim\limits_{x \to 0} \dfrac{e^{4x} - 1 - 4x}{x^2} \overset{\text{H}}{=} \lim\limits_{x \to 0} \dfrac{4e^{4x} - 4}{2x} \overset{\text{H}}{=} \lim\limits_{x \to 0} \dfrac{16e^{4x}}{2} = \lim\limits_{x \to 0} 8e^{4x} = 8 \cdot 1 = 8$

75. $\lim\limits_{x \to \infty} x^3 e^{-x} = \lim\limits_{x \to \infty} \dfrac{x^3}{e^x} \overset{\text{H}}{=} \lim\limits_{x \to \infty} \dfrac{3x^2}{e^x} \overset{\text{H}}{=} \lim\limits_{x \to \infty} \dfrac{6x}{e^x} \overset{\text{H}}{=} \lim\limits_{x \to \infty} \dfrac{6}{e^x} = 0$

77. $\lim\limits_{x \to 1^+} \left(\dfrac{x}{x - 1} - \dfrac{1}{\ln x}\right) = \lim\limits_{x \to 1^+} \left(\dfrac{x \ln x - x + 1}{(x - 1)\ln x}\right) \overset{\text{H}}{=} \lim\limits_{x \to 1^+} \dfrac{x \cdot (1/x) + \ln x - 1}{(x - 1) \cdot (1/x) + \ln x}$

$\qquad\qquad = \lim\limits_{x \to 1^+} \dfrac{\ln x}{1 - 1/x + \ln x} \overset{\text{H}}{=} \lim\limits_{x \to 1^+} \dfrac{1/x}{1/x^2 + 1/x} = \dfrac{1}{1 + 1} = \dfrac{1}{2}$

79. $y = f(x) = \tan^{-1}(1/x)$ **A.** $D = \{x \mid x \neq 0\}$ **B.** No intercept **C.** $f(-x) = -f(x)$, so the curve is symmetric about the origin. **D.** $\lim\limits_{x \to \pm\infty} \tan^{-1}(1/x) = \tan^{-1} 0 = 0$, so $y = 0$ is a HA. $\lim\limits_{x \to 0^+} \tan^{-1}(1/x) = \frac{\pi}{2}$

and $\lim\limits_{x \to 0^-} \tan^{-1}(1/x) = -\frac{\pi}{2}$ since $\dfrac{1}{x} \to \pm\infty$ as $x \to 0^{\pm}$.

H.

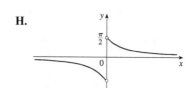

E. $f'(x) = \dfrac{1}{1 + (1/x)^2}\left(-1/x^2\right) = \dfrac{-1}{x^2 + 1}$ $\Rightarrow$ $f'(x) < 0$,

so f is decreasing on $(-\infty, 0)$ and $(0, \infty)$. **F.** No maximum nor minimum

G. $f''(x) = \dfrac{2x}{(x^2 + 1)^2} > 0$ $\Leftrightarrow$ $x > 0$, so f is CU on $(0, \infty)$ and CD on $(-\infty, 0)$.

81. $y = f(x) = x \ln x$ **A.** $D = (0, \infty)$ **B.** No y-intercept; x-intercept 1. **C.** No symmetry **D.** No asymptote

[Note that the graph approaches the point $(0,0)$ as $x \to 0^+$.]

H.

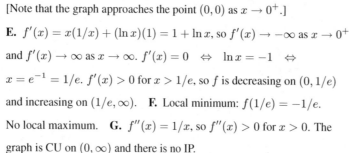
(1/e, −1/e)

E. $f'(x) = x(1/x) + (\ln x)(1) = 1 + \ln x$, so $f'(x) \to -\infty$ as $x \to 0^+$

and $f'(x) \to \infty$ as $x \to \infty$. $f'(x) = 0$ $\Leftrightarrow$ $\ln x = -1$ $\Leftrightarrow$

$x = e^{-1} = 1/e$. $f'(x) > 0$ for $x > 1/e$, so f is decreasing on $(0, 1/e)$

and increasing on $(1/e, \infty)$. **F.** Local minimum: $f(1/e) = -1/e$.

No local maximum. **G.** $f''(x) = 1/x$, so $f''(x) > 0$ for $x > 0$. The

graph is CU on $(0, \infty)$ and there is no IP.

83. $y = f(x) = e^x + e^{-3x}$ **A.** $D = \mathbb{R}$ **B.** y-intercept 2; no x-intercept **C.** No symmetry

D. $\lim\limits_{x \to \pm\infty} \left(e^x + e^{-3x}\right) = \infty$, no asymptote **E.** $y = f(x) = e^x + e^{-3x}$ $\Rightarrow$

$f'(x) = e^x - 3e^{-3x} = e^{-3x}\left(e^{4x} - 3\right) > 0$ $\Leftrightarrow$ $e^{4x} > 3$ $\Leftrightarrow$

$4x > \ln 3$ $\Leftrightarrow$ $x > \frac{1}{4}\ln 3 \approx 0.27$, so f is increasing on $\left(\frac{1}{4}\ln 3, \infty\right)$

and decreasing on $\left(-\infty, \frac{1}{4}\ln 3\right)$.

H.

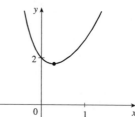

F. Absolute minimum value $f\left(\frac{1}{4}\ln 3\right) = 3^{1/4} + 3^{-3/4} \approx 1.75$.

G. $f''(x) = e^x + 9e^{-3x} > 0$, so f is CU on $(-\infty, \infty)$. No IP

85.

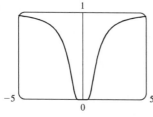

From the graph, we estimate the points of inflection to be about

$(\pm 0.82, 0.22)$. $f(x) = e^{-1/x^2}$ $\Rightarrow$ $f'(x) = 2x^{-3}e^{-1/x^2}$ $\Rightarrow$

$f''(x) = 2\left[x^{-3}\left(2x^{-3}\right)e^{-1/x^2} + e^{-1/x^2}\left(-3x^{-4}\right)\right]$

$= 2x^{-6}e^{-1/x^2}\left(2 - 3x^2\right)$.

This is 0 when $2 - 3x^2 = 0$ $\Leftrightarrow$ $x = \pm\sqrt{\frac{2}{3}}$, so the inflection points

are $\left(\pm\sqrt{\frac{2}{3}}, e^{-3/2}\right)$.

87. $s(t) = Ae^{-ct}\cos(\omega t + \delta) \quad \Rightarrow$

$$v(t) = s'(t) = A\{e^{-ct}\left[-\omega\sin(\omega t + \delta)\right] + \cos(\omega t + \delta)(-ce^{-ct})\}$$
$$= -Ae^{-ct}\left[\omega\sin(\omega t + \delta) + c\cos(\omega t + \delta)\right] \quad \Rightarrow$$

$$a(t) = v'(t) = -A\{e^{-ct}[\omega^2\cos(\omega t + \delta) - c\omega\sin(\omega t + \delta)] + [\omega\sin(\omega t + \delta) + c\cos(\omega t + \delta)](-ce^{-ct})\}$$
$$= -Ae^{-ct}[\omega^2\cos(\omega t + \delta) - c\omega\sin(\omega t + \delta) - c\omega\sin(\omega t + \delta) - c^2\cos(\omega t + \delta)]$$
$$= -Ae^{-ct}[(\omega^2 - c^2)\cos(\omega t + \delta) - 2c\omega\sin(\omega t + \delta)]$$
$$= Ae^{-ct}[(c^2 - \omega^2)\cos(\omega t + \delta) + 2c\omega\sin(\omega t + \delta)]$$

89. Let $P(t) = \dfrac{64}{1 + 31e^{-0.7944t}} = \dfrac{A}{1 + Be^{ct}} = A(1 + Be^{ct})^{-1}$, where $A = 64$, $B = 31$, and $c = -0.7944$.

$$P'(t) = -A(1 + Be^{ct})^{-2}(Bce^{ct}) = -ABce^{ct}(1 + Be^{ct})^{-2}$$

$$P''(t) = -ABce^{ct}\left[-2(1 + Be^{ct})^{-3}(Bce^{ct})\right] + (1 + Be^{ct})^{-2}(-ABc^2 e^{ct})$$

$$= -ABc^2 e^{ct}(1 + Be^{ct})^{-3}\left[-2Be^{ct} + (1 + Be^{ct})\right] = -\dfrac{ABc^2 e^{ct}(1 - Be^{ct})}{(1 + Be^{ct})^3}$$

The population is increasing most rapidly when its graph changes from CU to CD; that is,

when $P''(t) = 0$ in this case. $P''(t) = 0 \quad \Rightarrow \quad Be^{ct} = 1 \quad \Rightarrow \quad e^{ct} = \dfrac{1}{B} \quad \Rightarrow$

$ct = \ln\dfrac{1}{B} \quad \Rightarrow \quad t = \dfrac{\ln(1/B)}{c} = \dfrac{\ln(1/31)}{-0.7944} \approx 4.32$ days. Note that

$P\left(\dfrac{1}{c}\ln\dfrac{1}{B}\right) = \dfrac{A}{1 + Be^{c(1/c)\ln(1/B)}} = \dfrac{A}{1 + Be^{\ln(1/B)}} = \dfrac{A}{1 + B(1/B)} = \dfrac{A}{1 + 1} = \dfrac{A}{2}$, one-half the limit of P

as $t \to \infty$.

91. Let $u = -2y^2$. Then $du = -4y\,dy$ and

$$\int_0^1 ye^{-2y^2}\,dy = \int_0^{-2} e^u\left(-\tfrac{1}{4}\,du\right) = -\tfrac{1}{4}\left[e^u\right]_0^{-2} = -\tfrac{1}{4}(e^{-2} - 1) = \tfrac{1}{4}(1 - e^{-2}).$$

93. $\displaystyle\int_2^4 \dfrac{1 + x - x^2}{x^2}\,dx = \int_2^4\left(x^{-2} + \dfrac{1}{x} - 1\right)dx = \left[-\dfrac{1}{x} + \ln x - x\right]_2^4$

$$= \left(-\tfrac{1}{4} + \ln 4 - 4\right) - \left(-\tfrac{1}{2} + \ln 2 - 2\right) = \ln 2 - \tfrac{7}{4}$$

95. Let $u = \sqrt{x}$. Then $du = \dfrac{dx}{2\sqrt{x}} \quad \Rightarrow \quad \displaystyle\int \dfrac{e^{\sqrt{x}}}{\sqrt{x}}\,dx = 2\int e^u\,du = 2e^u + C = 2e^{\sqrt{x}} + C.$

97. Let $u = x^2 + 2x$. Then $du = (2x + 2)\,dx = 2(x + 1)\,dx$ and

$$\int \dfrac{x + 1}{x^2 + 2x}\,dx = \int \dfrac{\tfrac{1}{2}\,du}{u} = \dfrac{1}{2}\ln|u| + C = \dfrac{1}{2}\ln|x^2 + 2x| + C.$$

99. Let $u = \ln(\cos x)$. Then $du = \dfrac{-\sin x}{\cos x}\,dx = -\tan x\,dx \quad \Rightarrow$

$\int \tan x\ln(\cos x)\,dx = -\int u\,du = -\tfrac{1}{2}u^2 + C = -\tfrac{1}{2}[\ln(\cos x)]^2 + C.$

101. Let $u = \tan\theta$. Then $du = \sec^2\theta\,d\theta$ and $\displaystyle\int 2^{\tan\theta}\sec^2\theta\,d\theta = \int 2^u\,du = \dfrac{2^u}{\ln 2} + C = \dfrac{2^{\tan\theta}}{\ln 2} + C.$

103. Let $u = 1 + \sec\theta$, so $du = \sec\theta\tan\theta\,d\theta \ \Rightarrow\ \displaystyle\int \dfrac{\sec\theta\tan\theta}{1+\sec\theta}\,d\theta = \int \dfrac{1}{u}\,du = \ln|u| + C = \ln|1+\sec\theta| + C.$

105. $\cos x \le 1 \ \Rightarrow\ e^x\cos x \le e^x \ \Rightarrow\ \int_0^1 e^x\cos x\,dx \le \int_0^1 e^x\,dx = e^x\big]_0^1 = e - 1$

107. $f(x) = \displaystyle\int_1^{\sqrt{x}} \dfrac{e^s}{s}\,ds \ \Rightarrow\ f'(x) = \dfrac{d}{dx}\int_1^{\sqrt{x}} \dfrac{e^s}{s}\,ds = \dfrac{e^{\sqrt{x}}}{\sqrt{x}}\dfrac{d}{dx}\sqrt{x} = \dfrac{e^{\sqrt{x}}}{\sqrt{x}}\dfrac{1}{2\sqrt{x}} = \dfrac{e^{\sqrt{x}}}{2x}$

109. $f_{\text{ave}} = \dfrac{1}{4-1}\displaystyle\int_1^4 \dfrac{1}{x}\,dx = \dfrac{1}{3}\Big[\ln|x|\Big]_1^4 = \dfrac{1}{3}[\ln 4 - \ln 1] = \dfrac{1}{3}\ln 4$

111. $V = \displaystyle\int_0^1 \dfrac{2\pi x}{1+x^4}\,dx$ by cylindrical shells. Let $u = x^2 \ \Rightarrow\ du = 2x\,dx.$ Then

$$V = \int_0^1 \dfrac{\pi}{1+u^2}\,du = \pi\Big[\tan^{-1} u\Big]_0^1 = \pi\big(\tan^{-1}1 - \tan^{-1}0\big) = \pi\Big(\dfrac{\pi}{4}\Big) = \dfrac{\pi^2}{4}.$$

113. $f(x) = \ln x + \tan^{-1} x \ \Rightarrow\ f(1) = \ln 1 + \tan^{-1}1 = \frac{\pi}{4} \ \Rightarrow\ g\big(\frac{\pi}{4}\big) = 1.$

$f'(x) = \dfrac{1}{x} + \dfrac{1}{1+x^2}$, so $g'\big(\frac{\pi}{4}\big) = \dfrac{1}{f'(1)} = \dfrac{1}{3/2} = \dfrac{2}{3}.$

115.

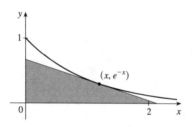

We find the equation of a tangent to the curve $y = e^{-x}$, so that we can find the x- and y-intercepts of this tangent, and then we can find the area of the triangle. The slope of the tangent at the point (a, e^{-a}) is given by $\dfrac{d}{dx}e^{-x}\bigg]_{x=a} = -e^{-a}$, and so the equation of the tangent is $y - e^{-a} = -e^{-a}(x - a) \ \Leftrightarrow\ y = e^{-a}(a - x + 1).$

The y-intercept of this line is $y = e^{-a}(a - 0 + 1) = e^{-a}(a + 1).$ To find the x-intercept we set

$y = 0 \ \Rightarrow\ e^{-a}(a - x + 1) = 0 \ \Rightarrow\ x = a + 1.$ So the area of the triangle is

$A(a) = \frac{1}{2}\big[e^{-a}(a+1)\big](a+1) = \frac{1}{2}e^{-a}(a+1)^2.$ We differentiate this with respect to a:

$A'(a) = \frac{1}{2}\big[e^{-a}(2)(a+1) + (a+1)^2 e^{-a}(-1)\big] = \frac{1}{2}e^{-a}(1 - a^2).$ This is 0 at $a = \pm 1$, and the root $a = 1$ gives a maximum, by the First Derivative Test. So the maximum area of the triangle is

$A(1) = \frac{1}{2}e^{-1}(1+1)^2 = 2e^{-1} = 2/e.$

117. $\displaystyle\lim_{x\to -1} F(x) = \lim_{x\to -1} \dfrac{b^{x+1} - a^{x+1}}{x+1} \overset{\text{H}}{=} \lim_{x\to -1} \dfrac{b^{x+1}\ln b - a^{x+1}\ln a}{1} = \ln b - \ln a = F(-1)$, so F is continuous at -1.

119. Differentiating both sides of the given equation, using the Fundamental Theorem for each side, gives

$$f(x) = e^{2x} + 2xe^{2x} + e^{-x}f(x). \text{ So } f(x)(1 - e^{-x}) = e^{2x} + 2xe^{2x}. \text{ Hence } f(x) = \dfrac{e^{2x}(1+2x)}{1 - e^{-x}}.$$

☐ PROBLEMS PLUS

1. Let $y = f(x) = e^{-x^2}$. The area of the rectangle under the curve from $-x$ to x is $A(x) = 2xe^{-x^2}$ where $x \geq 0$.

We maximize $A(x)$: $A'(x) = 2e^{-x^2} - 4x^2e^{-x^2} = 2e^{-x^2}(1 - 2x^2) = 0 \Rightarrow x = \frac{1}{\sqrt{2}}$. This gives a maximum

since $A'(x) > 0$ for $0 \leq x < \frac{1}{\sqrt{2}}$ and $A'(x) < 0$ for $x > \frac{1}{\sqrt{2}}$. We next determine the points of inflection of $f(x)$.

Notice that $f'(x) = -2xe^{-x^2} = -A(x)$. So $f''(x) = -A'(x)$ and hence, $f''(x) < 0$ for $-\frac{1}{\sqrt{2}} < x < \frac{1}{\sqrt{2}}$ and

$f''(x) > 0$ for $x < -\frac{1}{\sqrt{2}}$ and $x > \frac{1}{\sqrt{2}}$. So $f(x)$ changes concavity at $x = \pm\frac{1}{\sqrt{2}}$, and the two vertices of the

rectangle of largest area are at the inflection points.

3. Consider the statement that $\dfrac{d^n}{dx^n}(e^{ax} \sin bx) = r^n e^{ax} \sin(bx + n\theta)$. For $n = 1$,

$\dfrac{d}{dx}(e^{ax} \sin bx) = ae^{ax} \sin bx + be^{ax} \cos bx$, and

$$re^{ax} \sin(bx + \theta) = re^{ax}[\sin bx \cos \theta + \cos bx \sin \theta] = re^{ax}\left(\frac{a}{r}\sin bx + \frac{b}{r}\cos bx\right)$$

$$= ae^{ax} \sin bx + be^{ax} \cos bx$$

since $\tan \theta = \dfrac{b}{a} \Rightarrow \sin \theta = \dfrac{b}{r}$ and $\cos \theta = \dfrac{a}{r}$.

So the statement is true for $n = 1$. Assume it is true for $n = k$. Then

$$\frac{d^{k+1}}{dx^{k+1}}(e^{ax} \sin bx) = \frac{d}{dx}\left[r^k e^{ax} \sin(bx + k\theta)\right] = r^k ae^{ax} \sin(bx + k\theta) + r^k e^{ax}b\cos(bx + k\theta)$$

$$= r^k e^{ax}[a\sin(bx + k\theta) + b\cos(bx + k\theta)]$$

But

$$\sin[bx + (k + 1)\theta] = \sin[(bx + k\theta) + \theta] = \sin(bx + k\theta)\cos \theta + \sin \theta \cos(bx + k\theta)$$

$$= \frac{a}{r}\sin(bx + k\theta) + \frac{b}{r}\cos(bx + k\theta)$$

Hence, $a\sin(bx + k\theta) + b\cos(bx + k\theta) = r\sin[bx + (k + 1)\theta]$. So

$$\frac{d^{k+1}}{dx^{k+1}}(e^{ax} \sin bx) = r^k e^{ax}[a\sin(bx + k\theta) + b\cos(bx + k\theta)] = r^k e^{ax}[r\sin(bx + (k + 1)\theta)]$$

$$= r^{k+1}e^{ax}[\sin(bx + (k + 1)\theta)]$$

Therefore, the statement is true for all n by mathematical induction.

5. We first show that $\dfrac{x}{1+x^2} < \tan^{-1} x$ for $x > 0$. Let $f(x) = \tan^{-1} x - \dfrac{x}{1+x^2}$. Then

$$f'(x) = \frac{1}{1+x^2} - \frac{1(1+x^2) - x(2x)}{(1+x^2)^2} = \frac{(1+x^2) - (1-x^2)}{(1+x^2)^2} = \frac{2x^2}{(1+x^2)^2} > 0 \text{ for } x > 0. \text{ So } f(x) \text{ is}$$

increasing on $(0, \infty)$. Hence, $0 < x \;\Rightarrow\; 0 = f(0) < f(x) = \tan^{-1} x - \dfrac{x}{1+x^2}$. So $\dfrac{x}{1+x^2} < \tan^{-1} x$

for $0 < x$. We next show that $\tan^{-1} x < x$ for $x > 0$. Let $h(x) = x - \tan^{-1} x$. Then

$$h'(x) = 1 - \frac{1}{1+x^2} = \frac{x^2}{1+x^2} > 0. \text{ Hence, } h(x) \text{ is increasing on } (0, \infty). \text{ So for } 0 < x,$$

$0 = h(0) < h(x) = x - \tan^{-1} x$. Hence, $\tan^{-1} x < x$ for $x > 0$, and we conclude that $\dfrac{x}{1+x^2} < \tan^{-1} x < x$

for $x > 0$.

7. By the Fundamental Theorem of Calculus, $f(x) = \int_1^x \sqrt{1+t^3}\, dt \;\Rightarrow\; f'(x) = \sqrt{1+x^3} > 0$ for $x > -1$.

So f is increasing on $(-1, \infty)$ and hence is one-to-one. Note that $f(1) = 0$, so $f^{-1}(1) = 0 \;\Rightarrow$

$(f^{-1})'(0) = 1/f'(1) = \frac{1}{\sqrt{2}}$.

9. If $L = \displaystyle\lim_{x \to \infty} \left(\dfrac{x+a}{x-a}\right)^x$, then L has the indeterminate form 1^∞, so

$$\ln L = \lim_{x \to \infty} \ln\left(\frac{x+a}{x-a}\right)^x = \lim_{x \to \infty} x \ln\left(\frac{x+a}{x-a}\right) = \lim_{x \to \infty} \frac{\ln(x+a) - \ln(x-a)}{1/x}$$

$$\overset{\text{H}}{=} \lim_{x \to \infty} \frac{\dfrac{1}{x+a} - \dfrac{1}{x-a}}{-1/x^2} = \lim_{x \to \infty} \left[\frac{(x-a) - (x+a)}{(x+a)(x-a)} \cdot \frac{-x^2}{1}\right]$$

$$= \lim_{x \to \infty} \frac{2ax^2}{x^2 - a^2} = \lim_{x \to \infty} \frac{2a}{1 - a^2/x^2} = 2a.$$

Hence, $\ln L = 2a$, so $L = e^{2a}$. From the original equation, we want $L = e^1 \;\Rightarrow\; 2a = 1 \;\Rightarrow\; a = \frac{1}{2}$.

11. Both sides of the inequality are positive, so $\cosh(\sinh x) < \sinh(\cosh x) \;\Leftrightarrow\; \cosh^2(\sinh x) < \sinh^2(\cosh x)$

$\Leftrightarrow\; \sinh^2(\sinh x) + 1 < \sinh^2(\cosh x) \;\Leftrightarrow\; 1 < [\sinh(\cosh x) - \sinh(\sinh x)][\sinh(\cosh x) + \sinh(\sinh x)]$

$$\Leftrightarrow\; 1 < \left[\sinh\left(\frac{e^x + e^{-x}}{2}\right) - \sinh\left(\frac{e^x - e^{-x}}{2}\right)\right]\left[\sinh\left(\frac{e^x + e^{-x}}{2}\right) + \sinh\left(\frac{e^x - e^{-x}}{2}\right)\right]$$

$\Leftrightarrow\; 1 < [2\cosh(e^x/2)\sinh(e^{-x}/2)][2\sinh(e^x/2)\cosh(e^{-x}/2)]$ [use the addition formulas and cancel]

$\Leftrightarrow\; 1 < [2\sinh(e^x/2)\cosh(e^x/2)][2\sinh(e^{-x}/2)\cosh(e^{-x}/2)] \;\Leftrightarrow\; 1 < \sinh e^x \sinh e^{-x}$,

by the half-angle formula. Now both e^x and e^{-x} are positive, and $\sinh y > y$ for $y > 0$, since $\sinh 0 = 0$ and

$(\sinh y - y)' = \cosh y - 1 > 0$ for $x > 0$, so $1 = e^x e^{-x} < \sinh e^x \sinh e^{-x}$. So, following this chain of

reasoning backward, we arrive at the desired result.

13.

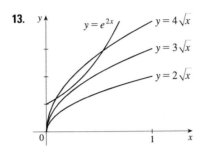

Let $f(x) = e^{2x}$ and $g(x) = k\sqrt{x}$ $(k > 0)$. From the graphs of f and g, we see that f will intersect g exactly once when f and g share a tangent line. Thus, we must have $f = g$ and $f' = g'$ at $x = a$. $f(a) = g(a)$ $\Rightarrow$

$e^{2a} = k\sqrt{a}$ **(1)** and $f'(a) = g'(a)$ $\Rightarrow$ $2e^{2a} = \dfrac{k}{2\sqrt{a}}$ $\Rightarrow$

$e^{2a} = \dfrac{k}{4\sqrt{a}}$. So we must have $k\sqrt{a} = \dfrac{k}{4\sqrt{a}}$ $\Rightarrow$ $(\sqrt{a})^2 = \dfrac{k}{4k}$ $\Rightarrow$

$a = \frac{1}{4}$. From **(1)**, $e^{2(1/4)} = k\sqrt{1/4}$ $\Rightarrow$ $k = 2e^{1/2} = 2\sqrt{e} \approx 3.297$.

15. Suppose that the curve $y = a^x$ intersects the line $y = x$. Then $a^{x_0} = x_0$ for some $x_0 > 0$, and hence $a = x_0^{1/x_0}$.

We find the maximum value of $g(x) = x^{1/x}$, > 0, because if a is larger than the maximum

value of this function, then the curve $y = a^x$ does not intersect the line $y = x$.

$g'(x) = e^{(1/x)\ln x}\left(-\dfrac{1}{x^2}\ln x + \dfrac{1}{x} \cdot \dfrac{1}{x}\right) = x^{1/x}\left(\dfrac{1}{x^2}\right)(1 - \ln x)$. This is 0 only where $x = e$, and for $0 < x < e$,

$f'(x) > 0$, while for $x > e$, $f'(x) < 0$, so g has an absolute maximum of $g(e) = e^{1/e}$. So if $y = a^x$ intersects

$y = x$, we must have $0 < a \le e^{1/e}$. Conversely, suppose that $0 < a \le e^{1/e}$. Then $a^e \le e$, so the graph of $y = a^x$

lies below or touches the graph of $y = x$ at $x = e$. Also $a^0 = 1 > 0$, so the graph of $y = a^x$ lies above that of

$y = x$ at $x = 0$. Therefore, by the Intermediate Value Theorem, the graphs of $y = a^x$ and $y = x$ must intersect

somewhere between $x = 0$ and $x = e$.

8 ☐ TECHNIQUES OF INTEGRATION

8.1 Integration by Parts

1. Let $u = \ln x$, $dv = x\,dx$ $\Rightarrow$ $du = dx/x$, $v = \frac{1}{2}x^2$. Then by Equation 2, $\int u\,dv = uv - \int v\,du$,

$$\int x \ln x\,dx = \frac{1}{2}x^2 \ln x - \int \frac{1}{2}x^2(dx/x) = \frac{1}{2}x^2 \ln x - \frac{1}{2}\int x\,dx = \frac{1}{2}x^2 \ln x - \frac{1}{2}\cdot\frac{1}{2}x^2 + C$$

$$= \frac{1}{2}x^2 \ln x - \frac{1}{4}x^2 + C$$

3. Let $u = x$, $dv = \cos 5x\,dx$ $\Rightarrow$ $du = dx$, $v = \frac{1}{5}\sin 5x$. Then by Equation 2,
$\int x \cos 5x\,dx = \frac{1}{5}x \sin 5x - \int \frac{1}{5}\sin 5x\,dx = \frac{1}{5}x \sin 5x + \frac{1}{25}\cos 5x + C$.

5. Let $u = r$, $dv = e^{r/2}\,dr$ $\Rightarrow$ $du = dr$, $v = 2e^{r/2}$. Then
$\int r e^{r/2}\,dr = 2r e^{r/2} - \int 2e^{r/2}\,dr = 2r e^{r/2} - 4e^{r/2} + C$.

7. Let $u = x^2$, $dv = \sin \pi x\,dx$ $\Rightarrow$ $du = 2x\,dx$ and $v = -\frac{1}{\pi}\cos \pi x$. Then
$I = \int x^2 \sin \pi x\,dx = -\frac{1}{\pi}x^2 \cos \pi x + \frac{2}{\pi}\int x \cos \pi x\,dx$ $(*)$.
Next let $U = x$, $dV = \cos \pi x\,dx$ $\Rightarrow$ $dU = dx$, $V = \frac{1}{\pi}\sin \pi x$, so
$\int x \cos \pi x\,dx = \frac{1}{\pi}x \sin \pi x - \frac{1}{\pi}\int \sin \pi x\,dx = \frac{1}{\pi}x \sin \pi x + \frac{1}{\pi^2}\cos \pi x + C_1$. Substituting for $\int x \cos \pi x\,dx$ in $(*)$,
we get $I = -\frac{1}{\pi}x^2 \cos \pi x + \frac{2}{\pi}\left(\frac{1}{\pi}x \sin \pi x + \frac{1}{\pi^2}\cos \pi x + C_1\right) = -\frac{1}{\pi}x^2 \cos \pi x + \frac{2}{\pi^2}x \sin \pi x + \frac{2}{\pi^3}\cos \pi x + C$,
where $C = \frac{2}{\pi}C_1$.

9. Let $u = \ln(2x+1)$, $dv = dx$ $\Rightarrow$ $du = \dfrac{2}{2x+1}\,dx$, $v = x$. Then

$$\int \ln(2x+1)\,dx = x\ln(2x+1) - \int \frac{2x}{2x+1}\,dx = x\ln(2x+1) - \int \frac{(2x+1)-1}{2x+1}\,dx$$

$$= x\ln(2x+1) - \int\left(1 - \frac{1}{2x+1}\right)dx = x\ln(2x+1) - x + \frac{1}{2}\ln(2x+1) + C$$

$$= \frac{1}{2}(2x+1)\ln(2x+1) - x + C$$

11. Let $u = \arctan 4t$, $dv = dt$ $\Rightarrow$ $du = \dfrac{4}{1+(4t)^2}\,dt = \dfrac{4}{1+16t^2}\,dt$, $v = t$. Then

$$\int \arctan 4t\,dt = t \arctan 4t - \int \frac{4t}{1+16t^2}\,dt = t \arctan 4t - \frac{1}{8}\int \frac{32t}{1+16t^2}\,dt$$

$$= t \arctan 4t - \frac{1}{8}\ln(1+16t^2) + C$$

13. First let $u = (\ln x)^2$, $dv = dx$ $\Rightarrow$ $du = 2\ln x \cdot \frac{1}{x}\,dx$, $v = x$. Then by Equation 2,
$I = \int (\ln x)^2\,dx = x(\ln x)^2 - 2\int x \ln x \cdot \frac{1}{x}\,dx = x(\ln x)^2 - 2\int \ln x\,dx$. Next let $U = \ln x$, $dV = dx$ $\Rightarrow$
$dU = 1/x\,dx$, $V = x$ to get $\int \ln x\,dx = x \ln x - \int x \cdot (1/x)\,dx = x \ln x - \int dx = x \ln x - x + C_1$. Thus,
$I = x(\ln x)^2 - 2(x \ln x - x + C_1) = x(\ln x)^2 - 2x \ln x + 2x + C$, where $C = -2C_1$.

15. First let $u = \sin 3\theta$, $dv = e^{2\theta}\,d\theta$ $\Rightarrow$ $du = 3\cos 3\theta\,d\theta$, $v = \frac{1}{2}e^{2\theta}$. Then
$I = \int e^{2\theta}\sin 3\theta\,d\theta = \frac{1}{2}e^{2\theta}\sin 3\theta - \frac{3}{2}\int e^{2\theta}\cos 3\theta\,d\theta$. Next let $U = \cos 3\theta$,
$dV = e^{2\theta}\,d\theta$ $\Rightarrow$ $dU = -3\sin 3\theta\,d\theta$, $V = \frac{1}{2}e^{2\theta}$ to get
$\int e^{2\theta}\cos 3\theta\,d\theta = \frac{1}{2}e^{2\theta}\cos 3\theta + \frac{3}{2}\int e^{2\theta}\sin 3\theta\,d\theta$. Substituting in the previous formula gives

$I = \frac{1}{2}e^{2\theta}\sin 3\theta - \frac{3}{4}e^{2\theta}\cos 3\theta - \frac{9}{4}\int e^{2\theta}\sin 3\theta\, d\theta = \frac{1}{2}e^{2\theta}\sin 3\theta - \frac{3}{4}e^{2\theta}\cos 3\theta - \frac{9}{4}I \Rightarrow$
$\frac{13}{4}I = \frac{1}{2}e^{2\theta}\sin 3\theta - \frac{3}{4}e^{2\theta}\cos 3\theta + C_1$. Hence, $I = \frac{1}{13}e^{2\theta}(2\sin 3\theta - 3\cos 3\theta) + C$, where $C = \frac{4}{13}C_1$.

17. Let $u = y$, $dv = \sinh y\, dy \Rightarrow du = dy$, $v = \cosh y$. Then
$\int y\sinh y\, dy = y\cosh y - \int \cosh y\, dy = y\cosh y - \sinh y + C$.

19. Let $u = t$, $dv = \sin 3t\, dt \Rightarrow du = dt$, $v = -\frac{1}{3}\cos 3t$. Then
$\int_0^\pi t\sin 3t\, dt = \left[-\frac{1}{3}t\cos 3t\right]_0^\pi + \frac{1}{3}\int_0^\pi \cos 3t\, dt = \left(\frac{1}{3}\pi - 0\right) + \frac{1}{9}\left[\sin 3t\right]_0^\pi = \frac{\pi}{3}$.

21. Let $u = \ln x$, $dv = x^{-2}\, dx \Rightarrow du = \frac{1}{x}\, dx$, $v = -x^{-1}$. By (6),
$\int_1^2 \frac{\ln x}{x^2}\, dx = \left[-\frac{\ln x}{x}\right]_1^2 + \int_1^2 x^{-2}\, dx = -\frac{1}{2}\ln 2 + \ln 1 + \left[-\frac{1}{x}\right]_1^2 = -\frac{1}{2}\ln 2 + 0 - \frac{1}{2} + 1 = \frac{1}{2} - \frac{1}{2}\ln 2$.

23. Let $u = y$, $dv = \dfrac{dy}{e^{2y}} = e^{-2y}dy \Rightarrow du = dy$, $v = -\dfrac{1}{2}e^{-2y}$. Then
$\int_0^1 \frac{y}{e^{2y}}\, dy = \left[-\frac{1}{2}ye^{-2y}\right]_0^1 + \frac{1}{2}\int_0^1 e^{-2y}dy = \left(-\frac{1}{2}e^{-2} + 0\right) - \frac{1}{4}\left[e^{-2y}\right]_0^1 = -\frac{1}{2}e^{-2} - \frac{1}{4}e^{-2} + \frac{1}{4} = \frac{1}{4} - \frac{3}{4}e^{-2}$.

25. Let $u = \cos^{-1} x$, $dv = dx \Rightarrow du = -\dfrac{dx}{\sqrt{1-x^2}}$, $v = x$. Then
$I = \int_0^{1/2} \cos^{-1} x\, dx = \left[x\cos^{-1} x\right]_0^{1/2} + \int_0^{1/2} \frac{x\, dx}{\sqrt{1-x^2}} = \frac{1}{2}\cdot\frac{\pi}{3} + \int_1^{3/4} t^{-1/2}\left[-\frac{1}{2}\, dt\right]$, where $t = 1 - x^2$
$\Rightarrow dt = -2x\, dx$. Thus, $I = \frac{\pi}{6} + \frac{1}{2}\int_{3/4}^1 t^{-1/2}\, dt = \frac{\pi}{6} + \left[\sqrt{t}\right]_{3/4}^1 = \frac{\pi}{6} + 1 - \frac{\sqrt{3}}{2} = \frac{1}{6}\left(\pi + 6 - 3\sqrt{3}\right)$.

27. Let $u = \ln(\sin x)$, $dv = \cos x\, dx \Rightarrow du = \dfrac{\cos x}{\sin x}\, dx$, $v = \sin x$. Then
$I = \int \cos x\ln(\sin x)\, dx = \sin x\ln(\sin x) - \int \cos x\, dx = \sin x\ln(\sin x) - \sin x + C$.
Another method: Substitute $t = \sin x$, so $dt = \cos x\, dx$. Then $I = \int \ln t\, dt = t\ln t - t + C$ (see Example 2) and
so $I = \sin x(\ln\sin x - 1) + C$.

29. Let $w = \ln x \Rightarrow dw = dx/x$. Then $x = e^w$ and $dx = e^w\, dw$, so
$$\int \cos(\ln x)\, dx = \int e^w \cos w\, dw = \frac{1}{2}e^w(\sin w + \cos w) + C \quad \text{[by the method of Example 4]}$$
$$= \frac{1}{2}x\left[\sin(\ln x) + \cos(\ln x)\right] + C$$

31. Let $u = (\ln x)^2$, $dv = x^4\, dx \Rightarrow du = 2\dfrac{\ln x}{x}\, dx$, $v = \dfrac{x^5}{5}$. By (6),
$\int_1^2 x^4(\ln x)^2\, dx = \left[\frac{x^5}{5}(\ln x)^2\right]_1^2 - 2\int_1^2 \frac{x^4}{5}\ln x\, dx = \frac{32}{5}(\ln 2)^2 - 0 - 2\int_1^2 \frac{x^4}{5}\ln x\, dx$.
Let $U = \ln x$, $dV = \dfrac{x^4}{5}\, dx \Rightarrow dU = \dfrac{1}{x}\, dx$, $V = \dfrac{x^5}{25}$.
Then $\int_1^2 \frac{x^4}{5}\ln x\, dx = \left[\frac{x^5}{25}\ln x\right]_1^2 - \int_1^2 \frac{x^4}{25}\, dx = \frac{32}{25}\ln 2 - 0 - \left[\frac{x^5}{125}\right]_1^2 = \frac{32}{25}\ln 2 - \left(\frac{32}{125} - \frac{1}{125}\right)$.
So $\int_1^2 x^4(\ln x)^2\, dx = \frac{32}{5}(\ln 2)^2 - 2\left(\frac{32}{25}\ln 2 - \frac{31}{125}\right) = \frac{32}{5}(\ln 2)^2 - \frac{64}{25}\ln 2 + \frac{62}{125}$.

33. Let $w = \sqrt{x}$, so that $x = w^2$ and $dx = 2w\, dw$. Thus, $\int \sin\sqrt{x}\, dx = \int 2w\sin w\, dw$. Now use parts with $u = 2w$,
$dv = \sin w\, dw$, $du = 2\, dw$, $v = -\cos w$ to get
$$\int 2w\sin w\, dw = -2w\cos w + \int 2\cos w\, dw = -2w\cos w + 2\sin w + C$$
$$= -2\sqrt{x}\cos\sqrt{x} + 2\sin\sqrt{x} + C = 2\left(\sin\sqrt{x} - \sqrt{x}\cos\sqrt{x}\right) + C$$

35. Let $x = \theta^2$, so that $dx = 2\theta\, d\theta$. Thus, $\int_{\sqrt{\pi/2}}^{\sqrt{\pi}} \theta^3 \cos(\theta^2)\, d\theta = \int_{\sqrt{\pi/2}}^{\sqrt{\pi}} \theta^2 \cos(\theta^2) \cdot \frac{1}{2}(2\theta\, d\theta) = \frac{1}{2}\int_{\pi/2}^{\pi} x\cos x\, dx$.

Now use parts with $u = x$, $dv = \cos x\, dx$, $du = dx$, $v = \sin x$ to get

$$\tfrac{1}{2}\int_{\pi/2}^{\pi} x\cos x\, dx = \tfrac{1}{2}\left([x\sin x]_{\pi/2}^{\pi} - \int_{\pi/2}^{\pi}\sin x\, dx\right) = \tfrac{1}{2}\,[x\sin x + \cos x]_{\pi/2}^{\pi}$$

$$= \tfrac{1}{2}(\pi\sin\pi + \cos\pi) - \tfrac{1}{2}\left(\tfrac{\pi}{2}\sin\tfrac{\pi}{2} + \cos\tfrac{\pi}{2}\right) = \tfrac{1}{2}(\pi\cdot 0 - 1) - \tfrac{1}{2}\left(\tfrac{\pi}{2}\cdot 1 + 0\right) = -\tfrac{1}{2} - \tfrac{\pi}{4}$$

In Exercises 37–40, let $f(x)$ denote the integrand and $F(x)$ its antiderivative (with $C = 0$).

37. Let $u = x$, $dv = \cos\pi x\, dx$ $\Rightarrow$ $du = dx$, $v = (\sin\pi x)/\pi$. Then

$$\int x\cos\pi x\, dx = x\cdot\frac{\sin\pi x}{\pi} - \int\frac{\sin\pi x}{\pi}\, dx = \frac{x\sin\pi x}{\pi} + \frac{\cos\pi x}{\pi^2} + C.$$

We see from the graph that this is reasonable, since F has extreme values where f is 0.

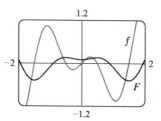

39. Let $u = 2x + 3$, $dv = e^x\, dx$ $\Rightarrow$ $du = 2\, dx$, $v = e^x$. Then
$\int(2x + 3)e^x\, dx = (2x + 3)e^x - 2\int e^x\, dx = (2x + 3)e^x - 2e^x + C = (2x + 1)e^x + C$. We see from the graph that this is reasonable, since F has a minimum where f changes from negative to positive.

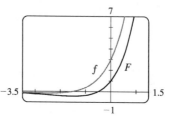

41. (a) Take $n = 2$ in Example 6 to get $\int\sin^2 x\, dx = -\frac{1}{2}\cos x\sin x + \frac{1}{2}\int 1\, dx = \frac{x}{2} - \frac{\sin 2x}{4} + C$.

(b) $\int\sin^4 x\, dx = -\frac{1}{4}\cos x\sin^3 x + \frac{3}{4}\int\sin^2 x\, dx = -\frac{1}{4}\cos x\sin^3 x + \frac{3}{8}x - \frac{3}{16}\sin 2x + C$.

43. (a) From Example 6, $\displaystyle\int\sin^n x\, dx = -\frac{1}{n}\cos x\sin^{n-1} x + \frac{n-1}{n}\int\sin^{n-2} x\, dx$. Using (6),

$$\int_0^{\pi/2}\sin^n x\, dx = \left[-\frac{\cos x\sin^{n-1} x}{n}\right]_0^{\pi/2} + \frac{n-1}{n}\int_0^{\pi/2}\sin^{n-2} x\, dx$$

$$= (0 - 0) + \frac{n-1}{n}\int_0^{\pi/2}\sin^{n-2} x\, dx = \frac{n-1}{n}\int_0^{\pi/2}\sin^{n-2} x\, dx$$

(b) Using $n = 3$ in part (a), we have $\int_0^{\pi/2}\sin^3 x\, dx = \frac{2}{3}\int_0^{\pi/2}\sin x\, dx = \left[-\frac{2}{3}\cos x\right]_0^{\pi/2} = \frac{2}{3}$.

Using $n = 5$ in part (a), we have $\int_0^{\pi/2}\sin^5 x\, dx = \frac{4}{5}\int_0^{\pi/2}\sin^3 x\, dx = \frac{4}{5}\cdot\frac{2}{3} = \frac{8}{15}$.

(c) The formula holds for $n = 1$ (that is, $2n + 1 = 3$) by (b). Assume it holds for some $k \geq 1$. Then

$$\int_0^{\pi/2}\sin^{2k+1} x\, dx = \frac{2\cdot 4\cdot 6\cdots(2k)}{3\cdot 5\cdot 7\cdots(2k+1)}.\text{ By Example 6,}$$

$$\int_0^{\pi/2}\sin^{2k+3} x\, dx = \frac{2k+2}{2k+3}\int_0^{\pi/2}\sin^{2k+1} x\, dx = \frac{2k+2}{2k+3}\cdot\frac{2\cdot 4\cdot 6\cdots(2k)}{3\cdot 5\cdot 7\cdots(2k+1)}$$

$$= \frac{2\cdot 4\cdot 6\cdots(2k)[2(k+1)]}{3\cdot 5\cdot 7\cdots(2k+1)[2(k+1)+1]},$$

so the formula holds for $n = k + 1$. By induction, the formula holds for all $n \geq 1$.

45. Let $u = (\ln x)^n$, $dv = dx$ $\Rightarrow$ $du = n(\ln x)^{n-1}(dx/x)$, $v = x$. By Equation 2,
$\int(\ln x)^n\, dx = x(\ln x)^n - \int nx(\ln x)^{n-1}(dx/x) = x(\ln x)^n - n\int(\ln x)^{n-1}\, dx$.

47. Let $u = \left(x^2 + a^2\right)^n$, $dv = dx$ $\Rightarrow$ $du = n\left(x^2 + a^2\right)^{n-1} 2x\,dx$, $v = x$. Then

$$\int \left(x^2 + a^2\right)^n dx = x\left(x^2 + a^2\right)^n - 2n \int x^2 \left(x^2 + a^2\right)^{n-1} dx$$

$$= x\left(x^2 + a^2\right)^n - 2n\left[\int \left(x^2 + a^2\right)^n dx - a^2 \int \left(x^2 + a^2\right)^{n-1} dx\right] \quad \text{[since } x^2 = \left(x^2 + a^2\right) - a^2\text{]}$$

$$\Rightarrow \quad (2n+1) \int \left(x^2 + a^2\right)^n dx = x\left(x^2 + a^2\right)^n + 2na^2 \int \left(x^2 + a^2\right)^{n-1} dx, \text{ and}$$

$$\int \left(x^2 + a^2\right)^n dx = \frac{x\left(x^2 + a^2\right)^n}{2n+1} + \frac{2na^2}{2n+1}\int \left(x^2 + a^2\right)^{n-1} dx \quad \text{[provided } 2n+1 \neq 0\text{]}.$$

49. Take $n = 3$ in Exercise 45 to get
$\int (\ln x)^3 dx = x(\ln x)^3 - 3\int (\ln x)^2 dx = x(\ln x)^3 - 3x(\ln x)^2 + 6x\ln x - 6x + C$ [by Exercise 13].
Or: Instead of using Exercise 13, apply Exercise 45 again with $n = 2$.

51. Area $= \int_0^5 xe^{-0.4x}dx$. Let $u = x$, $dv = e^{-0.4x}dx$ $\Rightarrow$

$du = dx$, $v = -2.5e^{-0.4x}$. Then

area $= \left[-2.5xe^{-0.4x}\right]_0^5 + 2.5\int_0^5 e^{-0.4x}dx$

$= -12.5e^{-2} + 0 + 2.5\left[-2.5e^{-0.4x}\right]_0^5$

$= -12.5e^{-2} - 6.25(e^{-2} - 1) = 6.25 - 18.75e^{-2}$ or $\frac{25}{4} - \frac{75}{4}e^{-2}$

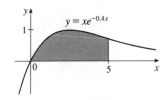

53. The curves $y = x\sin x$ and $y = (x-2)^2$ intersect at $a \approx 1.04748$ and
$b \approx 2.87307$, so

area $= \int_a^b \left[x\sin x - (x-2)^2\right] dx$

$= \left[-x\cos x + \sin x - \frac{1}{3}(x-2)^3\right]_a^b$ [by Example 1]

$\approx 2.81358 - 0.63075 = 2.18283$

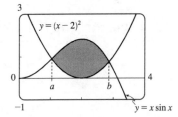

55. $V = \int_0^1 2\pi x\cos(\pi x/2)dx$. Let $u = x$, $dv = \cos(\pi x/2)dx$ $\Rightarrow$ $du = dx$, $v = \frac{2}{\pi}\sin(\pi x/2)$.

$V = 2\pi\left[\frac{2}{\pi}x\sin\left(\frac{\pi x}{2}\right)\right]_0^1 - 2\pi \cdot \frac{2}{\pi}\int_0^1 \sin\left(\frac{\pi x}{2}\right) dx = 2\pi\left(\frac{2}{\pi} - 0\right) - 4\left[-\frac{2}{\pi}\cos\left(\frac{\pi x}{2}\right)\right]_0^1$

$= 4 + \frac{8}{\pi}(0-1) = 4 - \frac{8}{\pi}$.

57. Volume $= \int_{-1}^0 2\pi(1-x)e^{-x} dx$. Let $u = 1-x$, $dv = e^{-x} dx$ $\Rightarrow$ $du = -dx$, $v = -e^{-x}$.

$V = 2\pi\left[(1-x)(-e^{-x})\right]_{-1}^0 - 2\pi\int_{-1}^0 e^{-x} dx = 2\pi\left[(x-1)(e^{-x}) + e^{-x}\right]_{-1}^0$

$= 2\pi\left[xe^{-x}\right]_{-1}^0 = 2\pi(0+e) = 2\pi e$

59. The average value of $f(x) = x^2\ln x$ on the interval $[1,3]$ is $f_{\text{ave}} = \dfrac{1}{3-1}\displaystyle\int_1^3 x^2\ln x\,dx = \frac{1}{2}I$.

Let $u = \ln x$, $dv = x^2 dx$ $\Rightarrow$ $du = (1/x)\,dx$, $v = \frac{1}{3}x^3$. So

$I = \left[\frac{1}{3}x^3\ln x\right]_1^3 - \int_1^3 \frac{1}{3}x^2 dx = (9\ln 3 - 0) - \left[\frac{1}{9}x^3\right]_1^3 = 9\ln 3 - \left(3 - \frac{1}{9}\right) = 9\ln 3 - \frac{26}{9}$.

Thus, $f_{\text{ave}} = \frac{1}{2}I = \frac{1}{2}\left(9\ln 3 - \frac{26}{9}\right) = \frac{9}{2}\ln 3 - \frac{13}{9}$.

61. Since $v(t) > 0$ for all t, the desired distance is $s(t) = \int_0^t v(w)dw = \int_0^t w^2 e^{-w}\, dw$.

First let $u = w^2$, $dv = e^{-w}\, dw$ $\Rightarrow$ $du = 2w\, dw$, $v = -e^{-w}$. Then $s(t) = \left[-w^2 e^{-w}\right]_0^t + 2\int_0^t w e^{-w}\, dw$.

Next let $U = w$, $dV = e^{-w}\, dw$ $\Rightarrow$ $dU = dw$, $V = -e^{-w}$. Then

$$s(t) = -t^2 e^{-t} + 2\left(\left[-we^{-w}\right]_0^t + \int_0^t e^{-w}\, dw\right) = -t^2 e^{-t} + 2\left(-te^{-t} + 0 + \left[-e^{-w}\right]_0^t\right)$$

$$= -t^2 e^{-t} + 2(-te^{-t} - e^{-t} + 1) = -t^2 e^{-t} - 2te^{-t} - 2e^{-t} + 2$$

$$= 2 - e^{-t}\left(t^2 + 2t + 2\right) \text{ meters}$$

63. For $I = \int_1^4 xf''(x)\, dx$, let $u = x$, $dv = f''(x)\, dx$ $\Rightarrow$ $du = dx$, $v = f'(x)$. Then

$I = \left[xf'(x)\right]_1^4 - \int_1^4 f'(x)\, dx = 4f'(4) - 1 \cdot f'(1) - [f(4) - f(1)] = 4 \cdot 3 - 1 \cdot 5 - (7 - 2) = 12 - 5 - 5 = 2$.

We used the fact that f'' is continuous to guarantee that I exists.

65. Using the formula for volumes of rotation and the figure, we see that

Volume $= \int_0^d \pi b^2\, dy - \int_0^c \pi a^2\, dy - \int_c^d \pi[g(y)]^2\, dy = \pi b^2 d - \pi a^2 c - \int_c^d \pi[g(y)]^2\, dy$. Let $y = f(x)$, which

gives $dy = f'(x)\, dx$ and $g(y) = x$, so that $V = \pi b^2 d - \pi a^2 c - \pi \int_a^b x^2 f'(x)\, dx$. Now integrate

by parts with $u = x^2$, and $dv = f'(x)\, dx$ $\Rightarrow$ $du = 2x\, dx$, $v = f(x)$, and

$\int_a^b x^2 f'(x)\, dx = \left[x^2 f(x)\right]_a^b - \int_a^b 2x f(x)\, dx = b^2 f(b) - a^2 f(a) - \int_a^b 2x f(x)\, dx$, but $f(a) = c$ and $f(b) = d$

$\Rightarrow$ $V = \pi b^2 d - \pi a^2 c - \pi\left[b^2 d - a^2 c - \int_a^b 2x f(x)\, dx\right] = \int_a^b 2\pi x f(x)\, dx$.

8.2 Trigonometric Integrals

The symbols $\overset{s}{=}$ and $\overset{c}{=}$ indicate the use of the substitutions $\{u = \sin x,\, du = \cos x\, dx\}$ and $\{u = \cos x,\, du = -\sin x\, dx\}$, respectively.

1. $\int \sin^3 x \cos^2 x\, dx = \int \sin^2 x \cos^2 x \sin x\, dx = \int (1 - \cos^2 x)\cos^2 x \sin x\, dx \overset{c}{=} \int (1 - u^2)u^2(-du)$

$\quad = \int (u^2 - 1)u^2\, du = \int (u^4 - u^2)\, du = \frac{1}{5}u^5 - \frac{1}{3}u^3 + C = \frac{1}{5}\cos^5 x - \frac{1}{3}\cos^3 x + C$

3. $\int_{\pi/2}^{3\pi/4} \sin^5 x \cos^3 x\, dx = \int_{\pi/2}^{3\pi/4} \sin^5 x \cos^2 x \cos x\, dx = \int_{\pi/2}^{3\pi/4} \sin^5 x\, (1 - \sin^2 x)\cos x\, dx$

$\quad \overset{s}{=} \int_1^{\sqrt{2}/2} u^5 (1 - u^2)\, du = \int_1^{\sqrt{2}/2} (u^5 - u^7)\, du = \left[\frac{1}{6}u^6 - \frac{1}{8}u^8\right]_1^{\sqrt{2}/2}$

$\quad = \left(\frac{1/8}{6} - \frac{1/16}{8}\right) - \left(\frac{1}{6} - \frac{1}{8}\right) = -\frac{11}{384}$

5. $\int \cos^5 x \sin^4 x\, dx = \int \cos^4 x \sin^4 x \cos x\, dx = \int (1 - \sin^2 x)^2 \sin^4 x \cos x\, dx \overset{s}{=} \int (1 - u^2)^2 u^4\, du$

$\quad = \int (1 - 2u^2 + u^4)u^4\, du = \int (u^4 - 2u^6 + u^8)\, du = \frac{1}{5}u^5 - \frac{2}{7}u^7 + \frac{1}{9}u^9 + C$

$\quad = \frac{1}{5}\sin^5 x - \frac{2}{7}\sin^7 x + \frac{1}{9}\sin^9 x + C$

7. $\int_0^{\pi/2} \cos^2 \theta\, d\theta = \int_0^{\pi/2} \frac{1}{2}(1 + \cos 2\theta)\, d\theta$ [half-angle identity]

$\quad = \frac{1}{2}\left[\theta + \frac{1}{2}\sin 2\theta\right]_0^{\pi/2} = \frac{1}{2}\left[\left(\frac{\pi}{2} + 0\right) - (0 + 0)\right] = \frac{\pi}{4}$

9. $\int_0^\pi \sin^4(3t)\, dt = \int_0^\pi \left[\sin^2(3t)\right]^2 dt = \int_0^\pi \left[\frac{1}{2}(1 - \cos 6t)\right]^2 dt = \frac{1}{4}\int_0^\pi (1 - 2\cos 6t + \cos^2 6t)\, dt$

$\quad = \frac{1}{4}\int_0^\pi \left[1 - 2\cos 6t + \frac{1}{2}(1 + \cos 12t)\right] dt = \frac{1}{4}\int_0^\pi \left(\frac{3}{2} - 2\cos 6t + \frac{1}{2}\cos 12t\right) dt$

$\quad = \frac{1}{4}\left[\frac{3}{2}t - \frac{1}{3}\sin 6t + \frac{1}{24}\sin 12t\right]_0^\pi = \frac{1}{4}\left[\left(\frac{3\pi}{2} - 0 + 0\right) - (0 - 0 + 0)\right] = \frac{3\pi}{8}$

11. $\int (1 + \cos\theta)^2 \, d\theta = \int (1 + 2\cos\theta + \cos^2\theta) \, d\theta = \theta + 2\sin\theta + \frac{1}{2}\int (1 + \cos 2\theta) \, d\theta$

$\qquad\qquad = \theta + 2\sin\theta + \frac{1}{2}\theta + \frac{1}{4}\sin 2\theta + C = \frac{3}{2}\theta + 2\sin\theta + \frac{1}{4}\sin 2\theta + C$

13. $\int_0^{\pi/4} \sin^4 x \cos^2 x \, dx = \int_0^{\pi/4} \sin^2 x \, (\sin x \cos x)^2 \, dx = \int_0^{\pi/4} \frac{1}{2}(1 - \cos 2x)\left(\frac{1}{2}\sin 2x\right)^2 \, dx$

$\qquad\qquad = \frac{1}{8}\int_0^{\pi/4}(1 - \cos 2x)\sin^2 2x \, dx = \frac{1}{8}\int_0^{\pi/4}\sin^2 2x \, dx - \frac{1}{8}\int_0^{\pi/4}\sin^2 2x \cos 2x \, dx$

$\qquad\qquad = \frac{1}{16}\int_0^{\pi/4}(1 - \cos 4x) \, dx - \frac{1}{16}\left[\frac{1}{3}\sin^3 2x\right]_0^{\pi/4} = \frac{1}{16}\left[x - \frac{1}{4}\sin 4x - \frac{1}{3}\sin^3 2x\right]_0^{\pi/4}$

$\qquad\qquad = \frac{1}{16}\left(\frac{\pi}{4} - 0 - \frac{1}{3}\right) = \frac{1}{192}(3\pi - 4)$

15. $\int \sin^3 x \sqrt{\cos x} \, dx = \int \left(1 - \cos^2 x\right)\sqrt{\cos x}\,\sin x \, dx \overset{c}{=} \int \left(1 - u^2\right)u^{1/2}\,(-du) = \int \left(u^{5/2} - u^{1/2}\right) du$

$\qquad\qquad = \frac{2}{7}u^{7/2} - \frac{2}{3}u^{3/2} + C = \frac{2}{7}(\cos x)^{7/2} - \frac{2}{3}(\cos x)^{3/2} + C$

$\qquad\qquad = \left(\frac{2}{7}\cos^3 x - \frac{2}{3}\cos x\right)\sqrt{\cos x} + C$

17. $\displaystyle\int \cos^2 x \tan^3 x \, dx = \int \frac{\sin^3 x}{\cos x} \, dx \overset{c}{=} \int \frac{(1 - u^2)(-du)}{u} = \int \left[\frac{-1}{u} + u\right] du$

$\qquad\qquad = -\ln|u| + \frac{1}{2}u^2 + C = \frac{1}{2}\cos^2 x - \ln|\cos x| + C$

19. $\displaystyle\int \frac{1 - \sin x}{\cos x} \, dx = \int (\sec x - \tan x) \, dx = \ln|\sec x + \tan x| - \ln|\sec x| + C$ $\quad\begin{bmatrix}\text{by (1) and the boxed}\\ \text{formula above it}\end{bmatrix}$

$\qquad\qquad = \ln|(\sec x + \tan x)\cos x| + C = \ln|1 + \sin x| + C$

$\qquad\qquad = \ln(1 + \sin x) + C \quad \text{since } 1 + \sin x \geq 0$

$\quad Or{:}\ \displaystyle\int \frac{1 - \sin x}{\cos x} \, dx = \int \frac{1 - \sin x}{\cos x} \cdot \frac{1 + \sin x}{1 + \sin x} \, dx = \int \frac{(1 - \sin^2 x)\,dx}{\cos x\,(1 + \sin x)} = \int \frac{\cos x\,dx}{1 + \sin x}$

$\qquad\qquad = \int \frac{dw}{w} \quad [\text{where } w = 1 + \sin x, \, dw = \cos x \, dx]$

$\qquad\qquad = \ln|w| + C = \ln|1 + \sin x| + C = \ln(1 + \sin x) + C$

21. Let $u = \tan x$, $du = \sec^2 x \, dx$. Then $\int \sec^2 x \tan x \, dx = \int u \, du = \frac{1}{2}u^2 + C = \frac{1}{2}\tan^2 x + C$.

$\quad Or{:}$ Let $v = \sec x$, $dv = \sec x \tan x \, dx$. Then $\int \sec^2 x \tan x \, dx = \int v \, dv = \frac{1}{2}v^2 + C = \frac{1}{2}\sec^2 x + C$.

23. $\int \tan^2 x \, dx = \int \left(\sec^2 x - 1\right) dx = \tan x - x + C$

25. $\int \sec^6 t \, dt = \int \sec^4 t \cdot \sec^2 t \, dt = \int (\tan^2 t + 1)^2 \sec^2 t \, dt = \int (u^2 + 1)^2 \, du \quad [u = \tan t, \, du = \sec^2 t \, dt]$

$\qquad\qquad = \int (u^4 + 2u^2 + 1) \, du = \frac{1}{5}u^5 + \frac{2}{3}u^3 + u + C = \frac{1}{5}\tan^5 t + \frac{2}{3}\tan^3 t + \tan t + C$

27. $\int_0^{\pi/3} \tan^5 x \sec^4 x \, dx = \int_0^{\pi/3} \tan^5 x \, (\tan^2 x + 1) \sec^2 x \, dx$

$\qquad\qquad = \int_0^{\sqrt{3}} u^5 (u^2 + 1) \, du \quad [u = \tan x, \, du = \sec^2 x \, dx]$

$\qquad\qquad = \int_0^{\sqrt{3}} (u^7 + u^5) \, du = \left[\frac{1}{8}u^8 + \frac{1}{6}u^6\right]_0^{\sqrt{3}} = \frac{81}{8} + \frac{27}{6} = \frac{81}{8} + \frac{9}{2} = \frac{81}{8} + \frac{36}{8} = \frac{117}{8}$

$\quad$*Alternate solution:*

$\quad \int_0^{\pi/3} \tan^5 x \sec^4 x \, dx = \int_0^{\pi/3} \tan^4 x \sec^3 x \sec x \tan x \, dx = \int_0^{\pi/3} (\sec^2 x - 1)^2 \sec^3 x \sec x \tan x \, dx$

$\qquad\qquad = \int_1^2 (u^2 - 1)^2 u^3 \, du \quad [u = \sec x, \, du = \sec x \tan x \, dx]$

$\qquad\qquad = \int_1^2 (u^4 - 2u^2 + 1)u^3 \, du = \int_1^2 (u^7 - 2u^5 + u^3) \, du$

$\qquad\qquad = \left[\frac{1}{8}u^8 - \frac{1}{3}u^6 + \frac{1}{4}u^4\right]_1^2 = \left(32 - \frac{64}{3} + 4\right) - \left(\frac{1}{8} - \frac{1}{3} + \frac{1}{4}\right) = \frac{117}{8}$

29. $\int \tan^3 x \sec x \, dx = \int \tan^2 x \sec x \tan x \, dx = \int \left(\sec^2 x - 1 \right) \sec x \tan x \, dx$

$\qquad = \int (u^2 - 1) \, du \qquad [u = \sec x, \, du = \sec x \tan x \, dx]$

$\qquad = \tfrac{1}{3} u^3 - u + C = \tfrac{1}{3} \sec^3 x - \sec x + C$

31. $\int \tan^5 x \, dx = \int \left(\sec^2 x - 1 \right)^2 \tan x \, dx = \int \sec^4 x \tan x \, dx - 2 \int \sec^2 x \tan x \, dx + \int \tan x \, dx$

$\qquad = \int \sec^3 x \sec x \tan x \, dx - 2 \int \tan x \sec^2 x \, dx + \int \tan x \, dx$

$\qquad = \tfrac{1}{4} \sec^4 x - \tan^2 x + \ln |\sec x| + C \quad [\text{or } \tfrac{1}{4} \sec^4 x - \sec^2 x + \ln |\sec x| + C \,]$

33. $\displaystyle \int \frac{\tan^3 \theta}{\cos^4 \theta} \, d\theta = \int \tan^3 \theta \sec^4 \theta \, d\theta = \int \tan^3 \theta \cdot (\tan^2 \theta + 1) \cdot \sec^2 \theta \, d\theta$

$\qquad = \int u^3 (u^2 + 1) \, du \qquad [u = \tan \theta, \, du = \sec^2 \theta \, d\theta]$

$\qquad = \int (u^5 + u^3) \, du = \tfrac{1}{6} u^6 + \tfrac{1}{4} u^4 + C = \tfrac{1}{6} \tan^6 \theta + \tfrac{1}{4} \tan^4 \theta + C$

35. $\int_{\pi/6}^{\pi/2} \cot^2 x \, dx = \int_{\pi/6}^{\pi/2} \left(\csc^2 x - 1 \right) dx = [-\cot x - x]_{\pi/6}^{\pi/2} = \left(0 - \tfrac{\pi}{2} \right) - \left(-\sqrt{3} - \tfrac{\pi}{6} \right) = \sqrt{3} - \tfrac{\pi}{3}$

37. $\int \cot^3 \alpha \csc^3 \alpha \, d\alpha = \int \cot^2 \alpha \csc^2 \alpha \cdot \csc \alpha \cot \alpha \, d\alpha = \int (\csc^2 \alpha - 1) \csc^2 \alpha \cdot \csc \alpha \cot \alpha \, d\alpha$

$\qquad = \int (u^2 - 1) u^2 \cdot (-du) \qquad [u = \csc \alpha, \, du = - \csc \alpha \cot \alpha \, d\alpha]$

$\qquad = \int (u^2 - u^4) \, du = \tfrac{1}{3} u^3 - \tfrac{1}{5} u^5 + C = \tfrac{1}{3} \csc^3 \alpha - \tfrac{1}{5} \csc^5 \alpha + C$

39. $\displaystyle I = \int \csc x \, dx = \int \frac{\csc x \, (\csc x - \cot x)}{\csc x - \cot x} \, dx = \int \frac{- \csc x \cot x + \csc^2 x}{\csc x - \cot x} \, dx.$ Let $u = \csc x - \cot x \;\; \Rightarrow$

$du = \left(- \csc x \cot x + \csc^2 x \right) dx.$ Then $I = \int du/u = \ln |u| = \ln |\csc x - \cot x| + C.$

41. Use Equation 2(b):

$\int \sin 5x \sin 2x \, dx = \int \tfrac{1}{2} [\cos(5x - 2x) - \cos(5x + 2x)] \, dx = \tfrac{1}{2} \int (\cos 3x - \cos 7x) \, dx$

$\qquad = \tfrac{1}{6} \sin 3x - \tfrac{1}{14} \sin 7x + C$

43. Use Equation 2(c):

$\int \cos 7\theta \cos 5\theta \, d\theta = \int \tfrac{1}{2} [\cos(7\theta - 5\theta) + \cos(7\theta + 5\theta)] \, d\theta = \tfrac{1}{2} \int (\cos 2\theta + \cos 12\theta) \, d\theta$

$\qquad = \tfrac{1}{2} \left(\tfrac{1}{2} \sin 2\theta + \tfrac{1}{12} \sin 12\theta \right) + C = \tfrac{1}{4} \sin 2\theta + \tfrac{1}{24} \sin 12\theta + C$

45. $\displaystyle \int \frac{1 - \tan^2 x}{\sec^2 x} \, dx = \int \left(\cos^2 x - \sin^2 x \right) dx = \int \cos 2x \, dx = \frac{1}{2} \sin 2x + C$

47. Let $u = \tan(t^2) \;\; \Rightarrow \;\; du = 2t \sec^2(t^2) \, dt.$ Then

$\int t \sec^2 \left(t^2 \right) \tan^4 \left(t^2 \right) \, dt = \int u^4 \left(\tfrac{1}{2} \, du \right) = \tfrac{1}{10} u^5 + C = \tfrac{1}{10} \tan^5(t^2) + C.$

49. Let $u = \cos x \;\; \Rightarrow \;\; du = - \sin x \, dx.$ Then

$\int \sin^5 x \, dx = \int \left(1 - \cos^2 x \right)^2 \sin x \, dx = \int \left(1 - u^2 \right)^2 (-du)$

$\qquad = \int \left(-1 + 2u^2 - u^4 \right) du = -\tfrac{1}{5} u^5 + \tfrac{2}{3} u^3 - u + C$

$\qquad = -\tfrac{1}{5} \cos^5 x + \tfrac{2}{3} \cos^3 x - \cos x + C$

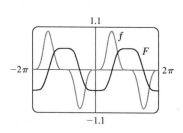

Notice that F is increasing when $f(x) > 0$, so the graphs serve as a check on our work.

51. $\int \sin 3x \sin 6x \, dx = \int \frac{1}{2}[\cos(3x - 6x) - \cos(3x + 6x)] \, dx$

$\qquad\qquad = \frac{1}{2} \int (\cos 3x - \cos 9x) \, dx$

$\qquad\qquad = \frac{1}{6} \sin 3x - \frac{1}{18} \sin 9x + C$

Notice that $f(x) = 0$ whenever F has a horizontal tangent.

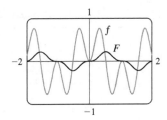

53. $f_{\text{ave}} = \frac{1}{2\pi} \int_{-\pi}^{\pi} \sin^2 x \cos^3 x \, dx = \frac{1}{2\pi} \int_{-\pi}^{\pi} \sin^2 x \left(1 - \sin^2 x\right) \cos x \, dx$

$\qquad = \frac{1}{2\pi} \int_{0}^{0} u^2 \left(1 - u^2\right) du \qquad [\text{where } u = \sin x]$

$\qquad = 0$

55. For $0 < x < \frac{\pi}{2}$, we have $0 < \sin x < 1$, so $\sin^3 x < \sin x$. Hence the area is

$\int_{0}^{\pi/2} \left(\sin x - \sin^3 x\right) dx = \int_{0}^{\pi/2} \sin x \left(1 - \sin^2 x\right) dx = \int_{0}^{\pi/2} \cos^2 x \sin x \, dx$. Now let $u = \cos x \quad \Rightarrow$

$du = -\sin x \, dx$. Then area $= \int_{1}^{0} u^2 \, (-du) = \int_{0}^{1} u^2 \, du = \left[\frac{1}{3}u^3\right]_{0}^{1} = \frac{1}{3}$.

57.

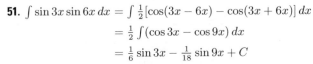

It seems from the graph that $\int_{0}^{2\pi} \cos^3 x \, dx = 0$, since the area below the x-axis and above the graph looks about equal to the area above the axis and below the graph. By Example 1, the integral is $\left[\sin x - \frac{1}{3}\sin^3 x\right]_{0}^{2\pi} = 0$. Note that due to symmetry, the integral of any odd power of $\sin x$ or $\cos x$ between limits which differ by $2n\pi$ (n any integer) is 0.

59. $V = \int_{\pi/2}^{\pi} \pi \sin^2 x \, dx = \pi \int_{\pi/2}^{\pi} \frac{1}{2}(1 - \cos 2x) \, dx = \pi \left[\frac{1}{2}x - \frac{1}{4}\sin 2x\right]_{\pi/2}^{\pi} = \pi \left(\frac{\pi}{2} - 0 - \frac{\pi}{4} + 0\right) = \frac{\pi^2}{4}$

61. Volume $= \pi \int_{0}^{\pi/2} \left[(1 + \cos x)^2 - 1^2\right] dx = \pi \int_{0}^{\pi/2} \left(2\cos x + \cos^2 x\right) dx$

$\qquad = \pi \left[2\sin x + \frac{1}{2}x + \frac{1}{4}\sin 2x\right]_{0}^{\pi/2} = \pi \left(2 + \frac{\pi}{4}\right) = 2\pi + \frac{\pi^2}{4}$

63. $s = f(t) = \int_{0}^{t} \sin \omega u \cos^2 \omega u \, du$. Let $y = \cos \omega u \quad \Rightarrow \quad dy = -\omega \sin \omega u \, du$. Then

$s = -\frac{1}{\omega} \int_{1}^{\cos \omega t} y^2 \, dy = -\frac{1}{\omega} \left[\frac{1}{3}y^3\right]_{1}^{\cos \omega t} = \frac{1}{3\omega}\left(1 - \cos^3 \omega t\right)$.

65. Just note that the integrand is odd $[f(-x) = -f(x)]$.

Or: If $m \neq n$, calculate

$$\int_{-\pi}^{\pi} \sin mx \cos nx \, dx = \int_{-\pi}^{\pi} \frac{1}{2}[\sin(m - n)x + \sin(m + n)x] \, dx$$

$$= \frac{1}{2}\left[-\frac{\cos(m - n)x}{m - n} - \frac{\cos(m + n)x}{m + n}\right]_{-\pi}^{\pi} = 0$$

If $m = n$, then the first term in each set of brackets is zero.

67. $\int_{-\pi}^{\pi} \cos mx \cos nx \, dx = \int_{-\pi}^{\pi} \frac{1}{2}[\cos(m - n)x + \cos(m + n)x] \, dx$. If $m \neq n$,

this is equal to $\frac{1}{2}\left[\frac{\sin(m - n)x}{m - n} + \frac{\sin(m + n)x}{m + n}\right]_{-\pi}^{\pi} = 0$. If $m = n$, we get

$\int_{-\pi}^{\pi} \frac{1}{2}[1 + \cos(m + n)x] \, dx = \left[\frac{1}{2}x\right]_{-\pi}^{\pi} + \left[\frac{\sin(m + n)x}{2(m + n)}\right]_{-\pi}^{\pi} = \pi + 0 = \pi$.

8.3 Trigonometric Substitution

1. Let $x = 3\sec\theta$, where $0 \le \theta < \frac{\pi}{2}$ or $\pi \le \theta < \frac{3\pi}{2}$. Then
$dx = 3\sec\theta\tan\theta\,d\theta$ and

$$\sqrt{x^2 - 9} = \sqrt{9\sec^2\theta - 9} = \sqrt{9(\sec^2\theta - 1)} = \sqrt{9\tan^2\theta}$$
$$= 3\,|\tan\theta| = 3\tan\theta \text{ for the relevant values of } \theta.$$

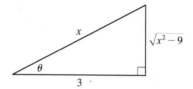

$$\int \frac{1}{x^2\sqrt{x^2 - 9}}\,dx = \int \frac{1}{9\sec^2\theta \cdot 3\tan\theta}3\sec\theta\tan\theta\,d\theta = \tfrac{1}{9}\int \cos\theta\,d\theta = \tfrac{1}{9}\sin\theta + C = \frac{1}{9}\frac{\sqrt{x^2 - 9}}{x} + C$$

Note that $-\sec(\theta + \pi) = \sec\theta$, so the figure is sufficient for the case $\pi \le \theta < \frac{3\pi}{2}$.

3. Let $x = 3\tan\theta$, where $-\frac{\pi}{2} < \theta < \frac{\pi}{2}$. Then $dx = 3\sec^2\theta\,d\theta$ and

$$\sqrt{x^2 + 9} = \sqrt{9\tan^2\theta + 9} = \sqrt{9(\tan^2\theta + 1)} = \sqrt{9\sec^2\theta}$$
$$= 3\,|\sec\theta| = 3\sec\theta \text{ for the relevant values of } \theta.$$

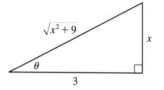

$$\int \frac{x^3}{\sqrt{x^2 + 9}}\,dx = \int \frac{3^3\tan^3\theta}{3\sec\theta}3\sec^2\theta\,d\theta = 3^3\int \tan^3\theta\sec\theta\,d\theta = 3^3\int \tan^2\theta\tan\theta\sec\theta\,d\theta$$
$$= 3^3\int (\sec^2\theta - 1)\tan\theta\sec\theta\,d\theta = 3^3\int (u^2 - 1)\,du \qquad [u = \sec\theta,\ du = \sec\theta\tan\theta\,d\theta]$$
$$= 3^3\left(\tfrac{1}{3}u^3 - u\right) + C = 3^3\left(\tfrac{1}{3}\sec^3\theta - \sec\theta\right) + C = 3^3\left[\frac{1}{3}\frac{(x^2 + 9)^{3/2}}{3^3} - \frac{\sqrt{x^2 + 9}}{3}\right] + C$$
$$= \tfrac{1}{3}(x^2 + 9)^{3/2} - 9\sqrt{x^2 + 9} + C \quad \text{or} \quad \tfrac{1}{3}(x^2 - 18)\sqrt{x^2 + 9} + C$$

5. Let $t = \sec\theta$, so $dt = \sec\theta\tan\theta\,d\theta$, $t = \sqrt{2} \ \Rightarrow \ \theta = \frac{\pi}{4}$, and $t = 2 \ \Rightarrow \ \theta = \frac{\pi}{3}$. Then

$$\int_{\sqrt{2}}^{2}\frac{1}{t^3\sqrt{t^2 - 1}}\,dt = \int_{\pi/4}^{\pi/3}\frac{1}{\sec^3\theta\tan\theta}\sec\theta\tan\theta\,d\theta = \int_{\pi/4}^{\pi/3}\frac{1}{\sec^2\theta}\,d\theta = \int_{\pi/4}^{\pi/3}\cos^2\theta\,d\theta$$
$$= \int_{\pi/4}^{\pi/3}\tfrac{1}{2}(1 + \cos 2\theta)\,d\theta = \tfrac{1}{2}\left[\theta + \tfrac{1}{2}\sin 2\theta\right]_{\pi/4}^{\pi/3}$$
$$= \tfrac{1}{2}\left[\left(\tfrac{\pi}{3} + \tfrac{1}{2}\tfrac{\sqrt{3}}{2}\right) - \left(\tfrac{\pi}{4} + \tfrac{1}{2}\cdot 1\right)\right] = \tfrac{1}{2}\left(\tfrac{\pi}{12} + \tfrac{\sqrt{3}}{4} - \tfrac{1}{2}\right) = \tfrac{\pi}{24} + \tfrac{\sqrt{3}}{8} - \tfrac{1}{4}$$

7. Let $x = 5\sin\theta$, so $dx = 5\cos\theta\,d\theta$. Then

$$\int \frac{1}{x^2\sqrt{25 - x^2}}\,dx = \int \frac{1}{5^2\sin^2\theta \cdot 5\cos\theta}5\cos\theta\,d\theta$$
$$= \tfrac{1}{25}\int \csc^2\theta\,d\theta = -\tfrac{1}{25}\cot\theta + C$$
$$= -\frac{1}{25}\frac{\sqrt{25 - x^2}}{x} + C$$

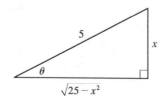

9. Let $x = 4\tan\theta$, where $-\frac{\pi}{2} < \theta < \frac{\pi}{2}$. Then $dx = 4\sec^2\theta\,d\theta$ and

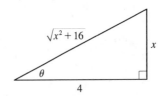

$$\sqrt{x^2 + 16} = \sqrt{16\tan^2\theta + 16} = \sqrt{16(\tan^2\theta + 1)}$$
$$= \sqrt{16\sec^2\theta} = 4\,|\sec\theta|$$
$$= 4\sec\theta \text{ for the relevant values of } \theta.$$

$$\int \frac{dx}{\sqrt{x^2 + 16}} = \int \frac{4\sec^2\theta\,d\theta}{4\sec\theta} = \int \sec\theta\,d\theta = \ln|\sec\theta + \tan\theta| + C_1$$
$$= \ln\left|\frac{\sqrt{x^2 + 16}}{4} + \frac{x}{4}\right| + C_1 = \ln\left|\sqrt{x^2 + 16} + x\right| - \ln|4| + C_1$$
$$= \ln\left(\sqrt{x^2 + 16} + x\right) + C, \text{ where } C = C_1 - \ln 4.$$

(Since $\sqrt{x^2 + 16} + x > 0$, we don't need the absolute value.)

11. Let $2x = \sin\theta$, where $-\frac{\pi}{2} \leq \theta \leq \frac{\pi}{2}$. Then $x = \frac{1}{2}\sin\theta$,

$dx = \frac{1}{2}\cos\theta\,d\theta$, and $\sqrt{1 - 4x^2} = \sqrt{1 - (2x)^2} = \cos\theta$.

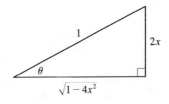

$$\int \sqrt{1 - 4x^2}\,dx = \int \cos\theta\left(\tfrac{1}{2}\cos\theta\right) d\theta = \tfrac{1}{4}\int (1 + \cos 2\theta)\,d\theta$$
$$= \tfrac{1}{4}\left(\theta + \tfrac{1}{2}\sin 2\theta\right) + C = \tfrac{1}{4}(\theta + \sin\theta\cos\theta) + C$$
$$= \tfrac{1}{4}\left[\sin^{-1}(2x) + 2x\sqrt{1 - 4x^2}\right] + C$$

13. Let $x = 3\sec\theta$, where $0 \leq \theta < \frac{\pi}{2}$ or $\pi \leq \theta < \frac{3\pi}{2}$. Then

$dx = 3\sec\theta\tan\theta\,d\theta$ and $\sqrt{x^2 - 9} = 3\tan\theta$, so

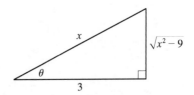

$$\int \frac{\sqrt{x^2 - 9}}{x^3}\,dx = \int \frac{3\tan\theta}{27\sec^3\theta}\,3\sec\theta\tan\theta\,d\theta = \frac{1}{3}\int \frac{\tan^2\theta}{\sec^2\theta}\,d\theta$$
$$= \tfrac{1}{3}\int \sin^2\theta\,d\theta = \tfrac{1}{3}\int \tfrac{1}{2}(1 - \cos 2\theta)\,d\theta = \tfrac{1}{6}\theta - \tfrac{1}{12}\sin 2\theta + C = \tfrac{1}{6}\theta - \tfrac{1}{6}\sin\theta\cos\theta + C$$
$$= \frac{1}{6}\sec^{-1}\left(\frac{x}{3}\right) - \frac{1}{6}\frac{\sqrt{x^2 - 9}}{x}\frac{3}{x} + C = \frac{1}{6}\sec^{-1}\left(\frac{x}{3}\right) - \frac{\sqrt{x^2 - 9}}{2x^2} + C$$

15. Let $x = a\sin\theta$, where $-\frac{\pi}{2} \leq \theta \leq \frac{\pi}{2}$. Then $dx = a\cos\theta\,d\theta$ and

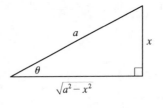

$$\int \frac{x^2\,dx}{(a^2 - x^2)^{3/2}} = \int \frac{a^2\sin^2\theta\,a\cos\theta\,d\theta}{a^3\cos^3\theta} = \int \tan^2\theta\,d\theta$$
$$= \int (\sec^2\theta - 1)\,d\theta = \tan\theta - \theta + C$$
$$= \frac{x}{\sqrt{a^2 - x^2}} - \sin^{-1}\frac{x}{a} + C$$

17. Let $u = x^2 - 7$, so $du = 2x\,dx$. Then $\displaystyle\int \frac{x}{\sqrt{x^2 - 7}}\,dx = \frac{1}{2}\int \frac{1}{\sqrt{u}}\,du = \frac{1}{2}\cdot 2\sqrt{u} + C = \sqrt{x^2 - 7} + C.$

19. Let $x = \tan\theta$, where $-\frac{\pi}{2} < \theta < \frac{\pi}{2}$. Then $dx = \sec^2\theta\,d\theta$

and $\sqrt{1+x^2} = \sec\theta$, so

$$\int \frac{\sqrt{1+x^2}}{x}\,dx = \int \frac{\sec\theta}{\tan\theta}\sec^2\theta\,d\theta = \int \frac{\sec\theta}{\tan\theta}(1+\tan^2\theta)\,d\theta$$

$$= \int (\csc\theta + \sec\theta\tan\theta)\,d\theta$$

$$= \ln|\csc\theta - \cot\theta| + \sec\theta + C \quad \text{[by Exercise 8.2.39]}$$

$$= \ln\left|\frac{\sqrt{1+x^2}}{x} - \frac{1}{x}\right| + \frac{\sqrt{1+x^2}}{1} + C = \ln\left|\frac{\sqrt{1+x^2}-1}{x}\right| + \sqrt{1+x^2} + C$$

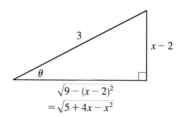

21. Let $u = 4 - 9x^2 \;\Rightarrow\; du = -18x\,dx$. Then $x^2 = \frac{1}{9}(4-u)$ and

$$\int_0^{2/3} x^3\sqrt{4-9x^2}\,dx = \int_4^0 \frac{1}{9}(4-u)u^{1/2}\left(-\frac{1}{18}\right)du = \frac{1}{162}\int_0^4 \left(4u^{1/2} - u^{3/2}\right)du$$

$$= \frac{1}{162}\left[\frac{8}{3}u^{3/2} - \frac{2}{5}u^{5/2}\right]_0^4 = \frac{1}{162}\left[\frac{64}{3} - \frac{64}{5}\right] = \frac{64}{1215}$$

Or: Let $3x = 2\sin\theta$, where $-\frac{\pi}{2} \le \theta \le \frac{\pi}{2}$.

23. $5 + 4x - x^2 = -(x^2 - 4x + 4) + 9 = -(x-2)^2 + 9$. Let

$x - 2 = 3\sin\theta$, $-\frac{\pi}{2} \le \theta \le \frac{\pi}{2}$, so $dx = 3\cos\theta\,d\theta$. Then

$$\int \sqrt{5+4x-x^2}\,dx = \int \sqrt{9-(x-2)^2}\,dx = \int \sqrt{9-9\sin^2\theta}\,3\cos\theta\,d\theta$$

$$= \int \sqrt{9\cos^2\theta}\,3\cos\theta\,d\theta = \int 9\cos^2\theta\,d\theta$$

$$= \frac{9}{2}\int(1+\cos 2\theta)\,d\theta = \frac{9}{2}\left(\theta + \frac{1}{2}\sin 2\theta\right) + C$$

$$= \frac{9}{2}\theta + \frac{9}{4}\sin 2\theta + C = \frac{9}{2}\theta + \frac{9}{4}(2\sin\theta\cos\theta) + C$$

$$= \frac{9}{2}\sin^{-1}\left(\frac{x-2}{3}\right) + \frac{9}{2}\cdot\frac{x-2}{3}\cdot\frac{\sqrt{5+4x-x^2}}{3} + C$$

$$= \frac{9}{2}\sin^{-1}\left(\frac{x-2}{3}\right) + \frac{1}{2}(x-2)\sqrt{5+4x-x^2} + C$$

25. $9x^2 + 6x - 8 = (3x+1)^2 - 9$, so let $u = 3x+1$, $du = 3dx$. Then $\displaystyle\int \frac{dx}{\sqrt{9x^2+6x-8}} = \int \frac{\frac{1}{3}du}{\sqrt{u^2-9}}$. Now

let $u = 3\sec\theta$, where $0 \le \theta < \frac{\pi}{2}$ or $\pi \le \theta < \frac{3\pi}{2}$. Then $du = 3\sec\theta\tan\theta\,d\theta$ and $\sqrt{u^2-9} = 3\tan\theta$, so

$$\int \frac{\frac{1}{3}du}{\sqrt{u^2-9}} = \int \frac{\sec\theta\tan\theta\,d\theta}{3\tan\theta} = \frac{1}{3}\int\sec\theta\,d\theta = \frac{1}{3}\ln|\sec\theta + \tan\theta| + C_1 = \frac{1}{3}\ln\left|\frac{u+\sqrt{u^2-9}}{3}\right| + C_1$$

$$= \frac{1}{3}\ln\left|u+\sqrt{u^2-9}\right| + C = \frac{1}{3}\ln\left|3x+1+\sqrt{9x^2+6x-8}\right| + C$$

27. $x^2 + 2x + 2 = (x+1)^2 + 1$. Let $u = x+1$, $du = dx$. Then

$$\int \frac{dx}{(x^2+2x+2)^2} = \int \frac{du}{(u^2+1)^2} = \int \frac{\sec^2\theta\,d\theta}{\sec^4\theta} \qquad \begin{bmatrix}\text{where } u = \tan\theta,\ du = \sec^2\theta\,d\theta,\\ \text{and } u^2+1 = \sec^2\theta\end{bmatrix}$$

$$= \int \cos^2\theta\,d\theta = \frac{1}{2}\int(1+\cos 2\theta)\,d\theta = \frac{1}{2}(\theta + \sin\theta\cos\theta) + C$$

$$= \frac{1}{2}\left[\tan^{-1}u + \frac{u}{1+u^2}\right] + C = \frac{1}{2}\left[\tan^{-1}(x+1) + \frac{x+1}{x^2+2x+2}\right] + C$$

29. Let $u = x^2$, $du = 2x\,dx$. Then

$$\int x\sqrt{1-x^4}\,dx = \int \sqrt{1-u^2}\left(\tfrac{1}{2}\,du\right) = \tfrac{1}{2}\int \cos\theta\cdot\cos\theta\,d\theta \quad \begin{bmatrix} \text{where } u=\sin\theta,\, du=\cos\theta\,d\theta, \\ \text{and } \sqrt{1-u^2}=\cos\theta \end{bmatrix}$$

$$= \tfrac{1}{2}\int \tfrac{1}{2}(1+\cos 2\theta)\,d\theta = \tfrac{1}{4}\theta + \tfrac{1}{8}\sin 2\theta + C = \tfrac{1}{4}\theta + \tfrac{1}{4}\sin\theta\cos\theta + C$$

$$= \tfrac{1}{4}\sin^{-1}u + \tfrac{1}{4}u\sqrt{1-u^2} + C = \tfrac{1}{4}\sin^{-1}(x^2) + \tfrac{1}{4}x^2\sqrt{1-x^4} + C$$

31. (a) Let $x = a\tan\theta$, where $-\tfrac{\pi}{2} < \theta < \tfrac{\pi}{2}$. Then $\sqrt{x^2+a^2} = a\sec\theta$ and

$$\int \frac{dx}{\sqrt{x^2+a^2}} = \int \frac{a\sec^2\theta\,d\theta}{a\sec\theta} = \int \sec\theta\,d\theta = \ln|\sec\theta + \tan\theta| + C_1 = \ln\left|\frac{\sqrt{x^2+a^2}}{a} + \frac{x}{a}\right| + C_1$$

$$= \ln\left(x + \sqrt{x^2+a^2}\right) + C \quad \text{where } C = C_1 - \ln|a|$$

(b) Let $x = a\sinh t$, so that $dx = a\cosh t\,dt$ and $\sqrt{x^2+a^2} = a\cosh t$. Then

$$\int \frac{dx}{\sqrt{x^2+a^2}} = \int \frac{a\cosh t\,dt}{a\cosh t} = t + C = \sinh^{-1}\frac{x}{a} + C.$$

33. The average value of $f(x) = \sqrt{x^2-1}/x$ on the interval $[1,7]$ is

$$\frac{1}{7-1}\int_1^7 \frac{\sqrt{x^2-1}}{x}\,dx = \frac{1}{6}\int_0^\alpha \frac{\tan\theta}{\sec\theta}\cdot\sec\theta\tan\theta\,d\theta \quad \begin{bmatrix} \text{where } x=\sec\theta,\, dx=\sec\theta\tan\theta\,d\theta, \\ \sqrt{x^2-1}=\tan\theta,\text{ and } \alpha=\sec^{-1}7 \end{bmatrix}$$

$$= \tfrac{1}{6}\int_0^\alpha \tan^2\theta\,d\theta = \tfrac{1}{6}\int_0^\alpha (\sec^2\theta - 1)\,d\theta$$

$$= \tfrac{1}{6}\Big[\tan\theta - \theta\Big]_0^\alpha = \tfrac{1}{6}(\tan\alpha - \alpha)$$

$$= \tfrac{1}{6}\left(\sqrt{48} - \sec^{-1}7\right)$$

35. Area of $\triangle POQ = \tfrac{1}{2}(r\cos\theta)(r\sin\theta) = \tfrac{1}{2}r^2\sin\theta\cos\theta$. Area of region $PQR = \int_{r\cos\theta}^r \sqrt{r^2-x^2}\,dx$. Let $x = r\cos u \;\Rightarrow\; dx = -r\sin u\,du$ for $\theta \le u \le \tfrac{\pi}{2}$. Then we obtain

$$\int \sqrt{r^2-x^2}\,dx = \int r\sin u\,(-r\sin u)\,du = -r^2\int \sin^2 u\,du = -\tfrac{1}{2}r^2(u - \sin u\cos u) + C$$

$$= -\tfrac{1}{2}r^2\cos^{-1}(x/r) + \tfrac{1}{2}x\sqrt{r^2-x^2} + C$$

so

$$\text{area of region } PQR = \tfrac{1}{2}\left[-r^2\cos^{-1}(x/r) + x\sqrt{r^2-x^2}\right]_{r\cos\theta}^r$$

$$= \tfrac{1}{2}\left[0 - (-r^2\theta + r\cos\theta\, r\sin\theta)\right]$$

$$= \tfrac{1}{2}r^2\theta - \tfrac{1}{2}r^2\sin\theta\cos\theta$$

and thus, (area of sector POR) = (area of $\triangle POQ$) + (area of region PQR) = $\tfrac{1}{2}r^2\theta$.

37. From the graph, it appears that the curve $y = x^2\sqrt{4 - x^2}$ and the line
$y = 2 - x$ intersect at about $x = 0.81$ and $x = 2$, with $x^2\sqrt{4 - x^2} > 2 - x$ on
$(0.81, 2)$. So the area bounded by the curve and the line is $A \approx$
$\int_{0.81}^{2} \left[x^2\sqrt{4 - x^2} - (2 - x)\right] dx = \int_{0.81}^{2} x^2\sqrt{4 - x^2}\, dx - \left[2x - \frac{1}{2}x^2\right]_{0.81}^{2}$.
To evaluate the integral, we put $x = 2\sin\theta$, where $-\frac{\pi}{2} \le \theta \le \frac{\pi}{2}$. Then

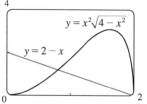

$dx = 2\cos\theta\, d\theta$, $x = 2 \Rightarrow \theta = \sin^{-1} 1 = \frac{\pi}{2}$, and $x = 0.81 \Rightarrow \theta = \sin^{-1} 0.405 \approx 0.417$. So

$\int_{0.81}^{2} x^2\sqrt{4 - x^2}\, dx \approx \int_{0.417}^{\pi/2} 4\sin^2\theta\,(2\cos\theta)(2\cos\theta\, d\theta) = 4\int_{0.417}^{\pi/2} \sin^2 2\theta\, d\theta = 4\int_{0.417}^{\pi/2} \frac{1}{2}(1 - \cos 4\theta)\, d\theta$

$\qquad = 2\left[\theta - \frac{1}{4}\sin 4\theta\right]_{0.417}^{\pi/2} = 2\left[\left(\frac{\pi}{2} - 0\right) - \left(0.417 - \frac{1}{4}(0.995)\right)\right] \approx 2.81$

Thus, $A \approx 2.81 - \left[\left(2 \cdot 2 - \frac{1}{2} \cdot 2^2\right) - \left(2 \cdot 0.81 - \frac{1}{2} \cdot 0.81^2\right)\right] \approx 2.10$.

39. Let the equation of the large circle be $x^2 + y^2 = R^2$. Then the equation of the small circle is $x^2 + (y - b)^2 = r^2$,
where $b = \sqrt{R^2 - r^2}$ is the distance between the centers of the circles. The desired area is

$$A = \int_{-r}^{r} \left[\left(b + \sqrt{r^2 - x^2}\right) - \sqrt{R^2 - x^2}\right] dx = 2\int_{0}^{r} \left(b + \sqrt{r^2 - x^2} - \sqrt{R^2 - x^2}\right) dx$$

$$= 2\int_{0}^{r} b\, dx + 2\int_{0}^{r} \sqrt{r^2 - x^2}\, dx - 2\int_{0}^{r} \sqrt{R^2 - x^2}\, dx$$

The first integral is just $2br = 2r\sqrt{R^2 - r^2}$. To evaluate the other two integrals, note that

$$\int \sqrt{a^2 - x^2}\, dx = \int a^2 \cos^2\theta\, d\theta \quad [x = a\sin\theta,\ dx = a\cos\theta\, d\theta] \quad = \frac{1}{2}a^2 \int (1 + \cos 2\theta)\, d\theta$$

$$= \frac{1}{2}a^2\left(\theta + \frac{1}{2}\sin 2\theta\right) + C = \frac{1}{2}a^2(\theta + \sin\theta\cos\theta) + C$$

$$= \frac{a^2}{2}\arcsin\left(\frac{x}{a}\right) + \frac{a^2}{2}\left(\frac{x}{a}\right)\frac{\sqrt{a^2 - x^2}}{a} + C = \frac{a^2}{2}\arcsin\left(\frac{x}{a}\right) + \frac{x}{2}\sqrt{a^2 - x^2} + C$$

so the desired area is

$$A = 2r\sqrt{R^2 - r^2} + \left[r^2 \arcsin(x/r) + x\sqrt{r^2 - x^2}\right]_{0}^{r} - \left[R^2 \arcsin(x/R) + x\sqrt{R^2 - x^2}\right]_{0}^{r}$$

$$= 2r\sqrt{R^2 - r^2} + r^2\left(\frac{\pi}{2}\right) - \left[R^2 \arcsin(r/R) + r\sqrt{R^2 - r^2}\right] = r\sqrt{R^2 - r^2} + \frac{\pi}{2}r^2 - R^2 \arcsin(r/R)$$

41. We use cylindrical shells and assume that $R > r$. $x^2 = r^2 - (y - R)^2 \Rightarrow x = \pm\sqrt{r^2 - (y - R)^2}$, so
$g(y) = 2\sqrt{r^2 - (y - R)^2}$ and

$$V = \int_{R-r}^{R+r} 2\pi y \cdot 2\sqrt{r^2 - (y - R)^2}\, dy = \int_{-r}^{r} 4\pi(u + R)\sqrt{r^2 - u^2}\, du \quad [\text{where } u = y - R]$$

$$= 4\pi \int_{-r}^{r} u\sqrt{r^2 - u^2}\, du + 4\pi R \int_{-r}^{r} \sqrt{r^2 - u^2}\, du \quad \begin{bmatrix} \text{where } u = r\sin\theta,\ du = r\cos\theta\, d\theta \\ \text{in the second integral} \end{bmatrix}$$

$$= 4\pi\left[-\frac{1}{3}\left(r^2 - u^2\right)^{3/2}\right]_{-r}^{r} + 4\pi R \int_{-\pi/2}^{\pi/2} r^2 \cos^2\theta\, d\theta = -\frac{4\pi}{3}(0 - 0) + 4\pi R r^2 \int_{-\pi/2}^{\pi/2} \cos^2\theta\, d\theta$$

$$= 2\pi R r^2 \int_{-\pi/2}^{\pi/2} (1 + \cos 2\theta)\, d\theta = 2\pi R r^2 \left[\theta + \frac{1}{2}\sin 2\theta\right]_{-\pi/2}^{\pi/2} = 2\pi^2 R r^2$$

Another method: Use washers instead of shells, so $V = 8\pi R \int_{0}^{r} \sqrt{r^2 - y^2}\, dy$ as in Exercise 6.2.61(a), but evaluate
the integral using $y = r\sin\theta$.

8.4 Integration of Rational Functions by Partial Fractions

1. (a) $\dfrac{2x}{(x+3)(3x+1)} = \dfrac{A}{x+3} + \dfrac{B}{3x+1}$

(b) $\dfrac{1}{x^3 + 2x^2 + x} = \dfrac{1}{x(x^2 + 2x + 1)} = \dfrac{1}{x(x+1)^2} = \dfrac{A}{x} + \dfrac{B}{x+1} + \dfrac{C}{(x+1)^2}$

3. (a) $\dfrac{2}{x^2 + 3x - 4} = \dfrac{2}{(x+4)(x-1)} = \dfrac{A}{x+4} + \dfrac{B}{x-1}$

(b) $x^2 + x + 1$ is irreducible, so $\dfrac{x^2}{(x-1)(x^2 + x + 1)} = \dfrac{A}{x-1} + \dfrac{Bx + C}{x^2 + x + 1}$.

5. (a) $\dfrac{x^4}{x^4 - 1} = \dfrac{(x^4 - 1) + 1}{x^4 - 1} = 1 + \dfrac{1}{x^4 - 1}$ [or use long division] $= 1 + \dfrac{1}{(x^2 - 1)(x^2 + 1)}$

$= 1 + \dfrac{1}{(x-1)(x+1)(x^2 + 1)} = 1 + \dfrac{A}{x-1} + \dfrac{B}{x+1} + \dfrac{Cx + D}{x^2 + 1}$

(b) $\dfrac{t^4 + t^2 + 1}{(t^2 + 1)(t^2 + 4)^2} = \dfrac{At + B}{t^2 + 1} + \dfrac{Ct + D}{t^2 + 4} + \dfrac{Et + F}{(t^2 + 4)^2}$

7. $\displaystyle\int \dfrac{x}{x-6}\, dx = \int \dfrac{(x-6) + 6}{x-6}\, dx = \int \left(1 + \dfrac{6}{x-6}\right) dx = x + 6\ln|x - 6| + C$

9. $\dfrac{x-9}{(x+5)(x-2)} = \dfrac{A}{x+5} + \dfrac{B}{x-2}$. Multiply both sides by $(x+5)(x-2)$ to get $x - 9 = A(x-2) + B(x+5)$.

Substituting 2 for x gives $-7 = 7B \iff B = -1$. Substituting -5 for x gives $-14 = -7A \iff A = 2$. Thus,

$$\int \dfrac{x-9}{(x+5)(x-2)}\, dx = \int \left(\dfrac{2}{x+5} + \dfrac{-1}{x-2}\right) dx = 2\ln|x+5| - \ln|x-2| + C$$

11. $\dfrac{1}{x^2 - 1} = \dfrac{1}{(x+1)(x-1)} = \dfrac{A}{x+1} + \dfrac{B}{x-1}$. Multiply both sides by $(x+1)(x-1)$ to get

$1 = A(x-1) + B(x+1)$. Substituting 1 for x gives $1 = 2B \iff B = \frac{1}{2}$.

Substituting -1 for x gives $1 = -2A \iff A = -\frac{1}{2}$. Thus,

$$\int_2^3 \dfrac{1}{x^2 - 1}\, dx = \int_2^3 \left(\dfrac{-1/2}{x+1} + \dfrac{1/2}{x-1}\right) dx = \left[-\tfrac{1}{2}\ln|x+1| + \tfrac{1}{2}\ln|x-1|\right]_2^3$$

$$= \left(-\tfrac{1}{2}\ln 4 + \tfrac{1}{2}\ln 2\right) - \left(-\tfrac{1}{2}\ln 3 + \tfrac{1}{2}\ln 1\right) = \tfrac{1}{2}(\ln 2 + \ln 3 - \ln 4) \quad \left[\text{or } \tfrac{1}{2}\ln\tfrac{3}{2}\right]$$

13. $\displaystyle\int \dfrac{ax}{x^2 - bx}\, dx = \int \dfrac{ax}{x(x-b)}\, dx = \int \dfrac{a}{x-b}\, dx = a\ln|x - b| + C$

15. $\dfrac{2x+3}{(x+1)^2} = \dfrac{A}{x+1} + \dfrac{B}{(x+1)^2} \Rightarrow 2x + 3 = A(x+1) + B$. Take $x = -1$ to get $B = 1$, and equate

coefficients of x to get $A = 2$. Now

$$\int_0^1 \dfrac{2x+3}{(x+1)^2}\, dx = \int_0^1 \left[\dfrac{2}{x+1} + \dfrac{1}{(x+1)^2}\right] dx = \left[2\ln(x+1) - \dfrac{1}{x+1}\right]_0^1$$

$$= 2\ln 2 - \tfrac{1}{2} - (2\ln 1 - 1) = 2\ln 2 + \tfrac{1}{2}$$

17. $\dfrac{4y^2 - 7y - 12}{y(y+2)(y-3)} = \dfrac{A}{y} + \dfrac{B}{y+2} + \dfrac{C}{y-3} \quad \Rightarrow \quad 4y^2 - 7y - 12 = A(y+2)(y-3) + By(y-3) + Cy(y+2).$

Setting $y = 0$ gives $-12 = -6A$, so $A = 2$. Setting $y = -2$ gives $18 = 10B$, so $B = \frac{9}{5}$. Setting $y = 3$ gives

$3 = 15C$, so $C = \frac{1}{5}$. Now

$$\int_1^2 \frac{4y^2 - 7y - 12}{y(y+2)(y-3)}\, dy = \int_1^2 \left(\frac{2}{y} + \frac{9/5}{y+2} + \frac{1/5}{y-3} \right) dy = \left[2\ln|y| + \tfrac{9}{5}\ln|y+2| + \tfrac{1}{5}\ln|y-3| \right]_1^2$$

$$= 2\ln 2 + \tfrac{9}{5}\ln 4 + \tfrac{1}{5}\ln 1 - 2\ln 1 - \tfrac{9}{5}\ln 3 - \tfrac{1}{5}\ln 2$$

$$= 2\ln 2 + \tfrac{18}{5}\ln 2 - \tfrac{1}{5}\ln 2 - \tfrac{9}{5}\ln 3 = \tfrac{27}{5}\ln 2 - \tfrac{9}{5}\ln 3 = \tfrac{9}{5}(3\ln 2 - \ln 3) = \tfrac{9}{5}\ln\tfrac{8}{3}$$

19. $\dfrac{1}{(x+5)^2(x-1)} = \dfrac{A}{x+5} + \dfrac{B}{(x+5)^2} + \dfrac{C}{x-1} \quad \Rightarrow \quad 1 = A(x+5)(x-1) + B(x-1) + C(x+5)^2.$ Setting

$x = -5$ gives $1 = -6B$, so $B = -\frac{1}{6}$. Setting $x = 1$ gives $1 = 36C$, so $C = \frac{1}{36}$. Setting $x = -2$ gives

$1 = A(3)(-3) + B(-3) + C(3^2) = -9A - 3B + 9C = -9A + \frac{1}{2} + \frac{1}{4} = -9A + \frac{3}{4}$, so $9A = -\frac{1}{4}$ and

$A = -\frac{1}{36}$. Now

$$\int \frac{1}{(x+5)^2(x-1)}\, dx = \int \left[\frac{-1/36}{x+5} - \frac{1/6}{(x+5)^2} + \frac{1/36}{x-1} \right] dx$$

$$= -\frac{1}{36}\ln|x+5| + \frac{1}{6(x+5)} + \frac{1}{36}\ln|x-1| + C$$

21. $\dfrac{5x^2 + 3x - 2}{x^3 + 2x^2} = \dfrac{5x^2 + 3x - 2}{x^2(x+2)} = \dfrac{A}{x} + \dfrac{B}{x^2} + \dfrac{C}{x+2}.$ Multiply by $x^2(x+2)$ to get

$5x^2 + 3x - 2 = Ax(x+2) + B(x+2) + Cx^2$. Set $x = -2$ to get $C = 3$, and take $x = 0$ to get

$B = -1$. Equating the coefficients of x^2 gives $5 = A + C \quad \Rightarrow \quad A = 2$. So

$$\int \frac{5x^2 + 3x - 2}{x^3 + 2x^2}\, dx = \int \left(\frac{2}{x} - \frac{1}{x^2} + \frac{3}{x+2} \right) dx = 2\ln|x| + \frac{1}{x} + 3\ln|x+2| + C.$$

23. $\dfrac{x^2}{(x+1)^3} = \dfrac{A}{x+1} + \dfrac{B}{(x+1)^2} + \dfrac{C}{(x+1)^3}.$ Multiply by $(x+1)^3$ to get $x^2 = A(x+1)^2 + B(x+1) + C.$

Setting $x = -1$ gives $C = 1$. Equating the coefficients of x^2 gives $A = 1$, and setting $x = 0$ gives $B = -2$.

Now $\displaystyle\int \frac{x^2\, dx}{(x+1)^3} = \int \left[\frac{1}{x+1} - \frac{2}{(x+1)^2} + \frac{1}{(x+1)^3} \right] dx = \ln|x+1| + \frac{2}{x+1} - \frac{1}{2(x+1)^2} + C.$

25. $\dfrac{10}{(x-1)(x^2+9)} = \dfrac{A}{x-1} + \dfrac{Bx+C}{x^2+9}.$ Multiply both sides by $(x-1)(x^2+9)$ to get

$10 = A(x^2+9) + (Bx+C)(x-1)$ $(*)$. Substituting 1 for x gives $10 = 10A \quad \Leftrightarrow \quad A = 1$. Substituting 0 for x

gives $10 = 9A - C \quad \Rightarrow \quad C = 9(1) - 10 = -1$. The coefficients of the x^2-terms in $(*)$ must be equal, so

$0 = A + B \quad \Rightarrow \quad B = -1$. Thus,

$$\int \frac{10}{(x-1)(x^2+9)}\, dx = \int \left(\frac{1}{x-1} + \frac{-x-1}{x^2+9} \right) dx = \int \left(\frac{1}{x-1} - \frac{x}{x^2+9} - \frac{1}{x^2+9} \right) dx$$

$$= \ln|x-1| - \tfrac{1}{2}\ln(x^2+9) \text{ [let } u = x^2 + 9] - \tfrac{1}{3}\tan^{-1}\left(\tfrac{x}{3}\right) \text{ [Formula 10] } + C$$

27. $\dfrac{x^3 + x^2 + 2x + 1}{(x^2 + 1)(x^2 + 2)} = \dfrac{Ax + B}{x^2 + 1} + \dfrac{Cx + D}{x^2 + 2}$. Multiply both sides by $(x^2 + 1)(x^2 + 2)$ to get

$x^3 + x^2 + 2x + 1 = (Ax + B)(x^2 + 2) + (Cx + D)(x^2 + 1) \quad \Leftrightarrow$

$x^3 + x^2 + 2x + 1 = (Ax^3 + Bx^2 + 2Ax + 2B) + (Cx^3 + Dx^2 + Cx + D) \quad \Leftrightarrow$

$x^3 + x^2 + 2x + 1 = (A + C)x^3 + (B + D)x^2 + (2A + C)x + (2B + D)$. Comparing coefficients gives us the

following system of equations:

$$A + C = 1 \quad \textbf{(1)} \qquad\qquad B + D = 1 \quad \textbf{(2)}$$
$$2A + C = 2 \quad \textbf{(3)} \qquad\qquad 2B + D = 1 \quad \textbf{(4)}$$

Subtracting equation **(1)** from equation **(3)** gives us $A = 1$, so $C = 0$. Subtracting equation **(2)** from equation **(4)**

gives us $B = 0$, so $D = 1$. Thus, $I = \displaystyle\int \dfrac{x^3 + x^2 + 2x + 1}{(x^2 + 1)(x^2 + 2)}\, dx = \int \left(\dfrac{x}{x^2 + 1} + \dfrac{1}{x^2 + 2} \right) dx$. For $\displaystyle\int \dfrac{x}{x^2 + 1}\, dx$,

let $u = x^2 + 1$ so $du = 2x\, dx$ and then $\displaystyle\int \dfrac{x}{x^2 + 1}\, dx = \dfrac{1}{2} \int \dfrac{1}{u}\, du = \dfrac{1}{2} \ln |u| + C = \dfrac{1}{2} \ln(x^2 + 1) + C$. For

$\displaystyle\int \dfrac{1}{x^2 + 2}\, dx$, use Formula 10 with $a = \sqrt{2}$. So $\displaystyle\int \dfrac{1}{x^2 + 2}\, dx = \int \dfrac{1}{x^2 + (\sqrt{2})^2}\, dx = \dfrac{1}{\sqrt{2}} \tan^{-1} \dfrac{x}{\sqrt{2}} + C$.

Thus, $I = \dfrac{1}{2} \ln(x^2 + 1) + \dfrac{1}{\sqrt{2}} \tan^{-1} \dfrac{x}{\sqrt{2}} + C$.

29. $\displaystyle\int \dfrac{x + 4}{x^2 + 2x + 5}\, dx = \int \dfrac{x + 1}{x^2 + 2x + 5}\, dx + \int \dfrac{3}{x^2 + 2x + 5}\, dx = \dfrac{1}{2} \int \dfrac{(2x + 2)\, dx}{x^2 + 2x + 5} + \int \dfrac{3\, dx}{(x + 1)^2 + 4}$

$\qquad = \dfrac{1}{2} \ln |x^2 + 2x + 5| + 3 \displaystyle\int \dfrac{2\, du}{4(u^2 + 1)} \qquad \begin{bmatrix} \text{where } x + 1 = 2u, \\ \text{and } dx = 2\, du \end{bmatrix}$

$\qquad = \dfrac{1}{2} \ln(x^2 + 2x + 5) + \dfrac{3}{2} \tan^{-1} u + C = \dfrac{1}{2} \ln(x^2 + 2x + 5) + \dfrac{3}{2} \tan^{-1} \left(\dfrac{x + 1}{2} \right) + C$

31. $\dfrac{1}{x^3 - 1} = \dfrac{1}{(x - 1)(x^2 + x + 1)} = \dfrac{A}{x - 1} + \dfrac{Bx + C}{x^2 + x + 1} \quad \Rightarrow \quad 1 = A(x^2 + x + 1) + (Bx + C)(x - 1)$.

Take $x = 1$ to get $A = \frac{1}{3}$. Equating coefficients of x^2 and then comparing the constant terms, we get $0 = \frac{1}{3} + B$,

$1 = \frac{1}{3} - C$, so $B = -\frac{1}{3}, C = -\frac{2}{3} \quad \Rightarrow$

$$\int \dfrac{1}{x^3 - 1}\, dx = \int \dfrac{\frac{1}{3}}{x - 1}\, dx + \int \dfrac{-\frac{1}{3}x - \frac{2}{3}}{x^2 + x + 1}\, dx = \tfrac{1}{3} \ln |x - 1| - \dfrac{1}{3} \int \dfrac{x + 2}{x^2 + x + 1}\, dx$$

$$= \tfrac{1}{3} \ln |x - 1| - \dfrac{1}{3} \int \dfrac{x + 1/2}{x^2 + x + 1}\, dx - \dfrac{1}{3} \int \dfrac{(3/2)\, dx}{(x + 1/2)^2 + 3/4}$$

$$= \tfrac{1}{3} \ln |x - 1| - \tfrac{1}{6} \ln(x^2 + x + 1) - \tfrac{1}{2} \left(\tfrac{2}{\sqrt{3}} \right) \tan^{-1} \left(\dfrac{x + \frac{1}{2}}{\sqrt{3}/2} \right) + K$$

$$= \tfrac{1}{3} \ln |x - 1| - \tfrac{1}{6} \ln(x^2 + x + 1) - \dfrac{1}{\sqrt{3}} \tan^{-1} \left(\tfrac{1}{\sqrt{3}}(2x + 1) \right) + K$$

33. Let $u = x^3 + 3x^2 + 4$. Then $du = 3(x^2 + 2x)\, dx \quad \Rightarrow$

$$\int_2^5 \dfrac{x^2 + 2x}{x^3 + 3x^2 + 4}\, dx = \dfrac{1}{3} \int_{24}^{204} \dfrac{du}{u} = \tfrac{1}{3} [\ln u]_{24}^{204} = \tfrac{1}{3}(\ln 204 - \ln 24) = \tfrac{1}{3} \ln \tfrac{204}{24} = \tfrac{1}{3} \ln \tfrac{17}{2}.$$

35. $\dfrac{1}{x^4 - x^2} = \dfrac{1}{x^2(x-1)(x+1)} = \dfrac{A}{x} + \dfrac{B}{x^2} + \dfrac{C}{x-1} + \dfrac{D}{x+1}$. Multiply by $x^2(x-1)(x+1)$ to get

$1 = Ax(x-1)(x+1) + B(x-1)(x+1) + Cx^2(x+1) + Dx^2(x-1)$. Setting $x = 1$ gives $C = \frac{1}{2}$, taking

$x = -1$ gives $D = -\frac{1}{2}$. Equating the coefficients of x^3 gives $0 = A + C + D = A$. Finally, setting $x = 0$ yields

$B = -1$. Now $\displaystyle\int \dfrac{dx}{x^4 - x^2} = \int \left[\dfrac{-1}{x^2} + \dfrac{1/2}{x-1} - \dfrac{1/2}{x+1} \right] dx = \dfrac{1}{x} + \frac{1}{2}\ln\left| \dfrac{x-1}{x+1} \right| + C$.

37. $\displaystyle\int \dfrac{x-3}{(x^2 + 2x + 4)^2}\, dx = \int \dfrac{x-3}{\left[(x+1)^2 + 3 \right]^2}\, dx = \int \dfrac{u-4}{(u^2+3)^2}\, du$ [with $u = x + 1$]

$\qquad = \displaystyle\int \dfrac{u\,du}{(u^2+3)^2} - 4\int \dfrac{du}{(u^2+3)^2} = \frac{1}{2}\int \dfrac{dv}{v^2} - 4\int \dfrac{\sqrt{3}\sec^2\theta\,d\theta}{9\sec^4\theta}$ $\begin{bmatrix} v = u^2 + 3 \text{ in the first integral;} \\ u = \sqrt{3}\tan\theta \text{ in the second} \end{bmatrix}$

$\qquad = \dfrac{-1}{(2v)} - \dfrac{4\sqrt{3}}{9}\displaystyle\int \cos^2\theta\,d\theta = \dfrac{-1}{2(u^2+3)} - \dfrac{2\sqrt{3}}{9}(\theta + \sin\theta\cos\theta) + C$

$\qquad = \dfrac{-1}{2(x^2+2x+4)} - \dfrac{2\sqrt{3}}{9}\left[\tan^{-1}\left(\dfrac{x+1}{\sqrt{3}} \right) + \dfrac{\sqrt{3}\,(x+1)}{x^2+2x+4} \right] + C$

$\qquad = \dfrac{-1}{2(x^2+2x+4)} - \dfrac{2\sqrt{3}}{9}\tan^{-1}\left(\dfrac{x+1}{\sqrt{3}} \right) - \dfrac{2(x+1)}{3(x^2+2x+4)} + C$

39. Let $u = \sqrt{x+1}$. Then $x = u^2 - 1$, $dx = 2u\,du$ $\Rightarrow$

$\displaystyle\int \dfrac{dx}{x\sqrt{x+1}} = \int \dfrac{2u\,du}{(u^2-1)\,u} = 2\int \dfrac{du}{u^2-1} = \ln\left| \dfrac{u-1}{u+1} \right| + C = \ln\left| \dfrac{\sqrt{x+1}-1}{\sqrt{x+1}+1} \right| + C$.

41. Let $u = \sqrt{x}$, so $u^2 = x$ and $dx = 2u\,du$. Thus,

$\displaystyle\int_9^{16} \dfrac{\sqrt{x}}{x-4}\, dx = \int_3^4 \dfrac{u}{u^2-4}\,2u\,du = 2\int_3^4 \dfrac{u^2}{u^2-4}\,du = 2\int_3^4 \left(1 + \dfrac{4}{u^2-4} \right) du$ [by long division]

$\qquad\qquad\qquad = 2 + 8\displaystyle\int_3^4 \dfrac{du}{(u+2)(u-2)}$. (*)

Multiply $\dfrac{1}{(u+2)(u-2)} = \dfrac{A}{u+2} + \dfrac{B}{u-2}$ by $(u+2)(u-2)$ to get $1 = A(u-2) + B(u+2)$. Equating

coefficients we get $A + B = 0$ and $-2A + 2B = 1$. Solving gives us $B = \frac{1}{4}$ and $A = -\frac{1}{4}$, so

$\dfrac{1}{(u+2)(u-2)} = \dfrac{-1/4}{u+2} + \dfrac{1/4}{u-2}$ and (*) is

$2 + 8\displaystyle\int_3^4 \left(\dfrac{-1/4}{u+2} + \dfrac{1/4}{u-2} \right) du = 2 + 8\left[-\frac{1}{4}\ln|u+2| + \frac{1}{4}\ln|u-2| \right]_3^4$

$\qquad\qquad\qquad\qquad = 2 + \left[2\ln|u-2| - 2\ln|u+2| \right]_3^4 = 2 + 2\left[\ln\left| \dfrac{u-2}{u+2} \right| \right]_3^4$

$\qquad\qquad\qquad\qquad = 2 + 2\left(\ln\frac{2}{6} - \ln\frac{1}{5} \right) = 2 + 2\ln\dfrac{2/6}{1/5}$

$\qquad\qquad\qquad\qquad = 2 + 2\ln\frac{5}{3}$ or $2 + \ln\left(\frac{5}{3} \right)^2 = 2 + \ln\frac{25}{9}$

43. Let $u = \sqrt[3]{x^2+1}$. Then $x^2 = u^3 - 1$, $2x\,dx = 3u^2\,du$ $\Rightarrow$

$\displaystyle\int \dfrac{x^3\,dx}{\sqrt[3]{x^2+1}} = \int \dfrac{(u^3-1)\frac{3}{2}u^2\,du}{u} = \frac{3}{2}\int \left(u^4 - u \right) du = \frac{3}{10}u^5 - \frac{3}{4}u^2 + C$

$\qquad\qquad\qquad = \frac{3}{10}\left(x^2+1 \right)^{5/3} - \frac{3}{4}\left(x^2+1 \right)^{2/3} + C$

45. If we were to substitute $u = \sqrt{x}$, then the square root would disappear but a cube root would remain. On the other hand, the substitution $u = \sqrt[3]{x}$ would eliminate the cube root but leave a square root. We can eliminate both roots by means of the substitution $u = \sqrt[6]{x}$. (Note that 6 is the least common multiple of 2 and 3.)

Let $u = \sqrt[6]{x}$. Then $x = u^6$, so $dx = 6u^5\, du$ and $\sqrt{x} = u^3$, $\sqrt[3]{x} = u^2$. Thus,

$$\int \frac{dx}{\sqrt{x} - \sqrt[3]{x}} = \int \frac{6u^5\, du}{u^3 - u^2} = 6\int \frac{u^5}{u^2(u-1)}\, du = 6\int \frac{u^3}{u-1}\, du$$

$$= 6\int \left(u^2 + u + 1 + \frac{1}{u-1} \right) du \qquad \text{[by long division]}$$

$$= 6\left(\tfrac{1}{3}u^3 + \tfrac{1}{2}u^2 + u + \ln|u-1|\right) + C = 2\sqrt{x} + 3\sqrt[3]{x} + 6\sqrt[6]{x} + 6\ln\left|\sqrt[6]{x} - 1\right| + C$$

47. Let $u = e^x$. Then $x = \ln u$, $dx = \dfrac{du}{u}$ $\Rightarrow$

$$\int \frac{e^{2x}\, dx}{e^{2x} + 3e^x + 2} = \int \frac{u^2\, (du/u)}{u^2 + 3u + 2} = \int \frac{u\, du}{(u+1)(u+2)} = \int \left[\frac{-1}{u+1} + \frac{2}{u+2}\right] du$$

$$= 2\ln|u+2| - \ln|u+1| + C = \ln\left[(e^x + 2)^2/(e^x + 1)\right] + C$$

49. Let $u = \ln(x^2 - x + 2)$, $dv = dx$. Then $du = \dfrac{2x-1}{x^2 - x + 2}\, dx$, $v = x$, and (by integration by parts)

$$\int \ln(x^2 - x + 2)\, dx = x\ln(x^2 - x + 2) - \int \frac{2x^2 - x}{x^2 - x + 2}\, dx = x\ln(x^2 - x + 2) - \int \left(2 + \frac{x-4}{x^2 - x + 2}\right) dx$$

$$= x\ln(x^2 - x + 2) - 2x - \int \frac{\tfrac{1}{2}(2x-1)}{x^2 - x + 2}\, dx + \frac{7}{2}\int \frac{dx}{(x - \tfrac{1}{2})^2 + \tfrac{7}{4}}$$

$$= x\ln(x^2 - x + 2) - 2x - \frac{1}{2}\ln(x^2 - x + 2) + \frac{7}{2}\int \frac{\frac{\sqrt{7}}{2}\, du}{\tfrac{7}{4}(u^2 + 1)} \qquad \begin{bmatrix} \text{where } x - \tfrac{1}{2} = \tfrac{\sqrt{7}}{2}u, \\ dx = \tfrac{\sqrt{7}}{2}\, du, \\ (x - \tfrac{1}{2})^2 + \tfrac{7}{4} = \tfrac{7}{4}(u^2 + 1) \end{bmatrix}$$

$$= (x - \tfrac{1}{2})\ln(x^2 - x + 2) - 2x + \sqrt{7}\tan^{-1} u + C$$

$$= (x - \tfrac{1}{2})\ln(x^2 - x + 2) - 2x + \sqrt{7}\tan^{-1}\frac{2x-1}{\sqrt{7}} + C$$

51.

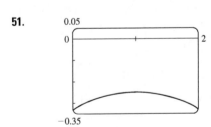

From the graph, we see that the integral will be negative, and we guess that the area is about the same as that of a rectangle with width 2 and height 0.3, so we estimate the integral to be $-(2 \cdot 0.3) = -0.6$. Now

$$\frac{1}{x^2 - 2x - 3} = \frac{1}{(x-3)(x+1)} = \frac{A}{x-3} + \frac{B}{x+1} \quad \Leftrightarrow$$

$1 = (A+B)x + A - 3B$, so $A = -B$ and $A - 3B = 1$ $\Leftrightarrow$ $A = \tfrac{1}{4}$

and $B = -\tfrac{1}{4}$, so the integral becomes

$$\int_0^2 \frac{dx}{x^2 - 2x - 3} = \frac{1}{4}\int_0^2 \frac{dx}{x-3} - \frac{1}{4}\int_0^2 \frac{dx}{x+1} = \frac{1}{4}\Big[\ln|x-3| - \ln|x+1|\Big]_0^2$$

$$= \frac{1}{4}\left[\ln\left|\frac{x-3}{x+1}\right|\right]_0^2 = \tfrac{1}{4}\left(\ln\tfrac{1}{3} - \ln 3\right) = -\tfrac{1}{2}\ln 3 \approx -0.55$$

53. $\displaystyle\int \frac{dx}{x^2 - 2x} = \int \frac{dx}{(x-1)^2 - 1} = \int \frac{du}{u^2 - 1}$ [put $u = x - 1$]

$$= \frac{1}{2} \ln\left|\frac{u-1}{u+1}\right| + C \quad \text{[by Equation 6]} \quad = \frac{1}{2} \ln\left|\frac{x-2}{x}\right| + C$$

55. (a) If $t = \tan\left(\dfrac{x}{2}\right)$, then $\dfrac{x}{2} = \tan^{-1} t$. The figure gives

$$\cos\left(\frac{x}{2}\right) = \frac{1}{\sqrt{1+t^2}} \text{ and } \sin\left(\frac{x}{2}\right) = \frac{t}{\sqrt{1+t^2}}.$$

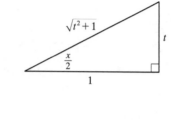

(b) $\cos x = \cos\left(2 \cdot \dfrac{x}{2}\right) = 2\cos^2\left(\dfrac{x}{2}\right) - 1$

$$= 2\left(\frac{1}{\sqrt{1+t^2}}\right)^2 - 1 = \frac{2}{1+t^2} - 1 = \frac{1-t^2}{1+t^2}$$

$$\sin x = \sin\left(2 \cdot \frac{x}{2}\right) = 2\sin\left(\frac{x}{2}\right)\cos\left(\frac{x}{2}\right) = 2\,\frac{t}{\sqrt{1+t^2}}\,\frac{1}{\sqrt{1+t^2}} = \frac{2t}{1+t^2}$$

(c) $\dfrac{x}{2} = \arctan t \;\Rightarrow\; x = 2\arctan t \;\Rightarrow\; dx = \dfrac{2}{1+t^2}\,dt$

57. Let $t = \tan(x/2)$. Then, using the expressions in Exercise 55, we have

$$\int \frac{1}{3\sin x - 4\cos x}\,dx = \int \frac{1}{3\left(\dfrac{2t}{1+t^2}\right) - 4\left(\dfrac{1-t^2}{1+t^2}\right)}\,\frac{2\,dt}{1+t^2} = 2\int \frac{dt}{3(2t) - 4(1-t^2)} = \int \frac{dt}{2t^2 + 3t - 2}$$

$$= \int \frac{dt}{(2t-1)(t+2)} = \int \left[\frac{2}{5}\frac{1}{2t-1} - \frac{1}{5}\frac{1}{t+2}\right]dt \quad \text{[using partial fractions]}$$

$$= \tfrac{1}{5}\left[\ln|2t-1| - \ln|t+2|\right] + C = \frac{1}{5}\ln\left|\frac{2t-1}{t+2}\right| + C = \frac{1}{5}\ln\left|\frac{2\tan(x/2)-1}{\tan(x/2)+2}\right| + C$$

59. Let $t = \tan(x/2)$. Then, by Exercise 55,

$$\int \frac{dx}{2\sin x + \sin 2x} = \frac{1}{2}\int \frac{dx}{\sin x + \sin x \cos x} = \frac{1}{2}\int \frac{2\,dt/(1+t^2)}{2t/(1+t^2) + 2t(1-t^2)/(1+t^2)^2}$$

$$= \frac{1}{2}\int \frac{(1+t^2)\,dt}{t(1+t^2) + t(1-t^2)} = \frac{1}{4}\int \frac{(1+t^2)\,dt}{t} = \frac{1}{4}\int \left(\frac{1}{t} + t\right)dt$$

$$= \tfrac{1}{4}\ln|t| + \tfrac{1}{8}t^2 + C = \tfrac{1}{4}\ln\left|\tan(\tfrac{1}{2}x)\right| + \tfrac{1}{8}\tan^2\left(\tfrac{1}{2}x\right) + C$$

61. $\dfrac{x+1}{x-1} = 1 + \dfrac{2}{x-1} > 0$ for $2 \le x \le 3$, so

$$\text{area} = \int_2^3 \left[1 + \frac{2}{x-1}\right]dx = \Big[x + 2\ln|x-1|\Big]_2^3 = (3 + 2\ln 2) - (2 + 2\ln 1) = 1 + 2\ln 2.$$

63. $\dfrac{P+S}{P\left[(r-1)P-S\right]} = \dfrac{A}{P} + \dfrac{B}{(r-1)P-S} \quad\Rightarrow\quad P+S = A\left[(r-1)P-S\right]+BP = \left[(r-1)A+B\right]P - AS$

$\Rightarrow\quad (r-1)A+B = 1,\ -A = 1 \quad\Rightarrow\quad A = -1,\ B = r.$ Now

$$t = \int \frac{P+S}{P\left[(r-1)P-S\right]}\,dP = \int \left[\frac{-1}{P} + \frac{r}{(r-1)P-S}\right]dP = -\int \frac{dP}{P} + \frac{r}{r-1}\int \frac{r-1}{(r-1)P-S}\,dP$$

so $t = -\ln P + \dfrac{r}{r-1}\ln|(r-1)P-S| + C.$ Here $r = 0.10$ and $S = 900$, so

$$t = -\ln P + \frac{0.1}{-0.9}\ln|-0.9P-900| + C = -\ln P - \tfrac{1}{9}\ln(|-1|\,|0.9P+900|)$$
$$= -\ln P - \tfrac{1}{9}\ln(0.9P+900) + C$$

When $t = 0$, $P = 10{,}000$, so $0 = -\ln 10{,}000 - \tfrac{1}{9}\ln(9900) + C$. Thus, $C = \ln 10{,}000 + \tfrac{1}{9}\ln 9900 \ [\approx 10.2326],$

so our equation becomes

$$t = \ln 10{,}000 - \ln P + \tfrac{1}{9}\ln 9900 - \tfrac{1}{9}\ln(0.9P+900) = \ln\frac{10{,}000}{P} + \frac{1}{9}\ln\frac{9900}{0.9P+900}$$

$$= \ln\frac{10{,}000}{P} + \frac{1}{9}\ln\frac{1100}{0.1P+100} = \ln\frac{10{,}000}{P} + \frac{1}{9}\ln\frac{11{,}000}{P+1000}$$

65. (a) In Maple, we define $f(x)$, and then use `convert(f,parfrac,x);` to obtain

$$f(x) = \frac{24{,}110/4879}{5x+2} - \frac{668/323}{2x+1} - \frac{9438/80{,}155}{3x-7} + \frac{(22{,}098x + 48{,}935)/260{,}015}{x^2+x+5}.$$

In Mathematica, we use the command `Apart`, and in Derive, we use `Expand`.

(b) $\displaystyle\int f(x)\,dx = \frac{24{,}110}{4879}\cdot\tfrac{1}{5}\ln|5x+2| - \frac{668}{323}\cdot\tfrac{1}{2}\ln|2x+1| - \frac{9438}{80{,}155}\cdot\tfrac{1}{3}\ln|3x-7|$

$$+ \frac{1}{260{,}015}\int \frac{22{,}098\left(x+\tfrac{1}{2}\right) + 37{,}886}{\left(x+\tfrac{1}{2}\right)^2 + \tfrac{19}{4}}\,dx + C$$

$$= \frac{24{,}110}{4879}\cdot\tfrac{1}{5}\ln|5x+2| - \frac{668}{323}\cdot\tfrac{1}{2}\ln|2x+1| - \frac{9438}{80{,}155}\cdot\tfrac{1}{3}\ln|3x-7|$$

$$+ \frac{1}{260{,}015}\left[22{,}098\cdot\tfrac{1}{2}\ln\left(x^2+x+5\right) + 37{,}886\cdot\sqrt{\tfrac{4}{19}}\,\tan^{-1}\left(\frac{1}{\sqrt{19/4}}\left(x+\tfrac{1}{2}\right)\right)\right] + C$$

$$= \frac{4822}{4879}\ln|5x+2| - \frac{334}{323}\ln|2x+1| - \frac{3146}{80{,}155}\ln|3x-7| + \frac{11{,}049}{260{,}015}\ln\left(x^2+x+5\right)$$

$$+ \frac{75{,}772}{260{,}015\sqrt{19}}\,\tan^{-1}\left[\tfrac{1}{\sqrt{19}}(2x+1)\right] + C$$

Using a CAS, we get

$$\frac{4822\ln(5x+2)}{4879} - \frac{334\ln(2x+1)}{323} - \frac{3146\ln(3x-7)}{80{,}155}$$

$$+ \frac{11{,}049\ln\left(x^2+x+5\right)}{260{,}015} + \frac{3988\sqrt{19}}{260{,}015}\,\tan^{-1}\left[\frac{\sqrt{19}}{19}(2x+1)\right]$$

The main difference in this answer is that the absolute value signs and the constant of integration have been omitted. Also, the fractions have been reduced and the denominators rationalized.

67. There are only finitely many values of x where $Q(x) = 0$ (assuming that Q is not the zero polynomial). At all other values of x, $F(x)/Q(x) = G(x)/Q(x)$, so $F(x) = G(x)$. In other words, the values of F and G agree at all except perhaps finitely many values of x. By continuity of F and G, the polynomials F and G must agree at those values of x too.

More explicitly: if a is a value of x such that $Q(a) = 0$, then $Q(x) \neq 0$ for all x sufficiently close to a. Thus,

$$F(a) = \lim_{x \to a} F(x) \text{ [by continuity of } F] = \lim_{x \to a} G(x) \quad \text{[whenever } Q(x) \neq 0]$$

$$= G(a) \quad \text{[by continuity of } G]$$

8.5 Strategy for Integration

1. $\displaystyle \int \frac{\sin x + \sec x}{\tan x}\, dx = \int \left(\frac{\sin x}{\tan x} + \frac{\sec x}{\tan x} \right) dx = \int (\cos x + \csc x)\, dx = \sin x + \ln|\csc x - \cot x| + C$

3. $\displaystyle \int_0^2 \frac{2t}{(t-3)^2}\, dt = \int_{-3}^{-1} \frac{2(u+3)}{u^2}\, du \ [u = t - 3,\ du = dt] = \int_{-3}^{-1} \left(\frac{2}{u} + \frac{6}{u^2} \right) du = \left[2\ln|u| - \frac{6}{u} \right]_{-3}^{-1}$

$$= (2\ln 1 + 6) - (2\ln 3 + 2) = 4 - 2\ln 3 \text{ or } 4 - \ln 9$$

5. Let $u = \arctan y$. Then $du = \dfrac{dy}{1 + y^2} \ \Rightarrow \ \displaystyle \int_{-1}^1 \frac{e^{\arctan y}}{1 + y^2}\, dy = \int_{-\pi/4}^{\pi/4} e^u\, du = [e^u]_{-\pi/4}^{\pi/4} = e^{\pi/4} - e^{-\pi/4}$.

7. $\displaystyle \int_1^3 r^4 \ln r\, dr \begin{bmatrix} u = \ln r, & dv = r^4\, dr, \\ du = \dfrac{dr}{r} & v = \dfrac{1}{5}r^5 \end{bmatrix} = \left[\frac{1}{5}r^5 \ln r \right]_1^3 - \int_1^3 \frac{1}{5}r^4\, dr = \frac{243}{5}\ln 3 - 0 - \left[\frac{1}{25}r^5 \right]_1^3$

$$= \tfrac{243}{5}\ln 3 - \left(\tfrac{243}{25} - \tfrac{1}{25} \right) = \tfrac{243}{5}\ln 3 - \tfrac{242}{25}$$

9. $\displaystyle \int \frac{x-1}{x^2 - 4x + 5}\, dx = \int \frac{(x-2)+1}{(x-2)^2 + 1}\, dx = \int \left(\frac{u}{u^2 + 1} + \frac{1}{u^2 + 1} \right) du \ [u = x - 2,\ du = dx]$

$$= \tfrac{1}{2}\ln(u^2 + 1) + \tan^{-1} u + C = \tfrac{1}{2}\ln(x^2 - 4x + 5) + \tan^{-1}(x - 2) + C$$

11. $\int \sin^3 \theta \cos^5 \theta\, d\theta = \int \cos^5 \theta \sin^2 \theta \sin \theta\, d\theta = -\int \cos^5 \theta (1 - \cos^2 \theta)(-\sin \theta)\, d\theta$

$$= -\int u^5 (1 - u^2)\, du \quad \begin{bmatrix} u = \cos \theta, \\ du = -\sin \theta\, d\theta \end{bmatrix}$$

$$= \int (u^7 - u^5)\, du = \tfrac{1}{8}u^8 - \tfrac{1}{6}u^6 + C = \tfrac{1}{8}\cos^8 \theta - \tfrac{1}{6}\cos^6 \theta + C$$

Another solution:

$\int \sin^3 \theta \cos^5 \theta\, d\theta = \int \sin^3 \theta (\cos^2 \theta)^2 \cos \theta\, d\theta = \int \sin^3 \theta (1 - \sin^2 \theta)^2 \cos \theta\, d\theta$

$$= \int u^3 (1 - u^2)^2\, du \quad \begin{bmatrix} u = \sin \theta, \\ du = \cos \theta\, d\theta \end{bmatrix} = \int u^3 (1 - 2u^2 + u^4)\, du$$

$$= \int (u^3 - 2u^5 + u^7)\, du = \tfrac{1}{4}u^4 - \tfrac{1}{3}u^6 + \tfrac{1}{8}u^8 + C = \tfrac{1}{4}\sin^4 \theta - \tfrac{1}{3}\sin^6 \theta + \tfrac{1}{8}\sin^8 \theta + C$$

13. Let $x = \sin \theta$, where $-\frac{\pi}{2} \leq \theta \leq \frac{\pi}{2}$. Then $dx = \cos \theta\, d\theta$ and

$(1 - x^2)^{1/2} = \cos \theta$, so

$$\int \frac{dx}{(1 - x^2)^{3/2}} = \int \frac{\cos \theta\, d\theta}{(\cos \theta)^3} = \int \sec^2 \theta\, d\theta$$

$$= \tan \theta + C = \frac{x}{\sqrt{1 - x^2}} + C$$

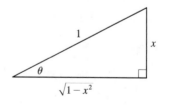

15. Let $u = 1 - x^2 \Rightarrow du = -2x\,dx$. Then

$$\int_0^{1/2} \frac{x}{\sqrt{1-x^2}}\,dx = -\frac{1}{2}\int_1^{3/4}\frac{1}{\sqrt{u}}\,du = \frac{1}{2}\int_{3/4}^1 u^{-1/2}\,du = \frac{1}{2}\Big[2u^{1/2}\Big]_{3/4}^1 = \Big[\sqrt{u}\Big]_{3/4}^1 = 1 - \frac{\sqrt{3}}{2}$$

17. $\int x\sin^2 x\,dx$ $\quad\begin{bmatrix} u = x, & dv = \sin^2 x\,dx, \\ du = dx & v = \int \sin^2 x\,dx = \int \frac{1}{2}(1-\cos 2x)\,dx = \frac{1}{2}x - \frac{1}{2}\sin x\cos x \end{bmatrix}$

$\quad = \frac{1}{2}x^2 - \frac{1}{2}x\sin x\cos x - \int\left(\frac{1}{2}x - \frac{1}{2}\sin x\cos x\right)dx$

$\quad = \frac{1}{2}x^2 - \frac{1}{2}x\sin x\cos x - \frac{1}{4}x^2 + \frac{1}{4}\sin^2 x + C = \frac{1}{4}x^2 - \frac{1}{2}x\sin x\cos x + \frac{1}{4}\sin^2 x + C$

Note: $\int \sin x\cos x\,dx = \int s\,ds = \frac{1}{2}s^2 + C$ [where $s = \sin x$, $ds = \cos x\,dx$].

A slightly different method is to write $\int x\sin^2 x\,dx = \int x\cdot\frac{1}{2}(1-\cos 2x)\,dx = \frac{1}{2}\int x\,dx - \frac{1}{2}\int x\cos 2x\,dx$. If we

evaluate the second integral by parts, we arrive at the equivalent answer $\frac{1}{4}x^2 - \frac{1}{4}x\sin 2x - \frac{1}{8}\cos 2x + C$.

19. Let $u = e^x$. Then $\int e^{x+e^x}\,dx = \int e^{e^x}e^x\,dx = \int e^u\,du = e^u + C = e^{e^x} + C$.

21. Integrate by parts three times, first with $u = t^3$, $dv = e^{-2t}\,dt$:

$$\int t^3 e^{-2t}\,dt = -\frac{1}{2}t^3 e^{-2t} + \frac{1}{2}\int 3t^2 e^{-2t}\,dt = -\frac{1}{2}t^3 e^{-2t} - \frac{3}{4}t^2 e^{-2t} + \frac{1}{2}\int 3t e^{-2t}\,dt$$

$$= -e^{-2t}\Big[\tfrac{1}{2}t^3 + \tfrac{3}{4}t^2\Big] - \frac{3}{4}t e^{-2t} + \frac{3}{4}\int e^{-2t}\,dt = -e^{-2t}\Big[\tfrac{1}{2}t^3 + \tfrac{3}{4}t^2 + \tfrac{3}{4}t + \tfrac{3}{8}\Big] + C$$

$$= -\frac{1}{8}e^{-2t}\big(4t^3 + 6t^2 + 6t + 3\big) + C$$

23. Let $u = 1 + \sqrt{x}$. Then $x = (u-1)^2$, $dx = 2(u-1)\,du \Rightarrow$

$$\int_0^1 (1+\sqrt{x})^8\,dx = \int_1^2 u^8\cdot 2(u-1)\,du = 2\int_1^2\big(u^9 - u^8\big)\,du = \Big[\tfrac{1}{5}u^{10} - 2\cdot\tfrac{1}{9}u^9\Big]_1^2$$

$$= \frac{1024}{5} - \frac{1024}{9} - \frac{1}{5} + \frac{2}{9} = \frac{4097}{45}$$

25. $\dfrac{3x^2 - 2}{x^2 - 2x - 8} = 3 + \dfrac{6x + 22}{(x-4)(x+2)} = 3 + \dfrac{A}{x-4} + \dfrac{B}{x+2} \Rightarrow 6x + 22 = A(x+2) + B(x-4)$. Setting

$x = 4$ gives $46 = 6A$, so $A = \frac{23}{3}$. Setting $x = -2$ gives $10 = -6B$, so $B = -\frac{5}{3}$. Now

$$\int \frac{3x^2 - 2}{x^2 - 2x - 8}\,dx = \int\left(3 + \frac{23/3}{x-4} - \frac{5/3}{x+2}\right)dx = 3x + \frac{23}{3}\ln|x-4| - \frac{5}{3}\ln|x+2| + C.$$

27. Let $u = \ln(\sin x)$. Then $du = \cot x\,dx \Rightarrow \int\cot x\ln(\sin x)\,dx = \int u\,du = \frac{1}{2}u^2 + C = \frac{1}{2}[\ln(\sin x)]^2 + C$.

29. $\displaystyle\int_0^5 \frac{3w-1}{w+2}\,dw = \int_0^5\left(3 - \frac{7}{w+2}\right)dw = \Big[3w - 7\ln|w+2|\Big]_0^5$

$\quad = 15 - 7\ln 7 + 7\ln 2 = 15 + 7(\ln 2 - \ln 7) = 15 + 7\ln\frac{2}{7}$

31. As in Example 5,

$$\int \sqrt{\frac{1+x}{1-x}}\,dx = \int \frac{\sqrt{1+x}}{\sqrt{1-x}}\cdot\frac{\sqrt{1+x}}{\sqrt{1+x}}\,dx = \int \frac{1+x}{\sqrt{1-x^2}}\,dx = \int \frac{dx}{\sqrt{1-x^2}} + \int \frac{x\,dx}{\sqrt{1-x^2}}$$

$$= \sin^{-1}x - \sqrt{1-x^2} + C$$

Another method: Substitute $u = \sqrt{(1+x)/(1-x)}$.

33. $3 - 2x - x^2 = -(x^2 + 2x + 1) + 4 = 4 - (x+1)^2$. Let
$x + 1 = 2\sin\theta$, where $-\frac{\pi}{2} \le \theta \le \frac{\pi}{2}$. Then $dx = 2\cos\theta\,d\theta$ and

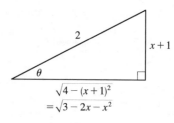

$$\int \sqrt{3 - 2x - x^2}\,dx = \int \sqrt{4 - (x+1)^2}\,dx = \int \sqrt{4 - 4\sin^2\theta}\,2\cos\theta\,d\theta$$
$$= 4\int \cos^2\theta\,d\theta = 2\int (1 + \cos 2\theta)\,d\theta$$
$$= 2\theta + \sin 2\theta + C = 2\theta + 2\sin\theta\cos\theta + C$$
$$= 2\sin^{-1}\left(\frac{x+1}{2}\right) + 2 \cdot \frac{x+1}{2} \cdot \frac{\sqrt{3 - 2x - x^2}}{2} + C$$
$$= 2\sin^{-1}\left(\frac{x+1}{2}\right) + \frac{x+1}{2}\sqrt{3 - 2x - x^2} + C$$

35. Because $f(x) = x^8 \sin x$ is the product of an even function and an odd function, it is odd. Therefore,
$\int_{-1}^{1} x^8 \sin x\,dx = 0$ [by (5.5.6)(b)].

37. $\int_0^{\pi/4} \cos^2\theta \tan^2\theta\,d\theta = \int_0^{\pi/4} \sin^2\theta\,d\theta = \int_0^{\pi/4} \frac{1}{2}(1 - \cos 2\theta)\,d\theta = \left[\frac{1}{2}\theta - \frac{1}{4}\sin 2\theta\right]_0^{\pi/4}$
$= \left(\frac{\pi}{8} - \frac{1}{4}\right) - (0 - 0) = \frac{\pi}{8} - \frac{1}{4}$

39. Let $u = 1 - x^2$. Then $du = -2x\,dx$ $\Rightarrow$

$$\int \frac{x\,dx}{1 - x^2 + \sqrt{1 - x^2}} = -\frac{1}{2}\int \frac{du}{u + \sqrt{u}} = -\int \frac{v\,dv}{v^2 + v} \quad [v = \sqrt{u},\, u = v^2,\, du = 2v\,dv]$$
$$= -\int \frac{dv}{v + 1} = -\ln|v + 1| + C = -\ln\left(\sqrt{1 - x^2} + 1\right) + C$$

41. Let $u = \theta$, $dv = \tan^2\theta\,d\theta = (\sec^2\theta - 1)\,d\theta$ $\Rightarrow$ $du = d\theta$ and $v = \tan\theta - \theta$. So

$$\int \theta \tan^2\theta\,d\theta = \theta(\tan\theta - \theta) - \int (\tan\theta - \theta)\,d\theta = \theta\tan\theta - \theta^2 - \ln|\sec\theta| + \frac{1}{2}\theta^2 + C$$
$$= \theta\tan\theta - \frac{1}{2}\theta^2 - \ln|\sec\theta| + C$$

43. Let $u = 1 + e^x$, so that $du = e^x\,dx$. Then
$\int e^x \sqrt{1 + e^x}\,dx = \int u^{1/2}\,du = \frac{2}{3}u^{3/2} + C = \frac{2}{3}(1 + e^x)^{3/2} + C$.
Or: Let $u = \sqrt{1 + e^x}$, so that $u^2 = 1 + e^x$ and $2u\,du = e^x\,dx$. Then
$\int e^x \sqrt{1 + e^x}\,dx = \int u \cdot 2u\,du = \int 2u^2\,du = \frac{2}{3}u^3 + C = \frac{2}{3}(1 + e^x)^{3/2} + C$.

45. Let $t = x^3$. Then $dt = 3x^2\,dx$ $\Rightarrow$ $I = \int x^5 e^{-x^3}\,dx = \frac{1}{3}\int te^{-t}\,dt$. Now integrate by parts with $u = t$,
$dv = e^{-t}\,dt$: $I = -\frac{1}{3}te^{-t} + \frac{1}{3}\int e^{-t}\,dt = -\frac{1}{3}te^{-t} - \frac{1}{3}e^{-t} + C = -\frac{1}{3}e^{-x^3}(x^3 + 1) + C$.

47. $\int \frac{x + a}{x^2 + a^2}\,dx = \frac{1}{2}\int \frac{2x\,dx}{x^2 + a^2} + a\int \frac{dx}{x^2 + a^2} = \frac{1}{2}\ln(x^2 + a^2) + a \cdot \frac{1}{a}\tan^{-1}\left(\frac{x}{a}\right) + C$
$= \ln\sqrt{x^2 + a^2} + \tan^{-1}(x/a) + C$

49. Let $u = \sqrt{4x + 1}$ $\Rightarrow$ $u^2 = 4x + 1$ $\Rightarrow$ $2u\,du = 4\,dx$ $\Rightarrow$ $dx = \frac{1}{2}u\,du$. So

$$\int \frac{1}{x\sqrt{4x + 1}}\,dx = \int \frac{\frac{1}{2}u\,du}{\frac{1}{4}(u^2 - 1)\,u} = 2\int \frac{du}{u^2 - 1} = 2\left(\frac{1}{2}\right)\ln\left|\frac{u - 1}{u + 1}\right| + C \quad \text{[by Formula 19]}$$
$$= \ln\left|\frac{\sqrt{4x + 1} - 1}{\sqrt{4x + 1} + 1}\right| + C$$

51. Let $2x = \tan\theta \;\Rightarrow\; x = \frac{1}{2}\tan\theta$, $dx = \frac{1}{2}\sec^2\theta\,d\theta$, $\sqrt{4x^2+1} = \sec\theta$, so

$$\int \frac{dx}{x\sqrt{4x^2+1}} = \int \frac{\frac{1}{2}\sec^2\theta\,d\theta}{\frac{1}{2}\tan\theta\sec\theta} = \int \frac{\sec\theta}{\tan\theta}\,d\theta = \int \csc\theta\,d\theta$$

$$= -\ln|\csc\theta + \cot\theta| + C \qquad [\text{or } \ln|\csc\theta - \cot\theta| + C]$$

$$= -\ln\left|\frac{\sqrt{4x^2+1}}{2x} + \frac{1}{2x}\right| + C \qquad \left[\text{or } \ln\left|\frac{\sqrt{4x^2+1}}{2x} - \frac{1}{2x}\right| + C\right]$$

53. $\displaystyle\int x^2\sinh(mx)\,dx = \frac{1}{m}x^2\cosh(mx) - \frac{2}{m}\int x\cosh(mx)\,dx$ $\qquad \begin{bmatrix} u = x^2, & dv = \sinh(mx)\,dx, \\ du = 2x\,dx & v = \frac{1}{m}\cosh(mx) \end{bmatrix}$

$$= \frac{1}{m}x^2\cosh(mx) - \frac{2}{m}\left(\frac{1}{m}x\sinh(mx) - \frac{1}{m}\int\sinh(mx)\,dx\right) \qquad \begin{bmatrix} U = x, & dV = \cosh(mx)\,dx, \\ dU = dx & V = \frac{1}{m}\sinh(mx) \end{bmatrix}$$

$$= \frac{1}{m}x^2\cosh(mx) - \frac{2}{m^2}x\sinh(mx) + \frac{2}{m^3}\cosh(mx) + C$$

55. Let $u = \sqrt{x+1}$. Then $x = u^2 - 1 \;\Rightarrow$

$$\int \frac{dx}{x + 4 + 4\sqrt{x+1}} = \int \frac{2u\,du}{u^2 + 3 + 4u} = \int\left[\frac{-1}{u+1} + \frac{3}{u+3}\right]du$$

$$= 3\ln|u+3| - \ln|u+1| + C = 3\ln\left(\sqrt{x+1}+3\right) - \ln\left(\sqrt{x+1}+1\right) + C$$

57. Let $u = \sqrt[3]{x+c}$. Then $x = u^3 - c \;\Rightarrow$

$$\int x\sqrt[3]{x+c}\,dx = \int (u^3 - c)u \cdot 3u^2\,du = 3\int(u^6 - cu^3)\,du = \frac{3}{7}u^7 - \frac{3}{4}cu^4 + C$$

$$= \frac{3}{7}(x+c)^{7/3} - \frac{3}{4}c(x+c)^{4/3} + C$$

59. Let $u = e^x$. Then $x = \ln u$, $dx = du/u \;\Rightarrow$

$$\int \frac{dx}{e^{3x} - e^x} = \int \frac{du/u}{u^3 - u} = \int \frac{du}{(u-1)u^2(u+1)} = \int\left[\frac{1/2}{u-1} - \frac{1}{u^2} - \frac{1/2}{u+1}\right]du$$

$$= \frac{1}{u} + \frac{1}{2}\ln\left|\frac{u-1}{u+1}\right| + C = e^{-x} + \frac{1}{2}\ln\left|\frac{e^x-1}{e^x+1}\right| + C$$

61. Let $u = x^5$. Then $du = 5x^4\,dx \;\Rightarrow$

$$\int \frac{x^4\,dx}{x^{10}+16} = \int \frac{\frac{1}{5}du}{u^2+16} = \frac{1}{5}\cdot\frac{1}{4}\tan^{-1}\left(\frac{1}{4}u\right) + C = \frac{1}{20}\tan^{-1}\left(\frac{1}{4}x^5\right) + C.$$

63. Let $y = \sqrt{x}$ so that $dy = \dfrac{1}{2\sqrt{x}}\,dx \;\Rightarrow\; dx = 2\sqrt{x}\,dy = 2y\,dy$. Then

$$\int \sqrt{x}\,e^{\sqrt{x}}\,dx = \int ye^y(2y\,dy) = \int 2y^2 e^y\,dy \qquad \begin{bmatrix} u = 2y^2, & dv = e^y\,dy, \\ du = 4y\,dy & v = e^y \end{bmatrix}$$

$$= 2y^2 e^y - \int 4ye^y\,dy \qquad \begin{bmatrix} U = 4y, & dV = e^y\,dy, \\ dU = 4\,dy & V = e^y \end{bmatrix}$$

$$= 2y^2 e^y - \left(4ye^y - \int 4e^y\,dy\right) = 2y^2 e^y - 4ye^y + 4e^y + C$$

$$= 2(y^2 - 2y + 2)e^y + C = 2(x - 2\sqrt{x} + 2)e^{\sqrt{x}} + C$$

65. $\displaystyle\int \frac{dx}{\sqrt{x+1}+\sqrt{x}} = \int \left(\frac{1}{\sqrt{x+1}+\sqrt{x}} \cdot \frac{\sqrt{x+1}-\sqrt{x}}{\sqrt{x+1}-\sqrt{x}} \right) dx = \int \left(\sqrt{x+1} - \sqrt{x} \right) dx$

$$= \tfrac{2}{3}\left[(x+1)^{3/2} - x^{3/2} \right] + C$$

67. Let $u = \sqrt{t}$. Then $du = dt/(2\sqrt{t}) \;\Rightarrow$

$$\int_1^3 \frac{\arctan\sqrt{t}}{\sqrt{t}}\, dt = \int_1^{\sqrt{3}} \tan^{-1}u\,(2\,du) = 2\left[u\tan^{-1}u - \tfrac{1}{2}\ln(1+u^2) \right]_1^{\sqrt{3}} \qquad \text{[Example 5 in Section 8.1]}$$

$$= 2\left[\left(\sqrt{3}\tan^{-1}\sqrt{3} - \tfrac{1}{2}\ln 4\right) - \left(\tan^{-1}1 - \tfrac{1}{2}\ln 2\right) \right]$$

$$= 2\left[\left(\sqrt{3}\cdot\tfrac{\pi}{3} - \ln 2\right) - \left(\tfrac{\pi}{4} - \tfrac{1}{2}\ln 2\right) \right] = \tfrac{2}{3}\sqrt{3}\,\pi - \tfrac{1}{2}\pi - \ln 2$$

69. Let $u = e^x$. Then $x = \ln u$, $dx = du/u \;\Rightarrow$

$$\int \frac{e^{2x}}{1+e^x}\, dx = \int \frac{u^2}{1+u}\frac{du}{u} = \int \frac{u}{1+u}\, du = \int \left(1 - \frac{1}{1+u} \right) du$$

$$= u - \ln|1+u| + C = e^x - \ln(1+e^x) + C$$

71. $\displaystyle \frac{x}{x^4 + 4x^2 + 3} = \frac{x}{(x^2+3)(x^2+1)} = \frac{Ax+B}{x^2+3} + \frac{Cx+D}{x^2+1} \;\Rightarrow$

$$x = (Ax+B)(x^2+1) + (Cx+D)(x^2+3) = \left(Ax^3 + Bx^2 + Ax + B\right) + \left(Cx^3 + Dx^2 + 3Cx + 3D\right)$$

$$= (A+C)x^3 + (B+D)x^2 + (A+3C)x + (B+3D) \;\Rightarrow$$

$A+C=0$, $B+D=0$, $A+3C=1$, $B+3D=0 \;\Rightarrow\; A = -\tfrac{1}{2}, C = \tfrac{1}{2}, B=0, D=0$. Thus,

$$\int \frac{x}{x^4 + 4x^2 + 3}\, dx = \int \left(\frac{-\tfrac{1}{2}x}{x^2+3} + \frac{\tfrac{1}{2}x}{x^2+1} \right) dx$$

$$= -\tfrac{1}{4}\ln\left(x^2+3\right) + \tfrac{1}{4}\ln\left(x^2+1\right) + C \quad \text{or} \quad \tfrac{1}{4}\ln\left(\frac{x^2+1}{x^2+3} \right) + C$$

73. $\displaystyle \frac{1}{(x-2)(x^2+4)} = \frac{A}{x-2} + \frac{Bx+C}{x^2+4} \;\Rightarrow$

$1 = A\left(x^2+4\right) + (Bx+C)(x-2) = (A+B)x^2 + (C-2B)x + (4A-2C)$. So $0 = A+B = C-2B$,

$1 = 4A - 2C$. Setting $x=2$ gives $A = \tfrac{1}{8} \;\Rightarrow\; B = -\tfrac{1}{8}$ and $C = -\tfrac{1}{4}$. So

$$\int \frac{1}{(x-2)(x^2+4)}\, dx = \int \left(\frac{\tfrac{1}{8}}{x-2} + \frac{-\tfrac{1}{8}x - \tfrac{1}{4}}{x^2+4} \right) dx = \frac{1}{8}\int \frac{dx}{x-2} - \frac{1}{16}\int \frac{2x\,dx}{x^2+4} - \frac{1}{4}\int \frac{dx}{x^2+4}$$

$$= \tfrac{1}{8}\ln|x-2| - \tfrac{1}{16}\ln\left(x^2+4\right) - \tfrac{1}{8}\tan^{-1}(x/2) + C$$

75. $\displaystyle\int \sin x \sin 2x \sin 3x\, dx = \int \sin x \cdot \tfrac{1}{2}[\cos(2x-3x) - \cos(2x+3x)]\, dx = \tfrac{1}{2}\int (\sin x \cos x - \sin x \cos 5x)\, dx$

$$= \tfrac{1}{4}\int \sin 2x\, dx - \tfrac{1}{2}\int \tfrac{1}{2}[\sin(x+5x) + \sin(x-5x)]\, dx$$

$$= -\tfrac{1}{8}\cos 2x - \tfrac{1}{4}\int (\sin 6x - \sin 4x)\, dx = -\tfrac{1}{8}\cos 2x + \tfrac{1}{24}\cos 6x - \tfrac{1}{16}\cos 4x + C$$

77. Let $u = x^{3/2}$ so that $u^2 = x^3$ and $du = \tfrac{3}{2}x^{1/2}\, dx \;\Rightarrow\; \sqrt{x}\, dx = \tfrac{2}{3}\, du$. Then

$$\int \frac{\sqrt{x}}{1+x^3}\, dx = \int \frac{\tfrac{2}{3}}{1+u^2}\, du = \frac{2}{3}\tan^{-1}u + C = \frac{2}{3}\tan^{-1}\left(x^{3/2}\right) + C.$$

79. Let $u = x$, $dv = \sin^2 x \cos x\, dx$ $\Rightarrow$ $du = dx$, $v = \frac{1}{3}\sin^3 x$. Then

$$\int x \sin^2 x \cos x\, dx = \frac{1}{3}x\sin^3 x - \int \frac{1}{3}\sin^3 x\, dx = \frac{1}{3}x\sin^3 x - \frac{1}{3}\int(1-\cos^2 x)\sin x\, dx$$

$$= \frac{1}{3}x\sin^3 x + \frac{1}{3}\int(1-y^2)\,dy \qquad \begin{bmatrix} y = \cos x, \\ dy = -\sin x\, dx \end{bmatrix}$$

$$= \frac{1}{3}x\sin^3 x + \frac{1}{3}y - \frac{1}{9}y^3 + C = \frac{1}{3}x\sin^3 x + \frac{1}{3}\cos x - \frac{1}{9}\cos^3 x + C$$

81. The function $y = 2xe^{x^2}$ *does* have an elementary antiderivative, so we'll use this fact to help evaluate the integral.

$$\int(2x^2+1)e^{x^2}\,dx = \int 2x^2 e^{x^2}\,dx + \int e^{x^2}\,dx = \int x(2xe^{x^2})\,dx + \int e^{x^2}\,dx$$

$$= xe^{x^2} - \int e^{x^2}\,dx + \int e^{x^2}\,dx \qquad \begin{bmatrix} u = x, & dv = 2xe^{x^2}\,dx, \\ du = dx & v = e^{x^2} \end{bmatrix} = xe^{x^2} + C$$

8.6 Integration Using Tables and Computer Algebra Systems

Keep in mind that there are several ways to approach many of these exercises, and different methods can lead to different forms of the answer.

1. We could make the substitution $u = \sqrt{2}\,x$ to obtain the radical $\sqrt{7-u^2}$ and then use Formula 33 with $a = \sqrt{7}$. Alternatively, we will factor $\sqrt{2}$ out of the radical and use $a = \sqrt{\frac{7}{2}}$.

$$\int \frac{\sqrt{7-2x^2}}{x^2}\,dx = \sqrt{2}\int \frac{\sqrt{\frac{7}{2}-x^2}}{x^2}\,dx \overset{33}{=} \sqrt{2}\left[-\frac{1}{x}\sqrt{\frac{7}{2}-x^2} - \sin^{-1}\frac{x}{\sqrt{\frac{7}{2}}}\right] + C$$

$$= -\frac{1}{x}\sqrt{7-2x^2} - \sqrt{2}\,\sin^{-1}\left(\sqrt{\frac{2}{7}}\,x\right) + C$$

3. Let $u = \pi x$ $\Rightarrow$ $du = \pi\,dx$, so

$$\int \sec^3(\pi x)\,dx = \frac{1}{\pi}\int \sec^3 u\,du \overset{71}{=} \frac{1}{\pi}\left(\frac{1}{2}\sec u \tan u + \frac{1}{2}\ln|\sec u + \tan u|\right) + C$$

$$= \frac{1}{2\pi}\sec \pi x \tan \pi x + \frac{1}{2\pi}\ln|\sec \pi x + \tan \pi x| + C$$

5. $\displaystyle\int_0^1 2x\cos^{-1}x\,dx \overset{91}{=} 2\left[\frac{2x^2-1}{4}\cos^{-1}x - \frac{x\sqrt{1-x^2}}{4}\right]_0^1 = 2\left[\left(\frac{1}{4}\cdot 0 - 0\right) - \left(-\frac{1}{4}\cdot\frac{\pi}{2} - 0\right)\right] = 2\left(\frac{\pi}{8}\right) = \frac{\pi}{4}$

7. By Formula 99 with $a = -3$ and $b = 4$,

$$\int e^{-3x}\cos 4x\,dx = \frac{e^{-3x}}{(-3)^2 + 4^2}(-3\cos 4x + 4\sin 4x) + C = \frac{e^{-3x}}{25}(-3\cos 4x + 4\sin 4x) + C.$$

9. Let $u = 2x$ and $a = 3$. Then $du = 2\,dx$ and

$$\int \frac{dx}{x^2\sqrt{4x^2+9}} = \int \frac{\frac{1}{2}\,du}{\frac{u^2}{4}\sqrt{u^2+a^2}} = 2\int \frac{du}{u^2\sqrt{a^2+u^2}} \overset{28}{=} -2\frac{\sqrt{a^2+u^2}}{a^2 u} + C$$

$$= -2\frac{\sqrt{4x^2+9}}{9\cdot 2x} + C = -\frac{\sqrt{4x^2+9}}{9x} + C$$

11. $\displaystyle\int_{-1}^0 t^2 e^{-t}\,dt \overset{97}{=} \left[\frac{1}{-1}t^2 e^{-t}\right]_{-1}^0 - \frac{2}{-1}\int_{-1}^0 te^{-t}\,dt = e + 2\int_{-1}^0 te^{-t}\,dt \overset{96}{=} e + 2\left[\frac{1}{(-1)^2}(-t-1)e^{-t}\right]_{-1}^0$

$$= e + 2\left[-e^0 + 0\right] = e - 2$$

13. $\displaystyle\int \frac{\tan^3(1/z)}{z^2}\,dz \quad \begin{bmatrix} u = 1/z, \\ du = -dz/z^2 \end{bmatrix} = -\int \tan^3 u\,du \overset{69}{=} -\frac{1}{2}\tan^2 u - \ln|\cos u| + C$

$$= -\frac{1}{2}\tan^2\left(\frac{1}{z}\right) - \ln\left|\cos\left(\frac{1}{z}\right)\right| + C$$

15. Let $u = e^x$. Then $du = e^x\,dx$, so $\int e^x \operatorname{sech}(e^x)\,dx = \int \operatorname{sech} u\,du \overset{107}{=} \tan^{-1}|\sinh u| + C = \tan^{-1}[\sinh(e^x)] + C$

17. Let $z = 6 + 4y - 4y^2 = 6 - (4y^2 - 4y + 1) + 1 = 7 - (2y - 1)^2$, $u = 2y - 1$, and $a = \sqrt{7}$. Then $z = a^2 - u^2$, $du = 2\,dy$, and

$$\int y\sqrt{6 + 4y - 4y^2}\,dy = \int y\sqrt{z}\,dy = \int \tfrac{1}{2}(u+1)\sqrt{a^2 - u^2}\,\tfrac{1}{2}\,du$$

$$= \tfrac{1}{4}\int u\sqrt{a^2 - u^2}\,du + \tfrac{1}{4}\int \sqrt{a^2 - u^2}\,du$$

$$= \tfrac{1}{4}\int \sqrt{a^2 - u^2}\,du - \tfrac{1}{8}\int (-2u)\sqrt{a^2 - u^2}\,du$$

$$\overset{30}{=} \frac{u}{8}\sqrt{a^2 - u^2} + \frac{a^2}{8}\sin^{-1}\left(\frac{u}{a}\right) - \frac{1}{8}\int \sqrt{w}\,dw \quad \begin{bmatrix} w = a^2 - u^2, \\ dw = -2u\,du \end{bmatrix}$$

$$= \frac{2y-1}{8}\sqrt{6 + 4y - 4y^2} + \frac{7}{8}\sin^{-1}\frac{2y-1}{\sqrt{7}} - \frac{1}{8}\cdot\frac{2}{3}w^{3/2} + C$$

$$= \frac{2y-1}{8}\sqrt{6 + 4y - 4y^2} + \frac{7}{8}\sin^{-1}\frac{2y-1}{\sqrt{7}} - \frac{1}{12}(6 + 4y - 4y^2)^{3/2} + C.$$

This can be rewritten as

$$\sqrt{6 + 4y - 4y^2}\left[\frac{1}{8}(2y - 1) - \frac{1}{12}(6 + 4y - 4y^2)\right] + \frac{7}{8}\sin^{-1}\frac{2y-1}{\sqrt{7}} + C$$

$$= \left(\frac{1}{3}y^2 - \frac{1}{12}y - \frac{5}{8}\right)\sqrt{6 + 4y - 4y^2} + \frac{7}{8}\sin^{-1}\left(\frac{2y-1}{\sqrt{7}}\right) + C$$

$$= \frac{1}{24}(8y^2 - 2y - 15)\sqrt{6 + 4y - 4y^2} + \frac{7}{8}\sin^{-1}\left(\frac{2y-1}{\sqrt{7}}\right) + C$$

19. Let $u = \sin x$. Then $du = \cos x\,dx$, so

$$\int \sin^2 x \cos x \ln(\sin x)\,dx = \int u^2 \ln u\,du \overset{101}{=} \frac{u^{2+1}}{(2+1)^2}[(2+1)\ln u - 1] + C = \tfrac{1}{9}u^3(3\ln u - 1) + C$$

$$= \tfrac{1}{9}\sin^3 x\,[3\ln(\sin x) - 1] + C$$

21. Let $u = e^x$ and $a = \sqrt{3}$. Then $du = e^x\,dx$ and

$$\int \frac{e^x}{3 - e^{2x}}\,dx = \int \frac{du}{a^2 - u^2} \overset{19}{=} \frac{1}{2a}\ln\left|\frac{u + a}{u - a}\right| + C = \frac{1}{2\sqrt{3}}\ln\left|\frac{e^x + \sqrt{3}}{e^x - \sqrt{3}}\right| + C.$$

23. $\int \sec^5 x\,dx \overset{77}{=} \tfrac{1}{4}\tan x \sec^3 x + \tfrac{3}{4}\int \sec^3 x\,dx \overset{77}{=} \tfrac{1}{4}\tan x \sec^3 x + \tfrac{3}{4}\left(\tfrac{1}{2}\tan x \sec x + \tfrac{1}{2}\int \sec x\,dx\right)$

$\overset{14}{=} \tfrac{1}{4}\tan x \sec^3 x + \tfrac{3}{8}\tan x \sec x + \tfrac{3}{8}\ln|\sec x + \tan x| + C$

25. Let $u = \ln x$ and $a = 2$. Then $du = \dfrac{dx}{x}$ and

$$\int \frac{\sqrt{4 + (\ln x)^2}}{x}\,dx = \int \sqrt{a^2 + u^2}\,du \overset{21}{=} \frac{u}{2}\sqrt{a^2 + u^2} + \frac{a^2}{2}\ln\left(u + \sqrt{a^2 + u^2}\right) + C$$

$$= \tfrac{1}{2}(\ln x)\sqrt{4 + (\ln x)^2} + 2\ln\left[\ln x + \sqrt{4 + (\ln x)^2}\right] + C$$

27. Let $u = e^x$. Then $x = \ln u$, $dx = du/u$, so

$$\int \sqrt{e^{2x} - 1}\,dx = \int \frac{\sqrt{u^2 - 1}}{u}\,du \overset{41}{=} \sqrt{u^2 - 1} - \cos^{-1}(1/u) + C = \sqrt{e^{2x} - 1} - \cos^{-1}\left(e^{-x}\right) + C.$$

29. $\displaystyle\int \frac{x^4\,dx}{\sqrt{x^{10}-2}} = \int \frac{x^4\,dx}{\sqrt{(x^5)^2-2}} = \frac{1}{5}\int \frac{du}{\sqrt{u^2-2}}$ $\qquad [u=x^5,\ du=5x^4\,dx]$

$\qquad\qquad \overset{43}{=} \frac{1}{5}\ln\left|u+\sqrt{u^2-2}\right|+C = \frac{1}{5}\ln\left|x^5+\sqrt{x^{10}-2}\right|+C$

31. Using cylindrical shells, we get

$$V = 2\pi\int_0^2 x\cdot x\sqrt{4-x^2}\,dx = 2\pi\int_0^2 x^2\sqrt{4-x^2}\,dx \overset{31}{=} 2\pi\left[\frac{x}{8}(2x^2-4)\sqrt{4-x^2}+\frac{16}{8}\sin^{-1}\frac{x}{2}\right]_0^2$$

$$= 2\pi\left[(0+2\sin^{-1}1)-(0+2\sin^{-1}0)\right] = 2\pi\left(2\cdot\frac{\pi}{2}\right) = 2\pi^2$$

33. (a) $\displaystyle\frac{d}{du}\left[\frac{1}{b^3}\left(a+bu-\frac{a^2}{a+bu}-2a\ln|a+bu|\right)+C\right] = \frac{1}{b^3}\left[b+\frac{ba^2}{(a+bu)^2}-\frac{2ab}{(a+bu)}\right]$

$\qquad\qquad = \frac{1}{b^3}\left[\frac{b(a+bu)^2+ba^2-(a+bu)2ab}{(a+bu)^2}\right] = \frac{1}{b^3}\left[\frac{b^3u^2}{(a+bu)^2}\right] = \frac{u^2}{(a+bu)^2}$

(b) Let $t=a+bu \Rightarrow dt=b\,du$. Note that $u=\dfrac{t-a}{b}$ and $du=\dfrac{1}{b}\,dt$.

$$\int\frac{u^2\,du}{(a+bu)^2} = \frac{1}{b^3}\int\frac{(t-a)^2}{t^2}\,dt = \frac{1}{b^3}\int\frac{t^2-2at+a^2}{t^2}\,dt$$

$$= \frac{1}{b^3}\int\left(1-\frac{2a}{t}+\frac{a^2}{t^2}\right)dt = \frac{1}{b^3}\left(t-2a\ln|t|-\frac{a^2}{t}\right)+C$$

$$= \frac{1}{b^3}\left(a+bu-\frac{a^2}{a+bu}-2a\ln|a+bu|\right)+C$$

35. Maple, Mathematica and Derive all give $\int x^2\sqrt{5-x^2}\,dx = -\frac{1}{4}x(5-x^2)^{3/2}+\frac{5}{8}x\sqrt{5-x^2}+\frac{25}{8}\sin^{-1}\left(\frac{1}{\sqrt5}x\right)$.

Using Formula 31, we get $\int x^2\sqrt{5-x^2}\,dx = \frac{1}{8}x(2x^2-5)\sqrt{5-x^2}+\frac{1}{8}(5^2)\sin^{-1}\left(\frac{1}{\sqrt5}x\right)+C$. But

$-\frac{1}{4}x(5-x^2)^{3/2}+\frac{5}{8}x\sqrt{5-x^2} = \frac{1}{8}x\sqrt{5-x^2}\left[5-2(5-x^2)\right] = \frac{1}{8}x(2x^2-5)\sqrt{5-x^2}$, and the $\sin^{-1}$ terms

are the same in each expression, so the answers are equivalent.

37. Maple and Derive both give $\int \sin^3 x\cos^2 x\,dx = -\frac{1}{5}\sin^2 x\cos^3 x - \frac{2}{15}\cos^3 x$ (although Derive factors the

expression), and Mathematica gives $\int \sin^3 x\cos^2 x\,dx = -\frac{1}{8}\cos x - \frac{1}{48}\cos 3x + \frac{1}{80}\cos 5x$. We can use a CAS to

show that both of these expressions are equal to $-\frac{1}{3}\cos^3 x + \frac{1}{5}\cos^5 x$. Using Formula 86, we write

$$\int \sin^3 x\cos^2 x\,dx = -\frac{1}{5}\sin^2 x\cos^3 x + \frac{2}{5}\int \sin x\cos^2 x\,dx = -\frac{1}{5}\sin^2 x\cos^3 x + \frac{2}{5}\left(-\frac{1}{3}\cos^3 x\right)+C$$

$$= -\frac{1}{5}\sin^2 x\cos^3 x - \frac{2}{15}\cos^3 x + C$$

39. Maple gives $\int x\sqrt{1+2x}\,dx = \frac{1}{10}(1+2x)^{5/2}-\frac{1}{6}(1+2x)^{3/2}$, Mathematica gives $\sqrt{1+2x}\left(\frac{2}{5}x^2+\frac{1}{15}x-\frac{1}{15}\right)$,

and Derive gives $\frac{1}{15}(1+2x)^{3/2}(3x-1)$. The first two expressions can be simplified to Derive's result. If we use

Formula 54, we get

$$\int x\sqrt{1+2x}\,dx = \frac{2}{15(2)^2}(3\cdot 2x-2\cdot 1)(1+2x)^{3/2}+C = \frac{1}{30}(6x-2)(1+2x)^{3/2}+C$$

$$= \frac{1}{15}(3x-1)(1+2x)^{3/2}$$

41. Maple gives $\int \tan^5 x \, dx = \frac{1}{4} \tan^4 x - \frac{1}{2} \tan^2 x + \frac{1}{2} \ln\left(1 + \tan^2 x\right)$, Mathematica

gives $\int \tan^5 x \, dx = \frac{1}{4}[-1 - 2\cos(2x)] \sec^4 x - \ln(\cos x)$, and Derive gives

$\int \tan^5 x \, dx = \frac{1}{4} \tan^4 x - \frac{1}{2} \tan^2 x - \ln(\cos x)$. These expressions are equivalent, and none includes absolute

value bars or a constant of integration. Note that Mathematica's and Derive's expressions suggest that the integral is

undefined where $\cos x < 0$, which is not the case.

Using Formula 75, $\int \tan^5 x \, dx = \frac{1}{5-1} \tan^{5-1} x - \int \tan^{5-2} x \, dx = \frac{1}{4} \tan^4 x - \int \tan^3 x \, dx$. Using Formula 69,

$\int \tan^3 x \, dx = \frac{1}{2} \tan^2 x + \ln|\cos x| + C$, so $\int \tan^5 x \, dx = \frac{1}{4} \tan^4 x - \frac{1}{2} \tan^2 x - \ln|\cos x| + C$.

43. Derive gives $I = \int 2^x \sqrt{4^x - 1} \, dx = \dfrac{2^{x-1} \sqrt{2^{2x} - 1}}{\ln 2} - \dfrac{\ln\left(\sqrt{2^{2x} - 1} + 2^x\right)}{2 \ln 2}$ immediately. Neither Maple nor

Mathematica is able to evaluate I in its given form. However, if we instead write I as $\int 2^x \sqrt{(2^x)^2 - 1} \, dx$, both

systems give the same answer as Derive (after minor simplification). Our trick works because the CAS now

recognizes 2^x as a promising substitution.

45. Maple gives the antiderivative

$$F(x) = \int \frac{x^2 - 1}{x^4 + x^2 + 1} \, dx = -\frac{1}{2} \ln\left(x^2 + x + 1\right) + \frac{1}{2} \ln\left(x^2 - x + 1\right).$$

We can see that at 0, this antiderivative is 0. From the graphs, it appears

that F has a maximum at $x = -1$ and a minimum at $x = 1$ [since

$F'(x) = f(x)$ changes sign at these x-values], and that F has inflection

points at $x \approx -1.7$, $x = 0$, and $x \approx 1.7$ [since $f(x)$ has extrema at these

x-values].

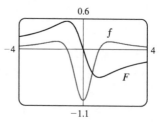

47. Since $f(x) = \sin^4 x \cos^6 x$ is everywhere positive, we know that its antiderivative F is increasing. Maple gives

$\int f(x) \, dx = -\frac{1}{10} \sin^3 x \cos^7 x - \frac{3}{80} \sin x \cos^7 x + \frac{1}{160} \cos^5 x \sin x + \frac{1}{128} \cos^3 x \sin x + \frac{3}{256} \cos x \sin x + \frac{3}{256} x$

and this expression is 0 at $x = 0$.

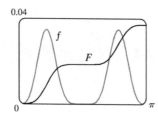

F has a minimum at $x = 0$ and a maximum at $x = \pi$. F has inflection points where f' changes sign, that is, at

$x \approx 0.7$, $x = \pi/2$, and $x \approx 2.5$.

8.7 Approximate Integration

1. (a) $\Delta x = (b - a)/n = (4 - 0)/2 = 2$

$$L_2 = \sum_{i=1}^{2} f(x_{i-1}) \, \Delta x = f(x_0) \cdot 2 + f(x_1) \cdot 2 = 2 \left[f(0) + f(2) \right] = 2(0.5 + 2.5) = 6$$

$$R_2 = \sum_{i=1}^{2} f(x_i) \, \Delta x = f(x_1) \cdot 2 + f(x_2) \cdot 2 = 2 \left[f(2) + f(4) \right] = 2(2.5 + 3.5) = 12$$

$$M_2 = \sum_{i=1}^{2} f(\overline{x}_i) \Delta x = f(\overline{x}_1) \cdot 2 + f(\overline{x}_2) \cdot 2 = 2 \left[f(1) + f(3) \right] \approx 2(1.6 + 3.2) = 9.6$$

(b)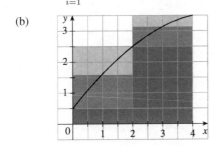

L_2 is an underestimate, since the area under the small rectangles is less than the area under the curve, and R_2 is an overestimate, since the area under the large rectangles is greater than the area under the curve. It appears that M_2 is an overestimate, though it is fairly close to I. See the solution to Exercise 45 for a proof of the fact that if f is concave down on $[a, b]$, then the Midpoint Rule is an overestimate of $\int_a^b f(x) \, dx$.

(c) $T_2 = \left(\frac{1}{2} \Delta x \right) [f(x_0) + 2f(x_1) + f(x_2)] = \frac{2}{2} [f(0) + 2f(2) + f(4)] = 0.5 + 2(2.5) + 3.5 = 9$.

This approximation is an underestimate, since the graph is concave down. Thus, $T_2 = 9 < I$. See the solution to Exercise 45 for a general proof of this conclusion.

(d) For any n, we will have $L_n < T_n < I < M_n < R_n$.

3. $f(x) = \cos(x^2)$, $\Delta x = \frac{1 - 0}{4} = \frac{1}{4}$

(a) $T_4 = \frac{1}{4 \cdot 2} \left[f(0) + 2f\left(\frac{1}{4} \right) + 2f\left(\frac{2}{4} \right) + 2f\left(\frac{3}{4} \right) + f(1) \right] \approx 0.895759$

(b) $M_4 = \frac{1}{4} \left[f\left(\frac{1}{8} \right) + f\left(\frac{3}{8} \right) + f\left(\frac{5}{8} \right) + f\left(\frac{7}{8} \right) \right] \approx 0.908907$

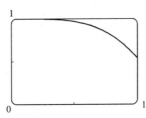

The graph shows that f is concave down on $[0, 1]$. So T_4 is an underestimate and M_4 is an overestimate. We can conclude that $0.895759 < \int_0^1 \cos(x^2) \, dx < 0.908907$.

5. $f(x) = x^2 \sin x$, $\Delta x = \dfrac{b - a}{n} = \dfrac{\pi - 0}{8} = \dfrac{\pi}{8}$

(a) $M_8 = \frac{\pi}{8} \left[f\left(\frac{\pi}{16} \right) + f\left(\frac{3\pi}{16} \right) + f\left(\frac{5\pi}{16} \right) + \cdots + f\left(\frac{15\pi}{16} \right) \right] \approx 5.932957$

(b) $S_8 = \frac{\pi}{8 \cdot 3} \left[f(0) + 4f\left(\frac{\pi}{8} \right) + 2f\left(\frac{2\pi}{8} \right) + 4f\left(\frac{3\pi}{8} \right) + 2f\left(\frac{4\pi}{8} \right) + 4f\left(\frac{5\pi}{8} \right) + 2f\left(\frac{6\pi}{8} \right) + 4f\left(\frac{7\pi}{8} \right) + f(\pi) \right]$
   ≈ 5.869247

Actual: $\int_0^\pi x^2 \sin x \, dx \overset{84}{=} \left[-x^2 \cos x \right]_0^\pi + 2 \int_0^\pi x \cos x \, dx \overset{83}{=} \left[-\pi^2 (-1) - 0 \right] + 2[\cos x + x \sin x]_0^\pi$
   $= \pi^2 + 2[(-1 + 0) - (1 + 0)] = \pi^2 - 4 \approx 5.869604$

Errors: $E_M = $ actual $- M_8 = \int_0^\pi x^2 \sin x \, dx - M_8 \approx -0.063353$

$E_S = $ actual $- S_8 = \int_0^\pi x^2 \sin x \, dx - S_8 \approx 0.000357$

7. $f(x) = \sqrt[4]{1+x^2}, \Delta x = \dfrac{2-0}{8} = \dfrac{1}{4}$

(a) $T_8 = \frac{1}{4 \cdot 2}\left[f(0) + 2f\left(\frac{1}{4}\right) + 2f\left(\frac{1}{2}\right) + \cdots + 2f\left(\frac{3}{2}\right) + 2f\left(\frac{7}{4}\right) + f(2)\right] \approx 2.413790$

(b) $M_8 = \frac{1}{4}\left[f\left(\frac{1}{8}\right) + f\left(\frac{3}{8}\right) + \cdots + f\left(\frac{13}{8}\right) + f\left(\frac{15}{8}\right)\right] \approx 2.411453$

(c) $S_8 = \frac{1}{4 \cdot 3}\left[f(0) + 4f\left(\frac{1}{4}\right) + 2f\left(\frac{1}{2}\right) + 4f\left(\frac{3}{4}\right) + 2f(1) + 4f\left(\frac{5}{4}\right) + 2f\left(\frac{3}{2}\right) + 4f\left(\frac{7}{4}\right) + f(2)\right] \approx 2.412232$

9. $f(x) = \dfrac{\ln x}{1+x}, \Delta x = \dfrac{2-1}{10} = \dfrac{1}{10}$

(a) $T_{10} = \frac{1}{10 \cdot 2}[f(1) + 2f(1.1) + 2f(1.2) + \cdots + 2f(1.8) + 2f(1.9) + f(2)] \approx 0.146879$

(b) $M_{10} = \frac{1}{10}[f(1.05) + f(1.15) + \cdots + f(1.85) + f(1.95)] \approx 0.147391$

(c) $S_{10} = \frac{1}{10 \cdot 3}[f(1) + 4f(1.1) + 2f(1.2) + 4f(1.3) + 2f(1.4) + 4f(1.5) + 2f(1.6) + 4f(1.7)$
$\qquad\qquad + 2f(1.8) + 4f(1.9) + f(2)]$

$\qquad \approx 0.147219$

11. $f(t) = \sin(e^{t/2}), \Delta t = \dfrac{\frac{1}{2} - 0}{8} = \dfrac{1}{16}$

(a) $T_8 = \frac{1}{16 \cdot 2}\left[f(0) + 2f\left(\frac{1}{16}\right) + 2f\left(\frac{2}{16}\right) + \cdots + 2f\left(\frac{7}{16}\right) + f\left(\frac{1}{2}\right)\right] \approx 0.451948$

(b) $M_8 = \frac{1}{16}\left[f\left(\frac{1}{32}\right) + f\left(\frac{3}{32}\right) + f\left(\frac{5}{32}\right) + \cdots + f\left(\frac{13}{32}\right) + f\left(\frac{15}{32}\right)\right] \approx 0.451991$

(c) $S_8 = \frac{1}{16 \cdot 3}\left[f(0) + 4f\left(\frac{1}{16}\right) + 2f\left(\frac{2}{16}\right) + \cdots + 4f\left(\frac{7}{16}\right) + f\left(\frac{1}{2}\right)\right] \approx 0.451976$

13. $f(x) = e^{1/x}, \Delta x = \dfrac{2-1}{4} = \dfrac{1}{4}$

(a) $T_4 = \frac{1}{4 \cdot 2}[f(1) + 2f(1.25) + 2f(1.5) + 2f(1.75) + f(2)] \approx 2.031893$

(b) $M_4 = \frac{1}{4}[f(1.125) + f(1.375) + f(1.625) + f(1.875)] \approx 2.014207$

(c) $S_4 = \frac{1}{4 \cdot 3}[f(1) + 4f(1.25) + 2f(1.5) + 4f(1.75) + f(2)] \approx 2.020651$

15. $f(x) = \dfrac{\cos x}{x}, \Delta x = \dfrac{5-1}{8} = \dfrac{1}{2}$

(a) $T_8 = \frac{1}{2 \cdot 2}\left[f(1) + 2f\left(\frac{3}{2}\right) + 2f(2) + \cdots + 2f(4) + 2f\left(\frac{9}{2}\right) + f(5)\right] \approx -0.495333$

(b) $M_8 = \frac{1}{2}\left[f\left(\frac{5}{4}\right) + f\left(\frac{7}{4}\right) + f\left(\frac{9}{4}\right) + f\left(\frac{11}{4}\right) + f\left(\frac{13}{4}\right) + f\left(\frac{15}{4}\right) + f\left(\frac{17}{4}\right) + f\left(\frac{19}{4}\right)\right] \approx -0.543321$

(c) $S_8 = \frac{1}{2 \cdot 3}\left[f(1) + 4f\left(\frac{3}{2}\right) + 2f(2) + 4f\left(\frac{5}{2}\right) + 2f(3) + 4f\left(\frac{7}{2}\right) + 2f(4) + 4f\left(\frac{9}{2}\right) + f(5)\right]$
$\qquad \approx -0.526123$

17. $f(y) = \dfrac{1}{1+y^5}, \Delta y = \dfrac{3-0}{6} = \dfrac{1}{2}$

(a) $T_6 = \frac{1}{2 \cdot 2}\left[f(0) + 2f\left(\frac{1}{2}\right) + 2f\left(\frac{2}{2}\right) + 2f\left(\frac{3}{2}\right) + 2f\left(\frac{4}{2}\right) + 2f\left(\frac{5}{2}\right) + f(3)\right] \approx 1.064275$

(b) $M_6 = \frac{1}{2}\left[f\left(\frac{1}{4}\right) + f\left(\frac{3}{4}\right) + f\left(\frac{5}{4}\right) + f\left(\frac{7}{4}\right) + f\left(\frac{9}{4}\right) + f\left(\frac{11}{4}\right)\right] \approx 1.067416$

(c) $S_6 = \frac{1}{2 \cdot 3}\left[f(0) + 4f\left(\frac{1}{2}\right) + 2f\left(\frac{2}{2}\right) + 4f\left(\frac{3}{2}\right) + 2f\left(\frac{4}{2}\right) + 4f\left(\frac{5}{2}\right) + f(3)\right] \approx 1.074915$

19. $f(x) = e^{-x^2}$, $\Delta x = \dfrac{2-0}{10} = \dfrac{1}{5}$

(a) $T_{10} = \frac{1}{5 \cdot 2}\{f(0) + 2[f(0.2) + f(0.4) + \cdots + f(1.8)] + f(2)\} \approx 0.881839$

$M_{10} = \frac{1}{5}[f(0.1) + f(0.3) + f(0.5) + \cdots + f(1.7) + f(1.9)] \approx 0.882202$

(b) $f(x) = e^{-x^2}$, $f'(x) = -2xe^{-x^2}$, $f''(x) = (4x^2 - 2)e^{-x^2}$, $f'''(x) = 4x(3 - 2x^2)e^{-x^2}$.

$f'''(x) = 0 \iff x = 0$ or $x = \pm\sqrt{\frac{3}{2}}$. So to find the maximum value of $|f''(x)|$ on $[0, 2]$, we need only

consider its values at $x = 0$, $x = 2$, and $x = \sqrt{\frac{3}{2}}$. $|f''(0)| = 2$, $|f''(2)| \approx 0.2564$ and $\left|f''\left(\sqrt{\frac{3}{2}}\right)\right| \approx 0.8925$.

Thus, taking $K = 2$, $a = 0$, $b = 2$, and $n = 10$ in Theorem 3, we get $|E_T| \leq 2 \cdot 2^3 / (12 \cdot 10^2) = \frac{1}{75} = 0.01\overline{3}$,

and $|E_M| \leq |E_T|/2 \leq 0.00\overline{6}$.

(c) Take $K = 2$ [as in part (b)] in Theorem 3. $|E_T| \leq \dfrac{K(b-a)^3}{12n^2} \leq 10^{-5} \iff \dfrac{2(2-0)^3}{12n^2} \leq 10^{-5} \iff$

$\frac{3}{4}n^2 \geq 10^5 \iff n \geq 365.1\ldots \iff n \geq 366$. Take $n = 366$ for T_n. For E_M, again take $K = 2$ in

Theorem 3 to get $|E_M| \leq 10^{-5} \iff \frac{3}{2}n^2 \geq 10^5 \iff n \geq 258.2 \Rightarrow n \geq 259$. Take $n = 259$ for M_n.

21. (a) $T_{10} = \frac{1}{10 \cdot 2}\{f(0) + 2[f(0.1) + f(0.2) + \cdots + f(0.9)] + f(1)\} \approx 1.71971349$

$S_{10} = \frac{1}{10 \cdot 3}[f(0) + 4f(0.1) + 2f(0.2) + 4f(0.3) + \cdots + 4f(0.9) + f(1)] \approx 1.71828278$

Since $I = \int_0^1 e^x\,dx = [e^x]_0^1 = e - 1 \approx 1.71828183$, $E_T = I - T_{10} \approx -0.00143166$ and

$E_S = I - S_{10} \approx -0.00000095$.

(b) $f(x) = e^x \Rightarrow f''(x) = e^x \leq e$ for $0 \leq x \leq 1$. Taking $K = e$, $a = 0$, $b = 1$, and $n = 10$ in Theorem 3, we

get $|E_T| \leq e(1)^3/(12 \cdot 10^2) \approx 0.002265 > 0.00143166$ [actual $|E_T|$ from (a)]. $f^{(4)}(x) = e^x < e$ for

$0 \leq x \leq 1$. Using Theorem 4, we have $|E_S| \leq e(1)^5/(180 \cdot 10^4) \approx 0.0000015 > 0.00000095$ [actual $|E_S|$

from (a)]. We see that the actual errors are about two-thirds the size of the error estimates.

(c) From part (b), we take $K = e$ to get $|E_T| \leq \dfrac{K(b-a)^3}{12n^2} \leq 0.00001 \Rightarrow n^2 \geq \dfrac{e(1^3)}{12(0.00001)} \Rightarrow$

$n \geq 150.5$. Take $n = 151$ for T_n. Now $|E_M| \leq \dfrac{K(b-a)^3}{24n^2} \leq 0.00001 \Rightarrow n \geq 106.4$. Take $n = 107$ for

M_n. Finally, $|E_S| \leq \dfrac{K(b-a)^5}{180n^4} \leq 0.00001 \Rightarrow n^4 \geq \dfrac{e(1^5)}{180(0.00001)} \Rightarrow n \geq 6.23$. Take $n = 8$ for S_n

(since n has to be even for Simpson's Rule).

23. (a) Using a CAS, we differentiate $f(x) = e^{\cos x}$ twice, and find that

$f''(x) = e^{\cos x}(\sin^2 x - \cos x)$. From the graph, we see that the

maximum value of $|f''(x)|$ occurs at the endpoints of the

interval $[0, 2\pi]$. Since $f''(0) = -e$, we can use $K = e$ or $K = 2.8$.

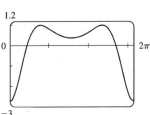

(b) A CAS gives $M_{10} \approx 7.954926518$. (In Maple, use `student[middlesum]`.)

(c) Using Theorem 3 for the Midpoint Rule, with $K = e$, we get $|E_M| \leq \dfrac{e(2\pi - 0)^3}{24 \cdot 10^2} \approx 0.280945995$. With

$K = 2.8$, we get $|E_M| \leq \dfrac{2.8(2\pi - 0)^3}{24 \cdot 10^2} = 0.289391916$.

(d) A CAS gives $I \approx 7.954926521$.

(e) The actual error is only about 3×10^{-9}, much less than the estimate in part (c).

(f) We use the CAS to differentiate twice more, and then graph

$$f^{(4)}(x) = e^{\cos x}\left(\sin^4 x - 6\sin^2 x \,\cos x + 3 - 7\sin^2 x + \cos x\right).$$

From the graph, we see that the maximum value of $\left|f^{(4)}(x)\right|$ occurs

at the endpoints of the interval $[0, 2\pi]$. Since $f^{(4)}(0) = 4e$, we can use

$K = 4e$ or $K = 10.9$.

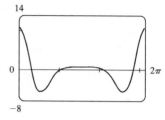

(g) A CAS gives $S_{10} \approx 7.953789422$. (In Maple, use `student[simpson]`.)

(h) Using Theorem 4 with $K = 4e$, we get $|E_S| \leq \dfrac{4e(2\pi - 0)^5}{180 \cdot 10^4} \approx 0.059153618$. With $K = 10.9$, we get

$|E_S| \leq \dfrac{10.9(2\pi - 0)^5}{180 \cdot 10^4} \approx 0.059299814$.

(i) The actual error is about $7.954926521 - 7.953789422 \approx 0.00114$. This is quite a bit smaller than the estimate in part (h), though the difference is not nearly as great as it was in the case of the Midpoint Rule.

(j) To ensure that $|E_S| \leq 0.0001$, we use Theorem 4: $|E_S| \leq \dfrac{4e(2\pi)^5}{180 \cdot n^4} \leq 0.0001 \quad \Rightarrow \quad \dfrac{4e(2\pi)^5}{180 \cdot 0.0001} \leq n^4 \quad \Rightarrow$

$n^4 \geq 5{,}915{,}362 \quad \Leftrightarrow \quad n \geq 49.3$. So we must take $n \geq 50$ to ensure that $|I - S_n| \leq 0.0001$. ($K = 10.9$ leads to the same value of n.)

25. $I = \int_0^1 x^3 \, dx = \left[\tfrac{1}{4}x^4\right]_0^1 = 0.25.\ f(x) = x^3.$

$n = 4$: $\quad L_4 = \tfrac{1}{4}\left[0^3 + \left(\tfrac{1}{4}\right)^3 + \left(\tfrac{2}{4}\right)^3 + \left(\tfrac{3}{4}\right)^3\right] = 0.140625$

$\qquad\quad R_4 = \tfrac{1}{4}\left[\left(\tfrac{1}{4}\right)^3 + \left(\tfrac{2}{4}\right)^3 + \left(\tfrac{3}{4}\right)^3 + 1^3\right] = 0.390625$

$\qquad\quad T_4 = \tfrac{1}{4 \cdot 2}\left[0^3 + 2\left(\tfrac{1}{4}\right)^3 + 2\left(\tfrac{2}{4}\right)^3 + 2\left(\tfrac{3}{4}\right)^3 + 1^3\right] = 0.265625,$

$\qquad\quad M_4 = \tfrac{1}{4}\left[\left(\tfrac{1}{8}\right)^3 + \left(\tfrac{3}{8}\right)^3 + \left(\tfrac{5}{8}\right)^3 + \left(\tfrac{7}{8}\right)^3\right] = 0.2421875,$

$\qquad\quad E_L = I - L_4 = \tfrac{1}{4} - 0.140625 = 0.109375,\ E_R = \tfrac{1}{4} - 0.390625 = -0.140625,$

$\qquad\quad E_T = \tfrac{1}{4} - 0.265625 = -0.015625,\ E_M = \tfrac{1}{4} - 0.2421875 = 0.0078125$

$n = 8$: $\quad L_8 = \tfrac{1}{8}\left[f(0) + f\left(\tfrac{1}{8}\right) + f\left(\tfrac{2}{8}\right) + \cdots + f\left(\tfrac{7}{8}\right)\right] \approx 0.191406$

$\qquad\quad R_8 = \tfrac{1}{8}\left[f\left(\tfrac{1}{8}\right) + f\left(\tfrac{2}{8}\right) + \cdots + f\left(\tfrac{7}{8}\right) + f(1)\right] \approx 0.316406$

$\qquad\quad T_8 = \tfrac{1}{8 \cdot 2}\left\{f(0) + 2\left[f\left(\tfrac{1}{8}\right) + f\left(\tfrac{2}{8}\right) + \cdots + f\left(\tfrac{7}{8}\right)\right] + f(1)\right\} \approx 0.253906$

$\qquad\quad M_8 = \tfrac{1}{8}\left[f\left(\tfrac{1}{16}\right) + f\left(\tfrac{3}{16}\right) + \cdots + f\left(\tfrac{13}{16}\right) + f\left(\tfrac{15}{16}\right)\right] = 0.248047$

$\qquad\quad E_L \approx \tfrac{1}{4} - 0.191406 \approx 0.058594,\ E_R \approx \tfrac{1}{4} - 0.316406 \approx -0.066406,$

$\qquad\quad E_T \approx \tfrac{1}{4} - 0.253906 \approx -0.003906,\ E_M \approx \tfrac{1}{4} - 0.248047 \approx 0.001953.$

[continued]

$n = 16$: $L_{16} = \frac{1}{16}\left[f(0) + f\left(\frac{1}{16}\right) + f\left(\frac{2}{16}\right) + \cdots + f\left(\frac{15}{16}\right)\right] \approx 0.219727$

$R_{16} = \frac{1}{16}\left[f\left(\frac{1}{16}\right) + f\left(\frac{2}{16}\right) + \cdots + f\left(\frac{15}{16}\right) + f(1)\right] \approx 0.282227$

$T_{16} = \frac{1}{16 \cdot 2}\left\{f(0) + 2\left[f\left(\frac{1}{16}\right) + f\left(\frac{2}{16}\right) + \cdots + f\left(\frac{15}{16}\right)\right] + f(1)\right\} \approx 0.250977$

$M_{16} = \frac{1}{16}\left[f\left(\frac{1}{32}\right) + f\left(\frac{3}{32}\right) + \cdots + f\left(\frac{31}{32}\right)\right] \approx 0.249512$

$E_L \approx \frac{1}{4} - 0.219727 \approx 0.030273,\ E_R \approx \frac{1}{4} - 0.282227 \approx -0.032227,$

$E_T \approx \frac{1}{4} - 0.250977 \approx -0.000977,\ E_M \approx \frac{1}{4} - 0.249512 \approx 0.000488.$

n	L_n	R_n	T_n	M_n
4	0.140625	0.390625	0.265625	0.242188
8	0.191406	0.316406	0.253906	0.248047
16	0.219727	0.282227	0.250977	0.249512

n	E_L	E_R	E_T	E_M
4	0.109375	−0.140625	−0.015625	0.007813
8	0.058594	−0.066406	−0.003906	0.001953
16	0.030273	−0.032227	−0.000977	0.000488

Observations:

1. E_L and E_R are always opposite in sign, as are E_T and E_M.

2. As n is doubled, E_L and E_R are decreased by about a factor of 2, and E_T and E_M are decreased by a factor of about 4.

3. The Midpoint approximation is about twice as accurate as the Trapezoidal approximation.

4. All the approximations become more accurate as the value of n increases.

5. The Midpoint and Trapezoidal approximations are much more accurate than the endpoint approximations.

27. $\int_1^4 \sqrt{x}\, dx = \left[\frac{2}{3}x^{3/2}\right]_1^4 = \frac{2}{3}(8 - 1) = \frac{14}{3} \approx 4.666667$

$n = 6$: $\Delta x = (4 - 1)/6 = \frac{1}{2}$

$T_6 = \frac{1}{2 \cdot 2}\left[\sqrt{1} + 2\sqrt{1.5} + 2\sqrt{2} + 2\sqrt{2.5} + 2\sqrt{3} + 2\sqrt{3.5} + \sqrt{4}\right] \approx 4.661488$

$M_6 = \frac{1}{2}\left[\sqrt{1.25} + \sqrt{1.75} + \sqrt{2.25} + \sqrt{2.75} + \sqrt{3.25} + \sqrt{3.75}\right] \approx 4.669245$

$S_6 = \frac{1}{2 \cdot 3}\left[\sqrt{1} + 4\sqrt{1.5} + 2\sqrt{2} + 4\sqrt{2.5} + 2\sqrt{3} + 4\sqrt{3.5} + \sqrt{4}\right] \approx 4.666563$

$E_T \approx \frac{14}{3} - 4.661488 \approx 0.005178,\quad E_M \approx \frac{14}{3} - 4.669245 \approx -0.002578,$

$E_S \approx \frac{14}{3} - 4.666563 \approx 0.000104.$

$n = 12$: $\Delta x = (4 - 1)/12 = \frac{1}{4}$

$T_{12} = \frac{1}{4 \cdot 2}\left(f(1) + 2\left[f(1.25) + f(1.5) + \cdots + f(3.5) + f(3.75)\right] + f(4)\right) \approx 4.665367$

$M_{12} = \frac{1}{4}\left[f(1.125) + f(1.375) + f(1.625) + \cdots + f(3.875)\right] \approx 4.667316$

$S_{12} = \frac{1}{4 \cdot 3}\left[f(1) + 4f(1.25) + 2f(1.5) + 4f(1.75) + \cdots + 4f(3.75) + f(4)\right] \approx 4.666659$

$E_T \approx \frac{14}{3} - 4.665367 \approx 0.001300,\quad E_M \approx \frac{14}{3} - 4.667316 \approx -0.000649,$

$E_S \approx \frac{14}{3} - 4.666659 \approx 0.000007.$

Note: These errors were computed more precisely and then rounded to six places. That is, they were not computed by comparing the rounded values of T_n, M_n, and S_n with the rounded value of the actual integral.

n	T_n	M_n	S_n
6	4.661488	4.669245	4.666563
12	4.665367	4.667316	4.666659

n	E_T	E_M	E_S
6	0.005178	−0.002578	0.000104
12	0.001300	−0.000649	0.000007

Observations:

1. E_T and E_M are opposite in sign and decrease by a factor of about 4 as n is doubled.

2. The Simpson's approximation is much more accurate than the Midpoint and Trapezoidal approximations, and seems to decrease by a factor of about 16 as n is doubled.

29. $\Delta x = (4 - 0)/4 = 1$

(a) $T_4 = \frac{1}{2}[f(0) + 2f(1) + 2f(2) + 2f(3) + f(4)] \approx \frac{1}{2}[0 + 2(3) + 2(5) + 2(3) + 1] = 11.5$

(b) $M_4 = 1 \cdot [f(0.5) + f(1.5) + f(2.5) + f(3.5)] \approx 1 + 4.5 + 4.5 + 2 = 12$

(c) $S_4 = \frac{1}{3}[f(0) + 4f(1) + 2f(2) + 4f(3) + f(4)] \approx \frac{1}{3}[0 + 4(3) + 2(5) + 4(3) + 1] = 11.\overline{6}$

31. (a) We are given the function values at the endpoints of 8 intervals of length 0.4, so we'll use the Midpoint Rule with $n = 8/2 = 4$ and $\Delta x = (3.2 - 0)/4 = 0.8$.

$$\int_0^{3.2} f(x)\,dx \approx M_4 = 0.8[f(0.4) + f(1.2) + f(2.0) + f(2.8)]$$
$$= 0.8[6.5 + 6.4 + 7.6 + 8.8]$$
$$= 0.8(29.3) = 23.44$$

(b) $-4 \leq f''(x) \leq 1 \Rightarrow |f''(x)| \leq 4$, so use $K = 4$, $a = 0$, $b = 3.2$, and $n = 4$ in Theorem 3. So

$$|E_M| \leq \frac{4(3.2 - 0)^3}{24(4)^2} = \frac{128}{375} = 0.341\overline{3}.$$

33. By the Net Change Theorem, the increase in velocity is equal to $\int_0^6 a(t)\,dt$. We use Simpson's Rule with $n = 6$ and $\Delta t = (6 - 0)/6 = 1$ to estimate this integral:

$$\int_0^6 a(t)\,dt \approx S_6 = \frac{1}{3}[a(0) + 4a(1) + 2a(2) + 4a(3) + 2a(4) + 4a(5) + a(6)]$$
$$\approx \frac{1}{3}[0 + 4(0.5) + 2(4.1) + 4(9.8) + 2(12.9) + 4(9.5) + 0] = \frac{1}{3}(113.2) = 37.7\overline{3} \text{ ft/s}$$

35. By the Net Change Theorem, the energy used is equal to $\int_0^6 P(t)\,dt$. We use Simpson's Rule with $n = 12$ and $\Delta t = (6 - 0)/12 = \frac{1}{2}$ to estimate this integral:

$$\int_0^6 P(t)\,dt \approx S_{12} = \frac{1/2}{3}[P(0) + 4P(0.5) + 2P(1) + 4P(1.5) + 2P(2) + 4P(2.5)$$
$$+ 2P(3) + 4P(3.5) + 2P(4) + 4P(4.5) + 2P(5) + 4P(5.5) + P(6)]$$
$$= \frac{1}{6}[1814 + 4(1735) + 2(1686) + 4(1646) + 2(1637) + 4(1609) + 2(1604)$$
$$+ 4(1611) + 2(1621) + 4(1666) + 2(1745) + 4(1886) + 2052]$$
$$= \frac{1}{6}(61,064) = 10,177.\overline{3} \text{ megawatt-hours.}$$

37. Let $y = f(x)$ denote the curve. Using cylindrical shells, $V = \int_2^{10} 2\pi x f(x)\,dx = 2\pi \int_2^{10} x f(x)\,dx = 2\pi I$.

Now use Simpson's Rule to approximate I:

$$I \approx S_8 = \frac{10-2}{3(8)}\left[2f(2) + 4\cdot 3f(3) + 2\cdot 4f(4) + 4\cdot 5f(5) + 2\cdot 6f(6)\right.$$
$$\left. + 4\cdot 7f(7) + 2\cdot 8f(8) + 4\cdot 9f(9) + 10f(10)\right]$$
$$\approx \tfrac{1}{3}[2(0) + 12(1.5) + 8(1.9) + 20(2.2) + 12(3.0) + 28(3.8) + 16(4.0) + 36(3.1) + 10(0)]$$
$$= \tfrac{1}{3}(395.2)$$

Thus, $V \approx 2\pi \cdot \tfrac{1}{3}(395.2) \approx 827.7$ or 828 cubic units.

39. Volume $= \pi \int_0^2 \left(\sqrt[3]{1+x^3}\right)^2 dx = \pi \int_0^2 \left(1+x^3\right)^{2/3} dx$. $V \approx \pi \cdot S_{10}$ where $f(x) = \left(1+x^3\right)^{2/3}$ and $\Delta x = (2-0)/10 = \tfrac{1}{5}$. Therefore,

$$V \approx \pi \cdot S_{10} = \pi \tfrac{1}{5\cdot 3}\left[f(0) + 4f(0.2) + 2f(0.4) + 4f(0.6) + 2f(0.8) + 4f(1)\right.$$
$$\left. + 2f(1.2) + 4f(1.4) + 2f(1.6) + 4f(1.8) + f(2)\right] \approx 12.325078$$

41. $I(\theta) = \dfrac{N^2 \sin^2 k}{k^2}$, where $k = \dfrac{\pi N d \sin\theta}{\lambda}$, $N = 10{,}000$, $d = 10^{-4}$, and $\lambda = 632.8 \times 10^{-9}$. So

$$I(\theta) = \dfrac{\left(10^4\right)^2 \sin^2 k}{k^2}, \text{ where } k = \dfrac{\pi\left(10^4\right)\left(10^{-4}\right)\sin\theta}{632.8 \times 10^{-9}}. \text{ Now } n = 10 \text{ and } \Delta\theta = \dfrac{10^{-6} - \left(-10^{-6}\right)}{10} = 2\times 10^{-7},$$

so $M_{10} = 2\times 10^{-7}[I(-0.0000009) + I(-0.0000007) + \cdots + I(0.0000009)] \approx 59.4$.

43. Consider the function f whose graph is shown. The area $\int_0^2 f(x)\,dx$
is close to 2. The Trapezoidal Rule gives
$$T_2 = \tfrac{2-0}{2\cdot 2}\left[f(0) + 2f(1) + f(2)\right] = \tfrac{1}{2}\left[1 + 2\cdot 1 + 1\right] = 2.$$
The Midpoint Rule gives
$$M_2 = \tfrac{2-0}{2}\left[f(0.5) + f(1.5)\right] = 1[0+0] = 0,$$
so the Trapezoidal Rule is more accurate.

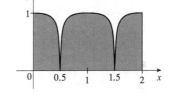

45. Since the Trapezoidal and Midpoint approximations on the interval $[a,b]$ are the sums of the Trapezoidal and Midpoint approximations on the subintervals $[x_{i-1}, x_i]$, $i = 1, 2, \ldots, n$, we can focus our attention on one such interval. The condition $f''(x) < 0$ for $a \le x \le b$ means that the graph of f is concave down as in Figure 5. In that figure, T_n is the area of the trapezoid $AQRD$, $\int_a^b f(x)\,dx$ is the area of the region $AQPRD$, and M_n is the area of the trapezoid $ABCD$, so $T_n < \int_a^b f(x)\,dx < M_n$. In general, the condition $f'' < 0$ implies that the graph of f on $[a,b]$ lies above the chord joining the points $(a, f(a))$ and $(b, f(b))$. Thus, $\int_a^b f(x)\,dx > T_n$. Since M_n is the area under a tangent to the graph, and since $f'' < 0$ implies that the tangent lies above the graph, we also have $M_n > \int_a^b f(x)\,dx$. Thus, $T_n < \int_a^b f(x)\,dx < M_n$.

47. $T_n = \frac{1}{2} \Delta x \left[f(x_0) + 2f(x_1) + \cdots + 2f(x_{n-1}) + f(x_n) \right]$ and

$M_n = \Delta x \left[f(\overline{x}_1) + f(\overline{x}_2) + \cdots + f(\overline{x}_{n-1}) + f(\overline{x}_n) \right]$, where $\overline{x}_i = \frac{1}{2}(x_{i-1} + x_i)$. Now

$$T_{2n} = \frac{1}{2} \left(\frac{1}{2} \Delta x \right) \left[f(x_0) + 2f(\overline{x}_1) + 2f(x_1) + 2f(\overline{x}_2) + 2f(x_2) + \cdots \right.$$

$$\left. + 2f(\overline{x}_{n-1}) + 2f(x_{n-1}) + 2f(\overline{x}_n) + f(x_n) \right]$$

so $\quad \frac{1}{2}(T_n + M_n) = \frac{1}{2} T_n + \frac{1}{2} M_n$

$$= \frac{1}{4} \Delta x \left[f(x_0) + 2f(x_1) + \cdots + 2f(x_{n-1}) + f(x_n) \right]$$

$$+ \frac{1}{4} \Delta x \left[2f(\overline{x}_1) + 2f(\overline{x}_2) + \cdots + 2f(\overline{x}_{n-1}) + 2f(\overline{x}_n) \right]$$

$$= T_{2n}$$

8.8 Improper Integrals

1. (a) Since $\int_1^\infty x^4 e^{-x^4} \, dx$ has an infinite interval of integration, it is an improper integral of Type I.

(b) Since $y = \sec x$ has an infinite discontinuity at $x = \frac{\pi}{2}$, $\int_0^{\pi/2} \sec x \, dx$ is a Type II improper integral.

(c) Since $y = \dfrac{x}{(x-2)(x-3)}$ has an infinite discontinuity at $x = 2$, $\displaystyle\int_0^2 \dfrac{x}{x^2 - 5x + 6} \, dx$ is a Type II improper integral.

(d) Since $\displaystyle\int_{-\infty}^0 \dfrac{1}{x^2 + 5} \, dx$ has an infinite interval of integration, it is an improper integral of Type I.

3. The area under the graph of $y = 1/x^3 = x^{-3}$ between $x = 1$ and $x = t$ is

$A(t) = \int_1^t x^{-3} \, dx = \left[-\frac{1}{2} x^{-2} \right]_1^t = -\frac{1}{2} t^{-2} - \left(-\frac{1}{2} \right) = \frac{1}{2} - 1/(2t^2)$. So the area for $1 \le x \le 10$ is

$A(10) = 0.5 - 0.005 = 0.495$, the area for $1 \le x \le 100$ is $A(100) = 0.5 - 0.00005 = 0.49995$, and the area for

$1 \le x \le 1000$ is $A(1000) = 0.5 - 0.0000005 = 0.4999995$. The total area under the curve for $x \ge 1$ is

$\displaystyle\lim_{t \to \infty} A(t) = \lim_{t \to \infty} \left[\frac{1}{2} - 1/(2t^2) \right] = \frac{1}{2}$.

5. $I = \displaystyle\int_1^\infty \dfrac{1}{(3x+1)^2} \, dx = \lim_{t \to \infty} \int_1^t \dfrac{1}{(3x+1)^2} \, dx$. Now

$$\int \dfrac{1}{(3x+1)^2} \, dx = \dfrac{1}{3} \int \dfrac{1}{u^2} \, du \quad [u = 3x+1, \, du = 3 \, dx]$$

$$= -\dfrac{1}{3u} + C = -\dfrac{1}{3(3x+1)} + C,$$

so $I = \displaystyle\lim_{t \to \infty} \left[-\dfrac{1}{3(3x+1)} \right]_1^t = \lim_{t \to \infty} \left[-\dfrac{1}{3(3t+1)} + \dfrac{1}{12} \right] = 0 + \dfrac{1}{12} = \dfrac{1}{12}$. Convergent

7. $\displaystyle\int_{-\infty}^{-1} \dfrac{1}{\sqrt{2-w}} \, dw = \lim_{t \to -\infty} \int_t^{-1} \dfrac{1}{\sqrt{2-w}} \, dw = \lim_{t \to -\infty} \left[-2\sqrt{2-w} \right]_t^{-1} \quad [u = 2 - w, \, du = -dw]$

$$= \lim_{t \to -\infty} \left[-2\sqrt{3} + 2\sqrt{2-t} \right] = \infty. \quad \text{Divergent}$$

9. $\int_4^\infty e^{-y/2}\,dy = \lim\limits_{t\to\infty}\int_4^t e^{-y/2}\,dy = \lim\limits_{t\to\infty}\left[-2e^{-y/2}\right]_4^t = \lim\limits_{t\to\infty}\left(-2e^{-t/2}+2e^{-2}\right) = 0+2e^{-2} = 2e^{-2}.$

Convergent

11. $\displaystyle\int_{-\infty}^\infty \frac{x\,dx}{1+x^2} = \int_{-\infty}^0 \frac{x\,dx}{1+x^2} + \int_0^\infty \frac{x\,dx}{1+x^2}$ and

$\displaystyle\int_{-\infty}^0 \frac{x\,dx}{1+x^2} = \lim\limits_{t\to-\infty}\left[\tfrac12\ln(1+x^2)\right]_t^0 = \lim\limits_{t\to-\infty}\left[0-\tfrac12\ln(1+t^2)\right] = -\infty.$ Divergent

13. $\int_{-\infty}^\infty xe^{-x^2}\,dx = \int_{-\infty}^0 xe^{-x^2}\,dx + \int_0^\infty xe^{-x^2}\,dx.$

$\int_{-\infty}^0 xe^{-x^2}\,dx = \lim\limits_{t\to-\infty}\left(-\tfrac12\right)\left[e^{-x^2}\right]_t^0 = \lim\limits_{t\to-\infty}\left(-\tfrac12\right)\left(1-e^{-t^2}\right) = -\tfrac12\cdot1 = -\tfrac12,$ and

$\int_0^\infty xe^{-x^2}\,dx = \lim\limits_{t\to\infty}\left(-\tfrac12\right)\left[e^{-x^2}\right]_0^t = \lim\limits_{t\to\infty}\left(-\tfrac12\right)\left(e^{-t^2}-1\right) = -\tfrac12\cdot(-1) = \tfrac12.$

Therefore, $\int_{-\infty}^\infty xe^{-x^2}\,dx = -\tfrac12+\tfrac12 = 0.$ Convergent

15. $\int_{2\pi}^\infty \sin\theta\,d\theta = \lim\limits_{t\to\infty}\int_{2\pi}^t \sin\theta\,d\theta = \lim\limits_{t\to\infty}\left[-\cos\theta\right]_{2\pi}^t = \lim\limits_{t\to\infty}(-\cos t+1).$ This limit does not exist, so the integral

is divergent. Divergent

17. $\displaystyle\int_1^\infty \frac{x+1}{x^2+2x}\,dx = \lim\limits_{t\to\infty}\int_1^t \frac{\tfrac12(2x+2)}{x^2+2x}\,dx = \tfrac12\lim\limits_{t\to\infty}\left[\ln(x^2+2x)\right]_1^t = \tfrac12\lim\limits_{t\to\infty}\left[\ln(t^2+2t)-\ln3\right]$

$= \infty.$ Divergent

19. $\displaystyle\int_0^\infty se^{-5s}\,ds = \lim\limits_{t\to\infty}\int_0^t se^{-5s}\,ds = \lim\limits_{t\to\infty}\left[-\tfrac15 se^{-5s}-\tfrac{1}{25}e^{-5s}\right]_0^t$ $\begin{bmatrix}\text{by integration by}\\\text{parts with }u=s\end{bmatrix}$

$= \lim\limits_{t\to\infty}\left(-\tfrac15 te^{-5t}-\tfrac{1}{25}e^{-5t}+\tfrac{1}{25}\right) = 0-0+\tfrac{1}{25}$ [by l'Hospital's Rule]

$= \tfrac{1}{25}.$ Convergent

21. $\displaystyle\int_1^\infty \frac{\ln x}{x}\,dx = \lim\limits_{t\to\infty}\left[\frac{(\ln x)^2}{2}\right]_1^t$ (by substitution with $u=\ln x$, $du=dx/x$) $= \lim\limits_{t\to\infty}\frac{(\ln t)^2}{2} = \infty.$ Divergent

23. $\displaystyle\int_{-\infty}^\infty \frac{x^2}{9+x^6}\,dx = \int_{-\infty}^0 \frac{x^2}{9+x^6}\,dx + \int_0^\infty \frac{x^2}{9+x^6}\,dx = 2\int_0^\infty \frac{x^2}{9+x^6}\,dx$ [since the integrand is even].

Now $\displaystyle\int \frac{x^2\,dx}{9+x^6}$ $\begin{bmatrix}u=x^3\\du=3x^2dx\end{bmatrix}$ $= \int \frac{\tfrac13 du}{9+u^2}$ $\begin{bmatrix}u=3v\\du=3\,dv\end{bmatrix}$ $= \int \frac{\tfrac13(3\,dv)}{9+9v^2} = \tfrac19\int \frac{dv}{1+v^2}$

$= \tfrac19\tan^{-1}v + C = \tfrac19\tan^{-1}\left(\tfrac{u}{3}\right) + C = \tfrac19\tan^{-1}\left(\tfrac{x^3}{3}\right) + C,$

so $\displaystyle 2\int_0^\infty \frac{x^2}{9+x^6}\,dx = 2\lim\limits_{t\to\infty}\int_0^t \frac{x^2}{9+x^6}\,dx = 2\lim\limits_{t\to\infty}\left[\tfrac19\tan^{-1}\left(\tfrac{x^3}{3}\right)\right]_0^t$

$= 2\lim\limits_{t\to\infty}\tfrac19\tan^{-1}\left(\tfrac{t^3}{3}\right) = \tfrac29\cdot\tfrac{\pi}{2} = \tfrac{\pi}{9}.$ Convergent

25. Integrate by parts with $u=\ln x$, $dv=dx/x^2 \Rightarrow du=dx/x$, $v=-1/x.$

$\displaystyle\int_1^\infty \frac{\ln x}{x^2}\,dx = \lim\limits_{t\to\infty}\int_1^t \frac{\ln x}{x^2}\,dx = \lim\limits_{t\to\infty}\left[-\frac{\ln x}{x}-\frac1x\right]_1^t = \lim\limits_{t\to\infty}\left(-\frac{\ln t}{t}-\frac1t+0+1\right)$

$= -0-0+0+1 = 1$

since $\lim\limits_{t\to\infty}\frac{\ln t}{t} \overset{H}{=} \lim\limits_{t\to\infty}\frac{1/t}{1} = 0.$ Convergent

27. There is an infinite discontinuity at the left endpoint of $[0, 3]$.

$$\int_0^3 \frac{dx}{\sqrt{x}} = \lim_{t \to 0^+} \int_t^3 \frac{dx}{\sqrt{x}} = \lim_{t \to 0^+} \left[2\sqrt{x} \right]_t^3 = \lim_{t \to 0^+} \left(2\sqrt{3} - 2\sqrt{t} \right) = 2\sqrt{3}. \quad \text{Convergent}$$

29. There is an infinite discontinuity at the right endpoint of $[-1, 0]$.

$$\int_{-1}^0 \frac{dx}{x^2} = \lim_{t \to 0^-} \int_{-1}^t \frac{dx}{x^2} = \lim_{t \to 0^-} \left[\frac{-1}{x} \right]_{-1}^t = \lim_{t \to 0^-} \left[-\frac{1}{t} + \frac{1}{-1} \right] = \infty. \quad \text{Divergent}$$

31. $\int_{-2}^3 \frac{dx}{x^4} = \int_{-2}^0 \frac{dx}{x^4} + \int_0^3 \frac{dx}{x^4}$, but $\int_{-2}^0 \frac{dx}{x^4} = \lim_{t \to 0^-} \left[-\frac{x^{-3}}{3} \right]_{-2}^t = \lim_{t \to 0^-} \left[-\frac{1}{3t^3} - \frac{1}{24} \right] = \infty$. Divergent

33. There is an infinite discontinuity at $x = 1$. $\int_0^{33} (x-1)^{-1/5}\, dx = \int_0^1 (x-1)^{-1/5}\, dx + \int_1^{33} (x-1)^{-1/5}\, dx$. Here

$$\int_0^1 (x-1)^{-1/5}\, dx = \lim_{t \to 1^-} \int_0^t (x-1)^{-1/5}\, dx = \lim_{t \to 1^-} \left[\tfrac{5}{4}(x-1)^{4/5} \right]_0^t = \lim_{t \to 1^-} \left[\tfrac{5}{4}(t-1)^{4/5} - \tfrac{5}{4} \right] = -\tfrac{5}{4} \text{ and}$$

$$\int_1^{33} (x-1)^{-1/5}\, dx = \lim_{t \to 1^+} \int_t^{33} (x-1)^{-1/5}\, dx = \lim_{t \to 1^+} \left[\tfrac{5}{4}(x-1)^{4/5} \right]_t^{33} = \lim_{t \to 1^+} \left[\tfrac{5}{4} \cdot 16 - \tfrac{5}{4}(t-1)^{4/5} \right] = 20.$$

Thus, $\int_0^{33} (x-1)^{-1/5}\, dx = -\tfrac{5}{4} + 20 = \tfrac{75}{4}$.   Convergent

35. $\int_0^\pi \sec x\, dx = \int_0^{\pi/2} \sec x\, dx + \int_{\pi/2}^\pi \sec x\, dx$. $\int_0^{\pi/2} \sec x\, dx = \lim_{t \to \pi/2^-} \int_0^t \sec x\, dx$

$$= \lim_{t \to \pi/2^-} \left[\ln|\sec x + \tan x| \right]_0^t = \lim_{t \to \pi/2^-} \ln|\sec t + \tan t| = \infty. \text{ Divergent}$$

37. There is an infinite discontinuity at $x = 0$. $\int_{-1}^1 \frac{e^x}{e^x - 1}\, dx = \int_{-1}^0 \frac{e^x}{e^x - 1}\, dx + \int_0^1 \frac{e^x}{e^x - 1}\, dx$.

$$\int_{-1}^0 \frac{e^x}{e^x - 1}\, dx = \lim_{t \to 0^-} \int_{-1}^t \frac{e^x}{e^x - 1}\, dx = \lim_{t \to 0^-} \left[\ln|e^x - 1| \right]_{-1}^t = \lim_{t \to 0^-} \left[\ln|e^t - 1| - \ln|e^{-1} - 1| \right] = -\infty,$$

so $\int_{-1}^1 \frac{e^x}{e^x - 1}\, dx$ is divergent. The integral $\int_0^1 \frac{e^x}{e^x - 1}\, dx$ also diverges since

$$\int_0^1 \frac{e^x}{e^x - 1}\, dx = \lim_{t \to 0^+} \int_t^1 \frac{e^x}{e^x - 1}\, dx = \lim_{t \to 0^+} \left[\ln|e^x - 1| \right]_t^1 = \lim_{t \to 0^+} \left[\ln|e - 1| - \ln|e^t - 1| \right] = \infty.$$

Divergent

39. $I = \int_0^2 z^2 \ln z\, dz = \lim_{t \to 0^+} \int_t^2 z^2 \ln z\, dz \overset{101}{=} \lim_{t \to 0^+} \left[\frac{z^3}{3^2}(3 \ln z - 1) \right]_t^2$

$$= \lim_{t \to 0^+} \left[\tfrac{8}{9}(3 \ln 2 - 1) - \tfrac{1}{9}t^3(3 \ln t - 1) \right] = \tfrac{8}{3} \ln 2 - \tfrac{8}{9} - \tfrac{1}{9} \lim_{t \to 0^+} \left[t^3(3 \ln t - 1) \right] = \tfrac{8}{3} \ln 2 - \tfrac{8}{9} - \tfrac{1}{9}L.$$

Now $L = \lim_{t \to 0^+} \left[t^3(3 \ln t - 1) \right] = \lim_{t \to 0^+} \frac{3 \ln t - 1}{t^{-3}} \overset{\text{H}}{=} \lim_{t \to 0^+} \frac{3/t}{-3/t^4} = \lim_{t \to 0^+} (-t^3) = 0$. Thus, $L = 0$ and

$I = \tfrac{8}{3} \ln 2 - \tfrac{8}{9}$.   Convergent

41.

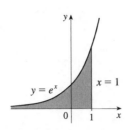

$$\text{Area} = \int_{-\infty}^{1} e^x \, dx = \lim_{t \to -\infty} [e^x]_t^1$$

$$= e - \lim_{t \to -\infty} e^t = e$$

43.

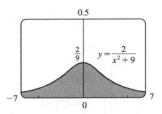

$$\text{Area} = \int_{-\infty}^{\infty} \frac{2}{x^2 + 9} \, dx = 2 \cdot 2 \int_0^{\infty} \frac{1}{x^2 + 9} \, dx$$

$$= 4 \lim_{t \to \infty} \int_0^t \frac{1}{x^2 + 9} \, dx = 4 \lim_{t \to \infty} \left[\frac{1}{3} \tan^{-1} \frac{x}{3} \right]_0^t$$

$$= \frac{4}{3} \lim_{t \to \infty} \left[\tan^{-1} \frac{t}{3} - 0 \right] = \frac{4}{3} \cdot \frac{\pi}{2} = \frac{2\pi}{3}$$

45.

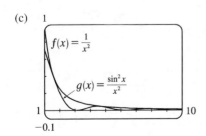

$$\text{Area} = \int_0^{\pi/2} \sec^2 x \, dx = \lim_{t \to (\pi/2)^-} \int_0^t \sec^2 x \, dx$$

$$= \lim_{t \to (\pi/2)^-} [\tan x]_0^t = \lim_{t \to (\pi/2)^-} (\tan t - 0)$$

$$= \infty$$

Infinite area

47. (a)

t	$\int_1^t g(x) \, dx$
2	0.447453
5	0.577101
10	0.621306
100	0.668479
1000	0.672957
10,000	0.673407

$$g(x) = \frac{\sin^2 x}{x^2}.$$

It appears that the integral is convergent.

(b) $-1 \le \sin x \le 1 \ \Rightarrow \ 0 \le \sin^2 x \le 1 \ \Rightarrow \ 0 \le \dfrac{\sin^2 x}{x^2} \le \dfrac{1}{x^2}$. Since $\displaystyle\int_1^{\infty} \frac{1}{x^2} \, dx$ is convergent

(Equation 2 with $p = 2 > 1$), $\displaystyle\int_1^{\infty} \frac{\sin^2 x}{x^2} \, dx$ is convergent by the Comparison Theorem.

(c)

Since $\int_1^{\infty} f(x) \, dx$ is finite and the area under $g(x)$ is less than the area under $f(x)$ on any interval $[1, t]$, $\int_1^{\infty} g(x) \, dx$ must be finite; that is, the integral is convergent.

49. For $x \geq 1$, $\dfrac{\cos^2 x}{1 + x^2} \leq \dfrac{1}{1 + x^2} < \dfrac{1}{x^2}$. $\displaystyle\int_1^\infty \dfrac{1}{x^2}\,dx$ is convergent by Equation 2 with $p = 2 > 1$, so $\displaystyle\int_1^\infty \dfrac{\cos^2 x}{1 + x^2}\,dx$

is convergent by the Comparison Theorem.

51. For $x \geq 1$, $x + e^{2x} > e^{2x} > 0$ $\Rightarrow$ $\dfrac{1}{x + e^{2x}} \leq \dfrac{1}{e^{2x}} = e^{-2x}$ on $[1, \infty)$.

$$\int_1^\infty e^{-2x}\,dx = \lim_{t \to \infty} \left[-\dfrac{1}{2}e^{-2x}\right]_1^t = \lim_{t \to \infty} \left[-\dfrac{1}{2}e^{-2t} + \dfrac{1}{2}e^{-2}\right] = \dfrac{1}{2}e^{-2}.$$ Therefore, $\displaystyle\int_1^\infty e^{-2x}\,dx$ is convergent,

and by the Comparison Theorem, $\displaystyle\int_1^\infty \dfrac{dx}{x + e^{2x}}$ is also convergent.

53. $\dfrac{1}{x \sin x} \geq \dfrac{1}{x}$ on $\left(0, \dfrac{\pi}{2}\right]$ since $0 \leq \sin x \leq 1$. $\displaystyle\int_0^{\pi/2} \dfrac{dx}{x} = \lim_{t \to 0^+} \int_t^{\pi/2} \dfrac{dx}{x} = \lim_{t \to 0^+} \left[\ln x\right]_t^{\pi/2}$.

But $\ln t \to -\infty$ as $t \to 0^+$, so $\displaystyle\int_0^{\pi/2} \dfrac{dx}{x}$ is divergent, and by the Comparison Theorem, $\displaystyle\int_0^{\pi/2} \dfrac{dx}{x \sin x}$ is also

divergent.

55. $\displaystyle\int_0^\infty \dfrac{dx}{\sqrt{x}\,(1 + x)} = \int_0^1 \dfrac{dx}{\sqrt{x}\,(1 + x)} + \int_1^\infty \dfrac{dx}{\sqrt{x}\,(1 + x)} = \lim_{t \to 0^+} \int_t^1 \dfrac{dx}{\sqrt{x}\,(1 + x)} + \lim_{t \to \infty} \int_1^t \dfrac{dx}{\sqrt{x}\,(1 + x)}$. Now

$$\int \dfrac{dx}{\sqrt{x}\,(1 + x)} = \int \dfrac{2u\,du}{u(1 + u^2)} \quad [u = \sqrt{x}, x = u^2, dx = 2u\,du]$$

$$= 2\int \dfrac{du}{1 + u^2} = 2\tan^{-1} u + C = 2\tan^{-1}\sqrt{x} + C,$$

so $\displaystyle\int_0^\infty \dfrac{dx}{\sqrt{x}\,(1 + x)} = \lim_{t \to 0^+} \left[2\tan^{-1}\sqrt{x}\right]_t^1 + \lim_{t \to \infty} \left[2\tan^{-1}\sqrt{x}\right]_1^t$

$$= \lim_{t \to 0^+} \left[2\left(\dfrac{\pi}{4}\right) - 2\tan^{-1}\sqrt{t}\right] + \lim_{t \to \infty} \left[2\tan^{-1}\sqrt{t} - 2\left(\dfrac{\pi}{4}\right)\right] = \dfrac{\pi}{2} - 0 + 2\left(\dfrac{\pi}{2}\right) - \dfrac{\pi}{2} = \pi.$$

57. If $p = 1$, then $\displaystyle\int_0^1 \dfrac{dx}{x^p} = \lim_{t \to 0^+} \int_t^1 \dfrac{dx}{x} = \lim_{t \to 0^+} \left[\ln x\right]_t^1 = \infty$. Divergent.

If $p \neq 1$, then $\displaystyle\int_0^1 \dfrac{dx}{x^p} = \lim_{t \to 0^+} \int_t^1 \dfrac{dx}{x^p}$ (note that the integral is not improper if $p < 0$)

$$= \lim_{t \to 0^+} \left[\dfrac{x^{-p+1}}{-p + 1}\right]_t^1 = \lim_{t \to 0^+} \dfrac{1}{1 - p}\left[1 - \dfrac{1}{t^{p-1}}\right]$$

If $p > 1$, then $p - 1 > 0$, so $\dfrac{1}{t^{p-1}} \to \infty$ as $t \to 0^+$, and the integral diverges.

If $p < 1$, then $p - 1 < 0$, so $\dfrac{1}{t^{p-1}} \to 0$ as $t \to 0^+$ and $\displaystyle\int_0^1 \dfrac{dx}{x^p} = \dfrac{1}{1 - p}\left[\lim_{t \to 0^+}\left(1 - t^{1-p}\right)\right] = \dfrac{1}{1 - p}$.

Thus, the integral converges if and only if $p < 1$, and in that case its value is $\dfrac{1}{1 - p}$.

59. First suppose $p = -1$. Then

$$\int_0^1 x^p \ln x \, dx = \int_0^1 \frac{\ln x}{x} \, dx = \lim_{t \to 0^+} \int_t^1 \frac{\ln x}{x} \, dx = \lim_{t \to 0^+} \left[\tfrac{1}{2}(\ln x)^2 \right]_t^1 = -\tfrac{1}{2} \lim_{t \to 0^+} (\ln t)^2 = -\infty,$$

so the integral diverges. Now suppose $p \neq -1$. Then integration by parts gives

$$\int x^p \ln x \, dx = \frac{x^{p+1}}{p+1} \ln x - \int \frac{x^p}{p+1} \, dx = \frac{x^{p+1}}{p+1} \ln x - \frac{x^{p+1}}{(p+1)^2} + C. \text{ If } p < -1, \text{ then } p+1 < 0, \text{ so}$$

$$\int_0^1 x^p \ln x \, dx = \lim_{t \to 0^+} \left[\frac{x^{p+1}}{p+1} \ln x - \frac{x^{p+1}}{(p+1)^2} \right]_t^1 = \frac{-1}{(p+1)^2} - \left(\frac{1}{p+1} \right) \lim_{t \to 0^+} \left[t^{p+1} \left(\ln t - \frac{1}{p+1} \right) \right] = \infty.$$

If $p > -1$, then $p+1 > 0$ and

$$\int_0^1 x^p \ln x \, dx = \frac{-1}{(p+1)^2} - \left(\frac{1}{p+1} \right) \lim_{t \to 0^+} \frac{\ln t - 1/(p+1)}{t^{-(p+1)}} \overset{\text{H}}{=} \frac{-1}{(p+1)^2} - \left(\frac{1}{p+1} \right) \lim_{t \to 0^+} \frac{1/t}{-(p+1)t^{-(p+2)}}$$

$$= \frac{-1}{(p+1)^2} + \frac{1}{(p+1)^2} \lim_{t \to 0^+} t^{p+1} = \frac{-1}{(p+1)^2}$$

Thus, the integral converges to $-\dfrac{1}{(p+1)^2}$ if $p > -1$ and diverges otherwise.

61. (a) $I = \int_{-\infty}^{\infty} x \, dx = \int_{-\infty}^{0} x \, dx + \int_0^{\infty} x \, dx$, and

$\int_0^{\infty} x \, dx = \lim_{t \to \infty} \int_0^t x \, dx = \lim_{t \to \infty} \left[\tfrac{1}{2}x^2 \right]_0^t = \lim_{t \to \infty} \left[\tfrac{1}{2}t^2 - 0 \right] = \infty$, so I is divergent.

(b) $\int_{-t}^{t} x \, dx = \left[\tfrac{1}{2}x^2 \right]_{-t}^{t} = \tfrac{1}{2}t^2 - \tfrac{1}{2}t^2 = 0$, so $\lim_{t \to \infty} \int_{-t}^{t} x \, dx = 0$. Therefore, $\int_{-\infty}^{\infty} x \, dx \neq \lim_{t \to \infty} \int_{-t}^{t} x \, dx$.

63. Volume $= \int_1^{\infty} \pi \left(\frac{1}{x} \right)^2 dx = \pi \lim_{t \to \infty} \int_1^t \frac{dx}{x^2} = \pi \lim_{t \to \infty} \left[-\frac{1}{x} \right]_1^t = \pi \lim_{t \to \infty} \left(1 - \frac{1}{t} \right) = \pi < \infty.$

65. Work $= \int_R^{\infty} F \, dr = \lim_{t \to \infty} \int_R^t \frac{GmM}{r^2} \, dr = \lim_{t \to \infty} GmM \left(\frac{1}{R} - \frac{1}{t} \right) = \frac{GmM}{R}$. The initial kinetic energy

provides the work, so $\tfrac{1}{2}mv_0^2 = \dfrac{GmM}{R} \quad \Rightarrow \quad v_0 = \sqrt{\dfrac{2GM}{R}}$.

67. (a) We would expect a small percentage of bulbs to burn out in the first few hundred hours, most of the bulbs to burn out after close to 700 hours, and a few overachievers to burn on and on.

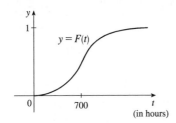

(b) $r(t) = F'(t)$ is the rate at which the fraction $F(t)$ of burnt-out bulbs increases as t increases. This could be interpreted as a fractional burnout rate.

(c) $\int_0^{\infty} r(t) \, dt = \lim_{x \to \infty} F(x) = 1$, since all of the bulbs will eventually burn out.

69. $I = \int_a^\infty \dfrac{1}{x^2 + 1}\, dx = \lim_{t\to\infty} \int_a^t \dfrac{1}{x^2+1}\, dx = \lim_{t\to\infty}\big[\tan^{-1} x\big]_a^t = \lim_{t\to\infty}\big(\tan^{-1} t - \tan^{-1} a\big) = \frac{\pi}{2} - \tan^{-1} a.$

$I < 0.001 \;\Rightarrow\; \frac{\pi}{2} - \tan^{-1} a < 0.001 \;\Rightarrow\; \tan^{-1} a > \frac{\pi}{2} - 0.001 \;\Rightarrow\; a > \tan\big(\frac{\pi}{2} - 0.001\big) \approx 1000.$

71. (a) $F(s) = \int_0^\infty f(t) e^{-st}\, dt = \int_0^\infty e^{-st}\, dt = \lim_{n\to\infty}\left[-\dfrac{e^{-st}}{s}\right]_0^n = \lim_{n\to\infty}\left(\dfrac{e^{-sn}}{-s} + \dfrac{1}{s}\right).$ This converges to $\dfrac{1}{s}$

only if $s > 0$. Therefore $F(s) = \dfrac{1}{s}$ with domain $\{s \mid s > 0\}$.

(b) $F(s) = \int_0^\infty f(t) e^{-st}\, dt = \int_0^\infty e^t e^{-st}\, dt = \lim_{n\to\infty}\int_0^n e^{t(1-s)}\, dt = \lim_{n\to\infty}\left[\dfrac{1}{1-s} e^{t(1-s)}\right]_0^n$

$= \lim_{n\to\infty}\left(\dfrac{e^{(1-s)n}}{1-s} - \dfrac{1}{1-s}\right)$

This converges only if $1 - s < 0 \;\Rightarrow\; s > 1$, in which case $F(s) = \dfrac{1}{s-1}$ with domain $\{s \mid s > 1\}$.

(c) $F(s) = \int_0^\infty f(t) e^{-st}\, dt = \lim_{n\to\infty}\int_0^n t e^{-st}\, dt.$ Use integration by parts: let $u = t,\ dv = e^{-st}\, dt \;\Rightarrow\;$

$du = dt,\ v = -\dfrac{e^{-st}}{s}.$ Then $F(s) = \lim_{n\to\infty}\left[-\dfrac{t}{s} e^{-st} - \dfrac{1}{s^2} e^{-st}\right]_0^n = \lim_{n\to\infty}\left(\dfrac{-n}{s e^{sn}} - \dfrac{1}{s^2 e^{sn}} + 0 + \dfrac{1}{s^2}\right) = \dfrac{1}{s^2}$

only if $s > 0$. Therefore, $F(s) = \dfrac{1}{s^2}$ and the domain of F is $\{s \mid s > 0\}$.

73. $G(s) = \int_0^\infty f'(t) e^{-st}\, dt.$ Integrate by parts with $u = e^{-st},\ dv = f'(t)\, dt \;\Rightarrow\; du = -s e^{-st},\ v = f(t)$:

$$G(s) = \lim_{n\to\infty}\big[f(t) e^{-st}\big]_0^n + s\int_0^\infty f(t) e^{-st}\, dt = \lim_{n\to\infty} f(n) e^{-sn} - f(0) + s F(s)$$

But $0 \le f(t) \le M e^{at} \;\Rightarrow\; 0 \le f(t) e^{-st} \le M e^{at} e^{-st}$ and $\lim_{t\to\infty} M e^{t(a-s)} = 0$ for $s > a$. So by the Squeeze

Theorem, $\lim_{t\to\infty} f(t) e^{-st} = 0$ for $s > a \;\Rightarrow\; G(s) = 0 - f(0) + s F(s) = s F(s) - f(0)$ for $s > a.$

75. We use integration by parts: let $u = x,\ dv = x e^{-x^2}\, dx \;\Rightarrow\; du = dx,\ v = -\frac{1}{2} e^{-x^2}.$ So

$$\int_0^\infty x^2 e^{-x^2}\, dx = \lim_{t\to\infty}\left[-\tfrac{1}{2} x e^{-x^2}\right]_0^t + \tfrac{1}{2}\int_0^\infty e^{-x^2}\, dx$$

$$= \lim_{t\to\infty}\left[-t\Big/\big(2 e^{t^2}\big)\right] + \tfrac{1}{2}\int_0^\infty e^{-x^2}\, dx = \tfrac{1}{2}\int_0^\infty e^{-x^2}\, dx$$

(The limit is 0 by l'Hospital's Rule.)

77. For the first part of the integral, let $x = 2\tan\theta \;\Rightarrow\; dx = 2\sec^2\theta\,d\theta$.

$$\int \frac{1}{\sqrt{x^2+4}}\,dx = \int \frac{2\sec^2\theta}{2\sec\theta}\,d\theta = \int \sec\theta\,d\theta = \ln|\sec\theta + \tan\theta|. \text{ From the}$$

figure, $\tan\theta = \dfrac{x}{2}$, and $\sec\theta = \dfrac{\sqrt{x^2+4}}{2}$. So

$$I = \int_0^\infty \left(\frac{1}{\sqrt{x^2+4}} - \frac{C}{x+2}\right) dx = \lim_{t\to\infty}\left[\ln\left|\frac{\sqrt{x^2+4}}{2} + \frac{x}{2}\right| - C\ln|x+2|\right]_0^t$$

$$= \lim_{t\to\infty}\left[\ln\frac{\sqrt{t^2+4}+t}{2} - C\ln(t+2) - (\ln 1 - C\ln 2)\right]$$

$$= \lim_{t\to\infty}\left[\ln\left(\frac{\sqrt{t^2+4}+t}{2\,(t+2)^C}\right) + \ln 2^C\right]$$

$$= \ln\left(\lim_{t\to\infty}\frac{t+\sqrt{t^2+4}}{(t+2)^C}\right) + \ln 2^{C-1}$$

Now $L = \lim\limits_{t\to\infty}\dfrac{t+\sqrt{t^2+4}}{(t+2)^C} \overset{\text{H}}{=} \lim\limits_{t\to\infty}\dfrac{1+t/\sqrt{t^2+4}}{C\,(t+2)^{C-1}} = \dfrac{2}{C\lim\limits_{t\to\infty}(t+2)^{C-1}}$.

If $C < 1$, $L = \infty$ and I diverges. If $C = 1$, $L = 2$ and I converges to $\ln 2 + \ln 2^0 = \ln 2$. If $C > 1$, $L = 0$ and I diverges to $-\infty$.

8 Review

——————————— CONCEPT CHECK ———————————

1. See Formula 8.1.1 or 8.1.2. We try to choose $u = f(x)$ to be a function that becomes simpler when differentiated (or at least not more complicated) as long as $dv = g'(x)\,dx$ can be readily integrated to give v.

2. See the Strategy for Evaluating $\int \sin^m x \cos^n x\,dx$ on page 520.

3. If $\sqrt{a^2 - x^2}$ occurs, try $x = a\sin\theta$; if $\sqrt{a^2 + x^2}$ occurs, try $x = a\tan\theta$, and if $\sqrt{x^2 - a^2}$ occurs, try $x = a\sec\theta$. See the Table of Trigonometric Substitutions on page 526.

4. See Equation 2 and Expressions 7, 9, and 11 in Section 8.4.

5. See the Midpoint Rule, the Trapezoidal Rule, and Simpson's Rule, as well as their associated error bounds, all in Section 8.7. We would expect the best estimate to be given by Simpson's Rule.

6. See Definitions 1(a), (b), and (c) in Section 8.8.

7. See Definitions 3(b), (a), and (c) in Section 8.8.

8. See the Comparison Theorem after Example 8 in Section 8.8.

--- TRUE-FALSE QUIZ ---

1. False.   Since the numerator has a higher degree than the denominator,

$$\frac{x(x^2+4)}{x^2-4} = x + \frac{8x}{x^2-4} = x + \frac{A}{x+2} + \frac{B}{x-2}.$$

3. False.   It can be put in the form $\dfrac{A}{x} + \dfrac{B}{x^2} + \dfrac{C}{x-4}$.

5. False.   This is an improper integral, since the denominator vanishes at $x = 1$.

$$\int_0^4 \frac{x}{x^2-1}\,dx = \int_0^1 \frac{x}{x^2-1}\,dx + \int_1^4 \frac{x}{x^2-1}\,dx \text{ and}$$

$$\int_0^1 \frac{x}{x^2-1}\,dx = \lim_{t\to 1^-} \int_0^t \frac{x}{x^2-1}\,dx = \lim_{t\to 1^-}\left[\tfrac{1}{2}\ln|x^2-1|\right]_0^t = \lim_{t\to 1^-} \tfrac{1}{2}\ln|t^2-1| = \infty$$

So the integral diverges.

7. False.   See Exercise 61 in Section 8.8.

9. (a) True.   See the end of Section 8.5.

   (b) False.   Examples include the functions $f(x) = e^{x^2}$, $g(x) = \sin(x^2)$, and $h(x) = \dfrac{\sin x}{x}$.

11. False.   If $f(x) = 1/x$, then f is continuous and decreasing on $[1,\infty)$ with $\lim\limits_{x\to\infty} f(x) = 0$, but $\int_1^\infty f(x)\,dx$
is divergent.

13. False.   Take $f(x) = 1$ for all x and $g(x) = -1$ for all x. Then $\int_a^\infty f(x)\,dx = \infty$ [divergent]   and
$\int_a^\infty g(x)\,dx = -\infty$ [divergent],   but $\int_a^\infty [f(x) + g(x)]\,dx = 0$ [convergent].

--- EXERCISES ---

1. $\displaystyle\int_0^5 \frac{x}{x+10}\,dx = \int_0^5 \left(1 - \frac{10}{x+10}\right) dx = \Big[x - 10\ln(x+10)\Big]_0^5$

$\qquad = 5 - 10\ln 15 + 10\ln 10 = 5 + 10\ln \frac{10}{15} = 5 + 10\ln \frac{2}{3}$

3. $\displaystyle\int_0^{\pi/2} \frac{\cos\theta}{1 + \sin\theta}\,d\theta = \Big[\ln(1 + \sin\theta)\Big]_0^{\pi/2} = \ln 2 - \ln 1 = \ln 2$

5. Let $u = \sec x$. Then $du = \sec x \tan x\,dx$, so

$\quad \int \tan^7 x \sec^3 x\,dx = \int \tan^6 x \sec^2 x \sec x \tan x\,dx = \int (u^2 - 1)^3 u^2\,du = \int (u^8 - 3u^6 + 3u^4 - u^2)\,du$

$\qquad = \tfrac{1}{9}u^9 - \tfrac{3}{7}u^7 + \tfrac{3}{5}u^5 - \tfrac{1}{3}u^3 + C = \tfrac{1}{9}\sec^9 x - \tfrac{3}{7}\sec^7 x + \tfrac{3}{5}\sec^5 x - \tfrac{1}{3}\sec^3 x + C$

7. Let $u = \ln t$, $du = dt/t$. Then $\displaystyle\int \frac{\sin(\ln t)}{t}\,dt = \int \sin u\,du = -\cos u + C = -\cos(\ln t) + C.$

9. $\displaystyle\int_1^4 x^{3/2}\ln x\,dx$ $\begin{bmatrix} u = \ln x, & dv = x^{3/2}\,dx, \\ du = dx/x & v = \tfrac{2}{5}x^{5/2} \end{bmatrix}$ $= \dfrac{2}{5}\Big[x^{5/2}\ln x\Big]_1^4 - \dfrac{2}{5}\int_1^4 x^{3/2}\,dx$

$\qquad\qquad\qquad = \tfrac{2}{5}(32\ln 4 - \ln 1) - \tfrac{2}{5}\Big[\tfrac{2}{5}x^{5/2}\Big]_1^4$

$\qquad\qquad\qquad = \tfrac{2}{5}(64\ln 2) - \tfrac{4}{25}(32 - 1)$

$\qquad\qquad\qquad = \tfrac{128}{5}\ln 2 - \tfrac{124}{25}$ $\left(\text{or } \tfrac{64}{5}\ln 4 - \tfrac{124}{25}\right)$

11. Let $x = \sec\theta$. Then

$$\int_1^2 \frac{\sqrt{x^2 - 1}}{x}\, dx = \int_0^{\pi/3} \frac{\tan\theta}{\sec\theta} \sec\theta \tan\theta\, d\theta = \int_0^{\pi/3} \tan^2\theta\, d\theta = \int_0^{\pi/3} \left(\sec^2\theta - 1\right) d\theta$$

$$= [\tan\theta - \theta]_0^{\pi/3} = \sqrt{3} - \tfrac{\pi}{3}$$

13. $\displaystyle\int \frac{dx}{x^3 + x} = \int \left(\frac{1}{x} - \frac{x}{x^2 + 1}\right) dx = \ln|x| - \tfrac{1}{2}\ln(x^2 + 1) + C$

15. $\int \sin^2\theta \cos^5\theta\, d\theta = \int \sin^2\theta \left(\cos^2\theta\right)^2 \cos\theta\, d\theta = \int \sin^2\theta \left(1 - \sin^2\theta\right)^2 \cos\theta\, d\theta$

$$= \int u^2 \left(1 - u^2\right)^2 du \quad [u = \sin\theta,\, du = \cos\theta\, d\theta] \ = \int u^2 \left(1 - 2u^2 + u^4\right) du$$

$$= \int \left(u^2 - 2u^4 + u^6\right) du = \tfrac{1}{3}u^3 - \tfrac{2}{5}u^5 + \tfrac{1}{7}u^7 + C = \tfrac{1}{3}\sin^3\theta - \tfrac{2}{5}\sin^5\theta + \tfrac{1}{7}\sin^7\theta + C$$

17. Integrate by parts with $u = x$, $dv = \sec x \tan x\, dx \quad \Rightarrow \quad du = dx$, $v = \sec x$:

$$\int x \sec x \tan x\, dx = x \sec x - \int \sec x\, dx \overset{14}{=} x \sec x - \ln|\sec x + \tan x| + C.$$

19. $\displaystyle\int \frac{x + 1}{9x^2 + 6x + 5}\, dx = \int \frac{x + 1}{(9x^2 + 6x + 1) + 4}\, dx = \int \frac{x + 1}{(3x + 1)^2 + 4}\, dx \quad \begin{bmatrix} u = 3x + 1, \\ du = 3\, dx \end{bmatrix}$

$$= \int \frac{\left[\tfrac{1}{3}(u - 1)\right] + 1}{u^2 + 4}\left(\tfrac{1}{3}\, du\right) = \frac{1}{3} \cdot \frac{1}{3}\int \frac{(u - 1) + 3}{u^2 + 4}\, du$$

$$= \frac{1}{9}\int \frac{u}{u^2 + 4}\, du + \frac{1}{9}\int \frac{2}{u^2 + 2^2}\, du = \frac{1}{9} \cdot \frac{1}{2}\ln(u^2 + 4) + \frac{2}{9} \cdot \frac{1}{2}\tan^{-1}\left(\tfrac{1}{2}u\right) + C$$

$$= \tfrac{1}{18}\ln(9x^2 + 6x + 5) + \tfrac{1}{9}\tan^{-1}\left[\tfrac{1}{2}(3x + 1)\right] + C$$

21.

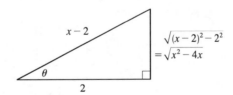

$$\int \frac{dx}{\sqrt{x^2 - 4x}} = \int \frac{dx}{\sqrt{(x^2 - 4x + 4) - 4}} = \int \frac{dx}{\sqrt{(x - 2)^2 - 2^2}}$$

$$= \int \frac{2\sec\theta \tan\theta\, d\theta}{2\tan\theta} \quad \begin{bmatrix} x - 2 = 2\sec\theta, \\ dx = 2\sec\theta \tan\theta\, d\theta \end{bmatrix} = \int \sec\theta\, d\theta = \ln|\sec\theta + \tan\theta| + C_1$$

$$= \ln\left|\frac{x - 2}{2} + \frac{\sqrt{x^2 - 4x}}{2}\right| + C_1 = \ln\left|x - 2 + \sqrt{x^2 - 4x}\right| + C, \text{ where } C = C_1 - \ln 2$$

23. Let $u = \cot 4x$. Then $du = -4\csc^2 4x\, dx \quad \Rightarrow$

$$\int \csc^4 4x\, dx = \int \left(\cot^2 4x + 1\right)\csc^2 4x\, dx = \int \left(u^2 + 1\right)\left(-\tfrac{1}{4}\, du\right)$$

$$= -\tfrac{1}{4}\left(\tfrac{1}{3}u^3 + u\right) + C = -\tfrac{1}{12}\left(\cot^3 4x + 3\cot 4x\right) + C$$

25. $\dfrac{3x^3 - x^2 + 6x - 4}{(x^2 + 1)(x^2 + 2)} = \dfrac{Ax + B}{x^2 + 1} + \dfrac{Cx + D}{x^2 + 2} \quad \Rightarrow$

$3x^3 - x^2 + 6x - 4 = (Ax + B)(x^2 + 2) + (Cx + D)(x^2 + 1)$. Equating the coefficients gives $A + C = 3$,

$B + D = -1$, $2A + C = 6$, and $2B + D = -4 \quad \Rightarrow \quad A = 3, C = 0, B = -3$, and $D = 2$. Now

$$\int \frac{3x^3 - x^2 + 6x - 4}{(x^2 + 1)(x^2 + 2)}\, dx = 3 \int \frac{x - 1}{x^2 + 1}\, dx + 2 \int \frac{dx}{x^2 + 2}$$

$$= \tfrac{3}{2} \ln(x^2 + 1) - 3 \tan^{-1} x + \sqrt{2} \tan^{-1}\left(\tfrac{1}{\sqrt{2}}x\right) + C$$

27. $\int_0^{\pi/2} \cos^3 x \sin 2x\, dx = \int_0^{\pi/2} \cos^3 x\, (2 \sin x \cos x)\, dx = \int_0^{\pi/2} 2 \cos^4 x \sin x\, dx = \left[-\tfrac{2}{5} \cos^5 x\right]_0^{\pi/2} = \tfrac{2}{5}$

29. The product of an odd function and an even function is an odd function, so $f(x) = x^5 \sec x$ is an odd function.

By Theorem 5.5.6(b), $\int_{-1}^1 x^5 \sec x\, dx = 0$.

31. Let $u = \sqrt{e^x - 1}$. Then $u^2 = e^x - 1$ and $2u\, du = e^x\, dx$. Also, $e^x + 8 = u^2 + 9$. Thus,

$$\int_0^{\ln 10} \frac{e^x \sqrt{e^x - 1}}{e^x + 8}\, dx = \int_0^3 \frac{u \cdot 2u\, du}{u^2 + 9} = 2 \int_0^3 \frac{u^2}{u^2 + 9}\, du = 2 \int_0^3 \left(1 - \frac{9}{u^2 + 9}\right) du$$

$$= 2\left[u - \frac{9}{3} \tan^{-1}\left(\frac{u}{3}\right)\right]_0^3 = 2\left[(3 - 3\tan^{-1} 1) - 0\right] = 2\left(3 - 3 \cdot \frac{\pi}{4}\right) = 6 - \frac{3\pi}{2}$$

33. Let $x = 2 \sin \theta \quad \Rightarrow \quad (4 - x^2)^{3/2} = (2 \cos \theta)^3, dx = 2 \cos \theta\, d\theta$, so

$$\int \frac{x^2}{(4 - x^2)^{3/2}}\, dx = \int \frac{4 \sin^2 \theta}{8 \cos^3 \theta}\, 2 \cos \theta\, d\theta$$

$$= \int \tan^2 \theta\, d\theta = \int \left(\sec^2 \theta - 1\right) d\theta$$

$$= \tan \theta - \theta + C = \frac{x}{\sqrt{4 - x^2}} - \sin^{-1}\left(\frac{x}{2}\right) + C$$

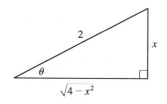

35. $\displaystyle\int \frac{1}{\sqrt{x + x^{3/2}}}\, dx = \int \frac{dx}{\sqrt{x\,(1 + \sqrt{x}\,)}} = \int \frac{dx}{\sqrt{x}\sqrt{1 + \sqrt{x}}} \quad \begin{bmatrix} u = 1 + \sqrt{x}, \\ du = \dfrac{dx}{2\sqrt{x}} \end{bmatrix} = \int \frac{2\, du}{\sqrt{u}} = \int 2u^{-1/2}\, du$

$$= 4\sqrt{u} + C = 4\sqrt{1 + \sqrt{x}} + C$$

37. $\int (\cos x + \sin x)^2 \cos 2x\, dx = \int \left(\cos^2 x + 2 \sin x \cos x + \sin^2 x\right) \cos 2x\, dx$

$\qquad = \int (1 + \sin 2x) \cos 2x\, dx = \int \cos 2x\, dx + \tfrac{1}{2} \int \sin 4x\, dx = \tfrac{1}{2} \sin 2x - \tfrac{1}{8} \cos 4x + C$

$\quad$ *Or:* $\int (\cos x + \sin x)^2 \cos 2x\, dx = \int (\cos x + \sin x)^2 \left(\cos^2 x - \sin^2 x\right) dx$

$\qquad = \int (\cos x + \sin x)^3 (\cos x - \sin x)\, dx = \tfrac{1}{4}(\cos x + \sin x)^4 + C_1$

39. We'll integrate $I = \displaystyle\int \frac{xe^{2x}}{(1+2x)^2}\,dx$ by parts with $u = xe^{2x}$ and $dv = \dfrac{dx}{(1+2x)^2}$. Then

$$du = (x \cdot 2e^{2x} + e^{2x} \cdot 1)\,dx \text{ and } v = -\frac{1}{2} \cdot \frac{1}{1+2x}, \text{ so}$$

$$I = -\frac{1}{2} \cdot \frac{xe^{2x}}{1+2x} - \int \left[-\frac{1}{2} \cdot \frac{e^{2x}(2x+1)}{1+2x} \right] dx = -\frac{xe^{2x}}{4x+2} + \frac{1}{2} \cdot \frac{1}{2} e^{2x} + C$$

$$= e^{2x}\left(\frac{1}{4} - \frac{x}{4x+2} \right) + C.$$

Thus, $\displaystyle\int_0^{1/2} \frac{xe^{2x}}{(1+2x)^2}\,dx = \left[e^{2x}\left(\frac{1}{4} - \frac{x}{4x+2} \right) \right]_0^{1/2} = e\left(\frac{1}{4} - \frac{1}{8} \right) - 1\left(\frac{1}{4} - 0 \right) = \frac{1}{8}e - \frac{1}{4}.$

41. $\displaystyle\int_1^\infty \frac{1}{(2x+1)^3}\,dx = \lim_{t\to\infty} \int_1^t \frac{1}{(2x+1)^3}\,dx = \lim_{t\to\infty} \int_1^t \tfrac{1}{2}(2x+1)^{-3}\,2\,dx$

$$= \lim_{t\to\infty} \left[-\frac{1}{4(2x+1)^2} \right]_1^t = -\frac{1}{4} \lim_{t\to\infty} \left[\frac{1}{(2t+1)^2} - \frac{1}{9} \right] = -\frac{1}{4}\left(0 - \frac{1}{9} \right) = \frac{1}{36}$$

43. $\displaystyle\int \frac{dx}{x\ln x} \quad \begin{bmatrix} u = \ln x, \\ du = \dfrac{dx}{x} \end{bmatrix} = \int \frac{du}{u} = \ln|u| + C = \ln|\ln x| + C$, so

$\displaystyle\int_2^\infty \frac{dx}{x\ln x} = \lim_{t\to\infty} \int_2^t \frac{dx}{x\ln x} = \lim_{t\to\infty} \left[\ln|\ln x| \right]_2^t = \lim_{t\to\infty} \left[\ln(\ln t) - \ln(\ln 2) \right] = \infty$, so the integral is divergent.

45. $\displaystyle\int_0^4 \frac{\ln x}{\sqrt{x}}\,dx = \lim_{t\to 0^+} \int_t^4 \frac{\ln x}{\sqrt{x}}\,dx \overset{*}{=} \lim_{t\to 0^+} \left[2\sqrt{x}\ln x - 4\sqrt{x} \right]_t^4$

$$= \lim_{t\to 0^+} \left[(2 \cdot 2\ln 4 - 4 \cdot 2) - (2\sqrt{t}\ln t - 4\sqrt{t}) \right] \overset{**}{=} (4\ln 4 - 8) - (0 - 0) = 4\ln 4 - 8$$

$(*)$ Let $u = \ln x$, $dv = \dfrac{1}{\sqrt{x}}\,dx \;\Rightarrow\; du = \dfrac{1}{x}\,dx$, $v = 2\sqrt{x}$. Then

$$\int \frac{\ln x}{\sqrt{x}}\,dx = 2\sqrt{x}\ln x - 2\int \frac{dx}{\sqrt{x}} = 2\sqrt{x}\ln x - 4\sqrt{x} + C$$

$(**)$ $\displaystyle\lim_{t\to 0^+} \left(2\sqrt{t}\ln t \right) = \lim_{t\to 0^+} \frac{2\ln t}{t^{-1/2}} \overset{\text{H}}{=} \lim_{t\to 0^+} \frac{2/t}{-\frac{1}{2}t^{-3/2}} = \lim_{t\to 0^+} \left(-4\sqrt{t} \right) = 0$

47. $\displaystyle\int_0^3 \frac{dx}{x^2 - x - 2} = \int_0^3 \frac{dx}{(x+1)(x-2)} = \int_0^2 \frac{dx}{(x+1)(x-2)} + \int_2^3 \frac{dx}{(x+1)(x-2)}$, and

$$\int_2^3 \frac{dx}{x^2 - x - 2} = \lim_{t\to 2^+} \int_t^3 \left[\frac{-1/3}{x+1} + \frac{1/3}{x-2} \right] dx = \lim_{t\to 2^+} \left[\frac{1}{3}\ln\left| \frac{x-2}{x+1} \right| \right]_t^3$$

$$= \lim_{t\to 2^+} \left[\tfrac{1}{3}\ln\tfrac{1}{4} - \frac{1}{3}\ln\left| \frac{t-2}{t+1} \right| \right] = \infty$$

so $\displaystyle\int_0^3 \frac{dx}{x^2 - x - 2}$ diverges.

49. Let $u = 2x + 1$. Then

$$\int_{-\infty}^{\infty} \frac{dx}{4x^2 + 4x + 5} = \int_{-\infty}^{\infty} \frac{\frac{1}{2}\,du}{u^2 + 4} = \frac{1}{2}\int_{-\infty}^{0} \frac{du}{u^2 + 4} + \frac{1}{2}\int_{0}^{\infty} \frac{du}{u^2 + 4}$$

$$= \tfrac{1}{2}\lim_{t\to-\infty}\left[\tfrac{1}{2}\tan^{-1}\left(\tfrac{1}{2}u\right)\right]_{t}^{0} + \tfrac{1}{2}\lim_{t\to\infty}\left[\tfrac{1}{2}\tan^{-1}\left(\tfrac{1}{2}u\right)\right]_{0}^{t}$$

$$= \tfrac{1}{4}\left[0 - \left(-\tfrac{\pi}{2}\right)\right] + \tfrac{1}{4}\left[\tfrac{\pi}{2} - 0\right] = \tfrac{\pi}{4}$$

51. We first make the substitution $t = x + 1$, so $\ln\left(x^2 + 2x + 2\right) = \ln\left[(x+1)^2 + 1\right] = \ln\left(t^2 + 1\right)$. Then we use parts with $u = \ln\left(t^2 + 1\right)$, $dv = dt$:

$$\int \ln\left(t^2 + 1\right)dt = t\,\ln\left(t^2 + 1\right) - \int \frac{t(2t)\,dt}{t^2 + 1} = t\,\ln\left(t^2 + 1\right) - 2\int \frac{t^2\,dt}{t^2 + 1}$$

$$= t\,\ln\left(t^2 + 1\right) - 2\int\left(1 - \frac{1}{t^2 + 1}\right)dt = t\,\ln\left(t^2 + 1\right) - 2t + 2\arctan t + C$$

$$= (x + 1)\ln\left(x^2 + 2x + 2\right) - 2x + 2\arctan(x + 1) + K, \text{ where } K = C - 2$$

[Alternatively, we could have integrated by parts immediately with $u = \ln\left(x^2 + 2x + 2\right)$.] Notice from the graph that $f = 0$ where F has a horizontal tangent. Also, F is always increasing, and $f \geq 0$.

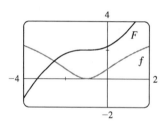

53. From the graph, it seems as though $\int_{0}^{2\pi} \cos^2 x \sin^3 x\,dx$ is equal to 0. To evaluate the integral, we write the integral as $I = \int_{0}^{2\pi} \cos^2 x \left(1 - \cos^2 x\right)\sin x\,dx$ and let $u = \cos x$ $\Rightarrow$ $du = -\sin x\,dx$. Thus, $I = \int_{1}^{1} u^2\left(1 - u^2\right)(-du) = 0$.

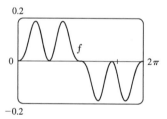

55. $u = e^x$ $\Rightarrow$ $du = e^x\,dx$, so

$$\int e^x\sqrt{1 - e^{2x}}\,dx = \int \sqrt{1 - u^2}\,du \overset{30}{=} \tfrac{1}{2}u\sqrt{1 - u^2} + \tfrac{1}{2}\sin^{-1}u + C = \tfrac{1}{2}\left[e^x\sqrt{1 - e^{2x}} + \sin^{-1}(e^x)\right] + C$$

57. $\displaystyle\int \sqrt{x^2 + x + 1}\,dx = \int \sqrt{x^2 + x + \tfrac{1}{4} + \tfrac{3}{4}}\,dx = \int \sqrt{\left(x + \tfrac{1}{2}\right)^2 + \tfrac{3}{4}}\,dx$

$$= \int \sqrt{u^2 + \left(\tfrac{\sqrt{3}}{2}\right)^2}\,du \quad [u = x + \tfrac{1}{2},\, du = dx]$$

$$\overset{21}{=} \tfrac{1}{2}u\sqrt{u^2 + \tfrac{3}{4}} + \tfrac{3}{8}\ln\left(u + \sqrt{u^2 + \tfrac{3}{4}}\right) + C$$

$$= \frac{2x + 1}{4}\sqrt{x^2 + x + 1} + \tfrac{3}{8}\ln\left(x + \tfrac{1}{2} + \sqrt{x^2 + x + 1}\right) + C$$

59. (a) $\dfrac{d}{du}\left[-\dfrac{1}{u}\sqrt{a^2-u^2}-\sin^{-1}\left(\dfrac{u}{a}\right)+C\right]=\dfrac{1}{u^2}\sqrt{a^2-u^2}+\dfrac{1}{\sqrt{a^2-u^2}}-\dfrac{1}{\sqrt{1-u^2/a^2}}\cdot\dfrac{1}{a}$

$$=\left(a^2-u^2\right)^{-1/2}\left[\dfrac{1}{u^2}\left(a^2-u^2\right)+1-1\right]=\dfrac{\sqrt{a^2-u^2}}{u^2}$$

(b) Let $u=a\sin\theta\ \Rightarrow\ du=a\cos\theta\,d\theta,\ a^2-u^2=a^2\left(1-\sin^2\theta\right)=a^2\cos^2\theta.$

$$\int\dfrac{\sqrt{a^2-u^2}}{u^2}\,du=\int\dfrac{a^2\cos^2\theta}{a^2\sin^2\theta}\,d\theta=\int\dfrac{1-\sin^2\theta}{\sin^2\theta}\,d\theta=\int\left(\csc^2\theta-1\right)d\theta=-\cot\theta-\theta+C$$

$$=-\dfrac{\sqrt{a^2-u^2}}{u}-\sin^{-1}\left(\dfrac{u}{a}\right)+C$$

61. For $n\geq 0$, $\int_0^\infty x^n\,dx=\lim\limits_{t\to\infty}\left[x^{n+1}/(n+1)\right]_0^t=\infty.$ For $n<0$, $\int_0^\infty x^n\,dx=\int_0^1 x^n\,dx+\int_1^\infty x^n\,dx.$ Both

integrals are improper. By (8.8.2), the second integral diverges if $-1\leq n<0$. By Exercise 8.8.57, the first integral

diverges if $n\leq -1$. Thus, $\int_0^\infty x^n\,dx$ is divergent for all values of n.

63. $f(x)=\sqrt{1+x^4},\ \Delta x=\dfrac{b-a}{n}=\dfrac{1-0}{10}=\dfrac{1}{10}.$

(a) $T_{10}=\dfrac{1}{10\cdot 2}\{f(0)+2\left[f(0.1)+f(0.2)+\cdots+f(0.9)\right]+f(1)\}\approx 1.090608$

(b) $M_{10}=\dfrac{1}{10}\left[f\left(\dfrac{1}{20}\right)+f\left(\dfrac{3}{20}\right)+f\left(\dfrac{5}{20}\right)+\cdots+f\left(\dfrac{19}{20}\right)\right]\approx 1.088840$

(c) $S_{10}=\dfrac{1}{10\cdot 3}\left[f(0)+4f(0.1)+2f(0.2)+\cdots+4f(0.9)+f(1)\right]\approx 1.089429$

f is concave upward, so the Trapezoidal Rule gives us an overestimate, the Midpoint Rule gives an underestimate,

and we cannot tell whether Simpson's Rule gives us an overestimate or an underestimate.

65. $f(x)=\left(1+x^4\right)^{1/2},\ f'(x)=\dfrac{1}{2}\left(1+x^4\right)^{-1/2}\left(4x^3\right)=2x^3\left(1+x^4\right)^{-1/2},\ f''(x)=\left(2x^6+6x^2\right)\left(1+x^4\right)^{-3/2}.$

A graph of f'' on $[0,1]$ shows that it has its maximum at $x=1$, so $|f''(x)|\leq f''(1)=\sqrt{8}$ on $[0,1]$. By taking

$K=\sqrt{8}$, we find that the error in Exercise 63(a) is bounded by $\dfrac{K(b-a)^3}{12n^2}=\dfrac{\sqrt{8}}{1200}\approx 0.0024$, and in (b) by about

$\dfrac{1}{2}(0.0024)=0.0012.$

Note: Another way to estimate K is to let $x=1$ in the factor $2x^6+6x^2$ (maximizing the numerator) and let $x=0$

in the factor $\left(1+x^4\right)^{-3/2}$ (minimizing the denominator). Doing so gives us $K=8$ and errors of $0.00\overline{6}$ and $0.00\overline{3}$.

Using $K=8$ for the Trapezoidal Rule, we have $|E_T|\leq\dfrac{K(b-a)^3}{12n^2}\leq 0.00001\ \Leftrightarrow\ \dfrac{8(1-0)^3}{12n^2}\leq\dfrac{1}{100,000}$

$\Leftrightarrow\ n^2\geq\dfrac{800,000}{12}\ \Leftrightarrow\ n\gtrsim 258.2,$ so we should take $n=259.$

For the Midpoint Rule, $|E_M|\leq\dfrac{K(b-a)^3}{24n^2}\leq 0.00001\ \Leftrightarrow\ n^2\geq\dfrac{800,000}{24}\ \Leftrightarrow\ n\gtrsim 182.6,$ so we should

take $n=183.$

67. $\Delta t = \left(\frac{10}{60} - 0\right) / 10 = \frac{1}{60}$.

Distance traveled $= \int_0^{10} v \, dt \approx S_{10}$

$$= \frac{1}{60 \cdot 3}[40 + 4(42) + 2(45) + 4(49) + 2(52) + 4(54) + 2(56) + 4(57) + 2(57) + 4(55) + 56]$$

$$= \frac{1}{180}(1544) = 8.5\overline{7} \text{ mi}$$

69. (a) $f(x) = \sin(\sin x)$. A CAS gives

$$f^{(4)}(x) = \sin(\sin x)\left[\cos^4 x + 7\cos^2 x - 3\right]$$

$$+ \cos(\sin x)\left[6\cos^2 x \sin x + \sin x\right]$$

From the graph, we see that $\left|f^{(4)}(x)\right| < 3.8$ for $x \in [0, \pi]$.

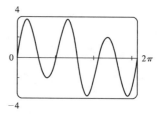

(b) We use Simpson's Rule with $f(x) = \sin(\sin x)$ and $\Delta x = \frac{\pi}{10}$:

$$\int_0^\pi f(x) \, dx \approx \frac{\pi}{10 \cdot 3}\left[f(0) + 4f\left(\frac{\pi}{10}\right) + 2f\left(\frac{2\pi}{10}\right) + \cdots + 4f\left(\frac{9\pi}{10}\right) + f(\pi)\right] \approx 1.786721$$

From part (a), we know that $\left|f^{(4)}(x)\right| < 3.8$ on $[0, \pi]$, so we use Theorem 8.7.4 with $K = 3.8$, and estimate the

error as $|E_S| \leq \dfrac{3.8(\pi - 0)^5}{180(10)^4} \approx 0.000646$.

(c) If we want the error to be less than 0.00001, we must have $|E_S| \leq \frac{3.8\pi^5}{180n^4} \leq 0.00001$, so

$n^4 \geq \frac{3.8\pi^5}{180(0.00001)} \approx 646{,}041.6 \quad \Rightarrow \quad n \geq 28.35$. Since n must be even for Simpson's Rule, we must have

$n \geq 30$ to ensure the desired accuracy.

71. $\dfrac{x^3}{x^5 + 2} \leq \dfrac{x^3}{x^5} = \dfrac{1}{x^2}$ for x in $[1, \infty)$. $\displaystyle\int_1^\infty \dfrac{1}{x^2} \, dx$ is convergent by (8.8.2) with $p = 2 > 1$. Therefore,

$\displaystyle\int_1^\infty \dfrac{x^3}{x^5 + 2} \, dx$ is convergent by the Comparison Theorem.

73. For x in $\left[0, \frac{\pi}{2}\right]$, $0 \leq \cos^2 x \leq \cos x$. For x in $\left[\frac{\pi}{2}, \pi\right]$, $\cos x \leq 0 \leq \cos^2 x$. Thus,

$$\text{area} = \int_0^{\pi/2}\left(\cos x - \cos^2 x\right) dx + \int_{\pi/2}^{\pi}\left(\cos^2 x - \cos x\right) dx$$

$$= \left[\sin x - \tfrac{1}{2}x - \tfrac{1}{4}\sin 2x\right]_0^{\pi/2} + \left[\tfrac{1}{2}x + \tfrac{1}{4}\sin 2x - \sin x\right]_{\pi/2}^{\pi}$$

$$= \left[\left(1 - \tfrac{\pi}{4}\right) - 0\right] + \left[\tfrac{\pi}{2} - \left(\tfrac{\pi}{4} - 1\right)\right] = 2$$

75. Using the formula for disks, the volume is

$$V = \int_0^{\pi/2} \pi\left[f(x)\right]^2 dx = \pi \int_0^{\pi/2}\left(\cos^2 x\right)^2 dx = \pi \int_0^{\pi/2}\left[\tfrac{1}{2}(1 + \cos 2x)\right]^2 dx$$

$$= \tfrac{\pi}{4}\int_0^{\pi/2}(1 + \cos^2 2x + 2\cos 2x)\, dx = \tfrac{\pi}{4}\int_0^{\pi/2}\left[1 + \tfrac{1}{2}(1 + \cos 4x) + 2\cos 2x\right] dx$$

$$= \tfrac{\pi}{4}\left[\tfrac{3}{2}x + \tfrac{1}{2}\left(\tfrac{1}{4}\sin 4x\right) + 2\left(\tfrac{1}{2}\sin 2x\right)\right]_0^{\pi/2} = \tfrac{\pi}{4}\left[\left(\tfrac{3\pi}{4} + \tfrac{1}{8}\cdot 0 + 0\right) - 0\right] = \tfrac{3\pi^2}{16}$$

77. By the Fundamental Theorem of Calculus,

$$\int_0^\infty f'(x)\,dx = \lim_{t\to\infty}\int_0^t f'(x)\,dx = \lim_{t\to\infty}\left[f(t) - f(0)\right] = \lim_{t\to\infty} f(t) - f(0) = 0 - f(0) = -f(0).$$

79. Let $u = 1/x \;\Rightarrow\; x = 1/u \;\Rightarrow\; dx = -\left(1/u^2\right)du.$

$$\int_0^\infty \frac{\ln x}{1 + x^2}\,dx = \int_\infty^0 \frac{\ln(1/u)}{1 + 1/u^2}\left(-\frac{du}{u^2}\right) = \int_\infty^0 \frac{-\ln u}{u^2 + 1}\,(-du) = \int_\infty^0 \frac{\ln u}{1 + u^2}\,du = -\int_0^\infty \frac{\ln u}{1 + u^2}\,du$$

Therefore, $\displaystyle\int_0^\infty \frac{\ln x}{1 + x^2}\,dx = -\int_0^\infty \frac{\ln x}{1 + x^2}\,dx = 0.$

☐ PROBLEMS PLUS

1.

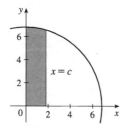 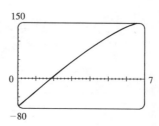

By symmetry, the problem can be reduced to finding the line $x = c$ such that the shaded area is one-third of the area

of the quarter-circle. The equation of the circle is $y = \sqrt{49 - x^2}$, so we require that $\int_0^c \sqrt{49 - x^2}\, dx = \frac{1}{3} \cdot \frac{1}{4}\pi(7)^2$

$\Leftrightarrow \left[\frac{1}{2}x\sqrt{49 - x^2} + \frac{49}{2}\sin^{-1}(x/7)\right]_0^c = \frac{49}{12}\pi$ [by Formula 30] $\Leftrightarrow$ $\frac{1}{2}c\sqrt{49 - c^2} + \frac{49}{2}\sin^{-1}(c/7) = \frac{49}{12}\pi$.

This equation would be difficult to solve exactly, so we plot the left-hand side as a function of c, and find that the

equation holds for $c \approx 1.85$. So the cuts should be made at distances of about 1.85 inches from the center of the

pizza.

3. The given integral represents the difference of the shaded areas, which appears

to be 0. It can be calculated by integrating with respect to either x or y, so we

find x in terms of y for each curve: $y = \sqrt[3]{1 - x^7}$ $\Rightarrow$ $x = \sqrt[7]{1 - y^3}$ and

$y = \sqrt[7]{1 - x^3}$ $\Rightarrow$ $x = \sqrt[3]{1 - y^7}$, so

$\int_0^1 \left(\sqrt[3]{1 - y^7} - \sqrt[7]{1 - y^3}\right) dy = \int_0^1 \left(\sqrt[7]{1 - x^3} - \sqrt[3]{1 - x^7}\right) dx$. But this

equation is of the form $z = -z$. So $\int_0^1 \left(\sqrt[3]{1 - x^7} - \sqrt[7]{1 - x^3}\right) dx = 0$.

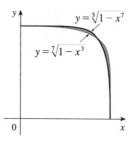

5. Recall that $\cos A \cos B = \frac{1}{2}[\cos(A + B) + \cos(A - B)]$. So

$$f(x) = \int_0^\pi \cos t \cos(x - t)\, dt = \frac{1}{2}\int_0^\pi [\cos(t + x - t) + \cos(t - x + t)]\, dt$$

$$= \frac{1}{2}\int_0^\pi [\cos x + \cos(2t - x)]\, dt = \frac{1}{2}\left[t\cos x + \frac{1}{2}\sin(2t - x)\right]_0^\pi$$

$$= \frac{\pi}{2}\cos x + \frac{1}{4}\sin(2\pi - x) - \frac{1}{4}\sin(-x) = \frac{\pi}{2}\cos x + \frac{1}{4}\sin(-x) - \frac{1}{4}\sin(-x)$$

$$= \frac{\pi}{2}\cos x$$

The minimum of $\cos x$ on this domain is -1, so the minimum value of $f(x)$ is $f(\pi) = -\frac{\pi}{2}$.

7. In accordance with the hint, we let $I_k = \int_0^1 \left(1 - x^2\right)^k \, dx$, and we find an expression for I_{k+1} in terms of I_k. We integrate I_{k+1} by parts with $u = \left(1 - x^2\right)^{k+1} \;\Rightarrow\; du = (k+1)\left(1 - x^2\right)^k(-2x), dv = dx \;\Rightarrow\; v = x$, and then split the remaining integral into identifiable quantities:

$$I_{k+1} = x(1 - x^2)^{k+1}\Big|_0^1 + 2(k+1)\int_0^1 x^2\left(1 - x^2\right)^k \, dx = (2k+2)\int_0^1 \left(1 - x^2\right)^k\left[1 - \left(1 - x^2\right)\right] dx$$

$$= (2k+2)(I_k - I_{k+1})$$

So $I_{k+1}[1 + (2k+2)] = (2k+2)I_k \;\Rightarrow\; I_{k+1} = \frac{2k+2}{2k+3} I_k$. Now to complete the proof, we use induction:

$I_0 = 1 = \dfrac{2^0(0!)^2}{1!}$, so the formula holds for $n = 0$. Now suppose it holds for $n = k$. Then

$$I_{k+1} = \frac{2k+2}{2k+3} I_k = \frac{2k+2}{2k+3}\left[\frac{2^{2k}(k!)^2}{(2k+1)!}\right] = \frac{2(k+1)2^{2k}(k!)^2}{(2k+3)(2k+1)!} = \frac{2(k+1)}{2k+2}\cdot\frac{2(k+1)2^{2k}(k!)^2}{(2k+3)(2k+1)!}$$

$$= \frac{[2(k+1)]^2\,2^{2k}(k!)^2}{(2k+3)(2k+2)(2k+1)!} = \frac{2^{2(k+1)}\,[(k+1)!]^2}{[2(k+1)+1]!}$$

So by induction, the formula holds for all integers $n \geq 0$.

9. $0 < a < b$. Now

$$\int_0^1 [bx + a(1-x)]^t \, dx = \int_a^b \frac{u^t}{(b-a)}\, du \quad [\text{put } u = bx + a(1-x)] \quad = \left[\frac{u^{t+1}}{(t+1)(b-a)}\right]_a^b = \frac{b^{t+1} - a^{t+1}}{(t+1)(b-a)}.$$

Now let $y = \lim_{t \to 0}\left[\dfrac{b^{t+1} - a^{t+1}}{(t+1)(b-a)}\right]^{1/t}$. Then $\ln y = \lim_{t \to 0}\left[\dfrac{1}{t}\ln\dfrac{b^{t+1} - a^{t+1}}{(t+1)(b-a)}\right]$. This limit is of the form $0/0$, so we can apply l'Hospital's Rule to get

$$\ln y = \lim_{t \to 0}\left[\frac{b^{t+1}\ln b - a^{t+1}\ln a}{b^{t+1} - a^{t+1}} - \frac{1}{t+1}\right] = \frac{b\ln b - a\ln a}{b-a} - 1 = \frac{b\ln b}{b-a} - \frac{a\ln a}{b-a} - \ln e = \ln\frac{b^{b/(b-a)}}{ea^{a/(b-a)}}.$$

Therefore, $y = e^{-1}\left(\dfrac{b^b}{a^a}\right)^{1/(b-a)}$.

11.

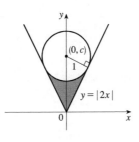

An equation of the circle with center $(0, c)$ and radius 1 is $x^2 + (y - c)^2 = 1^2$, so an equation of the lower semicircle is $y = c - \sqrt{1 - x^2}$. At the points of tangency, the slopes of the line and semicircle must be equal. For $x \geq 0$, we must have

$$y' = 2 \;\Rightarrow\; \frac{x}{\sqrt{1 - x^2}} = 2 \;\Rightarrow\; x = 2\sqrt{1 - x^2} \;\Rightarrow$$

$$x^2 = 4(1 - x^2) \;\Rightarrow\; 5x^2 = 4 \;\Rightarrow\; x^2 = \tfrac{4}{5} \;\Rightarrow\; x = \tfrac{2}{5}\sqrt{5}$$

and so $y = 2\left(\tfrac{2}{5}\sqrt{5}\right) = \tfrac{4}{5}\sqrt{5}$. The slope of the perpendicular line segment is $-\tfrac{1}{2}$, so an equation of the line segment is $y - \frac{4}{5}\sqrt{5} = -\frac{1}{2}\left(x - \frac{2}{5}\sqrt{5}\right) \Leftrightarrow y = -\frac{1}{2}x + \frac{1}{5}\sqrt{5} + \frac{4}{5}\sqrt{5} \Leftrightarrow y = -\frac{1}{2}x + \sqrt{5}$, so $c = \sqrt{5}$ and

an equation of the lower semicircle is $y = \sqrt{5} - \sqrt{1 - x^2}$. Thus, the shaded area is

$$2\int_0^{(2/5)\sqrt{5}}\left[\left(\sqrt{5} - \sqrt{1 - x^2}\right) - 2x\right]dx \overset{30}{=} 2\left[\sqrt{5}\,x - \frac{x}{2}\sqrt{1 - x^2} - \frac{1}{2}\sin^{-1}x - x^2\right]_0^{(2/5)\sqrt{5}}$$

$$= 2\left[2 - \frac{\sqrt{5}}{5}\cdot\frac{1}{\sqrt{5}} - \frac{1}{2}\sin^{-1}\left(\frac{2}{\sqrt{5}}\right) - \frac{4}{5}\right] - 2(0)$$

$$= 2\left[1 - \frac{1}{2}\sin^{-1}\left(\frac{2}{\sqrt{5}}\right)\right] = 2 - \sin^{-1}\left(\frac{2}{\sqrt{5}}\right)$$

13. We integrate by parts with $u = \dfrac{1}{\ln(1 + x + t)}$, $dv = \sin t\,dt$, so $du = \dfrac{-1}{(1 + x + t)[\ln(1 + x + t)]^2}$ and

$v = -\cos t$. The integral becomes

$$I = \int_0^\infty \frac{\sin t\,dt}{\ln(1 + x + t)} = \lim_{b\to\infty}\left(\left[\frac{-\cos t}{\ln(1 + x + t)}\right]_0^b - \int_0^b \frac{\cos t\,dt}{(1 + x + t)[\ln(1 + x + t)]^2}\right)$$

$$= \lim_{b\to\infty}\frac{-\cos b}{\ln(1 + x + b)} + \frac{1}{\ln(1 + x)} + \int_0^\infty \frac{-\cos t\,dt}{(1 + x + t)[\ln(1 + x + t)]^2} = \frac{1}{\ln(1 + x)} + J$$

where $J = \displaystyle\int_0^\infty \frac{-\cos t\,dt}{(1 + x + t)[\ln(1 + x + t)]^2}$. Now $-1 \le -\cos t \le 1$ for all t; in fact, the inequality is strict

except at isolated points. So $-\displaystyle\int_0^\infty \frac{dt}{(1 + x + t)[\ln(1 + x + t)]^2} < J < \int_0^\infty \frac{dt}{(1 + x + t)[\ln(1 + x + t)]^2} \Leftrightarrow$

$-\dfrac{1}{\ln(1 + x)} < J < \dfrac{1}{\ln(1 + x)} \Leftrightarrow 0 < I < \dfrac{2}{\ln(1 + x)}$.

9 □ FURTHER APPLICATIONS OF INTEGRATION

9.1 Arc Length

1. $y = 2 - 3x \quad \Rightarrow \quad L = \int_{-2}^{1} \sqrt{1 + (dy/dx)^2}\, dx = \int_{-2}^{1} \sqrt{1 + (-3)^2}\, dx = \sqrt{10}\,[1 - (-2)] = 3\sqrt{10}.$

The arc length can be calculated using the distance formula, since the curve is a line segment, so

$$L = [\text{distance from } (-2, 8) \text{ to } (1, -1)] = \sqrt{[1 - (-2)]^2 + [(-1) - 8]^2} = \sqrt{90} = 3\sqrt{10}$$

3.

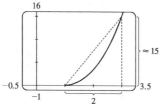

From the figure, the length of the curve is slightly larger than the hypotenuse of the triangle formed by the points $(1, 0)$, $(3, 0)$, and $(3, f(3)) \approx (3, 15)$, where $y = f(x) = \frac{2}{3}(x^2 - 1)^{3/2}$. This length is about $\sqrt{15^2 + 2^2} \approx 15$, so we might estimate the length to be 15.5. $y = \frac{2}{3}(x^2 - 1)^{3/2} \quad \Rightarrow \quad y' = (x^2 - 1)^{1/2}(2x) \quad \Rightarrow$

$1 + (y')^2 = 1 + 4x^2(x^2 - 1) = 4x^4 - 4x^2 + 1 = (2x^2 - 1)^2$, so, using the fact that $2x^2 - 1 > 0$ for $1 \le x \le 3$,

$$L = \int_{1}^{3} \sqrt{(2x^2 - 1)^2}\, dx = \int_{1}^{3} |2x^2 - 1|\, dx = \int_{1}^{3} (2x^2 - 1)\, dx = \left[\tfrac{2}{3}x^3 - x\right]_1^3$$

$$= (18 - 3) - \left(\tfrac{2}{3} - 1\right) = \tfrac{46}{3} = 15.\overline{3}$$

5. $y = 1 + 6x^{3/2} \quad \Rightarrow \quad dy/dx = 9x^{1/2} \quad \Rightarrow \quad 1 + (dy/dx)^2 = 1 + 81x.$ So

$L = \int_{0}^{1} \sqrt{1 + 81x}\, dx = \int_{1}^{82} u^{1/2}\left(\tfrac{1}{81}\, du\right) \qquad [\text{where } u = 1 + 81x \text{ and } du = 81\, dx]$

$= \tfrac{1}{81} \cdot \tfrac{2}{3} \left[u^{3/2}\right]_1^{82} = \tfrac{2}{243}\left(82\sqrt{82} - 1\right)$

7. $y = \dfrac{x^5}{6} + \dfrac{1}{10x^3} \quad \Rightarrow \quad \dfrac{dy}{dx} = \dfrac{5}{6}x^4 - \dfrac{3}{10}x^{-4} \quad \Rightarrow$

$1 + (dy/dx)^2 = 1 + \tfrac{25}{36}x^8 - \tfrac{1}{2} + \tfrac{9}{100}x^{-8} = \tfrac{25}{36}x^8 + \tfrac{1}{2} + \tfrac{9}{100}x^{-8} = \left(\tfrac{5}{6}x^4 + \tfrac{3}{10}x^{-4}\right)^2.$ So

$L = \int_{1}^{2} \sqrt{\left(\tfrac{5}{6}x^4 + \tfrac{3}{10}x^{-4}\right)^2}\, dx = \int_{1}^{2} \left(\tfrac{5}{6}x^4 + \tfrac{3}{10}x^{-4}\right) dx = \left[\tfrac{1}{6}x^5 - \tfrac{1}{10}x^{-3}\right]_1^2$

$= \left(\tfrac{32}{6} - \tfrac{1}{80}\right) - \left(\tfrac{1}{6} - \tfrac{1}{10}\right) = \tfrac{31}{6} + \tfrac{7}{80} = \tfrac{1261}{240}$

9. $x = \tfrac{1}{3}\sqrt{y}\,(y - 3) = \tfrac{1}{3}y^{3/2} - y^{1/2} \quad \Rightarrow \quad dx/dy = \tfrac{1}{2}y^{1/2} - \tfrac{1}{2}y^{-1/2} \quad \Rightarrow$

$1 + (dx/dy)^2 = 1 + \tfrac{1}{4}y - \tfrac{1}{2} + \tfrac{1}{4}y^{-1} = \tfrac{1}{4}y + \tfrac{1}{2} + \tfrac{1}{4}y^{-1} = \left(\tfrac{1}{2}y^{1/2} + \tfrac{1}{2}y^{-1/2}\right)^2.$ So

$L = \int_{1}^{9} \left(\tfrac{1}{2}y^{1/2} + \tfrac{1}{2}y^{-1/2}\right) dy = \tfrac{1}{2}\left[\tfrac{2}{3}y^{3/2} + 2y^{1/2}\right]_1^9 = \tfrac{1}{2}\left[\left(\tfrac{2}{3} \cdot 27 + 2 \cdot 3\right) - \left(\tfrac{2}{3} \cdot 1 + 2 \cdot 1\right)\right]$

$= \tfrac{1}{2}\left(24 - \tfrac{8}{3}\right) = \tfrac{1}{2}\left(\tfrac{64}{3}\right) = \tfrac{32}{3}$

11. $y = \ln(\sec x) \quad \Rightarrow \quad \dfrac{dy}{dx} = \dfrac{\sec x \tan x}{\sec x} = \tan x \quad \Rightarrow \quad 1 + \left(\dfrac{dy}{dx}\right)^2 = 1 + \tan^2 x = \sec^2 x,$ so

$L = \int_{0}^{\pi/4} \sqrt{\sec^2 x}\, dx = \int_{0}^{\pi/4} |\sec x|\, dx = \int_{0}^{\pi/4} \sec x\, dx = \left[\ln(\sec x + \tan x)\right]_0^{\pi/4}$

$= \ln\left(\sqrt{2} + 1\right) - \ln(1 + 0) = \ln\left(\sqrt{2} + 1\right)$

13. $y = \cosh x \;\Rightarrow\; y' = \sinh x \;\Rightarrow\; 1 + (y')^2 = 1 + \sinh^2 x = \cosh^2 x.$

So $L = \int_0^1 \cosh x \, dx = [\sinh x]_0^1 = \sinh 1 = \frac{1}{2}(e - 1/e).$

15. $y = e^x \;\Rightarrow\; y' = e^x \;\Rightarrow\; 1 + (y')^2 = 1 + e^{2x}.$ So

$$L = \int_0^1 \sqrt{1 + e^{2x}} \, dx = \int_1^e \sqrt{1 + u^2}\frac{du}{u} \qquad [u = e^x, \text{ so } x = \ln u, \, dx = du/u]$$

$$= \int_1^e \frac{\sqrt{1+u^2}}{u^2} u \, du = \int_{\sqrt{2}}^{\sqrt{1+e^2}} \frac{v}{v^2-1} v \, dv \qquad \left[v = \sqrt{1+u^2}, \text{ so } v^2 = 1 + u^2, \, v \, dv = u \, du\right]$$

$$= \int_{\sqrt{2}}^{\sqrt{1+e^2}} \left(1 + \frac{1/2}{v-1} - \frac{1/2}{v+1}\right) dv = \left[v + \frac{1}{2}\ln\frac{v-1}{v+1}\right]_{\sqrt{2}}^{\sqrt{1+e^2}}$$

$$= \sqrt{1+e^2} + \frac{1}{2}\ln\frac{\sqrt{1+e^2}-1}{\sqrt{1+e^2}+1} - \sqrt{2} - \frac{1}{2}\ln\frac{\sqrt{2}-1}{\sqrt{2}+1}$$

$$= \sqrt{1+e^2} - \sqrt{2} + \ln\left(\sqrt{1+e^2}-1\right) - 1 - \ln\left(\sqrt{2}-1\right)$$

Or: Use Formula 23 for $\int \left(\sqrt{1+u^2}/u\right) du$, or substitute $u = \tan\theta$.

17. $y = \cos x \;\Rightarrow\; dy/dx = -\sin x \;\Rightarrow\; 1 + (dy/dx)^2 = 1 + \sin^2 x.$ So $L = \int_0^{2\pi} \sqrt{1 + \sin^2 x} \, dx.$

19. $x = y + y^3 \;\Rightarrow\; dx/dy = 1 + 3y^2 \;\Rightarrow\; 1 + (dx/dy)^2 = 1 + (1 + 3y^2)^2 = 9y^4 + 6y^2 + 2.$

So $L = \int_1^4 \sqrt{9y^4 + 6y^2 + 2} \, dy.$

21. $y = xe^{-x} \;\Rightarrow\; dy/dx = e^{-x} - xe^{-x} = e^{-x}(1-x) \;\Rightarrow\; 1 + (dy/dx)^2 = 1 + e^{-2x}(1-x)^2.$ Let

$f(x) = \sqrt{1 + (dy/dx)^2} = \sqrt{1 + e^{-2x}(1-x)^2}.$ Then $L = \int_0^5 f(x) \, dx.$ Since $n = 10$, $\Delta x = \frac{5-0}{10} = \frac{1}{2}.$ Now

$$L \approx S_{10} = \frac{1/2}{3}\left[f(0) + 4f\left(\tfrac{1}{2}\right) + 2f(1) + 4f\left(\tfrac{3}{2}\right) + 2f(2) + 4f\left(\tfrac{5}{2}\right) + 2f(3)\right.$$
$$\left. + 4f\left(\tfrac{7}{2}\right) + 2f(4) + 4f\left(\tfrac{9}{2}\right) + f(5)\right] \approx 5.115840$$

The value of the integral produced by a calculator is 5.113568 (to six decimal places).

23. $y = \sec x \;\Rightarrow\; dy/dx = \sec x \tan x \;\Rightarrow\; L = \int_0^{\pi/3} f(x) \, dx$, where $f(x) = \sqrt{1 + \sec^2 x \tan^2 x}.$

Since $n = 10$, $\Delta x = \dfrac{\pi/3 - 0}{10} = \dfrac{\pi}{30}.$ Now

$$L \approx S_{10} = \frac{\pi/30}{3}\left[f(0) + 4f\left(\frac{\pi}{30}\right) + 2f\left(\frac{2\pi}{30}\right) + 4f\left(\frac{3\pi}{30}\right) + 2f\left(\frac{4\pi}{30}\right) + 4f\left(\frac{5\pi}{30}\right)\right.$$
$$\left. + 2f\left(\frac{6\pi}{30}\right) + 4f\left(\frac{7\pi}{30}\right) + 2f\left(\frac{8\pi}{30}\right) + 4f\left(\frac{9\pi}{30}\right) + f\left(\frac{\pi}{3}\right)\right] \approx 1.569619.$$

The value of the integral produced by a calculator is 1.569259 (to six decimal places).

25. (a)

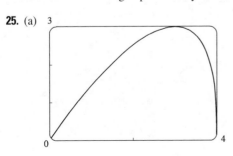

(b)

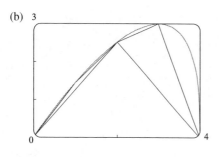

Let $f(x) = y = x\sqrt[3]{4-x}$. The polygon with one side is just the line segment joining the points $(0, f(0)) = (0,0)$ and $(4, f(4)) = (4,0)$, and its length is 4. The polygon with two sides joins the points $(0,0)$, $(2, f(2)) = (2, 2\sqrt[3]{2})$ and $(4,0)$.

Its length is

$$\sqrt{(2-0)^2 + \left(2\sqrt[3]{2} - 0\right)^2} + \sqrt{(4-2)^2 + \left(0 - 2\sqrt[3]{2}\right)^2} = 2\sqrt{4 + 2^{8/3}} \approx 6.43$$

Similarly, the inscribed polygon with four sides joins the points $(0,0)$, $(1, \sqrt[3]{3})$, $(2, 2\sqrt[3]{2})$, $(3,3)$, and $(4,0)$, so its length is

$$\sqrt{1 + \left(\sqrt[3]{3}\right)^2} + \sqrt{1 + \left(2\sqrt[3]{2} - \sqrt[3]{3}\right)^2} + \sqrt{1 + \left(3 - 2\sqrt[3]{2}\right)^2} + \sqrt{1+9} \approx 7.50$$

(c) Using the arc length formula with $\dfrac{dy}{dx} = x\left[\frac{1}{3}(4-x)^{-2/3}(-1)\right] + \sqrt[3]{4-x} = \dfrac{12 - 4x}{3(4-x)^{2/3}}$, the length of the

curve is $L = \displaystyle\int_0^4 \sqrt{1 + \left(\dfrac{dy}{dx}\right)^2}\, dx = \int_0^4 \sqrt{1 + \left[\dfrac{12 - 4x}{3(4-x)^{2/3}}\right]^2}\, dx.$

(d) According to a CAS, the length of the curve is $L \approx 7.7988$. The actual value is larger than any of the approximations in part (b). This is always true, since any approximating straight line between two points on the curve is shorter than the length of the curve between the two points.

27. $x = \ln(1 - y^2) \Rightarrow \dfrac{dx}{dy} = \dfrac{-2y}{1 - y^2} \Rightarrow 1 + \left(\dfrac{dx}{dy}\right)^2 = 1 + \dfrac{4y^2}{(1-y^2)^2} = \dfrac{(1 + y^2)^2}{(1 - y^2)^2}$. So

$$L = \int_0^{1/2} \sqrt{\dfrac{(1 + y^2)^2}{(1 - y^2)^2}}\, dy = \int_0^{1/2} \dfrac{1 + y^2}{1 - y^2}\, dy = \ln 3 - \tfrac{1}{2} \text{ [from a CAS]} \approx 0.599$$

29. $y^{2/3} = 1 - x^{2/3} \Rightarrow y = \left(1 - x^{2/3}\right)^{3/2} \Rightarrow$

$\dfrac{dy}{dx} = \tfrac{3}{2}\left(1 - x^{2/3}\right)^{1/2}\left(-\tfrac{2}{3}x^{-1/3}\right) = -x^{-1/3}\left(1 - x^{2/3}\right)^{1/2} \Rightarrow$

$\left(\dfrac{dy}{dx}\right)^2 = x^{-2/3}\left(1 - x^{2/3}\right) = x^{-2/3} - 1$. Thus

$L = 4\int_0^1 \sqrt{1 + (x^{-2/3} - 1)}\, dx = 4\int_0^1 x^{-1/3}\, dx = 4\lim_{t \to 0^+}\left[\tfrac{3}{2}x^{2/3}\right]_t^1 = 6.$

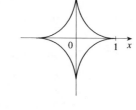

31. $y = 2x^{3/2} \Rightarrow y' = 3x^{1/2} \Rightarrow 1 + (y')^2 = 1 + 9x$. The arc length function with starting point $P_0(1,2)$ is

$$s(x) = \int_1^x \sqrt{1 + 9t}\, dt = \left[\tfrac{2}{27}(1 + 9t)^{3/2}\right]_1^x = \tfrac{2}{27}\left[(1 + 9x)^{3/2} - 10\sqrt{10}\right]$$

33. The prey hits the ground when $y = 0 \;\Leftrightarrow\; 180 - \frac{1}{45}x^2 = 0 \;\Leftrightarrow\; x^2 = 45 \cdot 180 \;\Rightarrow\; x = \sqrt{8100} = 90$, since x must be positive. $y' = -\frac{2}{45}x \;\Rightarrow\; 1 + (y')^2 = 1 + \frac{4}{45^2}x^2$, so the distance traveled by the prey is

$$L = \int_0^{90} \sqrt{1 + \frac{4}{45^2}x^2}\, dx = \int_0^4 \sqrt{1 + u^2}\left(\frac{45}{2}\,du\right) \qquad [u = \frac{2}{45}x,\ du = \frac{2}{45}\,dx]$$

$$\overset{21}{=} \frac{45}{2}\left[\frac{1}{2}u\sqrt{1 + u^2} + \frac{1}{2}\ln\left(u + \sqrt{1 + u^2}\right)\right]_0^4$$

$$= \frac{45}{2}\left[2\sqrt{17} + \frac{1}{2}\ln\left(4 + \sqrt{17}\right)\right] = 45\sqrt{17} + \frac{45}{4}\ln\left(4 + \sqrt{17}\right) \approx 209.1\ \text{m}$$

35. The sine wave has amplitude 1 and period 14, since it goes through two periods in a distance of 28 in., so its equation is $y = 1\sin\left(\frac{2\pi}{14}x\right) = \sin\left(\frac{\pi}{7}x\right)$. The width w of the flat metal sheet needed to make the panel is the arc length of the sine curve from $x = 0$ to $x = 28$. We set up the integral to evaluate w using the arc length formula with $\frac{dy}{dx} = \frac{\pi}{7}\cos\left(\frac{\pi}{7}x\right)$: $L = \int_0^{28}\sqrt{1 + \left[\frac{\pi}{7}\cos\left(\frac{\pi}{7}x\right)\right]^2}\,dx = 2\int_0^{14}\sqrt{1 + \left[\frac{\pi}{7}\cos\left(\frac{\pi}{7}x\right)\right]^2}\,dx$. This integral would be very difficult to evaluate exactly, so we use a CAS, and find that $L \approx 29.36$ inches.

37. $y = \int_1^x \sqrt{t^3 - 1}\,dt \;\Rightarrow\; \frac{dy}{dx} = \sqrt{x^3 - 1}$ [by FTC1] $\;\Rightarrow\; 1 + \left(\frac{dy}{dx}\right)^2 = 1 + \left(\sqrt{x^3 - 1}\right)^2 = x^3 \;\Rightarrow\;$

$$L = \int_1^4 \sqrt{x^3}\,dx = \int_1^4 x^{3/2}\,dx = \frac{2}{5}\left[x^{5/2}\right]_1^4 = \frac{2}{5}(32 - 1) = \frac{62}{5} = 12.4$$

9.2 Area of a Surface of Revolution

1. $y = \ln x \;\Rightarrow\; ds = \sqrt{1 + (dy/dx)^2}\,dx = \sqrt{1 + (1/x)^2}\,dx \;\Rightarrow\; S = \int_1^3 2\pi(\ln x)\sqrt{1 + (1/x)^2}\,dx$ [by (7)]

3. $y = \sec x \;\Rightarrow\; ds = \sqrt{1 + (dy/dx)^2}\,dx = \sqrt{1 + (\sec x \tan x)^2}\,dx \;\Rightarrow\;$
$S = \int_0^{\pi/4} 2\pi x\sqrt{1 + (\sec x \tan x)^2}\,dx$ [by (8)]

5. $y = x^3 \;\Rightarrow\; y' = 3x^2$. So

$$S = \int_0^2 2\pi y\sqrt{1 + (y')^2}\,dx = 2\pi\int_0^2 x^3\sqrt{1 + 9x^4}\,dx \qquad [u = 1 + 9x^4,\ du = 36x^3\,dx]$$

$$= \frac{2\pi}{36}\int_1^{145}\sqrt{u}\,du = \frac{\pi}{18}\left[\frac{2}{3}u^{3/2}\right]_1^{145} = \frac{\pi}{27}\left(145\sqrt{145} - 1\right)$$

7. $y = \sqrt{x} \;\Rightarrow\; 1 + (dy/dx)^2 = 1 + [1/(2\sqrt{x}\,)]^2 = 1 + 1/(4x)$. So

$$S = \int_4^9 2\pi y\sqrt{1 + \left(\frac{dy}{dx}\right)^2}\,dx = \int_4^9 2\pi\sqrt{x}\sqrt{1 + \frac{1}{4x}}\,dx = 2\pi\int_4^9 \sqrt{x + \frac{1}{4}}\,dx$$

$$= 2\pi\left[\frac{2}{3}\left(x + \frac{1}{4}\right)^{3/2}\right]_4^9 = \frac{4\pi}{3}\left[\frac{1}{8}(4x + 1)^{3/2}\right]_4^9 = \frac{\pi}{6}\left(37\sqrt{37} - 17\sqrt{17}\right)$$

9. $y = \cosh x \;\Rightarrow\; 1 + (dy/dx)^2 = 1 + \sinh^2 x = \cosh^2 x$. So

$$S = 2\pi\int_0^1 \cosh x \cosh x\,dx = 2\pi\int_0^1 \frac{1}{2}(1 + \cosh 2x)\,dx = \pi\left[x + \frac{1}{2}\sinh 2x\right]_0^1$$

$$= \pi\left(1 + \frac{1}{2}\sinh 2\right) \quad \text{or} \quad \pi\left[1 + \frac{1}{4}\left(e^2 - e^{-2}\right)\right]$$

11. $x = \frac{1}{3}\left(y^2 + 2\right)^{3/2} \;\Rightarrow\; dx/dy = \frac{1}{2}\left(y^2 + 2\right)^{1/2}(2y) = y\sqrt{y^2 + 2} \;\Rightarrow\;$
$1 + (dx/dy)^2 = 1 + y^2\left(y^2 + 2\right) = \left(y^2 + 1\right)^2$. So

$$S = 2\pi\int_1^2 y\left(y^2 + 1\right)dy = 2\pi\left[\frac{1}{4}y^4 + \frac{1}{2}y^2\right]_1^2 = 2\pi\left(4 + 2 - \frac{1}{4} - \frac{1}{2}\right) = \frac{21\pi}{2}$$

13. $y = \sqrt[3]{x} \;\Rightarrow\; x = y^3 \;\Rightarrow\; 1 + (dx/dy)^2 = 1 + 9y^4$. So

$$S = 2\pi \int_1^2 x \sqrt{1 + (dx/dy)^2}\, dy = 2\pi \int_1^2 y^3 \sqrt{1 + 9y^4}\, dy = \tfrac{2\pi}{36} \int_1^2 \sqrt{1 + 9y^4}\, 36y^3\, dy$$

$$= \tfrac{\pi}{18} \Big[\tfrac{2}{3}\big(1 + 9y^4\big)^{3/2} \Big]_1^2 = \tfrac{\pi}{27}\Big(145\sqrt{145} - 10\sqrt{10} \Big)$$

15. $x = \sqrt{a^2 - y^2} \;\Rightarrow\; dx/dy = \tfrac{1}{2}(a^2 - y^2)^{-1/2}(-2y) = -y/\sqrt{a^2 - y^2} \;\Rightarrow$

$$1 + (dx/dy)^2 = 1 + \frac{y^2}{a^2 - y^2} = \frac{a^2 - y^2}{a^2 - y^2} + \frac{y^2}{a^2 - y^2} = \frac{a^2}{a^2 - y^2} \;\Rightarrow$$

$$S = \int_0^{a/2} 2\pi \sqrt{a^2 - y^2}\, \frac{a}{\sqrt{a^2 - y^2}}\, dy = 2\pi \int_0^{a/2} a\, dy = 2\pi a \big[y\big]_0^{a/2} = 2\pi a\Big(\frac{a}{2} - 0\Big) = \pi a^2.$$ Note that this is

$\tfrac{1}{4}$ the surface area of a sphere of radius a, and the length of the interval $y = 0$ to $y = a/2$ is $\tfrac{1}{4}$ the length of the

interval $y = -a$ to $y = a$.

17. $y = \ln x \;\Rightarrow\; dy/dx = 1/x \;\Rightarrow\; 1 + (dy/dx)^2 = 1 + 1/x^2 \;\Rightarrow\; S = \int_1^3 2\pi \ln x \sqrt{1 + 1/x^2}\, dx$.

Let $f(x) = \ln x \sqrt{1 + 1/x^2}$. Since $n = 10$, $\Delta x = \frac{3-1}{10} = \tfrac{1}{5}$. Then

$$S \approx S_{10} = 2\pi \cdot \tfrac{1/5}{3}\, [f(1) + 4f(1.2) + 2f(1.4) + \cdots + 2f(2.6) + 4f(2.8) + f(3)] \approx 9.023754.$$

The value of the integral produced by a calculator is 9.024262 (to six decimal places).

19. $y = \sec x \;\Rightarrow\; dy/dx = \sec x \tan x \;\Rightarrow\; 1 + (dy/dx)^2 = 1 + \sec^2 x \tan^2 x \;\Rightarrow$

$S = \int_0^{\pi/3} 2\pi \sec x \sqrt{1 + \sec^2 x \tan^2 x}\, dx$. Let $f(x) = \sec x \sqrt{1 + \sec^2 x \tan^2 x}$.

Since $n = 10$, $\Delta x = \dfrac{\pi/3 - 0}{10} = \dfrac{\pi}{30}$. Then

$$S \approx S_{10} = 2\pi \cdot \tfrac{\pi/30}{3}\Big[f(0) + 4f\Big(\tfrac{\pi}{30}\Big) + 2f\Big(\tfrac{2\pi}{30}\Big) + \cdots + 2f\Big(\tfrac{8\pi}{30}\Big) + 4f\Big(\tfrac{9\pi}{30}\Big) + f\Big(\tfrac{\pi}{3}\Big) \Big] \approx 13.527296.$$

The value of the integral produced by a calculator is 13.516987 (to six decimal places).

21. $y = 1/x \;\Rightarrow\; ds = \sqrt{1 + (dy/dx)^2}\, dx = \sqrt{1 + (-1/x^2)^2}\, dx = \sqrt{1 + 1/x^4}\, dx \;\Rightarrow$

$$S = \int_1^2 2\pi \cdot \frac{1}{x}\sqrt{1 + \frac{1}{x^4}}\, dx = 2\pi \int_1^2 \frac{\sqrt{x^4 + 1}}{x^3}\, dx = 2\pi \int_1^4 \frac{\sqrt{u^2 + 1}}{u^2}\,\Big(\tfrac{1}{2}\, du\Big) \qquad [u = x^2,\ du = 2x\, dx]$$

$$= \pi \int_1^4 \frac{\sqrt{1 + u^2}}{u^2}\, du \stackrel{24}{=} \pi \Big[-\frac{\sqrt{1 + u^2}}{u} + \ln\Big(u + \sqrt{1 + u^2}\Big) \Big]_1^4$$

$$= \pi \Big[-\tfrac{\sqrt{17}}{4} + \ln\Big(4 + \sqrt{17}\Big) + \tfrac{\sqrt{2}}{1} - \ln\Big(1 + \sqrt{2}\Big) \Big] = \pi \Big[\sqrt{2} - \tfrac{\sqrt{17}}{4} + \ln\Big(\tfrac{4 + \sqrt{17}}{1 + \sqrt{2}}\Big) \Big]$$

23. $y = x^3$ and $0 \le y \le 1 \;\Rightarrow\; y' = 3x^2$ and $0 \le x \le 1$.

$$S = \int_0^1 2\pi x \sqrt{1 + (3x^2)^2}\, dx = 2\pi \int_0^3 \sqrt{1 + u^2}\, \tfrac{1}{6}\, du \qquad [u = 3x^2,\ du = 6x\, dx]$$

$$= \tfrac{\pi}{3} \int_0^3 \sqrt{1 + u^2}\, du \stackrel{21}{=} \text{[or use CAS]} \quad \tfrac{\pi}{3}\Big[\tfrac{1}{2} u\sqrt{1 + u^2} + \tfrac{1}{2}\ln\big(u + \sqrt{1 + u^2}\big) \Big]_0^3$$

$$= \tfrac{\pi}{3}\Big[\tfrac{3}{2}\sqrt{10} + \tfrac{1}{2}\ln\big(3 + \sqrt{10}\big) \Big] = \tfrac{\pi}{6}\Big[3\sqrt{10} + \ln\big(3 + \sqrt{10}\big) \Big]$$

25. $S = 2\pi \int_1^\infty y \sqrt{1 + \left(\dfrac{dy}{dx}\right)^2}\, dx = 2\pi \int_1^\infty \dfrac{1}{x}\sqrt{1 + \dfrac{1}{x^4}}\, dx = 2\pi \int_1^\infty \dfrac{\sqrt{x^4 + 1}}{x^3}\, dx$. Rather than trying to

evaluate this integral, note that $\sqrt{x^4 + 1} > \sqrt{x^4} = x^2$ for $x > 0$. Thus, if the area is finite,

$$S = 2\pi \int_1^\infty \dfrac{\sqrt{x^4 + 1}}{x^3}\, dx > 2\pi \int_1^\infty \dfrac{x^2}{x^3}\, dx = 2\pi \int_1^\infty \dfrac{1}{x}\, dx$$

But we know that this integral diverges, so the area S is infinite.

27. Since $a > 0$, the curve $3ay^2 = x(a - x)^2$ only has points with

$x \geq 0$. ($3ay^2 \geq 0 \;\Rightarrow\; x(a - x)^2 \geq 0 \;\Rightarrow\; x \geq 0$.) The

curve is symmetric about the x-axis (since the equation is

unchanged when y is replaced by $-y$). $y = 0$ when $x = 0$ or a,

so the curve's loop extends from $x = 0$ to $x = a$.

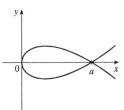

$\dfrac{d}{dx}(3ay^2) = \dfrac{d}{dx}\left[x(a-x)^2\right] \;\Rightarrow\; 6ay\dfrac{dy}{dx} = x \cdot 2(a-x)(-1) + (a-x)^2 \;\Rightarrow$

$\dfrac{dy}{dx} = \dfrac{(a-x)[-2x + a - x]}{6ay} \;\Rightarrow\; \left(\dfrac{dy}{dx}\right)^2 = \dfrac{(a-x)^2(a-3x)^2}{36a^2y^2} = \dfrac{(a-x)^2(a-3x)^2}{36a^2} \cdot \dfrac{3a}{x(a-x)^2}$

$\begin{bmatrix}\text{the last fraction} \\ \text{is } 1/y^2\end{bmatrix} = \dfrac{(a-3x)^2}{12ax} \;\Rightarrow$

$1 + \left(\dfrac{dy}{dx}\right)^2 = 1 + \dfrac{a^2 - 6ax + 9x^2}{12ax} = \dfrac{12ax}{12ax} + \dfrac{a^2 - 6ax + 9x^2}{12ax} = \dfrac{a^2 + 6ax + 9x^2}{12ax} = \dfrac{(a+3x)^2}{12ax}$ for $x \neq 0$.

(a) $S = \int_{x=0}^a 2\pi y\, ds = 2\pi \int_0^a \dfrac{\sqrt{x}(a-x)}{\sqrt{3a}} \cdot \dfrac{a+3x}{\sqrt{12ax}}\, dx = 2\pi \int_0^a \dfrac{(a-x)(a+3x)}{6a}\, dx$

$= \dfrac{\pi}{3a}\int_0^a (a^2 + 2ax - 3x^2)\, dx = \dfrac{\pi}{3a}\left[a^2x + ax^2 - x^3\right]_0^a = \dfrac{\pi}{3a}(a^3 + a^3 - a^3) = \dfrac{\pi}{3a} \cdot a^3 = \dfrac{\pi a^2}{3}$.

Note that we have rotated the top half of the loop about the x-axis. This generates the full surface.

(b) We must rotate the full loop about the y-axis, so we get double the area obtained by rotating the top half of

the loop:

$$S = 2 \cdot 2\pi \int_{x=0}^a x\, ds = 4\pi \int_0^a x\dfrac{a+3x}{\sqrt{12ax}}\, dx = \dfrac{4\pi}{2\sqrt{3a}}\int_0^a x^{1/2}(a+3x)\, dx$$

$$= \dfrac{2\pi}{\sqrt{3a}}\int_0^a (ax^{1/2} + 3x^{3/2})\, dx = \dfrac{2\pi}{\sqrt{3a}}\left[\dfrac{2}{3}ax^{3/2} + \dfrac{6}{5}x^{5/2}\right]_0^a = \dfrac{2\pi\sqrt{3}}{3\sqrt{a}}\left(\dfrac{2}{3}a^{5/2} + \dfrac{6}{5}a^{5/2}\right)$$

$$= \dfrac{2\pi\sqrt{3}}{3}\left(\dfrac{2}{3} + \dfrac{6}{5}\right)a^2 = \dfrac{2\pi\sqrt{3}}{3}\left(\dfrac{28}{15}\right)a^2 = \dfrac{56\pi\sqrt{3}\,a^2}{45}$$

29. $\dfrac{x^2}{a^2} + \dfrac{y^2}{b^2} = 1 \;\Rightarrow\; \dfrac{y\,(dy/dx)}{b^2} = -\dfrac{x}{a^2} \;\Rightarrow\; \dfrac{dy}{dx} = -\dfrac{b^2 x}{a^2 y} \;\Rightarrow$

$$1 + \left(\frac{dy}{dx}\right)^2 = 1 + \frac{b^4 x^2}{a^4 y^2} = \frac{b^4 x^2 + a^4 y^2}{a^4 y^2} = \frac{b^4 x^2 + a^4 b^2\left(1 - x^2/a^2\right)}{a^4 b^2\left(1 - x^2/a^2\right)} = \frac{a^4 b^2 + b^4 x^2 - a^2 b^2 x^2}{a^4 b^2 - a^2 b^2 x^2}$$

$$= \frac{a^4 + b^2 x^2 - a^2 x^2}{a^4 - a^2 x^2} = \frac{a^4 - \left(a^2 - b^2\right)x^2}{a^2\left(a^2 - x^2\right)}$$

The ellipsoid's surface area is twice the area generated by rotating the first quadrant portion of the ellipse about the x-axis. Thus,

$$S = 2\int_0^a 2\pi y \sqrt{1 + \left(\frac{dy}{dx}\right)^2}\, dx = 4\pi \int_0^a \frac{b}{a}\sqrt{a^2 - x^2}\,\frac{\sqrt{a^4 - (a^2 - b^2)x^2}}{a\sqrt{a^2 - x^2}}\, dx$$

$$= \frac{4\pi b}{a^2}\int_0^a \sqrt{a^4 - (a^2 - b^2)x^2}\, dx = \frac{4\pi b}{a^2}\int_0^{a\sqrt{a^2 - b^2}} \sqrt{a^4 - u^2}\,\frac{du}{\sqrt{a^2 - b^2}} \qquad [u = \sqrt{a^2 - b^2}\, x]$$

$$\overset{30}{=} \frac{4\pi b}{a^2\sqrt{a^2 - b^2}}\left[\frac{u}{2}\sqrt{a^4 - u^2} + \frac{a^4}{2}\sin^{-1}\frac{u}{a^2}\right]_0^{a\sqrt{a^2 - b^2}}$$

$$= \frac{4\pi b}{a^2\sqrt{a^2 - b^2}}\left[\frac{a\sqrt{a^2 - b^2}}{2}\sqrt{a^4 - a^2(a^2 - b^2)} + \frac{a^4}{2}\sin^{-1}\frac{\sqrt{a^2 - b^2}}{a}\right] = 2\pi\left[b^2 + \frac{a^2 b\sin^{-1}\dfrac{\sqrt{a^2 - b^2}}{a}}{\sqrt{a^2 - b^2}}\right]$$

31. The analogue of $f(x_i^*)$ in the derivation of (4) is now $c - f(x_i^*)$, so

$$S = \lim_{n\to\infty}\sum_{i=1}^n 2\pi[c - f(x_i^*)]\sqrt{1 + [f'(x_i^*)]^2}\,\Delta x = \int_a^b 2\pi[c - f(x)]\sqrt{1 + [f'(x)]^2}\, dx.$$

33. For the upper semicircle, $f(x) = \sqrt{r^2 - x^2}$, $f'(x) = -x/\sqrt{r^2 - x^2}$. The surface area generated is

$$S_1 = \int_{-r}^r 2\pi\left(r - \sqrt{r^2 - x^2}\right)\sqrt{1 + \frac{x^2}{r^2 - x^2}}\, dx = 4\pi\int_0^r \left(r - \sqrt{r^2 - x^2}\right)\frac{r}{\sqrt{r^2 - x^2}}\, dx$$

$$= 4\pi\int_0^r \left(\frac{r^2}{\sqrt{r^2 - x^2}} - r\right) dx$$

For the lower semicircle, $f(x) = -\sqrt{r^2 - x^2}$ and $f'(x) = \dfrac{x}{\sqrt{r^2 - x^2}}$, so $S_2 = 4\pi\displaystyle\int_0^r \left(\frac{r^2}{\sqrt{r^2 - x^2}} + r\right) dx$.

Thus, the total area is $S = S_1 + S_2 = 8\pi\displaystyle\int_0^r \left(\frac{r^2}{\sqrt{r^2 - x^2}}\right) dx = 8\pi\left[r^2\sin^{-1}\left(\frac{x}{r}\right)\right]_0^r = 8\pi r^2\left(\frac{\pi}{2}\right) = 4\pi^2 r^2$.

35. In the derivation of (4), we computed a typical contribution to the surface area to be $2\pi\dfrac{y_{i-1} + y_i}{2}\,|P_{i-1}P_i|$, the

area of a frustum of a cone. When $f(x)$ is not necessarily positive, the approximations $y_i = f(x_i) \approx f(x_i^*)$ and

$y_{i-1} = f(x_{i-1}) \approx f(x_i^*)$ must be replaced by $y_i = |f(x_i)| \approx |f(x_i^*)|$ and $y_{i-1} = |f(x_{i-1})| \approx |f(x_i^*)|$. Thus,

$2\pi\dfrac{y_{i-1} + y_i}{2}\,|P_{i-1}P_i| \approx 2\pi|f(x_i^*)|\sqrt{1 + [f'(x_i^*)]^2}\,\Delta x$. Continuing with the rest of the derivation as before, we

obtain $S = \int_a^b 2\pi|f(x)|\sqrt{1 + [f'(x)]^2}\, dx$.

9.3 Applications to Physics and Engineering

1. The weight density of water is $\delta = 62.5 \text{ lb/ft}^3$.

(a) $P = \delta d \approx \left(62.5 \text{ lb/ft}^3\right)(3 \text{ ft}) = 187.5 \text{ lb/ft}^2$

(b) $F = PA \approx \left(187.5 \text{ lb/ft}^2\right)(5 \text{ ft})(2 \text{ ft}) = 1875 \text{ lb}$. ($A$ is the area of the bottom of the tank.)

(c) As in Example 1, the area of the ith strip is $2\left(\Delta x\right)$ and the pressure is $\delta d = \delta x_i$. Thus,

$$F = \int_0^3 \delta x \cdot 2 \, dx \approx (62.5)(2) \int_0^3 x \, dx = 125\left[\tfrac{1}{2}x^2\right]_0^3 = 125\left(\tfrac{9}{2}\right) = 562.5 \text{ lb}$$

In Exercises 3–9, n is the number of subintervals of length Δx and x_i^* is a sample point in the ith subinterval $[x_{i-1}, x_i]$.

3. Set up a vertical x-axis as shown, with $x = 0$ at the water's surface and x

increasing in the downward direction. Then the area of the ith rectangular

strip is $6 \Delta x$ and the pressure on the strip is δx_i^* (where $\delta \approx 62.5 \text{ lb/ft}^3$).

Thus, the hydrostatic force on the strip is $\delta x_i^* \cdot 6 \Delta x$ and the total

hydrostatic force $\approx \sum_{i=1}^{n} \delta x_i^* \cdot 6 \Delta x$. The total force

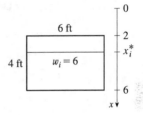

$$F = \lim_{n \to \infty} \sum_{i=1}^{n} \delta x_i^* \cdot 6 \Delta x = \int_2^6 \delta x \cdot 6 \, dx = 6\delta \int_2^6 x \, dx$$

$$= 6\delta\left[\tfrac{1}{2}x^2\right]_2^6 = 6\delta(18 - 2) = 96\delta \approx 6000 \text{ lb}$$

5. Since an equation for the shape is $x^2 + y^2 = 10^2$ ($x \geq 0$), we have

$y = \sqrt{100 - x^2}$. Thus, the area of the ith strip is $2\sqrt{100 - (x_i^*)^2}\, \Delta x$

and the pressure on the strip is $\rho g x_i^*$, so the hydrostatic force on the

strip is $\rho g x_i^* \cdot 2\sqrt{100 - (x_i^*)^2}\, \Delta x$ and the total force on the

plate $\approx \sum_{i=1}^{n} \rho g x_i^* \cdot 2\sqrt{100 - (x_i^*)^2}\, \Delta x$. The total force

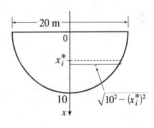

$$F = \lim_{n \to \infty} \sum_{i=1}^{n} \rho g x_i^* \cdot 2\sqrt{100 - (x_i^*)^2}\, \Delta x = \int_0^{10} 2\rho g x \sqrt{100 - x^2}\, dx$$

$$= -\rho g \int_0^{10} \left(100 - x^2\right)^{1/2} (-2x)\, dx = -\rho g\left[\tfrac{2}{3}(100 - x^2)^{3/2}\right]_0^{10} = -\tfrac{2}{3}\rho g(0 - 1000)$$

$$= \tfrac{2000}{3}\rho g \approx \tfrac{2000}{3} \cdot 1000 \cdot 9.8 \approx 6.5 \times 10^6 \text{ N} \quad \left[\rho \approx 1000 \text{ kg/m}^3 \text{ and } g \approx 9.8 \text{ m/s}^2.\right]$$

7. Using similar triangles, $\dfrac{4 \text{ ft wide}}{8 \text{ ft high}} = \dfrac{a \text{ ft wide}}{x_i^* \text{ ft high}}$, so $a = \frac{1}{2}x_i^*$ and the

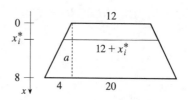

width of the ith rectangular strip is $12 + 2a = 12 + x_i^*$. The area of the

strip is $(12 + x_i^*)\,\Delta x$. The pressure on the strip is δx_i^*.

$$F = \lim_{n\to\infty} \sum_{i=1}^{n} \delta x_i^*(12 + x_i^*)\,\Delta x = \int_0^8 \delta x \cdot (12 + x)\,dx$$

$$= \delta \int_0^8 (12x + x^2)\,dx = \delta\left[6x^2 + \frac{x^3}{3}\right]_0^8 = \delta\left(384 + \frac{512}{3}\right)$$

$$= (62.5)\frac{1664}{3} \approx 3.47 \times 10^4 \text{ lb}$$

9. From the figure, the area of the ith rectangular strip is $2\sqrt{r^2 - (x_i^*)^2}\,\Delta x$

and the pressure on it is $\rho g(x_i^* + r)$.

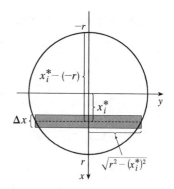

$$F = \lim_{n\to\infty} \sum_{i=1}^{n} \rho g(x_i^* + r)\,2\sqrt{r^2 - (x_i^*)^2}\,\Delta x$$

$$= \int_{-r}^{r} \rho g(x + r) \cdot 2\sqrt{r^2 - x^2}\,dx$$

$$= \rho g \int_{-r}^{r} \sqrt{r^2 - x^2}\,2x\,dx + 2\rho g r \int_{-r}^{r} \sqrt{r^2 - x^2}\,dx$$

The first integral is 0 because the integrand is an odd function. The second

integral can be interpreted as the area of a semicircular disk with radius r,

or we could make the trigonometric substitution $x = r\sin\theta$. Continuing:

$F = \rho g \cdot 0 + 2\rho g r \cdot \frac{1}{2}\pi r^2 = \rho g \pi r^3 = 1000 g \pi r^3$ N (SI units assumed).

11. By similar triangles, $\dfrac{8}{4\sqrt{3}} = \dfrac{w_i}{x_i^*} \;\Rightarrow\; w_i = \dfrac{2x_i^*}{\sqrt{3}}$. The area of the ith

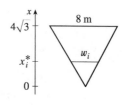

rectangular strip is $\dfrac{2x_i^*}{\sqrt{3}}\,\Delta x$ and the pressure on it is $\rho g(4\sqrt{3} - x_i^*)$.

$$F = \int_0^{4\sqrt{3}} \rho g\left(4\sqrt{3} - x\right)\frac{2x}{\sqrt{3}}\,dx = 8\rho g \int_0^{4\sqrt{3}} x\,dx - \frac{2\rho g}{\sqrt{3}} \int_0^{4\sqrt{3}} x^2\,dx$$

$$= 4\rho g\left[x^2\right]_0^{4\sqrt{3}} - \frac{2\rho g}{3\sqrt{3}}\left[x^3\right]_0^{4\sqrt{3}} = 192\rho g - \frac{2\rho g}{3\sqrt{3}}\,64 \cdot 3\sqrt{3}$$

$$= 192\rho g - 128\rho g = 64\rho g \approx 64(840)(9.8) \approx 5.27 \times 10^5 \text{ N}$$

13. (a) The top of the cube has depth $d = 1\text{ m} - 20\text{ cm} = 80\text{ cm} = 0.8\text{ m}$.

$$F = \rho g d A \approx (1000)(9.8)(0.8)(0.2)^2 = 313.6 \approx 314\text{ N}$$

(b) The area of a strip is $0.2\,\Delta x$ and the pressure on it is $\rho g x_i^*$.

$$F = \int_{0.8}^{1} \rho g x (0.2)\, dx = 0.2\rho g \left[\tfrac{1}{2}x^2\right]_{0.8}^{1} = (0.2\rho g)(0.18) = 0.036\rho g = 0.036(1000)(9.8)$$

$$= 352.8 \approx 353\text{ N}$$

15. (a) The area of a strip is $20\,\Delta x$ and the pressure on it is δx_i.

$$F = \int_{0}^{3} \delta x 20\, dx = 20\delta \left[\tfrac{1}{2}x^2\right]_{0}^{3} = 20\delta \cdot \frac{9}{2} = 90\delta$$

$$= 90(62.5) = 5625\text{ lb} \approx 5.63 \times 10^3\text{ lb}$$

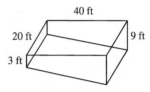

(b) $F = \int_{0}^{9} \delta x 20\, dx = 20\delta \left[\tfrac{1}{2}x^2\right]_{0}^{9} = 20\delta \cdot \frac{81}{2} = 810\delta = 810(62.5) = 50{,}625\text{ lb} \approx 5.06 \times 10^4\text{ lb.}$

(c) For the first 3 ft, the length of the side is constant at 40 ft. For $3 < x \le 9$, we can use similar triangles to find the

length a: $\dfrac{a}{40} = \dfrac{9-x}{6} \quad \Rightarrow \quad a = 40 \cdot \dfrac{9-x}{6}$.

$$F = \int_{0}^{3} \delta x 40\, dx + \int_{3}^{9} \delta x (40)\frac{9-x}{6}\, dx = 40\delta\left[\tfrac{1}{2}x^2\right]_{0}^{3} + \frac{20}{3}\delta \int_{3}^{9}\left(9x - x^2\right)dx$$

$$= 180\delta + \frac{20}{3}\delta\left[\tfrac{9}{2}x^2 - \tfrac{1}{3}x^3\right]_{3}^{9} = 180\delta + \frac{20}{3}\delta\left[\left(\tfrac{729}{2} - 243\right) - \left(\tfrac{81}{2} - 9\right)\right]$$

$$= 180\delta + 600\delta = 780\delta = 780(62.5) = 48{,}750\text{ lb} \approx 4.88 \times 10^4\text{ lb}$$

(d) For any right triangle with hypotenuse on the bottom,

$\csc\theta = \dfrac{\Delta x}{\text{hypotenuse}} \quad \Rightarrow$

$\text{hypotenuse} = \Delta x \csc\theta = \Delta x \dfrac{\sqrt{40^2 + 6^2}}{6} = \dfrac{\sqrt{409}}{3}\Delta x$.

$$F = \int_{3}^{9} \delta x 20 \frac{\sqrt{409}}{3}\, dx = \tfrac{1}{3}\left(20\sqrt{409}\right)\delta\left[\tfrac{1}{2}x^2\right]_{3}^{9}$$

$$= \tfrac{1}{3} \cdot 10\sqrt{409}\,\delta(81 - 9)$$

$$\approx 303{,}356\text{ lb} \approx 3.03 \times 10^5\text{ lb}$$

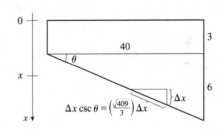

17. $F = \int_{2}^{5} \rho g x \cdot w(x)\, dx$, where $w(x)$ is the width of the plate at depth x. Since $n = 6$, $\Delta x = \frac{5-2}{6} = \frac{1}{2}$, and

$$F \approx S_6 = \rho g \cdot \frac{1/2}{3}[2 \cdot w(2) + 4 \cdot 2.5 \cdot w(2.5) + 2 \cdot 3 \cdot w(3) + 4 \cdot 3.5 \cdot w(3.5)$$

$$\qquad\qquad + 2 \cdot 4 \cdot w(4) + 4 \cdot 4.5 \cdot w(4.5) + 5 \cdot w(5)]$$

$$= \tfrac{1}{6}\rho g(2 \cdot 0 + 10 \cdot 0.8 + 6 \cdot 1.7 + 14 \cdot 2.4 + 8 \cdot 2.9 + 18 \cdot 3.3 + 5 \cdot 3.6)$$

$$= \tfrac{1}{6}(1000)(9.8)(152.4) \approx 2.5 \times 10^5\text{ N}$$

19. The moment M of the system about the origin is $M = \sum\limits_{i=1}^{2} m_i x_i = m_1 x_1 + m_2 x_2 = 40 \cdot 2 + 30 \cdot 5 = 230$.

The mass m of the system is $m = \sum\limits_{i=1}^{2} m_i = m_1 + m_2 = 40 + 30 = 70$. The center of mass of the system is

$M/m = \frac{230}{70} = \frac{23}{7}$.

21. $m = \sum\limits_{i=1}^{3} m_i = 6 + 5 + 10 = 21$. $M_x = \sum\limits_{i=1}^{3} m_i y_i = 6(5) + 5(-2) + 10(-1) = 10$;

$M_y = \sum\limits_{i=1}^{3} m_i x_i = 6(1) + 5(3) + 10(-2) = 1$. $\bar{x} = \dfrac{M_y}{m} = \dfrac{1}{21}$ and $\bar{y} = \dfrac{M_x}{m} = \dfrac{10}{21}$, so the center of mass of the

system is $\left(\frac{1}{21}, \frac{10}{21}\right)$.

23. Since the region in the figure is symmetric about the y-axis, we know

that $\bar{x} = 0$. The region is "bottom-heavy," so we know that $\bar{y} < 2$,

and we might guess that $\bar{y} = 1.5$.

$A = \int_{-2}^{2}(4 - x^2)\,dx = 2\int_{0}^{2}(4 - x^2)\,dx = 2\left[4x - \frac{1}{3}x^3\right]_{0}^{2}$

$\quad = 2\left(8 - \frac{8}{3}\right) = \frac{32}{3}$

$\bar{x} = \dfrac{1}{A}\int_{-2}^{2} x(4 - x^2)\,dx = 0$ since $f(x) = x(4 - x^2)$ is an odd

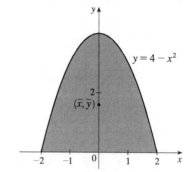

function (or since the region is symmetric about the y-axis).

$\bar{y} = \dfrac{1}{A}\int_{-2}^{2} \frac{1}{2}(4 - x^2)^2\,dx = \dfrac{3}{32} \cdot \dfrac{1}{2} \cdot 2\int_{0}^{2}(16 - 8x^2 + x^4)\,dx = \dfrac{3}{32}\left[16x - \dfrac{8}{3}x^3 + \dfrac{1}{5}x^5\right]_{0}^{2}$

$\quad = \frac{3}{32}\left(32 - \frac{64}{3} + \frac{32}{5}\right) = 3\left(1 - \frac{2}{3} + \frac{1}{5}\right) = 3\left(\frac{8}{15}\right) = \frac{8}{5}$

Thus, the centroid is $(\bar{x}, \bar{y}) = \left(0, \frac{8}{5}\right)$.

25. The region in the figure is "right-heavy" and "bottom-heavy," so we know

$\bar{x} > 0.5$ and $\bar{y} < 1$, and we might guess that $\bar{x} = 0.6$ and $\bar{y} = 0.9$.

$A = \int_{0}^{1} e^x\,dx = [e^x]_{0}^{1} = e - 1$,

$\bar{x} = \frac{1}{A}\int_{0}^{1} xe^x\,dx = \frac{1}{e-1}[xe^x - e^x]_{0}^{1}$ [by parts]

$\quad = \frac{1}{e-1}[0 - (-1)] = \frac{1}{e-1}$,

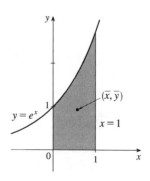

$\bar{y} = \frac{1}{A}\int_{0}^{1} \frac{1}{2}(e^x)^2\,dx = \frac{1}{e-1} \cdot \frac{1}{4}[e^{2x}]_{0}^{1} = \frac{1}{4(e-1)}(e^2 - 1) = \frac{e+1}{4}$.

Thus, the centroid is $(\bar{x}, \bar{y}) = \left(\frac{1}{e-1}, \frac{e+1}{4}\right) \approx (0.58, 0.93)$.

27. $A = \int_0^1 (\sqrt{x} - x)\, dx = \left[\frac{2}{3}x^{3/2} - \frac{1}{2}x^2\right]_0^1 = \frac{2}{3} - \frac{1}{2} = \frac{1}{6}$.

$\bar{x} = \frac{1}{A}\int_0^1 x(\sqrt{x} - x)\, dx = 6\int_0^1 (x^{3/2} - x^2)\, dx$

$\quad = 6\left[\frac{2}{5}x^{5/2} - \frac{1}{3}x^3\right]_0^1 = 6\left(\frac{2}{5} - \frac{1}{3}\right) = 6\left(\frac{1}{15}\right) = \frac{2}{5}$;

$\bar{y} = \frac{1}{A}\int_0^1 \frac{1}{2}\left[(\sqrt{x})^2 - x^2\right]\, dx = 6 \cdot \frac{1}{2}\int_0^1 (x - x^2)\, dx$

$\quad = 3\left[\frac{1}{2}x^2 - \frac{1}{3}x^3\right]_0^1 = 3\left(\frac{1}{2} - \frac{1}{3}\right) = \frac{1}{2}$.

Thus, the centroid is $(\bar{x}, \bar{y}) = \left(\frac{2}{5}, \frac{1}{2}\right)$.

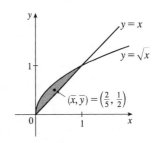

29. $A = \int_0^{\pi/4} (\cos x - \sin x)\, dx = [\sin x + \cos x]_0^{\pi/4} = \sqrt{2} - 1$,

$\bar{x} = A^{-1}\int_0^{\pi/4} x(\cos x - \sin x)\, dx$

$\quad = A^{-1}[x(\sin x + \cos x) + \cos x - \sin x]_0^{\pi/4} \quad$ [integration by parts]

$\quad = A^{-1}\left(\frac{\pi}{4}\sqrt{2} - 1\right) = \dfrac{\frac{1}{4}\pi\sqrt{2} - 1}{\sqrt{2} - 1}$

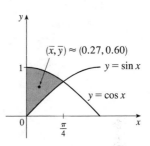

$\bar{y} = A^{-1}\int_0^{\pi/4} \frac{1}{2}\left(\cos^2 x - \sin^2 x\right)\, dx = \frac{1}{2A}\int_0^{\pi/4} \cos 2x\, dx = \frac{1}{4A}[\sin 2x]_0^{\pi/4} = \frac{1}{4A} = \frac{1}{4(\sqrt{2}-1)}$

Thus, the centroid is $(\bar{x}, \bar{y}) = \left(\dfrac{\pi\sqrt{2} - 4}{4(\sqrt{2} - 1)}, \dfrac{1}{4(\sqrt{2} - 1)}\right) \approx (0.27, 0.60)$.

31. From the figure we see that $\bar{y} = 0$. Now

$$A = \int_0^5 2\sqrt{5 - x}\, dx = 2\left[-\frac{2}{3}(5 - x)^{3/2}\right]_0^5$$

$$= 2\left(0 + \frac{2}{3} \cdot 5^{3/2}\right) = \frac{20}{3}\sqrt{5}$$

so

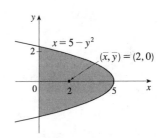

$\bar{x} = \frac{1}{A}\int_0^5 x\left[\sqrt{5 - x} - \left(-\sqrt{5 - x}\right)\right]\, dx = \frac{1}{A}\int_0^5 2x\sqrt{5 - x}\, dx$

$\quad = \frac{1}{A}\int_{\sqrt{5}}^0 2(5 - u^2)u(-2u)\, du \quad$ $[u = \sqrt{5 - x},\, x = 5 - u^2,\, u^2 = 5 - x,\, dx = -2u\, du]$

$\quad = \frac{4}{A}\int_0^{\sqrt{5}} u^2(5 - u^2)\, du = \frac{4}{A}\left[\frac{5}{3}u^3 - \frac{1}{5}u^5\right]_0^{\sqrt{5}} = \frac{3}{5\sqrt{5}}\left(\frac{25}{3}\sqrt{5} - 5\sqrt{5}\right) = 5 - 3 = 2$

Thus, the centroid is $(\bar{x}, \bar{y}) = (2, 0)$.

146

33. By symmetry, $M_y = 0$ and $\overline{x} = 0$. $A = \frac{1}{2}bh = \frac{1}{2} \cdot 2 \cdot 2 = 2$.

$$M_x = \rho \int_{-1}^{1} \tfrac{1}{2}(2 - 2x)^2 \, dx = 2\rho \int_{0}^{1} \tfrac{1}{2}(2 - 2x)^2 \, dx$$

$$= \left(2 \cdot 1 \cdot \tfrac{1}{2} \cdot 2^2\right) \int_{0}^{1} (1 - x)^2 \, dx$$

$$= 4 \int_{1}^{0} u^2(-du) \qquad [u = 1 - x, \ du = -dx]$$

$$= -4\left[\tfrac{1}{3}u^3\right]_{1}^{0} = -4\left(-\tfrac{1}{3}\right) = \tfrac{4}{3}$$

$\overline{y} = \frac{1}{m}M_x = \frac{1}{\rho A}M_x = \frac{1}{1 \cdot 2} \cdot \frac{4}{3} = \frac{2}{3}$. Thus, the centroid is $(\overline{x}, \overline{y}) = \left(0, \frac{2}{3}\right)$.

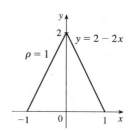

35. $A = \displaystyle\int_{0}^{2} \left(2^x - x^2\right) dx = \left[\dfrac{2^x}{\ln 2} - \dfrac{x^3}{3}\right]_{0}^{2}$

$$= \left(\dfrac{4}{\ln 2} - \dfrac{8}{3}\right) - \dfrac{1}{\ln 2} = \dfrac{3}{\ln 2} - \dfrac{8}{3} \approx 1.661418.$$

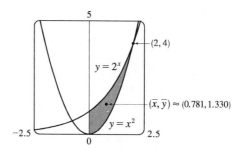

$\overline{x} = \dfrac{1}{A}\displaystyle\int_{0}^{2} x(2^x - x^2)\,dx = \dfrac{1}{A}\int_{0}^{2} (x2^x - x^3)\,dx$

$$= \dfrac{1}{A}\left[\dfrac{x2^x}{\ln 2} - \dfrac{2^x}{(\ln 2)^2} - \dfrac{x^4}{4}\right]_{0}^{2} \qquad \text{[use parts]}$$

$$= \dfrac{1}{A}\left[\dfrac{8}{\ln 2} - \dfrac{4}{(\ln 2)^2} - 4 + \dfrac{1}{(\ln 2)^2}\right]$$

$$= \dfrac{1}{A}\left[\dfrac{8}{\ln 2} - \dfrac{3}{(\ln 2)^2} - 4\right] \approx \dfrac{1}{A}(1.297453) \approx 0.781$$

$\overline{y} = \dfrac{1}{A}\displaystyle\int_{0}^{2} \tfrac{1}{2}\left[(2^x)^2 - (x^2)^2\right] dx = \dfrac{1}{A}\int_{0}^{2} \tfrac{1}{2}(2^{2x} - x^4)\,dx = \dfrac{1}{A} \cdot \dfrac{1}{2}\left[\dfrac{2^{2x}}{2\ln 2} - \dfrac{x^5}{5}\right]_{0}^{2}$

$$= \dfrac{1}{A} \cdot \dfrac{1}{2}\left(\dfrac{16}{2\ln 2} - \dfrac{32}{5} - \dfrac{1}{2\ln 2}\right) = \dfrac{1}{A}\left(\dfrac{15}{4\ln 2} - \dfrac{16}{5}\right) \approx \dfrac{1}{A}(2.210106) \approx 1.330$$

Since the position of a centroid is independent of density when the density is constant, we will assume for convenience that $\rho = 1$ in Exercises 36 and 37.

37. Choose x- and y-axes so that the base (one side of the triangle) lies along the x-axis with the other vertex along the positive y-axis as shown. From geometry, we know the medians intersect at a point $\frac{2}{3}$ of the way from each vertex (along the median) to the opposite side. The median from B goes to the midpoint $\left(\frac{1}{2}(a + c), 0\right)$ of side AC, so the point of intersection of the medians is $\left(\frac{2}{3} \cdot \frac{1}{2}(a + c), \frac{1}{3}b\right) = \left(\frac{1}{3}(a + c), \frac{1}{3}b\right)$.

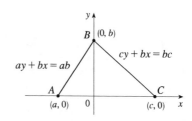

[continued]

This can also be verified by finding the equations of two medians, and solving them simultaneously to find their point of intersection. Now let us compute the location of the centroid of the triangle. The area is $A = \frac{1}{2}(c-a)b$.

$$\bar{x} = \frac{1}{A}\left[\int_a^0 x \cdot \frac{b}{a}(a-x)\,dx + \int_0^c x \cdot \frac{b}{c}(c-x)\,dx\right] = \frac{1}{A}\left[\frac{b}{a}\int_a^0 (ax-x^2)\,dx + \frac{b}{c}\int_0^c (cx-x^2)\,dx\right]$$

$$= \frac{b}{Aa}\left[\frac{1}{2}ax^2 - \frac{1}{3}x^3\right]_a^0 + \frac{b}{Ac}\left[\frac{1}{2}cx^2 - \frac{1}{3}x^3\right]_0^c = \frac{b}{Aa}\left[-\frac{1}{2}a^3 + \frac{1}{3}a^3\right] + \frac{b}{Ac}\left[\frac{1}{2}c^3 - \frac{1}{3}c^3\right]$$

$$= \frac{2}{a(c-a)} \cdot \frac{-a^3}{6} + \frac{2}{c(c-a)} \cdot \frac{c^3}{6} = \frac{1}{3(c-a)}(c^2 - a^2) = \frac{a+c}{3}$$

and

$$\bar{y} = \frac{1}{A}\left[\int_a^0 \frac{1}{2}\left(\frac{b}{a}(a-x)\right)^2\,dx + \int_0^c \frac{1}{2}\left(\frac{b}{c}(c-x)\right)^2\,dx\right]$$

$$= \frac{1}{A}\left[\frac{b^2}{2a^2}\int_a^0 (a^2 - 2ax + x^2)\,dx + \frac{b^2}{2c^2}\int_0^c (c^2 - 2cx + x^2)\,dx\right]$$

$$= \frac{1}{A}\left[\frac{b^2}{2a^2}\left[a^2 x - ax^2 + \frac{1}{3}x^3\right]_a^0 + \frac{b^2}{2c^2}\left[c^2 x - cx^2 + \frac{1}{3}x^3\right]_0^c\right]$$

$$= \frac{1}{A}\left[\frac{b^2}{2a^2}\left(-a^3 + a^3 - \frac{1}{3}a^3\right) + \frac{b^2}{2c^2}\left(c^3 - c^3 + \frac{1}{3}c^3\right)\right] = \frac{1}{A}\left[\frac{b^2}{6}(-a+c)\right] = \frac{2}{(c-a)b} \cdot \frac{(c-a)b^2}{6} = \frac{b}{3}$$

Thus, the centroid is $(\bar{x}, \bar{y}) = \left(\dfrac{a+c}{3}, \dfrac{b}{3}\right)$, as claimed.

Remarks: Actually the computation of $\bar{y}$ is all that is needed. By considering each side of the triangle in turn to be the base, we see that the centroid is $\frac{1}{3}$ of the way from each side to the opposite vertex and must therefore be the intersection of the medians.

The computation of $\bar{y}$ in this problem (and many others) can be simplified by using horizontal rather than vertical approximating rectangles. If the length of a thin rectangle at coordinate y is $\ell(y)$, then its area is $\ell(y)\,\Delta y$, its mass is $\rho\ell(y)\,\Delta y$, and its moment about the x-axis is $\Delta M_x = \rho y \ell(y)\,\Delta y$. Thus,

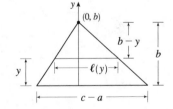

$$M_x = \int \rho y \ell(y)\,dy \quad\text{and}\quad \bar{y} = \frac{\int \rho y \ell(y)\,dy}{\rho A} = \frac{1}{A}\int y\ell(y)\,dy$$

In this problem, $\ell(y) = \dfrac{c-a}{b}(b-y)$ by similar triangles, so

$$\bar{y} = \frac{1}{A}\int_0^b \frac{c-a}{b}y(b-y)\,dy = \frac{2}{b^2}\int_0^b (by - y^2)\,dy = \frac{2}{b^2}\left[\frac{1}{2}by^2 - \frac{1}{3}y^3\right]_0^b = \frac{2}{b^2} \cdot \frac{b^3}{6} = \frac{b}{3}$$

Notice that only one integral is needed when this method is used.

39. Divide the lamina into two triangles and one rectangle with respective masses of 2, 2 and 4, so that the total mass is 8. Using the result of Exercise 37, the triangles have centroids $\left(-1, \frac{2}{3}\right)$ and $\left(1, \frac{2}{3}\right)$. The centroid of the rectangle (its center) is $\left(0, -\frac{1}{2}\right)$. So, using Formulas 5 and 7, we have

$$\bar{y} = \frac{M_x}{m} = \frac{1}{m} \sum_{i=1}^{3} m_i y_i = \frac{1}{8}\left[2\left(\frac{2}{3}\right) + 2\left(\frac{2}{3}\right) + 4\left(-\frac{1}{2}\right)\right] = \frac{1}{8}\left(\frac{2}{3}\right) = \frac{1}{12}, \text{ and } \bar{x} = 0, \text{ since the lamina is symmetric}$$

about the line $x = 0$. Thus, the centroid is $(\bar{x}, \bar{y}) = \left(0, \frac{1}{12}\right)$.

41. A cone of height h and radius r can be generated by rotating a right triangle about one of its legs as shown. By Exercise 37, $\bar{x} = \frac{1}{3}r$, so by the Theorem of Pappus, the volume of the cone is

$$V = Ad = \left(\frac{1}{2} \cdot \text{base} \cdot \text{height}\right) \cdot (2\pi\bar{x}) = \frac{1}{2}rh \cdot 2\pi\left(\frac{1}{3}r\right) = \frac{1}{3}\pi r^2 h.$$

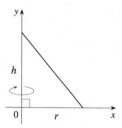

43. Suppose the region lies between two curves $y = f(x)$ and $y = g(x)$ where $f(x) \geq g(x)$, as illustrated in Figure 13. Choose points x_i with $a = x_0 < x_1 < \cdots < x_n = b$ and choose x_i^* to be the midpoint of the ith subinterval; that is, $x_i^* = \bar{x}_i = \frac{1}{2}(x_{i-1} + x_i)$. Then the centroid of the ith approximating rectangle R_i is its center $C_i = \left(\bar{x}_i, \frac{1}{2}[f(\bar{x}_i) + g(\bar{x}_i)]\right)$. Its area is $[f(\bar{x}_i) - g(\bar{x}_i)]\,\Delta x$, so its mass is

$\rho[f(\bar{x}_i) - g(\bar{x}_i)]\,\Delta x$. Thus, $M_y(R_i) = \rho[f(\bar{x}_i) - g(\bar{x}_i)]\,\Delta x \cdot \bar{x}_i = \rho\bar{x}_i\,[f(\bar{x}_i) - g(\bar{x}_i)]\,\Delta x$ and

$M_x(R_i) = \rho[f(\bar{x}_i) - g(\bar{x}_i)]\,\Delta x \cdot \frac{1}{2}[f(\bar{x}_i) + g(\bar{x}_i)] = \rho \cdot \frac{1}{2}\left[f(\bar{x}_i)^2 - g(\bar{x}_i)^2\right]\Delta x$. Summing over i and taking

the limit as $n \to \infty$, we get $M_y = \lim\limits_{n \to \infty} \sum_i \rho\bar{x}_i\,[f(\bar{x}_i) - g(\bar{x}_i)]\,\Delta x = \rho \int_a^b x[f(x) - g(x)]\,dx$ and

$M_x = \lim\limits_{n \to \infty} \sum_i \rho \cdot \frac{1}{2}\left[f(\bar{x}_i)^2 - g(\bar{x}_i)^2\right]\Delta x = \rho \int_a^b \frac{1}{2}\left[f(x)^2 - g(x)^2\right]dx$. Thus,

$$\bar{x} = \frac{M_y}{m} = \frac{M_y}{\rho A} = \frac{1}{A}\int_a^b x[f(x) - g(x)]\,dx \quad \text{and} \quad \bar{y} = \frac{M_x}{m} = \frac{M_x}{\rho A} = \frac{1}{A}\int_a^b \frac{1}{2}\left[f(x)^2 - g(x)^2\right]dx$$

9 Review

1. (a) The length of a curve is defined to be the limit of the lengths of the inscribed polygons, as described near Figure 3 in Section 9.1.

   (b) See Equation 9.1.2.

   (c) See Equation 9.1.4.

2. (a) $S = \int_a^b 2\pi f(x)\sqrt{1 + [f'(x)]^2}\,dx$

   (b) If $x = g(y)$, $c \leq y \leq d$, then $S = \int_c^d 2\pi y\sqrt{1 + [g'(y)]^2}\,dy$.

   (c) $S = \int_a^b 2\pi x\sqrt{1 + [f'(x)]^2}\,dx$ or $S = \int_c^d 2\pi g(y)\sqrt{1 + [g'(y)]^2}\,dy$

3. Let $c(x)$ be the cross-sectional length of the wall (measured parallel to the surface of the fluid) at depth x. Then the hydrostatic force against the wall is given by $F = \int_a^b \delta x c(x)\,dx$, where a and b are the lower and upper limits for x at points of the wall and δ is the weight density of the fluid.

4. (a) The center of mass is the point at which the plate balances horizontally.

   (b) See Equations 9.3.8.

5. If a plane region $\mathcal{R}$ that lies entirely on one side of a line ℓ in its plane is rotated about ℓ, then the volume of the resulting solid is the product of the area of $\mathcal{R}$ and the distance traveled by the centroid of $\mathcal{R}$.

6. See Figure 3 in Section 9.4, and the discussion which precedes it.

7. (a) See the definition in the first paragraph of the subsection *Cardiac Output* in Section 9.4.

   (b) See the discussion in the second paragraph of the subsection *Cardiac Output* in Section 9.4.

8. A probability density function f is a function on the domain of a continuous random variable X such that $\int_a^b f(x)\,dx$ measures the probability that X lies between a and b. Such a function f has nonnegative values and satisfies the relation $\int_D f(x)\,dx = 1$, where D is the domain of the corresponding random variable X. If $D = \mathbb{R}$, or if we define $f(x) = 0$ for real numbers $x \notin D$, then $\int_{-\infty}^{\infty} f(x)\,dx = 1$. (Of course, to work with f in this way, we must assume that the integrals of f exist.)

9. (a) $\int_0^{100} f(x)\,dx$ represents the probability that the weight of a randomly chosen female college student is less than 100 pounds.

(b) $\mu = \int_{-\infty}^{\infty} x f(x)\,dx = \int_0^{\infty} x f(x)\,dx$

(c) The median of f is the number m such that $\int_m^{\infty} f(x)\,dx = \frac{1}{2}$.

10. See the discussion near Equation 3 in Section 9.5.

--------- EXERCISES ---------

1. $y = \frac{1}{6}(x^2+4)^{3/2} \;\Rightarrow\; dy/dx = \frac{1}{4}(x^2+4)^{1/2}(2x) \;\Rightarrow$

$$1 + \left(\frac{dy}{dx}\right)^2 = 1 + \left[\frac{1}{2}x(x^2+4)^{1/2}\right]^2 = 1 + \frac{1}{4}x^2(x^2+4) = \frac{1}{4}x^4 + x^2 + 1 = \left(\frac{1}{2}x^2+1\right)^2.$$

Thus, $L = \int_0^3 \sqrt{\left(\frac{1}{2}x^2+1\right)^2}\,dx = \int_0^3 \left(\frac{1}{2}x^2+1\right)dx = \left[\frac{1}{6}x^3 + x\right]_0^3 = \frac{15}{2}$.

3. (a) $y = \dfrac{x^4}{16} + \dfrac{1}{2x^2} = \frac{1}{16}x^4 + \frac{1}{2}x^{-2} \;\Rightarrow\; \dfrac{dy}{dx} = \frac{1}{4}x^3 - x^{-3} \;\Rightarrow$

$$1 + (dy/dx)^2 = 1 + \left(\frac{1}{4}x^3 - x^{-3}\right)^2 = 1 + \frac{1}{16}x^6 - \frac{1}{2} + x^{-6} = \frac{1}{16}x^6 + \frac{1}{2} + x^{-6} = \left(\frac{1}{4}x^3 + x^{-3}\right)^2.$$

Thus, $L = \int_1^2 \left(\frac{1}{4}x^3 + x^{-3}\right)dx = \left[\frac{1}{16}x^4 - \frac{1}{2}x^{-2}\right]_1^2 = \left(1 - \frac{1}{8}\right) - \left(\frac{1}{16} - \frac{1}{2}\right) = \frac{21}{16}$.

(b) $S = \int_1^2 2\pi x\left(\frac{1}{4}x^3 + x^{-3}\right)dx = 2\pi \int_1^2 \left(\frac{1}{4}x^4 + x^{-2}\right)dx = 2\pi\left[\frac{1}{20}x^5 - \frac{1}{x}\right]_1^2$

$\qquad = 2\pi\left[\left(\frac{32}{20} - \frac{1}{2}\right) - \left(\frac{1}{20} - 1\right)\right] = 2\pi\left(\frac{8}{5} - \frac{1}{2} - \frac{1}{20} + 1\right) = 2\pi\left(\frac{41}{20}\right) = \frac{41}{10}\pi$

5. $y = e^{-x^2} \;\Rightarrow\; dy/dx = -2xe^{-x^2} \;\Rightarrow\; 1 + (dy/dx)^2 = 1 + 4x^2 e^{-2x^2}$.

Let $f(x) = \sqrt{1 + 4x^2 e^{-2x^2}}$. Then

$$L = \int_0^3 f(x)\,dx \approx S_6 = \frac{(3-0)/6}{3}[f(0) + 4f(0.5) + 2f(1) + 4f(1.5) + 2f(2) + 4f(2.5) + f(3)]$$

$$\approx 3.292287$$

7. $y = \displaystyle\int_1^x \sqrt{\sqrt{t}-1}\,dt \;\Rightarrow\; dy/dx = \sqrt{\sqrt{x}-1} \;\Rightarrow\; 1 + (dy/dx)^2 = 1 + (\sqrt{x}-1) = \sqrt{x}$.

Thus, $L = \int_1^{16} \sqrt{\sqrt{x}}\,dx = \int_1^{16} x^{1/4}\,dx = \frac{4}{5}\left[x^{5/4}\right]_1^{16} = \frac{4}{5}(32-1) = \frac{124}{5}$.

9. As in Example 1 of Section 9.3, $\dfrac{a}{2-x} = \dfrac{1}{2} \;\Rightarrow\; 2a = 2 - x$ and

$w = 2(1.5 + a) = 3 + 2a = 3 + 2 - x = 5 - x$. Thus,

$$F = \int_0^2 \rho g x(5-x)\,dx = \rho g\left[\frac{5}{2}x^2 - \frac{1}{3}x^3\right]_0^2 = \rho g\left(10 - \frac{8}{3}\right) = \frac{22}{3}\delta \;\; [\rho g = \delta] \approx \frac{22}{3}\cdot 62.5 \approx 458 \text{ lb}.$$

11. $A = \int_{-2}^{1} \left[(4 - x^2) - (x + 2) \right] dx = \int_{-2}^{1} \left(2 - x - x^2 \right) dx = \left[2x - \frac{1}{2}x^2 - \frac{1}{3}x^3 \right]_{-2}^{1}$

$= \left(2 - \frac{1}{2} - \frac{1}{3} \right) - \left(-4 - 2 + \frac{8}{3} \right) = \frac{9}{2} \quad \Rightarrow$

$\bar{x} = A^{-1} \int_{-2}^{1} x(2 - x - x^2) dx = \frac{2}{9} \int_{-2}^{1} \left(2x - x^2 - x^3 \right) dx = \frac{2}{9} \left[x^2 - \frac{1}{3}x^3 - \frac{1}{4}x^4 \right]_{-2}^{1}$

$= \frac{2}{9} \left[\left(1 - \frac{1}{3} - \frac{1}{4} \right) - \left(4 + \frac{8}{3} - 4 \right) \right] = -\frac{1}{2}$

and $\quad \bar{y} = A^{-1} \int_{-2}^{1} \frac{1}{2} \left[(4 - x^2)^2 - (x + 2)^2 \right] dx = \frac{1}{9} \int_{-2}^{1} \left(x^4 - 9x^2 - 4x + 12 \right) dx$

$= \frac{1}{9} \left[\frac{1}{5}x^5 - 3x^3 - 2x^2 + 12x \right]_{-2}^{1} = \frac{1}{9} \left[\left(\frac{1}{5} - 3 - 2 + 12 \right) - \left(-\frac{32}{5} + 24 - 8 - 24 \right) \right] = \frac{12}{5}$

Thus, the centroid is $(\bar{x}, \bar{y}) = \left(-\frac{1}{2}, \frac{12}{5} \right)$.

13. An equation of the line passing through $(0, 0)$ and $(3, 2)$ is $y = \frac{2}{3}x$. $A = \frac{1}{2} \cdot 3 \cdot 2 = 3$. Therefore, using

Equations 9.3.8, $\bar{x} = \frac{1}{3} \int_{0}^{3} x\left(\frac{2}{3}x \right) dx = \frac{2}{27} \left[x^3 \right]_{0}^{3} = 2$, and $\bar{y} = \frac{1}{3} \int_{0}^{3} \frac{1}{2} \left(\frac{2}{3}x \right)^2 dx = \frac{2}{81} \left[x^3 \right]_{0}^{3} = \frac{2}{3}$.

Thus, the centroid is $(\bar{x}, \bar{y}) = \left(2, \frac{2}{3} \right)$.

15. The centroid of this circle, $(1, 0)$, travels a distance $2\pi(1)$ when the lamina is rotated about the y-axis. The area of

the circle is $\pi(1)^2$. So by the Theorem of Pappus, $V = A(2\pi\bar{x}) = \pi(1)^2 2\pi(1) = 2\pi^2$.

17. $x = 100 \quad \Rightarrow \quad P = 2000 - 0.1(100) - 0.01(100)^2 = 1890$

$$\text{Consumer surplus} = \int_{0}^{100} [p(x) - P] \, dx = \int_{0}^{100} \left(2000 - 0.1x - 0.01x^2 - 1890 \right) dx$$

$$= \left[110x - 0.05x^2 - \frac{0.01}{3}x^3 \right]_{0}^{100} = 11,000 - 500 - \frac{10,000}{3} \approx \$7166.67$$

19. $f(x) = \begin{cases} \frac{\pi}{20} \sin\left(\frac{\pi}{10}x \right) & \text{if } 0 \leq x \leq 10 \\ 0 & \text{if } x < 0 \text{ or } x > 10 \end{cases}$

(a) $f(x) \geq 0$ for all real numbers x and

$$\int_{-\infty}^{\infty} f(x) \, dx = \int_{0}^{10} \frac{\pi}{20} \sin\left(\frac{\pi}{10}x \right) dx = \frac{\pi}{20} \cdot \frac{10}{\pi} \left[-\cos\left(\frac{\pi}{10}x \right) \right]_{0}^{10}$$

$$= \frac{1}{2}(-\cos \pi + \cos 0) = \frac{1}{2}(1 + 1) = 1$$

Therefore, f is a probability density function.

(b) $P(X < 4) = \int_{-\infty}^{4} f(x) \, dx = \int_{0}^{4} \frac{\pi}{20} \sin\left(\frac{\pi}{10}x \right) dx = \frac{1}{2} \left[-\cos\left(\frac{\pi}{10}x \right) \right]_{0}^{4} = \frac{1}{2} \left(-\cos \frac{2\pi}{5} + \cos 0 \right)$

$\approx \frac{1}{2}(-0.309017 + 1) \approx 0.3455$

(c) $\mu = \int_{-\infty}^{\infty} x f(x)\, dx = \int_0^{10} \frac{\pi}{20} x \sin\left(\frac{\pi}{10}x\right) dx$

$\qquad = \int_0^{\pi} \frac{\pi}{20} \cdot \frac{10}{\pi} u (\sin u)\left(\frac{10}{\pi}\right) du \quad [u = \frac{\pi}{10}x,\ du = \frac{\pi}{10}\, dx]$

$\qquad = \frac{5}{\pi} \int_0^{\pi} u \sin u\, du \overset{82}{=} \frac{5}{\pi}\left[\sin u - u \cos u\right]_0^{\pi} = \frac{5}{\pi}[0 - \pi(-1)] = 5$

This answer is expected because the graph of f is symmetric about

the line $x = 5$.

0.3

$y = \frac{\pi}{20}\sin\left(\frac{\pi x}{10}\right)$

0   10

−0.1

21. (a) The probability density function is $f(t) = \begin{cases} 0 & \text{if } t < 0 \\ \frac{1}{8}e^{-t/8} & \text{if } t \geq 0 \end{cases}$

$P(0 \leq X \leq 3) = \int_0^3 \frac{1}{8}e^{-t/8}\, dt = \left[-e^{-t/8}\right]_0^3 = -e^{-3/8} + 1 \approx 0.3127$

(b) $P(X > 10) = \int_{10}^{\infty} \frac{1}{8}e^{-t/8}\, dt = \lim_{x \to \infty}\left[-e^{-t/8}\right]_{10}^{x} = \lim_{x \to \infty}\left(-e^{-x/8} + e^{-10/8}\right) = 0 + e^{-5/4} \approx 0.2865$

(c) We need to find m such that $P(X \geq m) = \frac{1}{2} \;\Rightarrow\; \int_m^{\infty} \frac{1}{8}e^{-t/8}\, dt = \frac{1}{2} \;\Rightarrow\; \lim_{x \to \infty}\left[-e^{-t/8}\right]_m^{x} = \frac{1}{2} \;\Rightarrow\;$

$\lim_{x \to \infty}\left(-e^{-x/8} + e^{-m/8}\right) = \frac{1}{2} \;\Rightarrow\; e^{-m/8} = \frac{1}{2} \;\Rightarrow\; -m/8 = \ln\frac{1}{2} \;\Rightarrow\;$

$m = -8\ln\frac{1}{2} = 8\ln 2 \approx 5.55$ minutes.

10 □ DIFFERENTIAL EQUATIONS

10.1 Modeling with Differential Equations

1. $y = x - x^{-1}$ $\Rightarrow$ $y' = 1 + x^{-2}$. To show that y is a solution of the differential equation, we will substitute the expressions for y and y' in the left-hand side of the equation and show that the left-hand side is equal to the right-hand side.

$$\text{LHS} = xy' + y = x\left(1 + x^{-2}\right) + \left(x - x^{-1}\right) = x + x^{-1} + x - x^{-1} = 2x = \text{RHS}$$

3. (a) $y = \sin kt$ $\Rightarrow$ $y' = k \cos kt$ $\Rightarrow$ $y'' = -k^2 \sin kt$. $y'' + 9y = 0$ $\Rightarrow$
$-k^2 \sin kt + 9 \sin kt = 0$ for all t $\Leftrightarrow$ $\left(9 - k^2\right) \sin kt = 0$ for all t $\Leftrightarrow$ $9 - k^2 = 0$ $\Leftrightarrow$ $k = \pm 3$

(b) $y = A \sin kt + B \cos kt$ $\Rightarrow$ $y' = Ak \cos kt - Bk \sin kt$ $\Rightarrow$ $y'' = -Ak^2 \sin kt - Bk^2 \cos kt$.
Thus, $y'' + 9y = 0$ $\Rightarrow$ $-Ak^2 \sin kt - Bk^2 \cos kt + 9(A \sin kt + B \cos kt) = 0$ $\Rightarrow$
$\left(9 - k^2\right) A \sin kt + \left(9 - k^2\right) B \cos kt = 0$. The last equation is true for all values of A and B if $k = \pm 3$.

5. (a) $y = e^t$ $\Rightarrow$ $y' = e^t$ $\Rightarrow$ $y'' = e^t$. LHS $= y'' + 2y' + y = e^t + 2e^t + e^t = 4e^t \neq 0$, so $y = e^t$ is not a solution of the differential equation.

(b) $y = e^{-t}$ $\Rightarrow$ $y' = -e^{-t}$ $\Rightarrow$ $y'' = e^{-t}$. LHS $= y'' + 2y' + y = e^{-t} - 2e^{-t} + e^{-t} = 0 = $ RHS, so $y = e^{-t}$ is a solution.

(c) $y = te^{-t}$ $\Rightarrow$ $y' = t\left(-e^{-t}\right) + e^{-t}(1) = e^{-t}(1 - t)$ $\Rightarrow$ $y'' = e^{-t}(t - 2)$.

$$\text{LHS} = y'' + 2y' + y = e^{-t}(t - 2) + 2e^{-t}(1 - t) + te^{-t}$$
$$= e^{-t}[(t - 2) + 2(1 - t) + t] = e^{-t}(0) = 0 = \text{RHS},$$

so $y = te^{-t}$ is a solution.

(d) $y = t^2 e^{-t}$ $\Rightarrow$ $y' = te^{-t}(2 - t)$ $\Rightarrow$ $y'' = e^{-t}\left(t^2 - 4t + 2\right)$.

$$\text{LHS} = y'' + 2y' + y = e^{-t}\left(t^2 - 4t + 2\right) + 2te^{-t}(2 - t) + t^2 e^{-t}$$
$$= e^{-t}\left[\left(t^2 - 4t + 2\right) + 2t(2 - t) + t^2\right] = e^{-t}(2) \neq 0,$$

so $y = t^2 e^{-t}$ is not a solution.

7. (a) Since the derivative $y' = -y^2$ is always negative (or 0 if $y = 0$), the function y must be decreasing (or equal to 0) on any interval on which it is defined.

(b) $y = \dfrac{1}{x + C}$ $\Rightarrow$ $y' = -\dfrac{1}{(x + C)^2}$. LHS $= y' = -\dfrac{1}{(x + C)^2} = -\left(\dfrac{1}{x + C}\right)^2 = -y^2 = $ RHS

(c) $y = 0$ is a solution of $y' = -y^2$ that is not a member of the family in part (b).

(d) If $y(x) = \dfrac{1}{x + C}$, then $y(0) = \dfrac{1}{0 + C} = \dfrac{1}{C}$. Since $y(0) = 0.5$, $\dfrac{1}{C} = \dfrac{1}{2}$ $\Rightarrow$ $C = 2$, so $y = \dfrac{1}{x + 2}$.

9. (a) $\dfrac{dP}{dt} = 1.2P\left(1 - \dfrac{P}{4200}\right)$. Now $\dfrac{dP}{dt} > 0 \;\Rightarrow\; 1 - \dfrac{P}{4200} > 0$ [assuming that $P > 0$] $\;\Rightarrow\; \dfrac{P}{4200} < 1 \;\Rightarrow\;$

$P < 4200 \;\Rightarrow\;$ the population is increasing for $0 < P < 4200$.

(b) $\dfrac{dP}{dt} < 0 \;\Rightarrow\; P > 4200$

(c) $\dfrac{dP}{dt} = 0 \;\Rightarrow\; P = 4200$ or $P = 0$

11. (a) This function is increasing *and* also decreasing. But $dy/dt = e^t(y-1)^2 \geq 0$ for all t, implying that the graph of the solution of the differential equation cannot be decreasing on any interval.

(b) When $y = 1$, $dy/dt = 0$, but the graph does not have a horizontal tangent line.

13. (a) P increases most rapidly at the beginning, since there are usually many simple, easily-learned sub-skills associated with learning a skill. As t increases, we would expect dP/dt to remain positive, but decrease. This is because as time progresses, the only points left to learn are the more difficult ones.

(c)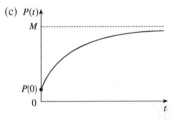

(b) $\dfrac{dP}{dt} = k(M - P)$ is always positive, so the level of performance P is increasing. As P gets close to M, dP/dt gets close to 0; that is, the performance levels off, as explained in part (a).

10.2 Direction Fields and Euler's Method

1. (a)

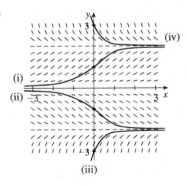

(b) It appears that the constant functions $y = 0$, $y = -2$, and $y = 2$ are equilibrium solutions. Note that these three values of y satisfy the given differential equation $y' = y\left(1 - \frac{1}{4}y^2\right)$.

3. $y' = y - 1$. The slopes at each point are independent of x, so the slopes are the same along each line parallel to the x-axis. Thus, IV is the direction field for this equation. Note that for $y = 1$, $y' = 0$.

5. $y' = y^2 - x^2 = 0 \implies y = \pm x$. There are horizontal tangents on these lines only in graph III, so this equation corresponds to direction field III.

7. (a) $y(0) = 1$ (b) $y(0) = 0$ (c) $y(0) = -1$

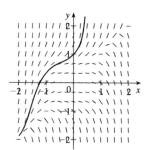 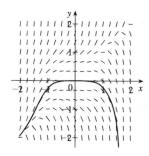 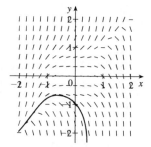

9.

x	y	$y' = 1 + y$
0	0	1
0	1	2
0	2	3
0	-3	-2
0	-2	-1

Note that for $y = -1$, $y' = 0$. The three solution curves sketched go through $(0, 0)$, $(0, -1)$, and $(0, -2)$.

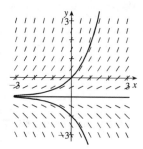

11.

x	y	$y' = y - 2x$
-2	-2	2
-2	2	6
2	2	-2
2	-2	-6

Note that $y' = 0$ for any point on the line $y = 2x$. The slopes are positive to the left of the line and negative to the right of the line. The solution curve in the graph passes through $(1, 0)$.

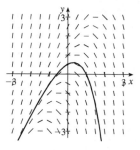

13.

x	y	$y' = y + xy$
0	± 2	± 2
1	± 2	± 4
-3	± 2	∓ 4

Note that $y' = y(x + 1) = 0$ for any point on $y = 0$ or on $x = -1$. The slopes are positive when the factors y and $x + 1$ have the same sign and negative when they have opposite signs. The solution curve in the graph passes through $(0, 1)$.

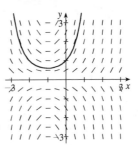

15. In Maple, we can use either `directionfield` (in Maple's share library) or `plots[fieldplot]` to plot the direction field. To plot the solution, we can either use the initial-value option in `directionfield`, or actually solve the equation. In Mathematica, we use `PlotVectorField` for the direction field, and the `Plot[Evaluate[...]]` construction to plot the solution, which

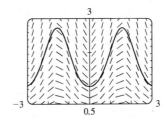

is $y = e^{(1 - \cos 2x)/2}$. In Derive, use `Direction_Field` (in utility file ODE_APPR) to plot the direction field. Then use `DSOLVE1(-y*SIN(2*x),1,x,y,0,1)` (in utility file ODE1) to solve the equation. Simplify each result.

17.

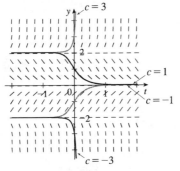

$L = \lim_{t \to \infty} y(t)$ exists for $-2 \le c \le 2$; $L = \pm 2$ for $c = \pm 2$ and $L = 0$ for $-2 < c < 2$. For other values of c, L does not exist.

19. (a) $y' = F(x, y) = y$ and $y(0) = 1 \quad \Rightarrow \quad x_0 = 0, y_0 = 1$.

    (i) $h = 0.4$ and $y_1 = y_0 + hF(x_0, y_0) \quad \Rightarrow \quad y_1 = 1 + 0.4 \cdot 1 = 1.4$. $x_1 = x_0 + h = 0 + 0.4 = 0.4$, so $y_1 = y(0.4) = 1.4$.

    (ii) $h = 0.2 \quad \Rightarrow \quad x_1 = 0.2$ and $x_2 = 0.4$, so we need to find y_2.

        $y_1 = y_0 + hF(x_0, y_0) = 1 + 0.2y_0 = 1 + 0.2 \cdot 1 = 1.2$,

        $y_2 = y_1 + hF(x_1, y_1) = 1.2 + 0.2y_1 = 1.2 + 0.2 \cdot 1.2 = 1.44$.

    (iii) $h = 0.1 \quad \Rightarrow \quad x_4 = 0.4$, so we need to find y_4. $y_1 = y_0 + hF(x_0, y_0) = 1 + 0.1y_0 = 1 + 0.1 \cdot 1 = 1.1$,

        $y_2 = y_1 + hF(x_1, y_1) = 1.1 + 0.1y_1 = 1.1 + 0.1 \cdot 1.1 = 1.21$,

        $y_3 = y_2 + hF(x_2, y_2) = 1.21 + 0.1y_2 = 1.21 + 0.1 \cdot 1.21 = 1.331$,

        $y_4 = y_3 + hF(x_3, y_3) = 1.331 + 0.1y_3 = 1.331 + 0.1 \cdot 1.331 = 1.4641$.

(b)

We see that the estimates are underestimates since they are all below the graph of $y = e^x$.

(c) (i) For $h = 0.4$: (exact value) $-$ (approximate value) $= e^{0.4} - 1.4 \approx 0.0918$

(ii) For $h = 0.2$: (exact value) $-$ (approximate value) $= e^{0.4} - 1.44 \approx 0.0518$

(iii) For $h = 0.1$: (exact value) $-$ (approximate value) $= e^{0.4} - 1.4641 \approx 0.0277$

Each time the step size is halved, the error estimate also appears to be halved (approximately).

21. $h = 0.5$, $x_0 = 1$, $y_0 = 0$, and $F(x, y) = y - 2x$.

Note that $x_1 = x_0 + h = 1 + 0.5 = 1.5$, $x_2 = 2$, and $x_3 = 2.5$.

$y_1 = y_0 + hF(x_0, y_0) = 0 + 0.5F(1, 0) = 0.5[0 - 2(1)] = -1$.

$y_2 = y_1 + hF(x_1, y_1) = -1 + 0.5F(1.5, -1) = -1 + 0.5[-1 - 2(1.5)] = -3$.

$y_3 = y_2 + hF(x_2, y_2) = -3 + 0.5F(2, -3) = -3 + 0.5[-3 - 2(2)] = -6.5$.

$y_4 = y_3 + hF(x_3, y_3) = -6.5 + 0.5F(2.5, -6.5) = -6.5 + 0.5[-6.5 - 2(2.5)] = -12.25$.

23. $h = 0.1$, $x_0 = 0$, $y_0 = 1$, and $F(x, y) = y + xy$.

Note that $x_1 = x_0 + h = 0 + 0.1 = 0.1$, $x_2 = 0.2$, $x_3 = 0.3$, and $x_4 = 0.4$.

$y_1 = y_0 + hF(x_0, y_0) = 1 + 0.1F(0, 1) = 1 + 0.1[1 + (0)(1)] = 1.1$.

$y_2 = y_1 + hF(x_1, y_1) = 1.1 + 0.1F(0.1, 1.1) = 1.1 + 0.1[1.1 + (0.1)(1.1)] = 1.221$.

$y_3 = y_2 + hF(x_2, y_2) = 1.221 + 0.1F(0.2, 1.221) = 1.221 + 0.1[1.221 + (0.2)(1.221)] = 1.36752$.

$y_4 = y_3 + hF(x_3, y_3) = 1.36752 + 0.1F(0.3, 1.36752) = 1.36752 + 0.1[1.36752 + (0.3)(1.36752)]$

$\qquad = 1.5452976$.

$y_5 = y_4 + hF(x_4, y_4) = 1.5452976 + 0.1F(0.4, 1.5452976)$

$\qquad = 1.5452976 + 0.1[1.5452976 + (0.4)(1.5452976)] = 1.761639264$.

Thus, $y(0.5) \approx 1.7616$.

25. (a) $dy/dx + 3x^2y = 6x^2 \Rightarrow y' = 6x^2 - 3x^2y$. Store this expression in Y_1 and use the following simple program to evaluate $y(1)$ for each part, using $H = h = 1$ and $N = 1$ for part (i), $H = 0.1$ and $N = 10$ for part (ii), and so forth.

$\qquad h \to H: 0 \to X: 3 \to Y:$

$\qquad$ For(I, 1, N): $Y + H \times Y_1 \to Y: X + H \to X:$

$\qquad$ End(loop):

$\qquad$ Display Y. [To see all iterations, include this statement in the loop.]

(i) $H = 1, N = 1 \Rightarrow y(1) = 3$

(ii) $H = 0.1, N = 10 \Rightarrow y(1) \approx 2.3928$

(iii) $H = 0.01, N = 100 \Rightarrow y(1) \approx 2.3701$

(iv) $H = 0.001, N = 1000 \Rightarrow y(1) \approx 2.3681$

(b) $y = 2 + e^{-x^3}$ $\Rightarrow$ $y' = -3x^2 e^{-x^3}$

$\text{LHS} = y' + 3x^2 y = -3x^2 e^{-x^3} + 3x^2\left(2 + e^{-x^3}\right) = -3x^2 e^{-x^3} + 6x^2 + 3x^2 e^{-x^3} = 6x^2 = \text{RHS}$

$y(0) = 2 + e^{-0} = 2 + 1 = 3$

(c) The exact value of $y(1)$ is $2 + e^{-1^3} = 2 + e^{-1}$.

(i) For $h = 1$: (exact value) − (approximate value) $= 2 + e^{-1} - 3 \approx -0.6321$

(ii) For $h = 0.1$: (exact value) − (approximate value) $= 2 + e^{-1} - 2.3928 \approx -0.0249$

(iii) For $h = 0.01$: (exact value) − (approximate value) $= 2 + e^{-1} - 2.3701 \approx -0.0022$

(iv) For $h = 0.001$: (exact value) − (approximate value) $= 2 + e^{-1} - 2.3681 \approx -0.0002$

In (ii)–(iv), it seems that when the step size is divided by 10, the error estimate is also divided by 10 (approximately).

27. (a) $R\dfrac{dQ}{dt} + \dfrac{1}{C}Q = E(t)$ becomes

$5Q' + \frac{1}{0.05}Q = 60$ or $Q' + 4Q = 12$.

(b) From the graph, it appears that the limiting value of the charge Q is about 3.

(c) If $Q' = 0$, then $4Q = 12$ $\Rightarrow$ $Q = 3$ is an equilibrium solution.

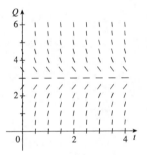

(d)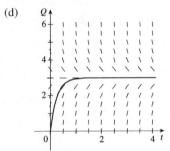

(e) $Q' + 4Q = 12$ $\Rightarrow$ $Q' = 12 - 4Q$. Now $Q(0) = 0$, so $t_0 = 0$ and $Q_0 = 0$.

$$Q_1 = Q_0 + hF(t_0, Q_0) = 0 + 0.1(12 - 4 \cdot 0) = 1.2$$
$$Q_2 = Q_1 + hF(t_1, Q_1) = 1.2 + 0.1(12 - 4 \cdot 1.2) = 1.92$$
$$Q_3 = Q_2 + hF(t_2, Q_2) = 1.92 + 0.1(12 - 4 \cdot 1.92) = 2.352$$
$$Q_4 = Q_3 + hF(t_3, Q_3) = 2.352 + 0.1(12 - 4 \cdot 2.352) = 2.6112$$
$$Q_5 = Q_4 + hF(t_4, Q_4) = 2.6112 + 0.1(12 - 4 \cdot 2.6112) = 2.76672$$

Thus, $Q_5 = Q(0.5) \approx 2.77$ C.

10.3 Separable Equations

1. $\dfrac{dy}{dx} = \dfrac{y}{x}$ $\Rightarrow$ $\dfrac{dy}{y} = \dfrac{dx}{x}$ $[y \neq 0]$ $\Rightarrow$ $\displaystyle\int \dfrac{dy}{y} = \int \dfrac{dx}{x}$ $\Rightarrow$ $\ln|y| = \ln|x| + C$ $\Rightarrow$

$|y| = e^{\ln|x|+C} = e^{\ln|x|}e^C = e^C|x|$ $\Rightarrow$ $y = Kx$, where $K = \pm e^C$ is a constant. (In our derivation, K was nonzero, but we can restore the excluded case $y = 0$ by allowing K to be zero.)

3. $(x^2 + 1)y' = xy$ $\Rightarrow$ $\dfrac{dy}{dx} = \dfrac{xy}{x^2 + 1}$ $\Rightarrow$ $\dfrac{dy}{y} = \dfrac{x\,dx}{x^2 + 1}$ $[y \neq 0]$ $\Rightarrow$ $\displaystyle\int \dfrac{dy}{y} = \int \dfrac{x\,dx}{x^2 + 1}$ $\Rightarrow$

$\ln|y| = \frac{1}{2}\ln(x^2 + 1) + C$ $[u = x^2 + 1, du = 2x\,dx]$ $= \ln(x^2 + 1)^{1/2} + \ln e^C = \ln\left(e^C\sqrt{x^2 + 1}\right)$ $\Rightarrow$

$|y| = e^C\sqrt{x^2 + 1}$ $\Rightarrow$ $y = K\sqrt{x^2 + 1}$, where $K = \pm e^C$ is a constant. (In our derivation, K was nonzero, but we can restore the excluded case $y = 0$ by allowing K to be zero.)

5. $(1 + \tan y)\,y' = x^2 + 1$ $\Rightarrow$ $(1 + \tan y)\dfrac{dy}{dx} = x^2 + 1$ $\Rightarrow$ $\left(1 + \dfrac{\sin y}{\cos y}\right)dy = (x^2 + 1)\,dx$ $\Rightarrow$

$\displaystyle\int \left(1 - \dfrac{-\sin y}{\cos y}\right)dy = \int (x^2 + 1)\,dx$ $\Rightarrow$ $y - \ln|\cos y| = \frac{1}{3}x^3 + x + C$. Note: The left side is equivalent to

$y + \ln|\sec y|$.

7. $\dfrac{dy}{dt} = \dfrac{te^t}{y\sqrt{1 + y^2}}$ $\Rightarrow$ $y\sqrt{1 + y^2}\,dy = te^t\,dt$ $\Rightarrow$ $\int y\sqrt{1 + y^2}\,dy = \int te^t\,dt$ $\Rightarrow$

$\frac{1}{3}\left(1 + y^2\right)^{3/2} = te^t - e^t + C$ [where the first integral is evaluated by substitution and the second by parts] $\Rightarrow$

$1 + y^2 = [3(te^t - e^t + C)]^{2/3}$ $\Rightarrow$ $y = \pm\sqrt{[3(te^t - e^t + C)]^{2/3} - 1}$

9. $\dfrac{du}{dt} = 2 + 2u + t + tu$ $\Rightarrow$ $\dfrac{du}{dt} = (1 + u)(2 + t)$ $\Rightarrow$ $\displaystyle\int \dfrac{du}{1 + u} = \int (2 + t)dt$ $[u \neq -1]$ $\Rightarrow$

$\ln|1 + u| = \frac{1}{2}t^2 + 2t + C$ $\Rightarrow$ $|1 + u| = e^{t^2/2 + 2t + C} = Ke^{t^2/2 + 2t}$, where $K = e^C$ $\Rightarrow$

$1 + u = \pm Ke^{t^2/2 + 2t}$ $\Rightarrow$ $u = -1 \pm Ke^{t^2/2 + 2t}$ where $K > 0$. $u = -1$ is also a solution, so

$u = -1 + Ae^{t^2/2 + 2t}$, where A is an arbitrary constant.

11. $\dfrac{dy}{dx} = y^2 + 1$, $y(1) = 0$. $\displaystyle\int \dfrac{dy}{y^2 + 1} = \int dx$ $\Rightarrow$ $\tan^{-1} y = x + C$. $y = 0$ when $x = 1$, so

$1 + C = \tan^{-1} 0 = 0$ $\Rightarrow$ $C = -1$. Thus, $\tan^{-1} y = x - 1$ and $y = \tan(x - 1)$.

13. $x\cos x = (2y + e^{3y})\,y'$ $\Rightarrow$ $x\cos x\,dx = (2y + e^{3y})\,dy$ $\Rightarrow$ $\int (2y + e^{3y})\,dy = \int x\cos x\,dx$ $\Rightarrow$

$y^2 + \frac{1}{3}e^{3y} = x\sin x + \cos x + C$ [where the second integral is evaluated using integration by parts]. Now

$y(0) = 0$ $\Rightarrow$ $0 + \frac{1}{3} = 0 + 1 + C$ $\Rightarrow$ $C = -\frac{2}{3}$. Thus, a solution is $y^2 + \frac{1}{3}e^{3y} = x\sin x + \cos x - \frac{2}{3}$.

We cannot solve explicitly for y.

15. $\dfrac{du}{dt} = \dfrac{2t + \sec^2 t}{2u}$, $u(0) = -5$. $\int 2u\,du = \int (2t + \sec^2 t)\,dt$ $\Rightarrow$ $u^2 = t^2 + \tan t + C$, where

$[u(0)]^2 = 0^2 + \tan 0 + C$ $\Rightarrow$ $C = (-5)^2 = 25$. Therefore, $u^2 = t^2 + \tan t + 25$, so $u = \pm\sqrt{t^2 + \tan t + 25}$.

Since $u(0) = -5$, we must have $u = -\sqrt{t^2 + \tan t + 25}$.

17. $y'\tan x = a + y$, $0 < x < \pi/2$ $\Rightarrow$ $\dfrac{dy}{dx} = \dfrac{a + y}{\tan x}$ $\Rightarrow$ $\dfrac{dy}{a + y} = \cot x\,dx$ $[a + y \neq 0]$ $\Rightarrow$

$\displaystyle\int \dfrac{dy}{a + y} = \int \dfrac{\cos x}{\sin x}\,dx$ $\Rightarrow$ $\ln|a + y| = \ln|\sin x| + C$ $\Rightarrow$

$|a + y| = e^{\ln|\sin x| + C} = e^{\ln|\sin x|} \cdot e^C = e^C|\sin x|$ $\Rightarrow$ $a + y = K\sin x$, where $K = \pm e^C$. (In our derivation,

K was nonzero, but we can restore the excluded case $y = -a$ by allowing K to be zero.) $y(\pi/3) = a$ $\Rightarrow$

$a + a = K\sin\left(\dfrac{\pi}{3}\right)$ $\Rightarrow$ $2a = K\dfrac{\sqrt{3}}{2}$ $\Rightarrow$ $K = \dfrac{4a}{\sqrt{3}}$. Thus, $a + y = \dfrac{4a}{\sqrt{3}}\sin x$ and so $y = \dfrac{4a}{\sqrt{3}}\sin x - a$.

19. $\dfrac{dy}{dx} = 4x^3 y$, $y(0) = 7$. $\dfrac{dy}{y} = 4x^3\,dx$ [if $y \neq 0$] $\Rightarrow$ $\displaystyle\int \dfrac{dy}{y} = \int 4x^3\,dx$ $\Rightarrow$ $\ln|y| = x^4 + C$ $\Rightarrow$

$e^{\ln|y|} = e^{x^4 + C}$ $\Rightarrow$ $|y| = e^{x^4}e^C$ $\Rightarrow$ $y = Ae^{x^4}$; $y(0) = 7$ $\Rightarrow$ $A = 7$ $\Rightarrow$ $y = 7e^{x^4}$.

21. (a) $y' = 2x\sqrt{1-y^2} \Rightarrow \dfrac{dy}{dx} = 2x\sqrt{1-y^2} \Rightarrow \dfrac{dy}{\sqrt{1-y^2}} = 2x\,dx \Rightarrow \displaystyle\int \dfrac{dy}{\sqrt{1-y^2}} = \int 2x\,dx \Rightarrow$

$\sin^{-1} y = x^2 + C$ for $-\frac{\pi}{2} \le x^2 + C \le \frac{\pi}{2}$.

(b) $y(0) = 0 \Rightarrow \sin^{-1} 0 = 0^2 + C \Rightarrow C = 0$, so $\sin^{-1} y = x^2$

and $y = \sin(x^2)$ for $-\sqrt{\pi/2} \le x \le \sqrt{\pi/2}$.

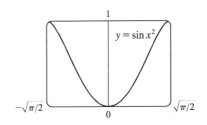

(c) For $\sqrt{1-y^2}$ to be a real number, we must have $-1 \le y \le 1$; that is, $-1 \le y(0) \le 1$. Thus, the initial-value

problem $y' = 2x\sqrt{1-y^2}$, $y(0) = 2$ does *not* have a solution.

23. $\dfrac{dy}{dx} = \dfrac{\sin x}{\sin y}$, $y(0) = \frac{\pi}{2}$. So $\int \sin y\,dy = \int \sin x\,dx \Leftrightarrow$

$-\cos y = -\cos x + C \Leftrightarrow \cos y = \cos x - C$. From the initial

condition, we need $\cos \frac{\pi}{2} = \cos 0 - C \Rightarrow 0 = 1 - C \Rightarrow C = 1$,

so the solution is $\cos y = \cos x - 1$. Note that we cannot take $\cos^{-1}$ of

both sides, since that would unnecessarily restrict the solution to the case

where $-1 \le \cos x - 1 \Leftrightarrow 0 \le \cos x$, as $\cos^{-1}$ is defined only on

$[-1, 1]$. Instead we plot the graph using Maple's

`plots[implicitplot]` or Mathematica's

`Plot[Evaluate[···]]`.

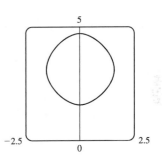

25. (a)

x	y	$y' = 1/y$	x	y	$y' = 1/y$
0	0.5	2	0	-2	-0.5
0	-0.5	-2	0	4	0.25
0	1	1	0	3	$0.\overline{3}$
0	-1	-1	0	0.25	4
0	2	0.5	0	$0.\overline{3}$	3

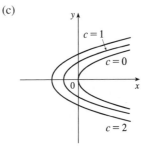

(b) $y' = 1/y \Rightarrow dy/dx = 1/y \Rightarrow$ (c)

$y\,dy = dx \Rightarrow \int y\,dy = \int dx \Rightarrow$

$\frac{1}{2}y^2 = x + c \Rightarrow y^2 = 2(x+c)$

or $y = \pm\sqrt{2(x+c)}$.

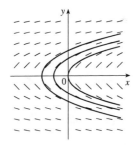

162

27. The curves $y = kx^2$ form a family of parabolas with axis the y-axis.
Differentiating gives $y' = 2kx$, but $k = y/x^2$, so $y' = 2y/x$. Thus, the
slope of the tangent line at any point (x, y) on one of the parabolas is
$y' = 2y/x$, so the orthogonal trajectories must satisfy $y' = -x/(2y)$
$\Leftrightarrow$ $2y\,dy = -x\,dx$ $\Leftrightarrow$ $y^2 = -x^2/2 + C_1$ $\Leftrightarrow$ $x^2 + 2y^2 = C$.
This is a family of ellipses.

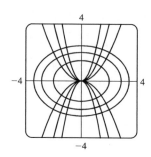

29. Differentiating $y = (x + k)^{-1}$ gives $y' = -\dfrac{1}{(x + k)^2}$, but $k = \dfrac{1}{y} - x$, so

$y' = -\dfrac{1}{(1/y)^2} = -y^2$. Thus, the orthogonal trajectories must satisfy

$y' = -\dfrac{1}{-y^2} = \dfrac{1}{y^2}$ $\Leftrightarrow$ $y^2\,dy = dx$ $\Leftrightarrow$ $\dfrac{y^3}{3} = x + C$ or

$y = [3(x + C)]^{1/3}$

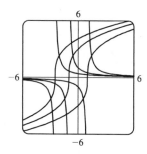

31. From Exercise 10.2.27, $\dfrac{dQ}{dt} = 12 - 4Q$ $\Leftrightarrow$ $\displaystyle\int \dfrac{dQ}{12 - 4Q} = \int dt$ $\Leftrightarrow$ $-\frac{1}{4}\ln|12 - 4Q| = t + C$ $\Leftrightarrow$

$\ln|12 - 4Q| = -4t - 4C$ $\Leftrightarrow$ $|12 - 4Q| = e^{-4t - 4C}$ $\Leftrightarrow$ $12 - 4Q = Ke^{-4t}$ $[K = \pm e^{-4C}]$ $\Leftrightarrow$

$4Q = 12 - Ke^{-4t}$ $\Leftrightarrow$ $Q = 3 - Ae^{-4t}$ $[A = K/4]$. $Q(0) = 0$ $\Leftrightarrow$ $0 = 3 - A$ $\Leftrightarrow$ $A = 3$ $\Leftrightarrow$

$Q(t) = 3 - 3e^{-4t}$. As $t \to \infty$, $Q(t) \to 3 - 0 = 3$ (the limiting value).

33. $\dfrac{dP}{dt} = k(M - P)$ $\Leftrightarrow$ $\displaystyle\int \dfrac{dP}{P - M} = \int (-k)\,dt$ $\Leftrightarrow$ $\ln|P - M| = -kt + C$ $\Leftrightarrow$ $|P - M| = e^{-kt + C}$

$\Leftrightarrow$ $P - M = Ae^{-kt}$ $[A = \pm e^C]$ $\Leftrightarrow$ $P = M + Ae^{-kt}$. If we assume that performance is at level 0 when

$t = 0$, then $P(0) = 0$ $\Leftrightarrow$ $0 = M + A$ $\Leftrightarrow$ $A = -M$ $\Leftrightarrow$ $P(t) = M - Me^{-kt}$.

$\displaystyle\lim_{t \to \infty} P(t) = M - M \cdot 0 = M$.

35. (a) If $a = b$, then $\dfrac{dx}{dt} = k(a - x)(b - x)^{1/2}$ becomes $\dfrac{dx}{dt} = k(a - x)^{3/2}$ $\Rightarrow$ $(a - x)^{-3/2}dx = k\,dt$ $\Rightarrow$

$\int(a - x)^{-3/2}dx = \int k\,dt$ $\Rightarrow$ $2(a - x)^{-1/2} = kt + C$ [by substitution] $\Rightarrow$ $\dfrac{2}{kt + C} = \sqrt{a - x}$ $\Rightarrow$

$\left(\dfrac{2}{kt + C}\right)^2 = a - x$ $\Rightarrow$ $x(t) = a - \dfrac{4}{(kt + C)^2}$. The initial concentration of HBr is 0, so $x(0) = 0$ $\Rightarrow$

$0 = a - \dfrac{4}{C^2}$ $\Rightarrow$ $\dfrac{4}{C^2} = a$ $\Rightarrow$ $C^2 = \dfrac{4}{a}$ $\Rightarrow$ $C = 2/\sqrt{a}$ (C is positive since

$kt + C = 2(a - x)^{-1/2} > 0$). Thus, $x(t) = a - \dfrac{4}{(kt + 2/\sqrt{a})^2}$.

(b) $\dfrac{dx}{dt} = k(a - x)(b - x)^{1/2}$ $\Rightarrow$ $\dfrac{dx}{(a - x)\sqrt{b - x}} = k\,dt$ $\Rightarrow$ $\displaystyle\int \dfrac{dx}{(a - x)\sqrt{b - x}} = \int k\,dt$ $(\star)$. From the

hint, $u = \sqrt{b - x}$ $\Rightarrow$ $u^2 = b - x$ $\Rightarrow$ $2u\,du = -dx$, so $\displaystyle\int \dfrac{dx}{(a - x)\sqrt{b - x}} = \int \dfrac{-2u\,du}{[a - (b - u^2)]u} =$

$-2\displaystyle\int \dfrac{du}{a - b + u^2} = -2\int \dfrac{du}{(\sqrt{a - b})^2 + u^2} \overset{17}{=} -2\left(\dfrac{1}{\sqrt{a - b}}\tan^{-1}\dfrac{u}{\sqrt{a - b}}\right)$. So $(\star)$ becomes

$$\frac{-2}{\sqrt{a-b}} \tan^{-1} \frac{\sqrt{b-x}}{\sqrt{a-b}} = kt + C. \text{ Now } x(0) = 0 \quad \Rightarrow \quad C = \frac{-2}{\sqrt{a-b}} \tan^{-1} \frac{\sqrt{b}}{\sqrt{a-b}}$$

and we have $\dfrac{-2}{\sqrt{a-b}} \tan^{-1} \dfrac{\sqrt{b-x}}{\sqrt{a-b}} = kt - \dfrac{2}{\sqrt{a-b}} \tan^{-1} \dfrac{\sqrt{b}}{\sqrt{a-b}} \quad \Rightarrow$

$$\frac{2}{\sqrt{a-b}} \left(\tan^{-1} \sqrt{\frac{b}{a-b}} - \tan^{-1} \sqrt{\frac{b-x}{a-b}} \right) = kt \quad \Rightarrow$$

$$t(x) = \frac{2}{k\sqrt{a-b}} \left(\tan^{-1} \sqrt{\frac{b}{a-b}} - \tan^{-1} \sqrt{\frac{b-x}{a-b}} \right).$$

37. (a) $\dfrac{dC}{dt} = r - kC \quad \Rightarrow \quad \dfrac{dC}{dt} = -(kC - r) \quad \Rightarrow \quad \displaystyle\int \dfrac{dC}{kC - r} = \int -dt \quad \Rightarrow \quad (1/k) \ln|kC - r| = -t + M_1$

$\Rightarrow \quad \ln|kC - r| = -kt + M_2 \quad \Rightarrow \quad |kC - r| = e^{-kt + M_2} \quad \Rightarrow \quad kC - r = M_3 e^{-kt} \quad \Rightarrow$

$kC = M_3 e^{-kt} + r \quad \Rightarrow \quad C(t) = M_4 e^{-kt} + r/k. \quad C(0) = C_0 \quad \Rightarrow \quad C_0 = M_4 + r/k \quad \Rightarrow$

$M_4 = C_0 - r/k \quad \Rightarrow \quad C(t) = (C_0 - r/k)e^{-kt} + r/k.$

(b) If $C_0 < r/k$, then $C_0 - r/k < 0$ and the formula for $C(t)$ shows that $C(t)$ increases and $\lim\limits_{t \to \infty} C(t) = r/k$.

As t increases, the formula for $C(t)$ shows how the role of C_0 steadily diminishes as that of r/k increases.

39. (a) Let $y(t)$ be the amount of salt (in kg) after t minutes. Then $y(0) = 15$. The amount of liquid in the tank is 1000 L at all times, so the concentration at time t (in minutes) is $y(t)/1000$ kg/L and

$$\frac{dy}{dt} = -\left[\frac{y(t)}{1000} \frac{\text{kg}}{\text{L}} \right] \left(10 \frac{\text{L}}{\text{min}} \right) = -\frac{y(t)}{100} \frac{\text{kg}}{\text{min}}. \int \frac{dy}{y} = -\frac{1}{100} \int dt \quad \Rightarrow \quad \ln y = -\frac{t}{100} + C, \text{ and}$$

$y(0) = 15 \quad \Rightarrow \quad \ln 15 = C$, so $\ln y = \ln 15 - \dfrac{t}{100}$. It follows that $\ln\left(\dfrac{y}{15}\right) = -\dfrac{t}{100}$ and $\dfrac{y}{15} = e^{-t/100}$, so

$y = 15e^{-t/100}$ kg.

(b) After 20 minutes, $y = 15e^{-20/100} = 15e^{-0.2} \approx 12.3$ kg.

41. Assume that the raindrop begins at rest, so that $v(0) = 0$. $dm/dt = km$ and $(mv)' = gm \quad \Rightarrow$

$mv' + vm' = gm \quad \Rightarrow \quad mv' + v(km) = gm \quad \Rightarrow \quad v' + vk = g \quad \Rightarrow \quad dv/dt = g - kv \quad \Rightarrow$

$\displaystyle\int \frac{dv}{g - kv} = \int dt \quad \Rightarrow \quad -(1/k)\ln|g - kv| = t + C \quad \Rightarrow \quad \ln|g - kv| = -kt - kC \quad \Rightarrow \quad g - kv = Ae^{-kt}.$

$v(0) = 0 \quad \Rightarrow \quad A = g.$ So $kv = g - ge^{-kt} \quad \Rightarrow \quad v = (g/k)\left(1 - e^{-kt}\right).$ Since $k > 0$, as $t \to \infty$, $e^{-kt} \to 0$

and therefore, $\lim\limits_{t \to \infty} v(t) = g/k.$

43. (a) The rate of growth of the area is jointly proportional to $\sqrt{A(t)}$ and $M - A(t)$; that is, the rate is proportional to the product of those two quantities. So for some constant k, $dA/dt = k\sqrt{A}\,(M - A)$. We are interested in the maximum of the function dA/dt (when the tissue grows the fastest), so we differentiate, using the Chain Rule and then substituting for dA/dt from the differential equation:

$$\frac{d}{dt}\left(\frac{dA}{dt}\right) = k\left[\sqrt{A}(-1)\frac{dA}{dt} + (M - A) \cdot \tfrac{1}{2}A^{-1/2}\frac{dA}{dt}\right] = \tfrac{1}{2}kA^{-1/2}\frac{dA}{dt}[-2A + (M - A)]$$

$$= \tfrac{1}{2}kA^{-1/2}\left[k\sqrt{A}(M - A)\right][M - 3A] = \tfrac{1}{2}k^2(M - A)(M - 3A)$$

This is 0 when $M - A = 0$ [this situation never actually occurs, since the graph of $A(t)$ is asymptotic to the line $y = M$, as in the logistic model] and when $M - 3A = 0 \quad \Leftrightarrow \quad A(t) = M/3$. This represents a maximum by the First Derivative Test, since $\dfrac{d}{dt}\left(\dfrac{dA}{dt}\right)$ goes from positive to negative when $A(t) = M/3$.

(b) From the CAS, we get $A(t) = M\left(\dfrac{Ce^{\sqrt{M}kt} - 1}{Ce^{\sqrt{M}kt} + 1}\right)^2$. To get C in terms of the initial area A_0 and the maximum

area M, we substitute $t = 0$ and $A = A_0 = A(0)$: $A_0 = M\left(\dfrac{C-1}{C+1}\right)^2 \quad \Leftrightarrow \quad (C+1)\sqrt{A_0} = (C-1)\sqrt{M}$

$\Leftrightarrow \quad C\sqrt{A_0} + \sqrt{A_0} = C\sqrt{M} - \sqrt{M} \quad \Leftrightarrow \quad \sqrt{M} + \sqrt{A_0} = C\sqrt{M} - C\sqrt{A_0} \quad \Leftrightarrow$

$\sqrt{M} + \sqrt{A_0} = C\left(\sqrt{M} - \sqrt{A_0}\right) \quad \Leftrightarrow \quad C = \dfrac{\sqrt{M} + \sqrt{A_0}}{\sqrt{M} - \sqrt{A_0}}$. (Notice that if $A_0 = 0$, then $C = 1$.)

10.4 Exponential Growth and Decay

1. The relative growth rate is $\dfrac{1}{P}\dfrac{dP}{dt} = 0.7944$, so $\dfrac{dP}{dt} = 0.7944P$ and, by Theorem 2,

$P(t) = P(0)e^{0.7944t} = 2e^{0.7944t}$. Thus, $P(6) = 2e^{0.7944(6)} \approx 234.99$ or about 235 members.

3. (a) By Theorem 2, $y(t) = y(0)e^{kt} = 500e^{kt}$. Now $y(3) = 500e^{k(3)} = 8000 \quad \Rightarrow \quad e^{3k} = \frac{8000}{500} \quad \Rightarrow$

$3k = \ln 16 \quad \Rightarrow \quad k = (\ln 16)/3$. So $y(t) = 500e^{(\ln 16)t/3} = 500 \cdot 16^{t/3}$

(b) $y(4) = 500 \cdot 16^{4/3} \approx 20{,}159$

(c) $dy/dt = ky \quad \Rightarrow \quad y'(4) = ky(4) = \frac{1}{3}\ln 16\left(500 \cdot 16^{4/3}\right)$ [from part (a)] $\approx 18{,}631$ cells/h

(d) $y(t) = 500 \cdot 16^{t/3} = 30{,}000 \quad \Rightarrow \quad 16^{t/3} = 60 \quad \Rightarrow \quad \frac{1}{3}t\ln 16 = \ln 60 \quad \Rightarrow \quad t = 3(\ln 60)/(\ln 16) \approx 4.4$ h

5. (a) Let the population (in millions) in the year t be $P(t)$. Since the initial time is the year 1750, we substitute

$t - 1750$ for t in Theorem 2, so the exponential model gives $P(t) = P(1750)e^{k(t-1750)}$. Then

$P(1800) = 980 = 790e^{k(1800-1750)} \quad \Rightarrow \quad \frac{980}{790} = e^{k(50)} \quad \Rightarrow \quad \ln\frac{980}{790} = 50k \quad \Rightarrow$

$k = \frac{1}{50}\ln\frac{980}{790} \approx 0.0043104$. So with this model, we have $P(1900) = 790e^{k(1900-1750)} \approx 1508$ million, and

$P(1950) = 790e^{k(1950-1750)} \approx 1871$ million. Both of these estimates are much too low.

(b) In this case, the exponential model gives $P(t) = P(1850)e^{k(t-1850)} \quad \Rightarrow$

$P(1900) = 1650 = 1260e^{k(1900-1850)} \quad \Rightarrow \quad \ln\frac{1650}{1260} = k(50) \quad \Rightarrow \quad k = \frac{1}{50}\ln\frac{1650}{1260} \approx 0.005393$. So with

this model, we estimate $P(1950) = 1260e^{k(1950-1850)} \approx 2161$ million. This is still too low, but closer than the

estimate of $P(1950)$ in part (a).

(c) The exponential model gives $P(t) = P(1900)e^{k(t-1900)} \quad \Rightarrow \quad P(1950) = 2560 = 1650e^{k(1950-1900)} \quad \Rightarrow$

$\ln\frac{2560}{1650} = k(50) \quad \Rightarrow \quad k = \frac{1}{50}\ln\frac{2560}{1650} \approx 0.008785$. With this model, we estimate

$P(2000) = 1650e^{k(2000-1900)} \approx 3972$ million. This is much too low. The discrepancy is explained by the fact

that the world birth rate (average yearly number of births per person) is about the same as always, whereas the

mortality rate (especially the infant mortality rate) is much lower, owing mostly to advances in medical science

and to the wars in the first part of the twentieth century. The exponential model assumes, among other things,

that the birth and mortality rates will remain constant.

7. (a) If $y = [N_2O_5]$ then by Theorem 2, $\dfrac{dy}{dt} = -0.0005y \quad \Rightarrow \quad y(t) = y(0)e^{-0.0005t} = Ce^{-0.0005t}$.

(b) $y(t) = Ce^{-0.0005t} = 0.9C \quad \Rightarrow \quad e^{-0.0005t} = 0.9 \quad \Rightarrow \quad -0.0005t = \ln 0.9 \quad \Rightarrow$

$t = -2000\ln 0.9 \approx 211$ s

9. (a) If $y(t)$ is the mass (in mg) remaining after t years, then $y(t) = y(0)e^{kt} = 100e^{kt}$. $y(30) = 100e^{30k} = \frac{1}{2}(100)$

$\Rightarrow \quad e^{30k} = \frac{1}{2} \quad \Rightarrow \quad k = -(\ln 2)/30 \quad \Rightarrow \quad y(t) = 100e^{-(\ln 2)t/30} = 100 \cdot 2^{-t/30}$

(b) $y(100) = 100 \cdot 2^{-100/30} \approx 9.92$ mg

(c) $100e^{-(\ln 2)t/30} = 1 \quad \Rightarrow \quad -(\ln 2)t/30 = \ln \frac{1}{100} \quad \Rightarrow \quad t = -30 \frac{\ln 0.01}{\ln 2} \approx 199.3$ years

11. Let $y(t)$ be the level of radioactivity. Thus, $y(t) = y(0)e^{-kt}$ and k is determined by using the half-life:

$y(5730) = \frac{1}{2}y(0) \quad \Rightarrow \quad y(0)e^{-k(5730)} = \frac{1}{2}y(0) \quad \Rightarrow \quad e^{-5730k} = \frac{1}{2} \quad \Rightarrow$

$-5730k = \ln \frac{1}{2} \quad \Rightarrow \quad k = -\frac{\ln \frac{1}{2}}{5730} = \frac{\ln 2}{5730}$. If 74% of the ^{14}C remains, then we know that $y(t) = 0.74y(0)$

$\Rightarrow \quad 0.74 = e^{-t(\ln 2)/5730} \quad \Rightarrow \quad \ln 0.74 = -\frac{t \ln 2}{5730} \quad \Rightarrow \quad t = -\frac{5730(\ln 0.74)}{\ln 2} \approx 2489 \approx 2500$ years.

13. (a) Using Newton's Law of Cooling, $\frac{dT}{dt} = k(T - T_s)$, we have $\frac{dT}{dt} = k(T - 75)$.

Now let $y = T - 75$, so $y(0) = T(0) - 75 = 185 - 75 = 110$, so y is a solution of the initial-value

problem $dy/dt = ky$ with $y(0) = 110$ and by Theorem 2 we have $y(t) = y(0)e^{kt} = 110e^{kt}$.

$y(30) = 110e^{30k} = 150 - 75 \quad \Rightarrow \quad e^{30k} = \frac{75}{110} = \frac{15}{22} \quad \Rightarrow \quad k = \frac{1}{30} \ln \frac{15}{22}$,

so $y(t) = 110e^{\frac{1}{30}t \ln\left(\frac{15}{22}\right)}$ and $y(45) = 110e^{\frac{45}{30} \ln\left(\frac{15}{22}\right)} \approx 62°$F. Thus, $T(45) \approx 62 + 75 = 137°$F.

(b) $T(t) = 100 \quad \Rightarrow \quad y(t) = 25$. $y(t) = 110e^{\frac{1}{30}t \ln\left(\frac{15}{22}\right)} = 25 \quad \Rightarrow \quad e^{\frac{1}{30}t \ln\left(\frac{15}{22}\right)} = \frac{25}{110} \quad \Rightarrow$

$\frac{1}{30}t \ln \frac{15}{22} = \ln \frac{25}{110} \quad \Rightarrow \quad t = \frac{30 \ln \frac{25}{110}}{\ln \frac{15}{22}} \approx 116$ min.

15. $\frac{dT}{dt} = k(T - 20)$. Letting $y = T - 20$, we get $\frac{dy}{dt} = ky$, so $y(t) = y(0)e^{kt}$.

$y(0) = T(0) - 20 = 5 - 20 = -15$, so $y(25) = y(0)e^{25k} = -15e^{25k}$, and

$y(25) = T(25) - 20 = 10 - 20 = -10$, so $-15e^{25k} = -10 \quad \Rightarrow \quad e^{25k} = \frac{2}{3}$. Thus, $25k = \ln\left(\frac{2}{3}\right)$ and

$k = \frac{1}{25} \ln\left(\frac{2}{3}\right)$, so $y(t) = y(0)e^{kt} = -15e^{(1/25) \ln(2/3)t}$. More simply, $e^{25k} = \frac{2}{3} \quad \Rightarrow \quad e^k = \left(\frac{2}{3}\right)^{1/25} \quad \Rightarrow$

$e^{kt} = \left(\frac{2}{3}\right)^{t/25} \quad \Rightarrow \quad y(t) = -15 \cdot \left(\frac{2}{3}\right)^{t/25}$.

(a) $T(50) = 20 + y(50) = 20 - 15 \cdot \left(\frac{2}{3}\right)^{50/25} = 20 - 15 \cdot \left(\frac{2}{3}\right)^2 = 20 - \frac{20}{3} = 13.\overline{3}°$C

(b) $15 = T(t) = 20 + y(t) = 20 - 15 \cdot \left(\frac{2}{3}\right)^{t/25} \quad \Rightarrow \quad 15 \cdot \left(\frac{2}{3}\right)^{t/25} = 5 \quad \Rightarrow \quad \left(\frac{2}{3}\right)^{t/25} = \frac{1}{3} \quad \Rightarrow$

$(t/25) \ln\left(\frac{2}{3}\right) = \ln\left(\frac{1}{3}\right) \quad \Rightarrow \quad t = 25 \ln\left(\frac{1}{3}\right) / \ln\left(\frac{2}{3}\right) \approx 67.74$ min.

17. (a) Let $P(h)$ be the pressure at altitude h. Then $dP/dh = kP \quad \Rightarrow \quad P(h) = P(0)e^{kh} = 101.3e^{kh}$.

$P(1000) = 101.3e^{1000k} = 87.14 \quad \Rightarrow \quad 1000k = \ln\left(\frac{87.14}{101.3}\right) \quad \Rightarrow$

$k = \frac{1}{1000} \ln\left(\frac{87.14}{101.3}\right) \quad \Rightarrow \quad P(h) = 101.3 \, e^{\frac{1}{1000}h \ln\left(\frac{87.14}{101.3}\right)}$, so $P(3000) = 101.3e^{3 \ln\left(\frac{87.14}{101.3}\right)} \approx 64.5$ kPa.

(b) $P(6187) = 101.3 \, e^{\frac{6187}{1000} \ln\left(\frac{87.14}{101.3}\right)} \approx 39.9$ kPa

19. (a) Using $A = A_0\left(1 + \dfrac{r}{n}\right)^{nt}$ with $A_0 = 3000$, $r = 0.05$, and $t = 5$, we have:

    (i) Annually: $n = 1$; $A = 3000\left(1 + \frac{0.05}{1}\right)^{1 \cdot 5} = \$3828.84$

    (ii) Semiannually: $n = 2$; $A = 3000\left(1 + \frac{0.05}{2}\right)^{2 \cdot 5} = \$3840.25$

    (iii) Monthly: $n = 12$; $A = 3000\left(1 + \frac{0.05}{12}\right)^{12 \cdot 5} = \$3850.08$

    (iv) Weekly: $n = 52$; $A = 3000\left(1 + \frac{0.05}{52}\right)^{52 \cdot 5} = \$3851.61$

    (v) Daily: $n = 365$; $A = 3000\left(1 + \frac{0.05}{365}\right)^{365 \cdot 5} = \$3852.01$

    (vi) Continuously: $A = 3000e^{(0.05)5} = \$3852.08$

(b) $dA/dt = 0.05A$ and $A(0) = 3000$.

21. (a) $\dfrac{dP}{dt} = kP - m = k\left(P - \dfrac{m}{k}\right)$. Let $y = P - \dfrac{m}{k}$, so $\dfrac{dy}{dt} = \dfrac{dP}{dt}$ and the differential equation becomes

    $\dfrac{dy}{dt} = ky$. The solution is $y = y_0 e^{kt} \;\Rightarrow\; P - \dfrac{m}{k} = \left(P_0 - \dfrac{m}{k}\right)e^{kt} \;\Rightarrow\; P(t) = \dfrac{m}{k} + \left(P_0 - \dfrac{m}{k}\right)e^{kt}$.

(b) Since $k > 0$, there will be an exponential expansion $\Leftrightarrow\; P_0 - \dfrac{m}{k} > 0 \;\Leftrightarrow\; m < kP_0$.

(c) The population will be constant if $P_0 - \dfrac{m}{k} = 0 \;\Leftrightarrow\; m = kP_0$. It will decline if $P_0 - \dfrac{m}{k} < 0 \;\Leftrightarrow$

    $m > kP_0$.

(d) $P_0 = 8{,}000{,}000$, $k = \alpha - \beta = 0.016$, $m = 210{,}000 \;\Rightarrow\; m > kP_0 \;(= 128{,}000)$, so by part (c), the

    population was declining.

10.5 The Logistic Equation

1. (a) $dP/dt = 0.05P - 0.0005P^2 = 0.05P(1 - 0.01P) = 0.05P(1 - P/100)$. Comparing to Equation 1,

    $dP/dt = kP(1 - P/K)$, we see that the carrying capacity is $K = 100$ and the value of k is 0.05.

(b) The slopes close to 0 occur where P is near 0 or 100. The largest slopes appear to be on the line $P = 50$. The

    solutions are increasing for $0 < P_0 < 100$ and decreasing for $P_0 > 100$.

(c)

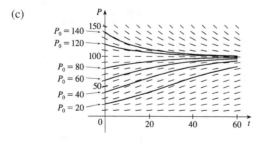

All of the solutions approach $P = 100$ as t increases. As in part (b), the solutions differ since for $0 < P_0 < 100$ they are increasing, and for $P_0 > 100$ they are decreasing. Also, some have an IP and some don't. It appears that the solutions which have $P_0 = 20$ and $P_0 = 40$ have inflection points at $P = 50$.

(d) The equilibrium solutions are $P = 0$ (trivial solution) and $P = 100$. The increasing solutions move away from

    $P = 0$ and all nonzero solutions approach $P = 100$ as $t \to \infty$.

3. (a) $\dfrac{dy}{dt} = ky\left(1 - \dfrac{y}{K}\right)$ $\Rightarrow$ $y(t) = \dfrac{K}{1 + Ae^{-kt}}$ with $A = \dfrac{K - y(0)}{y(0)}$. With $K = 8 \times 10^7$, $k = 0.71$, and

$y(0) = 2 \times 10^7$, we get the model $y(t) = \dfrac{8 \times 10^7}{1 + 3e^{-0.71t}}$, so $y(1) = \dfrac{8 \times 10^7}{1 + 3e^{-0.71}} \approx 3.23 \times 10^7$ kg.

(b) $y(t) = 4 \times 10^7$ $\Rightarrow$ $\dfrac{8 \times 10^7}{1 + 3e^{-0.71t}} = 4 \times 10^7$ $\Rightarrow$ $2 = 1 + 3e^{-0.71t}$ $\Rightarrow$ $e^{-0.71t} = \frac{1}{3}$ $\Rightarrow$

$-0.71t = \ln\frac{1}{3}$ $\Rightarrow$ $t = \dfrac{\ln 3}{0.71} \approx 1.55$ years

5. (a) We will assume that the difference in the birth and death rates is 20 million/year. Let $t = 0$ correspond to the

year 1990 and use a unit of 1 billion for all calculations. $k \approx \dfrac{1}{P}\dfrac{dP}{dt} = \dfrac{1}{5.3}(0.02) = \dfrac{1}{265}$, so

$$\frac{dP}{dt} = kP\left(1 - \frac{P}{K}\right) = \frac{1}{265}P\left(1 - \frac{P}{100}\right), P \text{ in billions}$$

(b) $A = \dfrac{K - P_0}{P_0} = \dfrac{100 - 5.3}{5.3} = \dfrac{947}{53} \approx 17.8679$. $P(t) = \dfrac{K}{1 + Ae^{-kt}} = \dfrac{100}{1 + \frac{947}{53}e^{-(1/265)t}}$, so

$P(10) \approx 5.49$ billion.

(c) $P(110) \approx 7.81$, and $P(510) \approx 27.72$. The predictions are 7.81 billion in the year 2100 and 27.72 billion

in 2500.

(d) If $K = 50$, then $P(t) = \dfrac{50}{1 + \frac{447}{53}e^{-(1/265)t}}$. So $P(10) \approx 5.48$, $P(110) \approx 7.61$, and $P(510) \approx 22.41$. The

predictions become 5.48 billion in the year 2000, 7.61 billion in 2100, and 22.41 billion in the year 2500.

7. (a) Our assumption is that $\dfrac{dy}{dt} = ky(1 - y)$, where y is the fraction of the population that has heard the rumor.

(b) Using the logistic equation (1), $\dfrac{dP}{dt} = kP\left(1 - \dfrac{P}{K}\right)$, we substitute $y = \dfrac{P}{K}$, $P = Ky$, and $\dfrac{dP}{dt} = K\dfrac{dy}{dt}$, to

obtain $K\dfrac{dy}{dt} = k(Ky)(1 - y)$ $\Leftrightarrow$ $\dfrac{dy}{dt} = ky(1 - y)$, our equation in part (a). Now the solution to (1) is

$P(t) = \dfrac{K}{1 + Ae^{-kt}}$, where $A = \dfrac{K - P_0}{P_0}$. We use the same substitution to obtain $Ky = \dfrac{K}{1 + \frac{K - Ky_0}{Ky_0}e^{-kt}}$

$\Rightarrow$ $y = \dfrac{y_0}{y_0 + (1 - y_0)e^{-kt}}$.

Alternatively, we could use the same steps as outlined in "The Analytic Solution," following Example 2.

(c) Let t be the number of hours since 8 A.M. Then $y_0 = y(0) = \frac{80}{1000} = 0.08$ and $y(4) = \frac{1}{2}$, so

$\dfrac{1}{2} = y(4) = \dfrac{0.08}{0.08 + 0.92e^{-4k}}$. Thus, $0.08 + 0.92e^{-4k} = 0.16$, $e^{-4k} = \dfrac{0.08}{0.92} = \dfrac{2}{23}$, and $e^{-k} = \left(\dfrac{2}{23}\right)^{1/4}$, so

$y = \dfrac{0.08}{0.08 + 0.92(2/23)^{t/4}} = \dfrac{2}{2 + 23(2/23)^{t/4}}$. Solving this equation for t, we get

$2y + 23y\left(\dfrac{2}{23}\right)^{t/4} = 2$ $\Rightarrow$ $\left(\dfrac{2}{23}\right)^{t/4} = \dfrac{2 - 2y}{23y}$ $\Rightarrow$ $\left(\dfrac{2}{23}\right)^{t/4} = \dfrac{2}{23}\cdot\dfrac{1 - y}{y}$ $\Rightarrow$

$\left(\dfrac{2}{23}\right)^{t/4 - 1} = \dfrac{1 - y}{y}$. It follows that $\dfrac{t}{4} - 1 = \dfrac{\ln[(1 - y)/y]}{\ln\frac{2}{23}}$, so $t = 4\left[1 + \dfrac{\ln((1 - y)/y)}{\ln\frac{2}{23}}\right]$.

When $y = 0.9$, $\dfrac{1 - y}{y} = \frac{1}{9}$, so $t = 4\left(1 - \dfrac{\ln 9}{\ln\frac{2}{23}}\right) \approx 7.6$ h or 7 h 36 min. Thus, 90% of the population will

have heard the rumor by 3:36 P.M.

9. (a) $\dfrac{dP}{dt} = kP\left(1 - \dfrac{P}{K}\right)$ $\Rightarrow$

$$\frac{d^2P}{dt^2} = k\left[P\left(-\frac{1}{K}\frac{dP}{dt}\right) + \left(1 - \frac{P}{K}\right)\frac{dP}{dt}\right] = k\frac{dP}{dt}\left(-\frac{P}{K} + 1 - \frac{P}{K}\right)$$

$$= k\left[kP\left(1 - \frac{P}{K}\right)\right]\left(1 - \frac{2P}{K}\right) = k^2P\left(1 - \frac{P}{K}\right)\left(1 - \frac{2P}{K}\right)$$

(b) P grows fastest when P' has a maximum, that is, when $P'' = 0$. From part (a), $P'' = 0$ $\Leftrightarrow$ $P = 0, P = K$, or $P = K/2$. Since $0 < P < K$, we see that $P'' = 0$ $\Leftrightarrow$ $P = K/2$.

11. (a) The term -15 represents a harvesting of fish at a constant rate—in this case, 15 fish/week. This is the rate at which fish are caught.

(b)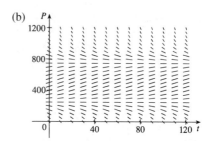

(c) From the graph in part (b), it appears that $P(t) = 250$ and $P(t) = 750$ are the equilibrium solutions. We confirm this analytically by solving the equation $dP/dt = 0$ as follows: $0.08P(1 - P/1000) - 15 = 0$ $\Rightarrow$ $0.08P - 0.00008P^2 - 15 = 0$ $\Rightarrow$ $-0.00008(P^2 - 1000P + 187{,}500) = 0$ $\Rightarrow$ $(P - 250)(P - 750) = 0$ $\Rightarrow$ $P = 250$ or 750.

(d)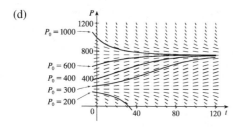

For $0 < P_0 < 250$, $P(t)$ decreases to 0. For $P_0 = 250$, $P(t)$ remains constant. For $250 < P_0 < 750$, $P(t)$ increases and approaches 750. For $P_0 = 750$, $P(t)$ remains constant. For $P_0 > 750$, $P(t)$ decreases and approaches 750.

(e) $\dfrac{dP}{dt} = 0.08P\left(1 - \dfrac{P}{1000}\right) - 15$ $\Leftrightarrow$ $-\dfrac{100{,}000}{8} \cdot \dfrac{dP}{dt} = \left(0.08P - 0.00008P^2 - 15\right) \cdot \left(-\dfrac{100{,}000}{8}\right)$ $\Leftrightarrow$

$-12{,}500\,\dfrac{dP}{dt} = P^2 - 1000P + 187{,}500$ $\Leftrightarrow$ $\dfrac{dP}{(P - 250)(P - 750)} = -\dfrac{1}{12{,}500}\,dt$ $\Leftrightarrow$

$\displaystyle\int\left(\dfrac{-1/500}{P - 250} + \dfrac{1/500}{P - 750}\right)dP = -\dfrac{1}{12{,}500}\,dt$ $\Leftrightarrow$ $\displaystyle\int\left(\dfrac{1}{P - 250} - \dfrac{1}{P - 750}\right)dP = \tfrac{1}{25}\,dt$ $\Leftrightarrow$

$\ln|P - 250| - \ln|P - 750| = \tfrac{1}{25}t + C$ $\Leftrightarrow$ $\ln\left|\dfrac{P - 250}{P - 750}\right| = \tfrac{1}{25}t + C$ $\Leftrightarrow$

$\left|\dfrac{P - 250}{P - 750}\right| = e^{t/25 + C} = ke^{t/25}$ $\Leftrightarrow$ $\dfrac{P - 250}{P - 750} = ke^{t/25}$ $\Leftrightarrow$ $P - 250 = Pke^{t/25} - 750ke^{t/25}$ $\Leftrightarrow$

$$P - Pke^{t/25} = 250 - 750ke^{t/25} \quad \Leftrightarrow \quad P(t) = \frac{250 - 750ke^{t/25}}{1 - ke^{t/25}}. \text{ If } t = 0 \text{ and } P = 200, \text{ then}$$

$$200 = \frac{250 - 750k}{1 - k} \quad \Leftrightarrow \quad 200 - 200k = 250 - 750k \quad \Leftrightarrow$$

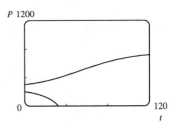

$$550k = 50 \quad \Leftrightarrow \quad k = \frac{1}{11}. \text{ Similarly, if } t = 0 \text{ and } P = 300, \text{ then}$$

$$k = -\frac{1}{9}. \text{ Simplifying } P \text{ with these two values of } k \text{ gives us}$$

$$P(t) = \frac{250\left(3e^{t/25} - 11\right)}{e^{t/25} - 11} \text{ and } P(t) = \frac{750\left(e^{t/25} + 3\right)}{e^{t/25} + 9}.$$

13. (a) $\dfrac{dP}{dt} = (kP)\left(1 - \dfrac{P}{K}\right)\left(1 - \dfrac{m}{P}\right)$. If $m < P < K$, then $dP/dt = (+)(+)(+) = + \quad \Rightarrow \quad P$ is increasing.

If $0 < P < m$, then $dP/dt = (+)(+)(-) = - \quad \Rightarrow \quad P$ is decreasing.

(b)

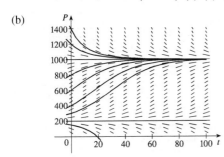

$k = 0.08$, $K = 1000$, and $m = 200 \quad \Rightarrow$

$$\frac{dP}{dt} = 0.08P\left(1 - \frac{P}{1000}\right)\left(1 - \frac{200}{P}\right)$$

For $0 < P_0 < 200$, the population dies out. For $P_0 = 200$, the population is steady. For $200 < P_0 < 1000$, the population increases and approaches 1000. For $P_0 > 1000$, the population decreases and approaches 1000.

The equilibrium solutions are $P(t) = 200$ and $P(t) = 1000$.

(c) $\dfrac{dP}{dt} = kP\left(1 - \dfrac{P}{K}\right)\left(1 - \dfrac{m}{P}\right) = kP\left(\dfrac{K - P}{K}\right)\left(\dfrac{P - m}{P}\right) = \dfrac{k}{K}(K - P)(P - m) \quad \Leftrightarrow$

$$\int \frac{dP}{(K - P)(P - m)} = \int \frac{k}{K} \, dt.$$

By partial fractions, $\dfrac{1}{(K - P)(P - m)} = \dfrac{A}{K - P} + \dfrac{B}{P - m}$, so $A(P - m) + B(K - P) = 1$.

If $P = m$, $B = \dfrac{1}{K - m}$; if $P = K$, $A = \dfrac{1}{K - m}$, so $\dfrac{1}{K - m}\displaystyle\int \left(\dfrac{1}{K - P} + \dfrac{1}{P - m}\right) dP = \int \dfrac{k}{K} \, dt \quad \Rightarrow$

$$\frac{1}{K - m}\left(-\ln|K - P| + \ln|P - m|\right) = \frac{k}{K}t + M \quad \Rightarrow \quad \frac{1}{K - m}\ln\left|\frac{P - m}{K - P}\right| = \frac{k}{K}t + M \quad \Rightarrow$$

$$\ln\left|\frac{P - m}{K - P}\right| = (K - m)\frac{k}{K}t + M_1 \quad \Leftrightarrow \quad \frac{P - m}{K - P} = De^{(K-m)(k/K)t} \quad [D = \pm e^{M_1}].$$

Let $t = 0$: $\dfrac{P_0 - m}{K - P_0} = D$. So $\dfrac{P - m}{K - P} = \dfrac{P_0 - m}{K - P_0}e^{(K-m)(k/K)t}$. Solving for P, we get

$$P(t) = \frac{m(K - P_0) + K(P_0 - m)e^{(K-m)(k/K)t}}{K - P_0 + (P_0 - m)e^{(K-m)(k/K)t}}.$$

(d) If $P_0 < m$, then $P_0 - m < 0$. Let $N(t)$ be the numerator of the expression for $P(t)$ in part (c). Then

$N(0) = P_0(K - m) > 0$, and $P_0 - m < 0 \quad \Leftrightarrow \quad \displaystyle\lim_{t \to \infty} K(P_0 - m)e^{(K-m)(k/K)t} = -\infty \quad \Rightarrow$

$\displaystyle\lim_{t \to \infty} N(t) = -\infty$. Since N is continuous, there is a number t such that $N(t) = 0$ and thus $P(t) = 0$. So the species will become extinct.

15. (a) $dP/dt = kP\cos(rt - \phi) \Rightarrow (dP)/P = k\cos(rt - \phi)\,dt \Rightarrow \int(dP)/P = k\int\cos(rt - \phi)\,dt \Rightarrow$
$\ln P = (k/r)\sin(rt - \phi) + C$. (Since this is a growth model, $P > 0$ and we can write $\ln P$ instead of $\ln|P|$.)
Since $P(0) = P_0$, we obtain $\ln P_0 = (k/r)\sin(-\phi) + C = -(k/r)\sin\phi + C \Rightarrow$
$C = \ln P_0 + (k/r)\sin\phi$. Thus, $\ln P = (k/r)\sin(rt - \phi) + \ln P_0 + (k/r)\sin\phi$, which we can rewrite as
$\ln(P/P_0) = (k/r)[\sin(rt - \phi) + \sin\phi]$ or, after exponentiation, $P(t) = P_0 e^{(k/r)[\sin(rt-\phi)+\sin\phi]}$.

(b) As k increases, the amplitude increases, but the minimum value stays the same.

As r increases, the amplitude and the period decrease.

A change in ϕ produces slight adjustments in the phase shift and amplitude.

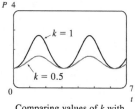

Comparing values of k with $P_0 = 1, r = 2$, and $\phi = \pi/2$

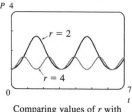

Comparing values of r with $P_0 = 1, k = 1$, and $\phi = \pi/2$

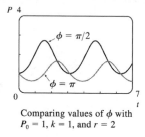

Comparing values of ϕ with $P_0 = 1, k = 1$, and $r = 2$

$P(t)$ oscillates between $P_0 e^{(k/r)(1+\sin\phi)}$ and $P_0 e^{(k/r)(-1+\sin\phi)}$ (the extreme values are attained when $rt - \phi$ is an odd multiple of $\frac{\pi}{2}$), so $\lim\limits_{t\to\infty} P(t)$ does not exist.

17. By Equation (4), $P(t) = \dfrac{K}{1 + Ae^{-kt}}$. By comparison, if $c = (\ln A)/k$ and $u = \frac{1}{2}k(t - c)$, then

$$1 + \tanh u = 1 + \frac{e^u - e^{-u}}{e^u + e^{-u}} = \frac{e^u + e^{-u}}{e^u + e^{-u}} + \frac{e^u - e^{-u}}{e^u + e^{-u}} = \frac{2e^u}{e^u + e^{-u}} \cdot \frac{e^{-u}}{e^{-u}} = \frac{2}{1 + e^{-2u}}$$

and $e^{-2u} = e^{-k(t-c)} = e^{kc}e^{-kt} = e^{\ln A}e^{-kt} = Ae^{-kt}$, so

$$\tfrac{1}{2}K\left[1 + \tanh\left(\tfrac{1}{2}k(t - c)\right)\right] = \frac{K}{2}[1 + \tanh u] = \frac{K}{2} \cdot \frac{2}{1 + e^{-2u}} = \frac{K}{1 + e^{-2u}} = \frac{K}{1 + Ae^{-kt}} = P(t).$$

10 Review

1. (a) A differential equation is an equation that contains an unknown function and one or more of its derivatives.

(b) The order of a differential equation is the order of the highest derivative that occurs in the equation.

(c) An initial condition is a condition of the form $y(t_0) = y_0$.

2. $y' = x^2 + y^2 \geq 0$ for all x and y. $y' = 0$ only at the origin, so there is a horizontal tangent at $(0,0)$, but nowhere else. The graph of the solution is increasing on every interval.

3. See the paragraph preceding Example 1 in Section 10.2.

4. See the paragraph after Figure 14 in Section 10.2.

5. A separable equation is a first-order differential equation in which the expression for dy/dx can be factored as a function of x times a function of y, that is, $dy/dx = g(x)f(y)$. We can solve the equation by integrating both sides of the equation $dy/f(y) = g(x)dx$ and solving for y.

6. A first-order linear differential equation is a differential equation that can be put in the form $\dfrac{dy}{dx} + P(x)\,y = Q(x)$, where P and Q are continuous functions on a given interval. To solve such an equation, multiply it by the integrating factor $I(x) = e^{\int P(x)dx}$ to put it in the form $[I(x)\,y]' = I(x)\,Q(x)$ and then integrate both sides to get $I(x)\,y = \int I(x)\,Q(x)\,dx$, that is, $e^{\int P(x)\,dx}y = \int e^{\int P(x)\,dx}Q(x)\,dx$. Solving for y gives us $y = e^{-\int P(x)\,dx}\int e^{\int P(x)\,dx}Q(x)\,dx$.

7. (a) $\dfrac{dy}{dt} = ky$; the relative growth rate, $\dfrac{1}{y}\dfrac{dy}{dt}$, is constant.

(b) The equation in part (a) is an appropriate model for population growth, assuming that there is enough room and nutrition to support the growth.

(c) If $y(0) = y_0$, then the solution is $y(t) = y_0 e^{kt}$.

8. (a) $dP/dt = kP(1 - P/K)$, where K is the carrying capacity.

(b) The equation in part (a) is an appropriate model for population growth, assuming that the population grows at a rate proportional to the size of the population in the beginning, but eventually levels off and approaches its carrying capacity because of limited resources.

9. (a) $dF/dt = kF - aFS$ and $dS/dt = -rS + bFS$.

(b) In the absence of sharks, an ample food supply would support exponential growth of the fish population, that is, $dF/dt = kF$, where k is a positive constant. In the absence of fish, we assume that the shark population would decline at a rate proportional to itself, that is, $dS/dt = -rS$, where r is a positive constant.

1. True.   Since $y^4 \geq 0$, $y' = -1 - y^4 < 0$ and the solutions are decreasing functions.

3. False. $x + y$ cannot be written in the form $g(x)f(y)$.

5. True. $e^x y' = y \;\Rightarrow\; y' = e^{-x}y \;\Rightarrow\; y' + (-e^{-x})y = 0$, which is of the form $y' + P(x)\,y = Q(x)$, so the equation is linear.

7. True.   By comparing $\dfrac{dy}{dt} = 2y\left(1 - \dfrac{y}{5}\right)$ with the logistic differential equation (10.5.1), we see that the carrying capacity is 5; that is, $\lim\limits_{t\to\infty} y = 5$.

--- EXERCISES ---

1. (a)

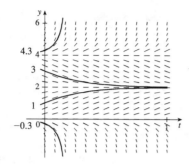

(b) $\lim_{t \to \infty} y(t)$ appears to be finite for $0 \le c \le 4$. In fact $\lim_{t \to \infty} y(t) = 4$ for $c = 4$, $\lim_{t \to \infty} y(t) = 2$ for $0 < c < 4$, and $\lim_{t \to \infty} y(t) = 0$ for $c = 0$. The equilibrium solutions are $y(t) = 0$, $y(t) = 2$, and $y(t) = 4$.

3. (a)

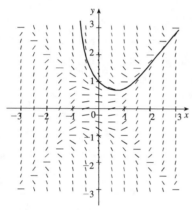

We estimate that when $x = 0.3$, $y = 0.8$, so $y(0.3) \approx 0.8$.

(b) $h = 0.1$, $x_0 = 0$, $y_0 = 1$ and $F(x, y) = x^2 - y^2$. So $y_n = y_{n-1} + 0.1(x_{n-1}^2 - y_{n-1}^2)$. Thus,

$y_1 = 1 + 0.1(0^2 - 1^2) = 0.9$,

$y_2 = 0.9 + 0.1(0.1^2 - 0.9^2) = 0.82$,

$y_3 = 0.82 + 0.1(0.2^2 - 0.82^2) = 0.75676$. This is close to our graphical estimate of $y(0.3) \approx 0.8$.

(c) The centers of the horizontal line segments of the direction field are located on the lines $y = x$ and $y = -x$. When a solution curve crosses one of these lines, it has a local maximum or minimum.

5. $y' = xe^{-\sin x} - y \cos x \quad \Rightarrow \quad y' + (\cos x) y = xe^{-\sin x}$ (∗). This is a linear equation and the integrating factor is $I(x) = e^{\int \cos x \, dx} = e^{\sin x}$. Multiplying (∗) by $e^{\sin x}$ gives $e^{\sin x} y' + e^{\sin x} (\cos x) y = x \quad \Rightarrow \quad (e^{\sin x} y)' = x$
$\Rightarrow \quad e^{\sin x} y = \frac{1}{2}x^2 + C \quad \Rightarrow \quad y = \left(\frac{1}{2}x^2 + C\right) e^{-\sin x}$.

7. $(3y^2 + 2y) y' = x \cos x \quad \Rightarrow \quad (3y^2 + 2y) \, dy = (x \cos x) \, dx \quad \Rightarrow \quad \int (3y^2 + 2y) \, dy = \int (x \cos x) \, dx \quad \Rightarrow$
$y^3 + y^2 = \cos x + x \sin x + C$. For the last step, use integration by parts or Formula 83 in the Table of Integrals.

9. $xyy' = \ln x \quad \Rightarrow \quad y \, dy = \frac{\ln x}{x} \, dx \quad \Rightarrow \quad \int y \, dy = \int \frac{\ln x}{x} \, dx$ (Make the substitution $u = \ln x$; then $du = dx/x$.) So $\int y \, dy = \int u \, du \quad \Rightarrow \quad \frac{1}{2}y^2 = \frac{1}{2}u^2 + C \quad \Rightarrow \frac{1}{2}y^2 = \frac{1}{2}(\ln x)^2 + C$. $y(1) = 2 \quad \Rightarrow$
$\frac{1}{2}2^2 = \frac{1}{2}(\ln 1)^2 + C = C \quad \Leftrightarrow \quad C = 2$. Therefore, $\frac{1}{2}y^2 = \frac{1}{2}(\ln x)^2 + 2$, or $y = \sqrt{(\ln x)^2 + 4}$. The negative square root is inadmissible, since $y(1) > 0$.

11. Since the equation is linear, let $I(x) = e^{\int dx} = e^x$. Then multiplying by $I(x)$ gives $e^x y' + e^x y = \sqrt{x} \quad \Rightarrow$
$(e^x y)' = \sqrt{x} \quad \Rightarrow \quad y(x) = e^{-x}\left(\int \sqrt{x} \, dx + c\right) = e^{-x}\left(\frac{2}{3}x^{3/2} + c\right)$. But $3 = y(0) = c$, so the solution to the initial-value problem is $y(x) = e^{-x}\left(\frac{2}{3}x^{3/2} + 3\right)$.

13. The curves $kx^2 + y^2 = 1$ form a family of ellipses for $k > 0$, a family of hyperbolas for $k < 0$, and two parallel lines $y = \pm 1$ for $k = 0$. Solving $kx^2 + y^2 = 1$ for k gives $k = \dfrac{1 - y^2}{x^2}$. Differentiating gives $2kx + 2yy' = 0$ $\Leftrightarrow$ $y' = -\dfrac{kx}{y} = -\left(1 - y^2\right)\dfrac{x}{yx^2} = \dfrac{y^2 - 1}{xy}$. Thus, for $k \neq 0$ the orthogonal trajectories must satisfy $y' = -\dfrac{xy}{y^2 - 1}$ $\Rightarrow$ $\dfrac{y^2 - 1}{y} \, dy = -x \, dx$ $\Rightarrow$ $\dfrac{y^2}{2} - \ln|y| = \dfrac{-x^2}{2} + K$ $\Rightarrow$ $y^2 - 2\ln|y| + x^2 = C$. For $k = 0$, the orthogonal trajectories are given by $x = C_1$ for C_1 an arbitrary constant.

15. (a) $y(t) = y(0)e^{kt} = 1000e^{kt}$ $\Rightarrow$ $y(2) = 1000e^{2k} = 9000$ $\Rightarrow$ $e^{2k} = 9$ $\Rightarrow$ $2k = \ln 9$ $\Rightarrow$ $k = \frac{1}{2}\ln 9 = \ln 3$ $\Rightarrow$ $y(t) = 1000e^{(\ln 3)t} = 1000 \cdot 3^t$

(b) $y(3) = 1000 \cdot 3^3 = 27{,}000$

(c) $y'(t) = 1000 \cdot 3^t \cdot \ln 3$, so $y'(3) = 27{,}000 \ln 3 \approx 29{,}663$ bacteria per hour

(d) $1000 \cdot 3^t = 2 \cdot 1000$ $\Rightarrow$ $3^t = 2$ $\Rightarrow$ $t \ln 3 = \ln 2$ $\Rightarrow$ $t = (\ln 2)/\ln 3 \approx 0.63$ h

17. (a) $C'(t) = -kC(t)$ $\Rightarrow$ $C(t) = C(0)e^{-kt}$ by Theorem 10.4.2. But $C(0) = C_0$, so $C(t) = C_0 e^{-kt}$.

(b) $C(30) = \frac{1}{2}C_0$ since the concentration is reduced by half. Thus, $\frac{1}{2}C_0 = C_0 e^{-30k}$ $\Rightarrow$ $\ln \frac{1}{2} = -30k$ $\Rightarrow$ $k = -\frac{1}{30}\ln\frac{1}{2} = \frac{1}{30}\ln 2$. Since 10% of the original concentration remains if 90% is eliminated, we want the value of t such that $C(t) = \frac{1}{10}C_0$. Therefore, $\frac{1}{10}C_0 = C_0 e^{-t(\ln 2)/30}$ $\Rightarrow$ $\ln 0.1 = -t(\ln 2)/30$ $\Rightarrow$ $t = -\frac{30}{\ln 2}\ln 0.1 \approx 100$ h.

19. (a) $\dfrac{dL}{dt} \propto L_\infty - L$ $\Rightarrow$ $\dfrac{dL}{dt} = k(L_\infty - L)$ $\Rightarrow$ $\displaystyle\int \dfrac{dL}{L_\infty - L} = \int k \, dt$ $\Rightarrow$ $-\ln|L_\infty - L| = kt + C$ $\Rightarrow$ $\ln|L_\infty - L| = -kt - C$ $\Rightarrow$ $|L_\infty - L| = e^{-kt-C}$ $\Rightarrow$ $L_\infty - L = Ae^{-kt}$ $\Rightarrow$ $L = L_\infty - Ae^{-kt}$. At $t = 0$, $L = L(0) = L_\infty - A$ $\Rightarrow$ $A = L_\infty - L(0)$ $\Rightarrow$ $L(t) = L_\infty - [L_\infty - L(0)]\,e^{-kt}$.

(b) $L_\infty = 53$ cm, $L(0) = 10$ cm, and $k = 0.2$ $\Rightarrow$ $L(t) = 53 - (53 - 10)e^{-0.2t} = 53 - 43e^{-0.2t}$.

21. Let P be the population and I be the number of infected people. The rate of spread dI/dt is jointly proportional to I and to $P - I$, so for some constant k, $dI/dt = kI(P - I)$ $\Rightarrow$ $I = \dfrac{I_0 P}{I_0 + (P - I_0)e^{-kPt}}$ (from the discussion of logistic growth in Section 10.5).

Now, measuring t in days, we substitute $t = 7$, $P = 5000$, $I_0 = 160$ and $I(7) = 1200$ to find k:

$1200 = \dfrac{160 \cdot 5000}{160 + (5000 - 160)e^{-5000 \cdot 7 \cdot k}}$ $\Leftrightarrow$ $k \approx 0.00006448$. So, putting $I = 5000 \times 80\% = 4000$, we solve

for t: $4000 = \dfrac{160 \cdot 5000}{160 + (5000 - 160)e^{-0.00006448 \cdot 5000 \cdot t}}$ $\Leftrightarrow$ $160 + 4840e^{-0.3224t} = 200$ $\Leftrightarrow$

$-0.3224t = \ln\frac{40}{4840}$ $\Leftrightarrow$ $t \approx 14.9$. So it takes about 15 days for 80% of the population to be infected.

23. $\dfrac{dh}{dt} = -\dfrac{R}{V}\left(\dfrac{h}{k + h}\right)$ $\Rightarrow$ $\displaystyle\int \dfrac{k + h}{h} \, dh = \int\left(-\dfrac{R}{V}\right) dt$ $\Rightarrow$ $\displaystyle\int\left(1 + \dfrac{k}{h}\right) dh = -\dfrac{R}{V}\int 1 \, dt$ $\Rightarrow$

$h + k\ln h = -\dfrac{R}{V}t + C$. This equation gives a relationship between h and t, but it is not possible to isolate h and express it in terms of t.

25. (a) $dx/dt = 0.4x(1 - 0.000005x) - 0.002xy$, $dy/dt = -0.2y + 0.000008xy$. If $y = 0$, then

$dx/dt = 0.4x(1 - 0.000005x)$, so $dx/dt = 0$ $\Leftrightarrow$ $x = 0$ or $x = 200{,}000$, which shows that the insect population increases logistically with a carrying capacity of 200,000. Since $dx/dt > 0$ for $0 < x < 200{,}000$ and $dx/dt < 0$ for $x > 200{,}000$, we expect the insect population to stabilize at 200,000.

(b) x and y are constant $\Rightarrow$ $x' = 0$ and $y' = 0$ $\Rightarrow$

$$\begin{cases} 0 = 0.4x(1 - 0.000005x) - 0.002xy \\ 0 = -0.2y + 0.000008xy \end{cases} \Rightarrow \begin{cases} 0 = 0.4x[(1 - 0.000005x) - 0.005y] \\ 0 = y(-0.2 + 0.000008x) \end{cases}$$

The second equation is true if $y = 0$ or $x = \frac{0.2}{0.000008} = 25{,}000$. If $y = 0$ in the first equation, then either $x = 0$ or $x = \frac{1}{0.000005} = 200{,}000$. If $x = 25{,}000$, then $0 = 0.4(25{,}000)[(1 - 0.000005 \cdot 25{,}000) - 0.005y]$ $\Rightarrow$

$0 = 10{,}000[(1 - 0.125) - 0.005y]$ $\Rightarrow$ $0 = 8750 - 50y$ $\Rightarrow$ $y = 175$.

Case (i): $y = 0$, $x = 0$: Zero populations

Case (ii): $y = 0$, $x = 200{,}000$: In the absence of birds, the insect population is always 200,000.

Case (iii): $x = 25{,}000$, $y = 175$: The predator/prey interaction balances and the populations are stable.

(c) The populations of the birds and insects fluctuate around 175 and 25,000, respectively, and eventually stabilize at those values.

(d)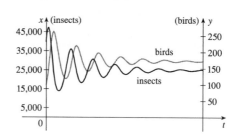

27. (a) $\dfrac{d^2y}{dx^2} = k\sqrt{1 + \left(\dfrac{dy}{dx}\right)^2}$. Setting $z = \dfrac{dy}{dx}$, we get $\dfrac{dz}{dx} = k\sqrt{1 + z^2}$ $\Rightarrow$ $\dfrac{dz}{\sqrt{1 + z^2}} = k\,dx$. Using

Formula 25 gives $\ln\left(z + \sqrt{1 + z^2}\right) = kx + c$ $\Rightarrow$ $z + \sqrt{1 + z^2} = Ce^{kx}$ (where $C = e^c$) $\Rightarrow$

$\sqrt{1 + z^2} = Ce^{kx} - z$ $\Rightarrow$ $1 + z^2 = C^2 e^{2kx} - 2Ce^{kx}z + z^2$ $\Rightarrow$ $2Ce^{kx}z = C^2 e^{2kx} - 1$ $\Rightarrow$

$z = \dfrac{C}{2}e^{kx} - \dfrac{1}{2C}e^{-kx}$. Now $\dfrac{dy}{dx} = \dfrac{C}{2}e^{kx} - \dfrac{1}{2C}e^{-kx}$ $\Rightarrow$ $y = \dfrac{C}{2k}e^{kx} + \dfrac{1}{2Ck}e^{-kx} + C'$. From the

diagram in the text, we see that $y(0) = a$ and $y(\pm b) = h$. $a = y(0) = \dfrac{C}{2k} + \dfrac{1}{2Ck} + C'$ $\Rightarrow$

$C' = a - \dfrac{C}{2k} - \dfrac{1}{2Ck}$ $\Rightarrow$ $y = \dfrac{C}{2k}\left(e^{kx} - 1\right) + \dfrac{1}{2Ck}\left(e^{-kx} - 1\right) + a$. From $h = y(\pm b)$, we find

$h = \dfrac{C}{2k}\left(e^{kb} - 1\right) + \dfrac{1}{2Ck}\left(e^{-kb} - 1\right) + a$ and $h = \dfrac{C}{2k}\left(e^{-kb} - 1\right) + \dfrac{1}{2Ck}\left(e^{kb} - 1\right) + a$. Subtracting the

second equation from the first, we get $0 = \dfrac{C}{k}\dfrac{e^{kb} - e^{-kb}}{2} - \dfrac{1}{Ck}\dfrac{e^{kb} - e^{-kb}}{2} = \dfrac{1}{k}\left(C - \dfrac{1}{C}\right)\sinh kb$.

Now $k > 0$ and $b > 0$, so $\sinh kb > 0$ and $C = \pm 1$. If $C = 1$, then

$y = \dfrac{1}{2k}\left(e^{kx} - 1\right) + \dfrac{1}{2k}\left(e^{-kx} - 1\right) + a = \dfrac{1}{k}\dfrac{e^{kx} + e^{-kx}}{2} - \dfrac{1}{k} + a = a + \dfrac{1}{k}(\cosh kx - 1)$. If $C = -1$, then $y = -\dfrac{1}{2k}\left(e^{kx} - 1\right) - \dfrac{1}{2k}\left(e^{-kx} - 1\right) + a = \dfrac{-1}{k}\dfrac{e^{kx} + e^{-kx}}{2} + \dfrac{1}{k} + a = a - \dfrac{1}{k}(\cosh kx - 1)$.

Since $k > 0$, $\cosh kx \geq 1$, and $y \geq a$, we conclude that $C = 1$ and $y = a + \dfrac{1}{k}(\cosh kx - 1)$, where

$h = y(b) = a + \dfrac{1}{k}(\cosh kb - 1)$. Since $\cosh(kb) = \cosh(-kb)$, there is no further information to extract from

the condition that $y(b) = y(-b)$. However, we could replace a with the expression $h - \dfrac{1}{k}(\cosh kb - 1)$,

obtaining $y = h + \dfrac{1}{k}(\cosh kx - \cosh kb)$. It would be better still to keep a in the expression for y, and use the expression for h to solve for k in terms of a, b, and h. That would enable us to express y in terms of x and the given parameters a, b, and h. Sadly, it is not possible to solve for k in closed form. That would have to be done by numerical methods when specific parameter values are given.

(b) The length of the cable is

$$L = \int_{-b}^{b} \sqrt{1 + (dy/dx)^2}\, dx = \int_{-b}^{b} \sqrt{1 + \sinh^2 kx}\, dx = \int_{-b}^{b} \cosh kx\, dx = 2\int_{0}^{b} \cosh kx\, dx$$

$$= 2\left[(1/k)\sinh kx\right]_{0}^{b} = (2/k)\sinh kb$$

☐ PROBLEMS PLUS

1. We use the Fundamental Theorem of Calculus to differentiate the given equation:

$$[f(x)]^2 = 100 + \int_0^x \left\{ [f(t)]^2 + [f'(t)]^2 \right\} dt \quad \Rightarrow \quad 2f(x)f'(x) = [f(x)]^2 + [f'(x)]^2 \quad \Rightarrow$$

$$[f(x)]^2 + [f'(x)]^2 - 2f(x)f'(x) = 0 \quad \Rightarrow \quad [f(x) - f'(x)]^2 = 0 \quad \Leftrightarrow \quad f(x) = f'(x). \text{ We can solve this as a}$$

separable equation, or else use Theorem 10.4.2 with $k = 1$, which says that the solutions are $f(x) = Ce^x$. Now $[f(0)]^2 = 100$, so $f(0) = C = \pm 10$, and hence $f(x) = \pm 10e^x$ are the only functions satisfying the given equation.

3. $f'(x) = \lim\limits_{h \to 0} \dfrac{f(x+h) - f(x)}{h} = \lim\limits_{h \to 0} \dfrac{f(x)\,[f(h) - 1]}{h}$ [since $f(x+h) = f(x)f(h)$]

$$= f(x) \lim_{h \to 0} \frac{f(h) - 1}{h} = f(x) \lim_{h \to 0} \frac{f(h) - f(0)}{h - 0} = f(x)f'(0) = f(x)$$

Therefore, $f'(x) = f(x)$ for all x and from Theorem 10.4.2 we get $f(x) = Ae^x$. Now $f(0) = 1 \quad \Rightarrow \quad A = 1 \quad \Rightarrow$ $f(x) = e^x$.

5. Let $y(t)$ denote the temperature of the peach pie t minutes after 5:00 P.M. and R the temperature of the room.

Newton's Law of Cooling gives us $dy/dt = k(y - R)$. Solving for y we get $\dfrac{dy}{y - R} = k\,dt \quad \Rightarrow$

$\ln|y - R| = kt + C \quad \Rightarrow \quad |y - R| = e^{kt+C} \quad \Rightarrow \quad y - R = \pm e^{kt} \cdot e^C \quad \Rightarrow \quad y = Me^{kt} + R$, where M is a nonzero constant. We are given temperatures at three times.

$$\begin{aligned}
y(0) &= 100 &\Rightarrow& \quad 100 = M + R &\Rightarrow& \quad R = 100 - M \\
y(10) &= 80 &\Rightarrow& \quad 80 = Me^{10k} + R &\textbf{(1)}& \\
y(20) &= 65 &\Rightarrow& \quad 65 = Me^{20k} + R &\textbf{(2)}&
\end{aligned}$$

Substituting $100 - M$ for R in **(1)** and **(2)** gives us

$$-20 = Me^{10k} - M \quad \textbf{(3)} \quad \text{and} \quad -35 = Me^{20k} - M \quad \textbf{(4)}$$

Dividing **(3)** by **(4)** gives us $\dfrac{-20}{-35} = \dfrac{M(e^{10k} - 1)}{M(e^{20k} - 1)} \quad \Rightarrow \quad \dfrac{4}{7} = \dfrac{e^{10k} - 1}{e^{20k} - 1} \quad \Rightarrow \quad 4e^{20k} - 4 = 7e^{10k} - 7 \quad \Rightarrow$

$4e^{20k} - 7e^{10k} + 3 = 0$. This is a quadratic equation in e^{10k}. $\left(4e^{10k} - 3\right)\left(e^{10k} - 1\right) = 0 \quad \Rightarrow \quad e^{10k} = \frac{3}{4}$ or 1

$\Rightarrow \quad 10k = \ln\frac{3}{4}$ or $\ln 1 \quad \Rightarrow \quad k = \frac{1}{10}\ln\frac{3}{4}$ since k is a nonzero constant of proportionality. Substituting $\frac{3}{4}$ for e^{10k} in **(3)** gives us $-20 = M \cdot \frac{3}{4} - M \quad \Rightarrow \quad -20 = -\frac{1}{4}M \quad \Rightarrow \quad M = 80$. Now $R = 100 - M$ so $R = 20\,°\text{C}$.

7. (a) While running from $(L, 0)$ to (x, y), the dog travels a distance

$$s = \int_x^L \sqrt{1 + (dy/dx)^2}\, dx = -\int_L^x \sqrt{1 + (dy/dx)^2}\, dx, \text{ so } \frac{ds}{dx} = -\sqrt{1 + (dy/dx)^2}.$$ The dog and rabbit

run at the same speed, so the rabbit's position when the dog has traveled a distance s is $(0, s)$. Since the dog runs

straight for the rabbit, $\dfrac{dy}{dx} = \dfrac{s - y}{0 - x}$ (see the figure).

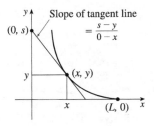

y↑ Slope of tangent line

$(0, s)$ $= \dfrac{s - y}{0 - x}$

y (x, y)

x $(L, 0)$ x

Thus, $s = y - x\dfrac{dy}{dx}$ $\Rightarrow$ $\dfrac{ds}{dx} = \dfrac{dy}{dx} - \left(x\dfrac{d^2y}{dx^2} + 1\dfrac{dy}{dx}\right) = -x\dfrac{d^2y}{dx^2}$. Equating the two expressions for $\dfrac{ds}{dx}$

gives us $x\dfrac{d^2y}{dx^2} = \sqrt{1 + \left(\dfrac{dy}{dx}\right)^2}$, as claimed.

(b) Letting $z = \dfrac{dy}{dx}$, we obtain the differential equation $x\dfrac{dz}{dx} = \sqrt{1 + z^2}$, or $\dfrac{dz}{\sqrt{1 + z^2}} = \dfrac{dx}{x}$. Integrating:

$\ln x = \displaystyle\int \dfrac{dz}{\sqrt{1 + z^2}} \overset{25}{=} \ln\left(z + \sqrt{1 + z^2}\right) + C$. When $x = L$, $z = dy/dx = 0$, so $\ln L = \ln 1 + C$.

Therefore, $C = \ln L$, so $\ln x = \ln\left(\sqrt{1 + z^2} + z\right) + \ln L = \ln\left[L\left(\sqrt{1 + z^2} + z\right)\right]$ $\Rightarrow$

$x = L\left(\sqrt{1 + z^2} + z\right)$ $\Rightarrow$ $\sqrt{1 + z^2} = \dfrac{x}{L} - z$ $\Rightarrow$ $1 + z^2 = \left(\dfrac{x}{L}\right)^2 - \dfrac{2xz}{L} + z^2$ $\Rightarrow$

$\left(\dfrac{x}{L}\right)^2 - 2z\left(\dfrac{x}{L}\right) - 1 = 0$ $\Rightarrow$ $z = \dfrac{(x/L)^2 - 1}{2(x/L)} = \dfrac{x^2 - L^2}{2Lx} = \dfrac{x}{2L} - \dfrac{L}{2}\dfrac{1}{x}$ [for $x > 0$]. Since $z = \dfrac{dy}{dx}$,

$y = \dfrac{x^2}{4L} - \dfrac{L}{2}\ln x + C_1$. Since $y = 0$ when $x = L$, $0 = \dfrac{L}{4} - \dfrac{L}{2}\ln L + C_1$ $\Rightarrow$ $C_1 = \dfrac{L}{2}\ln L - \dfrac{L}{4}$. Thus,

$y = \dfrac{x^2}{4L} - \dfrac{L}{2}\ln x + \dfrac{L}{2}\ln L - \dfrac{L}{4} = \dfrac{x^2 - L^2}{4L} - \dfrac{L}{2}\ln\left(\dfrac{x}{L}\right)$.

(c) As $x \to 0^+$, $y \to \infty$, so the dog never catches the rabbit.

9. (a) We are given that $V = \frac{1}{3}\pi r^2 h$, $dV/dt = 60{,}000\pi$ ft^3/h, and $r = 1.5h = \frac{3}{2}h$. So $V = \frac{1}{3}\pi\left(\frac{3}{2}h\right)^2 h = \frac{3}{4}\pi h^3$

$\Rightarrow \dfrac{dV}{dt} = \frac{3}{4}\pi \cdot 3h^2\,\dfrac{dh}{dt} = \frac{9}{4}\pi h^2\,\dfrac{dh}{dt}$. Therefore, $\dfrac{dh}{dt} = \dfrac{4(dV/dt)}{9\pi h^2} = \dfrac{240{,}000\pi}{9\pi h^2} = \dfrac{80{,}000}{3h^2}$ $(\star)$ $\Rightarrow$

$\int 3h^2\,dh = \int 80{,}000\,dt \quad\Rightarrow\quad h^3 = 80{,}000t + C$. When $t = 0$, $h = 60$. Thus, $C = 60^3 = 216{,}000$, so

$h^3 = 80{,}000t + 216{,}000$. Let $h = 100$. Then $100^3 = 1{,}000{,}000 = 80{,}000t + 216{,}000 \quad\Rightarrow$

$80{,}000t = 784{,}000 \quad\Rightarrow\quad t = 9.8$, so the time required is 9.8 hours.

(b) The floor area of the silo is $F = \pi \cdot 200^2 = 40{,}000\pi$ ft^2, and the area of the base of the pile is

$A = \pi r^2 = \pi\left(\frac{3}{2}h\right)^2 = \frac{9\pi}{4}h^2$. So the area of the floor which is not covered when $h = 60$ is

$F - A = 40{,}000\pi - 8100\pi = 31{,}900\pi \approx 100{,}217$ ft^2. Now $A = \frac{9\pi}{4}h^2 \quad\Rightarrow\quad dA/dt = \frac{9\pi}{4} \cdot 2h\,(dh/dt)$,

and from $(\star)$ in part (a) we know that when $h = 60$, $dh/dt = \dfrac{80{,}000}{3(60)^2} = \dfrac{200}{27}$ ft/h. Therefore,

$dA/dt = \frac{9\pi}{4}(2)(60)\left(\frac{200}{27}\right) = 2000\pi \approx 6283$ ft^2/h.

(c) At $h = 90$ ft, $dV/dt = 60{,}000\pi - 20{,}000\pi = 40{,}000\pi$ ft^3/h. From $(\star)$ in part (a),

$\dfrac{dh}{dt} = \dfrac{4(dV/dt)}{9\pi h^2} = \dfrac{4(40{,}000\pi)}{9\pi h^2} = \dfrac{160{,}000}{9h^2} \quad\Rightarrow\quad \int 9h^2\,dh = \int 160{,}000\,dt \quad\Rightarrow\quad 3h^3 = 160{,}000t + C$.

When $t = 0$, $h = 90$; therefore, $C = 3 \cdot 729{,}000 = 2{,}187{,}000$. So $3h^3 = 160{,}000t + 2{,}187{,}000$. At the top,

$h = 100 \quad\Rightarrow\quad 3(100)^3 = 160{,}000t + 2{,}187{,}000 \quad\Rightarrow\quad t = \frac{813{,}000}{160{,}000} \approx 5.1$. The pile reaches the top after

about 5.1 h.

11. Let $P(a, b)$ be any point on the curve. If m is the slope of the tangent line at P, then $m = y'(a)$, and

an equation of the normal line at P is $y - b = -\dfrac{1}{m}(x - a)$, or equivalently, $y = -\dfrac{1}{m}x + b + \dfrac{a}{m}$.

The y-intercept is always 6, so $b + \dfrac{a}{m} = 6 \quad\Rightarrow\quad \dfrac{a}{m} = 6 - b \quad\Rightarrow\quad m = \dfrac{a}{6-b}$.

We will solve the equivalent differential equation $\dfrac{dy}{dx} = \dfrac{x}{6-y} \quad\Rightarrow\quad (6-y)\,dy = x\,dx \quad\Rightarrow$

$\displaystyle\int(6-y)\,dy = \int x\,dx \quad\Rightarrow\quad 6y - \frac{1}{2}y^2 = \frac{1}{2}x^2 + C \quad\Rightarrow\quad 12y - y^2 = x^2 + K$. Since $(3, 2)$ is on the curve,

$12(2) - 2^2 = 3^2 + K \quad\Rightarrow\quad K = 11$. So the curve is given by $12y - y^2 = x^2 + 11 \quad\Rightarrow$

$x^2 + y^2 - 12y + 36 = -11 + 36 \quad\Rightarrow\quad x^2 + (y-6)^2 = 25$, a circle with center $(0, 6)$ and radius 5.

12 □ INFINITE SEQUENCES AND SERIES

12.1 Sequences

1. (a) A sequence is an ordered list of numbers. It can also be defined as a function whose domain is the set of positive integers.

   (b) The terms a_n approach 8 as n becomes large. In fact, we can make a_n as close to 8 as we like by taking n sufficiently large.

   (c) The terms a_n become large as n becomes large. In fact, we can make a_n as large as we like by taking n sufficiently large.

3. $a_n = 1 - (0.2)^n$, so the sequence is $\{0.8, 0.96, 0.992, 0.9984, 0.99968, \dots\}$.

5. $a_n = \dfrac{3(-1)^n}{n!}$, so the sequence is $\left\{ \dfrac{-3}{1}, \dfrac{3}{2}, \dfrac{-3}{6}, \dfrac{3}{24}, \dfrac{-3}{120}, \dots \right\} = \left\{ -3, \dfrac{3}{2}, -\dfrac{1}{2}, \dfrac{1}{8}, -\dfrac{1}{40}, \dots \right\}$.

7. $a_1 = 3$, $a_{n+1} = 2a_n - 1$. Each term is defined in terms of the preceding term.
   $a_2 = 2a_1 - 1 = 2(3) - 1 = 5$. $a_3 = 2a_2 - 1 = 2(5) - 1 = 9$. $a_4 = 2a_3 - 1 = 2(9) - 1 = 17$.
   $a_5 = 2a_4 - 1 = 2(17) - 1 = 33$. The sequence is $\{3, 5, 9, 17, 33, \dots\}$.

9. The numerators are all 1 and the denominators are powers of 2, so $a_n = \dfrac{1}{2^n}$.

11. $\{2, 7, 12, 17, \dots\}$. Each term is larger than the preceding one by 5, so
    $a_n = a_1 + d(n - 1) = 2 + 5(n - 1) = 5n - 3$.

13. $\left\{ 1, -\dfrac{2}{3}, \dfrac{4}{9}, -\dfrac{8}{27}, \dots \right\}$. Each term is $-\dfrac{2}{3}$ times the preceding one, so $a_n = \left(-\dfrac{2}{3} \right)^{n-1}$.

15. $a_n = n(n - 1)$. $a_n \to \infty$ as $n \to \infty$, so the sequence diverges.

17. $a_n = \dfrac{3 + 5n^2}{n + n^2} = \dfrac{(3 + 5n^2)/n^2}{(n + n^2)/n^2} = \dfrac{5 + 3/n^2}{1 + 1/n}$, so $a_n \to \dfrac{5 + 0}{1 + 0} = 5$ as $n \to \infty$. Converges

19. $a_n = \dfrac{2^n}{3^{n+1}} = \dfrac{1}{3} \left(\dfrac{2}{3} \right)^n$, so $\lim\limits_{n \to \infty} a_n = \dfrac{1}{3} \lim\limits_{n \to \infty} \left(\dfrac{2}{3} \right)^n = \dfrac{1}{3} \cdot 0 = 0$ by (8) with $r = \dfrac{2}{3}$. Converges

21. $a_n = \dfrac{(-1)^{n-1} n}{n^2 + 1} = \dfrac{(-1)^{n-1}}{n + 1/n}$, so $0 \leq |a_n| = \dfrac{1}{n + 1/n} \leq \dfrac{1}{n} \to 0$ as $n \to \infty$, so $a_n \to 0$ by the Squeeze Theorem and Theorem 6. Converges

23. $a_n = \cos(n/2)$. This sequence diverges since the terms don't approach any particular real number as $n \to \infty$. The terms take on values between -1 and 1.

25. $a_n = \dfrac{(2n - 1)!}{(2n + 1)!} = \dfrac{(2n - 1)!}{(2n + 1)(2n)(2n - 1)!} = \dfrac{1}{(2n + 1)(2n)} \to 0$ as $n \to \infty$. Converges

27. $a_n = \dfrac{e^n + e^{-n}}{e^{2n} - 1} \cdot \dfrac{e^{-n}}{e^{-n}} = \dfrac{1 + e^{-2n}}{e^n - e^{-n}} \to \dfrac{1 + 0}{e^n - 0} \to 0$ as $n \to \infty$. Converges

29. $a_n = n^2 e^{-n} = \dfrac{n^2}{e^n}$. Since $\lim\limits_{x \to \infty} \dfrac{x^2}{e^x} \overset{\text{H}}{=} \lim\limits_{x \to \infty} \dfrac{2x}{e^x} \overset{\text{H}}{=} \lim\limits_{x \to \infty} \dfrac{2}{e^x} = 0$, it follows from Theorem 3 that $\lim\limits_{n \to \infty} a_n = 0$. Converges

31. $0 \leq \dfrac{\cos^2 n}{2^n} \leq \dfrac{1}{2^n}$ [since $0 \leq \cos^2 n \leq 1$], so since $\lim\limits_{n \to \infty} \dfrac{1}{2^n} = 0$, $\left\{ \dfrac{\cos^2 n}{2^n} \right\}$ converges to 0 by the Squeeze Theorem.

33. $a_n = n \sin(1/n) = \dfrac{\sin(1/n)}{1/n}$. Since $\displaystyle\lim_{x \to \infty} \dfrac{\sin(1/x)}{1/x} = \lim_{t \to 0^+} \dfrac{\sin t}{t}$ [where $t = 1/x$] $= 1$, it follows from Theorem 3 that $\{a_n\}$ converges to 1.

35. $a_n = \left(1 + \dfrac{2}{n}\right)^{1/n} \quad \Rightarrow \quad \ln a_n = \dfrac{1}{n} \ln\left(1 + \dfrac{2}{n}\right)$. As $n \to \infty$, $\dfrac{1}{n} \to 0$ and $\ln\left(1 + \dfrac{2}{n}\right) \to 0$, so $\ln a_n \to 0$.

Thus, $a_n \to e^0 = 1$ as $n \to \infty$. Converges

37. $\{0, 1, 0, 0, 1, 0, 0, 0, 1, \dots\}$ diverges since the sequence takes on only two values, 0 and 1, and never stays arbitrarily close to either one (or any other value) for n sufficiently large.

39. $a_n = \dfrac{n!}{2^n} = \dfrac{1}{2} \cdot \dfrac{2}{2} \cdot \dfrac{3}{2} \cdot \dots \cdot \dfrac{(n-1)}{2} \cdot \dfrac{n}{2} \geq \dfrac{1}{2} \cdot \dfrac{n}{2}$ [for $n > 1$] $= \dfrac{n}{4} \to \infty$ as $n \to \infty$, so $\{a_n\}$ diverges.

41.

From the graph, we see that the sequence $\left\{(-1)^n \dfrac{n+1}{n}\right\}$ is divergent, since it oscillates between 1 and -1 (approximately).

43.

From the graph, it appears that the sequence converges to about 0.78.

$$\lim_{n \to \infty} \dfrac{2n}{2n+1} = \lim_{n \to \infty} \dfrac{2}{2 + 1/n} = 1, \text{ so}$$

$$\lim_{n \to \infty} \arctan\left(\dfrac{2n}{2n+1}\right) = \arctan 1 = \dfrac{\pi}{4}.$$

45.

From the graph, it appears that the sequence converges to 0.

$$0 < a_n = \dfrac{n^3}{n!} = \dfrac{n}{n} \cdot \dfrac{n}{(n-1)} \cdot \dfrac{n}{(n-2)} \cdot \dfrac{n}{(n-3)} \cdot \dots \cdot \dfrac{1}{3} \cdot \dfrac{1}{2} \cdot \dfrac{1}{1}$$

$$\leq \dfrac{n^2}{(n-1)(n-2)(n-3)} \quad [\text{for } n \geq 4]$$

$$= \dfrac{1/n}{(1 - 1/n)(1 - 2/n)(1 - 3/n)} \to 0 \text{ as } n \to \infty$$

So by the Squeeze Theorem, $\{n^3/n!\}$ converges to 0.

47.

From the graph, it appears that the sequence approaches 0.

$$0 < a_n = \frac{1 \cdot 3 \cdot 5 \cdots (2n-1)}{(2n)^n} = \frac{1}{2n} \cdot \frac{3}{2n} \cdot \frac{5}{2n} \cdots \frac{2n-1}{2n}$$

$$\leq \frac{1}{2n} \cdot (1) \cdot (1) \cdots (1) = \frac{1}{2n} \to 0 \text{ as } n \to \infty$$

So by the Squeeze Theorem, $\left\{ \dfrac{1 \cdot 3 \cdot 5 \cdots (2n-1)}{(2n)^n} \right\}$ converges to 0.

49. (a) $a_n = 1000(1.06)^n \Rightarrow a_1 = 1060$, $a_2 = 1123.60$, $a_3 = 1191.02$, $a_4 = 1262.48$, and $a_5 = 1338.23$.

(b) $\lim\limits_{n \to \infty} a_n = 1000 \lim\limits_{n \to \infty} (1.06)^n$, so the sequence diverges by (8) with $r = 1.06 > 1$.

51. If $|r| \geq 1$, then $\{r^n\}$ diverges by (8), so $\{nr^n\}$ diverges also, since $|nr^n| = n\,|r^n| \geq |r^n|$. If $|r| < 1$ then

$$\lim_{x \to \infty} xr^x = \lim_{x \to \infty} \frac{x}{r^{-x}} \overset{\text{H}}{=} \lim_{x \to \infty} \frac{1}{(-\ln r)\, r^{-x}} = \lim_{x \to \infty} \frac{r^x}{-\ln r} = 0, \text{ so } \lim_{n \to \infty} nr^n = 0, \text{ and hence } \{nr^n\} \text{ converges}$$

whenever $|r| < 1$.

53. Since $\{a_n\}$ is a decreasing sequence, $a_n > a_{n+1}$ for all $n \geq 1$. Because all of its terms lie between 5 and 8, $\{a_n\}$ is a bounded sequence. By the Monotonic Sequence Theorem, $\{a_n\}$ is convergent; that is, $\{a_n\}$ has a limit L. L must be less than 8 since $\{a_n\}$ is decreasing, so $5 \leq L < 8$.

55. $a_n = \dfrac{1}{2n+3}$ is decreasing since $a_{n+1} = \dfrac{1}{2(n+1)+3} = \dfrac{1}{2n+5} < \dfrac{1}{2n+3} = a_n$ for each $n \geq 1$. The sequence is bounded since $0 < a_n \leq \frac{1}{5}$ for all $n \geq 1$. Note that $a_1 = \frac{1}{5}$.

57. $a_n = \cos(n\pi/2)$ is not monotonic. The first few terms are $0, -1, 0, 1, 0, -1, 0, 1, \ldots$. In fact, the sequence consists of the terms $0, -1, 0, 1$ repeated over and over again in that order. The sequence is bounded since $|a_n| \leq 1$ for all $n \geq 1$.

59. $a_n = \dfrac{n}{n^2+1}$ defines a decreasing sequence since for $f(x) = \dfrac{x}{x^2+1}$,

$$f'(x) = \frac{(x^2+1)(1) - x(2x)}{(x^2+1)^2} = \frac{1-x^2}{(x^2+1)^2} \leq 0 \text{ for } x \geq 1. \text{ The sequence is bounded since } 0 < a_n \leq \frac{1}{2} \text{ for all}$$

$n \geq 1$.

61. $a_1 = 2^{1/2}$, $a_2 = 2^{3/4}$, $a_3 = 2^{7/8}$, $\ldots$, so $a_n = 2^{(2^n-1)/2^n} = 2^{1-(1/2^n)}$. $\lim\limits_{n \to \infty} a_n = \lim\limits_{n \to \infty} 2^{1-(1/2^n)} = 2^1 = 2$.

Alternate solution: Let $L = \lim\limits_{n \to \infty} a_n$. (We could show the limit exists by showing that $\{a_n\}$ is bounded and increasing.) Then L must satisfy $L = \sqrt{2 \cdot L} \Rightarrow L^2 = 2L \Rightarrow L(L-2) = 0$. $L \neq 0$ since the sequence increases, so $L = 2$.

63. We show by induction that $\{a_n\}$ is increasing and bounded above by 3.

Let P_n be the proposition that $a_{n+1} > a_n$ and $0 < a_n < 3$. Clearly P_1 is true. Assume that P_n is true.

Then $a_{n+1} > a_n \Rightarrow \dfrac{1}{a_{n+1}} < \dfrac{1}{a_n} \Rightarrow -\dfrac{1}{a_{n+1}} > -\dfrac{1}{a_n}$.

Now $a_{n+2} = 3 - \dfrac{1}{a_{n+1}} > 3 - \dfrac{1}{a_n} = a_{n+1} \Leftrightarrow P_{n+1}$. This proves that $\{a_n\}$ is increasing and bounded above by 3, so $1 = a_1 < a_n < 3$, that is, $\{a_n\}$ is bounded, and hence convergent by the Monotonic Sequence Theorem. If $L = \lim\limits_{n \to \infty} a_n$, then $\lim\limits_{n \to \infty} a_{n+1} = L$ also, so L must satisfy $L = 3 - 1/L \Rightarrow L^2 - 3L + 1 = 0 \Rightarrow$

$L = \dfrac{3 \pm \sqrt{5}}{2}$. But $L > 1$, so $L = \dfrac{3 + \sqrt{5}}{2}$.

65. (a) Let a_n be the number of rabbit pairs in the nth month. Clearly $a_1 = 1 = a_2$. In the nth month, each pair that is 2 or more months old (that is, a_{n-2} pairs) will produce a new pair to add to the a_{n-1} pairs already present. Thus, $a_n = a_{n-1} + a_{n-2}$, so that $\{a_n\} = \{f_n\}$, the Fibonacci sequence.

(b) $a_n = \dfrac{f_{n+1}}{f_n} \;\Rightarrow\; a_{n-1} = \dfrac{f_n}{f_{n-1}} = \dfrac{f_{n-1} + f_{n-2}}{f_{n-1}} = 1 + \dfrac{f_{n-2}}{f_{n-1}} = 1 + \dfrac{1}{f_{n-1}/f_{n-2}} = 1 + \dfrac{1}{a_{n-2}}$. If

$L = \lim\limits_{n \to \infty} a_n$, then $L = \lim\limits_{n \to \infty} a_{n-1}$ and $L = \lim\limits_{n \to \infty} a_{n-2}$, so L must satisfy $L = 1 + \dfrac{1}{L} \;\Rightarrow$

$L^2 - L - 1 = 0 \;\Rightarrow\; L = \frac{1+\sqrt{5}}{2}$ (since L must be positive).

67. (a)

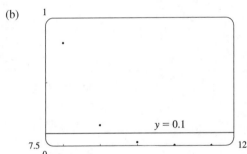

From the graph, it appears that the

sequence $\left\{ \dfrac{n^5}{n!} \right\}$ converges to 0, that is,

$$\lim_{n \to \infty} \frac{n^5}{n!} = 0.$$

(b)

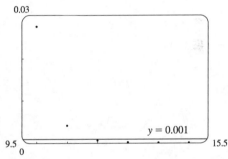

From the first graph, it seems that the smallest possible value of N corresponding to $\varepsilon = 0.1$ is 9, since $n^5/n! < 0.1$ whenever $n \geq 10$, but $9^5/9! > 0.1$. From the second graph, it seems that for $\varepsilon = 0.001$, the smallest possible value for N is 11.

69. If $\lim\limits_{n \to \infty} |a_n| = 0$ then $\lim\limits_{n \to \infty} -|a_n| = 0$, and since $-|a_n| \leq a_n \leq |a_n|$, we have that $\lim\limits_{n \to \infty} a_n = 0$ by the Squeeze Theorem.

71. (a) First we show that $a > a_1 > b_1 > b$.

$a_1 - b_1 = \frac{a+b}{2} - \sqrt{ab} = \frac{1}{2}\left(a - 2\sqrt{ab} + b\right) = \frac{1}{2}\left(\sqrt{a} - \sqrt{b}\right)^2 > 0$ (since $a > b$) $\;\Rightarrow\; a_1 > b_1$. Also

$a - a_1 = a - \frac{1}{2}(a + b) = \frac{1}{2}(a - b) > 0$ and $b - b_1 = b - \sqrt{ab} = \sqrt{b}\left(\sqrt{b} - \sqrt{a}\right) < 0$, so $a > a_1 > b_1 > b$.

In the same way we can show that $a_1 > a_2 > b_2 > b_1$ and so the given assertion is true for $n = 1$. Suppose it is true for $n = k$, that is, $a_k > a_{k+1} > b_{k+1} > b_k$. Then

$$a_{k+2} - b_{k+2} = \frac{1}{2}(a_{k+1} + b_{k+1}) - \sqrt{a_{k+1}b_{k+1}} = \frac{1}{2}\left(a_{k+1} - 2\sqrt{a_{k+1}b_{k+1}} + b_{k+1}\right)$$

$$= \frac{1}{2}\left(\sqrt{a_{k+1}} - \sqrt{b_{k+1}}\right)^2 > 0$$

$$a_{k+1} - a_{k+2} = a_{k+1} - \frac{1}{2}(a_{k+1} + b_{k+1}) = \frac{1}{2}(a_{k+1} - b_{k+1}) > 0$$

and $b_{k+1} - b_{k+2} = b_{k+1} - \sqrt{a_{k+1}b_{k+1}} = \sqrt{b_{k+1}}\left(\sqrt{b_{k+1}} - \sqrt{a_{k+1}}\right) < 0 \quad \Rightarrow$

$a_{k+1} > a_{k+2} > b_{k+2} > b_{k+1}$, so the assertion is true for $n = k + 1$. Thus, it is true for all n by mathematical induction.

(b) From part (a) we have $a > a_n > a_{n+1} > b_{n+1} > b_n > b$, which shows that both sequences, $\{a_n\}$ and $\{b_n\}$, are monotonic and bounded. So they are both convergent by the Monotonic Sequence Theorem.

(c) Let $\lim\limits_{n \to \infty} a_n = \alpha$ and $\lim\limits_{n \to \infty} b_n = \beta$. Then $\lim\limits_{n \to \infty} a_{n+1} = \lim\limits_{n \to \infty} \dfrac{a_n + b_n}{2} \quad \Rightarrow \quad \alpha = \dfrac{\alpha + \beta}{2} \quad \Rightarrow$

$2\alpha = \alpha + \beta \quad \Rightarrow \quad \alpha = \beta.$

73. (a) Suppose $\{p_n\}$ converges to p. Then $p_{n+1} = \dfrac{bp_n}{a + p_n} \quad \Rightarrow \quad \lim\limits_{n \to \infty} p_{n+1} = \dfrac{b \lim\limits_{n \to \infty} p_n}{a + \lim\limits_{n \to \infty} p_n} \quad \Rightarrow$

$p = \dfrac{bp}{a + p} \quad \Rightarrow \quad p^2 + ap = bp \quad \Rightarrow \quad p(p + a - b) = 0 \quad \Rightarrow \quad p = 0$ or $p = b - a.$

(b) $p_{n+1} = \dfrac{bp_n}{a + p_n} = \dfrac{\frac{b}{a}p_n}{1 + \frac{p_n}{a}} < \dfrac{b}{a}p_n$ since $1 + \dfrac{p_n}{a} > 1.$

(c) By part (b), $p_1 < \left(\dfrac{b}{a}\right)p_0$, $p_2 < \left(\dfrac{b}{a}\right)p_1 < \left(\dfrac{b}{a}\right)^2 p_0$, $p_3 < \left(\dfrac{b}{a}\right)p_2 < \left(\dfrac{b}{a}\right)^3 p_0$, etc. In general,

$p_n < \left(\dfrac{b}{a}\right)^n p_0$, so $\lim\limits_{n \to \infty} p_n \le \lim\limits_{n \to \infty} \left(\dfrac{b}{a}\right)^n \cdot p_0 = 0$ since $b < a$. [By result 8, $\lim\limits_{n \to \infty} r^n = 0$ if $-1 < r < 1$.

Here $r = \dfrac{b}{a} \in (0, 1).$]

(d) Let $a < b$. We first show, by induction, that if $p_0 < b - a$, then $p_n < b - a$ and $p_{n+1} > p_n$.

For $n = 0$, we have $p_1 - p_0 = \dfrac{bp_0}{a + p_0} - p_0 = \dfrac{p_0(b - a - p_0)}{a + p_0} > 0$ since $p_0 < b - a$. So $p_1 > p_0.$

Now we suppose the assertion is true for $n = k$, that is, $p_k < b - a$ and $p_{k+1} > p_k$. Then

$b - a - p_{k+1} = b - a - \dfrac{bp_k}{a + p_k} = \dfrac{a(b - a) + bp_k - ap_k - bp_k}{a + p_k} = \dfrac{a(b - a - p_k)}{a + p_k} > 0$ because $p_k < b - a.$

So $p_{k+1} < b - a$. And $p_{k+2} - p_{k+1} = \dfrac{bp_{k+1}}{a + p_{k+1}} - p_{k+1} = \dfrac{p_{k+1}(b - a - p_{k+1})}{a + p_{k+1}} > 0$ since $p_{k+1} < b - a.$

Therefore, $p_{k+2} > p_{k+1}$. Thus, the assertion is true for $n = k + 1$. It is therefore true for all n by mathematical induction. A similar proof by induction shows that if $p_0 > b - a$, then $p_n > b - a$ and $\{p_n\}$ is decreasing.

In either case the sequence $\{p_n\}$ is bounded and monotonic, so it is convergent by the Monotonic Sequence Theorem. It then follows from part (a) that $\lim\limits_{n \to \infty} p_n = b - a.$

12.2 Series

1. (a) A sequence is an ordered list of numbers whereas a series is the *sum* of a list of numbers.

(b) A series is convergent if the sequence of partial sums is a convergent sequence. A series is divergent if it is not convergent.

3.

n	s_n
1	-2.40000
2	-1.92000
3	-2.01600
4	-1.99680
5	-2.00064
6	-1.99987
7	-2.00003
8	-1.99999
9	-2.00000
10	-2.00000

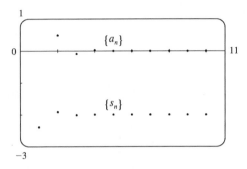

From the graph and the table, it seems that the series converges to -2. In fact, it is a geometric series with $a = -2.4$ and $r = -\frac{1}{5}$, so its sum is

$$\sum_{n=1}^{\infty} \frac{12}{(-5)^n} = \frac{-2.4}{1 - \left(-\frac{1}{5}\right)} = \frac{-2.4}{1.2} = -2.$$ Note that the dot corresponding to

$n = 1$ is part of both $\{a_n\}$ and $\{s_n\}$.

TI-86 Note: To graph $\{a_n\}$ and $\{s_n\}$, set your calculator to Param mode and DrawDot mode. (DrawDot is under GRAPH, MORE, FORMT (F3).) Now under E(t) = make the assignments: xt1=t, yt1=12/(-5)^t, xt2=t, yt2=sum seq(yt1,t,1,t,1). (sum and seq are under LIST, OPS (F5), MORE.) Under WIND use 1,10,1,0,10,1,-3,1,1 to obtain a graph similar to the one above. Then use TRACE (F4) to see the values.

5.

n	s_n
1	1.55741
2	-0.62763
3	-0.77018
4	0.38764
5	-2.99287
6	-3.28388
7	-2.41243
8	-9.21214
9	-9.66446
10	-9.01610

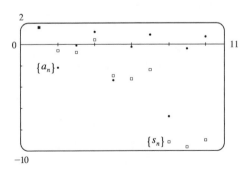

The series $\displaystyle\sum_{n=1}^{\infty} \tan n$ diverges, since its terms do not approach 0.

186

7.

n	s_n
1	0.64645
2	0.80755
3	0.87500
4	0.91056
5	0.93196
6	0.94601
7	0.95581
8	0.96296
9	0.96838
10	0.97259

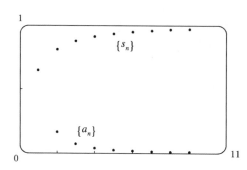

From the graph, it seems that the series converges to 1. To find the sum, we write

$$s_n = \sum_{i=1}^{n} \left(\frac{1}{i^{1.5}} - \frac{1}{(i+1)^{1.5}} \right)$$

$$= \left(1 - \frac{1}{2^{1.5}} \right) + \left(\frac{1}{2^{1.5}} - \frac{1}{3^{1.5}} \right) + \left(\frac{1}{3^{1.5}} - \frac{1}{4^{1.5}} \right) + \cdots + \left(\frac{1}{n^{1.5}} - \frac{1}{(n+1)^{1.5}} \right) = 1 - \frac{1}{(n+1)^{1.5}}$$

So the sum is $\lim\limits_{n \to \infty} s_n = 1 - 0 = 1$.

9. (a) $\lim\limits_{n \to \infty} a_n = \lim\limits_{n \to \infty} \dfrac{2n}{3n+1} = \dfrac{2}{3}$, so the *sequence* $\{a_n\}$ is convergent by (12.1.1).

(b) Since $\lim\limits_{n \to \infty} a_n = \frac{2}{3} \neq 0$, the *series* $\sum\limits_{n=1}^{\infty} a_n$ is divergent by the Test for Divergence (7).

11. $3 + 2 + \frac{4}{3} + \frac{8}{9} + \cdots$ is a geometric series with first term $a = 3$ and common ratio $r = \frac{2}{3}$. Since $|r| = \frac{2}{3} < 1$, the series converges to $\frac{a}{1-r} = \frac{3}{1-2/3} = \frac{3}{1/3} = 9$.

13. $-2 + \frac{5}{2} - \frac{25}{8} + \frac{125}{32} - \cdots$ is a geometric series with $a = -2$ and $r = \frac{5/2}{-2} = -\frac{5}{4}$. Since $|r| = \frac{5}{4} > 1$, the series diverges by (4).

15. $\sum\limits_{n=1}^{\infty} 5 \left(\frac{2}{3} \right)^{n-1}$ is a geometric series with $a = 5$ and $r = \frac{2}{3}$. Since $|r| = \frac{2}{3} < 1$, the series converges to

$$\frac{a}{1-r} = \frac{5}{1-2/3} = \frac{5}{1/3} = 15.$$

17. $\sum\limits_{n=1}^{\infty} \frac{(-3)^{n-1}}{4^n} = \frac{1}{4} \sum\limits_{n=1}^{\infty} \left(-\frac{3}{4} \right)^{n-1}$. The latter series is geometric with $a = 1$ and $r = -\frac{3}{4}$. Since $|r| = \frac{3}{4} < 1$, it converges to $\frac{1}{1-(-3/4)} = \frac{4}{7}$. Thus, the given series converges to $\left(\frac{1}{4} \right) \left(\frac{4}{7} \right) = \frac{1}{7}$.

19. $\sum\limits_{n=0}^{\infty} \frac{\pi^n}{3^{n+1}} = \frac{1}{3} \sum\limits_{n=0}^{\infty} \left(\frac{\pi}{3} \right)^n$ is a geometric series with ratio $r = \frac{\pi}{3}$. Since $|r| > 1$, the series diverges.

21. $\displaystyle\sum_{n=1}^{\infty} \frac{n}{n+5}$ diverges since $\displaystyle\lim_{n\to\infty} a_n = \lim_{n\to\infty} \frac{n}{n+5} = 1 \neq 0$. [Use (7), the Test for Divergence.]

23. Using partial fractions, the partial sums are

$$s_n = \sum_{i=2}^{n} \frac{2}{(i-1)(i+1)} = \sum_{i=2}^{n} \left(\frac{1}{i-1} - \frac{1}{i+1} \right)$$

$$= \left(1 - \frac{1}{3} \right) + \left(\frac{1}{2} - \frac{1}{4} \right) + \left(\frac{1}{3} - \frac{1}{5} \right) + \cdots + \left(\frac{1}{n-3} - \frac{1}{n-1} \right) + \left(\frac{1}{n-2} - \frac{1}{n} \right)$$

This sum is a telescoping series and $s_n = 1 + \dfrac{1}{2} - \dfrac{1}{n-1} - \dfrac{1}{n}$.

Thus, $\displaystyle\sum_{n=2}^{\infty} \frac{2}{n^2-1} = \lim_{n\to\infty} \left(1 + \frac{1}{2} - \frac{1}{n-1} - \frac{1}{n} \right) = \frac{3}{2}$.

25. $\displaystyle\sum_{k=2}^{\infty} \frac{k^2}{k^2-1}$ diverges by the Test for Divergence since $\displaystyle\lim_{k\to\infty} a_k = \lim_{k\to\infty} \frac{k^2}{k^2-1} = 1 \neq 0$.

27. Converges. $\displaystyle\sum_{n=1}^{\infty} \frac{3^n + 2^n}{6^n} = \sum_{n=1}^{\infty} \left(\frac{3^n}{6^n} + \frac{2^n}{6^n} \right) = \sum_{n=1}^{\infty} \left[\left(\frac{1}{2} \right)^n + \left(\frac{1}{3} \right)^n \right] = \frac{1/2}{1-1/2} + \frac{1/3}{1-1/3} = 1 + \frac{1}{2} = \frac{3}{2}$

29. $\displaystyle\sum_{n=1}^{\infty} \sqrt[n]{2} = 2 + \sqrt{2} + \sqrt[3]{2} + \sqrt[4]{2} + \cdots$ diverges by the Test for Divergence since

$$\lim_{n\to\infty} a_n = \lim_{n\to\infty} \sqrt[n]{2} = \lim_{n\to\infty} 2^{1/n} = 2^0 = 1 \neq 0.$$

31. $\displaystyle\lim_{n\to\infty} a_n = \lim_{n\to\infty} \arctan n = \frac{\pi}{2} \neq 0$, so the series diverges by the Test for Divergence.

33. The first series is a telescoping sum:

$$\sum_{n=1}^{\infty} \frac{3}{n(n+3)} = \sum_{n=1}^{\infty} \left(\frac{1}{n} - \frac{1}{n+3} \right) = \sum_{n=1}^{\infty} \left(\frac{1}{n} - \frac{1}{n+1} + \frac{1}{n+1} - \frac{1}{n+2} + \frac{1}{n+2} - \frac{1}{n+3} \right)$$

$$= \sum_{n=1}^{\infty} \left(\frac{1}{n} - \frac{1}{n+1} \right) + \sum_{n=1}^{\infty} \left(\frac{1}{n+1} - \frac{1}{n+2} \right) + \sum_{n=1}^{\infty} \left(\frac{1}{n+2} - \frac{1}{n+3} \right)$$

$$= 1 + \frac{1}{2} + \frac{1}{3} = \frac{11}{6}$$

The second series is geometric with first term $\dfrac{5}{4}$ and ratio $\dfrac{1}{4}$: $\displaystyle\sum_{n=1}^{\infty} \frac{5}{4^n} = \frac{5/4}{1-1/4} = \frac{5}{3}$. Thus,

$$\sum_{n=1}^{\infty} \left(\frac{3}{n(n+3)} + \frac{5}{4^n} \right) = \sum_{n=1}^{\infty} \frac{3}{n(n+3)} + \sum_{n=1}^{\infty} \frac{5}{4^n} \text{ [sum of two convergent series]} = \frac{11}{6} + \frac{5}{3} = \frac{7}{2}.$$

35. $0.\overline{2} = \dfrac{2}{10} + \dfrac{2}{10^2} + \cdots$ is a geometric series with $a = \dfrac{2}{10}$ and $r = \dfrac{1}{10}$. It converges to $\dfrac{a}{1-r} = \dfrac{2/10}{1-1/10} = \dfrac{2}{9}$.

37. $3.\overline{417} = 3 + \dfrac{417}{10^3} + \dfrac{417}{10^6} + \cdots = 3 + \dfrac{417/10^3}{1 - 1/10^3} = 3 + \dfrac{417}{999} = \dfrac{3414}{999} = \dfrac{1138}{333}$

39. $0.123\overline{456} = \dfrac{123}{1000} + \dfrac{0.000456}{1 - 0.001} = \dfrac{123}{1000} + \dfrac{456}{999,000} = \dfrac{123,333}{999,000} = \dfrac{41,111}{333,000}$

41. $\displaystyle\sum_{n=1}^{\infty} \frac{x^n}{3^n} = \sum_{n=1}^{\infty} \left(\frac{x}{3}\right)^n$ is a geometric series with $r = \dfrac{x}{3}$, so the series converges $\Leftrightarrow |r| < 1 \Leftrightarrow \dfrac{|x|}{3} < 1 \Leftrightarrow$

$|x| < 3$; that is, $-3 < x < 3$. In that case, the sum of the series is $\dfrac{a}{1 - r} = \dfrac{x/3}{1 - x/3} = \dfrac{x/3}{1 - x/3} \cdot \dfrac{3}{3} = \dfrac{x}{3 - x}$.

43. $\sum_{n=0}^{\infty} 4^n x^n = \sum_{n=0}^{\infty} (4x)^n$ is a geometric series with $r = 4x$, so the series converges $\Leftrightarrow |r| < 1 \Leftrightarrow$

$4|x| < 1 \Leftrightarrow |x| < \frac{1}{4}$. In that case, the sum of the series is $\dfrac{1}{1 - 4x}$.

45. $\displaystyle\sum_{n=0}^{\infty} \frac{\cos^n x}{2^n}$ is a geometric series with first term 1 and ratio $r = \dfrac{\cos x}{2}$, so it converges $\Leftrightarrow |r| < 1$. But

$|r| = \dfrac{|\cos x|}{2} \leq \dfrac{1}{2}$ for all x. Thus, the series converges for all real values of x and the sum of the series is

$\dfrac{1}{1 - (\cos x)/2} = \dfrac{2}{2 - \cos x}$.

47. After defining f, We use `convert(f,parfrac);` in Maple, `Apart` in Mathematica, or `Expand Rational`

and `Simplify` in Derive to find that the general term is $\dfrac{1}{(4n + 1)(4n - 3)} = -\dfrac{1/4}{4n + 1} + \dfrac{1/4}{4n - 3}$. So the

nth partial sum is

$$s_n = \sum_{k=1}^{n} \left(-\frac{1/4}{4k + 1} + \frac{1/4}{4k - 3}\right) = \frac{1}{4} \sum_{k=1}^{n} \left(\frac{1}{4k - 3} - \frac{1}{4k + 1}\right)$$

$$= \frac{1}{4}\left[\left(1 - \frac{1}{5}\right) + \left(\frac{1}{5} - \frac{1}{9}\right) + \left(\frac{1}{9} - \frac{1}{13}\right) + \cdots + \left(\frac{1}{4n - 3} - \frac{1}{4n + 1}\right)\right] = \frac{1}{4}\left(1 - \frac{1}{4n + 1}\right)$$

The series converges to $\lim\limits_{n \to \infty} s_n = \frac{1}{4}$. This can be confirmed by directly computing the sum using

`sum(f,1..infinity);` (in Maple), `Sum[f, {n,1,Infinity}]` (in Mathematica), or `Calculus Sum`

(from 1 to ∞) and `Simplify` (in Derive).

49. For $n = 1$, $a_1 = 0$ since $s_1 = 0$. For $n > 1$,

$$a_n = s_n - s_{n-1} = \frac{n - 1}{n + 1} - \frac{(n - 1) - 1}{(n - 1) + 1} = \frac{(n - 1)n - (n + 1)(n - 2)}{(n + 1)n} = \frac{2}{n(n + 1)}$$

Also, $\displaystyle\sum_{n=1}^{\infty} a_n = \lim_{n \to \infty} s_n = \lim_{n \to \infty} \frac{1 - 1/n}{1 + 1/n} = 1$.

51. (a) The first step in the chain occurs when the local government spends D dollars. The people who receive it spend a fraction c of those D dollars, that is, Dc dollars. Those who receive the Dc dollars spend a fraction c of it, that is, Dc^2 dollars. Continuing in this way, we see that the total spending after n transactions is

$$S_n = D + Dc + Dc^2 + \cdots + Dc^{n-1} = \frac{D(1-c^n)}{1-c} \text{ by (3).}$$

(b) $\displaystyle\lim_{n\to\infty} S_n = \lim_{n\to\infty} \frac{D(1-c^n)}{1-c} = \frac{D}{1-c} \lim_{n\to\infty}(1-c^n) = \frac{D}{1-c}$ (since $0 < c < 1 \;\Rightarrow\; \displaystyle\lim_{n\to\infty} c^n = 0$)

$= \dfrac{D}{s}$ (since $c + s = 1$) $= kD$ (since $k = 1/s$)

If $c = 0.8$, then $s = 1 - c = 0.2$ and the multiplier is $k = 1/s = 5$.

53. $\sum_{n=2}^{\infty} (1+c)^{-n}$ is a geometric series with $a = (1+c)^{-2}$ and $r = (1+c)^{-1}$, so the series converges when

$\left|(1+c)^{-1}\right| < 1 \;\Leftrightarrow\; |1+c| > 1 \;\Leftrightarrow\; 1+c > 1 \text{ or } 1+c < -1 \;\Leftrightarrow\; c > 0 \text{ or } c < -2.$ We calculate

the sum of the series and set it equal to 2: $\dfrac{(1+c)^{-2}}{1-(1+c)^{-1}} = 2 \;\Leftrightarrow\; \left(\dfrac{1}{1+c}\right)^2 = 2 - 2\left(\dfrac{1}{1+c}\right) \;\Leftrightarrow\;$

$1 = 2(1+c)^2 - 2(1+c) \;\Leftrightarrow\; 2c^2 + 2c - 1 = 0 \;\Leftrightarrow\; c = \frac{-2 \pm \sqrt{12}}{4} = \frac{\pm\sqrt{3}-1}{2}.$ However, the negative root is

inadmissible because $-2 < \frac{-\sqrt{3}-1}{2} < 0$. So $c = \frac{\sqrt{3}-1}{2}$.

55. Let d_n be the diameter of C_n. We draw lines from the centers of
the C_i to the center of D (or C), and using the Pythagorean

Theorem, we can write $1^2 + \left(1 - \frac{1}{2}d_1\right)^2 = \left(1 + \frac{1}{2}d_1\right)^2 \;\Leftrightarrow\;$

$1 = \left(1 + \frac{1}{2}d_1\right)^2 - \left(1 - \frac{1}{2}d_1\right)^2 = 2d_1$ (difference of squares)

$\Rightarrow\; d_1 = \frac{1}{2}$. Similarly,

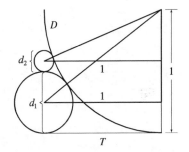

$1 = \left(1 + \frac{1}{2}d_2\right)^2 - \left(1 - d_1 - \frac{1}{2}d_2\right)^2 = 2d_2 + 2d_1 - d_1^2 - d_1 d_2$

$= (2 - d_1)(d_1 + d_2) \;\Leftrightarrow\;$

$d_2 = \dfrac{1}{2-d_1} - d_1 = \dfrac{(1-d_1)^2}{2-d_1}, \quad 1 = \left(1 + \frac{1}{2}d_3\right)^2 - \left(1 - d_1 - d_2 - \frac{1}{2}d_3\right)^2 \;\Leftrightarrow\; d_3 = \dfrac{[1-(d_1+d_2)]^2}{2-(d_1+d_2)},$ and

in general, $d_{n+1} = \dfrac{\left(1 - \sum_{i=1}^{n} d_i\right)^2}{2 - \sum_{i=1}^{n} d_i}$. If we actually calculate d_2 and d_3 from the formulas above, we find that they

are $\dfrac{1}{6} = \dfrac{1}{2 \cdot 3}$ and $\dfrac{1}{12} = \dfrac{1}{3 \cdot 4}$ respectively, so we suspect that in general, $d_n = \dfrac{1}{n(n+1)}$. To prove this, we use

induction: Assume that for all $k \leq n$, $d_k = \dfrac{1}{k(k+1)} = \dfrac{1}{k} - \dfrac{1}{k+1}$. Then

$$\sum_{i=1}^{n} d_i = 1 - \frac{1}{n+1} = \frac{n}{n+1} \quad \text{(telescoping sum). Substituting this into our formula for } d_{n+1}, \text{ we get}$$

$$d_{n+1} = \frac{\left[1 - \dfrac{n}{n+1}\right]^2}{2 - \left(\dfrac{n}{n+1}\right)} = \frac{\dfrac{1}{(n+1)^2}}{\dfrac{n+2}{n+1}} = \frac{1}{(n+1)(n+2)}, \text{ and the induction is complete.}$$

Now, we observe that the partial sums $\sum_{i=1}^{n} d_i$ of the diameters of the circles approach 1 as $n \to \infty$; that is,

$$\sum_{n=1}^{\infty} a_n = \sum_{n=1}^{\infty} \frac{1}{n(n+1)} = 1, \text{ which is what we wanted to prove.}$$

57. The series $1 - 1 + 1 - 1 + 1 - 1 + \cdots$ diverges (geometric series with $r = -1$) so we cannot say that

$0 = 1 - 1 + 1 - 1 + 1 - 1 + \cdots$.

59. $\sum_{n=1}^{\infty} ca_n = \lim_{n \to \infty} \sum_{i=1}^{n} ca_i = \lim_{n \to \infty} c \sum_{i=1}^{n} a_i = c \lim_{n \to \infty} \sum_{i=1}^{n} a_i = c \sum_{n=1}^{\infty} a_n$, which exists by hypothesis.

61. Suppose on the contrary that $\sum (a_n + b_n)$ converges. Then $\sum (a_n + b_n)$ and $\sum a_n$ are convergent series. So by Theorem 8, $\sum [(a_n + b_n) - a_n]$ would also be convergent. But $\sum [(a_n + b_n) - a_n] = \sum b_n$, a contradiction, since $\sum b_n$ is given to be divergent.

63. The partial sums $\{s_n\}$ form an increasing sequence, since $s_n - s_{n-1} = a_n > 0$ for all n. Also, the sequence $\{s_n\}$ is bounded since $s_n \le 1000$ for all n. So by Theorem 12.1.11, the sequence of partial sums converges, that is, the series $\sum a_n$ is convergent.

65. (a) At the first step, only the interval $\left(\frac{1}{3}, \frac{2}{3}\right)$ (length $\frac{1}{3}$) is removed. At the second step, we remove the intervals $\left(\frac{1}{9}, \frac{2}{9}\right)$ and $\left(\frac{7}{9}, \frac{8}{9}\right)$, which have a total length of $2 \cdot \left(\frac{1}{3}\right)^2$. At the third step, we remove 2^2 intervals, each of length $\left(\frac{1}{3}\right)^3$. In general, at the nth step we remove 2^{n-1} intervals, each of length $\left(\frac{1}{3}\right)^n$, for a length of $2^{n-1} \cdot \left(\frac{1}{3}\right)^n = \frac{1}{3}\left(\frac{2}{3}\right)^{n-1}$. Thus, the total length of all removed intervals is $\sum_{n=1}^{\infty} \frac{1}{3}\left(\frac{2}{3}\right)^{n-1} = \frac{1/3}{1 - 2/3} = 1$ (geometric series with $a = \frac{1}{3}$ and $r = \frac{2}{3}$). Notice that at the nth step, the leftmost interval that is removed is $\left(\left(\frac{1}{3}\right)^n, \left(\frac{2}{3}\right)^n\right)$, so we never remove 0, and 0 is in the Cantor set. Also, the rightmost interval removed is $\left(1 - \left(\frac{2}{3}\right)^n, 1 - \left(\frac{1}{3}\right)^n\right)$, so 1 is never removed. Some other numbers in the Cantor set are $\frac{1}{3}, \frac{2}{3}, \frac{1}{9}, \frac{2}{9}, \frac{7}{9}$, and $\frac{8}{9}$.

(b) The area removed at the first step is $\frac{1}{9}$; at the second step, $8 \cdot \left(\frac{1}{9}\right)^2$; at the third step, $(8)^2 \cdot \left(\frac{1}{9}\right)^3$. In general, the area removed at the nth step is $(8)^{n-1}\left(\frac{1}{9}\right)^n = \frac{1}{9}\left(\frac{8}{9}\right)^{n-1}$, so the total area of all removed squares is

$$\sum_{n=1}^{\infty} \frac{1}{9}\left(\frac{8}{9}\right)^{n-1} = \frac{1/9}{1 - 8/9} = 1.$$

67. (a) For $\sum_{n=1}^{\infty} \dfrac{n}{(n+1)!}$, $s_1 = \dfrac{1}{1 \cdot 2} = \dfrac{1}{2}$, $s_2 = \dfrac{1}{2} + \dfrac{2}{1 \cdot 2 \cdot 3} = \dfrac{5}{6}$, $s_3 = \dfrac{5}{6} + \dfrac{3}{1 \cdot 2 \cdot 3 \cdot 4} = \dfrac{23}{24}$,

$s_4 = \dfrac{23}{24} + \dfrac{4}{1 \cdot 2 \cdot 3 \cdot 4 \cdot 5} = \dfrac{119}{120}$. The denominators are $(n+1)!$, so a guess would be $s_n = \dfrac{(n+1)! - 1}{(n+1)!}$.

(b) For $n = 1$, $s_1 = \dfrac{1}{2} = \dfrac{2! - 1}{2!}$, so the formula holds for $n = 1$. Assume $s_k = \dfrac{(k+1)! - 1}{(k+1)!}$. Then

$$s_{k+1} = \dfrac{(k+1)! - 1}{(k+1)!} + \dfrac{k+1}{(k+2)!} = \dfrac{(k+1)! - 1}{(k+1)!} + \dfrac{k+1}{(k+1)!(k+2)}$$

$$= \dfrac{(k+2)! - (k+2) + k + 1}{(k+2)!} = \dfrac{(k+2)! - 1}{(k+2)!}$$

Thus, the formula is true for $n = k + 1$. So by induction, the guess is correct.

(c) $\lim_{n \to \infty} s_n = \lim_{n \to \infty} \dfrac{(n+1)! - 1}{(n+1)!} = \lim_{n \to \infty} \left[1 - \dfrac{1}{(n+1)!} \right] = 1$ and so $\sum_{n=1}^{\infty} \dfrac{n}{(n+1)!} = 1$.

12.3 The Integral Test and Estimates of Sums

1. The picture shows that $a_2 = \dfrac{1}{2^{1.3}} < \int_1^2 \dfrac{1}{x^{1.3}}\, dx$,

$a_3 = \dfrac{1}{3^{1.3}} < \int_2^3 \dfrac{1}{x^{1.3}}\, dx$, and so on, so $\sum_{n=2}^{\infty} \dfrac{1}{n^{1.3}} < \int_1^{\infty} \dfrac{1}{x^{1.3}}\, dx$. The

integral converges by (8.8.2) with $p = 1.3 > 1$, so the series converges.

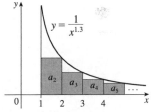

3. The function $f(x) = 1/x^4$ is continuous, positive, and decreasing on $[1, \infty)$, so the Integral Test applies.

$\int_1^{\infty} \dfrac{1}{x^4}\, dx = \lim_{t \to \infty} \int_1^t x^{-4}\, dx = \lim_{t \to \infty} \left[\dfrac{x^{-3}}{-3} \right]_1^t = \lim_{t \to \infty} \left(-\dfrac{1}{3t^3} + \dfrac{1}{3} \right) = \dfrac{1}{3}$. Since this improper integral is

convergent, the series $\sum_{n=1}^{\infty} \dfrac{1}{n^4}$ is also convergent by the Integral Test.

5. The function $f(x) = 1/(3x + 1)$ is continuous, positive, and decreasing on $[1, \infty)$, so the Integral Test applies.

$$\int_1^{\infty} \dfrac{dx}{3x + 1} = \lim_{b \to \infty} \int_1^b \dfrac{dx}{3x + 1} = \lim_{b \to \infty} \left[\tfrac{1}{3} \ln(3x + 1) \right]_1^b = \lim_{b \to \infty} \left[\tfrac{1}{3} \ln(3b + 1) - \tfrac{1}{3} \ln 4 \right] = \infty$$

so the improper integral diverges, and so does the series $\sum_{n=1}^{\infty} 1/(3n + 1)$.

7. $f(x) = xe^{-x}$ is continuous and positive on $[1, \infty)$. $f'(x) = -xe^{-x} + e^{-x} = e^{-x}(1 - x) < 0$ for $x > 1$, so f is decreasing on $[1, \infty)$. Thus, the Integral Test applies.

$$\int_1^{\infty} xe^{-x}\, dx = \lim_{b \to \infty} \int_1^b xe^{-x}\, dx = \lim_{b \to \infty} \left[-xe^{-x} - e^{-x} \right]_1^b \text{ (by parts)}$$

$$= \lim_{b \to \infty} \left[-be^{-b} - e^{-b} + e^{-1} + e^{-1} \right] = 2/e$$

since $\lim_{b \to \infty} be^{-b} = \lim_{b \to \infty} (b/e^b) \overset{H}{=} \lim_{b \to \infty} (1/e^b) = 0$ and $\lim_{b \to \infty} e^{-b} = 0$. Thus, $\sum_{n=1}^{\infty} ne^{-n}$ converges.

9. The series $\displaystyle\sum_{n=1}^{\infty} \frac{1}{n^{0.85}}$ is a p-series with $p = 0.85 \leq 1$, so it diverges by (1). Therefore, the series $\displaystyle\sum_{n=1}^{\infty} \frac{2}{n^{0.85}}$ must

also diverge, for if it converged, then $\displaystyle\sum_{n=1}^{\infty} \frac{1}{n^{0.85}}$ would have to converge (by Theorem 8(i) in Section 11.2).

11. $1 + \dfrac{1}{8} + \dfrac{1}{27} + \dfrac{1}{64} + \dfrac{1}{125} + \cdots = \displaystyle\sum_{n=1}^{\infty} \frac{1}{n^3}$. This is a p-series with $p = 3 > 1$, so it converges by (1).

13. $\displaystyle\sum_{n=1}^{\infty} \frac{5 - 2\sqrt{n}}{n^3} = 5 \sum_{n=1}^{\infty} \frac{1}{n^3} - 2 \sum_{n=1}^{\infty} \frac{1}{n^{5/2}}$ by Theorem 12.2.8, since $\displaystyle\sum_{n=1}^{\infty} \frac{1}{n^3}$ and $\displaystyle\sum_{n=1}^{\infty} \frac{1}{n^{5/2}}$ both converge by (1)

(with $p = 3 > 1$ and $p = \frac{5}{2} > 1$). Thus, $\displaystyle\sum_{n=1}^{\infty} \frac{5 - 2\sqrt{n}}{n^3}$ converges.

15. The function $f(x) = \dfrac{1}{x^2 + 4}$ is continuous, positive, and decreasing on $[1, \infty)$, so we can apply the Integral Test.

$$\int_1^{\infty} \frac{1}{x^2 + 4}\, dx = \lim_{t \to \infty} \int_1^t \frac{1}{x^2 + 4}\, dx = \lim_{t \to \infty} \left[\frac{1}{2} \tan^{-1} \frac{x}{2}\right]_1^t = \frac{1}{2} \lim_{t \to \infty} \left[\tan^{-1}\left(\frac{t}{2}\right) - \tan^{-1}\left(\frac{1}{2}\right)\right]$$

$$= \frac{1}{2}\left[\frac{\pi}{2} - \tan^{-1}\left(\frac{1}{2}\right)\right]$$

Therefore, the series $\displaystyle\sum_{n=1}^{\infty} \frac{1}{n^2 + 4}$ converges.

17. $f(x) = \dfrac{x}{x^2 + 1}$ is continuous and positive on $[1, \infty)$, and since

$$f'(x) = \frac{1 - x^2}{(x^2 + 1)^2} < 0 \text{ for } x > 1, f \text{ is also decreasing. Using the Integral Test,}$$

$$\int_1^{\infty} \frac{x}{x^2 + 1}\, dx = \lim_{t \to \infty} \int_1^t \frac{x}{x^2 + 1}\, dx = \lim_{t \to \infty} \left[\frac{\ln(x^2 + 1)}{2}\right]_1^t = \frac{1}{2} \lim_{t \to \infty} \left[\ln(t^2 + 1) - \ln 2\right] = \infty, \text{ so the series}$$

diverges.

19. $f(x) = xe^{-x^2}$ is continuous and positive on $[1, \infty)$, and since $f'(x) = e^{-x^2}\left(1 - 2x^2\right) < 0$ for

$x > 1, f$ is decreasing as well. Thus, we can use the Integral Test.

$\int_1^{\infty} xe^{-x^2}\, dx = \lim_{t \to \infty} \left[-\frac{1}{2}e^{-x^2}\right]_1^t = 0 - \left(-\frac{1}{2}e^{-1}\right) = 1/(2e)$. Since the integral converges, the series converges.

21. $f(x) = \dfrac{1}{x \ln x}$ is continuous and positive on $[2, \infty)$, and also decreasing since $f'(x) = -\dfrac{1 + \ln x}{x^2(\ln x)^2} < 0$ for $x > 2$,

so we can use the Integral Test. $\displaystyle\int_2^{\infty} \frac{1}{x \ln x}\, dx = \lim_{t \to \infty} \left[\ln(\ln x)\right]_2^t = \lim_{t \to \infty} \left[\ln(\ln t) - \ln(\ln 2)\right] = \infty$, so the series

diverges.

23. The function $f(x) = \dfrac{1}{x^3 + x}$ is continuous, positive, and decreasing on $[1, \infty)$, so the Integral Test applies. We use partial fractions to evaluate the integral:

$$\int_1^{\infty} \frac{1}{x^3 + x}\, dx = \lim_{t \to \infty} \int_1^t \left[\frac{1}{x} - \frac{x}{1 + x^2} \right] dx = \lim_{t \to \infty} \left[\ln x - \frac{1}{2} \ln(1 + x^2) \right]_1^t$$

$$= \lim_{t \to \infty} \left[\ln \frac{x}{\sqrt{1 + x^2}} \right]_1^t = \lim_{t \to \infty} \left(\ln \frac{t}{\sqrt{1 + t^2}} - \ln \frac{1}{\sqrt{2}} \right)$$

$$= \lim_{t \to \infty} \left(\ln \frac{1}{\sqrt{1 + 1/t^2}} + \frac{1}{2} \ln 2 \right) = \frac{1}{2} \ln 2$$

so the series $\displaystyle\sum_{n=1}^{\infty} \frac{1}{n^3 + n}$ converges.

25. We have already shown (in Exercise 21) that when $p = 1$ the series $\displaystyle\sum_{n=2}^{\infty} \frac{1}{n(\ln n)^p}$ diverges, so assume that $p \neq 1$.

$f(x) = \dfrac{1}{x(\ln x)^p}$ is continuous and positive on $[2, \infty)$, and $f'(x) = -\dfrac{p + \ln x}{x^2 (\ln x)^{p+1}} < 0$ if $x > e^{-p}$, so that f is eventually decreasing and we can use the Integral Test.

$$\int_2^{\infty} \frac{1}{x(\ln x)^p}\, dx = \lim_{t \to \infty} \left[\frac{(\ln x)^{1-p}}{1 - p} \right]_2^t \quad \text{(for } p \neq 1\text{)} \ = \lim_{t \to \infty} \left[\frac{(\ln t)^{1-p}}{1 - p} \right] - \frac{(\ln 2)^{1-p}}{1 - p}$$

This limit exists whenever $1 - p < 0 \ \Leftrightarrow \ p > 1$, so the series converges for $p > 1$.

27. Clearly the series cannot converge if $p \geq -\frac{1}{2}$, because then $\lim_{n \to \infty} n(1 + n^2)^p \neq 0$. Also, if $p = -1$ the series diverges (see Exercise 17). So assume $p < -\frac{1}{2}, p \neq -1$. Then $f(x) = x(1 + x^2)^p$ is continuous, positive, and eventually decreasing on $[1, \infty)$, and we can use the Integral Test.

$$\int_1^{\infty} x(1 + x^2)^p\, dx = \lim_{t \to \infty} \left[\frac{1}{2} \cdot \frac{(1 + x^2)^{p+1}}{p + 1} \right]_1^t = \lim_{t \to \infty} \frac{1}{2} \cdot \frac{(1 + t^2)^{p+1}}{p + 1} - \frac{2^p}{p + 1}.$$ This limit exists and is finite

$\Leftrightarrow \ p + 1 < 0 \ \Leftrightarrow \ p < -1$, so the series converges whenever $p < -1$.

29. Since this is a p-series with $p = x$, $\zeta(x)$ is defined when $x > 1$. Unless specified otherwise, the domain of a function f is the set of numbers x such that the expression for $f(x)$ makes sense and defines a real number. So, in the case of a series, it's the set of numbers x such that the series is convergent.

31. (a) $f(x) = \dfrac{1}{x^2}$ is positive and continuous and $f'(x) = -\dfrac{2}{x^3}$ is negative for $x > 0$, and so the Integral Test applies. $\displaystyle\sum_{n=1}^{\infty} \frac{1}{n^2} \approx s_{10} = \frac{1}{1^2} + \frac{1}{2^2} + \frac{1}{3^2} + \cdots + \frac{1}{10^2} \approx 1.549768$.

$$R_{10} \leq \int_{10}^{\infty} \frac{1}{x^2}\, dx = \lim_{t \to \infty} \left[\frac{-1}{x} \right]_{10}^t = \lim_{t \to \infty} \left(-\frac{1}{t} + \frac{1}{10} \right) = \frac{1}{10},$$ so the error is at most 0.1.

(b) $s_{10} + \int_{11}^{\infty} \frac{1}{x^2} \, dx \le s \le s_{10} + \int_{10}^{\infty} \frac{1}{x^2} \, dx \quad \Rightarrow \quad s_{10} + \frac{1}{11} \le s \le s_{10} + \frac{1}{10} \quad \Rightarrow$

$1.549768 + 0.090909 = 1.640677 \le s \le 1.549768 + 0.1 = 1.649768$, so we get $s \approx 1.64522$ (the average of 1.640677 and 1.649768) with error ≤ 0.005 (the maximum of $1.649768 - 1.64522$ and $1.64522 - 1.640677$, rounded up).

(c) $R_n \le \int_{n}^{\infty} \frac{1}{x^2} \, dx = \frac{1}{n}$. So $R_n < 0.001$ if $\frac{1}{n} < \frac{1}{1000} \quad \Leftrightarrow \quad n > 1000$.

33. $f(x) = x^{-3/2}$ is positive and continuous and $f'(x) = -\frac{3}{2} x^{-5/2}$ is negative for $x > 0$, so the Integral Test applies. From the end of Example 6, we see that the error is at most half the length of the interval. From (3), the interval is $\left(s_n + \int_{n+1}^{\infty} f(x)\,dx, \; s_n + \int_{n}^{\infty} f(x)\,dx \right)$, so its length is $\int_{n}^{\infty} f(x)\,dx - \int_{n+1}^{\infty} f(x)\,dx = \int_{n}^{n+1} f(x)\,dx$. Thus, we need n such that

$$0.01 > \frac{1}{2} \int_{n}^{n+1} x^{-3/2}\,dx = \frac{1}{2} \left[\frac{-2}{\sqrt{x}} \right]_{n}^{n+1} = \frac{1}{\sqrt{n}} - \frac{1}{\sqrt{n+1}}$$

$\Leftrightarrow \quad n > 13.08$ (use a graphing calculator to solve $1/\sqrt{x} - 1/\sqrt{x+1} < 0.01$). Again from the end of Example 6, we approximate s by the midpoint of this interval. In general, the midpoint is

$\frac{1}{2} \left[\left(s_n + \int_{n+1}^{\infty} f(x)\,dx \right) + \left(s_n + \int_{n}^{\infty} f(x)\,dx \right) \right] = s_n + \frac{1}{2} \left(\int_{n+1}^{\infty} f(x)\,dx + \int_{n}^{\infty} f(x)\,dx \right)$. So using $n = 14$,

we have $s \approx s_{14} + \frac{1}{2} \left(\int_{14}^{\infty} x^{-3/2}\,dx + \int_{15}^{\infty} x^{-3/2}\,dx \right) \approx 2.0872 + \frac{1}{\sqrt{14}} + \frac{1}{\sqrt{15}} \approx 2.6127 \approx 2.61$. Any larger

value of n will also work. For instance, $s \approx s_{30} + \frac{1}{\sqrt{30}} + \frac{1}{\sqrt{31}} \approx 2.6124$.

35. $\displaystyle\sum_{n=1}^{\infty} n^{-1.001} = \sum_{n=1}^{\infty} \frac{1}{n^{1.001}}$ is a convergent p-series with $p = 1.001 > 1$. Using (2), we get

$R_n \le \int_{n}^{\infty} x^{-1.001}\,dx = \lim_{t \to \infty} \left[\frac{x^{-0.001}}{-0.001} \right]_{n}^{t} = -1000 \lim_{t \to \infty} \left[\frac{1}{x^{0.001}} \right]_{n}^{t} = -1000 \left(-\frac{1}{n^{0.001}} \right) = \frac{1000}{n^{0.001}}$. We want

$R_n < 0.000\,000\,005 \quad \Leftrightarrow \quad \frac{1000}{n^{0.001}} < 5 \times 10^{-9} \quad \Leftrightarrow \quad n^{0.001} > \frac{1000}{5 \times 10^{-9}} \quad \Leftrightarrow$

$n > \left(2 \times 10^{11} \right)^{1000} = 2^{1000} \times 10^{11,000} \approx 1.07 \times 10^{301} \times 10^{11,000} = 1.07 \times 10^{11,301}$.

37. (a) From the figure, $a_2 + a_3 + \cdots + a_n \le \int_{1}^{n} f(x)\,dx$, so with

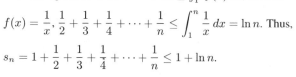

$f(x) = \frac{1}{x}, \; \frac{1}{2} + \frac{1}{3} + \frac{1}{4} + \cdots + \frac{1}{n} \le \int_{1}^{n} \frac{1}{x}\,dx = \ln n$. Thus,

$s_n = 1 + \frac{1}{2} + \frac{1}{3} + \frac{1}{4} + \cdots + \frac{1}{n} \le 1 + \ln n$.

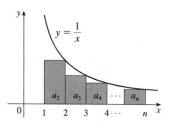

(b) By part (a), $s_{10^6} \le 1 + \ln 10^6 \approx 14.82 < 15$ and $s_{10^9} \le 1 + \ln 10^9 \approx 21.72 < 22$.

39. $b^{\ln n} = \left(e^{\ln b} \right)^{\ln n} = \left(e^{\ln n} \right)^{\ln b} = n^{\ln b} = \frac{1}{n^{-\ln b}}$. This is a p-series, which converges for all b such that $-\ln b > 1$

$\Leftrightarrow \quad \ln b < -1 \quad \Leftrightarrow \quad b < e^{-1} \quad \Leftrightarrow \quad b < 1/e$ [with $b > 0$].

12.4 The Comparison Tests

1. (a) We cannot say anything about $\sum a_n$. If $a_n > b_n$ for all n and $\sum b_n$ is convergent, then $\sum a_n$ could be convergent or divergent. (See the note after Example 2.)

(b) If $a_n < b_n$ for all n, then $\sum a_n$ is convergent. [This is part (i) of the Comparison Test.]

3. $\dfrac{1}{n^2 + n + 1} < \dfrac{1}{n^2}$ for all $n \geq 1$, so $\displaystyle\sum_{n=1}^{\infty} \dfrac{1}{n^2 + n + 1}$ converges by comparison with $\displaystyle\sum_{n=1}^{\infty} \dfrac{1}{n^2}$, which converges because it is a p-series with $p = 2 > 1$.

5. $\dfrac{5}{2 + 3^n} < \dfrac{5}{3^n}$ for all $n \geq 1$, so $\displaystyle\sum_{n=1}^{\infty} \dfrac{5}{2 + 3^n}$ converges by comparison with $\displaystyle\sum_{n=1}^{\infty} \dfrac{5}{3^n} = 5 \sum_{n=1}^{\infty} \dfrac{1}{3^n}$, which converges because $\displaystyle\sum_{n=1}^{\infty} \dfrac{1}{3^n}$ is a convergent geometric series with $r = \frac{1}{3}$ ($|r| < 1$).

7. $\dfrac{n + 1}{n^2} > \dfrac{n}{n^2} = \dfrac{1}{n}$ for all $n \geq 1$, so $\displaystyle\sum_{n=1}^{\infty} \dfrac{n + 1}{n^2}$ diverges by comparison with the harmonic series $\displaystyle\sum_{n=1}^{\infty} \dfrac{1}{n}$.

9. $\dfrac{\cos^2 n}{n^2 + 1} \leq \dfrac{1}{n^2 + 1} < \dfrac{1}{n^2}$, so the series $\displaystyle\sum_{n=1}^{\infty} \dfrac{\cos^2 n}{n^2 + 1}$ converges by comparison with the p-series $\displaystyle\sum_{n=1}^{\infty} \dfrac{1}{n^2}$ ($p = 2 > 1$).

11. If $a_n = \dfrac{n^2 + 1}{n^3 - 1}$ and $b_n = \dfrac{1}{n}$, then $\displaystyle\lim_{n\to\infty} \dfrac{a_n}{b_n} = \lim_{n\to\infty} \dfrac{n^3 + n}{n^3 - 1} = \lim_{n\to\infty} \dfrac{1 + 1/n^2}{1 - 1/n^3} = 1$, so $\displaystyle\sum_{n=2}^{\infty} \dfrac{n^2 + 1}{n^3 - 1}$ diverges by the Limit Comparison Test with the divergent (partial) harmonic series $\displaystyle\sum_{n=2}^{\infty} \dfrac{1}{n}$.

Or: Since $a_n = \dfrac{n^2 + 1}{n^3 - 1} > \dfrac{n^2 + 1}{n^3} > \dfrac{n^2}{n^3} = \dfrac{1}{n} = b_n$, we could use the Comparison Test.

13. $\dfrac{n - 1}{n4^n}$ is positive for $n > 1$ and $\dfrac{n - 1}{n4^n} < \dfrac{n}{n4^n} = \dfrac{1}{4^n}$, so $\displaystyle\sum_{n=1}^{\infty} \dfrac{n - 1}{n4^n}$ converges by comparison with the convergent geometric series $\displaystyle\sum_{n=1}^{\infty} \left(\dfrac{1}{4}\right)^n$.

15. $\dfrac{2 + (-1)^n}{n\sqrt{n}} \leq \dfrac{3}{n\sqrt{n}}$, and $\displaystyle\sum_{n=1}^{\infty} \dfrac{3}{n\sqrt{n}}$ converges because it is a constant multiple of the convergent p-series $\displaystyle\sum_{n=1}^{\infty} \dfrac{1}{n\sqrt{n}}$ ($p = \frac{3}{2} > 1$), so the given series converges by the Comparison Test.

17. Use the Limit Comparison Test with $a_n = \dfrac{1}{\sqrt{n^2 + 1}}$ and $b_n = \dfrac{1}{n}$:

$\displaystyle\lim_{n\to\infty} \dfrac{a_n}{b_n} = \lim_{n\to\infty} \dfrac{n}{\sqrt{n^2 + 1}} = \lim_{n\to\infty} \dfrac{1}{\sqrt{1 + (1/n^2)}} = 1 > 0$. Since the harmonic series $\displaystyle\sum_{n=1}^{\infty} \dfrac{1}{n}$ diverges, so does $\displaystyle\sum_{n=1}^{\infty} \dfrac{1}{\sqrt{n^2 + 1}}$.

19. $\dfrac{2^n}{1 + 3^n} < \dfrac{2^n}{3^n} = \left(\dfrac{2}{3}\right)^n$. $\displaystyle\sum_{n=1}^{\infty} \left(\dfrac{2}{3}\right)^n$ is a convergent geometric series ($|r| = \frac{2}{3} < 1$), so $\displaystyle\sum_{n=1}^{\infty} \dfrac{2^n}{1 + 3^n}$ converges by the Comparison Test.

21. Use the Limit Comparison Test with $a_n = \dfrac{1}{1+\sqrt{n}}$ and $b_n = \dfrac{1}{\sqrt{n}}$: $\displaystyle\lim_{n\to\infty} \dfrac{a_n}{b_n} = \lim_{n\to\infty} \dfrac{\sqrt{n}}{1+\sqrt{n}} = 1 > 0$. Since

$\displaystyle\sum_{n=1}^{\infty} \dfrac{1}{\sqrt{n}}$ is a divergent p-series $(p = \frac{1}{2} \le 1)$, $\displaystyle\sum_{n=1}^{\infty} \dfrac{1}{1+\sqrt{n}}$ also diverges.

23. Use the Limit Comparison Test with $a_n = \dfrac{5+2n}{(1+n^2)^2}$ and $b_n = \dfrac{1}{n^3}$:

$\displaystyle\lim_{n\to\infty} \dfrac{a_n}{b_n} = \lim_{n\to\infty} \dfrac{n^3(5+2n)}{(1+n^2)^2} = \lim_{n\to\infty} \dfrac{5n^3 + 2n^4}{(1+n^2)^2} \cdot \dfrac{1/n^4}{1/(n^2)^2} = \lim_{n\to\infty} \dfrac{\frac{5}{n} + 2}{\left(\frac{1}{n^2} + 1\right)^2} = 2 > 0$. Since $\displaystyle\sum_{n=1}^{\infty} \dfrac{1}{n^3}$ is a

convergent p-series $(p = 3 > 1)$, the series $\displaystyle\sum_{n=1}^{\infty} \dfrac{5+2n}{(1+n^2)^2}$ also converges.

25. If $a_n = \dfrac{1+n+n^2}{\sqrt{1+n^2+n^6}}$ and $b_n = \dfrac{1}{n}$, then

$\displaystyle\lim_{n\to\infty} \dfrac{a_n}{b_n} = \lim_{n\to\infty} \dfrac{n+n^2+n^3}{\sqrt{1+n^2+n^6}} = \lim_{n\to\infty} \dfrac{1/n^2 + 1/n + 1}{\sqrt{1/n^6 + 1/n^4 + 1}} = 1 > 0$, so $\displaystyle\sum_{n=1}^{\infty} \dfrac{1+n+n^2}{\sqrt{1+n^2+n^6}}$ diverges by the

Limit Comparison Test with the divergent harmonic series $\displaystyle\sum_{n=1}^{\infty} \dfrac{1}{n}$.

27. Use the Limit Comparison Test with $a_n = \left(1 + \dfrac{1}{n}\right)^2 e^{-n}$ and $b_n = e^{-n}$: $\displaystyle\lim_{n\to\infty} \dfrac{a_n}{b_n} = \lim_{n\to\infty} \left(1 + \dfrac{1}{n}\right)^2 = 1 > 0$.

Since $\displaystyle\sum_{n=1}^{\infty} e^{-n} = \sum_{n=1}^{\infty} \dfrac{1}{e^n}$ is a convergent geometric series $\left(|r| = \frac{1}{e} < 1\right)$, the series $\displaystyle\sum_{n=1}^{\infty} \left(1 + \dfrac{1}{n}\right)^2 e^{-n}$ also converges.

29. Clearly $n! = n(n-1)(n-2)\cdots(3)(2) \ge 2 \cdot 2 \cdot 2 \cdots\cdots 2 \cdot 2 = 2^{n-1}$, so $\dfrac{1}{n!} \le \dfrac{1}{2^{n-1}}$. $\displaystyle\sum_{n=1}^{\infty} \dfrac{1}{2^{n-1}}$ is a convergent

geometric series $\left(|r| = \frac{1}{2} < 1\right)$, so $\displaystyle\sum_{n=1}^{\infty} \dfrac{1}{n!}$ converges by the Comparison Test.

31. Use the Limit Comparison Test with $a_n = \sin\left(\dfrac{1}{n}\right)$ and $b_n = \dfrac{1}{n}$. Then $\sum a_n$ and $\sum b_n$ are series with positive

terms and $\displaystyle\lim_{n\to\infty} \dfrac{a_n}{b_n} = \lim_{n\to\infty} \dfrac{\sin(1/n)}{1/n} = \lim_{\theta\to 0} \dfrac{\sin\theta}{\theta} = 1 > 0$. Since $\sum_{n=1}^{\infty} b_n$ is the divergent harmonic series,

$\sum_{n=1}^{\infty} \sin(1/n)$ also diverges. (Note that we could also use l'Hospital's Rule to evaluate the limit:

$\displaystyle\lim_{x\to\infty} \dfrac{\sin(1/x)}{1/x} \overset{\text{H}}{=} \lim_{x\to\infty} \dfrac{\cos(1/x)\cdot\left(-1/x^2\right)}{-1/x^2} = \lim_{x\to\infty} \cos\dfrac{1}{x} = \cos 0 = 1$.)

33. $\displaystyle\sum_{n=1}^{10} \dfrac{1}{n^4+n^2} = \dfrac{1}{2} + \dfrac{1}{20} + \dfrac{1}{90} + \cdots + \dfrac{1}{10,100} \approx 0.567975$. Now $\dfrac{1}{n^4+n^2} < \dfrac{1}{n^4}$, so using the reasoning and

notation of Example 5, the error is $R_{10} \le T_{10} = \displaystyle\sum_{n=11}^{\infty} \dfrac{1}{n^4} \le \int_{10}^{\infty} \dfrac{dx}{x^4} = \lim_{t\to\infty} \left[-\dfrac{x^{-3}}{3}\right]_{10}^{t} = \dfrac{1}{3000} = 0.000\overline{3}$.

35. $\displaystyle\sum_{n=1}^{10} \dfrac{1}{1+2^n} = \dfrac{1}{3} + \dfrac{1}{5} + \dfrac{1}{9} + \cdots + \dfrac{1}{1025} \approx 0.76352$. Now $\dfrac{1}{1+2^n} < \dfrac{1}{2^n}$, so the error is

$R_{10} \le T_{10} = \displaystyle\sum_{n=11}^{\infty} \dfrac{1}{2^n} = \dfrac{1/2^{11}}{1 - 1/2}$ (geometric series) ≈ 0.00098.

37. Since $\dfrac{d_n}{10^n} \le \dfrac{9}{10^n}$ for each n, and since $\displaystyle\sum_{n=1}^{\infty} \dfrac{9}{10^n}$ is a convergent geometric series ($|r| = \frac{1}{10} < 1$),

$0.d_1 d_2 d_3 \ldots = \displaystyle\sum_{n=1}^{\infty} \dfrac{d_n}{10^n}$ will always converge by the Comparison Test.

39. Since $\sum a_n$ converges, $\displaystyle\lim_{n \to \infty} a_n = 0$, so there exists N such that $|a_n - 0| < 1$ for all $n > N$ $\Rightarrow$ $0 \le a_n < 1$

for all $n > N$ $\Rightarrow$ $0 \le a_n^2 \le a_n$. Since $\sum a_n$ converges, so does $\sum a_n^2$ by the Comparison Test.

41. (a) Since $\displaystyle\lim_{n \to \infty} \dfrac{a_n}{b_n} = \infty$, there is an integer N such that $\dfrac{a_n}{b_n} > 1$ whenever $n > N$. (Take $M = 1$ in

Definition 12.1.5.) Then $a_n > b_n$ whenever $n > N$ and since $\sum b_n$ is divergent, $\sum a_n$ is also divergent by the
Comparison Test.

(b) (i) If $a_n = \dfrac{1}{\ln n}$ and $b_n = \dfrac{1}{n}$ for $n \ge 2$, then

$$\lim_{n \to \infty} \dfrac{a_n}{b_n} = \lim_{n \to \infty} \dfrac{n}{\ln n} = \lim_{x \to \infty} \dfrac{x}{\ln x} \overset{\text{H}}{=} \lim_{x \to \infty} \dfrac{1}{1/x} = \lim_{x \to \infty} x = \infty, \text{ so by part (a), } \sum_{n=2}^{\infty} \dfrac{1}{\ln n} \text{ is divergent.}$$

(ii) If $a_n = \dfrac{\ln n}{n}$ and $b_n = \dfrac{1}{n}$, then $\displaystyle\sum_{n=1}^{\infty} b_n$ is the divergent harmonic series and

$$\lim_{n \to \infty} \dfrac{a_n}{b_n} = \lim_{n \to \infty} \ln n = \lim_{x \to \infty} \ln x = \infty, \text{ so } \sum_{n=1}^{\infty} a_n \text{ diverges by part (a).}$$

43. $\displaystyle\lim_{n \to \infty} n a_n = \lim_{n \to \infty} \dfrac{a_n}{1/n}$, so we apply the Limit Comparison Test with $b_n = \dfrac{1}{n}$. Since $\displaystyle\lim_{n \to \infty} n a_n > 0$ we know that

either both series converge or both series diverge, and we also know that $\displaystyle\sum_{n=0}^{\infty} \dfrac{1}{n}$ diverges (p-series with $p = 1$).

Therefore, $\sum a_n$ must be divergent.

45. Yes. Since $\sum a_n$ is a convergent series with positive terms, $\displaystyle\lim_{n \to \infty} a_n = 0$ by Theorem 12.2.6, and

$\sum b_n = \sum \sin(a_n)$ is a series with positive terms (for large enough n). We have

$\displaystyle\lim_{n \to \infty} \dfrac{b_n}{a_n} = \lim_{n \to \infty} \dfrac{\sin(a_n)}{a_n} = 1 > 0$ by Theorem 3.5.2. Thus, $\sum b_n$ is also convergent by the Limit Comparison
Test.

12.5 Alternating Series

1. (a) An alternating series is a series whose terms are alternately positive and negative.

(b) An alternating series $\sum_{n=1}^{\infty} (-1)^{n-1} b_n$ converges if $0 < b_{n+1} \le b_n$ for all n and $\displaystyle\lim_{n \to \infty} b_n = 0$. (This is the
Alternating Series Test.)

(c) The error involved in using the partial sum s_n as an approximation to the total sum s is the remainder
$R_n = s - s_n$ and the size of the error is smaller than b_{n+1}; that is, $|R_n| \le b_{n+1}$. (This is the Alternating Series
Estimation Theorem.)

3. $\dfrac{4}{7} - \dfrac{4}{8} + \dfrac{4}{9} - \dfrac{4}{10} + \dfrac{4}{11} - \cdots = \displaystyle\sum_{n=1}^{\infty} (-1)^{n-1} \dfrac{4}{n+6}$. Now $b_n = \dfrac{4}{n+6} > 0$, $\{b_n\}$ is decreasing, and

$\displaystyle\lim_{n \to \infty} b_n = 0$, so the series converges by the Alternating Series Test.

5. $b_n = \dfrac{1}{\sqrt{n}} > 0$, $\{b_n\}$ is decreasing, and $\lim\limits_{n \to \infty} b_n = 0$, so the series $\sum\limits_{n=1}^{\infty} \dfrac{(-1)^{n-1}}{\sqrt{n}}$ converges by the Alternating Series Test.

7. $\sum\limits_{n=1}^{\infty} a_n = \sum\limits_{n=1}^{\infty}(-1)^n \dfrac{3n-1}{2n+1} = \sum\limits_{n=1}^{\infty}(-1)^n b_n$. Now $\lim\limits_{n \to \infty} b_n = \lim\limits_{n \to \infty} \dfrac{3 - 1/n}{2 + 1/n} = \dfrac{3}{2} \neq 0$. Since $\lim\limits_{n \to \infty} a_n \neq 0$ (in fact the limit does not exist), the series diverges by the Test for Divergence.

9. $b_n = \dfrac{1}{4n^2 + 1} > 0$, $\{b_n\}$ is decreasing, and $\lim\limits_{n \to \infty} b_n = 0$, so the series $\sum\limits_{n=1}^{\infty} \dfrac{(-1)^{n+1}}{4n^2 + 1}$ converges by the Alternating Series Test.

11. $b_n = \dfrac{n^2}{n^3 + 4} > 0$ for $n \geq 1$. $\{b_n\}$ is decreasing for $n \geq 2$ since

$$\left(\dfrac{x^2}{x^3 + 4}\right)' = \dfrac{(x^3 + 4)(2x) - x^2(3x^2)}{(x^3 + 4)^2} = \dfrac{x(2x^3 + 8 - 3x^3)}{(x^3 + 4)^2} = \dfrac{x(8 - x^3)}{(x^3 + 4)^2} < 0 \text{ for } x > 2. \text{ Also,}$$

$\lim\limits_{n \to \infty} b_n = \lim\limits_{n \to \infty} \dfrac{1/n}{1 + 4/n^3} = 0$. Thus, the series $\sum\limits_{n=1}^{\infty}(-1)^{n+1} \dfrac{n^2}{n^3 + 4}$ converges by the Alternating Series Test.

13. $\sum\limits_{n=2}^{\infty}(-1)^n \dfrac{n}{\ln n}$. $\lim\limits_{n \to \infty} \dfrac{n}{\ln n} = \lim\limits_{x \to \infty} \dfrac{x}{\ln x} \overset{\text{H}}{=} \lim\limits_{x \to \infty} \dfrac{1}{1/x} = \infty$, so the series diverges by the Test for Divergence.

15. $\sum\limits_{n=1}^{\infty} \dfrac{\cos n\pi}{n^{3/4}} = \sum\limits_{n=1}^{\infty} \dfrac{(-1)^n}{n^{3/4}}$. $b_n = \dfrac{1}{n^{3/4}}$ is decreasing and positive and $\lim\limits_{n \to \infty} \dfrac{1}{n^{3/4}} = 0$, so the series converges by the Alternating Series Test.

17. $\sum\limits_{n=1}^{\infty}(-1)^n \sin \dfrac{\pi}{n}$. $b_n = \sin \dfrac{\pi}{n} > 0$ for $n \geq 2$ and $\sin \dfrac{\pi}{n} \geq \sin \dfrac{\pi}{n+1}$, and $\lim\limits_{n \to \infty} \sin \dfrac{\pi}{n} = \sin 0 = 0$, so the series converges by the Alternating Series Test.

19. $\dfrac{n^n}{n!} = \dfrac{n \cdot n \cdot \dots \cdot n}{1 \cdot 2 \cdot \dots \cdot n} \geq n \;\Rightarrow\; \lim\limits_{n \to \infty} \dfrac{n^n}{n!} = \infty \;\Rightarrow\; \lim\limits_{n \to \infty} \dfrac{(-1)^n n^n}{n!}$ does not exist. So the series diverges by the Test for Divergence.

21.

n	a_n	s_n
1	1	1
2	-0.35355	0.64645
3	0.19245	0.83890
4	-0.125	0.71390
5	0.08944	0.80334
6	-0.06804	0.73530
7	0.05399	0.78929
8	-0.04419	0.74510
9	0.03704	0.78214
10	-0.03162	0.75051

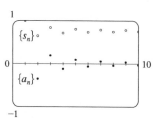

By the Alternating Series Estimation Theorem, the error in the approximation $\sum\limits_{n=1}^{\infty} \dfrac{(-1)^{n-1}}{n^{3/2}} \approx 0.75051$ is

$|s - s_{10}| \leq b_{11} = 1/(11)^{3/2} \approx 0.0275$ (to four decimal places, rounded up).

23. The series $\sum_{n=1}^{\infty} (-1)^{n-1} \dfrac{1}{n^2}$ satisfies (i) of the Alternating Series Test because $\dfrac{1}{(n+1)^2} < \dfrac{1}{n^2}$ and

(ii) $\lim\limits_{n \to \infty} \dfrac{1}{n^2} = 0$, so the series is convergent. Now $b_{10} = \dfrac{1}{10^2} = 0.01$ and $b_{11} = \dfrac{1}{11^2} = \dfrac{1}{121} \approx 0.008 < 0.01$, so

by the Alternating Series Estimation Theorem, $n = 10$. (That is, since the 11th term is less than the desired error, we need to add the first 10 terms to get the sum to the desired accuracy.)

25. The series $\sum_{n=1}^{\infty} \dfrac{(-2)^n}{n!} = \sum_{n=1}^{\infty} (-1)^n \dfrac{2^n}{n!}$ satisfies (i) of the Alternating Series Test

because $b_{n+1} = \dfrac{2^{n+1}}{(n+1)!} = \dfrac{2 \cdot 2^n}{(n+1)n!} = \dfrac{2}{n+1} \cdot \dfrac{2^n}{n!} = \dfrac{2}{n+1} \cdot b_n \le b_n$ and (ii)

$\lim\limits_{n \to \infty} \dfrac{2^n}{n!} = \dfrac{2}{n} \cdot \dfrac{2}{n-1} \cdot \cdots \cdot \dfrac{2}{2} \cdot \dfrac{2}{1} = 0$, so the series is convergent. Now $b_7 = 2^7/7! \approx 0.025 > 0.01$ and

$b_8 = 2^8/8! \approx 0.006 < 0.01$, so by the Alternating Series Estimation Theorem, $n = 7$. (That is, since the 8th term is less than the desired error, we need to add the first 7 terms to get the sum to the desired accuracy.)

27. $b_7 = \dfrac{1}{7^5} = \dfrac{1}{16{,}807} \approx 0.000\,059\,5$, so

$\sum_{n=1}^{\infty} \dfrac{(-1)^{n+1}}{n^5} \approx s_6 = \sum_{n=1}^{6} \dfrac{(-1)^{n+1}}{n^5} = 1 - \frac{1}{32} + \frac{1}{243} - \frac{1}{1024} + \frac{1}{3125} - \frac{1}{7776} \approx 0.972\,080$. Adding b_7 to s_6 does

not change the fourth decimal place of s_6, so the sum of the series, correct to four decimal places, is 0.9721.

29. $b_7 = \dfrac{7^2}{10^7} = 0.000\,004\,9$, so

$\sum_{n=1}^{\infty} \dfrac{(-1)^{n-1}n^2}{10^n} \approx s_6 = \sum_{n=1}^{6} \dfrac{(-1)^{n-1}n^2}{10^n} = \frac{1}{10} - \frac{4}{100} + \frac{9}{1000} - \frac{16}{10{,}000} + \frac{25}{100{,}000} - \frac{36}{1{,}000{,}000} = 0.067\,614$.

Adding b_7 to s_6 does not change the fourth decimal place of s_6, so the sum of the series, correct to four decimal places, is 0.0676.

31. $\sum_{n=1}^{\infty} \dfrac{(-1)^{n-1}}{n} = 1 - \frac{1}{2} + \frac{1}{3} - \frac{1}{4} + \cdots + \frac{1}{49} - \frac{1}{50} + \frac{1}{51} - \frac{1}{52} + \cdots$. The 50th partial sum of this series is an

underestimate, since $\sum_{n=1}^{\infty} \dfrac{(-1)^{n-1}}{n} = s_{50} + \left(\dfrac{1}{51} - \dfrac{1}{52} \right) + \left(\dfrac{1}{53} - \dfrac{1}{54} \right) + \cdots$, and the terms in parentheses are

all positive. The result can be seen geometrically in Figure 1.

33. Clearly $b_n = \dfrac{1}{n+p}$ is decreasing and eventually positive and $\lim\limits_{n \to \infty} b_n = 0$ for any p. So the series converges (by

the Alternating Series Test) for any p for which every b_n is defined, that is, $n + p \ne 0$ for $n \ge 1$, or p is not a negative integer.

35. $\sum b_{2n} = \sum 1/(2n)^2$ clearly converges (by comparison with the p-series for $p = 2$). So

suppose that $\sum (-1)^{n-1} b_n$ converges. Then by Theorem 12.2.8(ii), so does

$\sum \left[(-1)^{n-1} b_n + b_n \right] = 2 \left(1 + \frac{1}{3} + \frac{1}{5} + \cdots \right) = 2 \sum \dfrac{1}{2n-1}$. But this diverges by comparison with the

harmonic series, a contradiction. Therefore, $\sum (-1)^{n-1} b_n$ must diverge. The Alternating Series Test does not apply since $\{b_n\}$ is not decreasing.

12.6 Absolute Convergence and the Ratio and Root Tests

1. (a) Since $\lim\limits_{n\to\infty}\left|\dfrac{a_{n+1}}{a_n}\right| = 8 > 1$, part (b) of the Ratio Test tells us that the series $\sum a_n$ is divergent.

(b) Since $\lim\limits_{n\to\infty}\left|\dfrac{a_{n+1}}{a_n}\right| = 0.8 < 1$, part (a) of the Ratio Test tells us that the series $\sum a_n$ is absolutely convergent (and therefore convergent).

(c) Since $\lim\limits_{n\to\infty}\left|\dfrac{a_{n+1}}{a_n}\right| = 1$, the Ratio Test fails and the series $\sum a_n$ might converge or it might diverge.

3. $\displaystyle\sum_{n=0}^{\infty}\dfrac{(-10)^n}{n!}$. Using the Ratio Test, $\lim\limits_{n\to\infty}\left|\dfrac{a_{n+1}}{a_n}\right| = \lim\limits_{n\to\infty}\left|\dfrac{(-10)^{n+1}}{(n+1)!}\cdot\dfrac{n!}{(-10)^n}\right| = \lim\limits_{n\to\infty}\left|\dfrac{-10}{n+1}\right| = 0 < 1$, so the series is absolutely convergent.

5. $\displaystyle\sum_{n=1}^{\infty}\dfrac{(-1)^{n+1}}{\sqrt[4]{n}}$ converges by the Alternating Series Test, but $\displaystyle\sum_{n=1}^{\infty}\dfrac{1}{\sqrt[4]{n}}$ is a divergent p-series $\left(p = \tfrac{1}{4} \leq 1\right)$, so the given series is conditionally convergent.

7. $\lim\limits_{n\to\infty}|a_n| = \lim\limits_{n\to\infty}\dfrac{n}{5+n} = \lim\limits_{n\to\infty}\dfrac{1}{5/n+1} = 1$, so $\lim\limits_{n\to\infty}a_n \neq 0$. Thus, the given series is divergent by the Test for Divergence.

9. $\lim\limits_{n\to\infty}\left|\dfrac{a_{n+1}}{a_n}\right| = \lim\limits_{n\to\infty}\dfrac{1/(2n+2)!}{1/(2n)!} = \lim\limits_{n\to\infty}\dfrac{(2n)!}{(2n+2)!} = \lim\limits_{n\to\infty}\dfrac{(2n)!}{(2n+2)(2n+1)(2n)!}$

$= \lim\limits_{n\to\infty}\dfrac{1}{(2n+2)(2n+1)} = 0 < 1$, so the series $\displaystyle\sum_{n=1}^{\infty}\dfrac{1}{(2n)!}$ is absolutely convergent by the Ratio Test. Of course, absolute convergence is the same as convergence for this series, since all of its terms are positive.

11. Since $0 \leq \dfrac{e^{1/n}}{n^3} \leq \dfrac{e}{n^3} = e\left(\dfrac{1}{n^3}\right)$ and $\displaystyle\sum_{n=1}^{\infty}\dfrac{1}{n^3}$ is a convergent p-series $(p = 3 > 1)$, $\displaystyle\sum_{n=1}^{\infty}\dfrac{e^{1/n}}{n^3}$ converges, and so $\displaystyle\sum_{n=1}^{\infty}\dfrac{(-1)^n e^{1/n}}{n^3}$ is absolutely convergent.

13. $\lim\limits_{n\to\infty}\left|\dfrac{a_{n+1}}{a_n}\right| = \lim\limits_{n\to\infty}\left[\dfrac{(n+1)\,3^{n+1}}{4^n}\cdot\dfrac{4^{n-1}}{n\cdot 3^n}\right] = \lim\limits_{n\to\infty}\left(\dfrac{3}{4}\cdot\dfrac{n+1}{n}\right) = \dfrac{3}{4} < 1$, so the series $\displaystyle\sum_{n=1}^{\infty}\dfrac{n(-3)^n}{4^{n-1}}$ is absolutely convergent by the Ratio Test.

15. $\lim\limits_{n\to\infty}\left|\dfrac{a_{n+1}}{a_n}\right| = \lim\limits_{n\to\infty}\left[\dfrac{10^{n+1}}{(n+2)\,4^{2n+3}}\cdot\dfrac{(n+1)\,4^{2n+1}}{10^n}\right] = \lim\limits_{n\to\infty}\left(\dfrac{10}{4^2}\cdot\dfrac{n+1}{n+2}\right) = \dfrac{5}{8} < 1$, so the series $\displaystyle\sum_{n=1}^{\infty}\dfrac{10^n}{(n+1)4^{2n+1}}$ is absolutely convergent by the Ratio Test. Since the terms of this series are positive, absolute convergence is the same as convergence.

17. $\displaystyle\sum_{n=2}^{\infty} \frac{(-1)^n}{\ln n}$ converges by the Alternating Series Test since $\displaystyle\lim_{n\to\infty} \frac{1}{\ln n} = 0$ and $\left\{\dfrac{1}{\ln n}\right\}$ is decreasing. Now

$\ln n < n$, so $\dfrac{1}{\ln n} > \dfrac{1}{n}$, and since $\displaystyle\sum_{n=2}^{\infty} \frac{1}{n}$ is the divergent (partial) harmonic series, $\displaystyle\sum_{n=2}^{\infty} \frac{1}{\ln n}$ diverges by the

Comparison Test. Thus, $\displaystyle\sum_{n=2}^{\infty} \frac{(-1)^n}{\ln n}$ is conditionally convergent.

19. $\dfrac{|\cos(n\pi/3)|}{n!} \le \dfrac{1}{n!}$ and $\displaystyle\sum_{n=1}^{\infty} \frac{1}{n!}$ converges (use the Ratio Test or the result of Exercise 12.4.29), so the series

$\displaystyle\sum_{n=1}^{\infty} \frac{\cos(n\pi/3)}{n!}$ converges absolutely by the Comparison Test.

21. $\displaystyle\lim_{n\to\infty} \sqrt[n]{|a_n|} = \lim_{n\to\infty} \left(\frac{n^n}{3^{1+3n}}\right)^{1/n} = \lim_{n\to\infty} \frac{n}{\sqrt[n]{3} \cdot 3^3} = \infty$, so the series $\displaystyle\sum_{n=1}^{\infty} \frac{n^n}{3^{1+3n}}$ is divergent by the Root Test.

$Or:$ $\displaystyle\lim_{n\to\infty} \left|\frac{a_{n+1}}{a_n}\right| = \lim_{n\to\infty}\left[\frac{(n+1)^{n+1}}{3^{4+3n}} \cdot \frac{3^{1+3n}}{n^n}\right] = \lim_{n\to\infty}\left[\frac{1}{3^3} \cdot \left(\frac{n+1}{n}\right)^n (n+1)\right]$

$\displaystyle = \frac{1}{27}\lim_{n\to\infty}\left(1+\frac{1}{n}\right)^n \lim_{n\to\infty}(n+1) = \tfrac{1}{27}e \lim_{n\to\infty}(n+1) = \infty,$

so the series is divergent by the Ratio Test.

23. $\displaystyle\lim_{n\to\infty} \sqrt[n]{|a_n|} = \lim_{n\to\infty} \frac{n^2+1}{2n^2+1} = \lim_{n\to\infty} \frac{1+1/n^2}{2+1/n^2} = \frac{1}{2} < 1$, so the series $\displaystyle\sum_{n=1}^{\infty}\left(\frac{n^2+1}{2n^2+1}\right)^n$ is absolutely

convergent by the Root Test.

25. Use the Ratio Test with the series $1 - \dfrac{1\cdot3}{3!} + \dfrac{1\cdot3\cdot5}{5!} - \dfrac{1\cdot3\cdot5\cdot7}{7!} + \cdots + (-1)^{n-1}\dfrac{1\cdot3\cdot5\cdot\cdots\cdot(2n-1)}{(2n-1)!} + \cdots$

$\displaystyle = \sum_{n=1}^{\infty} (-1)^{n-1}\frac{1\cdot3\cdot5\cdot\cdots\cdot(2n-1)}{(2n-1)!}.$

$\displaystyle\lim_{n\to\infty}\left|\frac{a_{n+1}}{a_n}\right| = \lim_{n\to\infty}\left|\frac{(-1)^n \cdot 1\cdot3\cdot5\cdot\cdots\cdot(2n-1)[2(n+1)-1]}{[2(n+1)-1]!} \cdot \frac{(2n-1)!}{(-1)^{n-1}\cdot1\cdot3\cdot5\cdot\cdots\cdot(2n-1)}\right|$

$\displaystyle = \lim_{n\to\infty}\left|\frac{(-1)(2n+1)(2n-1)!}{(2n+1)(2n)(2n-1)!}\right|$

$\displaystyle = \lim_{n\to\infty}\frac{1}{2n} = 0 < 1,$

so the given series is absolutely convergent and therefore convergent.

27. $\displaystyle\sum_{n=1}^{\infty} \frac{2\cdot4\cdot6\cdot\cdots\cdot(2n)}{n!} = \sum_{n=1}^{\infty} \frac{(2\cdot1)\cdot(2\cdot2)\cdot(2\cdot3)\cdot\cdots\cdot(2\cdot n)}{n!} = \sum_{n=1}^{\infty}\frac{2^n n!}{n!} = \sum_{n=1}^{\infty} 2^n$, which diverges by the
Test for Divergence since $\displaystyle\lim_{n\to\infty} 2^n = \infty$.

29. By the recursive definition, $\displaystyle\lim_{n\to\infty}\left|\frac{a_{n+1}}{a_n}\right| = \lim_{n\to\infty}\left|\frac{5n+1}{4n+3}\right| = \frac{5}{4} > 1$, so the series diverges by the Ratio Test.

31. (a) $\lim\limits_{n\to\infty}\left|\dfrac{1/(n+1)^3}{1/n^3}\right| = \lim\limits_{n\to\infty}\dfrac{n^3}{(n+1)^3} = \lim\limits_{n\to\infty}\dfrac{1}{(1+1/n)^3} = 1$. Inconclusive.

(b) $\lim\limits_{n\to\infty}\left|\dfrac{(n+1)}{2^{n+1}}\cdot\dfrac{2^n}{n}\right| = \lim\limits_{n\to\infty}\dfrac{n+1}{2n} = \lim\limits_{n\to\infty}\left(\dfrac{1}{2}+\dfrac{1}{2n}\right) = \dfrac{1}{2}$. Conclusive (convergent).

(c) $\lim\limits_{n\to\infty}\left|\dfrac{(-3)^n}{\sqrt{n+1}}\cdot\dfrac{\sqrt{n}}{(-3)^{n-1}}\right| = 3\lim\limits_{n\to\infty}\sqrt{\dfrac{n}{n+1}} = 3\lim\limits_{n\to\infty}\sqrt{\dfrac{1}{1+1/n}} = 3$. Conclusive (divergent).

(d) $\lim\limits_{n\to\infty}\left|\dfrac{\sqrt{n+1}}{1+(n+1)^2}\cdot\dfrac{1+n^2}{\sqrt{n}}\right| = \lim\limits_{n\to\infty}\left[\sqrt{1+\dfrac{1}{n}}\cdot\dfrac{1/n^2+1}{1/n^2+(1+1/n)^2}\right] = 1$. Inconclusive.

33. (a) $\lim\limits_{n\to\infty}\left|\dfrac{a_{n+1}}{a_n}\right| = \lim\limits_{n\to\infty}\left|\dfrac{x^{n+1}}{(n+1)!}\cdot\dfrac{n!}{x^n}\right| = \lim\limits_{n\to\infty}\left|\dfrac{x}{n+1}\right| = |x|\lim\limits_{n\to\infty}\dfrac{1}{n+1} = |x|\cdot 0 = 0 < 1$, so by the Ratio

Test the series $\displaystyle\sum_{n=0}^{\infty}\dfrac{x^n}{n!}$ converges for all x.

(b) Since the series of part (a) always converges, we must have $\lim\limits_{n\to\infty}\dfrac{x^n}{n!} = 0$ by Theorem 12.2.6.

35. (a) $s_5 = \displaystyle\sum_{n=1}^{5}\dfrac{1}{n2^n} = \dfrac{1}{2}+\dfrac{1}{8}+\dfrac{1}{24}+\dfrac{1}{64}+\dfrac{1}{160} = \dfrac{661}{960} \approx 0.68854$. Now the ratios

$r_n = \dfrac{a_{n+1}}{a_n} = \dfrac{n2^n}{(n+1)2^{n+1}} = \dfrac{n}{2(n+1)}$ form an increasing sequence, since

$r_{n+1}-r_n = \dfrac{n+1}{2(n+2)} - \dfrac{n}{2(n+1)} = \dfrac{(n+1)^2-n(n+2)}{2(n+1)(n+2)} = \dfrac{1}{2(n+1)(n+2)} > 0$. So by Exercise 34(b),

the error in using s_5 is $R_5 \le \dfrac{a_6}{1-\lim\limits_{n\to\infty}r_n} = \dfrac{1/(6\cdot 2^6)}{1-1/2} = \dfrac{1}{192} \approx 0.00521$.

(b) The error in using s_n as an approximation to the sum is $R_n = \dfrac{a_{n+1}}{1-\frac{1}{2}} = \dfrac{2}{(n+1)2^{n+1}}$. We want

$R_n < 0.00005 \iff \dfrac{1}{(n+1)2^n} < 0.00005 \iff (n+1)2^n > 20{,}000$. To find such an n we can use trial

and error or a graph. We calculate $(11+1)2^{11} = 24{,}576$, so $s_{11} = \displaystyle\sum_{n=1}^{11}\dfrac{1}{n2^n} \approx 0.693109$ is within 0.00005 of

the actual sum.

37. Summing the inequalities $-|a_i| \le a_i \le |a_i|$ for $i = 1, 2, \ldots, n$, we get $-\sum_{i=1}^{n}|a_i| \le \sum_{i=1}^{n}a_i \le \sum_{i=1}^{n}|a_i|$

$\Rightarrow\ -\lim\limits_{n\to\infty}\sum_{i=1}^{n}|a_i| \le \lim\limits_{n\to\infty}\sum_{i=1}^{n}a_i \le \lim\limits_{n\to\infty}\sum_{i=1}^{n}|a_i|\ \Rightarrow\ -\sum_{n=1}^{\infty}|a_n| \le \sum_{n=1}^{\infty}a_n \le \sum_{n=1}^{\infty}|a_n|\ \Rightarrow$

$\left|\sum_{n=1}^{\infty}a_n\right| \le \sum_{n=1}^{\infty}|a_n|$.

39. (a) Since $\sum a_n$ is absolutely convergent, and since $|a_n^+| \le |a_n|$ and $|a_n^-| \le |a_n|$ (because a_n^+ and a_n^- each equal

either a_n or 0), we conclude by the Comparison Test that both $\sum a_n^+$ and $\sum a_n^-$ must be absolutely convergent.
(Or use Theorem 12.2.8.)

(b) We will show by contradiction that both $\sum a_n^+$ and $\sum a_n^-$ must diverge. For suppose that

$\sum a_n^+$ converged. Then so would $\sum\left(a_n^+ - \frac{1}{2}a_n\right)$ by Theorem 12.2.8. But

$\sum\left(a_n^+ - \frac{1}{2}a_n\right) = \sum\left[\frac{1}{2}\left(a_n + |a_n|\right) - \frac{1}{2}a_n\right] = \frac{1}{2}\sum|a_n|$, which diverges because $\sum a_n$ is only conditionally

convergent. Hence, $\sum a_n^+$ can't converge. Similarly, neither can $\sum a_n^-$.

12.7 Strategy for Testing Series

1. $\lim\limits_{n\to\infty} a_n = \lim\limits_{n\to\infty} \dfrac{n^2-1}{n^2+1} = \lim\limits_{n\to\infty} \dfrac{1-1/n^2}{1+1/n} = 1 \neq 0$, so the series $\sum\limits_{n=1}^{\infty} \dfrac{n^2-1}{n^2+1}$ diverges by the Test for Divergence.

3. $\dfrac{1}{n^2+n} < \dfrac{1}{n^2}$ for all $n \geq 1$, so $\sum\limits_{n=1}^{\infty} \dfrac{1}{n^2+n}$ converges by the Comparison Test with $\sum\limits_{n=1}^{\infty} \dfrac{1}{n^2}$, a p-series that converges because $p = 2 > 1$.

5. $\lim\limits_{n\to\infty} \left| \dfrac{a_{n+1}}{a_n} \right| = \lim\limits_{n\to\infty} \left| \dfrac{(-3)^{n+2}}{2^{3(n+1)}} \cdot \dfrac{2^{3n}}{(-3)^{n+1}} \right| = \lim\limits_{n\to\infty} \left| \dfrac{-3 \cdot 2^{3n}}{2^{3n} \cdot 2^3} \right| = \lim\limits_{n\to\infty} \dfrac{3}{2^3} = \dfrac{3}{8} < 1$, so the series

$\sum\limits_{n=1}^{\infty} \dfrac{(-3)^{n+1}}{2^{3n}}$ is absolutely convergent by the Ratio Test.

7. Let $f(x) = \dfrac{1}{x\sqrt{\ln x}}$. Then f is positive, continuous, and decreasing on $[2, \infty)$, so we can apply the Integral Test.

Since $\displaystyle\int \dfrac{1}{x\sqrt{\ln x}}\, dx \quad \begin{bmatrix} u = \ln x, \\ du = dx/x \end{bmatrix} = \int u^{-1/2}\, du = 2u^{1/2} + C = 2\sqrt{\ln x} + C$, we find

$\displaystyle\int_2^\infty \dfrac{dx}{x\sqrt{\ln x}} = \lim\limits_{t\to\infty} \int_2^t \dfrac{dx}{x\sqrt{\ln x}} = \lim\limits_{t\to\infty} \left[2\sqrt{\ln x} \right]_2^t = \lim\limits_{t\to\infty} \left(2\sqrt{\ln t} - 2\sqrt{\ln 2} \right) = \infty$. Since the integral

diverges, the given series $\sum\limits_{n=2}^{\infty} \dfrac{1}{n\sqrt{\ln n}}$ diverges.

9. $\sum\limits_{k=1}^{\infty} k^2 e^{-k} = \sum\limits_{k=1}^{\infty} \dfrac{k^2}{e^k}$. Using the Ratio Test, we get

$\lim\limits_{k\to\infty} \left| \dfrac{a_{k+1}}{a_k} \right| = \lim\limits_{k\to\infty} \left| \dfrac{(k+1)^2}{e^{k+1}} \cdot \dfrac{e^k}{k^2} \right| = \lim\limits_{k\to\infty} \left[\left(\dfrac{k+1}{k} \right)^2 \cdot \dfrac{1}{e} \right] = 1^2 \cdot \dfrac{1}{e} = \dfrac{1}{e} < 1$, so the series converges.

11. $b_n = \dfrac{1}{n\ln n} > 0$ for $n \geq 2$, $\{b_n\}$ is decreasing, and $\lim\limits_{n\to\infty} b_n = 0$, so the given series $\sum\limits_{n=2}^{\infty} \dfrac{(-1)^{n+1}}{n\ln n}$ converges by the Alternating Series Test.

13. $\lim\limits_{n\to\infty} \left| \dfrac{a_{n+1}}{a_n} \right| = \lim\limits_{n\to\infty} \left| \dfrac{3^{n+1}(n+1)^2}{(n+1)!} \cdot \dfrac{n!}{3^n n^2} \right| = \lim\limits_{n\to\infty} \left[\dfrac{3(n+1)^2}{(n+1)n^2} \right] = 3 \lim\limits_{n\to\infty} \dfrac{n+1}{n^2} = 0 < 1$, so the series

$\sum\limits_{n=1}^{\infty} \dfrac{3^n n^2}{n!}$ converges by the Ratio Test.

15. $\lim\limits_{n\to\infty} \left| \dfrac{a_{n+1}}{a_n} \right| = \lim\limits_{n\to\infty} \left| \dfrac{(n+1)!}{2\cdot 5\cdot 8\cdot\cdots\cdot(3n+2)[3(n+1)+2]} \cdot \dfrac{2\cdot 5\cdot 8\cdot\cdots\cdot(3n+2)}{n!} \right|$

$= \lim\limits_{n\to\infty} \dfrac{n+1}{3n+5} = \dfrac{1}{3} < 1$

so the series $\sum\limits_{n=0}^{\infty} \dfrac{n!}{2\cdot 5\cdot 8\cdot\cdots\cdot(3n+2)}$ converges by the Ratio Test.

17. $\lim\limits_{n\to\infty} 2^{1/n} = 2^0 = 1$, so $\lim\limits_{n\to\infty} (-1)^n 2^{1/n}$ does not exist and the series $\sum\limits_{n=1}^{\infty} (-1)^n 2^{1/n}$ diverges by the Test for Divergence.

19. Let $f(x) = \dfrac{\ln x}{\sqrt{x}}$. Then $f'(x) = \dfrac{2 - \ln x}{2x^{3/2}} < 0$ when $\ln x > 2$ or $x > e^2$, so $\dfrac{\ln n}{\sqrt{n}}$ is decreasing for $n > e^2$.

By l'Hospital's Rule, $\lim\limits_{n\to\infty} \dfrac{\ln n}{\sqrt{n}} = \lim\limits_{n\to\infty} \dfrac{1/n}{1/(2\sqrt{n})} = \lim\limits_{n\to\infty} \dfrac{2}{\sqrt{n}} = 0$, so the series $\sum\limits_{n=1}^{\infty} (-1)^n \dfrac{\ln n}{\sqrt{n}}$ converges by the Alternating Series Test.

21. $\sum\limits_{n=1}^{\infty} \dfrac{(-2)^{2n}}{n^n} = \sum\limits_{n=1}^{\infty} \left(\dfrac{4}{n}\right)^n$. $\lim\limits_{n\to\infty} \sqrt[n]{|a_n|} = \lim\limits_{n\to\infty} \dfrac{4}{n} = 0 < 1$, so the given series is absolutely convergent by the Root Test.

23. Using the Limit Comparison Test with $a_n = \tan\left(\dfrac{1}{n}\right)$ and $b_n = \dfrac{1}{n}$, we have

$$\lim_{n\to\infty} \frac{a_n}{b_n} = \lim_{n\to\infty} \frac{\tan(1/n)}{1/n} = \lim_{x\to\infty} \frac{\tan(1/x)}{1/x} \overset{\text{H}}{=} \lim_{x\to\infty} \frac{\sec^2(1/x)\cdot(-1/x^2)}{-1/x^2} = \lim_{x\to\infty} \sec^2(1/x) = 1^2 = 1 > 0.$$

Since $\sum_{n=1}^{\infty} b_n$ is the divergent harmonic series, $\sum_{n=1}^{\infty} a_n$ is also divergent.

25. Use the Ratio Test. $\lim\limits_{n\to\infty} \left|\dfrac{a_{n+1}}{a_n}\right| = \lim\limits_{n\to\infty} \left|\dfrac{(n+1)!}{e^{(n+1)^2}} \cdot \dfrac{e^{n^2}}{n!}\right| = \lim\limits_{n\to\infty} \dfrac{(n+1)n!\cdot e^{n^2}}{e^{n^2+2n+1}n!} = \lim\limits_{n\to\infty} \dfrac{n+1}{e^{2n+1}} = 0 < 1$, so

$$\sum_{n=1}^{\infty} \frac{n!}{e^{n^2}} \text{ converges.}$$

27. $\displaystyle\int_2^{\infty} \dfrac{\ln x}{x^2}\,dx = \lim\limits_{t\to\infty} \left[-\dfrac{\ln x}{x} - \dfrac{1}{x}\right]_1^t$ (using integration by parts) $\overset{\text{H}}{=} 1$. So $\sum\limits_{n=1}^{\infty} \dfrac{\ln n}{n^2}$ converges by the Integral Test,

and since $\dfrac{k\ln k}{(k+1)^3} < \dfrac{k\ln k}{k^3} = \dfrac{\ln k}{k^2}$, the given series $\sum\limits_{k=1}^{\infty} \dfrac{k\ln k}{(k+1)^3}$ converges by the Comparison Test.

29. $0 < \dfrac{\tan^{-1} n}{n^{3/2}} < \dfrac{\pi/2}{n^{3/2}}$. $\sum\limits_{n=1}^{\infty} \dfrac{\pi/2}{n^{3/2}} = \dfrac{\pi}{2}\sum\limits_{n=1}^{\infty} \dfrac{1}{n^{3/2}}$ which is a convergent p-series $(p = \tfrac{3}{2} > 1)$, so

$$\sum_{n=1}^{\infty} \frac{\tan^{-1} n}{n^{3/2}} \text{ converges by the Comparison Test.}$$

31. $\lim\limits_{k\to\infty} a_k = \lim\limits_{k\to\infty} \dfrac{5^k}{3^k + 4^k} = [\text{divide by } 4^k] \lim\limits_{k\to\infty} \dfrac{(5/4)^k}{(3/4)^k + 1} = \infty$ since $\lim\limits_{k\to\infty} \left(\dfrac{3}{4}\right)^k = 0$ and $\lim\limits_{k\to\infty} \left(\dfrac{5}{4}\right)^k = \infty$.

Thus, $\sum\limits_{k=1}^{\infty} \dfrac{5^k}{3^k + 4^k}$ diverges by the Test for Divergence.

33. Let $a_n = \dfrac{\sin(1/n)}{\sqrt{n}}$ and $b_n = \dfrac{1}{n\sqrt{n}}$. Then $\lim\limits_{n\to\infty} \dfrac{a_n}{b_n} = \lim\limits_{n\to\infty} \dfrac{\sin(1/n)}{1/n} = 1 > 0$, so $\sum\limits_{n=1}^{\infty} \dfrac{\sin(1/n)}{\sqrt{n}}$ converges by

limit comparison with the convergent p-series $\sum\limits_{n=1}^{\infty} \dfrac{1}{n^{3/2}}$ $(p = 3/2 > 1)$.

35. $\lim\limits_{n\to\infty} \sqrt[n]{|a_n|} = \lim\limits_{n\to\infty} \left(\dfrac{n}{n+1}\right)^{n^2/n} = \lim\limits_{n\to\infty} \dfrac{1}{[(n+1)/n]^n} = \dfrac{1}{\lim\limits_{n\to\infty}(1+1/n)^n} = \dfrac{1}{e} < 1$, so the series

$$\sum_{n=1}^{\infty} \left(\frac{n}{n+1}\right)^{n^2} \text{ converges by the Root Test.}$$

37. $\lim\limits_{n\to\infty} \sqrt[n]{|a_n|} = \lim\limits_{n\to\infty} \left(2^{1/n} - 1\right) = 1 - 1 = 0 < 1$, so the series $\sum\limits_{n=1}^{\infty} \left(\sqrt[n]{2} - 1\right)^n$ converges by the Root Test.

12.8 Power Series

1. A power series is a series of the form $\sum_{n=0}^{\infty} c_n x^n = c_0 + c_1 x + c_2 x^2 + c_3 x^3 + \cdots$, where x is a variable and the c_n's are constants called the coefficients of the series.

More generally, a series of the form $\sum_{n=0}^{\infty} c_n (x-a)^n = c_0 + c_1(x-a) + c_2(x-a)^2 + \cdots$ is called a power series in $(x-a)$ or a power series centered at a or a power series about a, where a is a constant.

3. If $a_n = \dfrac{x^n}{\sqrt{n}}$, then $\lim\limits_{n \to \infty} \left| \dfrac{a_{n+1}}{a_n} \right| = \lim\limits_{n \to \infty} \left| \dfrac{x^{n+1}}{\sqrt{n+1}} \cdot \dfrac{\sqrt{n}}{x^n} \right| = \lim\limits_{n \to \infty} \left| \dfrac{x}{\sqrt{n+1}/\sqrt{n}} \right| = \lim\limits_{n \to \infty} \dfrac{|x|}{\sqrt{1+1/n}} = |x|$.

By the Ratio Test, the series $\displaystyle\sum_{n=1}^{\infty} \dfrac{x^n}{\sqrt{n}}$ converges when $|x| < 1$, so the radius of convergence $R = 1$. Now we'll

check the endpoints, that is, $x = \pm 1$. When $x = 1$, the series $\displaystyle\sum_{n=1}^{\infty} \dfrac{1}{\sqrt{n}}$ diverges because it is a p-series with

$p = \frac{1}{2} \le 1$. When $x = -1$, the series $\displaystyle\sum_{n=1}^{\infty} \dfrac{(-1)^n}{\sqrt{n}}$ converges by the Alternating Series Test. Thus, the interval of

convergence is $I = [-1, 1)$.

5. If $a_n = \dfrac{(-1)^{n-1} x^n}{n^3}$, then $\lim\limits_{n \to \infty} \left| \dfrac{a_{n+1}}{a_n} \right| = \lim\limits_{n \to \infty} \left| \dfrac{(-1)^n x^{n+1}}{(n+1)^3} \cdot \dfrac{n^3}{(-1)^{n-1} x^n} \right| = \lim\limits_{n \to \infty} \left| \dfrac{(-1) x n^3}{(n+1)^3} \right|$

$= \lim\limits_{n \to \infty} \left[\left(\dfrac{n}{n+1} \right)^3 |x| \right] = 1^3 \cdot |x| = |x|$. By the Ratio Test, the series $\displaystyle\sum_{n=1}^{\infty} \dfrac{(-1)^{n-1} x^n}{n^3}$ converges when $|x| < 1$,

so the radius of convergence $R = 1$. Now we'll check the endpoints, that is, $x = \pm 1$. When $x = 1$, the series

$\displaystyle\sum_{n=1}^{\infty} \dfrac{(-1)^{n-1}}{n^3}$ converges by the Alternating Series Test. When $x = -1$, the series

$\displaystyle\sum_{n=1}^{\infty} \dfrac{(-1)^{n-1}(-1)^n}{n^3} = -\displaystyle\sum_{n=1}^{\infty} \dfrac{1}{n^3}$ converges because it is a constant multiple of a convergent p-series ($p = 3 > 1$).

Thus, the interval of convergence is $I = [-1, 1]$.

7. If $a_n = \dfrac{x^n}{n!}$, then $\lim\limits_{n \to \infty} \left| \dfrac{a_{n+1}}{a_n} \right| = \lim\limits_{n \to \infty} \left| \dfrac{x^{n+1}}{(n+1)!} \cdot \dfrac{n!}{x^n} \right| = \lim\limits_{n \to \infty} \left| \dfrac{x}{n+1} \right| = |x| \lim\limits_{n \to \infty} \dfrac{1}{n+1} = |x| \cdot 0 = 0 < 1$ for

all real x. So, by the Ratio Test, $R = \infty$, and $I = (-\infty, \infty)$.

9. $\lim\limits_{n \to \infty} \left| \dfrac{a_{n+1}}{a_n} \right| = \lim\limits_{n \to \infty} \dfrac{(n+1) 4^{n+1} |x|^{n+1}}{n 4^n |x|^n} = \lim\limits_{n \to \infty} \left(1 + \dfrac{1}{n} \right) 4 |x| = 4 |x|$. Now $4 |x| < 1 \iff |x| < \frac{1}{4}$, so by

the Ratio Test, $R = \frac{1}{4}$. When $x = \frac{1}{4}$, we get the divergent series $\sum_{n=1}^{\infty} (-1)^n n$, and when $x = -\frac{1}{4}$, we get the

divergent series $\sum_{n=1}^{\infty} n$. Thus, $I = \left(-\frac{1}{4}, \frac{1}{4} \right)$.

11. $a_n = \dfrac{(-2)^n x^n}{\sqrt[4]{n}}$, so $\lim\limits_{n \to \infty} \left| \dfrac{a_{n+1}}{a_n} \right| = \lim\limits_{n \to \infty} \dfrac{2^{n+1} |x|^{n+1}}{\sqrt[4]{n+1}} \cdot \dfrac{\sqrt[4]{n}}{2^n |x|^n} = \lim\limits_{n \to \infty} 2 |x| \sqrt[4]{\dfrac{n}{n+1}} = 2 |x|$, so by the

Ratio Test, the series converges when $2 |x| < 1 \iff |x| < \frac{1}{2}$, so $R = \frac{1}{2}$. When $x = -\frac{1}{2}$, we get the divergent

p-series $\displaystyle\sum_{n=1}^{\infty} \dfrac{1}{\sqrt[4]{n}}$ $(p = \frac{1}{4} \le 1)$. When $x = \frac{1}{2}$, we get the series $\displaystyle\sum_{n=1}^{\infty} \dfrac{(-1)^n}{\sqrt[4]{n}}$, which converges by the Alternating

Series Test. Thus, $I = \left(-\frac{1}{2}, \frac{1}{2} \right]$.

13. If $a_n = (-1)^n \dfrac{x^n}{4^n \ln n}$, then

$$\lim_{n \to \infty} \left| \frac{a_{n+1}}{a_n} \right| = \lim_{n \to \infty} \left| \frac{x^{n+1}}{4^{n+1} \ln(n+1)} \cdot \frac{4^n \ln n}{x^n} \right| = \frac{|x|}{4} \lim_{n \to \infty} \frac{\ln n}{\ln(n+1)} = \frac{|x|}{4} \cdot 1 \;\text{(by l'Hospital's Rule)} = \frac{|x|}{4}.$$

By the Ratio Test, the series converges when $\dfrac{|x|}{4} < 1 \quad \Leftrightarrow \quad |x| < 4$, so $R = 4$. When $x = -4$,

$$\sum_{n=2}^{\infty} (-1)^n \frac{x^n}{4^n \ln n} = \sum_{n=2}^{\infty} \frac{[(-1)(-4)]^n}{4^n \ln n} = \sum_{n=2}^{\infty} \frac{1}{\ln n}. \text{ Since } \ln n < n \text{ for } n \geq 2, \; \frac{1}{\ln n} > \frac{1}{n} \text{ and } \sum_{n=2}^{\infty} \frac{1}{n} \text{ is the}$$

divergent harmonic series (without the $n = 1$ term), $\displaystyle\sum_{n=2}^{\infty} \frac{1}{\ln n}$ is divergent by the Comparison Test. When $x = 4$,

$$\sum_{n=2}^{\infty} (-1)^n \frac{x^n}{4^n \ln n} = \sum_{n=2}^{\infty} (-1)^n \frac{1}{\ln n}, \text{ which converges by the Alternating Series Test. Thus, } I = (-4, 4].$$

15. If $a_n = \sqrt{n}\,(x-1)^n$, then $\displaystyle\lim_{n \to \infty} \left| \frac{a_{n+1}}{a_n} \right| = \lim_{n \to \infty} \left| \frac{\sqrt{n+1}\,|x-1|^{n+1}}{\sqrt{n}\,|x-1|^n} \right| = \lim_{n \to \infty} \sqrt{1 + \frac{1}{n}}\,|x-1| = |x-1|$. By

the Ratio Test, the series converges when $|x-1| < 1$ [so $R = 1$] $\quad \Leftrightarrow \quad -1 < x-1 < 1 \quad \Leftrightarrow \quad 0 < x < 2$.
When $x = 0$, the series becomes $\sum_{n=0}^{\infty} (-1)^n \sqrt{n}$, which diverges by the Test for Divergence. When $x = 2$, the
series becomes $\sum_{n=0}^{\infty} \sqrt{n}$, which also diverges by the Test for Divergence. Thus, $I = (0, 2)$.

17. If $a_n = (-1)^n \dfrac{(x+2)^n}{n2^n}$, then

$$\lim_{n \to \infty} \left| \frac{a_{n+1}}{a_n} \right| = \lim_{n \to \infty} \left[\frac{|x+2|^{n+1}}{(n+1)2^{n+1}} \cdot \frac{n2^n}{|x+2|^n} \right] = \lim_{n \to \infty} \frac{n}{n+1} \cdot \frac{|x+2|}{2} = \frac{|x+2|}{2}. \text{ By the Ratio Test, the}$$

series converges when $\dfrac{|x+2|}{2} < 1 \quad \Leftrightarrow \quad |x+2| < 2$ [so $R = 2$] $\quad \Leftrightarrow \quad -2 < x+2 < 2 \quad \Leftrightarrow \quad -4 < x < 0$.

When $x = -4$, the series becomes $\displaystyle\sum_{n=1}^{\infty} (-1)^n \frac{(-2)^n}{n2^n} = \sum_{n=1}^{\infty} \frac{2^n}{n2^n} = \sum_{n=1}^{\infty} \frac{1}{n}$, which is the divergent harmonic series.

When $x = 0$, the series is $\displaystyle\sum_{n=1}^{\infty} \frac{(-1)^n}{n}$, the alternating harmonic series, which converges by the Alternating Series
Test. Thus, $I = (-4, 0]$.

19. If $a_n = \dfrac{(x-2)^n}{n^n}$, then $\displaystyle\lim_{n \to \infty} \sqrt[n]{|a_n|} = \lim_{n \to \infty} \frac{|x-2|}{n} = 0$, so the series converges for all x (by the Root Test).
$R = \infty$ and $I = (-\infty, \infty)$.

21. $a_n = \dfrac{n}{b^n}(x-a)^n$, where $b > 0$.

$$\lim_{n \to \infty} \left| \frac{a_{n+1}}{a_n} \right| = \lim_{n \to \infty} \frac{(n+1)\,|x-a|^{n+1}}{b^{n+1}} \cdot \frac{b^n}{n\,|x-a|^n} = \lim_{n \to \infty} \left(1 + \frac{1}{n}\right) \frac{|x-a|}{b} = \frac{|x-a|}{b}.$$

By the Ratio Test, the series converges when $\dfrac{|x-a|}{b} < 1 \quad \Leftrightarrow \quad |x-a| < b \quad$ [so $R = b$] $\quad \Leftrightarrow$
$-b < x-a < b \quad \Leftrightarrow \quad a-b < x < a+b$. When $|x-a| = b$, $\displaystyle\lim_{n \to \infty} |a_n| = \lim_{n \to \infty} n = \infty$, so the series diverges.
Thus, $I = (a-b, a+b)$.

23. If $a_n = n!(2x-1)^n$, then $\displaystyle\lim_{n \to \infty} \left| \frac{a_{n+1}}{a_n} \right| = \lim_{n \to \infty} \left| \frac{(n+1)!(2x-1)^{n+1}}{n!(2x-1)^n} \right| = \lim_{n \to \infty} (n+1)\,|2x-1| \to \infty$

as $n \to \infty$ for all $x \neq \frac{1}{2}$. Since the series diverges for all $x \neq \frac{1}{2}$, $R = 0$ and $I = \left\{\frac{1}{2}\right\}$.

25. $\lim\limits_{n\to\infty}\left|\dfrac{a_{n+1}}{a_n}\right| = \lim\limits_{n\to\infty}\left[\dfrac{|4x+1|^{n+1}}{(n+1)^2} \cdot \dfrac{n^2}{|4x+1|^n}\right] = \lim\limits_{n\to\infty}\dfrac{|4x+1|}{(1+1/n)^2} = |4x+1|$, so by the Ratio Test, the

series converges when $|4x+1| < 1 \iff -1 < 4x+1 < 1 \iff -2 < 4x < 0 \iff -\frac{1}{2} < x < 0$, so

$R = \frac{1}{4}$. When $x = -\frac{1}{2}$, the series becomes $\sum\limits_{n=1}^{\infty}\dfrac{(-1)^n}{n^2}$, which converges by the Alternating Series Test. When

$x = 0$, the series becomes $\sum\limits_{n=1}^{\infty}\dfrac{1}{n^2}$, a convergent p-series ($p = 2 > 1$). $I = \left[-\frac{1}{2}, 0\right]$.

27. If $a_n = \dfrac{x^n}{(\ln n)^n}$, then $\lim\limits_{n\to\infty}\sqrt[n]{|a_n|} = \lim\limits_{n\to\infty}\dfrac{|x|}{\ln n} = 0 < 1$ for all x, so $R = \infty$ and $I = (-\infty, \infty)$ by the
Root Test.

29. (a) We are given that the power series $\sum_{n=0}^{\infty} c_n x^n$ is convergent for $x = 4$. So by Theorem 3, it must converge for
at least $-4 < x \le 4$. In particular, it converges when $x = -2$; that is, $\sum_{n=0}^{\infty} c_n(-2)^n$ is convergent.

(b) It does not follow that $\sum_{n=0}^{\infty} c_n(-4)^n$ is necessarily convergent. [See the comments after Theorem 3 about
convergence at the endpoint of an interval. An example is $c_n = (-1)^n / (n4^n)$.]

31. If $a_n = \dfrac{(n!)^k}{(kn)!}x^n$, then

$$\lim\limits_{n\to\infty}\left|\dfrac{a_{n+1}}{a_n}\right| = \lim\limits_{n\to\infty}\dfrac{[(n+1)!]^k\,(kn)!}{(n!)^k\,[k(n+1)]!}\,|x| = \lim\limits_{n\to\infty}\dfrac{(n+1)^k}{(kn+k)(kn+k-1)\cdots(kn+2)(kn+1)}\,|x|$$

$$= \lim\limits_{n\to\infty}\left[\dfrac{(n+1)}{(kn+1)}\dfrac{(n+1)}{(kn+2)}\cdots\dfrac{(n+1)}{(kn+k)}\right]|x|$$

$$= \lim\limits_{n\to\infty}\left[\dfrac{n+1}{kn+1}\right]\lim\limits_{n\to\infty}\left[\dfrac{n+1}{kn+2}\right]\cdots\lim\limits_{n\to\infty}\left[\dfrac{n+1}{kn+k}\right]|x| = \left(\dfrac{1}{k}\right)^k|x| < 1 \iff$$

$|x| < k^k$ for convergence, and the radius of convergence is $R = k^k$.

33. (a) If $a_n = \dfrac{(-1)^n\,x^{2n+1}}{n!(n+1)!\,2^{2n+1}}$, then

$$\lim\limits_{n\to\infty}\left|\dfrac{a_{n+1}}{a_n}\right| = \lim\limits_{n\to\infty}\left|\dfrac{x^{2n+3}}{(n+1)!(n+2)!\,2^{2n+3}} \cdot \dfrac{n!(n+1)!\,2^{2n+1}}{x^{2n+1}}\right| = \left(\dfrac{x}{2}\right)^2\lim\limits_{n\to\infty}\dfrac{1}{(n+1)(n+2)} = 0 \text{ for}$$

all x. So $J_1(x)$ converges for all x and its domain is $(-\infty, \infty)$.

(b), (c) The initial terms of $J_1(x)$ up to $n = 5$ are

$a_0 = \dfrac{x}{2}$, $a_1 = -\dfrac{x^3}{16}$, $a_2 = \dfrac{x^5}{384}$, $a_3 = -\dfrac{x^7}{18{,}432}$,

$a_4 = \dfrac{x^9}{1{,}474{,}560}$, and $a_5 = -\dfrac{x^{11}}{176{,}947{,}200}$. The

partial sums seem to approximate $J_1(x)$ well near

the origin, but as $|x|$ increases, we need to take a

large number of terms to get a good approximation.

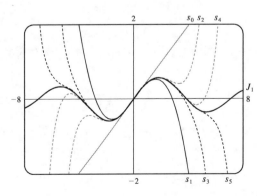

35. $s_{2n-1} = 1 + 2x + x^2 + 2x^3 + x^4 + 2x^5 + \cdots + x^{2n-2} + 2x^{2n-1}$

$$= 1(1 + 2x) + x^2(1 + 2x) + x^4(1 + 2x) + \cdots + x^{2n-2}(1 + 2x)$$

$$= (1 + 2x)(1 + x^2 + x^4 + \cdots + x^{2n-2})$$

$$= (1 + 2x)\frac{1 - x^{2n}}{1 - x^2} \text{ [by (12.2.3)] with } r = x^2] \to \frac{1 + 2x}{1 - x^2} \text{ as } n \to \infty \text{ [by (12.2.4)]},$$

when $|x| < 1$. Also $s_{2n} = s_{2n-1} + x^{2n} \to \dfrac{1 + 2x}{1 - x^2}$ since $x^{2n} \to 0$ for $|x| < 1$. Therefore,

$s_n \to \dfrac{1 + 2x}{1 - x^2}$ since s_{2n} and s_{2n-1} both approach $\dfrac{1 + 2x}{1 - x^2}$ as $n \to \infty$. Thus, the interval of convergence is $(-1, 1)$

and $f(x) = \dfrac{1 + 2x}{1 - x^2}$.

37. We use the Root Test on the series $\sum c_n x^n$. We need $\displaystyle\lim_{n\to\infty} \sqrt[n]{|c_n x^n|} = |x| \lim_{n\to\infty} \sqrt[n]{|c_n|} = c\,|x| < 1$ for

convergence, or $|x| < 1/c$, so $R = 1/c$.

39. For $2 < x < 3$, $\sum c_n x^n$ diverges and $\sum d_n x^n$ converges. By Exercise 12.2.61, $\sum (c_n + d_n) x^n$ diverges. Since

both series converge for $|x| < 2$, the radius of convergence of $\sum (c_n + d_n) x^n$ is 2.

12.9 Representations of Functions as Power Series

1. If $f(x) = \displaystyle\sum_{n=0}^{\infty} c_n x^n$ has radius of convergence 10, then $f'(x) = \displaystyle\sum_{n=1}^{\infty} n c_n x^{n-1}$ also has radius of convergence 10

by Theorem 2.

3. Our goal is to write the function in the form $\dfrac{1}{1 - r}$, and then use Equation (1) to represent the function as a sum of a

power series. $f(x) = \dfrac{1}{1 + x} = \dfrac{1}{1 - (-x)} = \displaystyle\sum_{n=0}^{\infty} (-x)^n = \displaystyle\sum_{n=0}^{\infty} (-1)^n x^n$ with $|-x| < 1 \Leftrightarrow |x| < 1$, so $R = 1$

and $I = (-1, 1)$.

5. Replacing x with x^3 in (1) gives $f(x) = \dfrac{1}{1 - x^3} = \displaystyle\sum_{n=0}^{\infty} (x^3)^n = \displaystyle\sum_{n=0}^{\infty} x^{3n}$. The series converges when $|x^3| < 1$

$\Leftrightarrow |x|^3 < 1 \Leftrightarrow |x| < \sqrt[3]{1} \Leftrightarrow |x| < 1$. Thus, $R = 1$ and $I = (-1, 1)$.

7. $f(x) = \dfrac{1}{x - 5} = -\dfrac{1}{5}\left(\dfrac{1}{1 - x/5}\right) = -\dfrac{1}{5} \displaystyle\sum_{n=0}^{\infty} \left(\dfrac{x}{5}\right)^n$ or equivalently, $-\displaystyle\sum_{n=0}^{\infty} \dfrac{1}{5^{n+1}} x^n$. The series converges when

$\left|\dfrac{x}{5}\right| < 1$; that is, when $|x| < 5$, so $I = (-5, 5)$.

9. $f(x) = \dfrac{x}{9 + x^2} = \dfrac{x}{9}\left[\dfrac{1}{1 + (x/3)^2}\right] = \dfrac{x}{9}\left[\dfrac{1}{1 - \{-(x/3)^2\}}\right] = \dfrac{x}{9} \displaystyle\sum_{n=0}^{\infty} \left[-\left(\dfrac{x}{3}\right)^2\right]^n$

$= \dfrac{x}{9} \displaystyle\sum_{n=0}^{\infty} (-1)^n \dfrac{x^{2n}}{9^n} = \displaystyle\sum_{n=0}^{\infty} (-1)^n \dfrac{x^{2n+1}}{9^{n+1}}$. The geometric series $\displaystyle\sum_{n=0}^{\infty} \left[-\left(\dfrac{x}{3}\right)^2\right]^n$ converges when

$\left|-\left(\dfrac{x}{3}\right)^2\right| < 1 \Leftrightarrow \dfrac{|x^2|}{9} < 1 \Leftrightarrow |x|^2 < 9 \Leftrightarrow |x| < 3$, so $R = 3$ and $I = (-3, 3)$.

11. $f(x) = \dfrac{3}{x^2 + x - 2} = \dfrac{3}{(x+2)(x-1)} = \dfrac{A}{x+2} + \dfrac{B}{x-1} \quad \Rightarrow \quad 3 = A(x-1) + B(x+2)$. Taking $x = -2$, we

get $A = -1$. Taking $x = 1$, we get $B = 1$. Thus,

$$\dfrac{3}{x^2 + x - 2} = \dfrac{1}{x-1} - \dfrac{1}{x+2} = -\dfrac{1}{1-x} - \dfrac{1}{2}\dfrac{1}{1+x/2} = -\sum_{n=0}^{\infty} x^n - \dfrac{1}{2}\sum_{n=0}^{\infty} \left(-\dfrac{x}{2}\right)^n$$

$$= \sum_{n=0}^{\infty}\left[-1 - \tfrac{1}{2}\left(-\tfrac{1}{2}\right)^n\right] x^n = \sum_{n=0}^{\infty}\left[-1 + \left(-\tfrac{1}{2}\right)^{n+1}\right] x^n = \sum_{n=0}^{\infty}\left[\dfrac{(-1)^{n+1}}{2^{n+1}} - 1\right] x^n$$

We represented the given function as the sum of two geometric series; the first converges for $x \in (-1, 1)$ and the

second converges for $x \in (-2, 2)$. Thus, the sum converges for $x \in (-1, 1) = I$.

13. (a) $f(x) = \dfrac{1}{(1+x)^2} = \dfrac{d}{dx}\left(\dfrac{-1}{1+x}\right) = -\dfrac{d}{dx}\left[\sum_{n=0}^{\infty}(-1)^n x^n\right]$ [from Exercise 3]

$$= \sum_{n=1}^{\infty}(-1)^{n+1} n x^{n-1} \text{ [from Theorem 2(i)]} = \sum_{n=0}^{\infty}(-1)^n(n+1)x^n \text{ with } R = 1.$$

In the last step, note that we *decreased* the initial value of the summation variable n by 1, and then *increased*

each occurrence of n in the term by 1 [also note that $(-1)^{n+2} = (-1)^n$].

(b) $f(x) = \dfrac{1}{(1+x)^3} = -\dfrac{1}{2}\dfrac{d}{dx}\left[\dfrac{1}{(1+x)^2}\right] = -\dfrac{1}{2}\dfrac{d}{dx}\left[\sum_{n=0}^{\infty}(-1)^n(n+1)x^n\right]$ [from part (a)]

$$= -\tfrac{1}{2}\sum_{n=1}^{\infty}(-1)^n(n+1)n x^{n-1} = \tfrac{1}{2}\sum_{n=0}^{\infty}(-1)^n(n+2)(n+1)x^n \text{ with } R = 1.$$

(c) $f(x) = \dfrac{x^2}{(1+x)^3} = x^2 \cdot \dfrac{1}{(1+x)^3} = x^2 \cdot \dfrac{1}{2}\sum_{n=0}^{\infty}(-1)^n(n+2)(n+1)x^n$ [from part (b)]

$$= \dfrac{1}{2}\sum_{n=0}^{\infty}(-1)^n(n+2)(n+1)x^{n+2}. \text{ To write the power series with } x^n \text{ rather than } x^{n+2},$$

we will *decrease* each occurrence of n in the term by 2 and *increase* the initial value of the summation variable

by 2. This gives us $\dfrac{1}{2}\sum_{n=2}^{\infty}(-1)^n(n)(n-1)x^n$.

15. $f(x) = \ln(5 - x) = -\displaystyle\int \dfrac{dx}{5-x} = -\dfrac{1}{5}\int \dfrac{dx}{1-x/5}$

$$= -\dfrac{1}{5}\int\left[\sum_{n=0}^{\infty}\left(\dfrac{x}{5}\right)^n\right] dx = C - \dfrac{1}{5}\sum_{n=0}^{\infty}\dfrac{x^{n+1}}{5^n(n+1)} = C - \sum_{n=1}^{\infty}\dfrac{x^n}{n5^n}$$

Putting $x = 0$, we get $C = \ln 5$. The series converges for $|x/5| < 1 \quad \Leftrightarrow \quad |x| < 5$, so $R = 5$.

17. $\dfrac{1}{2-x} = \dfrac{1}{2(1-x/2)} = \dfrac{1}{2}\sum_{n=0}^{\infty}\left(\dfrac{x}{2}\right)^n = \sum_{n=0}^{\infty}\dfrac{1}{2^{n+1}}x^n \text{ for } \left|\dfrac{x}{2}\right| < 1 \quad \Leftrightarrow \quad |x| < 2$. Now

$$\dfrac{1}{(x-2)^2} = \dfrac{d}{dx}\left(\dfrac{1}{2-x}\right) = \dfrac{d}{dx}\left(\sum_{n=0}^{\infty}\dfrac{1}{2^{n+1}}x^n\right) = \sum_{n=1}^{\infty}\dfrac{n}{2^{n+1}}x^{n-1} = \sum_{n=0}^{\infty}\dfrac{n+1}{2^{n+2}}x^n. \text{ So}$$

$$f(x) = \dfrac{x^3}{(x-2)^2} = x^3 \sum_{n=0}^{\infty}\dfrac{n+1}{2^{n+2}}x^n = \sum_{n=0}^{\infty}\dfrac{n+1}{2^{n+2}}x^{n+3} \text{ or } \sum_{n=3}^{\infty}\dfrac{n-2}{2^{n-1}}x^n \text{ for } |x| < 2. \text{ Thus, } R = 2 \text{ and}$$

$I = (-2, 2)$.

19. $f(x) = \ln(3 + x) = \displaystyle\int \frac{dx}{3 + x} = \frac{1}{3}\int \frac{dx}{1 + x/3} = \frac{1}{3}\int \frac{dx}{1 - (-x/3)} = \frac{1}{3}\int \sum_{n=0}^{\infty}\left(-\frac{x}{3}\right)^n dx$

$= C + \dfrac{1}{3}\displaystyle\sum_{n=0}^{\infty}\dfrac{(-1)^n}{(n+1)3^n}x^{n+1} = \ln 3 + \dfrac{1}{3}\sum_{n=1}^{\infty}\dfrac{(-1)^{n-1}}{n3^{n-1}}x^n \quad [C = f(0) = \ln 3]$

$= \ln 3 + \displaystyle\sum_{n=1}^{\infty}\dfrac{(-1)^{n-1}}{n3^n}x^n.$ The series converges when $|-x/3| < 1 \iff |x| < 3$, so $R = 3$.

The terms of the series are $a_0 = \ln 3, a_1 = \dfrac{x}{3}, a_2 = -\dfrac{x^2}{18}, a_3 = \dfrac{x^3}{81}, a_4 = -\dfrac{x^4}{324}, a_5 = \dfrac{x^5}{1215}, \dots.$

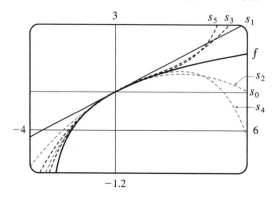

As n increases, $s_n(x)$ approximates f better on the interval of convergence, which is $(-3, 3)$.

21. $f(x) = \ln\left(\dfrac{1 + x}{1 - x}\right) = \ln(1 + x) - \ln(1 - x) = \displaystyle\int \frac{dx}{1 + x} + \int \frac{dx}{1 - x}$

$= \displaystyle\int \frac{dx}{1 - (-x)} + \int \frac{dx}{1 - x} = \int \left[\sum_{n=0}^{\infty}(-1)^n x^n + \sum_{n=0}^{\infty} x^n\right] dx$

$= \displaystyle\int \left[\left(1 - x + x^2 - x^3 + x^4 - \cdots\right) + \left(1 + x + x^2 + x^3 + x^4 + \cdots\right)\right] dx$

$= \displaystyle\int \left(2 + 2x^2 + 2x^4 + \cdots\right) dx = \int \sum_{n=0}^{\infty} 2x^{2n}\, dx = C + \sum_{n=0}^{\infty}\frac{2x^{2n+1}}{2n+1}$

But $f(0) = \ln\frac{1}{1} = 0$, so $C = 0$ and we have $f(x) = \displaystyle\sum_{n=0}^{\infty}\frac{2x^{2n+1}}{2n+1}$ with $R = 1$. If $x = \pm 1$, then

$f(x) = \pm 2\displaystyle\sum_{n=0}^{\infty}\frac{1}{2n+1}$, which both diverge by the Limit Comparison Test with $b_n = \dfrac{1}{n}$.

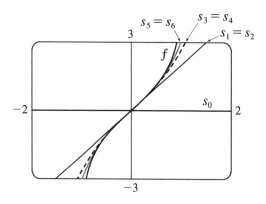

As n increases, $s_n(x)$ approximates f better on the interval of convergence, which is $(-1, 1)$.

23. $\dfrac{t}{1-t^8} = t \cdot \dfrac{1}{1-t^8} = t \displaystyle\sum_{n=0}^{\infty}(t^8)^n = \sum_{n=0}^{\infty} t^{8n+1} \quad\Rightarrow\quad \displaystyle\int \dfrac{t}{1-t^8}\,dt = C + \sum_{n=0}^{\infty}\dfrac{t^{8n+2}}{8n+2}.$ The series for $\dfrac{1}{1-t^8}$

converges when $\left|t^8\right| < 1 \quad\Leftrightarrow\quad |t| < 1$, so $R = 1$ for that series and also the series for $t/(1-t^8)$. By Theorem

2, the series for $\displaystyle\int \dfrac{t}{1-t^8}\,dt$ also has $R = 1$.

25. By Example 7, $\tan^{-1} x = \displaystyle\sum_{n=0}^{\infty}(-1)^n \dfrac{x^{2n+1}}{2n+1}$ with $R = 1$, so

$$x - \tan^{-1} x = x - \left(x - \dfrac{x^3}{3} + \dfrac{x^5}{5} - \dfrac{x^7}{7} + \cdots\right) = \dfrac{x^3}{3} - \dfrac{x^5}{5} + \dfrac{x^7}{7} - \cdots = \sum_{n=1}^{\infty}(-1)^{n+1}\dfrac{x^{2n+1}}{2n+1}$$

and $\dfrac{x - \tan^{-1} x}{x^3} = \displaystyle\sum_{n=1}^{\infty}(-1)^{n+1}\dfrac{x^{2n-2}}{2n+1}$, so

$$\int \dfrac{x - \tan^{-1} x}{x^3}\,dx = C + \sum_{n=1}^{\infty}(-1)^{n+1}\dfrac{x^{2n-1}}{(2n+1)(2n-1)} = C + \sum_{n=1}^{\infty}(-1)^{n+1}\dfrac{x^{2n-1}}{4n^2-1}. \text{ By Theorem 2, } R = 1.$$

27. $\dfrac{1}{1+x^5} = \dfrac{1}{1-(-x^5)} = \displaystyle\sum_{n=0}^{\infty}(-x^5)^n = \sum_{n=0}^{\infty}(-1)^n x^{5n} \quad\Rightarrow$

$$\int \dfrac{1}{1+x^5}\,dx = \int \sum_{n=0}^{\infty}(-1)^n x^{5n}\,dx = C + \sum_{n=0}^{\infty}(-1)^n \dfrac{x^{5n+1}}{5n+1}. \text{ Thus,}$$

$$I = \int_0^{0.2} \dfrac{1}{1+x^5}\,dx = \left[x - \dfrac{x^6}{6} + \dfrac{x^{11}}{11} - \cdots\right]_0^{0.2} = 0.2 - \dfrac{(0.2)^6}{6} + \dfrac{(0.2)^{11}}{11} - \cdots. \text{ The series is alternating, so}$$

if we use the first two terms, the error is at most $(0.2)^{11}/11 \approx 1.9 \times 10^{-9}$. So $I \approx 0.2 - (0.2)^6/6 \approx 0.199989$ to

six decimal places.

29. We substitute x^4 for x in Example 7, and find that

$$\int x^2 \tan^{-1}(x^4)\,dx = \int x^2 \sum_{n=0}^{\infty}(-1)^n \dfrac{(x^4)^{2n+1}}{2n+1}\,dx$$

$$= \int \sum_{n=0}^{\infty}(-1)^n \dfrac{x^{8n+6}}{2n+1}\,dx = C + \sum_{n=0}^{\infty}(-1)^n \dfrac{x^{8n+7}}{(2n+1)(8n+7)}$$

So $\displaystyle\int_0^{1/3} x^2 \tan^{-1}(x^4)\,dx = \left[\dfrac{x^7}{7} - \dfrac{x^{15}}{45} + \cdots\right]_0^{1/3} = \dfrac{1}{7 \cdot 3^7} - \dfrac{1}{45 \cdot 3^{15}} + \cdots.$ The series is alternating,

so if we use only one term, the error is at most $1/(45 \cdot 3^{15}) \approx 1.5 \times 10^{-9}$. So

$\int_0^{1/3} x^2 \tan^{-1}(x^4)\,dx \approx 1/(7 \cdot 3^7) \approx 0.000065$ to six decimal places.

31. Using the result of Example 6, $\ln(1-x) = -\sum_{n=1}^{\infty} \dfrac{x^n}{n}$, with $x = -0.1$, we have

$$\ln 1.1 = \ln[1-(-0.1)] = 0.1 - \frac{0.01}{2} + \frac{0.001}{3} - \frac{0.0001}{4} + \frac{0.00001}{5} - \cdots. \text{ The series is alternating, so if}$$

we use only the first four terms, the error is at most $\dfrac{0.00001}{5} = 0.000002$. So

$$\ln 1.1 \approx 0.1 - \frac{0.01}{2} + \frac{0.001}{3} - \frac{0.0001}{4} \approx 0.09531.$$

33. (a) $J_0(x) = \sum_{n=0}^{\infty} \dfrac{(-1)^n x^{2n}}{2^{2n}(n!)^2}$, $J_0'(x) = \sum_{n=1}^{\infty} \dfrac{(-1)^n 2nx^{2n-1}}{2^{2n}(n!)^2}$, and $J_0''(x) = \sum_{n=1}^{\infty} \dfrac{(-1)^n 2n(2n-1)x^{2n-2}}{2^{2n}(n!)^2}$, so

$$x^2 J_0''(x) + x J_0'(x) + x^2 J_0(x) = \sum_{n=1}^{\infty} \frac{(-1)^n 2n(2n-1)x^{2n}}{2^{2n}(n!)^2} + \sum_{n=1}^{\infty} \frac{(-1)^n 2nx^{2n}}{2^{2n}(n!)^2} + \sum_{n=0}^{\infty} \frac{(-1)^n x^{2n+2}}{2^{2n}(n!)^2}$$

$$= \sum_{n=1}^{\infty} \frac{(-1)^n 2n(2n-1)x^{2n}}{2^{2n}(n!)^2} + \sum_{n=1}^{\infty} \frac{(-1)^n 2nx^{2n}}{2^{2n}(n!)^2} + \sum_{n=1}^{\infty} \frac{(-1)^{n-1} x^{2n}}{2^{2n-2}[(n-1)!]^2}$$

$$= \sum_{n=1}^{\infty} \frac{(-1)^n 2n(2n-1)x^{2n}}{2^{2n}(n!)^2} + \sum_{n=1}^{\infty} \frac{(-1)^n 2nx^{2n}}{2^{2n}(n!)^2} + \sum_{n=1}^{\infty} \frac{(-1)^n(-1)^{-1} 2^2 n^2 x^{2n}}{2^{2n}(n!)^2}$$

$$= \sum_{n=1}^{\infty} (-1)^n \left[\frac{2n(2n-1) + 2n - 2^2 n^2}{2^{2n}(n!)^2} \right] x^{2n} = \sum_{n=1}^{\infty} (-1)^n \left[\frac{4n^2 - 2n + 2n - 4n^2}{2^{2n}(n!)^2} \right] x^{2n} = 0$$

(b) $\displaystyle \int_0^1 J_0(x)\,dx = \int_0^1 \left[\sum_{n=0}^{\infty} \frac{(-1)^n x^{2n}}{2^{2n}(n!)^2} \right] dx = \int_0^1 \left(1 - \frac{x^2}{4} + \frac{x^4}{64} - \frac{x^6}{2304} + \cdots \right) dx$

$$= \left[x - \frac{x^3}{3 \cdot 4} + \frac{x^5}{5 \cdot 64} - \frac{x^7}{7 \cdot 2304} + \cdots \right]_0^1 = 1 - \frac{1}{12} + \frac{1}{320} - \frac{1}{16{,}128} + \cdots$$

Since $\frac{1}{16{,}128} \approx 0.000062$, it follows from The Alternating Series Estimation Theorem that, correct to three

decimal places, $\int_0^1 J_0(x)\,dx \approx 1 - \frac{1}{12} + \frac{1}{320} \approx 0.920$.

35. (a) $f(x) = \sum_{n=0}^{\infty} \dfrac{x^n}{n!} \ \Rightarrow \ f'(x) = \sum_{n=1}^{\infty} \dfrac{nx^{n-1}}{n!} = \sum_{n=1}^{\infty} \dfrac{x^{n-1}}{(n-1)!} = \sum_{n=0}^{\infty} \dfrac{x^n}{n!} = f(x)$

(b) By Theorem 10.4.2, the only solution to the differential equation $df(x)/dx = f(x)$ is $f(x) = Ke^x$, but

$f(0) = 1$, so $K = 1$ and $f(x) = e^x$.

Or: We could solve the equation $df(x)/dx = f(x)$ as a separable differential equation.

37. If $a_n = \dfrac{x^n}{n^2}$, then by the Ratio Test, $\lim\limits_{n\to\infty}\left|\dfrac{a_{n+1}}{a_n}\right| = \lim\limits_{n\to\infty}\left|\dfrac{x^{n+1}}{(n+1)^2}\cdot\dfrac{n^2}{x^n}\right| = |x|\lim\limits_{n\to\infty}\left(\dfrac{n}{n+1}\right)^2 = |x| < 1$ for

convergence, so $R = 1$. When $x = \pm 1$, $\sum\limits_{n=1}^{\infty}\left|\dfrac{x^n}{n^2}\right| = \sum\limits_{n=1}^{\infty}\dfrac{1}{n^2}$ which is a convergent p-series ($p = 2 > 1$), so the

interval of convergence for f is $[-1, 1]$. By Theorem 2, the radii of convergence of f' and f'' are both 1, so we need

only check the endpoints. $f(x) = \sum\limits_{n=1}^{\infty}\dfrac{x^n}{n^2} \Rightarrow f'(x) = \sum\limits_{n=1}^{\infty}\dfrac{nx^{n-1}}{n^2} = \sum\limits_{n=0}^{\infty}\dfrac{x^n}{n+1}$, and this series diverges for

$x = 1$ (harmonic series) and converges for $x = -1$ (Alternating Series Test), so the interval of convergence

is $[-1, 1)$. $f''(x) = \sum\limits_{n=1}^{\infty}\dfrac{nx^{n-1}}{n+1}$ diverges at both 1 and -1 (Test for Divergence) since $\lim\limits_{n\to\infty}\dfrac{n}{n+1} = 1 \neq 0$, so its

interval of convergence is $(-1, 1)$.

39. By Example 7, $\tan^{-1}x = \sum\limits_{n=0}^{\infty}(-1)^n\dfrac{x^{2n+1}}{2n+1}$ for $|x| < 1$. In particular, for $x = \dfrac{1}{\sqrt{3}}$, we have

$$\dfrac{\pi}{6} = \tan^{-1}\left(\dfrac{1}{\sqrt{3}}\right) = \sum\limits_{n=0}^{\infty}(-1)^n\dfrac{(1/\sqrt{3})^{2n+1}}{2n+1} = \sum\limits_{n=0}^{\infty}(-1)^n\left(\dfrac{1}{3}\right)^n\dfrac{1}{\sqrt{3}}\dfrac{1}{2n+1}, \text{ so}$$

$$\pi = \dfrac{6}{\sqrt{3}}\sum\limits_{n=0}^{\infty}\dfrac{(-1)^n}{(2n+1)3^n} = 2\sqrt{3}\sum\limits_{n=0}^{\infty}\dfrac{(-1)^n}{(2n+1)3^n}.$$

12.10 Taylor and Maclaurin Series

1. Using Theorem 5 with $\sum\limits_{n=0}^{\infty}b_n(x-5)^n$, $b_n = \dfrac{f^{(n)}(a)}{n!}$, so $b_8 = \dfrac{f^{(8)}(5)}{8!}$.

3.

n	$f^{(n)}(x)$	$f^{(n)}(0)$
0	$\cos x$	1
1	$-\sin x$	0
2	$-\cos x$	-1
3	$\sin x$	0
4	$\cos x$	1
$\vdots$	$\vdots$	$\vdots$

We use Equation 7 with $f(x) = \cos x$.

$$\cos x = f(0) + f'(0)x + \dfrac{f''(0)}{2!}x^2 + \dfrac{f^{(3)}(0)}{3!}x^3 + \dfrac{f^{(4)}(0)}{4!}x^4 + \cdots$$

$$= 1 - \dfrac{x^2}{2!} + \dfrac{x^4}{4!} - \cdots = \sum\limits_{n=0}^{\infty}\dfrac{(-1)^n x^{2n}}{(2n)!}$$

If $a_n = \dfrac{(-1)^n x^{2n}}{(2n)!}$, then

$$\lim\limits_{n\to\infty}\left|\dfrac{a_{n+1}}{a_n}\right| = \lim\limits_{n\to\infty}\left|\dfrac{x^{2n+2}}{(2n+2)!}\cdot\dfrac{(2n)!}{x^{2n}}\right| = x^2\lim\limits_{n\to\infty}\dfrac{1}{(2n+2)(2n+1)} = 0 < 1 \text{ for all } x.$$

So $R = \infty$ (Ratio Test).

5.

n	$f^{(n)}(x)$	$f^{(n)}(0)$
0	$(1+x)^{-3}$	1
1	$-3(1+x)^{-4}$	-3
2	$12(1+x)^{-5}$	12
3	$-60(1+x)^{-6}$	-60
4	$360(1+x)^{-7}$	360
$\vdots$	$\vdots$	$\vdots$

$$(1+x)^{-3} = f(0) + f'(0)x + \frac{f''(0)}{2!}x^2 + \frac{f'''(0)}{3!}x^3 + \frac{f^{(4)}(0)}{4!}x^4 + \cdots$$

$$= 1 - 3x + \frac{4 \cdot 3}{2!}x^2 - \frac{5 \cdot 4 \cdot 3}{3!}x^3 + \frac{6 \cdot 5 \cdot 4 \cdot 3}{4!}x^4 - \cdots$$

$$= 1 - 3x + \frac{4 \cdot 3 \cdot 2}{2 \cdot 2!}x^2 - \frac{5 \cdot 4 \cdot 3 \cdot 2}{2 \cdot 3!}x^3 + \frac{6 \cdot 5 \cdot 4 \cdot 3 \cdot 2}{2 \cdot 4!}x^4 - \cdots$$

$$= \sum_{n=0}^{\infty} \frac{(-1)^n (n+2)! \, x^n}{2(n!)} = \sum_{n=0}^{\infty} \frac{(-1)^n (n+2)(n+1)x^n}{2}$$

$$\lim_{n \to \infty} \left| \frac{a_{n+1}}{a_n} \right| = \lim_{n \to \infty} \left| \frac{(n+3)(n+2)x^{n+1}}{2} \cdot \frac{2}{(n+2)(n+1)x^n} \right| = |x| \lim_{n \to \infty} \frac{n+3}{n+1} = |x| < 1 \text{ for convergence,}$$

so $R = 1$ (Ratio Test).

7.

n	$f^{(n)}(x)$	$f^{(n)}(0)$
0	e^{5x}	1
1	$5e^{5x}$	5
2	$5^2 e^{5x}$	25
3	$5^3 e^{5x}$	125
4	$5^4 e^{5x}$	625
$\vdots$	$\vdots$	$\vdots$

$$e^{5x} = \sum_{n=0}^{\infty} \frac{f^{(n)}(0)}{n!}x^n = \sum_{n=0}^{\infty} \frac{5^n}{n!}x^n.$$

$$\lim_{n \to \infty} \left| \frac{a_{n+1}}{a_n} \right| = \lim_{n \to \infty} \left[\frac{5^{n+1}|x|^{n+1}}{(n+1)!} \cdot \frac{n!}{5^n |x|^n} \right]$$

$$= \lim_{n \to \infty} \frac{5|x|}{n+1} = 0 < 1 \text{ for all } x, \text{ so } R = \infty.$$

9.

n	$f^{(n)}(x)$	$f^{(n)}(0)$
0	$\sinh x$	0
1	$\cosh x$	1
2	$\sinh x$	0
3	$\cosh x$	1
4	$\sinh x$	0
$\vdots$	$\vdots$	$\vdots$

$$f^{(n)}(0) = \begin{cases} 0 & \text{if } n \text{ is even} \\ 1 & \text{if } n \text{ is odd} \end{cases} \quad \text{so } \sinh x = \sum_{n=0}^{\infty} \frac{x^{2n+1}}{(2n+1)!}.$$

Use the Ratio Test to find R. If $a_n = \dfrac{x^{2n+1}}{(2n+1)!}$, then

$$\lim_{n \to \infty} \left| \frac{a_{n+1}}{a_n} \right| = \lim_{n \to \infty} \left| \frac{x^{2n+3}}{(2n+3)!} \cdot \frac{(2n+1)!}{x^{2n+1}} \right|$$

$$= x^2 \cdot \lim_{n \to \infty} \frac{1}{(2n+3)(2n+2)} = 0 < 1$$

for all x, so $R = \infty$.

11.

n	$f^{(n)}(x)$	$f^{(n)}(2)$
0	$1 + x + x^2$	7
1	$1 + 2x$	5
2	2	2
3	0	0
4	0	0
$\vdots$	$\vdots$	$\vdots$

$$f(x) = 7 + 5(x - 2) + \frac{2}{2!}(x - 2)^2 + \sum_{n=3}^{\infty} \frac{0}{n!}(x - 2)^n$$

$$= 7 + 5(x - 2) + (x - 2)^2$$

Since $a_n = 0$ for large n, $R = \infty$.

13. Clearly, $f^{(n)}(x) = e^x$, so $f^{(n)}(3) = e^3$ and $e^x = \sum_{n=0}^{\infty} \frac{e^3}{n!}(x - 3)^n$. If $a_n = \frac{e^3}{n!}(x - 3)^n$, then

$$\lim_{n \to \infty} \left| \frac{a_{n+1}}{a_n} \right| = \lim_{n \to \infty} \left| \frac{e^3(x - 3)^{n+1}}{(n + 1)!} \cdot \frac{n!}{e^3(x - 3)^n} \right| = \lim_{n \to \infty} \frac{|x - 3|}{n + 1} = 0 < 1 \text{ for all } x, \text{ so } R = \infty.$$

15.

n	$f^{(n)}(x)$	$f^{(n)}(\pi)$
0	$\cos x$	-1
1	$-\sin x$	0
2	$-\cos x$	1
3	$\sin x$	0
4	$\cos x$	-1
$\vdots$	$\vdots$	$\vdots$

$$\cos x = \sum_{k=0}^{\infty} \frac{f^{(k)}(\pi)}{k!}(x - \pi)^k = -1 + \frac{(x - \pi)^2}{2!} - \frac{(x - \pi)^4}{4!} + \frac{(x - \pi)^6}{6!} - \cdots = \sum_{n=0}^{\infty} (-1)^{n+1} \frac{(x - \pi)^{2n}}{(2n)!}.$$

$$\lim_{n \to \infty} \left| \frac{a_{n+1}}{a_n} \right| = \lim_{n \to \infty} \left[\frac{|x - \pi|^{2n+2}}{(2n + 2)!} \cdot \frac{(2n)!}{|x - \pi|^{2n}} \right] = \lim_{n \to \infty} \frac{|x - \pi|^2}{(2n + 2)(2n + 1)} = 0 < 1 \text{ for all } x, \text{ so } R = \infty.$$

17.

n	$f^{(n)}(x)$	$f^{(n)}(9)$
0	$x^{-1/2}$	$\frac{1}{3}$
1	$-\frac{1}{2}x^{-3/2}$	$-\frac{1}{2} \cdot \frac{1}{3^3}$
2	$\frac{3}{4}x^{-5/2}$	$-\frac{1}{2} \cdot \left(-\frac{3}{2}\right) \cdot \frac{1}{3^5}$
3	$-\frac{15}{8}x^{-7/2}$	$-\frac{1}{2} \cdot \left(-\frac{3}{2}\right) \cdot \left(-\frac{5}{2}\right) \cdot \frac{1}{3^7}$
$\vdots$	$\vdots$	$\vdots$

$$\frac{1}{\sqrt{x}} = \frac{1}{3} - \frac{1}{2 \cdot 3^3}(x - 9) + \frac{3}{2^2 \cdot 3^5}\frac{(x - 9)^2}{2!} - \frac{3 \cdot 5}{2^3 \cdot 3^7}\frac{(x - 9)^3}{3!} + \cdots$$

$$= \sum_{n=0}^{\infty} (-1)^n \frac{1 \cdot 3 \cdot 5 \cdot \cdots \cdot (2n - 1)}{2^n \cdot 3^{2n+1} \cdot n!}(x - 9)^n.$$

$$\lim_{n\to\infty}\left|\frac{a_{n+1}}{a_n}\right| = \lim_{n\to\infty}\left[\frac{1\cdot 3\cdot 5\cdot\cdots\cdot(2n-1)[2(n+1)-1]\,|x-9|^{n+1}}{2^{n+1}\cdot 3^{[2(n+1)+1]}\cdot(n+1)!}\cdot\frac{2^n\cdot 3^{2n+1}\cdot n!}{1\cdot 3\cdot 5\cdot\cdots\cdot(2n-1)\,|x-9|^n}\right]$$

$$= \lim_{n\to\infty}\left[\frac{(2n+1)\,|x-9|}{2\cdot 3^2(n+1)}\right] = \frac{1}{9}\,|x-9| < 1$$

for convergence, so $|x-9| < 9$ and $R = 9$.

19. If $f(x) = \cos x$, then $f^{(n+1)}(x) = \pm\sin x$ or $\pm\cos x$. In each case, $\left|f^{(n+1)}(x)\right| \le 1$, so by Formula 9 with $a = 0$

and $M = 1$, $|R_n(x)| \le \dfrac{1}{(n+1)!}\,|x|^{n+1}$. Thus, $|R_n(x)| \to 0$ as $n \to \infty$ by Equation 10. So $\lim\limits_{n\to\infty} R_n(x) = 0$ and,

by Theorem 8, the series in Exercise 3 represents $\cos x$ for all x.

21. If $f(x) = \sinh x$, then for all n, $f^{(n+1)}(x) = \cosh x$ or $\sinh x$. Since $|\sinh x| < |\cosh x| = \cosh x$ for all x, we

have $\left|f^{(n+1)}(x)\right| \le \cosh x$ for all n. If d is any positive number and $|x| \le d$, then $\left|f^{(n+1)}(x)\right| \le \cosh x \le \cosh d$,

so by Formula 9 with $a = 0$ and $M = \cosh d$, we have $|R_n(x)| \le \dfrac{\cosh d}{(n+1)!}\,|x|^{n+1}$. It follows that $|R_n(x)| \to 0$

as $n \to \infty$ for $|x| \le d$ (by Equation 10). But d was an arbitrary positive number. So by Theorem 8, the series

represents $\sinh x$ for all x.

23. $\cos x = \sum\limits_{n=0}^{\infty}(-1)^n\dfrac{x^{2n}}{(2n)!} \quad\Rightarrow\quad f(x) = \cos(\pi x) = \sum\limits_{n=0}^{\infty}\dfrac{(-1)^n(\pi x)^{2n}}{(2n)!} = \sum\limits_{n=0}^{\infty}\dfrac{(-1)^n\pi^{2n}x^{2n}}{(2n)!},\ R = \infty$

25. $\tan^{-1}x = \sum\limits_{n=0}^{\infty}(-1)^n\dfrac{x^{2n+1}}{2n+1} \quad\Rightarrow\quad f(x) = x\tan^{-1}x = x\sum\limits_{n=0}^{\infty}(-1)^n\dfrac{x^{2n+1}}{2n+1} = \sum\limits_{n=0}^{\infty}(-1)^n\dfrac{x^{2n+2}}{2n+1},\ R = 1$

27. $e^x = \sum\limits_{n=0}^{\infty}\dfrac{x^n}{n!} \quad\Rightarrow\quad f(x) = x^2 e^{-x} = x^2\sum\limits_{n=0}^{\infty}\dfrac{(-x)^n}{n!} = \sum\limits_{n=0}^{\infty}\dfrac{(-1)^n\,x^{n+2}}{n!},\ R = \infty$

29. $\sin^2 x = \dfrac{1}{2}(1-\cos 2x) = \dfrac{1}{2}\left[1 - \sum\limits_{n=0}^{\infty}\dfrac{(-1)^n(2x)^{2n}}{(2n)!}\right] = \dfrac{1}{2}\left[1 - 1 - \sum\limits_{n=1}^{\infty}\dfrac{(-1)^n(2x)^{2n}}{(2n)!}\right]$

$$= \sum\limits_{n=1}^{\infty}\dfrac{(-1)^{n+1}2^{2n-1}x^{2n}}{(2n)!},\ R = \infty$$

31. $\dfrac{\sin x}{x} = \dfrac{1}{x}\sum\limits_{n=0}^{\infty}\dfrac{(-1)^n x^{2n+1}}{(2n+1)!} = \sum\limits_{n=0}^{\infty}\dfrac{(-1)^n x^{2n}}{(2n+1)!}$ and this series also gives the required value at $x = 0$ (namely 1);

$R = \infty$.

33.

n	$f^{(n)}(x)$	$f^{(n)}(0)$
0	$(1+x)^{1/2}$	1
1	$\frac{1}{2}(1+x)^{-1/2}$	$\frac{1}{2}$
2	$-\frac{1}{4}(1+x)^{-3/2}$	$-\frac{1}{4}$
3	$\frac{3}{8}(1+x)^{-5/2}$	$\frac{3}{8}$
4	$-\frac{15}{16}(1+x)^{-7/2}$	$-\frac{15}{16}$
$\vdots$	$\vdots$	$\vdots$

So $f^{(n)}(0) = \dfrac{(-1)^{n-1}\,1 \cdot 3 \cdot 5 \cdots \cdots (2n-3)}{2^n}$ for $n \geq 2$, and

$$\sqrt{1+x} = 1 + \frac{x}{2} + \sum_{n=2}^{\infty} \frac{(-1)^{n-1}1 \cdot 3 \cdot 5 \cdots \cdots (2n-3)}{2^n n!} x^n. \text{ If } a_n = \frac{(-1)^{n-1}1 \cdot 3 \cdot 5 \cdots \cdots (2n-3)}{2^n n!} x^n,$$

then $\displaystyle\lim_{n\to\infty}\left|\frac{a_{n+1}}{a_n}\right| = \lim_{n\to\infty}\left|\frac{1 \cdot 3 \cdot 5 \cdots \cdots (2n-3)(2n-1)x^{n+1}}{2^{n+1}(n+1)!} \cdot \frac{2^n n!}{1 \cdot 3 \cdot 5 \cdots \cdots (2n-3)x^n}\right|$

$$= \frac{|x|}{2}\lim_{n\to\infty}\frac{2n-1}{n+1} = \frac{|x|}{2} \cdot 2 = |x| < 1 \text{ for convergence, so } R = 1.$$

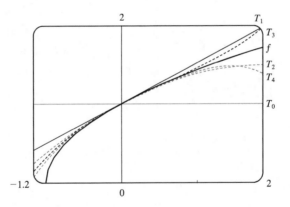

Notice that, as n increases, $T_n(x)$ becomes a better approximation to $f(x)$ for $-1 < x < 1$.

35. $\cos x = \displaystyle\sum_{n=0}^{\infty}(-1)^n\frac{x^{2n}}{(2n)!} \quad\Rightarrow\quad f(x) = \cos(x^2) = \sum_{n=0}^{\infty}\frac{(-1)^n\left(x^2\right)^{2n}}{(2n)!} = \sum_{n=0}^{\infty}\frac{(-1)^n x^{4n}}{(2n)!},\, R = \infty$

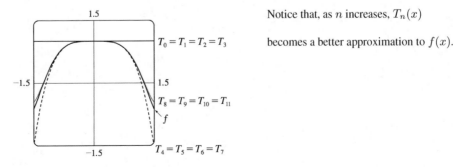

Notice that, as n increases, $T_n(x)$ becomes a better approximation to $f(x)$.

37. $e^x = \sum\limits_{n=0}^{\infty} \dfrac{x^n}{n!}$, so

$$e^{-0.2} = \sum_{n=0}^{\infty} \frac{(-0.2)^n}{n!} = 1 - 0.2 + \frac{1}{2!}(0.2)^2 - \frac{1}{3!}(0.2)^3 + \frac{1}{4!}(0.2)^4 - \frac{1}{5!}(0.2)^5 + \frac{1}{6!}(0.2)^6 - \cdots. \text{ But}$$

$\dfrac{1}{6!}(0.2)^6 = 8.\overline{8} \times 10^{-8}$, so by the Alternating Series Estimation Theorem, $e^{-0.2} \approx \sum\limits_{n=0}^{5} \dfrac{(-0.2)^n}{n!} \approx 0.81873$,

correct to five decimal places.

39. $\cos x \overset{(16)}{=} \sum\limits_{n=0}^{\infty} (-1)^n \dfrac{x^{2n}}{(2n)!} \quad \Rightarrow \quad \cos(x^3) = \sum\limits_{n=0}^{\infty} (-1)^n \dfrac{(x^3)^{2n}}{(2n)!} = \sum\limits_{n=0}^{\infty} (-1)^n \dfrac{x^{6n}}{(2n)!} \quad \Rightarrow$

$x \cos(x^3) = \sum\limits_{n=0}^{\infty} (-1)^n \dfrac{x^{6n+1}}{(2n)!} \quad \Rightarrow \quad \displaystyle\int x \cos(x^3)\, dx = C + \sum\limits_{n=0}^{\infty} (-1)^n \dfrac{x^{6n+2}}{(6n+2)(2n)!}$, with $R = \infty$.

41. Using the series from Exercise 33 and substituting x^3 for x, we get

$$\int \sqrt{x^3 + 1}\, dx = \int \left[1 + \frac{x^3}{2} + \sum_{n=2}^{\infty} \frac{(-1)^{n-1} 1 \cdot 3 \cdot 5 \cdot \cdots \cdot (2n-3)}{2^n n!} x^{3n} \right] dx$$

$$= C + x + \frac{x^4}{8} + \sum_{n=2}^{\infty} \frac{(-1)^{n-1} 1 \cdot 3 \cdot 5 \cdot \cdots \cdot (2n-3)}{2^n n! (3n+1)} x^{3n+1}$$

43. By Exercise 39, $\displaystyle\int x \cos(x^3)\, dx = C + \sum\limits_{n=0}^{\infty} (-1)^n \dfrac{x^{6n+2}}{(6n+2)(2n)!}$, so $\displaystyle\int_0^1 x \cos(x^3)\, dx$

$$= \left[\sum_{n=0}^{\infty} (-1)^n \frac{x^{6n+2}}{(6n+2)(2n)!} \right]_0^1 = \sum_{n=0}^{\infty} \frac{(-1)^n}{(6n+2)(2n)!} = \frac{1}{2} - \frac{1}{8 \cdot 2!} + \frac{1}{14 \cdot 4!} - \frac{1}{20 \cdot 6!} + \cdots, \text{ but}$$

$\dfrac{1}{20 \cdot 6!} = \dfrac{1}{14{,}400} \approx 0.000\,069$, so $\displaystyle\int_0^1 x \cos(x^3)\, dx \approx \dfrac{1}{2} - \dfrac{1}{16} + \dfrac{1}{336} \approx 0.440$ (correct to three decimal places)

by the Alternating Series Estimation Theorem.

45. We first find a series representation for $f(x) = (1+x)^{-1/2}$, and then substitute.

n	$f^{(n)}(x)$	$f^{(n)}(0)$
0	$(1+x)^{-1/2}$	1
1	$-\frac{1}{2}(1+x)^{-3/2}$	$-\frac{1}{2}$
2	$\frac{3}{4}(1+x)^{-5/2}$	$\frac{3}{4}$
3	$-\frac{15}{8}(1+x)^{-7/2}$	$-\frac{15}{8}$
$\vdots$	$\vdots$	$\vdots$

$$\frac{1}{\sqrt{1+x}} = 1 - \frac{x}{2} + \frac{3}{4}\left(\frac{x^2}{2!}\right) - \frac{15}{8}\left(\frac{x^3}{3!}\right) + \cdots \quad \Rightarrow \quad \frac{1}{\sqrt{1+x^3}} = 1 - \frac{1}{2}x^3 + \frac{3}{8}x^6 - \frac{5}{16}x^9 + \cdots \quad \Rightarrow$$

$$\int_0^{0.1} \frac{dx}{\sqrt{1+x^3}} = \left[x - \frac{1}{8}x^4 + \frac{3}{56}x^7 - \frac{1}{32}x^{10} + \cdots \right]_0^{0.1} \approx (0.1) - \frac{1}{8}(0.1)^4, \text{ by the Alternating Series}$$

Estimation Theorem, since $\frac{3}{56}(0.1)^7 \approx 0.000\,000\,005\,4 < 10^{-8}$, which is the maximum desired error. Therefore,

$$\int_0^{0.1} \frac{dx}{\sqrt{1+x^3}} \approx 0.099\,987\,50.$$

47. $\displaystyle\lim_{x\to0} \frac{x - \tan^{-1} x}{x^3} = \lim_{x\to0} \frac{x - \left(x - \frac{1}{3}x^3 + \frac{1}{5}x^5 - \frac{1}{7}x^7 + \cdots\right)}{x^3} = \lim_{x\to0} \frac{\frac{1}{3}x^3 - \frac{1}{5}x^5 + \frac{1}{7}x^7 - \cdots}{x^3}$

$$= \lim_{x\to0}\left(\tfrac{1}{3} - \tfrac{1}{5}x^2 + \tfrac{1}{7}x^4 - \cdots\right) = \tfrac{1}{3}$$

since power series are continuous functions.

49. $\displaystyle\lim_{x\to0} \frac{\sin x - x + \frac{1}{6}x^3}{x^5} = \lim_{x\to0} \frac{\left(x - \frac{1}{3!}x^3 + \frac{1}{5!}x^5 - \frac{1}{7!}x^7 + \cdots\right) - x + \frac{1}{6}x^3}{x^5}$

$$= \lim_{x\to0} \frac{\frac{1}{5!}x^5 - \frac{1}{7!}x^7 + \cdots}{x^5} = \lim_{x\to0}\left(\frac{1}{5!} - \frac{x^2}{7!} + \frac{x^4}{9!} - \cdots\right) = \frac{1}{5!} = \frac{1}{120}$$

since power series are continuous functions.

51. As in Example 8(a), we have $e^{-x^2} = 1 - \dfrac{x^2}{1!} + \dfrac{x^4}{2!} - \dfrac{x^6}{3!} + \cdots$ and we know that $\cos x = 1 - \dfrac{x^2}{2!} + \dfrac{x^4}{4!} - \cdots$

from Equation 16. Therefore, $e^{-x^2}\cos x = \left(1 - x^2 + \frac{1}{2}x^4 - \cdots\right)\left(1 - \frac{1}{2}x^2 + \frac{1}{24}x^4 - \cdots\right)$. Writing only the

terms with degree ≤ 4, we get $e^{-x^2}\cos x = 1 - \frac{1}{2}x^2 + \frac{1}{24}x^4 - x^2 + \frac{1}{2}x^4 + \frac{1}{2}x^4 + \cdots = 1 - \frac{3}{2}x^2 + \frac{25}{24}x^4 + \cdots$.

53.

$$
\begin{array}{r}
1 + \frac{1}{6}x^2 + \frac{7}{360}x^4 + \cdots \\
x - \frac{1}{6}x^3 + \frac{1}{120}x^5 - \cdots \overline{\smash{\big)}\, x } \\
\underline{x - \frac{1}{6}x^3 + \frac{1}{120}x^5 - \cdots} \\
\frac{1}{6}x^3 - \frac{1}{120}x^5 + \cdots \\
\underline{\frac{1}{6}x^3 - \frac{1}{36}x^5 + \cdots} \\
\frac{7}{360}x^5 + \cdots \\
\underline{\frac{7}{360}x^5 + \cdots} \\
\cdots
\end{array}
$$

$\dfrac{x}{\sin x} \overset{(15)}{=} \dfrac{x}{x - \frac{1}{6}x^3 + \frac{1}{120}x^5 - \cdots}$. From the long division above, $\dfrac{x}{\sin x} = 1 + \frac{1}{6}x^2 + \frac{7}{360}x^4 + \cdots$.

55. $\displaystyle\sum_{n=0}^{\infty}(-1)^n \frac{x^{4n}}{n!} = \sum_{n=0}^{\infty}\frac{\left(-x^4\right)^n}{n!} = e^{-x^4}$, by (11).

57. $\displaystyle\sum_{n=0}^{\infty}\frac{(-1)^n\,\pi^{2n+1}}{4^{2n+1}(2n+1)!} = \sum_{n=0}^{\infty}\frac{(-1)^n\left(\frac{\pi}{4}\right)^{2n+1}}{(2n+1)!} = \sin\frac{\pi}{4} = \frac{1}{\sqrt{2}}$, by (15).

59. $3 + \dfrac{9}{2!} + \dfrac{27}{3!} + \dfrac{81}{4!} + \cdots = \dfrac{3^1}{1!} + \dfrac{3^2}{2!} + \dfrac{3^3}{3!} + \dfrac{3^4}{4!} + \cdots = \displaystyle\sum_{n=1}^{\infty} \dfrac{3^n}{n!} = \sum_{n=0}^{\infty} \dfrac{3^n}{n!} - 1 = e^3 - 1$, by (11).

61. Assume that $|f'''(x)| \le M$, so $f'''(x) \le M$ for $a \le x \le a + d$. Now $\int_a^x f'''(t)\, dt \le \int_a^x M\, dt \quad \Rightarrow$

$f''(x) - f''(a) \le M(x - a) \quad \Rightarrow \quad f''(x) \le f''(a) + M(x - a)$. Thus, $\int_a^x f''(t)\, dt \le \int_a^x [f''(a) + M(t - a)]\, dt$

$\Rightarrow \quad f'(x) - f'(a) \le f''(a)(x - a) + \frac{1}{2}M(x - a)^2 \quad \Rightarrow \quad f'(x) \le f'(a) + f''(a)(x - a) + \frac{1}{2}M(x - a)^2 \quad \Rightarrow$

$\int_a^x f'(t)\, dt \le \int_a^x \left[f'(a) + f''(a)(t - a) + \frac{1}{2}M(t - a)^2 \right] dt \quad \Rightarrow$

$f(x) - f(a) \le f'(a)(x - a) + \frac{1}{2}f''(a)(x - a)^2 + \frac{1}{6}M(x - a)^3$. So

$f(x) - f(a) - f'(a)(x - a) - \frac{1}{2}f''(a)(x - a)^2 \le \frac{1}{6}M(x - a)^3$. But

$R_2(x) = f(x) - T_2(x) = f(x) - f(a) - f'(a)(x - a) - \frac{1}{2}f''(a)(x - a)^2$, so $R_2(x) \le \frac{1}{6}M(x - a)^3$.

A similar argument using $f'''(x) \ge -M$ shows that $R_2(x) \ge -\frac{1}{6}M(x - a)^3$. So $|R_2(x_2)| \le \frac{1}{6}M\,|x - a|^3$.

Although we have assumed that $x > a$, a similar calculation shows that this inequality is also true if $x < a$.

12 Review

———————————— CONCEPT CHECK ————————————

1. (a) See Definition 12.1.1.

(b) See Definition 12.2.2.

(c) The terms of the sequence $\{a_n\}$ approach 3 as n becomes large.

(d) By adding sufficiently many terms of the series, we can make the partial sums as close to 3 as we like.

2. (a) See Definition 12.1.10.

(b) A sequence is monotonic if it is either increasing or decreasing.

(c) By Theorem 12.1.11, every bounded, monotonic sequence is convergent.

3. (a) See (4) in Section 12.2.

(b) The p-series $\displaystyle\sum_{n=1}^{\infty} \frac{1}{n^p}$ is convergent if $p > 1$.

4. If $\sum a_n = 3$, then $\displaystyle\lim_{n \to \infty} a_n = 0$ and $\displaystyle\lim_{n \to \infty} s_n = 3$.

5. (a) See the Test for Divergence on page 754.

(b) See the Integral Test on page 760.

(c) See the Comparison Test on page 767.

(d) See the Limit Comparison Test on page 768.

(e) See the Alternating Series Test on page 772.

(f) See the Ratio Test on page 778.

(g) See the Root Test on page 780.

6. (a) A series $\sum a_n$ is called *absolutely convergent* if the series of absolute values $\sum |a_n|$ is convergent.

(b) If a series $\sum a_n$ is absolutely convergent, then it is convergent.

(c) A series $\sum a_n$ is called *conditionally convergent* if it is convergent but not absolutely convergent.

7. (a) Use (3) in Section 12.3.

(b) See Example 5 in Section 12.4.

(c) By adding terms until you reach the desired accuracy given by the Alternating Series Estimation Theorem on page 774.

8. (a) $\sum_{n=0}^{\infty} c_n (x - a)^n$

(b) Given the power series $\sum_{n=0}^{\infty} c_n (x - a)^n$, the radius of convergence is:

(i) 0 if the series converges only when $x = a$

(ii) ∞ if the series converges for all x, or

(iii) a positive number R such that the series converges if $|x - a| < R$ and diverges if $|x - a| > R$.

(c) The interval of convergence of a power series is the interval that consists of all values of x for which the series converges. Corresponding to the cases in part (b), the interval of convergence is: (i) the single point $\{a\}$, (ii) all real numbers, that is, the real number line $(-\infty, \infty)$, or (iii) an interval with endpoints $a - R$ and $a + R$ which can contain neither, either, or both of the endpoints. In this case, we must test the series for convergence at each endpoint to determine the interval of convergence.

9. (a), (b) See Theorem 12.9.2.

10. (a) $T_n(x) = \sum\limits_{i=0}^{n} \dfrac{f^{(i)}(a)}{i!}(x-a)^i$

(b) $\sum\limits_{n=0}^{\infty} \dfrac{f^{(n)}(a)}{n!}(x-a)^n$

(c) $\sum\limits_{n=0}^{\infty} \dfrac{f^{(n)}(0)}{n!}x^n$ [$a=0$ in part (b)]

(d) See Theorem 12.10.8.

(e) See Taylor's Inequality (12.10.9).

11. (a) – (e) See the table on page 803.

12. See the Binomial Series (12.11.2) for the expansion. The radius of convergence for the binomial series is 1.

TRUE-FALSE QUIZ

1. False.   See Note 2 after Theorem 12.2.6.

3. True.   If $\lim\limits_{n\to\infty} a_n = L$, then given any $\varepsilon > 0$, we can find a positive integer N such that $|a_n - L| < \varepsilon$ whenever $n > N$. If $n > N$, then $2n+1 > N$ and $|a_{2n+1} - L| < \varepsilon$. Thus, $\lim\limits_{n\to\infty} a_{2n+1} = L$.

5. False.   For example, take $c_n = (-1)^n / (n6^n)$.

7. False, since $\lim\limits_{n\to\infty} \left|\dfrac{a_{n+1}}{a_n}\right| = \lim\limits_{n\to\infty} \left|\dfrac{1}{(n+1)^3} \cdot \dfrac{n^3}{1}\right| = \lim\limits_{n\to\infty} \left|\dfrac{n^3}{(n+1)^3} \cdot \dfrac{1/n^3}{1/n^3}\right| = \lim\limits_{n\to\infty} \dfrac{1}{(1+1/n)^3} = 1$.

9. False.   See the note after Example 2 in Section 12.4.

11. True.   See (8) in Section 12.1.

13. True.   By Theorem 12.10.5 the coefficient of x^3 is $\dfrac{f'''(0)}{3!} = \dfrac{1}{3} \;\Rightarrow\; f'''(0) = 2$.

Or: Use Theorem 12.9.2 to differentiate f three times.

15. False.   For example, let $a_n = b_n = (-1)^n$. Then $\{a_n\}$ and $\{b_n\}$ are divergent, but $a_n b_n = 1$, so $\{a_n b_n\}$ is convergent.

17. True by Theorem 12.6.3. $\left[\sum (-1)^n a_n \text{ is absolutely convergent and hence convergent.}\right]$

EXERCISES

1. $\left\{\dfrac{2+n^3}{1+2n^3}\right\}$ converges since $\lim\limits_{n\to\infty} \dfrac{2+n^3}{1+2n^3} = \lim\limits_{n\to\infty} \dfrac{2/n^3 + 1}{1/n^3 + 2} = \dfrac{1}{2}$.

3. $\lim\limits_{n\to\infty} a_n = \lim\limits_{n\to\infty} \dfrac{n^3}{1+n^2} = \lim\limits_{n\to\infty} \dfrac{n}{1/n^2 + 1} = \infty$, so the sequence diverges.

5. $|a_n| = \left|\dfrac{n\sin n}{n^2+1}\right| \le \dfrac{n}{n^2+1} < \dfrac{1}{n}$, so $|a_n| \to 0$ as $n \to \infty$. Thus, $\lim\limits_{n\to\infty} a_n = 0$. The sequence $\{a_n\}$ is convergent.

7. $\left\{\left(1 + \dfrac{3}{n}\right)^{4n}\right\}$ is convergent. Let $y = \left(1 + \dfrac{3}{x}\right)^{4x}$. Then

$$\lim_{x\to\infty} \ln y = \lim_{x\to\infty} 4x\ln(1 + 3/x) = \lim_{x\to\infty} \frac{\ln(1 + 3/x)}{1/(4x)} \overset{\text{H}}{=} \lim_{x\to\infty} \frac{\dfrac{1}{1 + 3/x}\left(-\dfrac{3}{x^2}\right)}{-1/(4x^2)} = \lim_{x\to\infty} \frac{12}{1 + 3/x} = 12$$

so $\displaystyle\lim_{x\to\infty} y = \lim_{n\to\infty}\left(1 + \frac{3}{n}\right)^{4n} = e^{12}$.

Or: Use Exercise 7.7.54.

9. We use induction, hypothesizing that $a_{n-1} < a_n < 2$. Note first that $1 < a_2 = \frac{1}{3}(1 + 4) = \frac{5}{3} < 2$, so the hypothesis holds for $n = 2$. Now assume that $a_{k-1} < a_k < 2$. Then $a_k = \frac{1}{3}(a_{k-1} + 4) < \frac{1}{3}(a_k + 4) < \frac{1}{3}(2 + 4) = 2$. So $a_k < a_{k+1} < 2$, and the induction is complete. To find the limit of the sequence, we note that $L = \displaystyle\lim_{n\to\infty} a_n = \lim_{n\to\infty} a_{n+1} \Rightarrow L = \frac{1}{3}(L + 4) \Rightarrow L = 2$.

11. $\dfrac{n}{n^3 + 1} < \dfrac{n}{n^3} = \dfrac{1}{n^2}$, so $\displaystyle\sum_{n=1}^{\infty} \frac{n}{n^3 + 1}$ converges by the Comparison Test with the convergent p-series

$\displaystyle\sum_{n=1}^{\infty} \frac{1}{n^2}$ $(p = 2 > 1)$.

13. $\displaystyle\lim_{n\to\infty}\left|\frac{a_{n+1}}{a_n}\right| = \lim_{n\to\infty}\left[\frac{(n+1)^3}{5^{n+1}} \cdot \frac{5^n}{n^3}\right] = \lim_{n\to\infty}\left(1 + \frac{1}{n}\right)^3 \cdot \frac{1}{5} = \frac{1}{5} < 1$, so $\displaystyle\sum_{n=1}^{\infty} \frac{n^3}{5^n}$ converges by the Ratio Test.

15. Let $f(x) = \dfrac{1}{x\sqrt{\ln x}}$. Then f is continuous, positive, and decreasing on $[2, \infty)$, so the Integral Test applies.

$$\int_2^{\infty} f(x)\,dx = \lim_{t\to\infty}\int_2^t \frac{1}{x\sqrt{\ln x}}\,dx \quad \begin{bmatrix} u = \ln x, \\ du = \dfrac{1}{x}\,dx \end{bmatrix} = \lim_{t\to\infty}\int_{\ln 2}^{\ln t} u^{-1/2}\,du = \lim_{t\to\infty}\left[2\sqrt{u}\right]_{\ln 2}^{\ln t}$$

$$= \lim_{t\to\infty}(2\sqrt{\ln t} - 2\sqrt{\ln 2}) = \infty, \text{ so the series } \sum_{n=2}^{\infty} \frac{1}{n\sqrt{\ln n}} \text{ diverges.}$$

17. $|a_n| = \left|\dfrac{\cos 3n}{1 + (1.2)^n}\right| \le \dfrac{1}{1 + (1.2)^n} < \dfrac{1}{(1.2)^n} = \left(\dfrac{5}{6}\right)^n$, so $\displaystyle\sum_{n=1}^{\infty} |a_n|$ converges by comparison with the convergent

geometric series $\displaystyle\sum_{n=1}^{\infty}\left(\frac{5}{6}\right)^n$ $\left(r = \frac{5}{6} < 1\right)$. It follows that $\displaystyle\sum_{n=1}^{\infty} a_n$ converges (by Theorem 3 in Section 12.6).

19. $\displaystyle\lim_{n\to\infty}\left|\frac{a_{n+1}}{a_n}\right| = \lim_{n\to\infty}\frac{1 \cdot 3 \cdot 5 \cdot\cdots\cdot(2n-1)(2n+1)}{5^{n+1}(n+1)!} \cdot \frac{5^n n!}{1 \cdot 3 \cdot 5 \cdot\cdots\cdot(2n-1)} = \lim_{n\to\infty}\frac{2n+1}{5(n+1)} = \frac{2}{5} < 1$, so the series converges by the Ratio Test.

21. $b_n = \dfrac{\sqrt{n}}{n+1} > 0$, $\{b_n\}$ is decreasing, and $\displaystyle\lim_{n\to\infty} b_n = 0$, so the series $\displaystyle\sum_{n=1}^{\infty}(-1)^{n-1}\frac{\sqrt{n}}{n+1}$ converges by the Alternating Series Test.

23. Consider the series of absolute values: $\sum_{n=1}^{\infty} n^{-1/3}$ is a p-series with $p = \frac{1}{3} \le 1$ and is therefore divergent. But if we apply the Alternating Series Test, we see that $b_n = \dfrac{1}{\sqrt[3]{n}} > 0$, $\{b_n\}$ is decreasing, and $\displaystyle\lim_{n\to\infty} b_n = 0$, so the series

$\displaystyle\sum_{n=1}^{\infty}(-1)^{n-1}n^{-1/3}$ converges. Thus, $\displaystyle\sum_{n=1}^{\infty}(-1)^{n-1}n^{-1/3}$ is conditionally convergent.

25. $\left| \dfrac{a_{n+1}}{a_n} \right| = \left| \dfrac{(-1)^{n+1}\,(n+2)\,3^{n+1}}{2^{2n+3}} \cdot \dfrac{2^{2n+1}}{(-1)^n\,(n+1)\,3^n} \right| = \dfrac{n+2}{n+1} \cdot \dfrac{3}{4} = \dfrac{1+(2/n)}{1+(1/n)} \cdot \dfrac{3}{4} \to \dfrac{3}{4} < 1$ as $n \to \infty$, so

by the Ratio Test, $\displaystyle\sum_{n=1}^{\infty} \dfrac{(-1)^n\,(n+1)\,3^n}{2^{2n+1}}$ is absolutely convergent.

27. $\dfrac{2^{2n+1}}{5^n} = \dfrac{2^{2n} \cdot 2^1}{5^n} = \dfrac{(2^2)^n \cdot 2}{5^n} = 2\left(\dfrac{4}{5}\right)^n$, so $\displaystyle\sum_{n=1}^{\infty} \dfrac{2^{2n+1}}{5^n} = 2\sum_{n=1}^{\infty}\left(\dfrac{4}{5}\right)^n$ is a geometric series with $a = \dfrac{8}{5}$ and

$r = \dfrac{4}{5}$. Since $|r| = \dfrac{4}{5} < 1$, the series converges to $\dfrac{a}{1-r} = \dfrac{8/5}{1-4/5} = \dfrac{8/5}{1/5} = 8$.

29. $\displaystyle\sum_{n=1}^{\infty} \left[\tan^{-1}(n+1) - \tan^{-1} n \right] = \lim_{n\to\infty} s_n = \lim_{n\to\infty} \left[\left(\tan^{-1} 2 - \tan^{-1} 1\right) + \left(\tan^{-1} 3 - \tan^{-1} 2\right) + \cdots \right.$

$$\left. + \left(\tan^{-1}(n+1) - \tan^{-1} n\right)\right]$$

$$= \lim_{n\to\infty} \left[\tan^{-1}(n+1) - \tan^{-1} 1\right] = \tfrac{\pi}{2} - \tfrac{\pi}{4} = \tfrac{\pi}{4}$$

31. $1 - e + \dfrac{e^2}{2!} - \dfrac{e^3}{3!} + \dfrac{e^4}{4!} - \cdots = \displaystyle\sum_{n=0}^{\infty} (-1)^n \dfrac{e^n}{n!} = \sum_{n=0}^{\infty} \dfrac{(-e)^n}{n!} = e^{-e}$ since $e^x = \displaystyle\sum_{n=0}^{\infty} \dfrac{x^n}{n!}$ for all x.

33. $\cosh x = \dfrac{1}{2}(e^x + e^{-x}) = \dfrac{1}{2}\left(\displaystyle\sum_{n=0}^{\infty} \dfrac{x^n}{n!} + \sum_{n=0}^{\infty} \dfrac{(-x)^n}{n!} \right)$

$$= \dfrac{1}{2}\left[\left(1 + x + \dfrac{x^2}{2!} + \dfrac{x^3}{3!} + \dfrac{x^4}{4!} + \cdots \right) + \left(1 - x + \dfrac{x^2}{2!} - \dfrac{x^3}{3!} + \dfrac{x^4}{4!} - \cdots \right) \right]$$

$$= \dfrac{1}{2}\left(2 + 2 \cdot \dfrac{x^2}{2!} + 2 \cdot \dfrac{x^4}{4!} + \cdots \right)$$

$$= 1 + \dfrac{1}{2}x^2 + \sum_{n=2}^{\infty} \dfrac{x^{2n}}{(2n)!}$$

$$\geq 1 + \dfrac{1}{2}x^2 \quad \text{for all } x$$

35. $\displaystyle\sum_{n=1}^{\infty} \dfrac{(-1)^{n+1}}{n^5} = 1 - \dfrac{1}{32} + \dfrac{1}{243} - \dfrac{1}{1024} + \dfrac{1}{3125} - \dfrac{1}{7776} + \dfrac{1}{16{,}807} - \dfrac{1}{32{,}768} + \cdots$.

Since $b_8 = \dfrac{1}{8^5} = \dfrac{1}{32{,}768} < 0.000031$, $\displaystyle\sum_{n=1}^{\infty} \dfrac{(-1)^{n+1}}{n^5} \approx \sum_{n=1}^{7} \dfrac{(-1)^{n+1}}{n^5} \approx 0.9721$.

37. $\displaystyle\sum_{n=1}^{\infty} \dfrac{1}{2+5^n} \approx \sum_{n=1}^{8} \dfrac{1}{2+5^n} \approx 0.18976224$. To estimate the error, note that $\dfrac{1}{2+5^n} < \dfrac{1}{5^n}$, so the remainder term is

$R_8 = \displaystyle\sum_{n=9}^{\infty} \dfrac{1}{2+5^n} < \sum_{n=9}^{\infty} \dfrac{1}{5^n} = \dfrac{1/5^9}{1-1/5} = 6.4 \times 10^{-7}$ (geometric series with $a = \tfrac{1}{5^9}$ and $r = \tfrac{1}{5}$).

39. Use the Limit Comparison Test. $\displaystyle\lim_{n\to\infty} \left| \dfrac{\left(\frac{n+1}{n}\right) a_n}{a_n} \right| = \lim_{n\to\infty} \dfrac{n+1}{n} = \lim_{n\to\infty} \left(1 + \dfrac{1}{n} \right) = 1 > 0$.

Since $\sum |a_n|$ is convergent, so is $\displaystyle\sum \left| \left(\dfrac{n+1}{n} \right) a_n \right|$, by the Limit Comparison Test.

41. $\lim\limits_{n \to \infty} \left| \dfrac{a_{n+1}}{a_n} \right| = \lim\limits_{n \to \infty} \left[\dfrac{|x+2|^{n+1}}{(n+1)\,4^{n+1}} \cdot \dfrac{n4^n}{|x+2|^n} \right] = \lim\limits_{n \to \infty} \left[\dfrac{n}{n+1} \dfrac{|x+2|}{4} \right] = \dfrac{|x+2|}{4} < 1 \quad \Leftrightarrow \quad |x+2| < 4$,

so $R = 4$. $|x+2| < 4 \quad \Leftrightarrow \quad -4 < x+2 < 4 \quad \Leftrightarrow \quad -6 < x < 2$. If $x = -6$, then the series $\displaystyle\sum_{n=1}^{\infty} \dfrac{(x+2)^n}{n4^n}$

becomes $\displaystyle\sum_{n=1}^{\infty} \dfrac{(-4)^n}{n4^n} = \sum_{n=1}^{\infty} \dfrac{(-1)^n}{n}$, the alternating harmonic series, which converges by the Alternating Series

Test. When $x = 2$, the series becomes the harmonic series $\displaystyle\sum_{n=1}^{\infty} \dfrac{1}{n}$, which diverges. Thus, $I = [-6, 2)$.

43. $\lim\limits_{n \to \infty} \left| \dfrac{a_{n+1}}{a_n} \right| = \lim\limits_{n \to \infty} \left| \dfrac{2^{n+1}(x-3)^{n+1}}{\sqrt{n+4}} \cdot \dfrac{\sqrt{n+3}}{2^n (x-3)^n} \right| = 2\,|x-3| \lim\limits_{n \to \infty} \sqrt{\dfrac{n+3}{n+4}} = 2\,|x-3| < 1 \quad \Leftrightarrow$

$|x-3| < \frac{1}{2}$, so $R = \frac{1}{2}$. $|x-3| < \frac{1}{2} \quad \Leftrightarrow \quad -\frac{1}{2} < x-3 < \frac{1}{2} \quad \Leftrightarrow \quad \frac{5}{2} < x < \frac{7}{2}$. For $x = \frac{7}{2}$, the series

$\displaystyle\sum_{n=1}^{\infty} \dfrac{2^n (x-3)^n}{\sqrt{n+3}}$ becomes $\displaystyle\sum_{n=0}^{\infty} \dfrac{1}{\sqrt{n+3}} = \sum_{n=3}^{\infty} \dfrac{1}{n^{1/2}}$, which diverges ($p = \frac{1}{2} \le 1$), but for $x = \frac{5}{2}$, we get

$\displaystyle\sum_{n=0}^{\infty} \dfrac{(-1)^n}{\sqrt{n+3}}$, which is a convergent alternating series, so $I = \left[\frac{5}{2}, \frac{7}{2} \right)$.

45.

n	$f^{(n)}(x)$	$f^{(n)}\left(\frac{\pi}{6}\right)$
0	$\sin x$	$\frac{1}{2}$
1	$\cos x$	$\frac{\sqrt{3}}{2}$
2	$-\sin x$	$-\frac{1}{2}$
3	$-\cos x$	$-\frac{\sqrt{3}}{2}$
4	$\sin x$	$\frac{1}{2}$
$\vdots$	$\vdots$	$\vdots$

$\sin x = f\left(\frac{\pi}{6}\right) + f'\left(\frac{\pi}{6}\right)\left(x - \frac{\pi}{6}\right) + \dfrac{f''\left(\frac{\pi}{6}\right)}{2!}\left(x - \frac{\pi}{6}\right)^2 + \dfrac{f^{(3)}\left(\frac{\pi}{6}\right)}{3!}\left(x - \frac{\pi}{6}\right)^3 + \dfrac{f^{(4)}\left(\frac{\pi}{6}\right)}{4!}\left(x - \frac{\pi}{6}\right)^4 + \cdots$

$= \dfrac{1}{2}\left[1 - \dfrac{1}{2!}\left(x - \frac{\pi}{6}\right)^2 + \dfrac{1}{4!}\left(x - \frac{\pi}{6}\right)^4 - \cdots \right] + \dfrac{\sqrt{3}}{2}\left[\left(x - \frac{\pi}{6}\right) - \dfrac{1}{3!}\left(x - \frac{\pi}{6}\right)^3 + \cdots \right]$

$= \dfrac{1}{2}\displaystyle\sum_{n=0}^{\infty} (-1)^n \dfrac{1}{(2n)!}\left(x - \frac{\pi}{6}\right)^{2n} + \dfrac{\sqrt{3}}{2}\sum_{n=0}^{\infty} (-1)^n \dfrac{1}{(2n+1)!}\left(x - \frac{\pi}{6}\right)^{2n+1}$

47. $\dfrac{1}{1+x} = \dfrac{1}{1-(-x)} = \displaystyle\sum_{n=0}^{\infty} (-x)^n = \sum_{n=0}^{\infty} (-1)^n x^n$ for $|x| < 1 \quad \Rightarrow \quad \dfrac{x^2}{1+x} = \sum_{n=0}^{\infty} (-1)^n x^{n+2}$ with $R = 1$.

49. $\dfrac{1}{1-x} = \displaystyle\sum_{n=0}^{\infty} x^n$ for $|x| < 1 \quad \Rightarrow \quad \ln(1-x) = -\int \dfrac{dx}{1-x} = -\int \sum_{n=0}^{\infty} x^n \, dx = C - \sum_{n=0}^{\infty} \dfrac{x^{n+1}}{n+1}$.

$\ln(1-0) = C - 0 \quad \Rightarrow \quad C = 0 \quad \Rightarrow \quad \ln(1-x) = -\displaystyle\sum_{n=0}^{\infty} \dfrac{x^{n+1}}{n+1} = \sum_{n=1}^{\infty} \dfrac{-x^n}{n}$ with $R = 1$.

51. $\sin x = \sum\limits_{n=0}^{\infty} \dfrac{(-1)^n x^{2n+1}}{(2n+1)!} \quad \Rightarrow \quad \sin\left(x^4\right) = \sum\limits_{n=0}^{\infty} \dfrac{(-1)^n \left(x^4\right)^{2n+1}}{(2n+1)!} = \sum\limits_{n=0}^{\infty} \dfrac{(-1)^n x^{8n+4}}{(2n+1)!}$ for all x, so the radius of

convergence is ∞.

53. $f(x) = 1\big/\sqrt[4]{16-x} = 1\Big/\left(\sqrt[4]{16}\sqrt[4]{1-\tfrac{1}{16}x}\right) = \tfrac{1}{2}\left(1-\tfrac{1}{16}x\right)^{-1/4}$

$$= \frac{1}{2}\left[1 + \left(-\frac{1}{4}\right)\left(-\frac{x}{16}\right) + \frac{\left(-\frac{1}{4}\right)\left(-\frac{5}{4}\right)}{2!}\left(-\frac{x}{16}\right)^2 + \frac{\left(-\frac{1}{4}\right)\left(-\frac{5}{4}\right)\left(-\frac{9}{4}\right)}{3!}\left(-\frac{x}{16}\right)^3 + \cdots\right]$$

$$= \frac{1}{2} + \sum_{n=1}^{\infty} \frac{1\cdot 5\cdot 9\cdot\cdots\cdot(4n-3)}{2\cdot 4^n\cdot n!\cdot 16^n}x^n = \frac{1}{2} + \sum_{n=1}^{\infty} \frac{1\cdot 5\cdot 9\cdot\cdots\cdot(4n-3)}{2^{6n+1}\,n!}x^n$$

for $\left|-\dfrac{x}{16}\right| < 1 \quad \Leftrightarrow \quad |x| < 16$, so $R = 16$.

55. $e^x = \sum\limits_{n=0}^{\infty} \dfrac{x^n}{n!}$, so $\dfrac{e^x}{x} = \dfrac{1}{x} + \sum\limits_{n=1}^{\infty} \dfrac{x^{n-1}}{n!}$ and $\displaystyle\int \dfrac{e^x}{x}\,dx = C + \ln|x| + \sum\limits_{n=1}^{\infty} \dfrac{x^n}{n\cdot n!}$.

57. (a)

n	$f^{(n)}(x)$	$f^{(n)}(1)$
0	$x^{1/2}$	1
1	$\frac{1}{2}x^{-1/2}$	$\frac{1}{2}$
2	$-\frac{1}{4}x^{-3/2}$	$-\frac{1}{4}$
3	$\frac{3}{8}x^{-5/2}$	$\frac{3}{8}$
4	$-\frac{15}{16}x^{-7/2}$	$-\frac{15}{16}$
$\vdots$	$\vdots$	$\vdots$

$$\sqrt{x} \approx T_3(x) = 1 + \frac{1/2}{1!}(x-1) - \frac{1/4}{2!}(x-1)^2 + \frac{3/8}{3!}(x-1)^3$$
$$= 1 + \tfrac{1}{2}(x-1) - \tfrac{1}{8}(x-1)^2 + \tfrac{1}{16}(x-1)^3$$

(b)

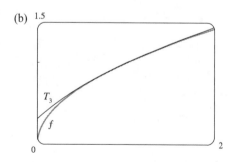

(c) $|R_3(x)| \le \dfrac{M}{4!}|x-1|^4$, where $\left|f^{(4)}(x)\right| \le M$ with

$f^{(4)}(x) = -\tfrac{15}{16}x^{-7/2}$. Now $0.9 \le x \le 1.1 \quad \Rightarrow$

$-0.1 \le x-1 \le 0.1 \quad \Rightarrow \quad (x-1)^4 \le (0.1)^4$,

and letting $x = 0.9$ gives $M = \dfrac{15}{16(0.9)^{7/2}}$, so

$$|R_3(x)| \le \frac{15}{16(0.9)^{7/2}4!}(0.1)^4 \approx 0.000\,005\,648$$
$$\approx 0.000\,006$$
$$= 6 \times 10^{-6}$$

(d)

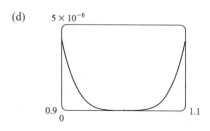

From the graph of $|R_3(x)| = |\sqrt{x} - T_3(x)|$, it appears

that the error is less than 5×10^{-6} on $[0.9, 1.1]$.

59. $\sin x = \sum\limits_{n=0}^{\infty} (-1)^n \dfrac{x^{2n+1}}{(2n+1)!} = x - \dfrac{x^3}{3!} + \dfrac{x^5}{5!} - \dfrac{x^7}{7!} + \cdots$, so $\sin x - x = -\dfrac{x^3}{3!} + \dfrac{x^5}{5!} - \dfrac{x^7}{7!} + \cdots$ and

$\dfrac{\sin x - x}{x^3} = -\dfrac{1}{3!} + \dfrac{x^2}{5!} - \dfrac{x^4}{7!} + \cdots$. Thus, $\lim\limits_{x \to 0} \dfrac{\sin x - x}{x^3} = \lim\limits_{x \to 0} \left(-\dfrac{1}{6} + \dfrac{x^2}{120} - \dfrac{x^4}{5040} + \cdots \right) = -\dfrac{1}{6}$.

61. $f(x) = \sum_{n=0}^{\infty} c_n x^n \quad \Rightarrow \quad f(-x) = \sum_{n=0}^{\infty} c_n (-x)^n = \sum_{n=0}^{\infty} (-1)^n c_n x^n$

(a) If f is an odd function, then $f(-x) = -f(x) \quad \Rightarrow \quad \sum_{n=0}^{\infty} (-1)^n c_n x^n = \sum_{n=0}^{\infty} -c_n x^n$. The coefficients of

any power series are uniquely determined (by Theorem 12.10.5), so $(-1)^n c_n = -c_n$. If n is even, then

$(-1)^n = 1$, so $c_n = -c_n \quad \Rightarrow \quad 2c_n = 0 \quad \Rightarrow \quad c_n = 0$. Thus, all even coefficients are 0, that is,

$c_0 = c_2 = c_4 = \cdots = 0$.

(b) If f is even, then $f(-x) = f(x) \quad \Rightarrow \quad \sum_{n=0}^{\infty} (-1)^n c_n x^n = \sum_{n=0}^{\infty} c_n x^n \quad \Rightarrow \quad (-1)^n c_n = c_n$.

If n is odd, then $(-1)^n = -1$, so $-c_n = c_n \quad \Rightarrow \quad 2c_n = 0 \quad \Rightarrow \quad c_n = 0$. Thus, all odd coefficients are 0,

that is, $c_1 = c_3 = c_5 = \cdots = 0$.

☐ **PROBLEMS PLUS**

1. It would be far too much work to compute 15 derivatives of f. The key idea is to remember that $f^{(n)}(0)$ occurs in the coefficient of x^n in the Maclaurin series of f. We start with the Maclaurin series for sin:

$$\sin x = x - \frac{x^3}{3!} + \frac{x^5}{5!} - \cdots. \text{ Then } \sin(x^3) = x^3 - \frac{x^9}{3!} + \frac{x^{15}}{5!} - \cdots, \text{ and so the coefficient of } x^{15} \text{ is}$$

$\dfrac{f^{(15)}(0)}{15!} = \dfrac{1}{5!}$. Therefore, $f^{(15)}(0) = \dfrac{15!}{5!} = 6 \cdot 7 \cdot 8 \cdot 9 \cdot 10 \cdot 11 \cdot 12 \cdot 13 \cdot 14 \cdot 15 = 10{,}897{,}286{,}400$.

3. (a) From Formula 14a in Appendix D, with $x = y = 0$, we get $\tan 2\theta = \dfrac{2 \tan \theta}{1 - \tan^2 \theta}$, so $\cot 2\theta = \dfrac{1 - \tan^2 \theta}{2 \tan \theta}$ $\Rightarrow$

$2 \cot 2\theta = \dfrac{1 - \tan^2 \theta}{\tan \theta} = \cot \theta - \tan \theta$. Replacing θ by $\frac{1}{2}x$, we get $2 \cot x = \cot \frac{1}{2}x - \tan \frac{1}{2}x$, or

$$\tan \tfrac{1}{2}x = \cot \tfrac{1}{2}x - 2 \cot x$$

(b) From part (a) with $\dfrac{x}{2^{n-1}}$ in place of x, $\tan \dfrac{x}{2^n} = \cot \dfrac{x}{2^n} - 2 \cot \dfrac{x}{2^{n-1}}$, so the nth partial sum of

$\displaystyle\sum_{n=1}^{\infty} \frac{1}{2^n} \tan \frac{x}{2^n}$ is

$$s_n = \frac{\tan(x/2)}{2} + \frac{\tan(x/4)}{4} + \frac{\tan(x/8)}{8} + \cdots + \frac{\tan(x/2^n)}{2^n}$$

$$= \left[\frac{\cot(x/2)}{2} - \cot x\right] + \left[\frac{\cot(x/4)}{4} - \frac{\cot(x/2)}{2}\right] + \left[\frac{\cot(x/8)}{8} - \frac{\cot(x/4)}{4}\right] + \cdots$$

$$+ \left[\frac{\cot(x/2^n)}{2^n} - \frac{\cot(x/2^{n-1})}{2^{n-1}}\right] = -\cot x + \frac{\cot(x/2^n)}{2^n} \quad \text{(telescoping sum)}$$

Now $\dfrac{\cot(x/2^n)}{2^n} = \dfrac{\cos(x/2^n)}{2^n \sin(x/2^n)} = \dfrac{\cos(x/2^n)}{x} \cdot \dfrac{x/2^n}{\sin(x/2^n)} \to \dfrac{1}{x} \cdot 1 = \dfrac{1}{x}$ as $n \to \infty$ since $x/2^n \to 0$

for $x \neq 0$. Therefore, if $x \neq 0$ and $x \neq k\pi$ where k is any integer, then

$$\sum_{n=1}^{\infty} \frac{1}{2^n} \tan \frac{x}{2^n} = \lim_{n\to\infty} s_n = \lim_{n\to\infty} \left(-\cot x + \frac{1}{2^n} \cot \frac{x}{2^n}\right) = -\cot x + \frac{1}{x}$$

If $x = 0$, then all terms in the series are 0, so the sum is 0.

5. (a) At each stage, each side is replaced by four shorter sides, each of
length $\frac{1}{3}$ of the side length at the preceding stage. Writing s_0 and ℓ_0
for the number of sides and the length of the side of the initial
triangle, we generate the table at right. In general, we have
$s_n = 3 \cdot 4^n$ and $\ell_n = \left(\frac{1}{3}\right)^n$, so the length of the perimeter at the nth
stage of construction is $p_n = s_n \ell_n = 3 \cdot 4^n \cdot \left(\frac{1}{3}\right)^n = 3 \cdot \left(\frac{4}{3}\right)^n$.

$s_0 = 3$	$\ell_0 = 1$
$s_1 = 3 \cdot 4$	$\ell_1 = 1/3$
$s_2 = 3 \cdot 4^2$	$\ell_2 = 1/3^2$
$s_3 = 3 \cdot 4^3$	$\ell_3 = 1/3^3$
$\cdots$	$\cdots$

(b) $p_n = \dfrac{4^n}{3^{n-1}} = 4\left(\dfrac{4}{3}\right)^{n-1}$. Since $\frac{4}{3} > 1$, $p_n \to \infty$ as $n \to \infty$.

(c) The area of each of the small triangles added at a given stage is one-ninth of the area of the triangle added at the preceding stage. Let a be the area of the original triangle. Then the area a_n of each of the small triangles added at stage n is $a_n = a \cdot \dfrac{1}{9^n} = \dfrac{a}{9^n}$. Since a small triangle is added to each side at every stage, it follows that the total area A_n added to the figure at the nth stage is

$$A_n = s_{n-1} \cdot a_n = 3 \cdot 4^{n-1} \cdot \frac{a}{9^n} = a \cdot \frac{4^{n-1}}{3^{2n-1}}.$$ Then the total area enclosed by the snowflake curve is

$$A = a + A_1 + A_2 + A_3 + \cdots = a + a \cdot \frac{1}{3} + a \cdot \frac{4}{3^3} + a \cdot \frac{4^2}{3^5} + a \cdot \frac{4^3}{3^7} + \cdots.$$ After the first term, this is a geometric series with common ratio $\frac{4}{9}$, so $A = a + \dfrac{a/3}{1 - \frac{4}{9}} = a + \dfrac{a}{3} \cdot \dfrac{9}{5} = \dfrac{8a}{5}$. But the area of the original equilateral triangle with side 1 is $a = \frac{1}{2} \cdot 1 \cdot \sin \frac{\pi}{3} = \frac{\sqrt{3}}{4}$. So the area enclosed by the snowflake curve is $\frac{8}{5} \cdot \frac{\sqrt{3}}{4} = \frac{2\sqrt{3}}{5}$.

7. (a) Let $a = \arctan x$ and $b = \arctan y$. Then, from Formula 14b in Appendix D,

$$\tan(a - b) = \frac{\tan a - \tan b}{1 + \tan a \tan b} = \frac{\tan(\arctan x) - \tan(\arctan y)}{1 + \tan(\arctan x)\tan(\arctan y)} = \frac{x - y}{1 + xy}.$$

Now $\arctan x - \arctan y = a - b = \arctan(\tan(a - b)) = \arctan \dfrac{x - y}{1 + xy}$ since $-\frac{\pi}{2} < a - b < \frac{\pi}{2}$.

(b) From part (a) we have

$$\arctan \tfrac{120}{119} - \arctan \tfrac{1}{239} = \arctan \frac{\frac{120}{119} - \frac{1}{239}}{1 + \frac{120}{119} \cdot \frac{1}{239}} = \arctan \frac{\frac{28{,}561}{28{,}441}}{\frac{28{,}561}{28{,}441}} = \arctan 1 = \frac{\pi}{4}$$

(c) Replacing y by $-y$ in the formula of part (a), we get $\arctan x + \arctan y = \arctan \dfrac{x + y}{1 - xy}$. So

$$4 \arctan \tfrac{1}{5} = 2\left(\arctan \tfrac{1}{5} + \arctan \tfrac{1}{5}\right) = 2 \arctan \frac{\frac{1}{5} + \frac{1}{5}}{1 - \frac{1}{5} \cdot \frac{1}{5}} = 2 \arctan \tfrac{5}{12} = \arctan \tfrac{5}{12} + \arctan \tfrac{5}{12}$$

$$= \arctan \frac{\frac{5}{12} + \frac{5}{12}}{1 - \frac{5}{12} \cdot \frac{5}{12}} = \arctan \tfrac{120}{119}$$

Thus, from part (b), we have $4 \arctan \frac{1}{5} - \arctan \frac{1}{239} = \arctan \frac{120}{119} - \arctan \frac{1}{239} = \frac{\pi}{4}$.

(d) From Example 7 in Section 12.9 we have $\arctan x = x - \dfrac{x^3}{3} + \dfrac{x^5}{5} - \dfrac{x^7}{7} + \dfrac{x^9}{9} - \dfrac{x^{11}}{11} + \cdots$, so

$$\arctan \frac{1}{5} = \frac{1}{5} - \frac{1}{3 \cdot 5^3} + \frac{1}{5 \cdot 5^5} - \frac{1}{7 \cdot 5^7} + \frac{1}{9 \cdot 5^9} - \frac{1}{11 \cdot 5^{11}} + \cdots$$

This is an alternating series and the size of the terms decreases to 0, so by the Alternating Series Estimation Theorem, the sum lies between s_5 and s_6, that is, $0.197395560 < \arctan \frac{1}{5} < 0.197395562$.

(e) From the series in part (d) we get $\arctan \dfrac{1}{239} = \dfrac{1}{239} - \dfrac{1}{3 \cdot 239^3} + \dfrac{1}{5 \cdot 239^5} - \cdots$. The third term is less than 2.6×10^{-13}, so by the Alternating Series Estimation Theorem, we have, to nine decimal places, $\arctan \frac{1}{239} \approx s_2 \approx 0.004184076$. Thus, $0.004184075 < \arctan \frac{1}{239} < 0.004184077$.

(f) From part (c) we have $\pi = 16 \arctan \frac{1}{5} - 4 \arctan \frac{1}{239}$, so from parts (d) and (e) we have

$16(0.197395560) - 4(0.004184077) < \pi < 16(0.197395562) - 4(0.004184075) \quad \Rightarrow$

$3.141592652 < \pi < 3.141592692$. So, to 7 decimal places, $\pi \approx 3.1415927$.

9. We start with the geometric series $\displaystyle\sum_{n=0}^{\infty} x^n = \dfrac{1}{1-x}$, $|x| < 1$, and differentiate:

$$\sum_{n=1}^{\infty} n x^{n-1} = \frac{d}{dx}\left(\sum_{n=0}^{\infty} x^n\right) = \frac{d}{dx}\left(\frac{1}{1-x}\right) = \frac{1}{(1-x)^2} \text{ for } |x| < 1 \quad \Rightarrow$$

$$\sum_{n=1}^{\infty} n x^n = x \sum_{n=1}^{\infty} n x^{n-1} = \frac{x}{(1-x)^2} \text{ for } |x| < 1. \text{ Differentiate again:}$$

$$\sum_{n=1}^{\infty} n^2 x^{n-1} = \frac{d}{dx}\frac{x}{(1-x)^2} = \frac{(1-x)^2 - x \cdot 2(1-x)(-1)}{(1-x)^4} = \frac{x+1}{(1-x)^3} \quad \Rightarrow \quad \sum_{n=1}^{\infty} n^2 x^n = \frac{x^2+x}{(1-x)^3} \quad \Rightarrow$$

$$\sum_{n=1}^{\infty} n^3 x^{n-1} = \frac{d}{dx}\frac{x^2+x}{(1-x)^3} = \frac{(1-x)^3(2x+1) - (x^2+x)3(1-x)^2(-1)}{(1-x)^6} = \frac{x^2+4x+1}{(1-x)^4} \quad \Rightarrow$$

$$\sum_{n=1}^{\infty} n^3 x^n = \frac{x^3+4x^2+x}{(1-x)^4}, \ |x| < 1. \text{ The radius of convergence is 1 because that is the radius of convergence for}$$

the geometric series we started with. If $x = \pm 1$, the series is $\sum n^3 (\pm 1)^n$, which diverges by the Test For Divergence, so the interval of convergence is $(-1, 1)$.

11. $\ln\left(1 - \dfrac{1}{n^2}\right) = \ln\left(\dfrac{n^2-1}{n^2}\right) = \ln\dfrac{(n+1)(n-1)}{n^2} = \ln[(n+1)(n-1)] - \ln n^2$

$= \ln(n+1) + \ln(n-1) - 2\ln n$

$= \ln(n-1) - \ln n - \ln n + \ln(n+1)$

$= \ln\dfrac{n-1}{n} - [\ln n - \ln(n+1)] = \ln\dfrac{n-1}{n} - \ln\dfrac{n}{n+1}.$

Let $s_k = \displaystyle\sum_{n=2}^{k} \ln\left(1 - \dfrac{1}{n^2}\right) = \sum_{n=2}^{k}\left(\ln\dfrac{n-1}{n} - \ln\dfrac{n}{n+1}\right)$ for $k \geq 2$. Then

$s_k = \left(\ln\dfrac{1}{2} - \ln\dfrac{2}{3}\right) + \left(\ln\dfrac{2}{3} - \ln\dfrac{3}{4}\right) + \cdots + \left(\ln\dfrac{k-1}{k} - \ln\dfrac{k}{k+1}\right) = \ln\dfrac{1}{2} - \ln\dfrac{k}{k+1}$, so

$\displaystyle\sum_{n=2}^{\infty} \ln\left(1 - \dfrac{1}{n^2}\right) = \lim_{k\to\infty} s_k = \lim_{k\to\infty}\left(\ln\dfrac{1}{2} - \ln\dfrac{k}{k+1}\right) = \ln\dfrac{1}{2} - \ln 1 = \ln 1 - \ln 2 - \ln 1 = -\ln 2.$

13. $u = 1 + \dfrac{x^3}{3!} + \dfrac{x^6}{6!} + \dfrac{x^9}{9!} + \cdots, \ v = x + \dfrac{x^4}{4!} + \dfrac{x^7}{7!} + \dfrac{x^{10}}{10!} + \cdots, \ w = \dfrac{x^2}{2!} + \dfrac{x^5}{5!} + \dfrac{x^8}{8!} + \cdots.$

Use the Ratio Test to show that the series for u, v, and w have positive radii of convergence (∞ in each case), so Theorem 12.9.2 applies, and hence, we may differentiate each of these series:

$$\frac{du}{dx} = \frac{3x^2}{3!} + \frac{6x^5}{6!} + \frac{9x^8}{9!} + \cdots = \frac{x^2}{2!} + \frac{x^5}{5!} + \frac{x^8}{8!} + \cdots = w$$

Similarly, $\dfrac{dv}{dx} = 1 + \dfrac{x^3}{3!} + \dfrac{x^6}{6!} + \dfrac{x^9}{9!} + \cdots = u$, and $\dfrac{dw}{dx} = x + \dfrac{x^4}{4!} + \dfrac{x^7}{7!} + \dfrac{x^{10}}{10!} + \cdots = v$.

So $u' = w$, $v' = u$, and $w' = v$. Now differentiate the left hand side of the desired equation:

$$\frac{d}{dx}\left(u^3 + v^3 + w^3 - 3uvw\right) = 3u^2u' + 3v^2v' + 3w^2w' - 3(u'vw + uv'w + uvw')$$

$$= 3u^2w + 3v^2u + 3w^2v - 3(vw^2 + u^2w + uv^2) = 0 \quad \Rightarrow$$

$u^3 + v^3 + w^3 - 3uvw = C$. To find the value of the constant C, we put $x = 0$ in the last equation and get

$1^3 + 0^3 + 0^3 - 3(1 \cdot 0 \cdot 0) = C \quad \Rightarrow \quad C = 1$, so $u^3 + v^3 + w^3 - 3uvw = 1$.

15. If L is the length of a side of the equilateral triangle, then the area is $A = \frac{1}{2}L \cdot \frac{\sqrt{3}}{2}L = \frac{\sqrt{3}}{4}L^2$ and so $L^2 = \frac{4}{\sqrt{3}}A$.

Let r be the radius of one of the circles. When there are n rows of circles, the figure shows that

$$L = \sqrt{3}r + r + (n-2)(2r) + r + \sqrt{3}r = r(2n - 2 + 2\sqrt{3}), \text{ so } r = \frac{L}{2(n + \sqrt{3} - 1)}.$$

The number of circles is $1 + 2 + \cdots + n = \dfrac{n(n+1)}{2}$, and so the total area of the circles is

$$A_n = \frac{n(n+1)}{2}\pi r^2 = \frac{n(n+1)}{2}\pi \frac{L^2}{4(n + \sqrt{3} - 1)^2} = \frac{n(n+1)}{2}\pi \frac{4A/\sqrt{3}}{4(n + \sqrt{3} - 1)^2}$$

$$= \frac{n(n+1)}{(n + \sqrt{3} - 1)^2}\frac{\pi A}{2\sqrt{3}} \quad \Rightarrow$$

$$\frac{A_n}{A} = \frac{n(n+1)}{(n + \sqrt{3} - 1)^2}\frac{\pi}{2\sqrt{3}}$$

$$= \frac{1 + 1/n}{[1 + (\sqrt{3} - 1)/n]^2}\frac{\pi}{2\sqrt{3}} \to \frac{\pi}{2\sqrt{3}} \text{ as } n \to \infty$$

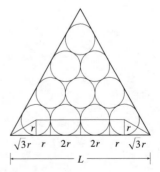

17. As in Section 12.9 we have to integrate the function x^x by integrating series. Writing $x^x = (e^{\ln x})^x = e^{x\ln x}$ and

using the Maclaurin series for e^x, we have $x^x = (e^{\ln x})^x = e^{x\ln x} = \displaystyle\sum_{n=0}^{\infty} \frac{(x\ln x)^n}{n!} = \sum_{n=0}^{\infty} \frac{x^n(\ln x)^n}{n!}.$

As with power series, we can integrate this series term-by-term:

$$\int_0^1 x^x \, dx = \sum_{n=0}^{\infty} \int_0^1 \frac{x^n (\ln x)^n}{n!} \, dx = \sum_{n=0}^{\infty} \frac{1}{n!} \int_0^1 x^n (\ln x)^n \, dx$$

We integrate by parts with $u = (\ln x)^n$, $dv = x^n \, dx$, so $du = \dfrac{n(\ln x)^{n-1}}{x} \, dx$ and $v = \dfrac{x^{n+1}}{n+1}$:

$$\int_0^1 x^n (\ln x)^n \, dx = \lim_{t \to 0^+} \int_t^1 x^n (\ln x)^n \, dx = \lim_{t \to 0^+} \left[\frac{x^{n+1}}{n+1} (\ln x)^n \right]_t^1 - \lim_{t \to 0^+} \int_t^1 \frac{n}{n+1} x^n (\ln x)^{n-1} \, dx$$

$$= 0 - \frac{n}{n+1} \int_0^1 x^n (\ln x)^{n-1} \, dx$$

(where l'Hospital's Rule was used to help evaluate the first limit).

Further integration by parts gives $\displaystyle\int_0^1 x^n (\ln x)^k \, dx = -\frac{k}{n+1} \int_0^1 x^n (\ln x)^{k-1} \, dx$ and, combining

these steps, we get $\displaystyle\int_0^1 x^n (\ln x)^n \, dx = \frac{(-1)^n n!}{(n+1)^n} \int_0^1 x^n \, dx = \frac{(-1)^n n!}{(n+1)^{n+1}} \quad \Rightarrow$

$$\int_0^1 x^x \, dx = \sum_{n=0}^{\infty} \frac{1}{n!} \int_0^1 x^n (\ln x)^n \, dx = \sum_{n=0}^{\infty} \frac{1}{n!} \frac{(-1)^n n!}{(n+1)^{n+1}} = \sum_{n=0}^{\infty} \frac{(-1)^n}{(n+1)^{n+1}} = \sum_{n=1}^{\infty} \frac{(-1)^{n-1}}{n^n}.$$

19. Let $f(x) = \sum_{m=0}^{\infty} c_m x^m$ and $g(x) = e^{f(x)} = \sum_{n=0}^{\infty} d_n x^n$. Then $g'(x) = \sum_{n=0}^{\infty} n d_n x^{n-1}$, so $n d_n$ occurs as the coefficient of x^{n-1}. But also

$$g'(x) = e^{f(x)} f'(x) = \left(\sum_{n=0}^{\infty} d_n x^n \right) \left(\sum_{m=1}^{\infty} m c_m x^{m-1} \right)$$

$$= \left(d_0 + d_1 x + d_2 x^2 + \cdots + d_{n-1} x^{n-1} + \cdots \right) \left(c_1 + 2c_2 x + 3c_3 x^2 + \cdots + n c_n x^{n-1} + \cdots \right)$$

so the coefficient of x^{n-1} is $c_1 d_{n-1} + 2c_2 d_{n-2} + 3c_3 d_{n-3} + \cdots + n c_n d_0 = \sum_{i=1}^{n} i c_i d_{n-i}$. Therefore, $n d_n = \sum_{i=1}^{n} i c_i d_{n-i}$.

21. Call the series S. We group the terms according to the number of digits in their denominators:

$$S = \underbrace{\left(\tfrac{1}{1} + \tfrac{1}{2} + \cdots + \tfrac{1}{8} + \tfrac{1}{9} \right)}_{g_1} + \underbrace{\left(\tfrac{1}{11} + \cdots + \tfrac{1}{99} \right)}_{g_2} + \underbrace{\left(\tfrac{1}{111} + \cdots + \tfrac{1}{999} \right)}_{g_3} + \cdots$$

Now in the group g_n, since we have 9 choices for each of the n digits in the denominator, there are 9^n terms. Furthermore, each term in g_n is less than $\frac{1}{10^{n-1}}$ [except for the first term in g_1]. So $g_n < 9^n \cdot \frac{1}{10^{n-1}} = 9 \left(\frac{9}{10} \right)^{n-1}$.

Now $\sum_{n=1}^{\infty} 9 \left(\frac{9}{10} \right)^{n-1}$ is a geometric series with $a = 9$ and $r = \frac{9}{10} < 1$. Therefore, by the Comparison Test,

$$S = \sum_{n=1}^{\infty} g_n < \sum_{n=1}^{\infty} 9 \left(\frac{9}{10} \right)^{n-1} = \frac{9}{1 - 9/10} = 90.$$